Control of Information in the United States

in the

United States

An Annotated Bibliography

Meckler Corporation's
Bibliographies on Communications
and First Amendment Law, no. 1

Control of Information
in the
United States
An Annotated Bibliography

James R. Bennett

Meckler

Library of Congress Cataloging-in-Publication Data

Bennett, James R., 1932-
    Control of information in the United States : an
annotated bibliography / by James R. Bennett.
        p.   cm.
    Includes indexes.
    ISBN 0-88736-082-3 : $59.00
    1. Censorship--United States--Bibliography   2. Communication
policy--United States--Bibliography.   I. Title.
Z658.U5B46 1987
016.3633'1'0973--dc19   87-16475
                                                                      CIP

Meckler Corporation, 11 Ferry Lane West, Westport, CT 06880.
Meckler Ltd., Grosvenor Gardens House, Grosvenor Gardens,
    London SW1W 0BS, UK.

Printed on acid-free paper and bound in the United States of America.

The surest way to corrupt a youth is to instruct him to hold in higher esteem those who think alike rather than those who think differently.

Nietzsche, *The Dawn*

It is only by a deliberate act of the imagination that we can "separate" ourselves from our culture and undertake to inspect what has become an organic part--perhaps the major part--of ourselves. The culture itself is blind; only its creatures are able to see, but they must have the courage to look. Those who do become the eyes of civilization and are no longer mere *creatures*.

Tom Vernon, "Great Infidels, Friedrich Wilhelm Nietzsche"

Contents

Acknowledgments ———————————————————— x
General Introduction ———————————————————— xi
List of Periodicals Cited ———————————————————— xvii
I.   Anticommunism and Anti-Sovietism ———————————— 1
    Introduction ———————————————————— 2
    A. General History, 1873-Present ———————————— 4
    B. Post-World War I ———————————————— 6
    C. Post-World War II ———————————————— 7
        1. Cold War ———————————————— 7
        2. Repression, Disinformation, and
            Conformity ———————————————— 16
        3. Senator Joseph McCarthy ———————————— 45
    D. The Reagan Years ———————————————— 48
II. The Complex ———————————————————— 69
    Introduction ———————————————————— 70
    A. Interlocking Power ———————————————— 75
    B. Military-Industrial Complex ———————————— 86
    C. Corporations and Government Regulation ——————— 98
    D. Media ———————————————————— 109
        1. Mass Media ———————————————— 109
        2. News ———————————————————— 120
    E. Education and Research ———————————————— 142
        1. Curriculum ———————————————— 142
        2. Research ———————————————————— 151
        3. Governing Boards and Officers ———————————— 155
    F. Secrecy, Censorship, Disinformation, Deceit ——————— 156
III. Corporations ———————————————————— 175
    Introduction ———————————————————— 176
    A. Concentration of Ownership ———————————— 180
    B. Lobbying and Campaigning ———————————— 194
    C. Sponsors, Product Advertising, Consumer Cul-
        ture ———————————————————— 200
    D. Public Relations, Image and Advocacy Adver-
        tising ———————————————————— 226
    E. Foundations ———————————————————— 240
    F. Secrecy, Censorship, Intelligence Activities ——————— 242
IV. Government ———————————————————— 249
    Introduction ———————————————————— 250

    A.   The Presidency _____ 255
        1.   Public Relations, News Manage-
                ment, Media Access _____ 255
        2.   Presidential Secrecy, Censorship,
                Cover-up, Surveillance, Repression _____ 266
        3.   Presidential Disinformation _____ 273
        4.   Presidential Elections, Campaign-
                ing _____ 278
    B.   Watergate _____ 282
    C.   Bureaucracy _____ 283
        1.   Secrecy, Classification,
                Censorship, Self-Censorship, Cov-
                er-up _____ 283
        2.   Bureaucratic Disinformation _____ 303
        3.   Bureaucratic Surveillance,
                Repression _____ 307
    D.   Congress _____ 312
    E.   Think Tanks _____ 314
    F.   Washington Press Corps _____ 317
    G.   Wars _____ 320
        1.   Post-World War II _____ 320
        2.   Vietnam War _____ 323
             a.   Government Disinformation,
                      Secrecy, and Censorship _____ 323
             b.   Media and Education _____ 328
    H.   Latin America _____ 337
        1.   Central and South America _____ 337
        2.   Central America and the Caribbean _____ 338
             a.   Nicaragua _____ 349
             b.   El Salvador _____ 356
        3.   South America _____ 359
V.   Pentagon _____ 361
    Introduction _____ 362
    A.   Militarism _____ 365
    B.   Public Relations, Media, Recruiting _____ 373
    C.   Education and Research _____ 383
    D.   Secrecy, Censorship, Disinformation, Cover-up _____ 385

VI.   Intelligence Agencies ———————————————— 395
       Introduction ———————————————————— 396
       A.   The Apparatuses ——————————————— 399
       B.   Federal Bureau of Investigation ——————— 417
       C.   CIA ————————————————————— 428
       D.   National Security Agency ———————————— 450
VII. Global ———————————————————————— 453
       Introduction ———————————————————— 454
       A.   United States Information Order, Multinational
             Communications Corporations, Global Cultu-
             ral Domination ————————————————— 456
       B.   New World Information Order,
             "Free Flow" Controversy, UNESCO ——————— 469
       C.   Propaganda, United States Information Agency,
             Cold War ————————————————————— 476
       D.   Foundations ———————————————————— 482
Contributors Index ———————————————————— 485
Subject Index ——————————————————————— 523

Acknowledgments

The inter-library loan, reference, and documents staffs of the Mullins Library at the University of Arkansas were helpful and efficient. Phoebe Haddad, Julie Phelan, and Ken Smedley provided capable research assistance. My students in "Language and Public Policy" provided stimulation. Karen Hodges and Tim Garvin saved me from some errors. Jo shared as always. Above all, I learned to honor the contributors to this bibliography for their skepticism toward power and their love of truth and justice. This book is dedicated to them and to all who know that totalitarianism, if not opposed, can triumph anywhere.

General Introduction

The process of creating and sustaining a national consensus in the United States is the subject of this bibliography. Whatever its label--America, land of the free, democratic capitalism, corporate state, national security state, monopoly capitalism, Pentagon state, or warfare state--it is the result of many social, economic, political, and religious factors in the history of the country. It is the result of a long historical and human struggle out of which one set of perspectives has triumphed over others. Some of the books and articles collected here reach back even into the nineteenth century to explain the origins of this long conflict, but most of the entries deal with the post-World War II period.

Power has been defined as the ability to impose one's will over others. John Kenneth Galbraith examines three ways by which power is enforced. The first two--condign power, or the threat or reality of punishment, and compensatory power, or reward--figure importantly in this bibliography. But my chief focus is upon conditional power, or persuasion or appeal to belief. Most of the contributions to this compilation investigate how information functions to enforce power in a democratic country like the US. Coercive and pecuniary power involve awareness by the people submitting. The conditioning power of access, communication, media, and education, in contrast, because it affects belief regarding what seems natural, proper, and right, is not recognized as enforcement. To Galbraith this power "is central" (6) to the functioning of the modern polity like that of the US. This book is dedicated to that proposition.

Galbraith links these three instruments of power to three sources of power: leadership, wealth, and organization. Organization is the "most important source of power in modern societies." Conditioned power is the primary strength of organizations. Wealth and leadership reinforce organized, conditioning power. In Subliminal Politics Dan Nimmo and James Combs examine "the taken-for-granted set of assumptions, conceptions, and ideas about American politics that lies below the threshhold of consciousness." Theirs is "a book about myths of American politics and the persons who make and help plant them in our subconscious--politicians, political press agents, popular entertainers, journalists, pollsters, and political scientists." The contributors to Control of Information share this framework of understanding, although many use the term "ideology" instead of myth, and together they greatly enlarge the categories of organizations engaged in consensus-making: corporations, advertisers, the Pentagon, the intelligence agencies, think tanks, foundations. A nation's ideology, its set of generally assumed beliefs, has two functions: to create consensus and to minimize challenge from competing beliefs--to make people know and act upon certain values and to prevent them from knowing and acting upon other values. Information control is thus an essential function of the agencies and agents of ideology.

This means in practice that people "make and help plant" beliefs within certain constraints. Nimmo and Combs study several of the mechanisms that maintain the "substantial realm" of the unifying process, from politicians to political scientists. This bibliography reflects their formulation of the American way, but reshapes it in order to emphasize and clarify its systemic realities. In creating his categories, Galbraith always recognized, what the contributors to this bibliography well know, that the sources of power and the instruments by which power is exercised are interrelated in complex ways. The contributors tend to ask, What are the primary sources of power in the US? And how are they connected? Many political scientists and sociologists have pursued these questions, as this bibliography amply shows. Many other scholars have investigated the influence of power over the multifarious modes of communication. This bibliography is the first to bring together research on the system as a whole, the network from banks and White House and Pentagon to education and the media.

Arrangement

The seven categories begin with anticommunism and anti-Sovietism because they seem to energize the system more than any-other single factor. The second section emphasizes the system without forgetting that all seven areas together convey the anti-Soviet-corporate-government-military-intelligence-global complex in its actual entirety, in which education and the media play significant roles. This section stresses the interlocking power of the military-industrial complex. Section three focuses upon some of the specific modes of corporate influence. As the items throughout all seven sections indicate, however, corporate values and power are never far from the other institutions that maintain the consensus, and many of the contributors, indeed perhaps most, would give corporate power primary place in the system. Section four addresses the importance of the presidency to the consolida-tion of national unity and patriotism. It departs slightly from the categories of other sections by its attention to US wars since 1945 (as projections of the system). Section five attends first to the trend toward militarism as the partial consequence of forty years of Cold War and hot wars, before tracing some aspects of Pentagon public relations. Section six establishes the role of the intelligence agencies in containing the system within and, in conjunction with multinational corporations, the Pentagon, and other institutions, expanding it abroad. And sec-tion seven sketches out the international projection through com-munications of the system described in the preceding sections. The interchangeability of many of the subjects covered in the bibliography reflects the closely interlocking process of the system.
The contributors to the bibliography concentrate on descrip-tion and diagnosis of information control. Many offer remedies, a subject deserving a separate, equally large bibliography.
The bibliography contains 2,943 entries. The two indexes both facilitate their use and emphasize the complexity of the system. Over 2000 observers of the system contributed to the bibliography. The subject index contains some 3,700 topics.

Bibliographical Resources

This compilation offers the tip of the iceberg. Reynolds and
Henslin characterize the economic, political, and military orders
as the "master institutions of market society." I have concentrated my efforts upon these three institutions in seven parts.
Of the institutions of power which they consider to be secondary-
-"scientific, religious, medical, educational, familial, and
legal" (xi), I have given most attention to science and education. Religion in the US as both an appendage of the master
orders and as critic of that interlocking power deserves a separate bibliography. Each of my seven major subject divisions also
deserves its own bibliographical study. Several important sub-
topics--e.g., control of broadcasting (not discussed by Reynolds
and Henslin as a secondary power)--also. Many topics by their
inherent nature (secrecy in all areas, the Pentagon) resist
investigation.

Space limitation was a necessary constraint. I have scanned
the following biliographies and indexes and omitted as much or
more as I chose, trying always to select the best.

Blackstock, Paul and Frank Schaf. Intelligence, Espionage,
Counter-Espionage, and Covert Operations: A Guide to Information
Sources. Detroit: Gale, 1978. 225.

Cline, Marjorie, et al., eds. Scholar's Guide to Intelligence Literature: Bibliography of the Russell J. Bowen Collection. Frederick, MD: U Pub. of America, 1983. 236.

Free Speech Yearbook, annual bibliography.

Kittross, John. A Bibliography of Theses and Dissertations
in Broadcasting 1920-1973. Broadcast Education Assoc., 1978.
240.

Kraus, Sidney and Dennis Davis. The Effects of Mass Communication on Political Behavior. Univ. Park, PA: Pennsylvania
State UP, 1976. 308.

Marxism and the Mass Media: Towards a Basic Bibliography.
Bagnolet, Fr.: International Mass Media Research Center (IMMRC),
1972-.

McCavitt, William, comp. Radio and Television: A Selected,
Annotated Bibliography. Metuchen, NJ: Scarecrow, 1978. 229.

McCavitt, William, comp. Radio and Television: A Selected
Annotated Bibliography Supplement One: 1977-1981. Metuchen, NJ:
Scarecrow, 1982. 155.

McCoy, Ralph. Freedom of the Press: An Annotated Bibliography. Carbondale: Southern Illinois UP, 1968. 526.

McKerns, Joseph, comp. News Media & Public Policy: An Annotated Bibliography. New York: Garland, 1985. 250.

Miles, William. The Image Makers: Bibliography of American
Presidential Campaign Biographies. Metuchen, NJ: Scarecrow,
1979. 254.

Smith, Myron, Jr. U.S. Television Network News: A Guide to
Sources in English. Jefferson, NC: McFarland, 1984. 233.

Television in Government and Politics: A Bibliography. New
York: Television Information Office, 1964. 62.

These sources were useful, but I found more effective a
direct survey of many of the magazines listed later by acronym.
Many of these magazines were so rich in relevant material (Bul-

letin of the Atomic Scientists, Common Cause, Chicago Journalism Review, Columbia Journalism Review, Civil Liberties Review, Counterspy, Edcentric, First Principles, The Guardian, Inquiry) that the task of selection challenged time and judgment.

Surveying magazines committed to examining power and control has a distinctive advantage over using standard bibliographies and indexes, for the simple reason that you do not find many of these magazines in those sources. The 1985 IMS/Ayer Directory of Publications (newspapers, magazines, journals, and newsletters published in the US, Canada, Bahamas, Bermuda, and the Philippines) omits over sixty of the print media important to my study. It does cite Ceramics International, but not Business and Professional Ethics Journal, Common Cause, Counterspy, Deadline, Free Speech, Freedom of Speech Newsletter, Investigative Reporters and Editors Journal, Journal of Business Ethics, Jump Cut, Lucha, Multinational Monitor, Nicaraguan Perspectives, Nuclear Times, Peace and Change, Public Citizen, Radical Teacher, Science for the People, Sojourners, or Washington Spectator. The Reader's Guide to Periodical Literature, widely used in public schools and libraries, does not survey most of the periodicals I found useful. It does cover the Christian Century, The Center Magazine, Consumer Reports, The Nation, The Progressive, Rolling Stone, and the Washington Monthly, all able and willing to call corporate and government actions to account, a few of them, occasionally, radically. But not too radically. None of these journals is socialist in perspective. Most of the magazines surveyed by Reader's Guide uphold the status quo, and whenever critical of power, only of technique and seldom of structure and system.

The importance of the Directory and of Reader's Guide as one more instrument of social control is that, as one public school librarian explained to me, whatever is not indexed might as well not exist. Speaking generally, indexers choose sources--they provide a reality for students--within orthodox boundaries. A remedy is available, which was helpful to me in discovering perspectives challenging the system and offering the range of options fundamental to freedom: the Alternative Press Index. But it is difficult to find.

Annotations

James J. Harner in On Compiling an Annotated Bibliography distinguishes between the "paraphrase" and the "commentary" approaches, the former a miniaturized transcription of the original, the latter a statement of what it is about. Because my goal was to reveal the quantity and range of publications on the subject of information control, generally I chose the more succinct commentary method. I have further and frequently condensed the commentary form by expressing the thesis or perspective or major concern of the item as though the author were speaking directly. Thus, instead of writing "The author surveys press coverage of" or using a subjectless sentence, "Surveys press coverage of," I write, "Mainstream press coverage of Nicaraguan Contra atrocities is inadequate," or "The press has underreported Nicaraguan Contra atrocities." This method has two advantages. It is brief, and it reduces the repetition of annotation verbs,

xiv

such as "surveys," "suggests," "demonstrates," "asserts," "discusses," and "examines." This style is not to be confused with
my own voice, which appears in brackets. My chief aim is to
present the thesis or theses of the work. Sometimes, however, I
add the contents of the book when its scope and diversity warrant.

Works Cited

Galbraith, John Kenneth. The Anatomy of Power. Boston:
Houghton, 1983. 206.

List of Periodicals Cited
(in alphabetical
order by acronym)

Acronym	Title
AAPSS-A	American Academy of Political and Social Science Annals
A&S	Administration and Society
ABAJ	American Bar Association Journal
AD	Arkansas Democrat
AF	American Film
AG	Arkansas Gazette
AJ	Amicus Journal
AJS	American Journal of Sociology
AM	Atlantic Monthly
AmT	American Teacher
AP	American Psychologist
APSR	American Political Science Review
ArT	Army Times
ASR	American Sociological Review
AT	Arkansas Traveler
Au	Audubon
AULR	American U Law Review
BAS	Bulletin of the Atomic Scientists
BCAS	Bulletin of Concerned Asian Scholars
Bf	Blackfriars
BI	Barricada Internacional
BoB	Bulletin of Bibliography
BR	The Brookings Review
BPEJ	Business and Professional Ethics Journal
Br	Broadcasting
BS	Brazilian Studies
BSR	Business and Society Review
BT	Business Today
Bth	Breakthrough
CAA	Central America Alert
CAB	Central America Bulletin
CAIB	Covert Action Information Bulletin
C&C	Christianity and Crisis
CAR	Central America Report
CarlJR	Carleton Journalism Review
CC	Common Cause Magazine
CCR	Center for Constitutional Rights

CE	College English
CEAF	The CEA Forum
CFL	Conservation Foundation Newslettter
Cg	Change
Ch	Channels
ChC	Christian Century
CHE	Chronicle of Higher Education
ChJR	Chicago Journalism Review (1968-1975)
CHm	The Churchman
CJR	Columbia Journalism Review
CL	Civil Liberties
CLR	Civil Liberties Review (1973-1979)
CLRv	Columbia Law Review
CM	Center Magazine
CMJ	Critical Mass Journal (later, Critical Mass Energy Journal) (1977-1983)
CNN	CCCO News Notes
Cog	Cogito
CongQ	Congressional Quarterly
CQ	Communication Quarterly (formerly Today's Speech)
CR	Consumer Reports
CRPV	Current Research on Peace and Violence (formerly Instant Research on Peace and Violence
CS	CounterSpy (now The National Reporter)
CSM	Christian Science Monitor
Ct	Cubatimes (1974-1985)
CulC	Cultural Critique
Current	Current: For People in Public Telecommunications
Da	Daedalus
DAI	Dissertation Abstracts International
DC	Daily Camera
Dead	Deadline: The Press and the Arms Race
DJ	The Democratic Journalist
DM	The Defense Monitor
EA	Environmental Action
E&P	Editor and Publisher
Ed	Edcentric (1971-1979)

EF	Educational Forum
EJ	English Journal
EL	Educational Leadership
ELJ	Emory Law Journal
En	Envio
Esq	Esquire
ETC	Etcetera
EW	Education Week
FC	FCNL Washington Newsletter
Feed	Feedback
Fel	Fellowship
FfA	Facts for Action
FI	Free Inquiry
FiC	Film Comment
FM	Focus Midwest
FoM	Food Monitor (1976-1984) (1986-)
For	Fortune
ForP	Foreign Policy
FP	First Principles: National Security and Civil Liberties
FS	Free Speech
FSN	Freedom of Speech Newsletter
FSULR	Florida State U Law Review
FSY	Free Speech Yearbook
Fu	The Futurist
Gaz	Gazette: International Journal for Mass Communication Studies
GLR	Georgetown Law Journal
Gma	Granma
GR	The Green Revolution
GrE	Greenpeace Examiner
Gu	Guatamala!
Guard	The Guardian
GZ	Ground Zero
HA	Health Affairs
HAM	Harvard Alumni Magazine
Har	Harper's
HCLQ	Hastings Constitutuonal Law Quarterly
HER	Harvard Educational Review
HI	Humanities International
HL	Health Letter
HLJ	Hastings Law Journal
HR	Human Rights
HRQ	Human Rights Quarterly
HS	Humanities in the South
IBCB	Interracial Books for Children Bulletin

IC	Index on Censorship
IJWP	Internation Journal on World Peace
ILJ	Indiana Law Journal
IM	Index Magazine
Independent	The Independent Film and Video Monthly
Inq	Inquiry (1978-1982)
IPSR	International Political Science Review
IR	Islamic Revolution
IREJ	The IRE Journal
IRPV	Instant Research on Peace and Violence (now Current Research on Peace and Violence)
IS	The Insurgent Sociologist
ItS	Inside the System
ITT	In These Times
IW	Industry Week
JA	Journalists' Affairs
JACR	Journal of Applied Communications Research
JAE	Journal of Aesthetic Education
JBE	Journal of Business Ethics
JC	Jump Cut: A Review of Contemporary Media
JCA	Journal of Contemporary Asia
JEL	Journal of Economic Literature
JFAS	Journal of the Federation of American Scientists
JIA	Journal of International Affairs
JM	Journalism Monographs
JoB	Journal of Broadcasting and Electronic Media (formerly Journal of Broadcasting)
JoC	Journal of Communication
JPHP	Journal of Public Health Policy
JPR	Journal of Peace Research
JQ	Journalism Quarterly
JSR	Journal of Social Reconstruction
LAER	Latin America and Empire Report
LAP	Latin American Perspectives
LARR	Latin American Research Review
LASAF	Latin American Studies Association Forum
LAWR	Latin American Weekly Report
LCP	Law and Contemporary Problems
LJ	Library Journal

Lu	Lucha
Mam	Mesoamerica
M&M	Media and Methods
MCS	Media, Culture and Society
MGW	Manchester Guardian Weekly
MJ	Mother Jones
MLR	Michigan Law Review
MM	Multinational Monitor
MORE	MORE (1971-1978)
MQR	Michigan Quarterly Review
MW	Media Watch (1976-1981)
Na	The Nation
NA	The Nonviolent Activist
NACLA	NACLA Newsletter (Report on the Americas)
NaR	The National Reporter (formerly CounterSpy)
NAT	Northwest Arkansas Times
NB	Nation's Business
NCLR	North Carolina Law Review
NCTVN	National Coalition on Television Violence News
NEAT	The NEA Today
NHEJ	The NEA Higher Education Journal
NicP	Nicaraguan Perspectives
NJ	National Journal
NLR	Nebraska Law Review
NMA	Not Man Apart
NMPN	The New Manhattan Project Newsletter
NmR	Nieman Reports
NNN	No Nuclear News (1977-1984)
NP	New Politics
NPS	New Political Science◆
NR	New Republic
NRDCN	Natural Resources Defense Council Newsline
NRJ	Newspaper Research Journal
NSEN	New Schools Exchange Newsletter (1969-1976)
NT	Nuclear Times
NuA	Nutrition Action
NULR	Northwestern University Law Review
NUT	New University Thought
NYT	The New York Times
NYTM	New York Times Magazine
NYTRB	New York Times Review of Books

NYUJLP	New York U Journal of International Law & Politics
Ob	The Observer
ON	Organizing Notes (1977-1983)
OOB	Off Our Backs
ORK	Our Right To Know
PA	Political Affairs
Pa	Parade
PacS	Pacific Spectator
Pan	Pandora
P&C	Peace and Change: A Journal of Peace Research
PaR	Partisan Review
PAR	Propaganda Analysis Review
Pb	Playboy
PC	Public Citizen
PCP	Political Communication and Persuasion
PDK	Phi Delta Kappan
PE	Politics and Education
PI	Philadelphia Enquirer
PLR	Pepperdine Law Review
Pn	Panorama
PolSQ	Political Science Quarterly
POQ	Public Opinion Quarterly
Pr	The Press
PRJ	Public Relations Journal
Prog	The Progressive
PS	Political Studies
PSQ	Presidential Studies Quarterly
PTR	Public Telecommunications Review (1973-1980)
QRD	Quarterly Review of Doublespeak
QREB	Quarterly Review of Economics and Business
RA	Report on the Americas (NACLA)
RadA	Radical America
RadS	Radical Software
RadSc	Radical Science
Ram	Ramparts (1962-1975)
Rep	The Reporter (1949-1968)
RHR	Radical History Review
RMN	Rocky Mountain News
Rn	Reason
RoP	Review of Politics
RP	Radical Philosophy
RS	Rolling Stone
RT	Radical Teacher

SANE	Sane World
S&D	Socialism and Democracy
S&S	School and Society
SAR	Soviet-American Review
Sc	Science
Sc&S	Science and Society
SCLR	Santa Clara law Review
ScP	Science for the People
SD	Seven Days (1977-1980)
SEP	Saturday Evening Post
SLJR	St. Louis Journalism Review
SLULJ	St. Louis U Law Journal
SM	Stanford Magazine
SocR	Socialist Review
Soj	Sojourners
SP	Social Problems
SocP	Social Policy
SPE	Studies in Political Economy
SQ	The Sociological Quarterly
SR	Saturday Review
SSQ	Social Science Quarterly
ST	Social Text
STP	Social Theory and Practice
TA	Thought and Action
TE	Today's Education
Telos	Telos: A Quarterly Journal of Critical Thought
TO	Texas Observer
TQ	Television Quarterly
TR	Technology Review
TRA	Television/Radio Age
Trans	Transaction
TS	Today's Speech (now Communication Quarterly)
TVG	TV Guide
TW	Tulsa World
UCLALR	UCLA Law Review
Un	Unity
USNW	U. S. News and World Report
Voice	A Voice of the Voiceless
VV	Village Voice
Win	Win (1965-1984)
Wit	The Witness
WJR	Washington Journalism Review
WM	Washington Monthly
WoP	World Politics
WP	Working Papers (1973-1983)
WPJ	World Policy Journal

WPR	World Press Review
WRH	Washington Report on the Hemisphere
WS	Washington Spectator
WSJ	Wall Street Journal
WULQ	Washington U Law Quarterly
WQ	Wilson Quarterly
YLJ	Yale Law Journal

I. ANTICOMMUNISM AND ANTI-SOVIETISM 1-413

Introduction

A. General History, 1873-Present 1-10

B. Post-World War I 11-17

C. Post-World War II 18-273
   1. Cold War 18-68
   2. Repression, Disinformation, and Conformity 69-252
   3. Senator Joseph McCarthy 253-273

D. The Reagan Years 274-413

ANTICOMMUNISM

INTRODUCTION

Sovietphobia

The question of whether anticommunism and anti-Sovietism function to reinforce the institutions of the United States is answered by recalling with Reynolds and Henslin what the main institutions are: the economic, political, and military orders. Within the upper echelons of these three institutions reside the real power, with first and foremost the corporate bureaucracy. Russet and Hanson maintain that this economic bureaucracy is the most anticommunist of elite groups. In foreign policy, economic interests take second place to anticommunist ideology. Second, that every president since Roosevelt--Democrat or Republican--has been militantly anticommunist/anti-USSR, needs no demonstration. The last national effort to debate the basic anti-Soviet assumptions of US policy took place in 1948 when Henry Wallace lost his race for the presidency under the Progressive Party. Third, as for the Pentagon, every weapon, every missile, every combat exercise has the Soviet Union immediately or ultimately in mind.

Less obvious are the cultural means and proceses by which this powerful force gained and retained sway over all the leaders through eight administrations and over most of the population. The writers in this section argue that big-power Soviet belligerance and threatening are only part of the Cold War. The United States must share the blame. So how were the parameters of legitimate thought and debate successfully defined as anticommunist/anti-Soviet so exclusively for so long by so many? On most major issues perhaps the majority of the public lacks a well-defined attitude. But regarding communism and the Soviet Union (hereafter SU) these same people know their enemy. How has this occurred? And how is it perpetuated?

Much more than is listed in this section and in related sections probably is yet to be published. The most recent effort at assimilation is the second half of Michael Parenti's Inventing Reality. Six chapters give an account of the creation of a right-wing mood in the country: discrediting protest, red-baiting the peace movement, McCarthy, building up the external "threat," derogatory reporting of the SU, distortion of Billy Graham's trip to Russia, portrayal of leftists as evil, downplaying US illegalities abroad, etc. One of these chapters gives "major examples of the big lie" toward the SU: "yellow rain," KAL 007, and the attempted assassination of the Pope, all disinformation campaigns by the US government with media compliance.

Many plausible explanations for this US/SU conflict have been developed: that both sides suffer from what Freud labeled the repetition compulsion--intensifying a course of action which only enhances the danger; that both are as untrustworthy as each perceives the other to be, each a mirror-image of the other, in self-fulfilling prophecy. A recent work on the psychology of bigotry and hatred, Keen's Faces of the Enemy, offers a Jungian explanation. Herbert Altschull in Agents of Power observes that the conflict "between Us and Them is driven into the belief sys-

tem of journalists as thoroughly as it is into that of their
fellow citizens. It is part of their ideology." But he also
recognizes that some journalists and citizens manage "to free
themselves of their ideological straitjackets and go beyond the
conflictual norms that dominate their culture" (ix). The contributors to this bibliography are among those who have managed
to do so.

Arrangement

This section differs organizationally from the other cate-
gorically arranged sections. I did at first select the anticommunist and anti-Soviet readings according to the familiar and
complementary culturalizing methods of absence of information and
alternative views, direct inculcation (propaganda), and repression (censorship, blacklisting). Public ignorance about the SU,
Marxism, and Marx is well documented, as is its utility in maintaining fear and hostility. As Robin Wood observes, a chief
means of suppression in the US is the baseless assumption that
"Marxism is either identical with, or inevitably results in,
Stalinism," or what Cragan refers to as the rhetoric of "red
fascism," the myth that all Soviet leaders replicate Hitler.
Ignorance enables indoctrination and repression. The nation's
long campaign of vilification of the USSR beginning in 1919 and
its resort to direct police intervention (destruction of US
socialist parties and radical groups, global intervention) to
counter communism and the SU are equally well researched.
Eventually, however, I chose a historical arrangement to lead
off the book, for the temporal context, but the three kinds of
culturalizing control--reduction of alternatives, propaganda, and
police action--connect the chronological events here and throughout the seven parts. This history is essential to the credibility of Stephen Cohen's distinction in Sovieticus between "the
real but manageable Soviet threat to our national security and
international interests" and the increasingly more serious problem of "`Sovietphobia', or exaggerated fear" of that threat (see
Schilling's critique).
The first two sub-sections offer a minute selection of writings on the over-all history and pre-World War II anticommunism
and anti-USSR. Knowledge of the long enmity felt against the SU,
except during the brief years of World War II, is essential to
understanding how deeply entrenched are the methods of control.
Most of the selections are to be found in the third sub-section,
which traces the Cold War and McCarthyite years from 1945 to
1980. The final sub-section brings the history up to 1985.

Works Cited

Keen, Sam. Faces of the Enemy: The Psychology of Enmity.
San Francisco: Harper, 1986.
Schilling, David. "The Peace Movement: Who We Are, What We
Can Do." C&C 46.4 (1986) 85-87.

I. ANTICOMMUNISM AND ANTI-SOVIETISM 1-413

I. A. General History, 1873-Present 1-10

1.   Anatomy of Anti-Communism. New York: Hill,
    1969. 138.
    "Anti-Communism, in one form or another, has been tried,
and tried, and tried--and has failed. The ultimate penalty of
doctrinaire anti-communism is our own destruction--along with
that of the Communists." One chapter examines the destructive
consequences of anticommunism to the US, including press and
mass media cover up of the excesses or mistakes of the
government in the name of national security, the weakening of
Congressional and public restraints on the Presidency, growing
militarism, and the decline of individual liberties.

2.   Auerbach, Jerold S. "Pursuit of Liberty." Prog 43.4
    (1979) 54-5.
    The narrow consensus and limits of political toleration are
largely the result of repression, which has undermined socialism
and other forms of left dissent since the earliest days of
industrial corporate capitalism.

3.   Avrich, Paul. The Haymarket Tragedy. Princeton,
    NJ: Princeton UP, 1984. 535.
    An account of the first "Red Scare" episode in American
history (1886), in which four anarchists were hanged for a
bombing in spite of the prosecution's failure to produce hard
evidence. Behind this miscarriage of justice was a widespread
and intense fear of foreigners and foreign "radical" ideas.

4.   DeSantis, Hugh. The Diplomacy of Silence: The
    American Foreign Service, the Soviet Union, and the Cold
    War, 1933-1947. Chicago: Chicago UP, 1979. 270.
    The diplomats' "cultural values and beliefs" and other
factors "blurred their memory of interwar Eastern Europe and
narrowed their vision of Soviet objectives, which . . . were not
globalistic, as American diplomats believed, at least for the
immediate postwar period, but rather cautious and limited in
both strategy and tactics" (Introduction).

5.   Fleming, D. F. The Cold War and Its Origins, 1917
    -1960. 2 vols. New York: Doubleday, 1961. 1,158.
    Vol. I: Part I, "Enemies and Allies, 1917-1945," Part II,
"The Cold War in Europe, 1945-1950;" Vol. II: Part III, "The
Cold War in East Asia, 1945-1955," Part IV, "The Second Cold
War, 1955-1959." In his final chapter, the author gives ten
reasons "Why the West Lost the Cold War." 1. "We refused to
accept the consequences of World War II." 2. "We relied on our
atomic monopoly and discounted Soviet science and industry far
too heavily." 3. "We equated Stalin with Hitler." 4. "We
equated communism with fascism." 5. "We disregarded the power
of education and evolution in the communist lands." 6. "We
embraced negativism in defeating other peoples' purposes"

4

(counter-revolution). 7. "We copied some of the worst features of our rival's system" (silencing dissenters, etc.). 8. "We overcompensated for our isolationist fiasco." 9. "We did not know that cold wars cannot be won." 10. "Our attempts to encircle and confine the Red giants helped to generate the power we feared."

6.   Foner, Philip S. "Anti-Communism in US Labor History." The United States Educational System: Marxist Approaches. Ed. Marvin J. Berlowitz and Frank E. Chapman, Jr. Studies in Marxism 6. Minneapolis: Marxist Educational P, 1980. 201-211.
A Cold War point of view toward the Communist Party and the American labor movement "still prevails."

7.   Fontaine, Andre. History of the Cold War, from the October Revolution to the Korean War, 1917-1950. D. D. Paige, trans. New York: Pantheon, 1968. 432.
"However one views both sides, it would be ridiculous to reduce the Cold War to a struggle between Good and Evil. Like all of humanity's great conflicts, it has given rise to the highest sacrifices and the basest crimes. Had they been born elsewhere, the heroes of one camp could often have been the heroes of the other. . . .Just as there would have been no 1789 if the leaders of the Ancien Regime had not betrayed their trust, there would have been no 1917 or any Cold War if capitalist society had discovered social justice before it was forced to--in too few places--by pressure from the masses. . . . Each side has fallen into the habit of seeing the adversary as an outlaw against whom no holds were barred. . . .If, in fact, there is a lesson to be drawn from this history, it is above all one of modesty. Neither so-called scientific socialism nor so-called liberal capitalism furnishes a ready-made solution to the problems of our poor world" (Introduction).

8.   Goldstein, Robert. Political Repression in Modern America From 1870 to the Present. Cambridge, MA: Schenkman, 1978. 682.
"The purpose of this study is to demonstrate that political repression . . . has frequently interfered with the free market of ideas in modern American history. . . .The holders of certain ideas in the United States have been systematically and gravely discriminated against and subjected to extraordinary treatment by governmental authorities, such as physical assaults, denials of freedom of speech and assembly, political deportation and firings, dubious and discriminatory arrests, intense police surveillance, and illegal burglaries, wiretaps and interception of mail." The repression has destroyed radical labor and political movements and imposed widespread self-censorship upon the American people, so that "the spectrum of what might be termed "'acceptable' political opinion in the United States, especially with regard to radical labor or explicitly socialist ideologies, is and has been narrower than that of perhaps any other industrialized democracy" (Introduction). Much on

5

Sovietphobia: Ch. 2, "The Development of Repressive Techniques, 1873-1900" (entirely about "red scares"), Ch. 5, "The Great Red Scare of 1919-1920," "The Abortive Red Scare of 1934-1935" (213-16), Ch. 9, "Truman-McCarthyism, 1946-1954)," and Ch. 11 on the Vietnam War era.

9.   Kahn, Albert. High Treason: The Plot Against the
        People. New York: Lear, 1950. 372.
        "This book deals with treason against the American people" by the "privileged minority" who attain power at "the expense and suffering of the great majority"--by oppression, exploitation, despoilment, impoverishment, fraudulent propaganda, and the making of wars. Book 1 gives an account of the illegal and unconstitutional actions of the government during the fabricated "Red Scare" of 1919-20, Book 2 the 1920s, Book 3 the struggles between President Roosevelt and business interests, and Book 4 deals with the post-WWII anticommunist period: suppression of ideas, loyalty oaths, witchhunts, and fear.

10.   Lens, Sidney. The Futile Crusade: Anti-Communism as
        American Credo. Chicago: Quadrangle, 1964. 256.
        "By the 1960's, an entire generation of Americans has been born into the belligerency of Anti-Communism. . . . Anti-Communism today is no longer a stance, but a credo" (13 & 18). A world-wide history and survey of US belligerence and its destructive consequences. Chs. on the history of the national phobia, an analysis of its chief elements, its manifestations abroad, its effects upon the Soviet Union, etc. "Fear of communism has persisted in American life with varying intensity ever since the Russian Revolution a half century ago".

I. B. Post-World War I 11-17

11.   Kriesberg, Martin. "Soviet News in the New York
        Times." POQ 10 (1946) 540-64.
        Covers the period from 1914 through May 1946. "The Times' reporting, found partisan during the early Soviet years, proved markedly more objective in later periods although evidence is found that a relapse occurred after V-E Day."

12.   Levin, Murray B. Political Hysteria in America: The
        Democratic Capacity for Repression. New York: Basic,
        1971. 312.
        Political hysteria is "a technique used by elites to manage social tension and maintain the system that provides them with power." This study of "the underlying forces that can produce hysteria and the repression it breeds" uses the Red Scare of 1919-1920 as illustration: a "Bolshevik conspiracy in America, which, in fact, did not exist."

13.   Lippmann, Walter, and Charles Merz. "A Test of the
        News." NR 23.296 (August 4, 1920) (supplement) 1-42.
        This study of over 1000 issues of The New York Times

coverage of the SU found mainly rumor, bias, falsehood, and wishful thinking. "On every essential question the net effect of the news was almost invariably misleading."

14.   Mitchell, David. 1919: Red Mirage. New York: Macmillian, 1970. 385.
    Ch. 6, sects. 1-2, treat the crushing of socialist and union organizations by corporations and the government.

15.   Murray, Robert. Red Scare: A Study of National Hysteria, 1919-1920. New York: McGraw, 1955. 337.
    During WWI a business and government sponsored "Americanism" campaign widely supported by the press, and sedition and espionage legislation, taught intolerance and hatred. In this atmosphere, along with certain economic and social conditions, the Great Red Scare occurred.

16.   Post, Louis F. The Deportations Delirium of 1920: A _ Personal Narrative of an Historic Official Experience. New York: DaCapo, 1970. 338. Orig. pub. Chicago: Kerr, 1923.
    An expose of the Department of Justice's campaign to imprison thousands of innocent people and to deport hundreds under the false claim that they were part of a Communist plot to overthrow the government. By the former Assist. Sect. of Labor, 1913-1921.

17.   To the American People-Report Upon the Illegal Practices of the United States Department of Justice. May, 1920. 63.
    A protest against the unconstitutional Palmer raids by distinguished jurists, professors of law, and practicing lawyers. The Justice Department created and disseminated false claims of a "Red plot" against the government and then systematically broke laws in suppressing the non-existent plot.

I. C. Post-World War II   18-273
I. C. 1. Cold War   18-68

18.   Alperovitz, Gar. Atomic Diplomacy: Hiroshima and Potsdam, The Use of the Atomic Bomb and the American Confrontation with Soviet Power. New York: Simon, 1965. 317. Rpt. Penguin, 1985. 426.
    "It is often believed that American policy followed a conciliatory course, changing--in reaction to Soviet intransigence--only in 1947 with the Truman Doctrine and the Marshall Plan." But "it is now evident that, far from following his predecessor's policy of cooperation, shortly after taking office Truman launched a powerful foreign policy initiative aimed at reducing or eliminating Soviet influence from Europe," using the atomic bomb "in the formulation" of that policy. The reissue contains a new introduction adducing new evidence from recently released diaries of Truman, Eisenhower, and others showing that the primary reason for bombing Hiroshima and

7

Nagasaki was not to end the war in Japan, but "to make the Russians more manageable."

19.   Altschull, J. Herbert. "Kruschev and the Berlin
            'Ultimatum'; The Jackal Syndrome and the Cold War."
         JQ 54.3 (1977) 545-51, 565.
    Historians (jackals) followed the media and the goverment
(lions) in heightening a hint in Kruschev's note on Berlin of
Nov. 27, 1958, into a threat and a crisis. Yet the note was a
"masterpiece" of "diplomatic innuendo," a proposal, not a
demand.

20.   Baker, Dorothy G. "Truman's Decision." BAS 42.1
         (1986) 56-57.
    Dropping the bombs on Hiroshima and Nagasaki was not
favored "by most of Truman's advisors." But President Truman
ordered the bombs to get "Japan to surrender to America rather
than to the Soviet Union."

21.   Bass, Cyrus. "Politics from a Different Position."
         Na 242.11 (1986) 420-21.
    The first major act of post-WWII hostility toward the
Russians was our secrecy with the atomic bomb at Potsdam (July,
1945); the second was the Marshall Plan, which excluded Eastern
Europe.

22.   Bernstein, Barton J. "Onus for the Cold War." Prog
         41.10 (1977) 54-55.
    The US is more responsible for the Cold War than the SU,
because Truman relied on the wrong assumptions (the "Riga
axioms") and the wrong advisors.

23.   Bernstein, Barton J., ed. Politics and Policies of
         the Truman Administration. Chicago: Quadrangle, 1970.
         330.
    Seven essays. In "American Foreign Policy and the Origins
of the Cold War," the editor argues that American leaders, by
seeking to reshape much of the world according to American needs
and standards, "contributed significantly to the origins of the
Cold War." Athan Theoharis in "The Rhetoric of Politics"
describes how Truman administration propaganda claimed American
innocence and omnipotence, with destructive consequences. The
same author in "The Escalation of the Loyalty Program" "charts
the administration's erosion of civil liberties."

24.   Bernstein, Barton J. "Truman at the Helm." Prog
         42.7 (1978) 41-43.
    A rev. of Robert Donovan's Conflict and Crisis. "The
Truman Administration significantly shaped the Cold War
consensus . . . and comfortably exploited anti-Soviet
sentiment."

25.   Bottome, Edgar. The Balance of Terror: Nuclear
         Weapons and the Illusion of Security, 1945-1985. Rev.

Boston: Beacon, 1986. 291.
An updated version of <u>The Balance of Terror: A Guide to the
Arms Race</u> (1971). Examines "the development of the balance of
terror and the concurrent arms race between the United States
and the Soviet Union. . . .Since 1945 US policy has never
deviated from its support of the status quo in all noncommunist
and nonsocialist countries. This policy is designed to maintain
control over the allocation of world-wide resources and
available labor and to ensure US access to market and investment
areas. No alternative forms of government could be allowed to
replace existing friendly governments, since successful
alternatives could demonstrate that there were different paths
to national economic development from those approved by the
United States."

26.   Brown, Pamela A. "Constructing the Cultural Curtain:
         The Meaning of Cold War in York, Pennsylvania Daily
         Newspapers, 1947-1962." Diss. U of Iowa, 1983.
These two newspapers, one liberal the other conservative,
shared the basic definition and "mission" of the US in
"obsessively measuring itself against its avowed enemy." Both
"helped to construct the American version of an iron curtain
designating common understandings of what was and was not
important and appropriate to U.S. life under Cold War."

27.   "Carter's Phoney Neutrality." <u>Inq</u> 2.8 (1979) 2-3.
The US plays the game of condemning acts that the SU
carries out but approves of the same acts by China.

28.   Chomsky, Noam. <u>Towards a New Cold War: Essays on the
         Current Crisis and How We Got There</u>. New York: Pantheon,
         1982. 498.
Thirteen essays written from 1973 through 1981 on diverse
topics make the basic argument that the Soviet threat against
the US is exaggerated to conceal the desire by those in power to
maintain hegemony in the world and to control public opinion in
the US for that expansionist policy. "Those who have a dominant
position in the domestic economy command substantial means to
influence public opinion. It would be surprising indeed if this
power were not reflected in the mass media--themselves major
corporations--and the schools and universities; if it did not,
in short, shape the prevailing ideology to a considerable
extent."

29.   Chomsky, Noam and Fred Halliday. "The New Cold War's
         Meaning." <u>ITT</u> 9.39 (1985) 16-17, 22.
An edited transcript of a radio debate between these two
critics of the arms race. Chomsky explains the Cold War as the
result of the US post-WWII desire to exploit the world
economically, but found the SU an impediment to its plans. The
Soviet threat was then used to justify the militarization of the
US in order to defend the expansion, on an endless cycle.

30.   Cohen, Stephen. <u>Rethinking the Soviet Experience</u>.

New York: Oxford UP, 1985. 235.
The Cold War shaped the academic study of the Soviet Union
in wrong and fundamentally ahistorical ways, particularly by
viewing history of the SU through the Stalinist context, when
there were and are alternatives.

31.   Cragan, John. "The Cold War Rhetorical Vision, 1946
        -1972." U of Minnesota. Diss, 1972. 210. DAI 33 (1973)
        5865-A.
A study of the "Red Fascist" perception embedded in popular
fantasies which contributed to the creation of "a very pervasive
and monolithic Cold War rhetorical vision."

32.   Draper, Theodore. "Contaminated News of the Dominican
        Republic." Mass Media and Mass Man. Ed. Alan Casty.
        New York: Holt, 1968. 212-214.
Details about the lies our ambassador to the Dominican
Republic and President Lyndon Johnson told reporters and the
American people to whitewash the US illegal invasion of that
country in 1965 in order to install its choice as head of the
government.

33.   Eisenberg, Carolyn. "New Left Writers and the Nuclear
        Arms Race." RHR 33 (1985) 61-90.
An assessment of "the two major theoretical positions
proposed by left writers" to explain the nuclear arms race --
imperialist and internalist -- and a proposal of "an alternative
methodology" for "resolving interpretive difficulties." Richard
Barnet and E. P. Thompson illustrate the "internalist
formulation" of a self-reproducing, military-industrial
bureaucracy which exaggerates the Soviet threat to justify
constant expansion of the system. Noam Chomsky represents the
"imperialist formulation," the US seeking to dominate the world
for overseas markets, outlets for investment, and profits, and
using the Soviet threat and its own nuclear arsenal to control
people and nations in its sphere of hegemony.

34.   Etzioni, Amitai. "Anatomy of an Incident." CJR 3.2
        (1964) 27-30.
The press reacted to the downing of a US plane over East
Germany in a hostile Cold War spirit even though the State Dept.
declared the pilot to blame and not Moscow.

35.   Franck, Thomas, and Edward Weisband. Word Politics:
        Verbal Strategy Among the Superpowers. New York: Oxford
        UP, 1972. 176.
"Our method is to compare the concepts which United States
strategists developed vis-a-vis Guatemala, Cuba, and the
Dominican Republic with those Soviet leaders developed vis-a-vis
Hungary and Czechoslovakia. . . .We show that the ways we chose
to conceptualize our national and regional rights and privileges
in the Western Hemisphere are precisely indistinguishable from
those most recently given prominence by the Soviet Union in the
Brezhnev Doctrine. We show that Russia and its Warsaw Pact

10

'family' were able to provide logically and legally impeccable
cover for the brutalization of Czechoslovakia without stepping
one word or phrase beyond the conceptual parameters the United
States and, at our urging, the Organization of American States
had devised, expressed, and put into practice between 1953 and
1965" (Preface).

36.   Gardner, Lloyd C. Architects of Illusion: Men and
         Ideas in American Foreign Policy, 1941-1949. Chicago:
         Quadrangle, 1970. 365.
     At the end of WWII, "none" of the "architects of American
policy" "wanted communist doctrine to spread--even into Eastern
Europe. When it did, or seemed to be doing so, most American
leaders assumed it was a question of ideological warfare, not
Russian national interests. . . .The book is premised on the
assumption that the United States was more responsible for the
way in which the Cold War developed" (Preface). "At the end of
the war it had much greater opportunity and far more options to
influence the course of events than the Soviet Union, whose
situation in victory was worse in some ways that that of the
defeated countries." But US policy quickly became inflexibly
anti-Soviet (317).

37.   Gaut, Greg. "Revisionist History Breaks Through Cold
         War Biases." ITT 9.36 (1985) 13.
     A rev. of Rethinking the Soviet Experience: Politics and
History Since 1917 by Stephen Cohen, and The Making of the
Soviet System: Essays in the Social History of Interwar Russia
by Moshe Lewin, both of which challenge the "totalitarian" Cold
War school of historians.

38.   Gould, Christopher, and James R. Bennett. "A
         Comparison of Press Coverage of Communist and Pro-Western
         Dictatorships." FSN 6 (June, 1980) 3-11.
     A study of the presentation of the Cold War in American
newspapers in 1979. The press consistently downplayed
totalitarian excesses by governments allied to the US, while
foregrounding communist wrongs often in a mood of rancor.

39.   Grosscup, Beau. "Kissinger's Africa Policy: What
         Else Is New?" Prog 40.10 (1976) 41-43.
     "The goal (of American strategy) is still to maintain
Africa as a Western capitalist preserve and keep socialist
influence out of the continent, or at least hold it to a
minimum."

40.   Hall, Francoise. "The United States' Search for
         Security: A Psychotherapist's Viewpoint." JPR 20.4
         (1983) 299-309.
     The US pursues ever more efficient violent means of
"defense" despite the increasing risk of self-destruction
possibly because its leaders do not understand that the real
threat is ecological and not the USSR. But global problems are
difficult to understand, while the SU is "a more manageable

11

target."

41.   Halliday, Fred. <u>The Making of the Second Cold War</u>.
       London: Verso; New York: Schocken, 1983. 280.
       "If the First Cold War was clearly anti-communist, this
Second Cold War was more specifically directed against the USSR"
(20). A history of the "Second" Cold War during the 1970s and
early 1980s.

42.   Helmreich, Jonathan. <u>Gathering Rare Ores: The
       Diplomacy of Uranium Acquisition, 1943-1954</u>. Princeton,
       NJ: Princeton UP, 1986. 312.
       The US and the UK attempted to monopolize the West's supply
of uranium and thorium during and immediately following WWII.
The campaign was conducted in great secrecy by soldiers and
businessmen during which representative bodies were only
partially informed. The efforts furthered the Cold War.

43.   Herken, Gregg. <u>The Winning Weapon: The Atomic Bomb
       in the Cold War, 1945-1950</u>. New York: Knopf, 1980. 425.
       A negative assessment of US secrecy and military security
doctrine concerning the bomb after WWII. The policy of secrecy
and monopoly undermined the option of international control of
the bomb and resulted in the victory of conservative forces over
atomic energy.

44.   Horowitz, David. <u>The Free World Colossus: A Critique
       of American Foreign Policy in the Cold War</u>. New York:
       Hill, 1965. 451.
       "America's cold war program" cannot be explained "as an
attempt to contain a Soviet expansionary threat. The evidence
for the existence of this threat has never been impressive."
The real containment was "containment of Communist revolution
(or election) rather than Russian expansion. . . .American cold
war policy had, in fact, a counter-revolutionary rather than a
counter-expansionary character," the "rhetoric of opposition to
aggression" a "mere cover for containing internal change" world
wide (411-413). "In 1964, as in 1947, America was . . . the
leader of a world-wide anti-revolutionary movement in defense of
vested interests. . . .When America set out on her post-war path
to contain revolution throughout the world, and threw her
immense power and influence into the balance against the rising
movement for social justice among the poverty stricken two-
thirds of the world's population, the first victims of her deed
were the very ideals for a better world--liberty, equality and
self-determination--which she herself, in her infancy, had done
so much to foster" (434).

45.   Kennan, George. <u>The Nuclear Delusion: Soviet-American
       Relations in the Atomic Age</u>. New York: Pantheon, 1982.
       208.
       A collection of Kennan's essays "written over the course of
some thirty years," organized in three topics: "The Nuclear
Problem in Its Infancy," "East-West Relations Under the Shadow

of the Nuclear Bomb," and "The Nuclear Age in Crisis." He makes a case for nuclear disarmament generally by the argument that the arms race was never based on a realistic assessment of the Soviet Union.

46.   Jones, J. Harry, Jr. The Minutemen. Garden City, NY: Doubleday, 1968. 426.
An account of the rise of an anticommunist organization calling themselves the "Minutemen" and arming against invasion by the Russians or Chinese or against an internal, treasonous takeover by a "Communist-Socialist" conspiracy. The author treats them not as different in kind from other anticommunist people but only different in degree, since, for example, the Republican party voted at its national convention in 1964 against condemning the John Birch Society.

47.   Kuklick, Bruce. "Tradition and Diplomatic Talent: The Case of the Cold Warriors." Recycling the Past: Popular Uses of American History. Ed. Leila Zenderland. Philadelphia: U Pennsylvania P, 1978. 116-131.
A study of the set of beliefs, key words, and metaphors of US Cold Warriors during the quarter of a century following the end of WWII, to explain their policies of "neo-imperialism, global expansionism, the explosion of military spending, the support of reaction around the world, and the growth of clandestine intelligence agencies."

48.   Lasch, Robert. "War Fever." Prog 44.7 (1980) 14-18.
Detente and "sour memories of Vietnam" have not ended US commitment to the Cold War, a policy based on the potential use of military force abroad which has ceased to be rational.

49.   Lens, Sidney. "What Makes Nitze Run?: The Committee on the Present Danger Pursues a Thirty-Year-Old Dream of Victory." Prog 43.9 (1979) 19-21.
"There is a strategy, developed first in 1950 and still pursued today, which holds that negotiations with the Soviet Union should not be regarded as a means of settling disputes or achieving detente, but as a stepping stone toward 'victory.'"

50.   Lynch, Joe. "Breaking the Habit." Soj 12.9 (1983) 36-38.
Rev. of The Nuclear Delusion: Soviet-American Relations in the Atomic Age (1982) and Beyond the Cold War; A New Approach to the Arms Race and Nuclear Annihilation (1982). Kennan warns that "the ideology of the West blinds it from seeing the Soviets as they really are" (seeking security not expansion). "Thompson calls for a politics whose banner is internationalism and whose task is to mend the divide between the European peoples in the East and West."

51.   McWilliams, Carey. The Education of Carey McWilliams. New York: Simon, 1979. 363.
Most of this book deals with McWilliams' and The Nation's

criticism of the Cold War and McCarthyism and support of civil liberties and the free flow of information uncolored by bigotry or jingoism.

52.   Miliband, Ralph, et al., eds. The Uses of Anti-
         Communism. New York: Monthly, 1985. 372.
     An analysis of the deep-seated anticommunism in the US and the West and the factors which have nourished it. Some topics: the ideological and intellectual origins of the Cold War, the relationship between anticommunism and the Catholic church, the ideological nature of current US policy in Central America, American intervention in Greece, anticommunism in the Korean War, Washington's alliance with Guatemalan death squads.

53.   Mills, C. Wright. The Causes of World War Three. New
         York: Simon, 1958. 172.
     Behind the lethal US policy of threatening nuclear war is the equally dangerous and absurd belief that eventually the Soviets will submit to Washington's ultimatums. "The doctrine of violence, and the inept opportunism based upon it, are substitutes for political and economic programs. That doctrine has been and is the fundamental basis of U. S. policy. And U. S. policy is now bankrupt."

54.   Perkovich, George. "Beyond the Cold War: Can
         America Shed 70 Years of Anti-Sovietism?" NT 5.3
         (1987) 12-20, 41.
     A survey of the destructive power of ignorance and intolerance of the USSR not merely in right wing groups but in the news media, the entertainment industry, scholarly specialists, politicians and policymakers, the public at large, and even in the peace movement. The author urges the leaders of the peace movement to tackle Sovietphobia head-on as the only way to end the arms race.

55.   Pruessen, Ronald W. "Revisionism 2." RHR 33 (1985)
         155-164.
     A review of five books that locate the rise of the Cold War partly or mainly in the aggressive US search for economic and political advantages: Cook, The Declassified Eisenhower; Kaufman, Eisenhower's Foreign Economic Policy; Immerman, The CIA in Guatemala; Schlesinger and Kinzer, The Untold Story of the American Coup in Guatemala; Wittner, American Intervention in Greece.

56.   Raskin, Marcus. The Politics of National Security.
         New York: Transaction, 1979. 211.
     After WWII American ruling elites created a national security apparatus to ensure national stability, to mute class conflicts, and to secure the domestic economy. This state then became the basis around the world for covert and overt imperialism.

57.   Sartre, Jean-paul. "The Chances of Peace." Na 171.27

(1950) 696-700.
A critique of US anti-Soviet policies -- its "Manicheism," its threats of using the atomic bomb, etc. The US is dangerously "obsessed by fear of communism."

58.   Sayre, Nora. Running Time: Films of the Cold War.
       New York: Dial, 1982. 243.
A selective survey of anticommunist and anti-Soviet films of the 1950s and Eisenhower years, "a time when Ferdinand the Bull was denounced as left-wing propaganda because the bull refused to fight the matador, when those who failed to embrace the status quo were often called unhealthy . . . when anxieties about fallout near an atomic testing site in Nevada were dismissed by a local senator as 'Communist-inspired scare stories' even after small children began to die of leukemia, when everything evil was somehow imported from Moscow" (29).

59.   Schuman, Frederick. The Cold War: Retrospect and
       Prospect. Baton Rouge: Louisiana State UP, 1967. 134.
By the mid 1960s, "power had passed in the USA to spokesmen of the 'military-industrial complex,'" and "most of these policy-makers, with the support of most patriots, were committed to seeking safety by armed violence."

60.   "Soviet Geopolitical Momentum: Myth or Menace?
       Trends of Soviet Influence Around the World from 1945 to
       1986." DM 15.5 (1986). 32.
The SU is not nor ever has been the threat US leaders and fearmongers have claimed. It had "significant influence" in 15% of the world's nations at its peak of world power in "the late 1950s," "dropping back to 11% today." "With the exception of Eastern Europe and Mongolia," the SU "has been unable to sustain influence in foreign countries over long periods of time."

61.   Stern, Laurence. The Wrong Horse: The Politics of
       Intervention and the Failure of American Diplomacy.
       New York: Times, 1978. 170.
US anti-Soviet/anticommunist policy in the eastern Mediterranean was misguided because Greece, Turkey, and Cyprus were never likely to go Communist, the area dominated by local and nationalist issues, not the threat of the SU.

62.   Stiglin, Peter. "Apocalyptic Theology and the Right."
       Wit 69.10 (1986) 6-9.
The forty years of post-WWII US Sovietphobia include a hardening "holy war" against the godless Communists by Evangelical fundamentalists preaching the imminent second coming of Christ and the destruction of the forces of evil in the world by US nuclear bombs.

63.   Toynbee, Arnold. "Supersam." Ram 4.8 (1965) 42-48.
       Toynbee examines American attitudes toward Communism.
"Sooner or later, the United States will have to recognize that Russia and China are her equals."

64.   "Warmongering: Council on Foreign Relations." CS 5.4
         (1981) 25-27.
     A review of The Soviet Challenge: A Policy Framework for
the 1980s, pub. by the CFR and paid for by the Ford
Foundation. The study is "a call to war and unrestrained
intervention wherever US private economic or strategic interests
are threatened."

65.   Weisskopf, Victor F. "The Task for a New Peace
         Movement." BAS 43.1 (1987) 26-32.
     "The public must recognize that there are no good reasons
for the United States and the Soviet Union to be enemies: no
territorial conflicts, and no significant economic conflicts."

66.   Welch, Richard, Jr. Response to Revolution: The
         United States and the Cuban Revolution, 1959-1961.
         Chapel Hill, NC: U of North Carolina P, 1985. 244.
     US response to Cuba was a mirror of our Cold War
assumptions and frustrations and of our apprehensions about
revolutionary movements abroad. Four sections: Castro's
revolution, responses of the Eisenhower and Kennedy
administrations, US public opinion, and the larger context of
the Cold War.

67.   Williams, William A. The Tragedy of American
         Diplomacy. 2nd ed. New York: Delta, 1972. 312.
     A critique of US economic and military global expansion and
its "myopic" anti-Sovietism. The US should above all commit
itself to an "open door for revolutions," if the tragedy of the
cold war is to be transcended.

68.   Wittner, Lawrence S. American Intervention in
         Greece, 1943-1949. New York: Columbia UP, 1982. 445.
     "America's dealings with wartime and postwar Greece are not
very pretty" for they were laced with "official lying, cynicism,
and cruelty." The US "is not unique in villainy" but "the
nastiness of numerous 'great powers' in world affairs--their
wars, their secret police, and their bullying of smaller
nations" is no justification "for tidying up this nation's
record in accordance with patriotic norms" (xi).

I. C. 2. Repression, Disinformation, and Conformity 69-252

69.   Adamic, Louis. "Confessions Of A 33d-Degree
         Subversive." Na 174.26 (1952) 637-638.
     A defense of subversiveness, in contrast to the uniformity
and "loyalty" as defined by the Un-American Activites Committee.

70.   Andrews, Bert. Washington Witch Hunt. New York:
         Random, 1948. 218.
     A reporter documents federal repression related to the "red
scare" after WWII. "The threat to civil liberties, as America
has known them, is as serious at this moment as it has ever been

in history," because of anticommunist hysteria.

71.   Aptheker, Herbert. The Era of McCarthyism. 2nd ed.
         New York: Marzani, 1962. 288. (Orig. History and
         Reality, 1955.)
     A selection of the author's essays published between 1948
and 1955. The essays especially focus upon conformity in the US
and the government's efforts to produce a country of certified-
one-hundred-percent-pure Americans purified against socialist
and Marxist ideas.

72.   Aronson, James. The Press and the Cold War.
         Indianapolis: Bobbs, 1970. 308.
     A double argument for an activist interpretation of the
First Amendment and against the self-censorship of the press by
which it has abdicated its duty to censor government, especially
on the issues of communism and the Soviet Union.

73.   Barth, Alan. Government by Investigation. New York:
         Viking, 1955. 231.
     "Congress has, increasingly during the last decade,
ominously during the past five years, used its indispensable
investigating power" in ways "that usurp and corrupt the special
functions of the judicial branch; and, most dangerous of all, it
has used this power in ways that extend the authority of the
government into vital areas of American life traditionally
reserved" for private control. Ch. 8, "Congress and the Fourth
Estate," offers a defense of a press immune from government
censorship.

74.   Barth, Alan. The Loyalty of Free Men. New York:
         Viking, 1951. 253.
     The author describes actions taken by the federal
government and citizens during the "Red Scare." "The principle
purpose of this book has been to show that tolerance of
diversity is now being vitiated in ways dangerous to national
security."

75.   Barton, Laurence. "Coverage of the 1980 Olympic
         Boycott: A Cross-Network Comparison." Television
         Coverage of International Affairs. Ed. William Adams.
         Norwood, NJ: Ablex, 1982. 129-142.
     "The manner in which the White House tested and then
ultimately embraced American public opinion on the boycott
proposal [because of the Soviet invasion of Afganistan] is a
fascinating instance of mobilization and manipulation" (129).

76.   Belfrage, Cedric. The American Inquisition, 1945-
         1960. Indianapolis: Bobbs, 1973. 316.
     Part One explains the background which led to the rise of
McCarthyism. Parts Two through Four give yearly accounts of the
effects of the anticommunist movement, with a plea for Americans
to be more tolerant.

17

77.   Belfrage, Cedric. "On Political Exile." Prog 41.8
        (1977) 20-21.
     An indictment of Section 212(a)(17) of the McCarran-Walter
Act by the former editor of The Nation Guardian, who was
deported in 1955 for invoking the Fifth Amendment before Senator
McCarthy's Subcommittee.

78.   Belfrage, Cedric, and James Aronson. Something to
        Guard: The Stormy Life of the National Guardian
        1948-1967. New York: Columbia UP, 1979. 362.
     This radical newspaper was not only persecuted by the
McCarthy committee, but more or less thrown to the wolves by the
rest of the press, none of whom defended its rights under the
First Amendment.

79.   Belknap, Michal. Cold War Political Justice: The
        Smith Act, the Communist Party, and American Civil
        Liberties. Westport, CT: Greenwood, 1977. 322.
     A history of the suppression of the Communist Party point
of view under the anti-Bill of Rights Smith Act, or Alien
Registration Act of 1940. "The nation paid a high price for the
debilitation of a small radical organization."

80.   Bell, Daniel, ed. The Radical Right. Garden City,
        NY: Doubleday, 1964. 468.
     Several of the fourteen essays discuss the anticommunism
and the anti-Sovietism of the John Birch Society, the
McCarthyites, etc.

81.   Bendiner, Robert. "Communists on Trial." Na 168.5
        (1949) 118-119.
     The 1949 trial of eleven communist leaders is an attempt at
"thought-control" based upon the questionably constitutional
Smith Act.

82.   Bentley, Eric, ed. Thirty Years of Treason: Excerpts
        from Hearings Before the House Committee on Un-American
        Activities, 1938-1968. New York: Viking, 1971. 991.
     A selection from what would be several dozen volumes like
this one to suggest the human fullness of the efforts of the
Committee to extirpate communism from the US.

83.   Bernstein, Barton J. "The Oppenheimer Conspiracy."
        ORK (Fall-Winter 1984-85) 9-13.
     FBI director J. Edgar Hoover and Admiral Lewis Strauss
conspired to end J. Robert Oppenheimer's influence because of
his communist associations.

84.   Biddle, Francis. The Fear of Freedom: A Discussion of
        the Contemporary Obsession of Anxiety and Fear in the
        United States, Its Historical Background and Present
        Expression, and Its Effect on National Security and on
        Free American Institutions. Garden City, NY: Doubleday,
        1951. 263.

Anticommunistic behavior shows how Americans "discard our freedoms, substituting sedition laws and investigations and loyalty tests and loyalty oaths for the give-and-take of uncontrolled thought." The author urges an end to the hysteria by "holding tight to our freedoms, insisting on fair play, and keeping unblocked the open roads of the mind."

85.   Birnbaum, Jon. "Classroom Struggle." PE 1.4 (1978) 22-23.
Examples are given of qualified professors who were denied appointment or tenure by university governing boards for their Marxist beliefs.

86.   Biskind, Peter. "The Way They Were." JC 1 (1974) 24-28.
A review of three books on the Cold War and blacklisting in Hollywood: Cogley, Report on Blacklisting, Bentley, Thirty Years of Treason, and Kanfer, A Journal of the Plague Years.

87.   Blair, William. "U. S. Court Rules Socialist Group Was Target of F.B.I. Harassment." NYT (August 26, 1986) 16.
A federal judge awarded $264,000 to the Socialist Workers Party because from 1958 to 1976 the FBI "violated the party's First Amendment rights of free speech and assembly" and its "Fourth Amendment protections against unreasonable searches and seizures."

88.   Bontecou, Eleanor. The Federal Loyalty-Security Program. Ithaca: Cornell UP, 1953. 377.
Criticism of the government's program to examine the "loyalty" of actual and prospective federal employees.

89.   Bordewich, Fergus M. "The Press Harmonizes On A Presidential Theme." CJR 16.4 (1977) 36-37.
Press concentration on the subject of dissidents in the Soviet Union during 1977 matched and mirrored President Carter's anti-Soviet campaign, and grossly distorted the reality of the USSR as a whole.

90.   Boyer, Paul. By the Bomb's Early Light: American Thought and Culture at the Dawn of the Atomic Age. New York: Pantheon, 1985. 441.
An assessment of "the bomb's effects on American culture and consciousness" and the lack of attention to its "pervasive impact" from 1945 through 1950. The bomb's "corrosive impact on the externals of life pales in comparison to its effect on the interior realm of consciousness and memory." The author was "struck" at "how uncannily familiar much of the early response to the bomb seems: the visions of atomic devastation, the earnest efforts to rouse people to resist such a fate, the voices seeking to soothe or deflect these fears, the insistence that security lay in greater technical expertise and in more and bigger weaponry." Chs. on the atomic scientists, utopian

19

fantasies, atomic energy, the morality of the bomb, the Cold War, etc.

91.   Brown, Ralph S. Loyalty and Security. New Haven:
         Yale UP, 1958. 524.
     Treats particularly the wrongs done to some of the victims of the federal loyalty-security program.

92.   Brown, Ralph S., Jr. "6,000,000 Second-Class
         Citizens." Na 174.26 (1952) 644-647.
     On destructive consequences of President Truman's Executive Order 9835, the loyalty program for government employees.

93.   Cade, Dozier C. "Witch-Hunting, 1952: The Role of
         the Press." JQ 29 (1952) 396-407.
     "Today, witch-hunters are on the prowl again," it is not safe to express your opinion, and freedom is in danger. Fear of "Russian Communism," "approaching hysteria, is dominating our national life." The author presents seven ways the press can counteract this hysteria and "lead the fight for a free country."

94.   Carleton, Don. Red Scare! Right-Wing Hysteria,
         Fifties Fanaticism, and Their Legacy in Texas. Austin:
         Texas Monthly, 1985. 390.
     A study of "America's second Red Scare" of the 1950s as manifested in Houston, Texas. The "power elite" there wished "to return the Republican party to power in Washington, purge the federal government of its New Deal-Fair Deal inheritance, and keep the Russians, blacks, and labor unions in their respective places. This power elite was willing to Red-bait and print scare stories in the newspapers it controlled to achieve its goals." "Because the public school system represented an intellectual pathway into Houston for the beliefs and ideas of the outside world, these true believers focused much of their attention on it" (Prologue). Ch. 3 contains analysis of media behavior: spreading fear through exposure and thus enforcing conformity.

95.   Carr, Robert K. The House Committee on Un-American
         Activities, 1945-1950. Ithaca, NY: Cornell UP, 1952.
         489.
     "This volume deals with the first six years " of the Un-American Activities Committee of the House of Representatives after it became a permanent agency. Ch. 10, "Press Treatment of the Un-American Activities Investigations" (364-405), generalizes that "the press is not likely to rise above the level" of a Congressional investigation or "to help save the people against the ever-present temptation to search out and persecute nonconformists or heretics." When a society "insists upon hunting witches and doubting its own integrity" its press "will play along with such insistence and doubts and give the people what they seemingly want to read" (405).

96.   Caute, David. <u>The Great Fear: The Anti-Communist</u>
        <u>Purge Under Truman and Eisenhower</u>. New York: Touchstone,
        1978. 697.
        The section headings exhibit the contents of the book: 1,
"The Politics of Hysteria," 2, "The Machinery of Repression," 3,
"The Assault on the Left," 4, "Purge of the Civil Service," 5,
"Pacification of the Working Class," 6, "Purge of the
Professions," 7, "Show Business: the Blacklists." In the summer
of 1954, "the high summer of the great fear," the Emergency
Civil Liberties Committee warned that "'the threat to civil
liberties in the United States today is the most serious in the
history of our country.'" The book is a study of "the most far-
reaching and corrosive (if not the most 'explosive and
violent')" of the "succession of 'red scares'" which have
plagued the country.

97.   Ceplair, Larry, and Steven Englund. <u>The Inquisition</u>
        <u>in Hollywood: Politics in the Film Community, 1930-1960</u>.
        Garden City, NY: Doubleday, 1980. 536.
        A history of the persecution of a small number of movie
people, most of them screenwriters, for their "long-term
membership in the progressive movement."

98.   Chafee, Zachariah, Jr. "The Encroachments on
        Freedom." <u>AM</u> 197 (1956) 39-44.
        The loyalty programs of Truman and Eisenhower have
interfered with the freedom of the citizens in ten areas.

99.   Chambers, John W. "A Journalist's History." <u>CJR</u> 17.4
        (1978) 66-71.
        Review of Theodore H. White's <u>In Search of History: A</u>
<u>Personal Adventure</u> (1978). "He fails to assess the dynamics of
power or ethics involved in Luce's decision deliberately to
misrepresent the news filed from the field. . . .Particularly
poignant is White's victimization by the virulent anti-communism
of the McCarthy era."

100.   Clubb, O. Edmund. <u>The Witness and I</u>. New York:
        Columbia UP, 1975. 314.
        An account by this former State Department official of his
experiences as a victim of the "red scare" of the McCarthy era.
"Given the sweep of the official 'anti-Communism' and the
frenzies of a partially contrived fear for the 'national
security,' there were instituted new procedures for the close
surveillance of government employees; and with the formal
identification of a new, ultimate enemy who might totally
annihilate us before we might obliterate him there was a
progressive militarization of thinking, policies, and processes"
(Preface).

101.   Cobb, Jean. "The Cold War Revisited." <u>CC</u> 11.5 (1985)
        10.
        Criticism of the McCarran-Walter Act (Section 212 of the
Immigration Code) which denies visas to writers, artists, and

political figures because of ideological views or political associations.

102.   Cogley, John. Report on Blacklisting. New York: Fund
         for the Republic, 1956. 312. Rpt. Arno, 1972.
    The first documented and systematic effort to show that the
blacklist existed.

103.   The Cold War Against Labor. Berkeley, CA: Meiklejohn
         Civil Liberties Institute, 1987.
    "A look at how attacks on labor in the 1940s and '50s made
possible the plant closures, the flight of jobs and capital, and
the high permanent employment we face today" (Publisher's
description).

104.   Cole, Lester. Hollywood Red: The Autobiography of
         Lester Cole. Palo Alto: Ramparts, 1981. 440.
    A memoir by one of the "Hollywood Ten" screenwriters and
directors jailed for defying the House Un-American Activities
Committee's attempt to impose an ideological orthodoxy upon the
US.

105.   Collum, Danny. "Anti-Communism." Soj 11.10 (1982)
         19-21.
    "The anticommunist ideology has in effect become our state
religion," and its utility to those in power for the maintenance
of their powers is enormous.

106.   Commager, Henry Steele. "Washington Witch-Hunt." Na
         164.14 (1947) 385-388.
    Witch-hunting in and by organizations.

107.   Cook, Bruce. "The Black Years of Dalton Trumbo." AF
         1.1 (1975) 30-36.
    Trumbo's activities during the 15 years he was blacklisted
from film production as one of the Hollywood Ten convicted for
Contempt of Congress after a hearing with the House Committee on
Un-American Activities.

108.   Cook, Fred J. "On Being an Enemy of the F.B.I."
         Na 242.11 (1986) 426-9.
    After the author wrote a "critical analysis" of the FBI in
1958, that organization launched a campaign to label him a
Communist.

109.   Countryman, Vern. "The Bigots And The Professionals."
         Na 174.26 (1952) 641-643.
    The House Un-American Activities Committee and other bigots
have focused on labor, entertainment, and government. Now
lawyers, ministers, doctors, and newspapermen are their victims.

110.   Cox, Arthur M. The Myths of National Security: The
         Peril of Secret Government. Boston: Beacon, 1975. 231.
    "But democracy and secrecy are incompatible, and it has now

become clear that secret powers should never have been delegated without guarantees of accountability to the people's representatives in the Congress. The peril of inadequate accountability is intensified because the American public is often gullible, especially in matters of national security" and the Soviet Union.

111.   Crane, Sylvia E. "Dawn of A New Day: Requiem for HISC/HUAC." CS 2.3 (1975) 34-40.
A summary essay on the consequences of anticommunism in the US: McCarthyism, Cold War subversion of foreign governments, counterrevolution and intervention abroad, secrecy, a conspiracy mentality, loyalty oaths, obsession with national security, the arms race, illegal wiretapping and bugging. The author calls for increased Congressional oversight to "contain the repressive tendencies."

112.   Davidon, Ann. "They Left the Party." Prog 41.11 (1977) 53-5.
"Among those coming out of the closet and into print these days are a number of former communists -- not in order to denounce communism, as in the 1950s, but to tell us how it was."

113.   Davis, Elmer H. But We Were Born Free. Indianapolis: Bobbs, 1954. 229.
Ch. 1, "Through the Perilous Night" is an attack on McCarthyism and a defense of freedom of thought.

114.   "The Deportation Cases." The Nation 166.11 (1948) 291-292.
Deportation cases are pending against several immigrants who came to America as young children and who became political radicals or Communists years later.

115.   Dixon, Marlene. Things Which Are Done in Secret. Montreal: Black Rose, 1976. 290.
A case study of the ways that radical and Marxist thought have been purged from North American universities.

116.   Dorman, William. "The Media: Playing the Government's Game." BAS 41 (1985) 118-124.
"US journalists are accustomed to accepting the dictates of 'national security' and Washington's view of the world, while remaining unshakably certain of their own objectivity." "In many significant ways . . . the return to peacetimes assumptions and practices did not occur after 1945. Instead, the mass media came to embrace the nuclear confrontation's fundamental assumption that the United States now faced a permanent, ruthless, and intractable enemy. Given such a presupposition, not surprisingly, the mainstream news media . . . have performed during the Cold War as they always have during the hot ones."

117.   Duncan, Donald. "The Whole Thing Was a Lie." Ram 4.10 (1966) 13-24.

Special forces master sergeant Donald Duncan explains his militant anticommunism as "due in part to my being Roman Catholic, in part to the stories in the news media about communism, and in part to the fact that my stepfather was born in Budapest, Hungary."

118.   Durr, Clifford J. "How To Measure Loyalty." Na
         168.17 (1949) 470-473.
"In the name of our 'democratic process,' certain men are empowered, in secret hearings, to render judgment against others, depriving them of their jobs, their reputations . . . without even giving the reason for their actions."

119.   Eggleston, Arthur. "Labor And Civil Liberties."
         Na 174.26 (1952) 647-650.
The witch-hunt against organized labor endangers the civil liberties of all citizens.

120.   Engel, Leonard. "Warning All Scientists." Na 165.5
         (1947) 117-19.
Commerce Secretary Henry Wallace's appointees are the victims of red-baiting.

121.   Evans, Frank. "The Meaning of Liberty." Na
         167.10 (1948) 255-257.
"The present Supreme Court is dodging the responsibility of facing and deciding the Constitutional issues" involved in the House Committee on Un-American Activities, the black-listing of left pressure groups, and the persecution of Communist Party members and fellow travelers.

122.   Faulk, John. Fear on Trial. New York: Simon, 1964.
         308.
The personal account by a former CBS commentator of being blacklisted for six years during the late 1950s and early 1960s following pro-communist allegations by a right-wing group. He sued for libel and eventually won. "To me, the most sinister aspect of that whole period was the systematic way respectable educators, ministers, artists, writers, librarians--Americans from every walk of life--were hauled in by some committee or publicly denounced by some vigilante group. . . .And we all kept quiet" (398).

123.   Forest, Marsha. "Why I'm Becoming a Marxist." MR 26
         (1974) 31-35.
First-hand observations on the persistent anti-Marxist biases at one leading university.

124.   Forster, Arnold, and Benjamin R. Epstein. Danger on
         the Right. New York: Random, 1964. 294.
A study of the "radical right," at present "some 20 percent of the American electorate."

125.   Foster, Douglas Zoloth. "Photos of 'Horror' in

Cambodia: Fake or Real?" CJR 16.6 (1978) 46-47.
Widely used photographic evidence of Khmer Rouge atrocities are doubtfully authentic.

126.   Freeland, Richard. The Truman Doctrine and the Origins of McCarthyism: Foreign Policy, Domestic Politics and Internal Security, 1946-1948. New York: Knopf, 1972. 419.
The section on "Education for Security" describes the Truman Administration's educational programs to propagate a deeper commitment to patriotism, democracy, internationalism, fairness, decency, etc., as an intimate part of the campaign for a Cold War foreign policy.

127.   Gellhorn, Walter. Security, Loyalty, and Science. Ithaca: Cornell UP, 1950. 300.
"The world's polarization into opposing forces has cast a shadow upon the traditionally accepted values of scientists. . . .Today science has come to be regarded somewhat in the nature of a national war plant in which a fortune has been invested. . . . The prevailing emphasis is on studies related somehow to war." This enormous effort results in elaborate security measures, not only physical barriers to guard access to work areas, but security for "ideas and information." This book is about devices to secure ideas and information and their consequences--the extensive classification system and the consequent restriction of the interchange of ideas between one scientist and another. The author believes that the US "is purchasing security at the price of progress," and he challenges the practicality, the constitutionality, and the morality of the classification and loyalty programs designed to protect the US from an alleged Soviet threat but which damage the US itself.

128.   Gilliam, Dorothy Butler. Paul Robeson: All-American. Washington, D.C.: New Republic, 1977. 216.
Includes an account of Robeson's communist sympathies that led to his persecution by the FBI, the State Department, and Congressional witch hunters.

129.   Goodman, Walter. The Committee: The Extraordinary Career of the House Committee on Un-American Activities. New York: Farrar, 1968. 564.
A history of the anticommunist hunt by the Committee, with its underlying enmity against the social changes which occurred under Pres. Roosevelt and the Democratic Party: "[Martin] Dies was out to get the New Deal," and guilt became "by extension." "Between the Committee and the liberal spirit no reconciliation is possible, for the Committee embodies the drive to ban, censor, forbid, jail that has cursed the land for two hundred years" (494).

130.   Green, Gil. Cold War Fugitive: A Personal Story of the McCarthy Years. New York: International, 1974. 275.

Green was one of the US Communist Party leaders sentenced to prison under the Smith Act who chose to go underground. His book gives an account of the enormous FBI hunt for him and its consequences to himself, his family, and his friends.

131.   Griffith, Robert, and Athan Theoharis, eds. The Specter: Original Essays on the Cold War and the Origins of McCarthyism. New York: New Viewpoints, 1974. 368.
A reassessment of the intensified anticommunism after WWII less in terms of McCarthy himself and his demagogic exploitation of lower-class resentments, and more in terms of conventional political institutions--"interest groups, parties, the presidency, the Congress." Of special interest is the Ch. on the process leading to internal security legislation, which profoundly deepened secrecy and surveillance in the US.

132.   Guilbaut, Serge. How New York Stole the Idea of Modern Art: Abstract Expressionism, Freedom, and the Cold War. Chicago: U of Chicago P, 1983. 277.
The art of Pollock, Rothko, Motherwell, and others was co-opted by the major institutions as a weapon against the Soviet Union. "What does interest me is the way in which the public reacted to the image of the Soviet threat forged by the government and the media," and the role played by abstract expressionism.

133.   Gwyn, Robert. "Political Dissent and the Free Market of Ideas: An Eight-Nation Study." Gaz 12 (1966) 187-200.
The San Francisco to Moscow Peace Walk conducted by the Committee for Non-Violent Action "received little attention in the press" and the coverage it did receive "was placed in the context of the Cold War." "No news media of any nation--whether Capitalist or Communist--will act as a 'common carrier' of ideas and proposals that radically challenge established policy on issues critical to the nation. It would seem then that the 'Establishment' in both the West and the East enjoys a monopolistic communications position at least in the area of foreign policy."

134.   Harper, Fowler. "The Fifth Freedom -- Our Paper Curtain." Na 174.9 (1952) 198-200.
On US restrictions on freedom of travel.

135.   Hayakawa, S. I. "The Use and Misuse of Language: Thoughts on Thermonuclear Gamesmanship." ETC 19 (May 1962) 39-58.
How the US and other peoples are trapped in misleading language like "defense" and "security" and "national survival" when such words "have either radically changed their meanings or lost their meanings altogether because of the fantastic destructive power released by our new weapons technology." The people of both the SU and the US are "victims of the process of abstraction," and the result is that what we think of the Russians is a mirror image of what they think of us, each side

perpetually confirming the other side's suspicions and hostility.

136.   Hearings Before the President's Commission on Immigration and Naturalization. HR, 82nd Congress, 2d Session, 1952.
Full of protests against the McCarran-Walter Act, visa denial, etc.

137.   Hellman, Lillian. Scoundrel Time. Boston: Little, 1976. 155.
An account of the author's successful defense before the witch-hunting House Committee on Un-American Activities (HUAC) in 1952.

138.   Herman, Edward. "Diversity of News: 'Marginalizing' The Opposition." JoC 35.3 (1985) 135-46.
Analysis of coverage of the strife in Cambodia and East Timor and the elections in El Salvador and Nicaragua reveals "selective use of criteria and attention in line with national political agendas." Criticized by William Adams, with reply by Herman, JoC 36.1 (1986) 189-92.

139.   "HISC's Last Hiccup." CLR 2.2 (1975) 117-123.
Correspondence between Congressman Edward Koch and the Chairman of the House Internal Security Committee (formerly the House Committee on Un-American Activities [HUAC]) regarding Koch's efforts to obtain secret files maintained on Mr. Nat Hentoff and the eventual revelation that the Committee had tracked him around the world and placed erroneous information in his file.

140.   Hobbs, Malcolm. "The Subversive Drugstore." Na 169.22 (1949) 517-518.
How investigation by the House Committee on Un-American Activities caused the ruination financially and eventual relocation of the owner of a major Washington, D. C. pharmacy.

141.   Horne, Gerald. Black and Red: W. E. B. DuBois and the Afro-American Response to the Cold War, 1944-1963. Albany, NY: State U of NY P, 1986. 457.
A study particularly of DuBois' last years, a critique of "the unconstitutional squelching of civil liberties" brought about by the bigotry of anticommunism in the US, a favorable assessment of the "role of the left--particularly the Communist Party-USA," and an exploration of "why Afro-Americans tended to be more progressive, generally, than Euro-Americans." "This study will show that there was a close identification between the antiBlack and antiRed" and that "Blacks harbored fewer Cold War attitudes than their white counterparts."

142.   The "I. F. Stone's Weekly" Reader. Ed. Neil Middleton. New York: Vintage, 1974. 321.
The essays on "McCarthy and the Cold War" discuss the

destructiveness of both to individuals and institutions.

143.   Jaffe, Louis. "American Education and International
        Tensions (1949)." HER 20 (Winter, 1950) 1-10.
    The author disagrees with the Report of the Educational
Policies Commission which presents the viewpoint the classroom
should reflect national policy including the Cold War.

144.   Josephson, Matthew. "The Battle Of The Books."
        Na 174.26 (1952) 619-624.
    Book censorship on political grounds threatens "one of the
last outposts of free inquiry and opinion."

145.   Kahn, Albert E. The Game of Death: Effects of the
        Cold War on Our Children. New York: Cameron & Kahn,
        1953. 256.
    The Cold War has had a "dire impact" upon the children:
"ravaging their security, deforming their characters and
imperiling their lives," stultifying their minds with "thought
control, repression and fear," brutalizing them with images of
destruction and arguments and slogans of enmity, teaching them
that war is inevitable, and that hatred and killing are natural.

146.   Kamen, Martin D. Radiant Science, Dark Politics: A
        Memoir of the Nuclear Age. Berkeley: U of California P,
        1985. 350.
    The author was fired from his post in the Berkeley
Radiation Laboratory in 1944. He focuses particularly upon his
struggles against the government's security and secrecy
regulations and the political attacks upon him during the
McCarthy era.

147.   Kanfer, Stefan. A Journal of the Plague Years. New
        York: Atheneum, 1973. 306.
    The story of the Hollywood Ten.

148.   Kaplan, Fred. The Wizards of Armageddon. New York:
        Simon, 1983. 452.
    This book about the development of US Cold War and arms
policies reveals the false information fed to the US public
regarding bomber and missile gaps--the result of the paranoid
assumption "that the Soviets were planning to use their nuclear
weapons to launch a devastating preemptive strike against SAC
and other important targets." This assumption "had corrupted
intelligence estimates for six years" (288). The main subject
of the book is the powerful influence of the RAND Corporation in
making US counterforce nuclear policy.

149.   Kelly, John. "Washington Post--Speaking for Whom?"
        CS 5.3 (1981) 13-19.
    On the close association between the Post and the CIA in
1950 in seeking to root out "subversives" against "national
security."

150.   Kenny, Robert W. "Congress Shall Make No Law . . ."
          Na 165.19 (1947) 494-495.
Compares the witch-hunting of the Committee on Un-American
Activities to Nazi behavior.

151.   Kirchwey, Frieda. "The Communist Arrests." Na 167.5
          (1948) 117-118.
Several American Communist leaders have been arrested in a
manner "comparable to those used in police states the world
over: the preliminary investigations were secret, the
indictments were sealed, the charges were general."

152.   Kirchwey, Frieda. "How Free Is Free?" Na 174.26
          (1952) 615-618.
Intro. to an entire issue on the political intolerance
ravaging the nation.

153.   Kirchwey, Frieda. "The President's Message." Na
          166.13 (1948) 341-342.
President Truman increased militarism by introducing to
Congress an emergency war preparation program during a time of
peace and without first consulting Congressional leaders.

154.   Klare, Michael. "Arms and the Democrats." Na 243.15
          (1986) 474, 488-91.
Democratic party leaders try to outdo Republicans in
decrying US military "inferiority" to the SU.

155.   Klausen, Paul. "Social Science College: A Fight for
          Democracy in Education." PA 58 (1979) 22-27.
On the suppression of the Social Sciences College at the
State University of New York at Buffalo because of the Marxist
commitment of many of the faculty.

156.   Kutler, Stanley. The American Inquisition: Justice
          and Injustice in the Cold War. New York: Hill, 1982.
          285.
Eight case studies of how office holders used their power
to pursue their own political and social goals by repressing the
freedom of others in violation of the constitutional recognition
of political diversity and due process. "The essays in this
book depict events largely dictated by the loyalty and security
demands of the post-World War II period. The Cold War of the
late 1940s and 1950s evoked official repression on an
unprecedented scale" (xii).

157.   Kwitny, Jonathan. Endless Enemies: The Making of an
          Unfriendly World. New York: Congdon, 1984. 435.
Ch. 21, "Lies: The Government and the Press," stresses the
damage done to truth by the four decades of anticommunism and
endless war. The lying "started well before Johnson's time.
But not until 1964 did government lies affect public safety so
profoundly" (357).

158.   Landis, Fred. "Robert Moss, Arnaud de Borchgrave, and Right-Wing Disinformation." CAIB 10 (Aug-Sept. 1980) 37-44.
A critique of the authors of The Spike, a novel which purports to describe a massive left-wing disinformation plot preliminary to Soviet domination of the world. "We have shown how Moss, acting in concert with a CIA network of think-tanks, businessmen, and intelligence officers, has spread disinformation at critical periods in Chile and Britain, which has led to the installation of his allies in power."

159.   Lardner, Ring, Jr. "Who's Doing What to Whom?" Na 170.20 (1950) 471.
Lardner maintains that he and nine colleagues questioned by the Un-American Activities Committee were being subjected to censorship and illegal imprisonment.

160.   Lasch, Christopher. "The Cultural Cold War: A Short History of the Congress for Cultural Freedom." Towards a New Past. Ed. Barton Bernstein. New York: Pantheon, 1968. 322-59.
Prominent American intellectuals "for nearly two decades defined much of their purpose by their anticommunism" (xii-xiii). The US subsidiary of the CCF, the American Committee for Cultural Freedom, founded in 1951, was "in effect" in the service of "whatever best served the interests of the United States government" (339).

161.   Laski, Harold J. "Liberty on the American Campus." Na 169.7 (1949) 149-151.
Relates specific incidents of anticommunist action on college campuses, including dismissals of professors and bias towards guest lecturers.

162.   Lasswell, Harold D. National Security and Individual Freedom. New York: McGraw-Hill, 1950. 259.
The US can avoid an authoritarian system, brought about by anticommunist and anti-Soviet hysteria, through civilian supremacy, the free flow of information, civil liberties, and a free economy. Ch. 2 warns of "The Threat Inherent in the Garrison-Police State" (secrecy, suspicion, a weak Congress, etc.). Chs. 5 & 6 discuss what Congress and the courts can do about the totalitarian danger. Ch. 7, "What the Public Can Do," discusses a free press, community councils on human rights, fostering unofficial sources of information, etc.

163.   Latham, Earl. The Communist Controversy in Washington: From the New Deal to McCarthy. Cambridge: Harvard UP, 1966. 446.
Part 4, "The Politics of Hysteria," recounts over-reaction of Senator McCarthy and the White House.

164.   Lazarsfeld, Paul F., and Wagner Thielens, Jr. The Academic Mind: Social Scientists in a Time of Crisis.

30

Glencoe, IL: Free, 1958. 460.
About the fearful reactions of professors to McCarthyism in
the 1950s, based upon personal interviews. One of the
conclusions of the study is that the "effective scope" of higher
education in America has been restricted because "a number of
social scientists . . . have withdrawn from participation in
community activities, and some have confined themselves to a
narrower sphere of teaching and research" (264).

165.   Leab, Daniel J. "Cold War Comics." CJR 3.4 (1965)
          42-47.
Certain comic strips portray their characters participating
in the Cold War by fighting a communist menace or supporting
armed forces propaganda.

166.   Lifschultz, Lawrence. "Could Karl Marx Teach
          Economics in America?" Ram 12 (1974) 27-30, 52-59.
Karl Marx would never gain tenure in an economics
department in the US so biased and narrow is the system.

167.   Lightman, Richard. "The University: Mask for
          Privilege?" CM 1 (1968) 2-17.
"The national attempt at defense against these threats to
the United States world hegemony [the threats of China, the
Soviet Union, and the Third World] produced the hysteria of the
last twenty yeas of rabid anti-communism and cold-war
containment--the euphemism for America's self-righteousness in
domination."

168.   Lubasch, Arnold. "Marxist Group Charges Conspiracy as
          $40 Million Suit Goes to Trial." NYT (April 3, 1981)
          A 12.
The Socialist Workers Party's suit against the government's
forty-year "campaign of disruption and defamation." As part of
the government's policy of elimination or crippling socialist
ideas in America, the government used informers, burglaries,
wiretaps and mail monitoring in violation of law and the Bill of
Rights.

169.   Lukas, J. Anthony. "Watergate Revisited: Dismantling
          Cold War Confidentiality." CLR 2.4 (1975) 74-81.
A review of "the major skirmishes" in the "battle between
confidentiality and disclosure." People like Nixon invoke the
need for secrecy. In opposition, the press, congressional
committees, and prosecutors stress the public's right to know
how the public's business is being conducted.

170.   "MacArthur Says No." Na 169.26 (1949) 609-611.
Reporter Andrew Roth was not admitted into Japan because
Roth had previously indicated some socialist beliefs.

171.   Mailer, Norman. "The CIA vs. Democracy." CS 2.3
          (1975) 41.
"In fighting Communism, we have come to a point where we

have been destroying our own potential," and "one agent of that destruction has been the CIA."

172.   Maland, Charles. "Dr. Strangelove (1964): Nightmare Comedy and the Ideology of Liberal Consensus." AQ 31 (1979) 697-717.
The film is a satire of the US Cold War bipartisan consensus characterized by (1) paranoid anticommunism and Sovietphobia, (2) aggressive competitiveness, (3) obsessive male sexual domination, (4) secrecy, (5) destruction of language (e.g., euphemisms) and thence of values, (6) easy acceptance of holocaust, (7) preference for violent solutions to international rivalry instead of diplomacy, (8) blind faith in technological progress, and (9) failure to see that nuclear weapons have changed warfare.

173.   Manoff, Robert Karl. "Covering the Bomb: The Nuclear Story and the News." WP 10 (1983) 19-27.
During the first weeks after the bombing of Hiroshima and Nagasaki (August 6 and 9, 1945), the "statist" and "civil" (moral) perspectives vied for acceptance in the media, but by early September the Cold War anti-Soviet attitude was gaining ascendancy. By October cooperation with the SU was rejected when President Truman created the Atomic Energy Commission and announced that the US would not share atom bomb secrets. Subsequent history has seen a hardening of the state control of the press in matters of national security and nuclearism.

174.   Manoff, Robert K. "Covering the Bomb: Press and State in the Shadow of Nuclear War." War, Peace and the News Media. Ed. David Rubin and Ann Cunningham. New York: New York UP, 1983. 197-237.
The state establishes the parameters of reporting and dissent. "The press may discover these limits for itself, but it does not set them. Nothing better illustrates this process than the handling of nuclear strategy over the last three decades."

175.   Marchino, Michael L. "No Place to Hide." Prog 42.4 (1978) 27.
A recent series of programs which portray the US civil defense system as vastly inferior to the Soviet Union's distorts reality and perpetuates the myth of a nuclear war as "inevitable, tolerable, and even winnable."

176.   Markowitz, Norman. "Reds and Red Scares: The Treatment of Communism in U.S. History Textbooks." The United States Educational System: Marxist Approaches. Ed. Marvin J. Berlowitz and Frank E. Chapman, Jr. Studies in Marxism 6. Minneapolis: Marxist Educational P, 1980. 185-200.
College texts generally present the history of Marxism and the Communist Party in the US as "inconsequential or comical" or "producing 'Red Scares,'" stereotypes like those applied to Afro-

Americans by racist scholars before WWII.

177.   Mather, Kirtley. "Scientists In The Doghouse." <u>Na</u>
        174 (June 28, 1952) 638-641.
        Scientists as targets of the anticommunist witch-hunters.

178.   Matthews, Herbert L. <u>A World in Revolution: A
        Newspaperman's Memoir</u>. New York: Scribner's, 1971. 462.
        The <u>New York Times</u> kept "my information out of the
newspapers" because of its anti-Castro and anti-Soviet biases.

179.   May, Gary. <u>China Scapegoat: The Diplomatic Ordeal of
        John Carter Vincent</u>. Washington, DC: New Republic,
        1980. 370.
        John Carter Vincent was fired from his diplomatic post in
China because he was falsely accused of being too sympathetic to
Mao-Tse-tung and too critical of Chiang Kai-shek. He was the
victim of rabid anticommunism.

180.   McAuliffe, Mary. <u>Crisis on the Left: Cold War
        Politics and American Liberals, 1947-1954</u>. Amherst:
        U of Massachusetts P, 1978. 204.
        "An examination of the response of the left, especially
liberals, to the Cold War and to the anti-Communist politics of
America's second great Red Scare" (2). "The attack of the
McCarthyite right and the inner civil war on the left had
combined to produce a decade in which the left was in virtual
eclipse" (145).

181.   McClellan, Jim, and David Anderson. "Lips That Sink
        Ships." <u>Prog</u> 41.5 (1977) 47-49.
        "The Red-Hunting era is alive and well at the Department of
Health, Education, and Welfare."

182.   McGovern, George. "The Russians Are Coming -- Again."
        <u>Prog</u> 41.5 (1977) 17-23.
        "The latest scare reports are -- like earlier versions --
both unwarranted and irresponsible. They escalate the risk of
nuclear war and give the world a totally false picture of
American weakness and unreliability."

183.   McIntyre, Thomas, and John Obert. <u>The Fear Brokers</u>.
        New York: Pilgrim, 1979. 350.
        An account of the author's struggle against the New Right
Wing particularly in his own State of New Hampshire. Much of
the book is about the anticommunism underlying right-wing
thinking and politics.

184.   McWilliams, Carey. "The Berkeley Debacle." <u>Na</u> 171.11
        (1950) 228.
        The Regents of the U of California ordered the dismissal of
32 faculty members, all on tenure, because they refused to sign
a loyalty statement.

185.   McWilliams, Carey. "The Registration Of Heretics."
         Na 171 (December 9, 1950) 526-528.
   Analysis of the "underlying pathology" of the "loyalty"
oath and registration of "subversives" in Los Angeles County,
the first county to require the oath (1947) and the registration
(1950).

186.   McWilliams, Carey. "The White House Under
         Surveillance." Na 174.7 (1952) 150-152.
   "No American is beyond the reach of witch-hunters or the
vicious activities of informers," and behind them, behind
Senator McCarthy is J. Edgar Hoover and the FBI.

187.   McWilliams, Carey. Witch Hunt: The Revival of
         Heresy. Boston: Little, 1950. 361.
   Bk. 1 studies "certain forms of modern heresy," Bk. 2 deals
with academic freedom at U of Washington, Bk. 3, the delusions
from which accusations of heresy arise.

188.   Meeropol, Robert and Michael. We Are Your Sons: The
         Legacy of Ethel and Julius Rosenberg. 2nd ed. Urbana,
         IL: Illinois UP, 1986. 450.
   A study of the Rosenberg case itself and the destructive
impact of the Cold War on US society.

189.   Meyer, Karl. "Fear on Trial at CBS." MORE 5 (1975)
         16-17, 22.
   Discusses CBS's prime-time TV movie about "how CBS bowed to
the blacklisters at the tail end of the McCarthy era by firing a
broadcaster named John Henry Faulk after he had been accused of
pro-Communism by a vigilante outfit known as AWARE, Inc." (16).
Faulk sued and won $3.5 million in damages.

190.   Miles, Michael W. The Odyssey of the American Right.
         New York: Oxford UP, 1980. 371.
   Sect. II deals with the McCarthy Era, III with the New
Right, Nixon, etc.

191.   Miller, Merle. The Judges and the Judged. Garden
         City, NY: Doubleday, 1952. 220.
   A study of "black lists in radio and television" following
WWII distributed by the magazine Counterattack and its booklet
Red Channels listing the names of 151 broadcasting employees
with alleged Communist connections.

192.   Miller, Merle. "Trouble On Madison Avenue, N.Y."
         Na 174.26 (1952) 631-636.
   Smear tactics and blacklists against people in the
entertainment industry.

193.   Moraes, Maria, and George Lawton. "Images of Chile in
         the U. S. Press." BS 4 (1974) 1-57.
   US press coverage of the 1973 Chilean coup followed the
anticommunist US line.

194.   Morgan, Carol E. "Textbook Portrayals of the Origins of the Cold War." The United States Educational System: Marxist Approaches. Ed. Marvin J. Berlowitz and Frank E. Chapman, Jr. Studies in Marxism 6. Minneapolis: Marxist Educational P, 1980. 173-183.
Because "U. S. aims had always been expansionist and motivated by economic interests," "the West bears a major share of the responsibility for the atmosphere of international conflict which emerged after the War." Examination reveals that "serious McCarthyite distortions continue to be prevalent." "An uncritical analysis of the Cold War period continues to prevail in Western Civilization textbooks."

195.   Morgan, Edward. P. "Never for Mundey." Prog 41.5 (1977) 9.
The US State Department refused a visa to Australian trade unionist Jack Mundey because he was a Communist, despite President Carter's pledge to "ease international travel restrictions."

196.   Myerson, Michael, and Mark Solomon. Stopping World War III. New York: US Peace Council, 1981. 142.
Ch. 4, "Lies My Government Told Me: 'The Soviet Threat'" (89-109).

197.   Navasky, Victor. Naming Names. New York: Viking, 1980. 482.
"What follows is less a history than a moral detective story. After an introduction to the way in which the informer and what I call the Informer Principle--the naming of names as a test of virtue--determined and defined the cold war environment, I focus on the role of the informer in Hollywood."

198.   Nelson, Jack, and Gene Roberts, Jr. The Censors and the Schools. Boston: Little, 1963. 208.
The authors discuss several cases of attacks on school texts and schools for alleged communist subversion: the "communist conspiracy" in Meriden, CT, the Daughters of the American Revolution's campaign against "Reds," E. Merrill Root's war on "communist brainwashing" in the public schools, etc. The authors oppose the efforts of pressure groups to control the content of texts, which they equate with Hitler's Nazi Germany and Soviet Russia.

199.   Norrgard, Lee, and Joe Rosenbloom. "The Cold Warriors." CC 11.4 (1985) 14-19.
The right-wing, anticommunist American Security Council is "a voice for the nation's defense establishment." "Born in the McCarthyism of the 1950s" it has "pushed aggressively for ever-increasing Pentagon budgets." Part of the weapons of the Council is its "jingoistic" films "bankrolled partly by $100,000 contributions from large defense contractors such as Lockheed Corporation." It also buys full-page ads in support of weapons

systems, and it publishes books.

200.   O'Connor, Tom. "News Tailored to Fit." <u>Na</u> 168.16
         (1949) 438-440.
     Newspaper accounts of the leftist-based Cultural and
Scientific Conference for World Peace "were slanted, headlines
were loaded, incidents were invented, wild and absurd charges
were played up, outright lies were printed as solemn fact."

201.   Osnos, Peter. "Soviet Dissidents and the American
         Press." <u>CJR</u> 16.4 (1977) 32-36.
     The American press presents a distorted picture of the
Soviet Union by overplaying the stories of dissidents.

202.   Ott, George. "Now It's a 'Naval Gap'." <u>Prog</u> 42.9
         (1978) 22-24.
     Once again, the Pentagon is overselling the Soviet threat
in order to build public support for increased defense spending,
this time for the Navy.

203.   Packer, Herbert. <u>Ex-Communist Witnesses: Four Studies
         in Fact Finding</u>. Stanford, CA: Stanford UP, 1962. 279.
     A study of the weaknesses in "the process of eliciting and
testing the information about Communist penetration in the US
contributed by former members of the Communist Party."
Whittaker Chambers mainly told the truth about Alger Hiss;
Elizabeth Bentley's story inspired disbelief; Louis Budenz'
testimony is "in the main, of a hearsay nature;" and John
Lautner's inconsistencies "appear relatively minor."

204.   Parenti, Michael. <u>The Anti-Communist Impulse</u>. New
         York: Random, 1969. 333.
     "Thousands of volumes have been written about the ideology,
history, and evils of communism, but not very much about anticommunism. Yet anti-communism is the most powerful political
force in the world. Endowed with an imposing ideology, and a
set of vivid images and sacred dogmas, it commands the psychic
and material resources of the most potent industrial-military
arsenal in the history of mankind." If America has an ideology,
or a national purpose, "it is anti-communism" (3-4).

205.   Parenti, Michael. <u>Inventing Reality: The Politics of
         the Mass Media</u>. New York: St. Martin's, 1986. 258.
     US media are dominated by two powers: corporatism and anti-
Sovietism. Chs. 6-9 focus upon the latter: Ch. 7, "The Media
Fight the Red Menace," 8, "The Russians Are Coming, the Russians
Are Collapsing," 9, "Soviet Terrorists, Bulgarian Pope Killers,
and Other Big Lies."

206.   Perry, Ralph. "Academic Freedom." <u>HER</u> 23 (Spring,
         1953) 71-76.
     Congressional investigations and dismissal for refusing to
testify are questioned.

207.   Pringle, Peter, and William Arkin. <u>S.I.O.P.: The</u>
      <u>Secret U. S. Plan for Nuclear War</u>. New York: Norton,
      1983. 287.
      A history of the Pentagon's most secret war plan, the
Single Integrated Operating Plan, which includes a multi-billion
dollar communications system and underground bunkers for
fighting an extended nuclear war. Nuclear war planning "was
conceived in the utmost secrecy after World War II, and people
have been so conditioned by the past that merely to ask what has
been going on is considered by many a 'seditious' act" (13).

208.   Rader, Melvin. <u>False Witness</u>. Seattle: U of
      Washington P, 1969. 209.
      An account of the witch-hunt for communists on the UW
campus by a legislative committee called the Canwell Committee.
Rader was a professor there at the time and an active
participant.

209.   Ransom, Harry. <u>Can American Democracy Survive Cold</u>
      <u>War</u>? New York: Doubleday, 1963. 270.
      Four of the nine chs. deal with secrecy. "My greatest
concern is that in periods of obsessive fear or true national
emergency, radical changes will occur in our institutions--in
the name of national security--that will severely damage the
democratic framework."

210.   Redekop, John. <u>The American Far Right: A Case Study</u>
      <u>of Billy James Hargis and Christian Crusade</u>. Grand
      Rapids, MI: Eerdmans, 1968. 232.
      "The Far Right has been successfully united by a well-
designed, well-financed, and persistent campaign of fear. The
fear of Communism is both the fire and fuel of the Far Right
movement. And the continual fanning of this fear by the Billy
James Hargises and other 'crusaders' has created such a
distortion in the perceptions of some adherents of the Far Right
that they can no longer distinguish between fantasy and
reality" (from Senator Mark Hatfield's Foreword).

211.   Reinhard, David W. <u>The Republican Right Since 1945</u>.
      Lexington, KY: Kentucky UP, 1983. 294.
      The major focus of this work (chs. 1-10) is the period from
1945 through 1965. The final two chs. "cover the period from
1965 to the inauguration of Ronald Reagan." "Generally,
conservative Republicans" opposed the policies of Roosevelt and
Johnson and favored "a foreign policy that allowed the United
States to 'go it alone' in the pursuit of its own national
interest. Fierce anticommunism was also a hallmark of
conservative republicanism." Yet "other Republicans, and indeed
other Americans (Democrats included), embraced many of these
same conservative positions."

212.   Ritt, Martin, interviewed by Pat McGilligan. "Ritt
      Large." <u>FC</u> 22.1 (Jan.-Feb., 1986) 32-37.
      Fifties blacklist victim film director Ritt recalls his

experiences as one of the censored directors.

213.   Roediger, David R. "Paul Robeson Rediscovered."
         <u>Prog</u> 43.3 (1979) 54-55.
     Rev. of Philip Foner, ed., <u>Paul Robeson Speaks</u> and <u>Paul
Robeson: The Great Forerunner</u> by Editors of Freedomways.
Robeson's reputation as "a major Afro-American thinker" was
repressed by Senator McCarthy, the State Department, and a
complicit press because of Robeson's attacks on capitalism,
colonialism, and racism and his defense of the SU.

214.   Roediger, David R. "The Radical Heritage of W.E.B.
         DuBois." <u>Prog</u> 42.10 (1978) 52-3.
     "As DuBois continued to support the Progressive Party and
other third-party candidates, and as he persisted in campaigning
for peace and against colonialism, his troubles multiplied."

215.   Rogge, O. John. <u>Our Vanishing Civil Liberties</u>. New
         York: Gaer, 1949. 287.
     In his foreword, Thomas Emerson believes that the country
has "succumbed to fear" and is "seeking a false and impossible
security in repression and cold war," but that Rogge's book
"should serve to shock" people into awareness of the dangers of
the present course. The book deals with the major anti-
democratic aspects of the US: anti-Soviet fanaticism combined
with the concentration of wealth in giant corporations.

216.   "<u>The Rosenberg File</u> Is a Cold War Fraud." <u>ITT</u> 7.38
         (1983) 11.
     Attacks <u>The Rosenberg File: A Search for the Truth</u> by
Ronald Radosh and Joyce Milton and Jim Weinstein's defense of it
in <u>ITT</u> (Sept. 14, 1983), including a statement from six
professors of history declaring the book to be guilty of
"countless misrepresentations."

217.   Roubatis, Yiannis, and Elias Vlanton. "Who Killed
         George Polk?" MORE 7.5 (1977) 12-23.
     CBS correspondent George Polk was murdered in Greece in
1948. There followed a "massive cover-up" of the death "by the
right-wing Greek government, by U. S. officials, and by members
of the American press." The authors undertake to reconstruct
the episode.

218.   Rubin, David, and Ann Cunningham, eds. <u>War, Peace and
         the News Media</u>. New York: New York UP, 1983. 285.
     Papers presented at a conference held at NYU on March 18
and 19, 1983: Sidney Drell, "How the Press Covers Nuclear
Weapons"; Ralph Earle, "How the Press Covers Arms Talks";
William Dorman, "The Image of the Soviet Union in the American
News Media: Coverage of Brezhnev, Andropov and MX"; Stephen
Hess, "The Golden Triangle: Press Relations at the White House,
State Department and Department of Defense"; Robert Manoff,
"Covering the Bomb: Press and State in the Shadow of Nuclear
War." Responses to each paper by diverse people. All of the

papers support the conviction that the US government controls
the press on military policy. As Robert Manoff argues, national
security journalism is fully "statist," helping the state
"sustain political inattention and popular indifference"
essential to the management of information and the retention of
power. "By the middle of the 1940s" the state and the press
"shared an elective affinity which had allowed the former to
fight wars and the latter to report them," a relationship which
became constant.

219.   Russett, Bruce M. and Elizabeth C. Hanson. Interest
      and Ideology: The Foreign Policy Beliefs of American
      Businessmen. San Francisco: Freeman, 1975. 296.
      An empirical investigation of a variety of hypotheses
concerning businessmen as compared to other elites. The authors
traced "aggressive foreign policies to imperatives of the
capitalist system in general. . . .The needs of a capitalist
system probably do make some contribution to producing an
activist, globalist, interventionalist United States foreign
policy." Of greater importance than economics, "our evidence
indicates that ideology--whether of the anticommunist variety,or
a more comprehensive kind of conservatism embracing restrictive
views on civil rights and civil liberties as well as capitalist
values--has a strong and, in important ways, independent
influence on foreign policy preference." In general, the
authors find that "military officers and businessmen--along with
substantial segments of the Republican party leadership--
constitute the most hawkish of the American elite groups" (249-
53).

220.   Ryan, Geoffrey. "Un-American Activities." IC 2.1
      (Spring 1973) 25-38.
      The first of three articles on the House Committee on Un-
American Activities. Part One 1938-45, plus an extract from its
hearings (35-38). The year 1938 "began two decades of the most
intense and widespread witch-hunting America has ever known,"
inspired by "the fear of Communism" and exploited by the Dies
Committee. See IC 2.2 (1946-50) & 2.3 (1950-59).

221.   Ryan, Geoffrey. "Un-American Activities." IC 2.2
      (Summer 1973) 77-90.
      The second of three articles on the Un-American Activities
Committee of Congress, Part Two: 1946-50.

222.   Ryan, Geoffrey. "Un-American Activities." IC 2.3
      (Autumn 1973) 81-93.
      The last of three articles, Part Three: "The McCarthy and
post-McCarthy eras 1950-59." "The McCarthys are the
subversives, the saboteurs and traitors of the democratic way of
life. Spouting the rhetoric of national interest, they brought
the United States as close to tyranny as it had come since the
Alien and Sedition Acts threatened to destroy the infant, still
experimental Constitutional government in the dawn of its
existence" (93).

223.   Sanders, Jane. <u>Cold War on the Campus: Academic</u>
         <u>Freedom at the University of Washington, 1946-64.</u>
         Seattle: U of Washington P, 1979. 243.
     An account of the Canwell Committee's witch-hunt for
communists at UW and its traumatic effects on the faculty, and
an analysis of speakers' bans, loyalty oaths, and disclaimer
oaths. "I believe much of the record must be judged
deplorable. The choices confronting the university faculty and
administration were problematic, but their failure to clearly
enunciate the necessity of an untrammeled atmosphere for the
pursuit of truth in the midst of a social crisis must stand as a
violation of the ideal of academic freedom."

224.   Sanders, Jerry. <u>Peddlers of Crisis: The Committee on</u>
         <u>the Present Danger and the Politics of Containment.</u>
         Boston: South End, 1983. 371.
     A history of one of the chief sources of pro-military, anti-
Soviet propaganda in the US. "Peddling crisis is not an
especially complicated business. . . .One first gathers the
required number of 'experts' from the vast network of think-
tanks, universities, corporations, and scientific associations
involved with military matters to coordinate the positions to be
taken. Then one constructs the appropriate slogan--bomber gap,
missile gap, window of vulnerability. . . .Tapping anticommunist
and rightwing funding sources, one then mounts a full-scale
propaganda effort involving direct-mail, op-ed pieces, talk
shows, seminars for policymakers, films, and all the other
paraphernalia of fear" (3-4, Foreword by Alan Wolfe).

225.   Schrecker, Ellen. <u>No Ivory Tower: McCarthyism and the</u>
         <u>Universities</u>. New York: Oxford UP, 1986. 437.
     McCarthyism was fed by the complicity of the institutions
it chose as its targets. At most universities the guiding
principle was guilty until proven innocent, and the punishment
was unemployment. "The academy did not fight McCarthyism. It
contributed to it. The dismissal, the blacklists, and above all
the almost universal acceptance of the legitimacy of what the
congressional committees and other official investigators were
doing conferred respectability upon the most repressive elements
of the anti-Communist crusade." Almost with out exception,
critical, independent radicalism was silenced on the campus.

226.   Seaman, John. "Style and Perspective in Anticommunist
         Polemic." <u>L&S</u> 1 (1968) 49-61.
     The exaggeration, polarization, and rigidity in the sermons
of Billy James Hargis.

227.   Selcraig, James. <u>The Red Scare in the Midwest,</u>
         <u>1945-55: A State and Local Study</u>. Ann Arbor, MI: UMI
         Research P, 1982. 208.
     A study of anticommunist and anti-Soviet zeal in five
midwestern states--Wisconsin, Illinois, Indiana, Ohio, and
Michigan. "Basically, the Scare was formed by the conservative

movement, which in turn drew strength from the rise of the
loyalty issue. . . .McCarthyism, which formed one segment of
this movement, has been accurately interpreted as a partisan
vehicle used by Republicans in their drive for power."

228.	Seldes, George. The People Don't Know: The American
	Press and the Cold War. New York: Gaer, 1949. 342.
	"My conclusion, as the following chapters hope to show, is
that when a cold war is declared, Truth is also the first
casualty." The American people, "who are not well informed
about American affairs, have never been well informed about
world affairs, and in this dangerous era of half-war, or a
political war which may be the forerunner of armed war, the
front pages of our newspapers are filled with war scares, with
great falsehoods, with half-truths, with more bias and hate and
corrupt headlines than at any time in history" (1-2). Much of
the book "deals with war preparations, war propaganda, war
talk,the conditioning of the American people for World War III"
(7).

229.	Simmons, George. "The 'Cold War' in Large-City
	Dailies of the United States." JQ 25 (1948) 354-60.
	"One of the more notable observations in the 'cold war' is
the extent to which conservative and middle-of-the-road
newspapers have led the United States' offensive against Russia
and Communism." "One weakness of news in the 'cold war' is due
to the extensive reliance upon statements from unnamed
sources." The author focuses upon one week in July, 1948, when
news of the Berlin blockade reached a peak of interest.

230.	Simmons, George. "The Communist Conspiracy Case:
	Views of 72 Daily Newspapers." JQ 27 (1950) 3-11.
	"The newspapers of this country are intent, under present
conditions of the world ideological conflict, to attack
communism. As a group, they do not knowingly overlook such
opportunities. But their struggle against communism in this
instance [the trial of US Communist leaders in 1949] tended to
run counter to their traditional defense of the freedoms
specified in the Bill of Rights. . . .Many loyal non-Communists
recognized and cited the dangers which they regarded as implicit
in application of the Smith Act during peace."

231.	Smith, Craig. The Fight for Freedom of Expression:
	Three Case Studies. Washington, DC: Institute for
	Freedom of Communication, 1985. 103.
	Examines the Alien and Sedition crisis (1798-1801), the
Reconstruction Acts following the Civil War (1865-1876), and the
McCarthy era (1950-54), beginning with the passage of the
Subversive Activities Control Act of 1950. Freedom of
expression was critical in the battle against reactionary people
who would deprive citizens of their civil liberties.

232.	Sorkin, Michael. "Timespeak: Hidden Persuaders."
	MORE 8.5 (1978) 29-32.

Time magazine's biased March 13 cover story of socialism
simplified argument, subtly distorted quotations, reduced
socialist theory to slogans, eliminated the history of
socialism, and gave misleading statistics and taxonomy. Time
writers marshaled a wide range of rhetorical devices to
depreciate socialism and exalt capitalism.

233.   Steif, William. "On the 'Objective' Press."
        Prog 43.1 (1979) 23-5.
US opposition to the UNESCO draft declaration on the press
is motivated by "business interests," anticommunism, and other
nationalistic motives. "The American pretension of objectivity
is a convention that reinforces our institutions, but it doesn't
have much more to do with the whole truth than Pravda."

234.   Stone, I. F. "The Grand Inquisition." Na 165.19
        (1947) 492-494.
The purpose of the anticommunist witch-hunt is "to
terrorize all leftists, liberals, and intellectuals; to make
them fearful in the film, the theater, the press, and any school
of advanced ideas the Thomas Committee can stigmatize as
'red.'"

235.   Stone, I. F. "Is The Constitution Un-American?"
        Na 165.10 (1947) 223-226.
Congressional Un-American Activities Committee contempt
proceedings against the Joint Anti-Facist Refugee Committee
(JAFRC).

236.   Stone, I. F. "A New Weapon For Witch-Hunters."
        Na 165.2 (July 12, 1947) 33-35.
"The Marzani case must be seen against the background of
the anti-red hysteria which is driving intellectuals of all
sorts out of government."

237.   Stone, I. F. The Truman Era. London: Turnstile; New
        York: Monthly Rev., 1953. 226.
Includes analysis of five reports on communism produced by
the US Chamber of Commerce as part of the Cold War consensus
created by corporations and anticommunist politicians. The post-
WWII witch-hunts were generated by the Establishment (80-82).

238.   Suall, Irwin. The American Ultras: The Extreme Right
        and the Military Industrial Complex. New York: New
        America, 1962. 64.
There is "a significant, and most dangerous, tendency for
an important section of the military-industrial complex to put
its enormous power behind right wing extremism. The source of
this development is in the Cold War."

239.   Theoharis, Athan. Seeds of Repression: Harry S.
        Truman and the Origins of McCarthyism. Chicago:
        Quadrangle, 1971. 238.
The emergence of McCarthyism "dramatized the connection

between foreign policy and domestic politics--specifically, the way in which a suspicious, militaristic approach to foreign policy, emphasizing the subversive character of the Soviet threat, substantively altered the domestic political climate."

240.   Theoharis, Athan, ed. The Truman Presidency: The Origins of the Imperial Presidency and the National Security State. Stanfordville, NY: Coleman, 1979. 396.
"The Truman years . . . witnessed two fundamental developments warranting the description of Truman's as a formative presidency--the evolution of an Imperial Presidency and of a National Security State. No longer were presidents and intelligence bureaucrats accountable" to the Congress, the public, or the law. Chs. on the creation and rise of the national security bureaucracy, executive privilege, secrecy, and classification system, the federal employee loyalty program, and the FBI surveillance and the detention programs, etc.

241.   Tucker, Nancy B. Patterns in the Dust: Chinese-American Relations and the Recognition Controversy, 1949-1950. New York: Columbia UP, 1983. 396.
Ch. 8, "Journalists and the Media," and Ch. 9, "The Public, Congress, Scholars," stress the profound ignorance that blighted the debate, which a hard core of anticommunists lobbied for the Kuomintang.

242.   "Twice in a Life Time." NT 4.3 (1986) 6.
In 1958 Life labeled as propaganda the Soviet decision to suspend nuclear testing. Now the Reagan Administration calls the Soviet test ban of August, 1985, a "propaganda ploy."

243.   Vaughn, Robert. Only Victims: A Study of Show Business Blacklisting. New York: Putnam's, 1972. 355.
The House Committee on Un-American Activities "blamed the nation's troubles on foreign subversion or alien ideologies" and adopted "totalitarian strategies to rid us of the threat they alone perceived--to set their own standards for what is and is not good American thought." The Committee resorted "with almost total abandon" to "trial by accusation, publicity, and presumption of guilt" and "innuendo" and "wanton" abuse of "the contempt power" (Foreword by Senator George McGovern).

244.   Walton, Richard. Henry Wallace, Harry Truman and the Cold War. New York: Viking, 1976. 388.
Concentrates on Wallace as presidential candidate of the Progressive Party in 1948, "the last time that the basic assumptions of American foreign policy were questioned until the mid-1060s. Not until five Presidential elections later did American voters begin to re-examine the anticommunism that had been the motivating force of American foreign policy since the death of Franklin D. Roosevelt in April 1945." "It was a forceful challenge, and brave, for by 1948 the clouds of that Dark Age later known as McCarthyism had already begun to lower

ANTICOMMUNISM

over the land."

245.   Watson, Goodwin. "The Public Schools Retreat From
         Freedom." Na 174.26 (1952) 653-657.
     Censorship, smear campaigns, and self-censorship are some
of the ways teachers are being compelled to conform to a pattern
established by bigots.

246.   Wechsler, James A. The Age of Suspicion. New York:
         Random, 1953. 333.
     The author's "exploration" of his life from a member of the
Communist Party to editor of the Washington Post and object of
Senator McCarthy's investigation.

247.   Weisberger, Bernard. Cold War, Cold Peace: The United
         States and Russia Since 1945. New York: American
         Heritage, Houghton, 1984. 341.
     The effects of the Cold War on the US include the rise of
McCarthyism, the burgeoning of our whole national security/
surveillance apparatus, and the increase in the power of the
presidency.

248.   Westin, Alan. "Wire-tapping: Supreme Court vs.
         FBI." Na 174.8 (1952) 172-174.
     Illegal federal, state, and private wire-tapping is
proliferating, particularly in "loyalty" cases.

249.   Wexley, John. The Judgment of Julius and Ethel
         Rosenberg. New York: Ballantine, 1977. 564. (Different
         version orig. pub. Cameron & Kahn, 1955.)
     This new edition contains more evidence in support of the
author's belief that the execution of the Rosenberg's was a
political frame-up in a climate of fear.

250.   Wilcox, Clair, ed. Civil Liberties Under Attack.
         Freeport, NY: Books for Libraries, 1968. 155.
     Fears of communism have undermined civil liberties by
"foolishly insisting that dissent be suppressed and conformity
coerced."

251.   Wittner, Lawrence S. Cold War America: From Hiroshima
         to Watergate. New York: Praeger, 1974. 403.
     American public policy since 1945 has ignored issues of
"war, poverty, and human freedom" in favor of corporate profit
and anticommunism. "Indeed, as an integral part of their
defense of corporate power, U. S. policy makers drove the nation
to the point of crisis, invading other countries, neglecting the
needs of American society, and finally, in fear of their own
citizens, leading an assault upon free institutions." The Cold
War must be ended, in favor of "freedom, justice, and
reconciliation with mankind."

252.   Wolfe, Alan. The Rise and Fall of the "Soviet
         Threat": Domestic Sources of the Cold War Consensus.

Washington, DC: Institute for Policy Studies, 1979. 94.
"Much of the recent hysteria about the Soviet military
build-up has much more to do with <u>domestic</u> politics that it does
with the security of the United States." What is at stake are
perceptions which are "determined politically." US perceptions
of hostile Soviet intentions derive not so much from their
behavior but from "the peculiar features of the American
political system."

I. C. 3. Senator Joseph McCarthy 253-273

253.   Anderson, Jack, and Ronald May. <u>McCarthy: The Man,
    the Senator, the "Ism."</u> Beacon, 1952. 431.
"Too many people wanted quick yes-or-no answers to the
troubles that confronted the nation: thus they created a market
for the hate-peddlers, the myth-mongers, and the fear-
spreaders." Fifty-five chapters cover the subjects indicated in
the title.

254.   <u>The AP McCarthy Series</u>. New York: Associated Press,
    1954. 94.
Covers eighteen topics, such as, "57, 81, or 205
Communists?" and "How McCarthy Operates."

255.   Bayley, Edwin R. <u>Joe McCarthy and the Press</u>.
    Madison, WI: U of Wisconsin P, 1981. 220.
McCarthy knew how to manipulate the press, which reported
what he said whether it was true or not. He played the wire
services like they were "puppets." Broadcasters and ad agencies
gave him free air time almost for the asking. Ch. 1 gives
background and appraises the coverage of his Lincoln Day
speeches that began at Wheeling; 2, news coverage from
Washington, conflict with President Truman, the Tydings
subcommittee; 3, the wire services; 4, the 1952 Wisconsin
senatorial election; 5, relations with newspaper and magazine
friends; 6, his relations with television and with the
Eisenhower administration, and four critical television events;
7, summary.

256.   Cook, Fred J. <u>The Nightmare Decade: The Life and
    Times of Senator Joe McCarthy</u>. New York: Random, 1971.
    626.
"It was a period dominated by the most effective demagogue
ever to practice the arts of mass passion on this continent--
Senator Joseph R. McCarthy of Wisconsin." In the Presidential
election of 1952, "he was loosed by the Republican hierarchy to
pin the label of 'twenty years of treason' on every Democrat in
sight," and "there was no gale of unfavorable publicity, no cry
of public outrage."

257.   Feuerlicht, Roberta Strauss. <u>Joe McCarthy and
    McCarthyism: The Hate That Haunts America</u>. New York:
    McGraw-Hill, 1972. 160.
Senator Joe McCarthy "exploited the issue of Communism in

government in a five-year rampage of political smear attacks, unsupported allegations, and personal vilification." The roots of McCarthyism lie in "attitudes of the Cold War" found not only in Republicans but in Democrats too. McCarthyism did not die with McCarthy but continues to poison the US.

258.   Ford, Sherman, Jr. The McCarthy Menace: An Evaluation of the Facts and an Interpretation of the Evidence. New York: William-Frederick, 1954. 94.
"The nation will never be able to calculate the amount of damage McCarthy has done to innocent people, the poison of fear he has spread . . . and the allies he has caused the United States to lose."

259.   The Fort Monmouth Security Investigations. Washington, DC: Fed. of Am. Sci., 1954. 68.
A critique of Senator Joe McCarthy and McCarthyism.

260.   Fried, Richard M. Men Against McCarthy. New York: Columbia UP, 1976. 428.
"Focuses upon the McCarthy problem as his political foes perceived it and examines their strategy and tactics. . . .Because McCarthyism was preeminently a partisan weapon deployed by Republicans to end the Democratic hegemony, the bulk of the coverage of McCarthy's opposition is devoted to the Democrats" and the "vast energies" applied by them to counter McCarthy and equally to avoid confronting him."

261.   Goldston, Robert C. The American Nightmare: Senator Joe McCarthy and the Politics of Hate. Indianapolis: Bobbs-Merrill, 1973. 202.
Since the triumph of the Bolshevik revolution in Russia in 1917, "the nightmare conspiracy that has most troubled the sleep of politically paranoid Americans has been the international Communist movement," particularly "the suspicion of plots and treasons at home." Joseph McCarthy, "one of the greatest demagogues this country has ever known," exploited a time of upheaval and crisis "to manipulate the politically paranoid minority to serve his own ends" (2-5).

262.   Griffith, Robert. The Politics of Fear: Joseph R. McCarthy and the Senate. Lexington: Kentucky UP, 1970. 362.
McCarthy "rose to power because of a political dynamic created during the late 1940s by a band of Republican partisans as they scrapped and clawed their way toward power. The broad issue of American policy toward Communist nations and the more specific issue of 'communism in government' were, to be sure, made viable by the cold war, but they were made dynamic by these partisans for whom they represented success or a means to success." Special attention to the Senate, which "did not serve this country well during those years," failing "to exercise those restraints necessary to halt McCarthy's excesses."

263.   Investigation of Senator Joseph R. McCarthy.
         Hearings before the Subcommittee on Privileges and
         Elections of the Committee on Rules and Administration,
         US Senate, 82nd Congress on S. Res. 187 to Investigate
         Senator Joseph R. McCarthy to Determine Whether Expulsion
         Proceedings Should Be Instituted Against Him. Part I,
         Sept. 28, 1951, May 12-16, 1952. Washington DC: GPO,
         1952. 320.

264.   Lattimore, Owen. Ordeal by Slander. Boston: Little,
         1950. 236.
The author's account of his experiences following Senator
Joe McCarthy's false accusation that he was the "top Russian
espionage agent" in the US.

265.   Matusow, Allen J., ed. Joseph R. McCarthy. Englewood
         Cliffs, NJ: Prentice, 1970. 181.
"The great irony of McCarthyism is that it developed in the
absence of any real internal Communist menace; for by 1950
communism in America had lost whatever influence it once
possessed." The editor wrote Part One, "McCarthy's Anti-
Communist Crusade, 1950-1954." Part two, "McCarthy Appraised."
five essays; Part Three, "Who Were the McCarthyites?" six
essays.

266.   Oshinsky, David. A Conspiracy So Immense: The World
         of Joe McCarthy. New York: Free, 1983. 597.
A biography of a man who "above all" offered "a simple
explanation for America's 'decline--'" the "massive internal
conspiracy, directed by Communists and abetted by government
officials." Yet "he never uncovered a Communist" (507).

267.   Oshinsky, David. Senator Joseph McCarthy and the
         American Labor Movement. Columbia, MO: Missouri UP,
         1976. 206.
The "dogmas of McCarthyism" caused labor leaders and rank-
and-file to swing to the right, though "they retained the
perception to differentiate between liberal anticommunism and
the reactionary doctrines of McCarthyism" (pro-Taft-Hartley Act,
against a higher federal minimum wage, etc.).

268.   Potter, Charles E., Senator. Days of Shame. New
         York: Coward, 1965. 304.
An account of Joe McCarthy's rise and fall by one of the
Republican senators on the Senate Government Operations
Committee which conducted the hearings over the McCarthy-Army
controversy. It was a period of "strange and hysterical
nonsense, brought on by a haunted man who had an overpowering
need to be the center of attraction but whose ambitions had no
substance."

269.   Reeves, Thomas. The Life and Times of Joe McCarthy: A
         Biography. New York: Stein, 1982. 819.
McCarthy was not "the grave threat to the Constitution and
to the nation he has seemed by some to be," for he had "no

ideology or program of any significance," and he was only a part of the "second Red Scare" for which others were as much or more to blame. "From any standpoint, it seems clear the McCarthy's life was profoundly tragic. His native intelligence and his formidable energy were largely squandered. He brought far more pain into the world than any man should. He was above all a reckless adventurer, an improvisor, a bluffer."

270.   Rogin, Michael P. The Intellectuals and McCarthy: The
          Radical Spectre. Cambridge, MA: M. I. T., 1967. 366.
     An attack on "the notion that McCarthy had agrarian radical roots." He was rather "a traditional conservative." The author studies American reform movements in order to show their difference from McCarthyism and right-wing Republicanism.

271.   Rorty, James, and Moshe Decter. McCarthy and the
          Communists. Boston: Beacon, 1954. 163.
     McCarthy is a demagogue but not a totalitarian. The real issue is how to combat communism responsibly.

272.   Rovere, Richard H. Senator Joe McCarthy. New York:
          Harcourt, 1959. 280.
     Joseph McCarthy "was in many ways the most gifted demagogue ever bred on these shores. No bolder seditionist ever moved among us--nor any politician with a surer, swifter access to the dark places of the American mind." He did not bring down American democracy, but "we cannot put aside our memories of the day when 50 percent of the people had a 'favorable opinion' of this bully and fraud and another 21 percent had 'no opinion' of him."

273.   Watkins, Arthur V. Enough Rope. Englewood Cliffs,
          NJ: Prentice, and Utah UP, 1969. 302.
     The story of the censure of Senator Joe McCarthy by his colleagues, by former Senator and Chairman of The Select Committee to Study Censure Charges Against Senator McCarthy. McCarthy never "presented sufficiently credible evidence against a single one of the 205, 81, or 57 'communists' he at various times declared himself ready to name. . . .The apprehensions raised by Senator McCarthy were largely destructive."

I. D. The Reagan Years 274-413

274.   Bennett, James R. "Anti-Sovietism." ORK (Winter 1986-
          87).
     This compilation is part of a four-part bibliography on Ronald Reagan published serially beginning in the Spring 1986 issue under the general title of "Presidential Control of Information: A Bibliography." A few of these items are repeated here, with annotations shortened.

[See IV. H. for items dealing with Latin America.]

275.   The Anatomy of a Slander Campaign. Sofia, Bulgaria:
         Sofia Press, 1983. 107.
A refutation of allegations by Claire Sterling and other
Western journalists that Bulgaria was behind the attempted
assassination of Pope John Paul II by Mehmet Ali Agca. Such
accusations derived from a desire to associate Eastern European
countries with terrorism.

276.   Anderson, Scott, and Jon Anderson. Inside the League:
         The Shocking Expose of How Terrorists, Nazis, and Latin
         American Death Squads Have Infiltrated the World Anti-
         Communist League. New York: Dodd, 1986. 322.
Rightists have taken over this international organization
with more than ninety branches on six continents.

277.   Aufderheide, Pat. "Ideological Aerobics." ITT 10.5
         (1985) 24.
Baryshnikov in White Nights "celebrates his freedom in an
atmosphere so clammy with Cold Warriorism that even his
spectacular dance scenes have a chill on them. The film forms
part of a wave of paranoid patriotism in Christmas movies
(Invasion USA, Rocky IV, Revolution, even The Stuff)."

278.   Beban, Richard, and Joy Mastroberardino. "Landau,
         Board Nix Soviet Trip in Wake of Explosive Debate."
         Current 4.10 (1985) 1, 4.
A routine trade delegation to the USSR was voted down by
the anti-Soviet majority of the Corporation for Public
Broadcasting. [Subsequent numbers of the magazine returned to
the issue. The delegation eventually went under the auspices of
PBS.]

279.   Bello, Walden. "Little Reagans: Liberal Democrats
         Re-enlist in the Cold War." Prog 50.1 (1986) 25-27.
"In the current campaign of anticommunism sweeping
Congress," it is the Democrats leading the troops.

280.   Bennett, James R. "Oceania and the United States in
         1984: The Selling of the Soviet Threat." STP 10 (1984)
         301-318.
By projecting an ever-threatening, diabolical Enemy through
constant "Two Minutes Hate" and recurrent "Hate Weeks" the
Reagan Administration imitates Orwell's Oceania.

281.   Bennett, James R. "Terrorism." SLJR 13.84 (1986) 2,
         10.
The meaning of the word "terrorism" has been torn from its
dictionary definition by contemporary politicians, newsmen, and
scholars, and transformed into a weapon in the Cold War.

282.   Bennett, James R. "TV Guide Bozzles America." QRD 9
         (1982) 3-4.
John Weismen's article in TV Guide, "Why American TV Is So
Vulnerable to Foreign Propaganda" (June 12, 1982) illustrates

49

the techniques he attacks: irrelevant conclusion, ignoring the
issue, diversion, and red herring.

283.   Bishop, Dale. "Lebanon: Everybody's Battleground."
     C&C 43.16 (1983) 370, 390.
     "In the days preceding the announcement of the national
conference on reconciliation, the Reagan administration
increasingly stressed the East-West aspect of the Lebanese
conflict."

284.   Black, George, and Robert Matthews. "Arms From The
     U.S.S.R.--Or From Nobody." Na 241.5 (1985) 129, 148-149.
     The Reagan administration blocked the Nicaraguans from
acquiring arms from Western allies, and then denounced them for
seeking arms from the SU.

285.   Boot, William. "Beating the Tribal Drums." CJR 22.4
     (1983) 27-30.
     Initial media reports of the downing of the K. A. L. flight
007 were "a veritable stampede" of the official Reagan anti-
Soviet charges of deliberate destruction of a civilian plane.

286.   Boot, William. "Operation Spy Dust." CJR 24.4 (1985)
     20-23.
     On the attempt by the Reagan administration to inflate the
significance of the KGB use of a fingerprint powder, another
example of how "highly vulnerable" the press is to "being used"
by the government.

287.   Bright, Charles. "On the Road to War with the Soviet
     Union: Strategic Consensus for the 1990s." SocR 16.1
     (1986) 7-44.
     "The Reagan administration took office in 1981 with neither
a grand strategy nor a geopolitical vision beyond a fathomless
suspicion of the Soviet Union."

288.   Broad, William. Star Warriors. New York: Simon,
     1985. 236.
     A portrait of a group of young weaponeers, known as "O
Group," at the Livermore National Laboratory who work on the
Strategic Defense Initiative (SDI), specifically to create super-
computers and future nuclear and laser weapons. Livermore was
founded in 1953 by one of the most obsessed of all Sovietphobes,
Dr. Edward Teller. These scientists share his views about
superpower conflict and the threat of the Soviet Union, and
perceive nuclear technologies to be central to the resolution of
the Cold War.

289.   Brodhead, Frank. "'Democratic Revolution' or Plain
     Old Counterrevolution?" Guard 38.28 (1986) 19.
     Reagan's call for "democratic revolution" in his March 14
speech "is simply an attempt to place human rights and reform
clothing on his long-term strategy of Counterrevolution Without
Frontiers."

290.   Brodhead, Frank, Howard Friel, and Edward Herman.
        "The 'Bulgarian Connection' Revisited." CAIB 23 (1985)
        3-38.
In an analysis of the massive western disinformation
campaign to convince the world that the Turkish fascist who shot
Pope Paul II was a Bulgarian (and therefore Soviet) agent, the
authors accuse such writers as Claire Sterling, Michael Ledeen,
and Paul Henze of much distortion and some lying, and they
indict the media for purveying their false explanations of the
case.

291.   "Cave-in at ABC." Na 242.10 (1986) 292.
Pressure on ABC News by the White House over Soviet
spokesman Vladimir Posner's critique of a speech by President
Reagan.

292.   Chace, James. Solvency: The Price of Survival. New
        York: Random, 1981. 115.
One of the theses of the book is that a foreign policy based
primarily on anti-Sovietism is self-destructive. "An anti-
Soviet consensus leading to a new crusade of global containment
will not only strain our resources to such a degree that we will
have to live with an enormous military establishment and a
continuing reduction in our standard of living, but will also
stretch our alliances to the breaking point" (106).

293.   Clarkson, Fred. "Pak in the Saddle Again." CAIB 20
        (Winter 1984) 38-9.
Contains some details about the anticommunist media empire
being built by Sun Myung Moon's Unification Church.

294.   Cockburn, Alexander. "'Amerika' the Beautiful." Na
        241.10 (1985) 302.
The ABC network is spending $40 million on a mini-series
entitled "Amerika" about the take-over of the US by the SU.

295.   Cockburn, Alexander. "The Gospel According to Ali
        Agca." Na 241.1 (1985) 1, 6-7.
The attempted assassination of the Pope was not a KGB-
inspired plot but "a right-wing conspiracy to bring off a major
propaganda coup in the cold war," and the "unwitting" agents of
this attempt are The New York Times, The Wall Street Journal,
NBC, PBS and Reader's Digest.

296.   Cockburn, Andrew. "Graphic Evidence . . . of Nuclear
        Confusion." CJR 22.1 (1983) 38-41.
The graphs used by the government to prove that the
"Soviets are out in front" in weapons are misleading.

297.   Cockburn, Alexander. "The Story of a Test Ban."
        Na 242.2 (1986) 38.
The Reagan Administration has dismissed Gorbachev's
proposed test ban as propaganda and some sort of a trick; the

press, like sheep, have more or less followed.

298.   Cohen, Stephen F. "Sovieticus." <u>Na</u> 241.11 (1985)
          335.
"President Reagan's cold war policy has gone essentially
unchallenged in the political mainstream for almost five years"
because believers in detente "are intimidated by the renewed
cold war climate of political intolerance, especially on Soviet
affairs."

299.   Cohen, Stephen F. "Sovieticus." <u>Na</u> 242.17 (1986)
          607.
"For many years media coverage of the Soviet Union has
attributed virtuous qualities almost only to dissidents, emigres
and would-be emigres, leaving the impression that the entire
Soviet establishment is conformist, cynical, corrupt or worse."

300.   Cohen, Stephen F. <u>Sovieticus: American Perceptions
          and Soviet Realities</u>. New York: Norton, 1985. 160.
Makes the distinction between "the real but manageable
Soviet threat to our national security and international
interests" and the "increasingly more serious problem" of
"Sovietphobia, or exaggerated fear of that Soviet threat" (19).
The press coverage of the SU is "so inadequate" because of
"official Soviet secretiveness and censorship, the lack of a
full time American press corps of specialists in Soviet affairs,
and the media's tendency to assume the worst about the Soviet
Union" (11).

301.   "Congress Inquiry Urged of PBS Documentaries." <u>AG</u>
          (January 23, 1986) 6A.
The conservative group Accuracy in Media is attacking PBS
for producing "leftist and often pro-Communist" documentaries.

302.   Cooper, Marc. "The Wild Man of Anaheim." <u>CJR</u> 23.1
          (1984) 14.
A description of the Sovietphobic talk show host Wally
George.

303.   Cox, Arthur M. <u>Russian Roulette: The Superpower
          Game</u>. New York: Times, 1982. 248.
Americans have been "hypnotized." "They have been told
that the Soviets are acquiring nuclear superiority over the
United States. They have been told that there is no point in
serious negotiations with the Soviet Union until we have
restored our 'margin of safety' (a euphemism for superiority) so
that we can bargain from strength. They have been told that the
Soviet Union is opposed to deep, verifiable cuts in the two
nuclear arsenals. All these assertions are false, but . . . it
has not been difficult for American advocates of military
supremacy to manipulate public opinion" (202).

304.   Crowell, George H. "After Geneva Sleight-of-Hand:
          Still a Chance for CTB." <u>C&C</u> 45.21 (1985) 510-511.

"The facts of the summit story reveal more clearly than ever before that the Soviet Union is open to nuclear disarmament, while the U. S. is not. Tragically the media have failed to emphasize the key facts, leaving the public in confusion."

305.   Dallek, Robert. <u>Ronald Reagan: The Politics of</u> <u>Symbolism</u>. Cambridge: Harvard UP, 1984. 221.
"The organizing principle of Ronald Reagan's defense and foreign policies is anti-Sovietism--the need to confront and overcome the Soviet Communist danger in every part of the globe. Reagan "sees almost no room for reasonable compromise with the Soviets and looks forward to the day when the West 'will transcend Communism.'"

306.   Dallin, Alexander. <u>Black Box: KAL 007 and the</u> <u>Superpowers</u>. Berkeley: U of California P, 1985. 130.
The Reagan administration denounced the SU for shooting down an off-course aircraft over its territory in contempt for human life. The Soviets claimed the plane was engaged in a spying mission. The author believes that a satisfactory explanation of the incident has not yet been provided, but he does not accept the idea that the pilots made a navigational error.

307.   Dallin, Alexander, and Condoleezza Rice, eds. <u>The</u> <u>Gorbachev Era</u>. Stanford, CA: Stanford UP, 1986. 194.
An analysis of various US myths about the SU, particularly its alleged expansionism. The notion of a Soviet master plan is "one of the most pernicious misconceptions we have entertained."

308.   Davis, Rod. "Bad Marx for Media." <u>MJ</u> 8.9 (1985) 4.
The deepest cause of "U. S. media misinterpretation of the Soviet Union" is reporters ignorant of Marx and Marxism who "pass along, indirectly, the wildest sorts of lies."

309.   DeMause, Lloyd. <u>Reagan's America</u>. New York, London: Creative Roots, 1984. 193.
A psychological explanation of America's anticommunism based upon the externalization of anger, fear, and guilt, and the connections of Reagan's life-long phobias with his anti-communist crusade.

310.   Denison, Dave. "The Current Illness." <u>TO</u> 77.22 (1985) 5-6.
Ronald Reagan has raised far-right militant anticommunism "to new respectability."

311.   Denison, Dave. "Rumble on the Far Right." <u>TO</u> 77.19 (1985) 10-14.
An account of the 4-day 1985 World Anti-Communist League convention in Dallas. WACL was founded by Nationalist Chinese in Taiwan in 1967 and is now neo-Nazi, anti-Semitic, and pro-dictatorship.

312.   Denison, Dave. "San Antonio Ponders Captive Nations
      Park." TO 77.20 (1985) 7-8.
On the efforts by the far-right World Anti-Communist League
to establish a "captive Nations Memorial Park" in San Antonio.

313.   "Disinformation." CS 7 (1983) 7-32.
Six articles on the Reagan administration's lies and
distortions of information: CIA and the Pope Plot, CIA and
missiles in Europe, the Pentagon's Soviet Military Power, 1983,
disinformation and Canadian peace groups, and reporting Northern
Ireland.

314.   Dixon, Marlene, ed. Omens of Darkness: The Rise
      of Reaction in the United States. San Francisco:
      Synthesis, 1985. 304.
The symptoms are many: Ronald Reagan, the militarization
of Central America, the revival of a virulent Cold War ideology,
nuclear provocation of the Soviet Union, an aggressive rollback
strategy against the socialist world, and increased repression
in the US in the name of "law and order." The rise of right-
wing politics is linked to the world capitalist crisis and the
demise of US hegemony.

315.   Donner, Frank. "The Return of the Red Squads." Na
      241.11 (1985) 329, 339-342.
"Police surveillance of political groups exercising their
right to dissent is now on the rise."

316.   Dorman, William. "The Image of the Soviet Union in
      the American News Media: Coverage of Brezhnev, Andropov,
      and MX." War, Peace & and the News Media. David Rubin
      and Ann Cunningham, eds. New York: New York U, 1983.
      44-76.
"[T]he mainstream media have closed many more questions in
the 65 years since the Bolshevik Revolution than they have
opened." Whether it is 1917 or 1982, "Russian intentions and
behavior continue to be painted in the darkest possible shades,
journalistic themes persist in echoing those of official
Washington, Americans' worst fears go unchallenged in the press,
and labels continue to be substituted for analysis." Evidence
based upon a survey of five newspapers, Time and Newsweek,
selected stories from UPI and AP, and the evening news programs
of the three television networks. Rptd. SLJR 9.56 (1983) 17-20.

317.   Dorman, William. "Soviets Seen Through Red-Tinted
      Glasses." BAS 41.2 (1985) 18-22.
The US media establishment, which continually proclaims its
"objectivity," is often biased in reporting about the Soviet
Union.

318.   Douglass, Jim. "The Parable of the Good Communist."
      GZ 4.4 (1986) 2-3.
Premier Gorbachev halted nuclear testing August 6, 1985,

yet the Reagan administration has convinced the media and the public the peace initiative is merely a propaganda ploy.

319.   Draper, Theodore. "Neoconservative History," NYRB 32.21 & 22 (1986) 5-15.
Accusations that the Yalta conference toward the end of WWII treasonably aided "Communist enslavements" "envenomed American politics throughout the McCarthy period" and are being revived today.

320.   Duffy, Gloria. "Administration Redefines Soviet 'Violations.'" BAS 3.5 (1986) 13-17.
The Weinberger Report on supposed Soviet non-compliance with arms control agreements is inflammatory and "fraught with contradictions and intellectual dishonesty."

321.   Dugger, Ronnie. On Reagan: The Man & His Presidency. New York: McGraw, 1983. 616.
Ch. 15, "Reagan's McCarthyism," especially and several other chs.--Ch. 13, "The Liberties of the People," Ch. 20, "Reagan and Nuclear War"--reveal Reagan's blinding antagonism toward communism and the SU.

322.   Dugger, Ronnie. "The President's Favorite Book." Na 239.13 (1984) 413-16.
Gen. Sir John Hackett's novel The Third World War teaches that the Russians may invade Europe and use nuclear weapons against cities, the US should retaliate against one Soviet bomb with numerous bombs, and the result will be the end of the SU and victory for the West.

323.   Dugger, Ronnie. "The State as Terrorist." TO 77.22 (1985) 6-7.
Reagan "would have us condemn only the torture and murders that are committed by the leftist states" and denies the invasion of Grenada or the mining of Nicaragua's harbors are state terrorism.

324.   Ebert, Allan. "Tracking a Poet in Exile." NaR 10.1 (1986) 32-33.
The Immigration and Naturalization Service classified South African poet and anti-apartheid activist Dennis Brutus an excludable alien for alleged communist association and ideas.

325.   Ege, Konrad. "Reagan's 'Misstatements': Fueling the Push for Military Superiority." CS 7 (1983) 15-20.
In its campaign to garner support for a 10 percent hike in the military budget, the Reagan administration falsifies facts about the US and Soviet military budgets.

326.   Ege, Konrad. "Soviet 'Slave Labor' Charges Examined." CS 7.3 (1983) 28-32.
Part of Reagan's "economic war against the Soviet Union" are his allegations that the Soviet Union was using slave labor

to build the Yamal natural gas pipeline. These allegations are based upon "flimsy" and even "fabricated" evidence.

327.   Ericson, Edward L. American Freedom and the Radical
          Right. New York: Ungar, 1982. 117.
      Ch. 1, "Resurgent McCarthyism: Today's Threat to Freedom,"
discusses the "witch hunt" against secular humanism "conducted
in the name of preserving the family, of protecting youth from
corrupting influences, of fighting communism and godlessness,
and of securing the Christian character of American
institutions." Ch. 7, "The Great Arms Race: The Holy War
Against Communism," denounces the "recklessness and sheer
hubris" of the right-wing ideologue's bellicosity.

328.   Evangelista, Matthew. "Exploiting the Soviet 'Threat'
          to Europe." BAS 43.1 (1987) 14-18.
      "Support for a European version of Star Wars is based on
unreliable evaluations of the Soviet Threat."

329.   Finder, Joseph. "Reporting from Russia: Three
          Correspondents in Moscow." WJR 7.6 (1985) 54-63.
      Dusko Doder of the Washington Post comments: "'Americans
really aren't interested in Russia. They think of Russia as a
military power and not much else. The average guy just wants to
hear how bad it is; that makes him feel good. It's the negative
stories that get the front-page play. . . .I'm glad I wasn't
here during the Korean Air Lines crisis. I was in Washington,
thank God. There was such hysteria in the U. S., and I know I
would have been expected to fulfill Americans' expectations.'"

330.   Gardner, Corinna. "Uncovering Nuclear Illusion." NT
          4.4 (1986) 21.
      An account of Steven Kull's interviews of government and
military leaders in both the US and SU to ascertain their
rationales for supporting the arms race. He concludes that both
sides are remarkably irrational.

331.   Garrison, Jim and Pyare Shivpuri. The Russian
          Threat: Its Myths and Realities. London: Gateway, 1983.
          344.
      An examination of "two main issues:" "Are the Russians
really bent upon dominating the world? Or is the White House
using the threat of Russian domination to itself dominate the
world?" The authors found "a lot of 'mis' in both the education
and the information about the Russians and about ourselves. . .
It is fear on both sides that compels the Russians to brand the
Americans as the imperialists and compels the Americans to paint
the Russians as the expansionists. Both are divided by
ignorance but deep down, they are both united in their fear"
(Preface).

332.   Gavshon, Arthur. "The Power and Influence Behind
          America's Right." MGW (Dec. 1, 1985) 9.
      How right wing Sovietphobia assaults civil liberty.

Concerned primarily with The Heritage Foundation.

333.   Gervasi. Tom. "Charting the Double Standard in the
        Coverage of Chernobyl." Dead 1.3 (1986) 1-5.
The self-righteous tone of media coverage of the Chernobyl
nuclear disaster reflected "a double standard that overlooked
much of our own nuclear record." US newsrooms "turned a tragic
accident and powerful warning into a shrill exercise in Cold War
journalism."

334.   Gluck, Sidney, ed. "The New Far Right Attack on the
        Campuses." New York: Scholars Against the Escalating
        Danger of the Far Right, 1986. 16.
A collection of articles exposing the repressive aims of
Accuracy in Academia.

335.   Goldberg, Donald. "War Without Guns." NaR 9.2
        (1985) 9-11.
The Federal Emergency Management Agency (FEMA) is planning
"economic warfare" in response "to a real or potential threat
from a hostile state," specifically, the Soviet Union.

336.   Gordon, Michael R., and Roger P. Labrie. "The Press
        Rewrites Salt II." CJR 22.2 (1983) 39-40.
Because journalists generally misunderstand or have not
read the SALT II treaty document they erroneously and unfairly
have accused the SU of violating it.

337.   Gordon, Suzanne. "Impaired Faculties." Prog 47.10
        (1983) 18-21.
Examples of attacks on radical activist academics.

338.   Gulden, Bob. "American Myths and New Soviet
        Realities." Guard 38.38 (1986) 5.
Review of Cohen's Sovieticus and Hough's The Struggle for
the Third World. Both books "help to dismantle" stereotypes
about the Soviet Union. For example, Hough shows that the SU
"does not inspire (or even predict) many revolutions that
occur."

339.   Halliday, Fred. "Managing the News in the East and
        West." ITT 9.37 (1985) 17.
Well-reported stories of Soviet military superiority and
support of revolutions are myths created and sustained by US
officials, academics, and journalists.

340.   Hentoff, Nat. "Treason in the Stacks." Prog 49.5
        (1985) 28-30.
Harry Kenneth Clark, a reshelver at the Library of
Congress, was the subject of a large scale FBI investigation
after attending meetings of socialist political parties and was
subsequently denied promotion.

341.   Herman, Edward, and Frank Brodhead. The Rise and Fall

of the Bulgarian Connection. New York: Sheridan, 1986. 255.

The "main thesis" of the book is that "the only Bulgarian Connection in the plot to assassinate Pope John Paul II existed in the minds of its originators and spokespersons in the West and in the selective coverage of the topic in the Western mass media. The story of the 'rise' of the Connection is therefore the tale of how and why this politically useful story was put over by a small coterie of U. S. journalists who we believe to be propagandists and disinformationists, most notably Claire Sterling, Paul Henze, and Michael Ledeen. More broadly, The Rise and Fall of the Bulgarian Connection is a case study of how the mass media of the Free World function as a propaganda system" (Preface xi). Ch. 7, "The Dissemination of the Bulgarian Connection Plot," examines the media propaganda system: Reader's Digest, NBC, CBS, New York Times, Wall Street Journal, PBS, Christian Science Monitor, Time, Newsweek, etc.

342.   Hersh, Seymour. The Target Is Destroyed: What Really Happened to Flight 007 and What America Knew About It. New York: Random, 1986. 288.

The KAL 007 aircraft shot down over Soviet territory was not a spy plane, but US military tracking posts did know the airline was far off course and in danger, but for many reasons warnings were not sent. After the plane was shot down various anti-Soviet officials charged the Russians with deliberately and wantonly shooting down what they knew to be a civilian aircraft. This story was immediately accepted by most of the US press. But in fact Soviet air defense forces confused the KAL 007 with a military RC-135 that had been gathering electronic intelligence along the periphery of Soviet airspace.

343.   Hertsgaard, Mark. "How Reagan Seduced Us." VV (Sept. 18, 1984) 42.

Analysis of a speech by the President in March, 1984, full of "one-sided interpretations" and "demonstrably false statements" against the SU, yet the networks, the NY Times and the Washington Post failed to condemn the disinformation.

344.   Heuvel, Katrina. "No Free Speech at Radio Liberty." Na 241.19 (1985) 612-15.

A Soviet defector was fired from his job with Radio Liberty, the US government funded anti-Soviet station in Munich, for criticizing "anti-democratic and anti-Semitic broadcasts."

345.   Hoffman, Stanley. Dead Ends: American Foreign Policy in the New Cold War. Cambridge, MA: Ballinger, 1983. 299.

"I deeply deplore the new orthodoxy [and the new Cold War that it tries to wage], not because I believe that the Soviet Union is a benevolent or conservative state, nor because I underestimate the scope and depth of the superpowers' rivalry, but because a cold war strategy rests on an incomplete analysis of the international system and is capable of leading only to

confrontations that heighten the risks for world order and
international security" (2).

346.   "Hollywood's New Bad Guy." MacNeil-Lehrer News Hour,
          Nov. 1, 1985.
      An increasing number of movies and television shows feature
"Eastern European or Soviet villains."

347.   "It's As Simple As ABC to the Cold Warriors." ITT
          10.14 (1986) 14.
      As "Reagan continues to define national independence and
self-determination as a Communist plot orchestrated by the Evil
Empire, he helps guarantee that every movement against existing
Third World tyrannies can expect aid only from the Soviets."

348.   Johnson, Michael W. "Debunking the Window of
          Vulnerability: A Comparison of Soviet and American
          Military Forces." TR 85 (1982) 58-65, 70.
      The US government claims that, in the 1980s, the Soviets
will have achieved military nuclear superiority, but quality,
not quantity, is one of the major reasons the US has and will
maintain nuclear superiority.349.

349.   Johnson, R. W. Shootdown: Flight 007 and the American
          Connection. New York: Viking, 1986. 335.
      The book makes a qualified case that Korean Air Lines
Flight 007, shot down over Soviet territory, was on some sort of
intelligence mission when it was destroyed. Events following
the disaster were orchestrated by US officials to obscure the
truth and to denigrate the Soviet Union. And attempts to track
down the full story are still being frustrated: data erased,
employees gagged, etc.

350.   Johnstone, Diana. "Dressed to Kill in Cozy Arms
          Race." ITT 10.5 (1985) 7.
      The 12th post-war US/SU summit was a media event. Reagan
maintained his Strategic Defense Initiative ("Star Wars") to
give the "U. S. military-industrial complex a new wind" and to
crush the Soviets economically.

351.   Johnstone, Diana. "Rome's Verdict: A Qualified
          Acquittal." ITT 10.20 (1986) 9, 15.
      The Italian prosecutor alleged that Moscow through Bulgaria
"must have directed the assassination attempt" on Pope John Paul
II by Mehmet Ali Agca, but "it became clear" that the
prosecution "had no material evidence."

352.   Jones, Jeff. "Margaret Randall To Be Deported."
          Guard 38.5 (1985) 5.
      She has been denied alien resident status on ideological
grounds under the McCarthy-era McCarran-Walter Act, because she
has lived in Cuba and Nicaragua and has written sympathetically
about those countries.

353.   "KAL 007: Many Questions Still Unanswered." <u>Bth</u> 7.1-2
         (1986) 36.
     Because "there are serious questions unanswered," an "open,
public investigation is clearly needed."

354.   Kaye, Tony. "The 27th Soviet Party Congress As Seen
         on U. S. Television." <u>Dead</u> 1.2 (1986) 10-11.
     ABC and CBS were particularly biased in their presentations
of the SU's 27th Congress.

355.   Kaye, Tony. "Playing Musical Chairs on the Network
         News Interview Shows." <u>Dead</u> 1.1 (March/April, 1986) 2-4.
     The "range of groups represented" on network news interview
shows dealing with arms control and US/SU relations "was
numbingly narrow," composed mainly of current and former US
government officials. "During the Reagan era . . . the whole
spectrum has moved so far to the right that Robert McNamara now
represents the left wing of the nuclear debate in official
circles and on the news talk shows."

356.   Kaye, Tony. "We Keep America on Top of the World."
         <u>Dead</u> 1.4 (1986) 5.
     CBS news consistently reports the SU in a negative manner.

357.   Kirkhorn, Michael. "Gorbachev As Corporate CEO: The
         Making and Trashing of an Image." <u>Dead</u> 1.2 (1986) 5-6.
     In innumerable ways US media tries to discredit the premier
of the SU. "This dismissive attitude was particularly
noticeable in network reporting."

358.   Knelman, F. H. <u>Reagan, God and the Bomb: From Myth to
         Policy in the Nuclear Arms Race</u>. Buffalo, NY:
         Prometheus, 1985. 343.
     A "holy nuclear crusade supported by a 'holocaust lobby'
and based on a mythology of nuclear warfighting now occupies
Washington."

359.   Konrad, George. <u>Antipolitics: An Essay</u>. New York:
         Harcourt, 1984. 243.
     "The East-West dichotomy doesn't depict the world
realistically; it works ideologically, to justify the bipolar
Holy Alliance of the Cold War. In the realms of ideological
war, everything becomes uncertain; agreements no longer have
validity, and all declarations become propaganda statements.
People hear what the foreign ministers say in public, but not
what they say to one another in private. The ideological war
calls into being societies that are half-formed, banal,
accustomed to thinking in cliches" (34).

360.   Kovel, Joel. <u>Against the State of Nuclear Terror</u>.
         Boston: South End, 1984. (Rev. and updated 1983 British
         ed.). 250.
     "The state needs an enemy. The whole system would collapse
like a house of cards unless it could focus on something made to

seem worse than itself." The anticommunism "that has so dominated U. S. life in recent times is one of the most spectacular exercises of the mechanism of projection in human history." Moreover, "it is essential that such indoctrination not take place solely through the state itself, or the corporations directly behind it." The state "can count on the press to hammer away at the basic themes of nuclear terror--to distort the reality of the bomb, to overemphasize the state's role as a protector from it, to underemphasize the state's lawlessness, and always to make the Soviets out to be worse than they are" (51-58).

361.   Landau, Saul. "Dress Rehearsal for a Red Scare." Na 242.13 (1986) 482-4.
    While teaching at the University of California, Davis, the author was the victim of a smear campaign by the right-wing Students for a Better America, part of a national Sovietphobic campaign.

362.   Landis, Fred. "Moscow Rules Moss's Mind." CAIB 2 (1985) 36-38.
    Robert Moss, a leading Sovietphobe, has written books on KGB plots to take over South America, to take over Europe, to take over the US (The Spike and Monimbo, with Arnaud de Borchgrave) and to take over the world (Death Beam). He has now written Moscow Rules about the collapse of the SU.

363.   Law, Steven. "Neo-con Noggin-banging Session." Guard 38.11 (1985) 3.
    On the meeting in Washington of anticommunist intellectuals from around the world sponsored by the Committee for the Free World, which receives most of its money from the right-wing Scaife and Olin foundations.

364.   Ledbetter, James. "I Was a Spy for Accuracy in Academia: Campus Double Agent." NR 193.27 (1985) 14-16.
    In an attempt to weed out Marxists on college campuses, AIA sent informants into the classroom.

365.   Lewis, Anthony. "New Conservatives Prefer Foreign Policy Crusades to Caution." AG (Dec. 19, 1985) 19A.
    Certain neoconservatives want the US to intervene everywhere against communism.

366.   "Limits of Dissent." Na 241.19 (1985) 603-04.
    On the US government's efforts to deport Margaret Randall because of her criticism of US policies.

367.   Mahler, Richard. "Anti-Communism Soaped Up In ABC's Amerika." ITT 10.26 (1986) 20-21.
    ABC's film about the Soviet takeover of the US is mainly a paranoid attack on liberals and leftists who, the film alleges, allowed the Russians to conquer.

368.   Makhijani, Arjun. "The Anti-Communists Are Coming!"
     NaR 9 (1986) 8.
An account of the World Anti-Communist League meeting held
in Dallas in the fall of 1985. The Rev. Sun Myung Moon, contra
leaders, wealthy right-wing Americans, and similar rightists
attended.

369.   Manley, John F. "Who Judges Accuracy in America?"
     ITT 10.5 (1985) 16.
Accuracy in Academia is "a threat to academic freedom" for
trying to root out professors of left orientation.

370.   Manoff, Robert K. "What Is the Real Message That
     Rocky and Dan Rather Send?" Dead 1.2 (1986) 8-9.
The widespread ignorance of Americans about the SU is part
of the anti-Soviet cognitive environment "created by political
leadership" and "then ramified and elaborated on by the entire
apparatus of culture," so that powerful anti-Soviet messages
"are often contained in news stories that seem peripheral."

371.   Manzione, Elton. "The Private Spy Agency." NaR 9.2
     (1985) 34-39.
The Western Goals Foundation, founded by former Congressman
Larry McDonald and headed by Roy Cohn, is "dedicated to spying
on the left." The Foundation is supported by corporations,
other right-wing foundations, and wealthy individual like Nelson
Bunker Hunt.

372.   McMahan, Jeff. Reagan and the World: Imperial Policy
     in the New Cold War. New York: Monthly, 1985. 300.
The overriding aim of the Reagan administration has been to
ensure control over the world in order to meet the threat to the
American Way posed by the menace of international communism and
by nationalist movements in the third world. For this aim the
administration has mounted an "unremitting campaign" and
"propaganda offensive" to "purge the Vietnam syndrome from the
body politic" and to portray the SU as the ultimate evil
threatening the very existence of the US.

373.   Miles, Sara. "The War at Home." RA 20.2 (1986)
     40-46.
The US anticommunist leaders seek "to recreate the sense of
a wartime situation" in order to manipulate the public and to
justify global intervention. They accomplish this aim partly by
the creation of "a new vocabulary" of "terrorism" or
"international terrorism," "low-intensity conflict," and
"humanitarian aid." These subterfuges are fundamental to the
administration's propaganda successes.

374.   Miller, Steven. "Salt Shakers: Are the Soviets
     Cheating?" NR 193 (July 8, 1985) 11-15.
Allegations of Soviet cheating on arms control agreements
reveal upon examination some plausibility in Soviet explanations
and eventual compliance where cheating actually occurred.

375.   Mische, Patricia. "Do the Soviets Cheat at Arms
          Control?" East Orange, NJ: Global Education
          Associates, 1985. (No. 21, The Whole Earth Paper).
Administration allegations of Soviet arms control
noncompliance contain no substantive evidence of Soviet
cheating.

376.   Moberg, David. "Media Turn Deaf Ear to the Peace
          Movement." ITT 10.11 (1985) 6.
"The Soviet Union's unilateral five-month moratorium on
nuclear testing, recently extended for three more months, seems
to have disappeared into a black hole of American
consciousness."

377.   "Mystery of Yellow Rain." NOVA (April 16, 1985).
An analysis of US government accusations that Vietnam with
the help of the Soviet Union dropped poisonous chemicals in
Southeast Asia reveals that swarms of bees are responsible for
the "yellow rain."

378.   Pally, Marcia. "Red Faces." FC 22.1 (1986) 32-37.
Hollywood hits like Rambo, Rocky IV, and White Nights seem
to be "training films for World War III, or anyway Cold War II"
(Contents page). "The media are trying to soothe our crisis in
self-image with the hate that dares to blare its name: Nuke the
Russians" (32).

379.   Peterzell, Jay. "The New Afganistanism." CJR 19.6
          (1981) 5-7.
A 60 Minutes broadcast, "Inside Afganistan," by Dan Rather
and many other news sources denied the US was supplying arms to
the rebels when in fact it was.

380.   Pieragostini, Karl. "Soviet Cheating? Reagan's Rush
          to Judgment." ADIU Report 6.1 (1984) 1-5.
Examination of allegations of Soviet arms control cheating
in four main areas finds the evidence "less than wholly
convincing."

381.   Pike, John, and Jonathan Rich. "Charges of Treaty
          Violations: Much Less Than Meets the Eye." JFAS 37.3
          (1984) 1-20.
Analysis of five of the seven allegations the Reagan
administration made of Soviet arms control violations, all well
reported in the media. "Given the ambiguity of some of the
treaty provisions, as well as the inconclusive nature of U. S.
evidence, few, if any, of the alleged violations can be proven."

382.   "Resignation Explained." AG (March 18, 1985) 6A.
The president of the Corporation for Public Broadcasting
resigned because the CPB Board banned travel to the Soviet Union
by public broadcasters.

383.   Reuben, William A. "The Documents That Weren't
         There." Na 241.2 (1985) 44-47.
Several recent spy cases, including the Walker and
Shevchenko cases, have "fueled the Administration's campaign to
restrict freedom in the name of security."

384.   Richelson, Jeffrey. "U. S. Intelligence and Soviet
         Star Wars." BAS 42.5 (1986) 12-14.
"Claims that Star Wars is a necessary U. S. response to a
vigorous Soviet space-based defense effort must be examined in
the light of earlier misleading intelligence predictions of
Soviet strategic programs."

385.   Ridgeway, James. "Invasion of the Classroom." TO
         77.18 (1985) 7-8.
Accuracy in Media (AIM) has launched a new group, Accuracy
in Academia (AIA), to root out Marxism in the classrooms of the
US.

386.   Rosen, Jay. "Ted Turner: 'Captain Outrageous' Or an
         Ambassador of Goodwill?" Dead 1.4 (1986) 6-8.
Turner's Goodwill Games were reported mainly by sports
reporters and disregarded by Pentagon, arms, and foreign policy
reporters.

387.   Rothmyer, Karen. "Mapping Out Moon's Media Empire."
         CJR 23.4 (1984) 23-31.
Unification Church leader Reverend Sung Myung Moon has
extensive holdings in the news media, but the real impact of
such ownership on individual news sources has yet to be
determined. His News World Communications organization helps
spread the church's anticommunist, anti-Soviet doctrine.

388.   Rowan, Carl. "Spy Panic Threatens Freedom." AG (June
         14, 1985) 21A.
The danger of the "panic and passion" over recent Soviet
espionage in the US is that it "will provoke us to emulate them,
meaning we will become a secretive and totalitarian society,
embracing more and more police state trappings in the foolish
belief that more secrecy and surveillance will keep us free."

389.   Rubin, David. "'A Range of Opinion as Narrow as
         Scarlett O'Hara's Waist.'" Dead (March/April, 1986) 1-2.
The Reagan administration's scornful treatment of Soviet
arms control proposals was retailed by the press.

390.   Rubin, David. "Why Not Declare the N. Y. Times a
         Nuclear Proliferation Zone?" Dead 1.2 (1986) 2-3.
With certain exceptions (Tom Wicker, and a few other
columnists) the Times supports the Reagan administration's
nuclear policies.

391.   Scheer, Robert. With Enough Shovels: Reagan, Bush and
         Nuclear War. New York: Random, 1982. 285.

An account "of how a handful of Cold War ideologues--led by the President himself--have reversed the longstanding American assumption that nuclear war means mutual suicide" and have "now chosen to fight and win a nuclear war--in fact, a protracted nuclear war with many nuclear exchanges," in the belief that "once such a war is won the U. S. will return to normal."

392.   Shapiro, Bruce. "Teaching Cops About Terrorism." Na 241.11 (1985) 344, 346.
Terrorism workshops "are spiced with rabid anti-Communism and cover such subjects as infiltrating protest movements, gathering intelligence and controlling political rallies."

393.   Sloyan, Patrick. "The Warnings Reagan Ignored." Na 239.13 (1984) 410-13.
Because Reagan saw the showdown in Beirut between Christians and Moslems in rigid Cold War patterns, he refused to withdraw the marines.

394.   Smock, William. "The Unhappy Warriors." ITT 10.7 (1985) 19.
A review of William J. Broad's book Star Warriors about the scientists at the Lawrence Livermore National Laboratory who are working on missile defense and lasers to win, not preclude, nuclear wars, and to bankrupt the Soviet Union.

395.   "Sneak Previews." Chicago: WTTW, January 23, 1986.
This program on recent anti-Soviet films from Hollywood suggests that films about the SU "try to evoke sympathy for people who are oppressed by communism inside Russia" and "show horrible atrocities perpetrated by communists beyond Soviet Union borders." The films are popular, in contrast to films which criticize the US or express appreciation for the SU, such as Reds, Daniel, Missing, and Under Fire.

396.   Soloman, Norman. "Americans Shouldn't Be So Quick To Mock Soviet Peace Groups." ITT 9.36 (1985) 12.
Few people in the West believe "that much good can come from an institution [the Soviet Peace committee] sponsored by the Soviet state." Yet "the five-month unilateral moratorium on nuclear test explosions put into effect on August 6 by Gorbachev, and rejected by President Reagan, indicates that the Soviet Union's current nuclear policies are less irresponsible than the Reagan policies being unsuccessfully challenged by the American [peace] movement."

397.   Stoloff, Samuel J. "Campus Red Scare." Na 233.8 (1981) 229-30.
At the University of Texas and other institutions of higher learning there is a growing tendency to "eliminate people with leftist convictions."

398.   "Summit Fallout." Na 243.13 (1986) 395-6.
"Reagan's attempt to disinform the American public about

the negotiation record at Iceland cannot undo the fact, as many American participants observed, that the Russians offered sweeping compromises."

399.   "A Surreal Policy Makes Us 'Victims Of Fear'." C&C
          45.15 (1985) 363-364.
     US foreign policy is determined by "ideological anticommunism, not by real pursuit of democratic goals. Anticommunism as a substitute for making wise choices in a complex world" characterizes President Reagan, who divides the world into friends and enemies.

400.   Talbott, Strobe. Deadly Gambits: The Reagan
          Administration and the Stalemate in Nuclear Arms Control.
          New York: Knopf, 1984. 380.
     "The U. S. would do best with gambits at the negotiating table that would lead to diplomatic stalemate; that the U. S. might more freely acquire and deploy new pieces on its side of the board and position itself, if necessary, to make winning military moves against the Soviet Union" (xii).

401.   Trinkl, John. "The Red Scare As a Way of Life."
          Guard 38.13 (Dec. 1985) 20, 17.
     A book review of The Uses of Anti-Communism, the Socialist Register 1984 by Miliband, Saville, and Liebman. Concerned with the prevailing public attitude toward the Soviets: "Anti-Communism is deeply embedded in our body politic. From the right wing paranoid fantasy film Red Dawn to the liberal anti-communist portrayal of the Soviet Union in Moscow on the Hudson, to the current Rocky IV where Rambo goes toe to toe with the Russkies, anti-communism is not so much an attitude as a part of many people's definition of the world."

402.   "The Unilateral Soviet Union Moratorium and the U. S.
          Response." NMPN (Nov.-Dec., 1985) 3-4.
     Criticism of US failure to join with the Soviet Union moratorium on the testing of nuclear warheads and refutation of US arguments for rejecting the moratorium.

403.   "Universities Urged to Join in Fighting AIA Threat."
          SLJR 13.84 (1986) 12.
     A report of the letter sent by the American Civil Liberties Union to 123 major universities and 36 educational organizations denouncing the efforts of Accuracy in Academia to monitor the ideological "errors" of instructors as part of a larger movement to censor and restrict information in universities, public schools, and libraries.

404.   Weaver, Maureen. "Cold War Charges and the Nuclear
          Freeze." ON 6.8 (1982) 3, 11.
     Ronald Reagan's McCarthyite claim that Soviet agents had infiltrated the peace movement is part of a right-wing smear campaign by Far-Right publicists, think-tanks and lobbyists who push the idea that citizens who work for peace and disarmament

are the dupes of manipulative Soviet agents.

405.   Weiss, Ted. "Honorable Members?" <u>Na</u> 237.11 (1983)
        328.
   On recent McCarthyism in Congress by Republican Congressmen
in a reprise of the early 1950s. "In the Reagan years,
McCarthylike charges . . . seem to be occurring with greater
frequency and vehemence."

406.   Wenger, Martha. "Caution, Yellow Rainmakers." <u>CS</u> 8.1
        (1983) 24.
   Further refutation of the Reagan administration's charge
that Laos, Vietnam, and the SU are killing people in Southeast
Asia with a new chemical warfare agent called "yellow rain."

407.   Wheaton, Philip. "'Attack on the Americas,' A
        Critique." <u>CAIB</u> 12 (1981) 22-23.
   The film produced by the American Security Council for the
Coalition for Peace Through Strength is a piece of "pure cold
war paranoia."

408.   "Where East Meets West." <u>Soj</u> 16.2 (1987).
   Several articles on US/SU hostility, "the great divide of
our time."

409.   Wolf, Louis, and Fred Clarkson. "Arnaud de Borchgrave
        Boards Moon's Ship." <u>CAIB</u> 24 (1985) 34-35.
   The new editor-in-chief of the <u>Washington Times</u>, owned by
Reverend Sun Myung Moon, "is a driven man, consumed by his mania
that disinformation is being foisted on the world by forces
ranging from the KGB in Moscow, through the international
communist conspiracy, to the myriad of peace, anti-intervention,
and anti-nuclear groups and individuals in the United States and
Europe."

410.   Woodmansee, Dave. "There." <u>SLJR</u> 14.88 (September
        1986) 2.
   Thee print media have covered military involvement in the
space shuttle program vey poorly.

411.   Yates, Michael. "South Africa, Anti-Communism, and
        Value-Free Science." <u>CHE</u> 32.11 (May 14, 1986) 84.
   "Nowhere in the industrialized world is anti-communism more
the official, state-sponsored ideology than it is in the United
States, and nowhere are academics as subservient to state
interests as they are here. The range of ideological debate in
this country is extremely narrow; anything 'radical' is by
definition off limits. Members of the media--and of academe--
exercise rigorous self-censorship, lest they be accused of
harboring subversive ideas."

412.   "'Yellow Rain': Bee Feces." <u>Bth</u> 7.1-2 (1986) 36.
   US allegations of Soviet use of chemical and biological
warfare in Southeast Asia are false. The "yellow rain" was bee
excrement.

413.   Yoffe, Emily. "New Weapon Unleashed by Irvine, AIM."
     WJR 1.4 (1978) 9, 12.
     Reed Irvine "and a group of anti-communist friends started
the Washington Press to combat imbalanced press coverage." This
is the latest undertaking by Irvine's Accuracy in Media
organization.

II. THE COMPLEX   414-1005

Introduction

A. Interlocking Power   415-470

B. Military-Industrial Complex   471-534

C. Corporations and Government Regulation   535-605

D. Media   606-787
    1.   Mass Media   606-665
    2.   News   666-787

E. Education and Research   788-887
    1.   Curriculum   789-858
    2.   Research   859-881
    3.   Governing Boards and Officers   882-887

F. Secrecy, Censorship, Disinformation, Deceit   888-1005

THE COMPLEX

INTRODUCTION

Interlocking Power

The ultimate questions the writers in this bibliography
address are those Edward Greenberg raises throughout his book on
The American Political System: "Is America just? Is America
democratic?" But these writers search for answers indirectly by
stalking the powers and processes which define reality. They
seek to understand how the prevailing views of justice and democracy have been created and sustained. How is the system legitimated? How does the system engender and maintain the belief that
the existing institutions are the most appropriate ones?
(Denitch). What are the links between economic and military
power and communications conceived in the broadest sense to
include elementary education and satellites? James Reston
asserted in lectures published by the Council on Foreign Relations that "'the responsible government official and the responsible reporter in the field of foreign affairs are not really in
conflict ninety per cent of the time'" (quot. in Downing). Shoup
shows how concentrated and interconnected is the control of "the
most influential media corporations of the United States" by the
"Eastern Establishment" (305). How has this unity occurred? How
is it perpetuated? What are its effects?
     A complete analysis must begin with fundamental institutions
and processes of domination and dependency. Robert Heilbroner
explores the relationships of the drive for wealth and the
attainment of power to the evolution of attitudes toward wealth
favorable to "the regime of capital": greed became "interest,"
with God and logic on its side, until now the legitimacy of capitalism, profits, and self-gain is seldom questioned and the
notions of surplus and exploitation suppressed from orthodox discourse.
     Clark and Dear in State Apparatus show how "the state appara-
tus operates as a complex system to ensure the political legitimacy of capitalist society." They ground their analysis fundamentally in language, how the system structures political discourse "bound by rules of inclusion and exclusion" to facilitate
"accumulation and social control." The language of politics "can
be thought of as the lingua franca of the state apparatus. For
example, the formalization of political discourse embodies a language of 'proper'or acceptable political behavior, and 'deligi-
timizes' other competing or unacceptable modes of political activity."
     G. William Domhoff in his many books focuses on the process
of rule. In The Powers That Be, for example, he examines four
components of the process. First, the means by which the wealthy
and influential persons and corporations "obtain tax breaks,
favors, subsidies and procedural rulings" beneficial to their
interests (25). Second, ways elites select and elect candidates
for high office, the personal and institutional connections among
individual corporations, parties, and the media. Third, the process by which controlling individuals, families, and companies

maintain a favorable ideology--e.g., the Council on Foreign Relations shaping foreign policy, the Committee on Economic Development advocating f: ~ enterprise. Fourth, how long-range policy strategies are for. ! by a network of wealthy people, corporations, and law firms, with the assistance of university expertise--issues such as telecommunications ownership in the year 2000. Financial resources provide research, which validates decisions, which prepare public opinion, and creates laws.

The Military-Industrial Complex

President Eisenhower has become as famous for his Farewell Address warning about the MIC as for anything else he said as President. Since that time, Seymour Melman, Sidney Lens, and many other scholars have established the history, the mechanisms, and the consequences of the complex in impressive detail. By the 1960s Melman was explaining the Pentagon-capitalist-war economy, the union of government, finance, and industry, and their depradations on resources and quality of life. Adams, Caldicott, and others have shown how the "iron triangle" works: military contractors, Executive branch (Pentagon, DOE, NASA), and Congress functioning as the "national security state." By 1986 military contracts accounted for 28 percent of all federal funds given to universities; two-thirds of all research at Johns Hopkins University was funded by the Pentagon; high tech industries had become partners with the Pentagon; Congress generally rubber-stamped the arms budgets; and the President had become the chief manager of the Corporate-Pentagon State.

Government Regulation

It has been in the natural interest of the elites both to have government intervene for stability in economic affairs and to control that intervention (Kolko). The control has been sometimes easy and sometimes not, depending upon the particular political party and president in power or the agency administrator. But in general there has developed a close cooperation between the economic, the political, and the communications institutions, which explains why so many of these writers refer to the system as state capitalism. Citizen groups in the 1970s struggled strenuously for access to media and to compel the regulatory agencies to defend the public. But the intimate association of businessmen and regulators was never significantly interrupted. One complicated issue continues to defy solution: whether broadcasting should be regulated--specifically whether the Fairness Doctrine should be abolished. The problem of how to make broadcasting more responsive to the needs of the people and to democracy, in greater balance with capital accumulation, is one of the most urgently discussed by the contributors to this bibliography. As these studies show, the drive to eliminate the regulatory structures, perhaps necessary in some cases, eliminates laws and agencies essential to social justice and the provision of information for an enlightened citizenry. (See VI on regulation of the intelligence agencies.)

Mass Media

We are experiencing a cultural revolution in the shift from communication by printed word to communication by electronics (radio, motion pictures, television). It is a revolution having profound implications for a democracy, since the freedoms asserted by the Bill of Rights are based upon the assumption that a democratic system depends upon an informed and critically independent people. The new power of electronic communications makes the old danger of undue influence by concentrated power even more alarming than it is for the print media. For it is increasingly felt that control of the electronic media means control of the population. The issues thus resolve into this question: If there is a dominating ideology which represents the interests of an identifiable group, does it determine the content and structure of the mass media? Excellent scholarship by Epstein, Gans and others have demonstrated how crucial are organizational factors in shaping reality. Internal pressures of profits, advertisers, and censorship occur within standardized ways of working and professionalism. But most of the contributors emphasize how much these are also external pressures. Not all go so far as Noam Chomsky's perception of the United States as a state religion governed through the media by setting the terms of debate, particularly through the technique of systematically marginalizing certain ideas and options. But most believe that the internal organization is only part of the construction of reality we find in mainstream magazines, comic strips, soaps, game shows, sit-coms, or news programs, and that to understand the "reality" projected by the mass media we must begin with the patterns of interconnected ownership in the U.S., from banks and industry to networks and publishing companies--the entire indoctrinating iceberg, not only the organizational tip but the underlying economic and political structure and process.

News

Carl Jensen's Project Censored, which celebrated its tenth anniversary in 1985, is one of the most significant media research organizations in the US. A national panel of media experts annually selects the major under-reported news stories of the year. While the mainstream news organizations stressed "junk food journalism"--in 1984 Clara Peller and "where's the beef?" in 1985 Coca-Cola, new, old, classic, and cherry--Jensen's panel for 1985 focused on media neglect of the aerial bombardment of rural El Salvador, "the most intense aerial war in western hemisphere" history, military toxic wastes, and the tenth year of genocide in East Timor.

The contributors to this bibliography are keenly interested in the superficiality of news, its causes, and its uses for the status quo. W. Lance Bennett believes the problem is "too deeply rooted" for remedy. Since influence in a democratic society depends on control of information, and as long as people in power fear an informed populace, the public will never be able to compel elites to reveal their dealings or to acquire sufficient access for successful political struggle. There are conflicts

within the system. A General Westmoreland sued CBS star Mike
Wallace. Paramount Pictures, owned by the conglomerate Gulf +
Western, produced the film <u>Reds</u> about Soviet sympathizer John
Reed. But although critics see opportunities for resistance and
change in the internal openings and contradictions, they agree on
the existence of a system of ownership and power which controls
the boundaries of expression and even of thought--and therefore
of "news." <u>The New York Times</u>, <u>Time</u>, and other major media are
"intimately linked with each other and with many leading corporations as well as with the most important policy planning organizations of upper-class America" (Shoup, 309), and this structure,
though not monolithic, not seamless, does condition what is
acceptable as true, good, and natural. Journalism schools teach
and good journalists strive for objectivity and a balance of competing viewpoinsts. But as William Dorman shows, the Pruning
Hook dissidents against U.S. nuclear missiles are barely reported
and never called political prisoners, while Sakharov and Soviet
dissidents and "political prisoners" receive lavish coverage. And
this is not organizational but is ideological: Kansas City,
where the Pruning Hook defendents were prosecuted, is less remote
than Gorki. The contributors to this bibliography make a persuasive case, in Tuchman's tactful words, for a recognition of news
"as an artful accomplishment attuned to specific understandings
of social reality" which "legitimate the status quo" (1978, 216).
Perhaps this reality is the supreme under-reported story.

Education and Research

The selections in this section describe the multifarious and
complex ways education and research contribute to economic and
cultural reinforcement. Many articles expose the obvious methods.
For example, in <u>A Time for Truth</u> former Treasure Secretary William Simon exhorted businessmen to give money only to clearly
pro-business, pro-capitalist, colleges and universities. To
effectuate that appeal, Simon and Irving Kristol created the
Institute for Educational Affairs (IEA) with business and foundation funds (Olin, Smith Richardson, Scaife) to serve as a clear-
inghouse between wealthy individuals, corporations, and educational institutions (Stone). But such explicit organization and
advocacy of the corporate state represents only the tip of the
iceberg. The US capitalist national security state--just as it
manifests itself in interlocking economic power, the MIC, corporate-government regulatory symbiosis, and the media--thoroughly
informs the schools. The eduational system, as part of the overall system, generally inculcates values favorable to vested
interests and conceals the contradictions and limitations within
it. The sciences, fragmented, empirical, and abstract, protect
and perpetuate the ruling ideology. Even the Humanities, now
specialized and isolated, only feebly performs its traditional
encouragement of the critical thinking a democratic society so
deeply depends upon. Both curriculum and research help defuse
and depoliticize potential challenges to the system and channel
youth into the niches in life required by corporate needs.

Secrecy

The case made by most of the writers on the system is that control is exerted via a multitude of persuasive and indoctrination methods. Created democratic illusions perpetuate concentrated power. But power and interest also thrive through concealment and sometimes by repression, particularly during crises, real or fabricated, when the public's guard is down, as Section VI on the Intelligence Agencies explains.

The contributors to this bibliography fear a "democratic dictatorship" or "friendly fascism" which would arise through a ruling elite gaining control of communication and information. But many of them also find hope in the diversity still possible, the mechanisms for change still functioning, and the contradictions within the State which provide opportunities for those who seek democratic and just alternatives to oligopoly, indoctrination, and secrecy. As Mosco and Herman point out, the system does not always work well for ruling elites; conflicts disturb their interests; government possesses some independence "to shape some measure of coherence"; resistance from below does exert pressure; there is class struggle.

Works Cited

Clark, Gordon and Michael Dear. State Apparatus: Structures and Language of Legitimacy. Boston: Allen, 1984.

Denitch, Bogdan, ed. Legitimation of Regimes: International Frameworks for Analysis. Beverly Hills, CA: Sage, 1979.

Downing, John. Radical Media: The Political Experience of Alternative Communication. Boston: South End, 1984.

Greenberg, Edward. The American Political System: A Radical Approach. 2nd ed. Cambridge, MA: U of Colorado/Winthrop, 1980.

Heilbroner, Robert. The Nature and Logic of Capitalism. New York: Norton, 1985.

Jensen, Carl. "Uncovering the Real News with Project Censored." APME News 163 (October 1986) 19-20.

Stone, Peter. "The I.E.A.--Teaching the `Right' Stuff." Na 233 (September 19, 1981) 231-5.

II. COMPLEX

414.   Bennett, James R. "Domination of Information in the
          United States: An Annotated Bibliography of Selected
          Books." BoB 43.2 (1986) 82-89.
     Almost 200 entries divided into six categories: the
complex, anticommunism, corporations, government, military,
intelligence establishment. Most of these books are included in
the present collection, annotations revised.

II. A. Interlocking Power 415-470

415.   Aronowitz, Stanley. Food, Shelter and the American
          Dream. New York: Seabury, 1974. 188.
     "We are on the road to what Bertram Gross has called
'friendly fascism.'" The foundation of fascism "has already
been laid in the consolidation of political and economic power
in incredibly few hands. The strengthening of the executive
branch of government to the point of almost dictatorial power
has taken place without the traditional symbols of repression."
The "distinctions between executive, legislative and corporate
spheres have been blurred if not completely obliterated" (166-
67).

416.   Ballard, Hoyt, and G. William Domhoff. C. Wright
          Mills and "The Power Elite." Boston: Beacon, 1968.
          478.
     A collection of reviews of Mills' The Power Elite which
described and indicted the ruling system in America: the people
at the head of the great corporations, the armed forces, the
state, and the mass media, who make the big decisions and have
the power to ensure acquiescence by the mass of society.

416a   Boylan, James. "Whose Press Is Free?" CJR 22.6
          (1984) 53-54.
     A favorable review of Altschull's Agents of Power.
Journalists are ethnocentric, "econocentric," and act for those
in power. They tend to believe the system in which they operate
the best one, and "in the long run" they "believe and write what
the system would like to have them believe and write."

417.   Bupp, Irvin and Jean-Claude Derian. Light Water: How
          the Nuclear Dream Dissolved. New York: Basic, 1978.
          241.
     "The way that the innovation process for light water
reactors was managed by business and government in the U.S. and
Western Europe contributed to the identification of nuclear
power technology with something that many citizens in these
countries dislike and distrust about their societies."

418.   Burnham, Walter. The Current Crisis in American
          Politics. Oxford UP, 1983. 330.
     Essays on the causes and consequences of the tension
between capitalism and democracy and the ascendancy of

capitalism. Only the political parties can mobilize the electorate, and they are declining in influence; consequently fewer and fewer people even vote.

419.   Domhoff, G. William. The Bohemian Grove and Other
        Retreats: A Study in Ruling-Class Cohesiveness. New
        York: Harper, 1974. 250.
    "It is my hypothesis that there is a ruling social class in the United States. This class is made up of the owners and managers of large corporations" (82). Analysis of three of its exclusive social clubs, their membership and activities, illustrates his thesis: the Bohemian Grove and Club of San Francisco and the Rancheros Visitadores and the Roundup Riders of the Rockies. [Cf. J. Van der Zee's The Greatest Men's Party on Earth: Inside the Bohemian Grove.]

420.   Domhoff, G. William. Fat Cats and Democrats: the
        Role of the Big Rich in the Party of the Common Man.
        Englewood Cliffs, NJ: Prentice, 1972. 203.
    Democratic Party financial support which determines government policy.

421.   Domhoff, G. William. The Powers That Be: Processes
        of Ruling Class Domination in America. New York:
        Vintage, 1979. 206.
    Domhoff discusses four processes, including the "Ideology Process," "through which members of the power elite attempt to shape the beliefs, attitudes and opinions of the underlying population" (170). The corporate power elite has spent "tens of millions of dollars" to create an ideology network and to shape economic attitudes in the U.S. The Joint Council on Economic Education, for example, funded by corporations and "the major organization in the field of economic education, "publishes books, pamphlets, teaching aids, curriculum guides and "most importantly, perhaps, it attempts to shape college programs in teacher training." The result: "most people state a belief in free enterprise and profits" (182).

422.   Domhoff, G. William. "State and Ruling Class in
        Corporate America." IS 4 (1974) 3-16.
    The country is dominated by a ruling class. The policy-making process employed by this "power elite" controls the flow of foreign policy ideology from the leaders to the general public.

423.   Domhoff, G. William. Who Rules America Now? A View
        for the '80s. Englewood Cliffs, NJ: Prentice, 1984.
        230.
    An up-dating of Who Rules America? (1967). "It is the purpose of this book to present systematic evidence that suggests there is a social upper class in the United States that is a ruling class by virtue of its dominant role in the economy and government. It will be shown that this ruling class is socially cohesive, has its basis in the large corporations and

banks, plays a major role in shaping the social and political climate, and dominates the federal government through a variety of organizations and methods."

424.   Dye, Thomas R. Who's Running America? The Reagan
         Years. 3rd ed. Englewood Cliffs, NJ: Prentice, 1983.
         285.
     The author's oligarchic model of national policy-making assumes that the planning and implementation of national policies derive from corporate and personal wealth. The ideas of the wealth-holding elites are channeled into the foundations, universities, and policy-planning institutions for the determination of national policies and for consensus building among the elites--"bringing together individuals at the top of corporate and financial institutions, the universities, the foundations, and the top law firms, as well as the leading intellectuals, the mass media, and influential figures in government." Out of this process come action recommendations which are then channeled into federal agencies (274-5).

425.   Ehrenreich, Barbara. "Who Owns America?" SD 2.2
         (1978) 29.
     Government/corporate "economic democracy" resembles "old fashioned oligarchy."

426.   Elliott, Dave, et al. The Politics of Nuclear Power.
         London: Pluto, 1978. 141.
     Nuclear technology reflects "the goals and values of the dominant class." This class seeks both profit and the stability for making profit, which means on occasion "resorting to force," or, usually, "developing organizational and technological arrangements which act as direct or indirect social controls." Because the author believes nuclear technology is neither profitable nor socially healthy, he analyzes why it is being "forced upon us."

427.   Gandy, Oscar. Beyond Agenda Setting: Information
         Subsidies and Public Policy. Norwood, NJ: Ablex, 1982.
         243.
     The power and methods utilized by corporate government participants in the public-policy process to influence the decisions of others through systematic reduction of the costs of access to self-serving information," especially through "their skillful manipulation of the mass media or other information channels." The opening chs. discuss agenda setting and subsidized information. Five chs. focus on information subsidies in various specific policy areas: health, education, science and technology, and national economic planning.

428.   Green, Mark, et al. The Closed Enterprise System.
         New York: Grossman, 1972. 488.
     An indictment of monopoly capitalism, the failure of federal antitrust enforcement, and "crime in the suites." Part I describes the economic and political setting in which

antitrust enforcement occurs. Part II on the Department of Justice and III on the Federal Trade Commission describe the "political interventions into the enforcement process."

429.   Gross, Bertram. Friendly Fascism: The New Face of Power in America. Boston: South End, 1982. 410.
The author perceives "a slow and powerful drift toward greater concentration of power and wealth in a repressive Big Business - Big Government partnership." This complex of power includes the manipulation of ruling myths that camouflage the growth of the power. "As shown in 'The Friendly Fascist Establishment' (Chapter 9) and 'Managing Information and Minds' (Chapter 12), these myths establish "America's symbolic environment. The Reagan administration has triggered a great leap forward in the mobilization and deployment of corporaatist myths" (from the Preface to the paperback ed.). The schools and media play "a major role." Indeed, "friendly fascism in the United States is unthinkable without the thorough integration of knowledge, information, and communication complexes into the Establishment" (255).

430.   Guerra, Joe. "Promoting Nuclear Power DOE-Style." CMJ 7.6 (1981) 5, 14.
The Department of Energy plans to conduct an expensive public relations advertising campaign to justify the administration's plans to continue nuclear subsidies.

431.   Halberstam, David. The Powers That Be. New York: Knopf, 1979. 771.
A study of Time, the Washington Post, the Los Angeles Times, and CBS, their owners (Luce, the Grahams, the Chandlers, and Paley), and corporate, government, media, and personal alliances and conflicts.

432.   Hartz, Louis. The Liberal Tradition in America: An Interpretation of American Political Thought Since the Revolution. New York: Harcourt, 1955. 329.
A history and appraisal of "the American liberal absolutism," the orthodoxy of both political parties and the basis for their opposition to socialism. "The redscare mentality displays the American absolutism in its purest form" (301), a reflection of "the irrational inward passion of 'Americanism'" which is "as grave a threat to domestic freedom as any we have ever faced" (303).

433.   Heilbroner, Robert. The Nature and Logic of Capitalism. New York: Norton, 1985. 225.
The capitalist economic system requires partnership with the state. And its legitimacy thrives upon control of ideology and therefore of information, redefining attitudes toward wealth, turning acquisitiveness into a virtue and liberty into doing what one wants, teaching the public not to question the "inevitable" and "natural" system, and not to intrude morality in the drive to amass wealth.

434.   Hochman, Sandra and Sybil Wong. <u>Satellite Spies: The Frightening Impact of a New Technology</u>. Indianapolis: Bobbs, 1976. 212.
The American people have had "no role in determining the domestic applications of satellites" even though satellites would "centralize control of society's information resources" and "boundlessly extend the government's capacity for surveillance." Chap. 7, "Corporate Control," tells the story of the government's give-away of satellite technology to a few giant corporations, the public paying all the way, "one more triumph for American capitalism."

435.   Jezer, Marty. <u>The Dark Ages: Life in the United States, 1945-1960</u>. Boston: South End, 1982. 335.
A survey of broad social problems and themes "in the context of monopolistic tendencies endemic to American capitalism as a whole." Part One, "Repression at Home and Abroad," treats the Cold War and military-industrial complex; Chap. 4 focuses upon anticommunism and political repression in the U.S. Part Two covers various aspects of life in the country, the section unified by "how the large corporations used their wealth, power and influence to shape the quality of life in virtually every social sphere." Part Three discusses the participatory and democratic currents that develop in the 1960s and early 1970s.

436.   Karp, Walter. <u>Indispensable Enemies: The Politics of Misrule in America</u>. New York: Saturday Review, 1973. 308.
"The near-monopoly of American politics by two collusive party syndicates is not one problem among many. It is the first and fundamental one as well as the wellspring of most of the others. As long as the present oligarchy rules, we will not have a restrained and peaceable foreign policy; we will not see racism languish and mutual respect grow among the citizenry. We will not see special interests curbed, economic dependence diminished nor special privilege stripped from the overprivileged," etc. (278). Chap. 14, "The Restoration of Self-Government," urges Americans to break up the ruling dynasty, "to break up party control of politics and strip the usurpers of their corrupt and corrupting power."

437.   Karp, Walter. "The Life of TV's Political Power." <u>CH</u> 3 (May/June 1983) 37-40.
"The notion that television wields political power, shapes our history and undermines the political establishment is a preposterous and pernicious fiction." In fact, television's power derives from those in power. It and "the parties are the closest of collaborators."

438.   Katznelson, Ira, and Mark Kesselman. <u>The Politics of Power: A Critical Introduction to American Government</u>. 2nd ed. New York: Harcourt, 1979. 435.
A study of the "fundamental inequalities--political, economic, social, and educational--which exist "among groups and

classes in the United States" and of "what these inequalities mean in terms of a democratic order." The authors place primary emphasis on the relationship between American capitalism and politics, since "the requirements of capitalism limit democratic practice and relegate democracy largely to the sphere of selecting government officials" (Preface). Sample ch. titles: "Ideology and the Creation of Consciousness," "Capitalism as Private Government," "The President as Manager of Corporate America." The ch. on ideology expresses the belief that "the power to define reality, just as economic and political power, is unequally distributed" (22), that there exists a dominant ideology in the US "more powerful . . . than in any other capitalist democracy" and which contains "most political debates" (29), and that the dominant ideology is perpetuated through "key institutions"--the schools, media, presidential press conferences, congressional elections, etc. (32-33).

439.   Kolko, Gabriel. The Triumph of Conservatism: A Reinterpretation of American History 1900-1916. New York: Free, 1963. 344.
On the drive of many of the largest corporations during the Progressive era to have the government intervene in economic matters to assure stability in marketing and financial affairs. "Political Capitalism"--the big business control over politics-- was the result.

440.   Lappe, Frances, and Joseph Collins. Food First: Beyond the Myth of Scarcity. Boston: Houghton, 1977. 466.
"It is the land monopolizers, both the traditional landed elites and corporate agribusiness, that have proved themselves to be the most inefficient, unreliable and destructive users of food resources. The only guarantee of long-term productivity and food security is for people to take control of food resources here and in other countries" (9).

441.   Larkin, Ralph, and Daniel A. Foss. Beyond Revolution: A New Theory of Social Movements. South Hadley, MA: Bergin, 1986. 256.
A critical review of the major theories in social movements as a basis for analysis of the mechanisms of the reproduction of social privilege, including the relations of exploitation, domination, and cultural domination, and the rise of dissidence.

442.   Lernoux, Penny. In Banks We Trust. New York: Anchor, 1984. 310.
On bank crimes and escapades: Chase Manhattan lost $1.12 billion in bad loans, the CIA uses banks to finance drug traffic in the name of anticommunism, banks frequently evade federal regulations, bank regulators rarely punish the big banks, etc.

443.   Lipsitz, George. Class and Culture in Cold War America: "A Rainbow at Midnight." New York: Praeger, 1981. 254.

American workers "helped build the concentration of power currently wielded by business and government." Ernest Tubb's song "A Rainbow at Midnight," recorded in 1946, expressed the hope for a loving and democratic future in contrast to a "totalitarian oligarchy."

444.   Melman, Seymour. "Priorities and the State Machine." NUT 4 (Winter 1966-67) 14-24.
"We have created in the executive branch of the federal government, with some participation by members of Congress, a managerial team that now dominates as the top management of the largest single unit sector of the American industrial system" (16).

445.   Mills, C. Wright. The Power Elite. New York: Oxford UP, 1959. 423.
An analysis of how the "leading men in each of the three domains of power--the warlords, the corporation chieftains, the political directorate--tend to come together, to form the power elite of America" (9).

446.   Mintz, Morton and Jerry Cohen. America, Inc.: Who Owns and Operates the United States. New York: Dial, 1971. 424.
The authors argue that much of governmental power derives from corporate power, that government functions to serve that power, and that this relationship permits technological violence against the public and subverts the integrity of government, whose original purpose was to serve the people rather than power. The authors advocate a deconcentration of corporate power through antitrust action and the federal chartering of corporations in order to redirect corporate resources toward the public good in a society of consumer sovereignty.

447.   Mintz, Morton, and Jerry Cohen. Power, Inc.: Public and Private Rulers and How to Make Them Accountable. New York: Viking, 1976. 831.
An exposé of the methods used "by the powerful in both public and private sectors to avoid accountability." Chaps. on the "obsolete Constitution," government and corporate secrecy, the "unaudited power" of the press, etc. The Constitution was designed to keep government responsive to public opinion, but it is inadequate. Furthermore, it includes little provision for nongovernment responsibility. What is needed is an accountability amendment to the Constitution to make all power centers accountable to the people. Section VIII, "The Press: Unaudited Power," includes chs. on "Setting the Agenda," "Overseeing the Overseer of the Overseer," and "Flacking."

448.   Mueller, Claus. The Politics of Communication: A Study in the Political Sociology of Language, Socialization, and Legitimation. New York: Oxford UP, 1973. 226.

"The unparallelled wealth and productivity of advanced industrial society is managed by a political system that relegates the citizen to a passive spectator whose identity is cloaked in the freedom to consume and whose communication is subverted by forces beyond his control." Consumerism and affluence "serve as substitutes for self-direction and social responsibility. The productivity of advanced industrial society and the strictures of constrained political communication, reinforced by the accommodative (and presumably lucrative) policies of the mass media and the pragmatic slant of education, eliminate any questioning by most of the population of those interests that govern society" (178-9).

449.   Nimmo, Dan. Subliminal Politics: Myths and
         Mythmakers in America. Englewood Cliffs, NJ: Prentice,
         1980. 265.
    "This is a book about myths of American politics and the persons who make and help plant them in our subconscious--politicians, political press agents, popular entertainers, journalists, pollsters, and political scientists."

450.   Peele, Gillian. Revival and Reaction: The Right in
         Contemporary America. New York: Oxford UP, 1984. 266.
    The convergence of the "new" right, the religious right, and the Republican Party in the 1970s produced the victory of Ronald Reagan in 1980. Ch. 1, "Neo-conservatism," 2 "The New Right," 3 "The Religious Right," 4 "Republicans and the Right," 5 "Reagan, the Right, and Social Policy," and 6 "Reagan, the Right, and Foreign Policy."

451.   Pember, Don. Mass Media in America. 2nd ed.
         Chicago: Science Res., 1977. 389.
    Ch. 10, "Mass Media and Government," includes sections on government and especially presidential power over the news. Chap. 11, "The Business of Mass Media," discusses concentration, access, antitrust, etc. "In the long run, the threat posed to the people by government attacks on our media system will probably be less than the threat posed by increased concentration, monopolization, and conglomerization" (335).

452.   Preston, William, Jr. "Is America Still a Company
         Town?" CLR 4.5 (1978) 54-58.
    The US has a "vast array of systems designed to modify or control the behavior of its people." With reference to 1984, "behavior modification has always been subtle, persuasive, powerful and often clothed in legal or pseudo-legal trappings." Only resistance to it opens "an avenue for constitutional redress."

453.   Reich, Charles. The Greening of America. New York:
         Random, 1970. 399.
    "The American Corporate State today can be thought of as a single vast corporation, with every person as an involuntary member and employee. It consists primarily of large industrial

organizations, plus nonprofit institutions such as foundations and the educational system, all related to the whole as divisions to a business corporation. Government is only a part of the state, but government coordinates it and provides a variety of needed services. The Corporate State is a complete reversal of the original American ideal and plan" (89). But the author hopes for a new society and consciousness responsive to the rich diversity of individuals.

454.   Reynolds, Larry and James Henslin, eds. American Society: A Critical Analysis. New York: McKay, 1973. 337.
Nine essays and an Introduction present the thesis that "the economic institution is the master institution of American society." Three essays deal with the "three master institutions of market society": corporations, politics, military; and six essays with the "secondary institutions as supportive appendages of the market": science, religion, medicine, education, family, and law. The editors agree with C. Wright Mills' thesis that "the highest reaches of the economic, military, and political orders interlock and overlap to form a military-industrial-political complex or what Mills termed The Power Elite." The editors explain that they use the term "market" only because of its familiarity, when in fact a "free market" society is a fiction: "we live in a corporate capitalistic society of organizational bureaucracy," and it is this system which rules America.

455.   Ridgeway, James. The Last Play: The Struggle to Monopolize the World's Energy Resources. New York: New American, 1973. 373.
About the takeover of the nation's energy economy by a handful of energy conglomerates. "In recent years the oil companies and their consorts in the utilities business have bombarded the public" with their perception of the "energy crisis," while quietly "staking out control over the remaining natural resources of the world" with "the cooperation, indeed encouragement" of the federal government, while the general public remains in ignorance.

456.   Roszak, Theodore. The Making of a Counter Culture: Reflections on the Technocratic Society and Its Youthful Opposition. Garden City, NY: Doubleday, 1968. 303.
"Whatever enlightening and beneficial 'spin-off' the universal research explosion of our time produces, the major interest of those who lavishly finance that research will continue to be in weapons, in techniques of social control, in commercial gadgetry, in market manipulation, and in the subversion of democratic processes by way of information monopoly and engineered consensus" (270).

457.   Rydell, Robert. All the World's a Fair: Visions of Empire at American International Expositions, 1876-1916. Chicago: Chicago UP, 1984. 328.
Brief accounts of each fair. The ruling elites controlled

and dominated economics and politics partly through cultural
actions, such as these fairs, that made expansive capitalism and
imperialism legitimate and prestigious to the public. The fairs
also expressed above all the inferiority of dark peoples and the
superiority of whites.

458.   Sallach, David. "Class Domination and Ideological
         Hegemony." SQ 15 (1974) 38-50. Rpt. Tuchman, The TV
         Establishment.
An exposition and defense of the Marxist view of social order
as elaborated by Antonio Gramsci that 1) a dominant class exists
and has privileged access to cultural institutions, 2) debate
within these institutions is circumscribed, and 3) popular beliefs
reflect such ideological constraints. "[T]he thesis that
ideological hegemony is an integral component of a larger system
of social control "is consistent with the available empirical
evidence."

459.   Schiller, Dan. Telematics and Government. Norwood,
         NJ: Ablex, 1982. 237.
Big corporations, demanding advanced computer services, have
mustered government policymakers' support effectually, "so as to
enhance their private control over not merely information
technology--but our economy and society as a whole" (xv).

460.   Schiller, Herbert. The Mind Managers. Boston: Beacon,
         1973. 214.
"A national communications pageant is orchestrated by the
surrogates of the state-capitalist economy, resident in the
Executive Offices of the White House and in Madison Avenue public
relations and advertising agency offices. As the following
chapters suggest, there is good reason to believe that information
management will be even more highly organized by media controllers
in the years ahead" (6). Chap. 1, the five myths by which the
people in power package consciousness, 2 and 3 the "knowledge
industry" run by the government/corporate complex, 4 TV Guide,
National Geographic, and Disney as reinforcers of the status quo,
5 polling, 6 "mind management overseas," 7 the diverse economic
and political pressures ensuring media conformity, and the final
chap. the new technologies of information. Schiller urges the
public to become aware of the growing control of information by
the giant corporations, the Pentagon, and the governmental
bureaucracy, in order to resist and gain control for the people.

461.   Shaffer, Butler. Calculated Chaos: Institutional
         Threats to Peace and Human Survival. Toluca Lake, CA:
         Autonomy, 1985. 338.
Wars, political oppression, racial and religious strife,
industrial rivalries, ideological confrontations, and other
conflicts are produced by institutions that define and direct
society.

462.   Shoup, Laurence. The Carter Presidency and Beyond:
         Power and Politics in the 1980s. Palo Alto, CA:

Ramparts, 1980. 319.
An analysis of the structures of power that are the real
government of the US. "This is a book about the real sources of
political power in the United States. Who the real power
wielders of the United States are and how they operate both behind
the scenes and openly in the media are explored by means of a
concrete case study of Jimmy Carter's political roots, presidency
and 1980 election prospects." The author undertakes to explain
how a candidate makes "contact with" and becomes "acceptable to
the key power centers of this society" and how their support gives
the candidate "the financial wherewithal and necessary favorable
coverage in the mass communications media to become President."
The author goes behind the "party politics" level of political
process to the "more important" "ruling class" level. "This term
refers to the ways in which power brokers representing the upper
class can and do control the political process." Chap. 3 deals
with "Carter and the Media Establishment": "What Carter had that
his opponents did not was the acceptance and support of elite
sectors of the mass communications media." Appendix II,
"Ownership and Control of the Influential Media."

463.   Slack, Jennifer. "The Information Revolution as
        Ideology." MCS 6 (1984) 247-256.
Challenges certain ideological assumptions of the corporate-
government-education-media hegemonic system and appeals to the
public to struggle to build an information system responsive to
the needs of people rather than to the ruling elite.

464.   Trachtenberg, Alan. The Incorporation of America:
        Culture and Society in the Gilded Age. New York: Hill,
        1982. 247.
Gives an analysis of the Columbian Exposition in Chicago in
1893, the main message of which was "a corporate alliance of
business, culture and the state" and a rejection of populist,
participatory democracy.

465.   Von Hoffman, Nicholas. Make Believe Presidents:
        Illusions of Power from McKinley to Carter. New York:
        Pantheon, 1978. 260.
A picture of the presidency as increasingly captive to
special interests, particularly to the leaders of corporate
capitalism, who have desired a "petrified and repetitive" society.
Chap. 7 US imperialism; 8 America first patriotism; 9 repression
in the US; 10 anti-communism, "the Red Monolith versus the Red,
White and Blue Monolith"; 11 the rise of the two-party consensus,
until "after Wallace there were no significant names to enter a
demurral on foreign-policy questions." Chap. 12 attacks the "one-
party state."

466.   Wallis, Jim. "A Wolf in Sheep's Clothing." Soj 15.5
        (1986) 20-23).
The traditional Jesus-oriented, other-worldly, anti-
materialistic, countercultural evangelicalism has been widely
altered into a civil religion by the Far Right--consumerist,

nationalistic, militaristic.

467.   Weinstein, James. The Corporate Ideal in the Liberal
         State 1900-1918. Boston: Beacon, 1968. 263.
"The ideal of a liberal corporate social order [known by
such names as the New Freedom, the New Deal, the New Frontier,
and the Great Society] was formulated and developed under the
aegis and supervision of those who then, as now, enjoyed
ideological and political hegemony in the United States: the
more sophisticated leaders of America's largest corporations and
financial institutions. This book is not based upon a
conspiracy theory of history, but it does posit a conscious and
successful effort to guide and control the economic and social
policies of federal, state, and municipal governments by various
business groupings in their own long-range interest as they
perceived it."

468.   Wolfe, Alan. The Seamy Side of Democracy: Repression
         in America. New York: McKay, 1973. 306.
Wolfe sees the control by a "national ruling class"
increasing through increasing centralization and indoctrination.
"The Educational System" (159-165).

469.   Young, T. R. "Information, Ideology and Political
         Reality Against Toffler." RFI 86 (Apr. 1982) 1-36.
The flow of information and new technology "tend to
reinforce the structures of wealth, power, and privilege"
through large, multinational corporations and state
functionaries.

470.   Zinn, Howard. A People's History of the United
         States. New York: Harper, 1980. 614.
Parts of this book reveal the long collusion between the US
government and the giant corporations. For example, underlying
US WWII policy was the intention "to make sure when the war
ended, American economic power would be second to none in the
world. United States business would penetrate areas that up to
this time had been dominated by England" (404).

II. B. Military-Industrial Complex 471-534
         (See I., II. E., V. A. & C.)

471.   Adams, Gordon. The Politics of Defense Contracting:
         The Iron Triangle. NJ: Transaction, 1982. 465.
How the military-industrial complex works, including Chap.
13, "Moving the Public: Advertising and the Grass Roots." This
study of the political power of the arms industry focuses upon
eight major contractors. "A powerful flow of people and money
moves between the defense contractors, the Executive branch (DoD
and NASA), and Congress, creating an 'iron triangle' on defense
policy and procurement that excludes outsiders and alternative
perspectives." The final ch. suggests how the public might
"penetrate" the triangle and reclaim some democratic control.

472.   Allegations of Improper Lobbying by Department of
          Defense Personnel of the C-5B and B-1B Aircraft and Sale
          to Saudi Arabia of the Airborne Warning and Control
          System. Hearings Before the Investigations Subcommittee
          of the Committee on Armed Services, HR, 97th Cong., 2nd
          Sess., 1982. Washington: GPO, 1983. 434.
Focuses on Pentagon and Lockheed Corporation efforts to lobby
HR members about Lockheed's C-5B cargo aircraft following S action
to procure Boeing 747 cargo aircraft.

473.   Archer, Dane. "University Management of Weapons Labs?
          No." BAS 42.1 (1986) 41-44.
Decries university weapons production and research. Secrecy
and government control "make meaningful university governance
impossible." Severance of the connection "could set in motion a
series of forces that would make meaningful arms control much more
likely."

474.   Arkin, William, and Richard Fieldhouse. Nuclear
          Battlefields: Global Links in the Arms Race. Cambridge:
          Ballinger, 1985. 328.
A study of the nuclear systems of the five nations admitting
to owning nuclear weapons--the US, the SU, Britain, France, and
China. These "infrastructures" include bases, research,
production, surveillance and communication networks, and civil
defense.

475.   Bean, Kevin. "Cozy Nuclear Camaraderie." Wit 69.9
          (1986) 6-8.
Connecticut is the most military-dependent state in the
country and United Technologies Corporation is its most powerful
contractor. UTC denies any moral responsibility for its devotion
to arms. Connecticut deceives itself about the job-value of
military contractors.

476.   Bertsch, Kenneth, and Linda Shaw. The Nuclear Weapons
          Industry. Investor Responsibility Research Center,
          1984. 405.
Chap. 4 deals with industry influence over nuclear weapons
policy. "Clearly, industrial political activities and the
important corporate role in developing new weapons systems gives
the defense industry an important voice in shaping the nation's
defense posture. It is also clear that other factors, including
ideological considerations and the nature and perception of the
Soviet and other foreign threats play important roles as well"
(79).

477.   Caldicott, Helen. Missile Envy: The Arms Race and
          Nuclear War. New York: Morrow, 1984. 365.
The ch. on "The Iron Triangle" explores the "societal
processes which sustained and motivated this enormous industry
of death. I discovered that the answer lay at the feet of the
scientists and the three arms of the 'Iron Triangle'--Congress,
the Pentagon, and the military-industrial complex" (p. 204).

The ch. discusses the scientists, the universities, and the military-industrial complex, including the Washington offices of the military corporations and the public relations campaigns by the companies and the military and lay press.

478.   "CC Asks Congress to Conduct Ethics Probe." CC 12.1
         (1986) 55.
Common Cause requested an investigation of congressional affiliations with military contractors.

479.   Diamond, Sara. "Politics New Aim of Religious Right."
         SLJR 13.84 (1986) 19.
The 43rd annual National Religious Broadcasters Convention revealed a "new foreign and military emphasis" in support of the Reagan administration's anti-Soviet and anti-Nicaraguan policies and its arms proposals.

480.   The DoD Revolving Door. Washington, DC: GAO, 1986.
A statistical study of the close relationship between the Pentagon and the defense contractors. Representative Gerry Sikorski (Dem-MN) commented that the contractors were "using the allure of lucrative jobs to manipulate the procurement process for their own gain" (AG, August 31, 1986, 1A).

481.   Doi, Kathy. "College Weapons Laboratories." CMJ 7.11
         (1982) 5.
The centrality the U of California's Lawrence Livermore National Laboratory and the Los Alamos Scientific Laboratory to the US nuclear weapon program. The UC Nuclear Weapons Labs Conversion Project has criticized the priorities of the labs and the safety of LLNL.

482.   Duker, Laurie. "Rites of Spring: The Swarming of the
         Arms Lobbyists." SANE 24 (April 1985) 6.
Lobbyists from arms contractors, the Pentagon, and the White House labored to win the MX program—20 fulltime lobbyists from the Pentagon, 200 liaison officers from the services, Reagan's team, and last-minute flights of key Congressmen back to Washington by the Pentagon.

483.   Farrell, James J. The Nuclear Devil's Dictionary.
         Minneapolis, MN: Usonia, 1985. 125.
A handbook on "how to read between the lies" of nuclear-age jargon, the doublespeak of nuclear war, weapons, and energy.

484.   Fitzgerald, A. Ernest. The High Priests of Waste.
         New York: Norton, 1972. 398.
An indictment of the Pentagon's deliberate policy of waste in military budgets shrouded in secrecy and of the docility of the American taxpayers, "the most docile in the world," who have been brainwashed into having complete trust and faith in the military establishment." We are "confronted with great concentrated, unaccountable, privileged power." Citizens "must learn to control the military spending juggernaut before they

are robbed of their resources and their freedoms."

485.   Friedman, Robert. "How America Gets Up in Arms." <u>NT</u>
         1 (March 1983) 19.
The military contractors are spending considerable money on
corporate image and advocacy advertising and "then writing off
the cost of these ads."

486.   Friel, Howard. "Covert Propaganda in <u>Time</u> and
         <u>Newsweek</u>." <u>CAIB</u> 21 (1984) 14-23.
The use of advertising, news stories, and news photographs
by <u>Time</u> and <u>Newsweek</u> in support of the vested interests of the
corporate-military establishment.

487.   Galbraith, John K. <u>The Anatomy of Power</u>. Boston:
         Houghton, 1983. 206.
A study mainly of the two most important modern
manifestations of power--organization and conditioning. "The
young are taught that in a democracy all power resides in the
people. And that in a free enterprise system all authority
rests with the sovereign consumer operating through the
impersonal mechanism of the market. Thus is hidden the public
power of organization--of the Pentagon, the weapons firms, and
other corporations and lobbyists. Similarly concealed by the
mystique of the market and consumer sovereignty is the power of
corporations to set or influence prices and costs, to suborn or
subdue politicians, and to manipulate consumer response" (12).
Chap. 14, "The Age of Organization," 15, "Organization and the
State," 16, "The Military Power."

488.   Gitlin, Todd. "Masters of War." <u>PE</u> 2.1 (1979)
         24-25.
The Department of Energy U of California's nuclear weapons
development labs claim they are safe, although they are built on
earthquake faults and may cause cancer.

489.   Gollon, Peter J. "SDI Funds Costly for Scientists."
         <u>BAS</u> 42.1 (1986) 24-27.
Part of the price to be paid by institutions accepting Star
Wars research money will be "an increase in secrecy and
dissimulation--hardly what we have come to expect at our best
scientific institutions, and not the qualities which have
contributed to their present excellence."

490.   Goulden, Joseph, and Marshall Singer. "Dial-A-Bomb:
         AT&T and the ABM." <u>RAM</u> 8 (1969) 29-37.
An account of AT&T and its subsidiary Western Electric's
manipulation of government agencies in order to obtain lucrative
defense contracts.

491.   Hartman, Thomas. "Reporting for Service: The Big
         Guns of the Military Press." <u>WJR</u> 6 (July-Aug. 1984) 29-
         32.
Distinguishes between the publications which function as

mouthpieces for the military-industrial-media complex and more
critical journals such as Defense Week, but reveals indirectly
how much all the publications operate within the boundaries
established by the weapons establishment.

492.   Hartzell, Grace. "Academics Protest Reagan's Plan
        Despite Threats to Their Funding." Guard 37.45 (Sept.
        18, 1985) 5.
University scientists opposed to "Star Wars" fear
opposition will result in the cutoff of federal research money.

493.   Hitchens, Christopher. "Minority Report." Na 240.18
        (1985) 551.
"The top twenty military contractors have doubled their
political donations since Reagan took office."

494.   Horowitz, David. "Sinews of Empire." Ram 8 (October
        1969) 32-42.
"The universities were once thought to constitute a vita,
independent, countervailing estate, but the modern university
has been converted into an Office of External Research for the
State Department, the Pentagon and the international
corporations" (33).

495.   Horowitz, David, and Reese Erlich. "Big Brother as a
        Holding Company." Ram (Nov. 30, 1968) 44-52.
The Litton Industry's connections with government and
military organizations.

496.   Horowitz, David, and Reese Erlich. "Litton
        Industries: Poverty Pays." Ram (Nov. 14-28, 1968) 40-
        49.
"Government agencies depend on the political influence of
business to help them compete for funds and authority."

497.   Howard, Bruce. "The Advertising Council: Selling
        Lies . . ." Ram 13 (Dec. 1974-Jan. 1975) 25-26,
        28-32.
The Advertising Council, funded and directed by America's
"Captains of Industry," monopolizes most of public service time
on television and free space in print media. No public interest
group is represented on the Council. The Ad Council is just one
more instrument of the military-industrial complex.

497a.   Koistinen, Paul. The Military-Industrial Complex: A
        Historical Perspective. New York: Praeger, 1980. 168.
A study of how the MIC came about from the colonial period
to the present, following a theoretical framework for analyzing
institutional interaction "which over time has produced the MIC
of today."

498.   Lasch, Christopher. The Culture of Narcissism:
        American Life in an Age of Diminishing Expectations.
        New York: Norton, 1978. 268.

Several chs. touch on the power of the military-industrial
complex through advertising (the worship of commodities) and the
capture of sports, the schools, and the family.

499.   Lens, Sidney, The Military-Industrial Complex.
            Philadelphia: United Church, 1970. 183.
The present military-industrial complex has upset the
tradition of Congressional control of the military and now
threatens the nation "with a political monopoly many times more
ominous than economic monopolies. If global expansion brings us
repeatedly to the brink of war, the domestic effect of
militarism drives us toward the monolithic state. For if there
is one thing that stands out in the military-industrial complex
it is a trend to "internal imperialism" (34). "Out of this
confluence of interests [Pentagon, military corporations, the
Administration, etc.] has evolved a refashioned power elite in
America, more formidable than any ever known before. At the
base of the military-industrial complex pyramid, naturally, is
the Pentagon itself, the fountainhead, though not the brainpower
of the complex. Above the base, not necessarily in the order of
importance" are: the militarist faction in Congress, the large
corporate contractors, organizations that act as liaison between
industry and the military, such as the National Security
Industrial Assoc., Pentagon-subsidized research organizations
called "think-tanks" often headed by former Pentagon officials,
private research and educational organizations, such as the
Hoover Institution on War and the American Security Council, the
leadership of the AFL-CIO, the academic community tied to the
Pentagon, etc.

500.   Levi, Michael. "A Look at America's 'Other'
            Reactors." CMJ 7.11 (1982) 4-5.
Criticism of the lack of information about non-power/non-
commercial reactors, many of which are located at universities.

501.   Lewis, Anthony. "Is U.S. Hooked on Arms?" AG (Dec.
            5, 1985) 21A.
Loss of lucrative contracts as the result of arms control
"worries" the weapons industry.

502.   Lindee, Susan, and Dorothy Nelkin. "Challenger: the
            High Cost of Hype." BAS 42.9 (1986) 16-18.
"NASA and the news media had a long-time, comfortable
relationship before the Challenger explosion," the press seldom
questioning "the program's necessity, importance, or ultimate
benefits."

503.   Loader, Jayne, and Keven and Pierce Rafferty. The
            Atomic Cafe. Arlington, VA: Archives Project, 1982.
A 90-minute documentary film revealing how the American
public was sold the atomic bomb.

504.   Loeb, Paul. Nuclear Culture: Living and Working in
            the World's Largest Atomic Complex. New York: Coward,

1982. 255.
A study of the people who live and work in the Hanford
Nuclear Reservation in Washington State. The employees and
other members of the community "have abdicated responsibility on
the most important questions" surrounding the production of
plutonium. To the author, Hanford epitomizes the public at
large who blindly evade nuclear realities especially by
trivializing the nuclear risks.

505.   Long, Franklin A. "Government Dollars for University
         Research." BAS 42.3 (1986) 45-49.
A look at the escalation under the Reagan administration of
government money for military research and development.

506.   McDougall, Walter. The Heavens and the Earth: A
         Political History of the Space Age. New York: Basic,
         1985. 555.
An attack on the ideology of technocracy and the technocracy
of politicians--the belief that a Project Apollo, for example,
could serve as a model for the state in solving problems. The
danger is that the US is becoming more like the SU.

507.   Melman, Seymour. "Economics of Armament and
         Disarmament." NUT 2 (Spring 1962) 79-92.
Businesses that contract government military work have
become so dependent upon the military that if the contracts were
taken from them, the businesses would probably be forced to lay
off thousands of their employees. "Twelve to 15 million jobs
now depend on military activity" (80-81). Instead of using
industry to prepare for war, we should make the changes
necessary in production to make industry instrumental in the
challenge of finding peace.

507a.   Melman, Seymour. Pentagon Capitalism: The Political
         Economy of War. New York: McGraw, 1970. 290.
A "diagnosis of the new central control system that was
installed under Robert McNamara, and the depleting consequences
for American economy and society from the operations of that
system" (viii). "In the name of defense, and without
announcement or debate, a basic alteration has been effected in
the governing institutions of the United States. An industrial
management has been installed in the federal government, under
the Secretary of Defense, to control the nation's largest
network of industrial enterprises" "Government is business.
That is state capitalism." "The true cost is measured by what
has been foregone, by the accumulated deterioration in many
facets of life, by the inability to alleviate human wretchedness
of long duration," and "by the industrial-technological
depletion caused by the concentration of technical manpower and
capital on military technology and in military industry" (1-3).

507b.   Melman, Seymour, ed. The War Economy of the United
         States: Readings on Military Industry and Economy. New
         York: St. Martin's, 1971. 247.

The 34 essays grapple with such propositions as: the military firm is controlled by state management, it does not minimize cost (as did entrepreneurial enterprise), and the military firms lack flexibility for conversion to civilian work.

508.   Millis, Walter. <u>An End to Arms</u>. New York: Atheneum, 1965. 301.
An "inquiry into possible demilitarization of the international politics system" on the basis of a distinction between militarization and armaments and the argument that demilitarization must precede disarmament. The author sees the test ban agreement of 1963 as "of overwhelming importance as a first faint recognition of the fact that brute military power is no longer the <u>ultima ratio</u> in international politics." But the book is not a technical study of arms limitations or reductions but an assessment of "the factors that have stultified all disarmament conferences for the past sixty or seventy years." After chapters on the problem and history of war, the author focuses on the contemporary problems of the Cold War, the language and myths which impede understanding, the pursuit of power, the lack of adequate international law, etc.

509.   Morrison, David. "Energy Department's Weapons Conglomerate." <u>BAS</u> 41 (April 1985) 32-37.
"The weapons establishment's nuclear promotion--plus a campaign against a nuclear freeze similar to the one that has stymied the comprehensive test ban--combines hard-sell lobbying with the promise of new technologies."

510.   Norrgard, Lee. "So That's How It's Done." <u>CC</u> 12.1 (1986) 12.
"General Dynamics led Pentagon sales with contract awards totaling more than $25 billion." Corporation lobbyists treat influential members of Congress to lavish expenditures.

511.   Norrgard, Lee. "Special Ed." <u>CC</u> 11.3 (1985) 11.
Funding for the MX Education Bureau comes from MX contractors and the pro-military American Security Council.

512.   Paine, Christopher. "The Selling of the B-1." <u>CC</u> 8 (October 1982) 16-23.
How Rockwell International and the Pentagon forced through the B-1 bomber through a lengthy, intensive, and expensive lobbying and public relations campaign.

513.   Patterson, Walter. <u>The Plutonium Business and the Spread of the Bomb</u>. San Francisco: Sierra, 1985. 272.
"By the turn of the century" companies and nations will be trafficking in plutonium fuel "sufficient to build about 100,000 atomic bombs" if "those who would make a business out of plutonium get their way" (Preface). "The proposed use of this potential nuclear explosive as a fuel is not only dangerous but unnecessary." Yet, "despite all, plutonium promoters have succeeded, for three decades, in exerting extraordinary

93

influence on the energy planning and decision-making of national governments everywhere in the world" (Introduction).

514.   Phee, Molly. "The Write Stuff." WJR (Jan. 1986) 9.
     Journalist space shuttle astronauts create ethical conflict of interest problems.

515.   Piller, Charles. "Biological Warfare and the New Genetic Technologies." SciP 17.3 (1985) 10-15.
     The new genetic research has great potential for application to biological warfare.

516.   Pringle, Peter, and James Spigelman. The Nuclear Barons. New York: Holt, 1981. 578.
     An international elite of scientists, technocrats, politicians, military officers, and businessmen have for more than four decades controlled the world's destiny. Radiation hazards, prohibitively costly energy, waste-disposal problems, plant safety, weapons proliferation, secrecy, lies--the nuclear nightmare is the direct result of choices made by a few men that were never thought through to their logical conclusions and never opened to public debate. "The atomic institutions became almost totalitarian in their powers, often requiring scientists and engineers to suppress information that stood in the way of nuclear revolution" (xii).

517.   Pyadyshev, B. The Military-Industrial Complex of the USA. Tr. Yuri Sdobnikov. Moscow: Progress, 1977. 187.
     The author gives Leonid Brezhnev's definition of the complex as "the alliance of the largest monopolies and the military in the state apparatus," asserts the "class substance of the MIC" and the conditions which have led to its emergence, and considers the structure, forms, and methods of its operation. Chap. 1, "The MIC and the State" (the corridors of power in Washington, the White House, the Pentagon, Congress); 2, "The MIC and the Economy"; 3, "The Ideology of Force" ("Cold War Dogmas," the "Pentagon's Propaganda Machine"); and 4, "The MIC and Foreign Policy" ("empire" and "militarism").

518.   Reich, Robert, et al. The Militarization of High Technology. Cambridge, MA: Ballinger, 1984. 247.
     A collection of essays on the partnership between the Pentagon and high-tech industries.

519.   Ridgeway, James. The Closed Corporation, America's Universities in Crisis. New York: Random, 1968. 273.
     "It was through the Defense Department that the universities and business first worked together in consortia arrangements to develop complicated weapons systems. This troika arrangement is slowly evolving into a new sort of corporate machine, or more precisely, machine parts which engage or disengage depending on the job to be done. Basically, the parts consist of the university, where products or processes are conceived, the government, which finances their development, and

private business which makes and sells the finished item" (7-10).

520.   Roose, Diana. "Top Dogs and Top Brass: An Inside
      Look at a Government Advisory Committee." IS 5
      (1975) 53-63.
      This article describes the activities of the Industry
Advisory Council (IAC) to the Pentagon. The IAC was a group of
business executives whose purpose "was to insure that business
had access to the vast bureaucracy of the Pentagon at the
highest policy levels" (53). The companies represented are
among the largest military contractors in the US. The IAC also
worked to "promote the Administration's point of view on
controversial issues" (58). Meetings of the IAC were secret, so
secret that when Congress insisted the meetings be opened to the
public, the council disbanded rather than comply with the order.

521.   Rumors of Peace (film). Washington, DC: Christic
      Institute, 1984.
      Examines the military-industrial complex pro-nuclear
propaganda which has made the arms race seem rational and has
whittled away our ability to imagine peace by labeling
peacemaking as naive and dangerous.

522.   Salzman, George. "11:39:12 am EST." SciP 18.2 (1986)
      27, 31.
      The coverage of the Challenger shuttle disaster is another
example of US media distortion of reality. For example, "U.S.-
supported killing of 100,000 East Timorese" has received
"negligible media attention." "The real tragedy of Challenger"
is . . . that it is widely perceived as tragedy and is used to
obscure our perception of what the world might be if human
intelligence and compassion were directed to solving social
problems."

523.   Sarkesian, Sam, ed. The Military-Industrial Complex:
      A Reassessment. Beverly Hills: Sage, 1972. 340.
      "The authors of the papers in this volume do not postulate
a unified view of the military-industrial complex"; rather they
"present a fundamental critique of military-industrial
interpenetrations." The first essay by Charles Moskos, for
example, identifies three elements of the complex: a military
hierarchy, administrative bureaucracy, and corporate wealth.

524.   Schiller, Herbert. "Information for What Kind of
      Society?" Telecommunications: Issues and Choices for
      Society. Ed. J. L. Salvaggio. New York: Longman, 1983.
      24-33.
      The elite of the military-industrial complex will use the
communication technologies for purposes of surveillance and
control over access to information, over production of
information, and over the data necessary for production. "The
question to be considered is not what may happen if a new
communication technology runs amok . . . . It is, how do we

check a communication technology that is already running amok
and that has had this tendency to do so built into it from the
outset?" (25)

525.   Schiller, Herbert I. and Joseph D. Phillips, eds.
         Super State: Readings in the Military-Industrial
         Complex. Chicago: U of Illinois, 1970. 353.
    The book is dedicated "to those Americans, particularly the
young, who are challenging the Super-state." Of the eleven
sections (26 essays), two are of special interest: 6 "The
Military-Industrial Complex and Communications", and 7 "Science
and the Universities in the Military-Industrial Complex."
President Eisenhower's Farewell Address, Jan. 17, 1961, is printed
in full.

526.   Shore, Elliott, et. al. Alternative Papers:
         Selections from the Alternative Press, 1979-1980.
         Philadelphia: Temple UP, 1982. 521.
    These articles offer "a view of reality that differs both
in scope and emphasis from that presented by the corporate
media." What the mass media tell us about our society
"conditions our experience, narrows our choices, and channels
our responses." Television, radio, and the daily and weekly
press "depend in one way or another on industry and government,
which inevitably trade in conservative information. They
therefore present a version of reality designed to reinforce
rather than challenge the social and political consensus." In
contrast, these articles question or attack corporate power,
nuclear power, hierarchy, racism, sexism, the warfare state,
i.e., the basic structures of the US corporate-military state.
Sections on the press, nukes, technology, the Third World,
corporations, repression, women, etc.

527.   Smith, Merritt R. Military Enterprise and
         Technological Change: Perspectives on the American
         Experience. Cambridge, MA: MIT P, 1985. 400.
    A history of the military-industrial complex via a variety
of case studies--e.g., the Army's first large-scale employment
of social scientists during World War II and their role in
shaping the postwar research agenda; the Army Signal Corp's
entrepreneurial role in the development of the transistor; and
the social implications of military and scientific management
styles.

528.   Smith, Michael. "Selling the Moon: The U.S. Space
         Program and the Triumph of Commodity Scientism." The
         Culture of Consumption. Ed. Richard Fox and T. J.
         Jackson Lears. New York: Pantheon, 1983. 175-209.
    During and after WWII, policy elites orchestrated their
scientific programs with manipulable images in order to sell
government science to taxpayers and to persuade the world the US
is Number One. The manned space program is the most dramatic
example of "commodity scientism." The astronauts became space-
age "Marlboro men" even though ironically all individuality was

immersed in the bureaucratic collectivity.

529.   Spiegelman, Robert. "Media Manipulation of the
     Movement." SocP 13.1 (1982) 9-16.
     The media fail to cover the antinuclear movement adequately
as a deliberate strategy to preserve and enhance the profit
status-quo, for example, the interlocking power of Morgan
Guaranty Trust in the arms industry and the media.

530.   Trager, Frank, and Philip Kronenburg, eds. National
     Security and American Society: Theory, Process, and
     Policy. Lawrence, Kansas: UP of Kansas, 1973. 612.
     Section V "emphasizes the consequences for society of the
actions taken in the implementation of national security
policy," with chapters on the garrison-state, the military-
industrial complex, secrecy vs. disclosure, classified military
research and the university, loyalty and dissent, etc. James
Reston in "The Influence of the Press" discusses the press as
ally and critic of the government (235).

531.   Tyrrell, C. Merton. Pentagon Partners, The New
     Nobility. New York: Grossman, 1970. 233.
     The author's "thesis that the military contract community
constitutes a new privileged class in American society should
command the attention of thoughtful people everywhere." The New
Nobility is the Pentagon-corporate contractors-Presidential-
Congressional sympathizers-university complex "which control or
influence most of the positions of power in our society, and
they are utterly ruthless in disposing of opposition" (Foreword
by A. E. Fitzgerald). The public gives its support to this new
elite partly because of the Nobility's successful creation of
the appearance of infallibility and partly because of the
intimidating complexity of military technology. The author has
set out to reveal the ineptitude rampant in the nation's
military acquisition process in order to puncture the appearance
of infallibility and to hearten the public to participate in the
process (Introduction).

532.   "Well-placed Few Get SDI Contracts." AG (October 27,
     1986) 6A.
     A report by the Council on Economic Priorities reveals that
"more than 90 percent of the 'Star Wars' contracts awarded in
fiscal 1985 and 1986 went to contractors located in states with
senators who sit on the two key Senate committees.

533.   Wicklein, John. Electronic Nightmare: The New
     Communications and Freedom. New York: Viking, 1981.
     282.
     The increasing unity of our electronic system "puts us in
immediate danger of losing our privacy and our individual
liberty." The author explores these dangers in detail, but also
presents numerous alternatives to a corporate/military takeover
of communication. "Without intervention by people concerned
primarily with human welfare, such technological changes will

continue to be pressed upon us when commercial and military
managers decide it will be best for their own interests to do
so" (7).

534.   Wofsy, Leon. "Can the Cold War Be Ended Peacefully?"
          ITT 9.22 (1985) 11-12.
     The author observes "how deeply militarism and the arms
program are entrenched in the current economic structure of our
society. The corporate system depends on mammoth military
expenditures, and commitments made in 1985 reach far into the
future.

II. C. Corporations and Government Regulation 535-605

535.   Ajemian, Peter. "The Hypocrisy of J. Peter Grace."
          PC (July-Aug. 1985) 10-15.
     The Grace Commission's task force on the EPA proposed
changes "that would lead to less stringent federal regulation."

536.   Ajemian, Peter, and Joan Claybrook. Deceiving the
          Public: The Story Behind J. Peter Grace and His
          Campaign. Washington, DC: Public Citizen, 1985. 110.
     President Reagan appointed Grace to head a commission to
eliminate waste in the federal government. The Commission's
report actually outlined new ways for corporations to wield
greater power and make more profits.

537.   "An Alar Apple a Day . . . May Be One Too Many." HL
          2.3 (1986) 14-15.
     In spite of the known danger of daminozide, the EPA refuses
to ban or label daminozide-containing foods ("Alar" is
Uniroyal's brand name for the chemical).

538.   Alvarez, Robert. "Radiation Workers." SciP 18.2
          (1986) 6-11.
     Epidemiological findings of excess cancer mortality among
radiation workers "are not being taken seriously by the
regulatory agencies."

539.   Arieff, Irwin. "Profits or a Free Press: The Effects
          of Broadcast Regulation." WJR 1.1 (1977) 40-44.
     Government regulation has provided the networks more
profits and less diversity of opinion. "For broadcasters [with
their vested interest in regulation], the First Amendment is an
operating expense they can't afford."

540.   Atkin, Kenward. "Federal Regulation of Broadcast
          Advertising." JB 3 (1959) 326-340.
     The Federal Communications Commission, which can determine
the acceptability of television programming, should work with
the FTC to regulate corporate advertisements.

541.   Aufderheide, Pat. "Shut Up and Watch." ITT 10.13
          (1986) 14.

"The premise implicit in the First Amendment--that access
to information is crucial to informed judgment on public affairs
in a democracy--seems to have slipped by the guardian of the
public interest," Mark Fowler, FCC head.

542.   Barron, Jerome. Freedom of the Press for Whom? The
      Right of Access to Mass Media. Bloomington: Indiana UP,
      1973. 368.
The book "chronicles the struggle to open the media" and
"states the case for access," because private censorship
dominates "both the print and the broadcast media." "The First
Amendment should be restored to its true proprietors--the
reader, the viewer, the listener. Freedom of the press must be
something more than a guarantee of the property rights of media
owners."

543.   Baughman, James L. Television's Guardians: The FCC
      and the Politics of Programming, 1958-1967. Knoxville:
      U of Tennessee P, 1985. 311.
The FCC's power to regulate television programming was
weakened by opposition from the executive and legislative
branches of the federal government which objected to policies
inimical to the interests of broadcasters, such as limiting the
number of commercials. And the "public never rallied to the
champions of the public interest"--Newton Minow and E. William
Henry. The author believes restraints on the FCC were proper
because of the "risk that one day men and women not concerned
with social betterment" would use the "instrumentalities of a
strong state to destroy liberty."

544.   Bennett, Jonathan. "An Expert for OSHA or Just
      Another Hack?" Guard 38.32 (1986) 6.
The new head of OSHA, John Pendergrass, has a serious
conflict of interest problem, for he worked and lobbied for the
3M Corporation which manufactures virtually useless disposable
dust masks.

545.   Bollier, David. "The Strange Politics of 'Fairness'."
      Ch 5.5 (1986) 47-49, 52.
Overview of the Fairness Doctrine in television news.

546.   Brenner, Daniel, and William Rivers. Free But
      Regulated: Conflicting Traditions in Media Law.
      Ames, IA: Iowa State UP, 1982. 283.
Sections on "Access to Information: Protecting the
Gatherer," "Access to Information: What Should Be Available,"
"Distributing Information: When the Executive Tries to Stop
Release" (the Pentagon Papers), "'Unprotected' Expression: One-
Sided, Deceptive, Unfair Speech," and similar topics. Brenner
in the final ch. makes some recommendations for a true
marketplace of ideas.

547.   Brown, Les. "The Buck Starts Here." Ch 3 (Sept./Oct.
      1983) 22.

The "flow of FCC officials to the industries they regulate, or to the law firms representing those industries" reflects the close relationship between the regulating agency and the money of the corporations.

548.   Brown, Les. "Fear of Fowler." Ch 1.5 (1981-82) 21-
         22.
FCC chairman Mark Fowler is "in control of an agency that is supposed to look after the public's stake," but is an "ideologue who believes free markets are the answer to everything."

549.   Brown, Les. "The New Impresarios of Politics." Ch 4
         (Mar./Apr. 1984) 21-22.
The FCC's revision of the "Aspen Rule" will weaken the Equal Time Rule, which exists to make broadcasting more democratic, by erasing the Equal Time Rule's guarantees for third-party and independent candidates.

550.   Brown, Les. "Reagan and the Unseen Network." Chd 1.4
         (1981) 17-18.
Reagan helped the broadcast industry persuade Congress to lengthen broadcast license terms, which "drastically reduces" accountability.

551.   Brown, Les. "Throwing the Bull in Barcelona." Ch 3
         (Sept./Oct. 1983) 21-22.
The US government sent its own spokesman to a conference on television in Barcelona in order to offset the "wayward" views of some of the American participants, such as Nicholas Johnson. The Reagan government argues against the Fairness Doctrine because "most station licensees are solid conservative businessmen and pillars of the Establishment."

552.   Brown, Les. "Who's Really Running the FCC--and Is It
         Legal?" Ch 3 (Jan./Feb. 1984) 38-39.
President Reagan "has his hand on the controls" of the FCC, having "effectively emasculated" the agency by treating its chairman, Mark Fowler, as a "toady."

553.   Carpenter, Tom. "Zimmer Fight May Be Just Beginning."
         CMJ 8.3 (1982) 4-5, 14.
Tom Applegate's investigation of the Zimmer Nuclear Power Plant led to the Nuclear Regulatory Commission's charges against the Cincinnati Gas & Electric Co. of "falsification of quality control documents, harassment and intimidation of quality control inspectors and a myriad of hardware problems from welds to piping and valves, so severe that it is questionable as to whether or not they are repairable." A record fine was levied.

554.   Cole, Barry, and Mal Oettinger. Reluctant Regulators:
         The FCC and the Broadcast Audience. Reading, MA:
         Addison-Wesley, 1978. 310.
On the struggles of citizen groups during the 1970s to make

the FCC more responsive to public needs in order to make
broadcasters more responsive to their audiences. Three chs.
deal with children's television.

555.   Cook, Fred. Maverick: Fifty Years of Investigative
         Reporting. New York: Putnam, 1984. 320.
     The autobiography of a four-time winner of the Newspaper
Guild Award for Investigative Journalism and other high awards.
He was among the first to challenge John Edgar Hoover; he
exposed the CIA ten years before the Senate inspected its
illegalities; he wrote a book on the military-industrial complex
before the expression became current. Studs Turkel says the
book "should be mandatory reading for any college journalism
class" (Introduction, 14).

556.   Cox, Edward, et al. The Nadar Report on the Federal
         Trade Commission. New York: Baron, 1969. 241.
     A protest against the failure of this agency to protect the
public from deceptive business practices hiding shoddy and
harmful products and fraudulent services by the disuse and
misuse of its vast information-procurement powers, the secrecy
of its meetings, the neglect of its enforcement tools, and in
general its close association with business interests.

557.   Emery, Walter B. "The Craven Dissent on Proposed
         Rule-Making." JoB 3 (1959) 153-160.
     FCC Commissioner T. A. M. Craven argues that proposals to
amend Section 4 of the Commission's Renewal Application would
increase censorship by advocating commission-established program
categories as "guides" for licensees.

558.   "Fairness & Equal Time: Should We Scrap the Rules?"
         Ch 1.5 (1981-1982) 6-7.
     Gene Jankowski, president of the CBS Broadcast Group, takes
the affirmative position, Rep. John Dingell the negative.

559.   Ford, Daniel. The Cult of the Atom: The Secret
         Papers of the Atomic Energy Commission. New York:
         Simon, 1982. 273.
     "By the late 1950s, the AEC began to acquire frightening
data about the potential hazards of nuclear technology."
Nevertheless, it pushed ahead "with ambitious plans to make
nuclear energy the dominant source of the nation's electric
power," authorizing the construction "of larger and larger
nuclear reactors all round the country, the dangers
notwithstanding." Senior officials at the AEC suppressed
warnings from their own scientists, while offering the public
"soothing reassurances about safety" (Foreword).

560.   Fore, William F. "Deregulation Is the Name, Grand
         Larceny the Game." C&C 43.15 (1983) 355-359.
     Deregulation of broadcasting is "a venal strategy, born out
of avarice, purposely deceptive and confusing, clothed in
patriotic appeal while jeopardizing the very freedom of

expression which lies at the heart of our cultural pluralism and our democratic system of governance." After deregulation stations will have no public service obligations and will be completely free to do whatever makes the most money.

561.   Fromartz, Samuel, and Francis Wilkinson.
        "Pesticides: The Other Side of Paradise." ITT 9.22
        (1985) 5.
    The Dept. of Agriculture knew about the toxic chemical heptachlor contamination of milk in Hawaii and "tried to keep it quiet."

562.   Geller, Henry. A Modest Proposal to Reform the
        Federal Communications Commission. Santa Monica, CA:
        Rand, 1974. 52.
    The chief weakness of the FCC is its "'over-identification with the industries regulated,'" that is, with "the powerful, entrenched elements of the industries regulated, in contrast to new emerging facets or technologies."

563.   Geller, Henry. "Two Ideal Notions for CPB."
        Current 4.15 (1985) 5, 8.
    Analysis of the flawed structure and financing of CPB which can be corrected through "two reform notions."

564.   Graeddon, Joe. "FDA Backs Off on Requiring
        Caution Labels." AG (May 26, 1985) 3B.
    Instances of the FDA caving in to industry pressure to deny or limit information to the public via label warnings or patient package inserts (PPIs).

565.   Gravois, John, and Walt Potter. "How the Press
        Misses the Beat." WJR 4.1 (1982) 29-32.
    Because the press often ignores federal regulatory agencies, the public misses important decisions, such as the FCC's 1981 deregulation package.

566.   Hill, Doug. "Don't Make Your Bath Water Too Hot
        . . . ." TVG (April 5, 1986) 32-4.
    A bill by the House Subcommittee on Telecommunications requiring TV stations to balance their alcohol commercials with spots on the dangers of drinking was tabled after the broadcasters promised better self-regulation. But the show of balance has already declined. Also, public service announcements have declined since the FCC decreased proof of station public service efforts.

567.   Jencks, Richard, and Robert Lewis Shayon. "Does the
        Fairness Doctrine Violate the First Amendment?" PTR 2
        (December 1974) 46-55.
    A debate between Jencks, VP of CBS (affirmative), and Shayon, a prof. of communications (negative).

568.   Kaidy, Mitchell. "Prime-Time Numbers" Na 239 (Sept.

22, 1984) 226.
"Together with the Reagan Administration's desire for
deregulation of radio and television, the longer licensing
periods [from three to five years] mean that licensees now can
offer no public affairs programming, yet still have up to seven
years to milk a station's profits before reselling the
property."

569.   Kotch, Jonathan W.   "The FCC and The First Amendment
          Facade: A Rejoinder." PTR 6.2 (1978) 34-37.
     A defense of government regulation of television
programming for children because censorship "is already taking
place, in the guise of free enterprise" or "censorship for
profit."

570.   Krasnow, Erwin and Lawrence Longley.   The Politics of
          Broadcast Regulation. 2nd ed. New York: St. Martin's,
          1978.   213.
     The authors feel that in general the FCC serves the public
interest only by the process of incremental and marginal
changes.   Part One evaluates the regulatory process.   Part Two
presents five case studies.   National Association of
Broadcasters' point of view.

571.   Krasnow, Erwin, and Samuel Simon.   "Does the Public
          Own the Airwaves?" Ch 2 (Sept.-Oct. 1982) 66-67.
     Krasnow, representing the National Association of
Broadcasters, presents the negative, Simon of the National
Citizens Committee for Broadcasting presents the affirmative.
Simon: the "government is obligated under the First Amendment
to protect our interest in an effective and democratic public
communications system.   The government is not free, therefore,
to turn the system over to private interests and market forces."

572.   Labunski, Richard.   The First Amendment Under Siege:
          The Politics of Broadcast Regulation. Westport, CT:
          Greenwood, 1981.   184.
     A defense of limited regulation of broadcasting in the name
of the First Amendment.   "Until programming that informs and
educates is more prevalent, it would be inappropriate and
premature to abolish the fairness doctrine" (158).   Ch. 1
considers whether electronic and print media are
constitutionally parallel; 2 and 3 examine case law in
broadcasting First Amendment rights; 4 FCC, Congress, White
House, etc., the political environment; 5 First Amendment
concepts of public interest, diversity, and access, fairness
doctrine; 6 current rewrite of the Communications Act of 1934
before Congress.

573.   Levin, Harvey.   "U.S. Broadcast Deregulation: A Case
          of Dubious Evidence." JoC 36.1 (Winter 1986) 25-40.
     The FCC proposal to increase the allowable number of radio
and TV stations owned by one group "raises large questions about
quality, diversity, and competition in programming."

574.   Lewis, Carolyn. "A Reporter Feels the Heat." CJR
         18.5 (1980) 34-37.
         An account of the inner workings of President Carter's
Three Mile Island Commission, its failure to recommend a
moratorium on nuclear power construction, its public relations
emphasis, and the failure of the press to probe into the biases
and abilities of the commissioners and the process.

575.   Lewis, Richard. The Nuclear-Power Rebellion:
         Citizens vs. the Atomic Industrial Establishment. New
         York: Viking, 1972. 313.
         An account of how private citizens successfully confronted
the AEC in "the only real challenge to a reckless nuclear-energy
policy" promoted by the AEC. "On the theory of a power
shortage, the AEC, the Joint Committee [on Atomic Energy], and
the White House had promoted quick, interim licensing of new
plants, overriding environmental and safety concerns. . . .It
was clear that if the environment were to be protected, citizens
would have to do it."

576.   Marine, Gene, and Judith Van Allen. Food Pollution:
         The Violation of Our Inner Ecology. New York: Holt,
         1972. 385.
         "The [food] industry owns the FDA, and the FDA does what
the industry wants it to do."

577.   Massing, Michael. "In Philly, Fair is Foul." CJR
         18.4 (1979) 8-10.
         Many television stations have used the fairness doctrine to
refuse to deal with controversial matters, including the
rejection of advocacy ads.

577a.   Mintz, Morton. "The Pill: Press and Public at the
         Experts' Mercy." CJR 7.4 (1968-69) 4-10.
         Evidence of "non-feasance, misfeasance, and malfeasance" on
the part of the FDA, the medical profession, and the
pharmaceutical companies have gone virtually unreported by the
media.

578.   Mosco, Vincent. Broadcasting in the United States:
         Innovative Challenge and Organizational Control.
         Norwood, NJ: Ablex, 1979. 153.
         A study of the "powerful people" who "brought us
television--who decided what we see and, more importantly, what
we don't see. This book focuses on the fate of attempts to
expand the radio/television world--on innovations that carried
the hope of remaking that world only to be weakened by the
structure that governs it. Specifically, I show how the
regulatory system has helped maintain the dominance of AM radio
and VHF television stations--and the profits of the companies
that own these stations--at the expense of such innovations as
FM radio, UHF, cable, and subscription television."

579.   Mosher, James, and Lawrence Wallack. "Government

Regulation of Alcohol Advertising: Protecting Industry
Profits versus Promoting the Public Health." <u>JPHP</u> 2
(1981) 333-353.
The Federal Bureau of Alcohol, Tobacco, and Firearms has
overridden public opinion and health concerns and has allowed
the alcohol industry to continue presenting commercials which
show alcohol as socially and sexually positive.

580.　　Owen, Bruce, and Ronald Braeutigam. <u>The Regulation
Game: Strategic Use of the Administrative Process</u>.
Cambridge: Ballinger, 1978. 271.
"Regulatory policy is increasingly made with participation
of experts, especially academics. A regulated firm or industry
should be prepared whenever possible to co-opt these experts.
This is most effectively done by identifying the leading experts
in each relevant field and hiring them as consultants or
advisors, or giving them research grants and the like. This
activity requires a modicum of finesse; it must not be too
blatant, for the experts themselves must not recognize that they
have lost their objectivity and freedom of action."

581.　　Packwood, Senator Bob. "Protecting First Amendment
Freedoms in the Age of Electronic Revolution." <u>TQ</u> 20.4
(1984) 51-55.
Packwood calls for repeal of the FCC "Fairness Doctrine,"
which requires that television networks give equal time to all
filed political candidates and to all counter-opinions to an
editorial. In this way he hopes to encourage competition and
airing of controversial issues.

582.　　"Pesticide Policy Steadfast Despite Worries." <u>AG</u>
(June 9, 1985) 2D.
Environmental groups are pushing for stronger laws and an
EPA capable of providing the information and action the public
needs, but the Reagan administration backed by the chemical
industry is pushing to extend the present weak law.

583.　　Piven, Frances, and Richard Cloward. <u>The New Class
War: Reagan's Attack on the Welfare State and Its
Consequences</u>. New York: Pantheon, 1982. 163.
One purpose of this essay is to explain why the business-
oriented leaders who came to power with the election of Reagan
in 1980 are trying to dismantle "welfare protections." The book
explains how the "virtually complete domination of state policy
by business" came about.

584.　　Pollock, Richard. "Conflict of Interest in the NRC."
<u>CMJ</u> 2.11 (1977) 1, 10.
In 1977, twelve of the fourteen members of the federal
Advisory Committee on Reactor Safeguards were taken from the
nuclear industry or laboratories working primarily with the
nuclear industry.

585.　　Pollock, Richard. "Industry-Government Collusion."

CMJ 2.9 (1976) 1, 10.
Standards of safety used by the Nuclear Regulatory
Commission are obtained to a large degree from a committee of
the American National Standards Institute. The committee, the
"National Standards Management Board," is made up primarily of
corporate executives in the nuclear industry, with no public
interest or labor representation.

586.   Pollock, Richard. "Trouble Brews Within Nuclear
      Agency." CMJ 2.10 (1977) 1, 10.
Five witnesses, representing over a dozen engineers and
technicians in the Nuclear Regulatory Commission, presented
specific incidents to a Senate Government Operations Committee
in which "their technical views have been stifled or suppressed
to favor industry."

587.   Pool, Ithiel de Sola. Technologies of Freedom.
      Cambridge, MA: Belknap, 1983. 299.
Advocates deregulation of electronic technologies on the
basis of the First Amendment to the US Constitution as the great
guarantor of freedom of communication. [Nicholas Garnham, MCS 7
(1985) 263-4: Because the First Amendment does not cope with
the concentration of power in corporations and fails to
distinguish between individual and corporate rights, de Sola
Pool places too much hope in electronic technologies as
expanders of choice.]

588.   Rapoport, Roger. "Oops!. . . The Story of Nuclear
      Power Plants." Ram 10 (March 1972) 49-57.
Several documented accidents show that already low Atomic
Energy Commission standards for nuclear power plant safety were
not being regularly followed. Nonetheless, the Nixon
administration joined with the utility industry in backing
further development.

589.   Read, William. "The First Amendment Meets the
      Information Society." Telecommunications: Issues and
      Choices for Society. Ed. Jerry Salvaggio. New York:
      Longman, 1983. 78-84.
An argument for the extension of First Amendment free press
protection to broadcasting, and consequently the elimination of
government regulation of broadcasting.

590.   "Researchers Assert Pesticide Laws Too Weak to Protect
      Farm Workers." AG (July 15, 1985) 6A.
"Despite four decades of regulation, authorities still lack
the information needed to determine the precise extent of risk
to as many as 5 million farm workers exposed to the chemicals."

591.   Rosenthal, Bruce. "Rasmussen's Conflict of Interest
      Revealed." CMJ 2.4 (1976) 3.
Consultants for government agencies are also working for
the industries regulated by the agencies.

592.   Rothschild, Matthew. "Death by Prescription." Prog
          50.6 (1986) 18-22.
     The FDA still permits the sale of the deadly drug Feldene
aggressively marketed by Pfizer with misleading ads.

593.   Ruby, Robert. "Withholding Nuclear Plant Accident
          Information 'Knowingly' Is Okay." Pr 10.2 (1982) 15-16.
     The Nuclear Regulatory Commission ruled that the engineers
of the Three Mile Island nuclear plant after the 1979 accident
did withhold information "knowingly," which is not punishable,
but they did not withhold the information "willfully," which is
against the law.

594.   Salzman, Lorna. "Nuclear Cover-up. Part One.
          Censorship in USA?" IC 7.5 (1978) 36-42.
     The "major responsibility for keeping the public poorly
informed" about nuclear dangers "lies with the nuclear power
industry and, more disturbingly, with the agencies of the United
States government which have been charged with regulating the
nuclear industry."

595.   Schmidt, Benno, Jr. Freedom of the Press Versus
          Public Access. New York: Praeger, 1976. 296.
     An analysis of "whether private publications, such as
newspapers, magazines, radio and television stations, and
conceivably even books, should be obligated by law to present
the viewpoint of some person or entity that the publisher would
not present as a matter of editorial discretion" (3). Part I
summarizes the Supreme Court decisions dealing with access.
Part II concerns recent related developments in First Amendment
law. Part III examines access obligations in the legal
regulation of broadcasting and possible extension to print
media. Part IV analyzes Supreme Court response to this
possibility.

596.   Schneider, Keith. "The Data Gap: What We Don't Know
          About Chemicals." AJ 6.3 (1985) 15-24.
     Poor quality data "threatens the scientific basis of the
nation's regulatory system."

597.   Sibbison, Jim. "Cancer Is a Dirty Word at EPA." CC
          9.1 (1983) 7.
     The EPA is ignoring the dangers of toxic chemicals "partly
because many" of its top officials "hail from the very
industries they're supposed to regulate"--Rita Lavelle and
others.

598.   Siepmann, Charles. "Radio's Operation Crossroads."
          Na 163.23 (December 7, 1946) 644-645.
     "Justin Miller, President of the National Association of
Broadcasters, has stumped the country for some weeks, inveighing
against the supporters of the FCC's 'Blue Book'."

599.   Simmons, Steven. The Fairness Doctrine and the Media.

Berkeley: California UP, 1979. 285.
A collection mainly of the author's law review articles
that chronicle the development of fairness doctrine law. The
author concludes that the doctrine should be repealed.
[Nicholas Johnson attacks the author's indifference to the First
Amendment and to the goals of the doctrine in CJR (May-June
1979) 63-66.]

600.   Smith, R. Jeffrey. "Covering the EPA, or, Wake Me Up
         if Anything Happens." CJR 22.3 (1983) 29-34.
The press was negligently slow in 1981 and 1982 in
investigating the scandalous behavior of Reagan's EPA, the close
ties between its top officials and regulated industries, and
neglect of pesticide, water pollution, radiation, noise, and
toxic waste problems.

600a.   Soloman, Goody L. "Food Pages: Is the Heyday Over?"
         CJR 20.5 (1982) 41-44.
The trend toward strong consumer-oriented reporting on food
politics "seems to have come to a rather abrupt halt." The
Reagan administration's "undoing of consumer protections" is
receiving "a near-starvation diet of stories." The food
industry has its way, and the press is virtually silent about
it.

601.   Steinberg, Charles S., ed. Broadcasting: The
         Critical Challenges. New York: Hastings, 1974. 315.
The book is organized by a series of "challenges" for the
seventies. The editor believes that the air-waves, "a national
resource, belong to the people" and must be regulated for the
"public interest." But the problem is to define that interest.
Sections also focus upon UHF, international broadcasting, public
television, etc.

602.   Stranahan, Susan Q. "TMI: The Real Story Leaks Out."
         CMJ 8.10 (1983) 7-8.
Evidence of mishandling, falsified reports, and
contradictory statements which occurred at Three Mile Island
before its 1979 accident.

603.   Streeter, Thomas. "Policy Discourse and Broadcast
         Practice: The FCC, the US Broadcast Networks and the
         Discourse of the Marketplace." MCS 5 (July/Oct. 1983)
         247-62.
Broadly, a study of "American network broadcasting as the
product of an integrated oligopolistic co-ordination between the
major broadcast corporations and the government"; specifically,
an examination of "the 'teeth-gritting harmony' between the FCC
and the Broadcast corporations in which the structure and power
of network broadcasting is constituted."

604.   Taylor, Peter. The Smoke Ring: Tobacco, Money, &
         Multi-National Politics. New York: Pantheon, 1984.
         328.

An exposé of the combination of tobacco money and right-wing lobbying that perpetuates this multi-billion dollar lethal industry. "My purpose is to consider why governments place wealth before health, and to examine the political and economic mechanisms of the power of tobacco." Several chapters deal with aspects of information control.

605.   Tolchin, Susan, and Martin Tolchin. <u>Dismantling</u>
        <u>America: The Rush to Deregulate</u>. Boston: Houghton,
        1983. 323.
An account of how the regulation balancing consumer and business interests is being shredded by deregulation.

605a.   Traub, James. "Radio Without Rules." <u>CJR</u> 20.5 (1982)
        36-38.
Deregulation will mean less public affairs programs. Instead of a public trust, radio will be just another market commodity.

II. D. Media 606-787

II. D. 1. Mass Media 606-665

606.   Aldrich, Pearl. <u>The Impact of Mass Media</u>. Rochelle
        Park, NJ: Hayden, 1975. 179.
"<u>The</u> MAJORITY <u>of material</u> [in the mass media] <u>is chosen or</u>
<u>designed to produce a predetermined response</u>. Even that part of media output called "entertainment" is chosen to keep you quiet, unquestioning, available, and receptive to commercial messages inserted throughout. . . .The journalism, news, or information-giving portion of media output is selected, edited, produced, placed in time slots or positioned in the newspaper or magazine to reflect and support the owner's policies. These policies are sometimes intricate and interwoven strands, difficult to isolate individually, because ownership is a giant conglomerate made up of intertwining sections of the current commercial-military-governmental complex" (5).

607.   Aufderheide, Pat. "An Irreverent Look at Media." <u>ITT</u>
        9 (March 13-19, 1985) 21.
In praise of Paper Tiger TV, "one of the best-established anti-establishment shows on public access TV." Paper Tiger "places this country's printed media under rigorous scrutiny," revealing especially the economic basis of each medium examined.

608.   Aufderheide, Pat. "NPR: Drifting Rightward or Simply
        Adrift?" <u>ITT</u> 9 (July 24/Aug. 6, 1985) 20-21.
Because National Public Radio is under intense attack from the right, it is suffering from a "bad case of caution."

609.   Ball-Rokeach, Sandra J., Milton Rokeach, and Joel W.
        Grube. <u>The Great American Values Test: Influencing</u>
        <u>Behavior and Belief Through Television</u>. New York: Free,
        1984. 190.

109

The authors' 30-minute television program "The Great American Values Test" "significantly affected the beliefs and behaviors of large numbers of people" and suggests that manipulation and brainwashing through television are distinctly possible.

610.   Barmash, Isadore. The World Is Full of It: How We Are Oversold, Overinfluenced, and Overwhelmed by the Communications Manipulators. New York: Delacorte, 1974. 269.
Deception is being practiced massively daily against Americans, compelling them to respond to the wrong things for the wrong reasons. The play on sex and violence supports spurious claims by business about its products and services, in blatant disregard of public welfare. The press is muzzled and not allowed to report clandestine activities and political chicanery. "Our society seems increasingly to function in a self-induced and accepted communications behavior consisting of sham, lies, posturing, image-making and a vast ploy of hoodwink" (7).

611.   Barnouw, Erik. A Tower of Babel: A History of Broadcasting in the United States. Vol. I--to 1933. New York: Oxford UP, 1966. 344.
The radio industry developed what became known as the American system of broadcasting, "which made the salesman the trustee of the public interest, with minimal supervision by a commission" (281).

612.   Barnouw, Erik. The Golden Web: A History of Broadcasting in the United States. Vol. II--1933 to 1953. New York: Oxford UP, 1968. 391.
Traces the rise of the American networks and their "world-wide ramifications" in "an age of American hegemony." "This would usher in an era dominated by television and the pax Americana, to be chronicled in a third volume."

613.   Barnouw, Erik. The Image Empire: A History of Broadcasting in the United States. Volume III--from 1953. New York: Oxford UP, 1970. 396.
"The role of broadcasters in this American expansion [an involvement of imperial scope] and in the era that produced it is the subject matter" of this last of three volumes. The power of broadcasting in the modern world lends "urgency to the study of television and radio and the forces and mechanisms that guide and control them." The three volumes reveal numerous details of corporate and government domination of information in the US via the conversion of a public trust--the air waves--"into a private power system firmly based on advertising" for personal profit. During the post-World War II period "a consumer goods era put the accent first on big-money quizzes, then on action melodrama, which became an international phenomenon as business-military interests spread worldwide. These interests, often using the weapon of political blacklists, narrowed the zone of permitted

conflict in ideas, and tended to thrust dissent into other media. The dominance of business-military interests became all-pervasive, leaving mainly news programming of various sorts, along with noncommercial broadcasting, as areas of comparative independence." Even here "there were constant pressures to get into line" (337).

614.   Barnouw, Erik. <u>Tube of Plenty: The Evolution of</u> <u>American Television</u>. New York: Oxford UP, 1975. 520.
A condensation and updating of Barnouw's three-volume <u>A</u> <u>History of Broadcasting in the United States</u>. The US commercial system, principally invented by AT&T, came to mean "a conduit dominated by forces known as the 'establishment'. . . the large corporations and the government, closely linked." Instead of looking closely at the problems facing society, television worsened such problems as inflation, energy, environment, and violence in the drive for corporate profits and the "world-wide thrust of American business and military power" (468-70).

615.   Barrett, John R.   "Will Bureaucracy Finally Kill Art?" <u>TQ</u> 8.3 (1969) 16-21.
Governmental and corporate control of television has caused it to focus upon the past and the bland.

616.   Biryukov, N. S. <u>Television in the West and Its</u> <u>Doctrines</u>. Trans. Yuri Sviridov. Moscow: Progress, 1981. 207.
A skeptical view of the impartiality and "free flow of information" of capitalist television. "The rich variety of forms, genres, techniques used by programme-makers reveals a set of definite ideological guidelines and principles of Western television, i.e., the main tasks assigned to it by the ruling class in the ideological sphere" (88).

617.   Burroughs, William. <u>Ah Pook Is Here and Other Texts</u>. London: Calder, 1982. 157.
Three essays, two of them about the necessity of freeing imagination from Control, under whatever ideology (a frequent theme of Burroughs' novels). Burroughs links death, power, and media. The third essay, "The Electronic Revolution," instructs us in the use of an electronic device to scramble conventional media contents in order to expose the illusions fostered by them.

618.   Chenoweth, Lawrence. <u>The American Dream of Success:</u> <u>The Search for the Self in the Twentieth Century</u>. North Scituate, MA: Duxbury, Wadsworth, 1974. 237.
A study of the <u>Reader's Digest</u> from 1926 through 1969, <u>The</u> <u>Saturday Evening Post</u> from 1917 through 1967, and 47 best-selling self-help books published between 1917 and 1969 to determine "how the concept of free will has been distorted into a device which encourages obedience to political and corporate leaders" and why "individual citizens" have become "increasingly passive even as the nation has become domestically more violent

and internationally more arrogant" (viii).

619.   Chomsky, Noam.   "The Bounds of Thinkable Thought."
     Prog 49.10 (1985) 28-31.
     "Democratic systems, unlike totalitarian ones, ensure
control not by force but by establishing a framework for
possible thought. The principles of the state religion need not
be asserted; it is better that they be presupposed.

620   Cirino, Robert. We're Being More Than Entertained.
     Honolulu: Lighthouse, 1977. 224.
     The author begins with the assumption that all media
messages are political, including entertainment programs, and
his book is intended to help readers "discover and then counter
the underlying political biases" in mass media entertainment,
the purpose of which is to make money for sponsors. He
discusses Kojak, All My Children, the L.A. Times sports pages,
Playboy, host shows, top 40, Tournament of Thrills,
Sesame Street, comic books, radio news, cartoons, and network
live coverage news. At the end he sets forth a proposal for a
multispectral political broadcasting system.

621.   Cox, Harvey. "The Consciousness Industry: A
     Theological View of the Media." PTR 1 (October 1973) 8-
     15.
     The author contrasts the biblical and mass-media notions of
"communication" and suggests ways of reconciling them.

622.   Cross, Donna. Mediaspeak: How Television Makes Up
     Your Mind. New York: Putnam, 1983. 254.
     Television's program content, including that of news shows,
promotes establishment values, stereotypes, the status quo, and
imprisons the viewers in a narcotized, pervasive sameness of
appearances.

623.   D'Agostino, Peter. Transmission: Theory and Practice
     for a New Television Aesthetics. New York: Tanam, 1985.
     336.
     This general collection includes "Nuclear Consciousness on
Television" by James Welsh, "The Case of the A-Bomb Footage" by
Erik Barnouw, and "Meet the Press: On Paper Tiger Television"
by Martha Gever.

624.   Dahl, Robert. Political Opposition in Western
     Democracies. New Haven, CT: Yale UP, 1966. 458.
     "The amount of time and space devoted to the mass media to
views openly hostile to the prevailing ideology is negligible."
Hence "the general effect of the mass media is to reinforce the
existing institutions and ideology" (47-48).

625.   DeMott, Benjamin. "The Trouble with Public Television."
     Atlantic 243 (Feb. 1979) 42-47.
     PBS and CPB are a "sea of corporate mayonnaise" best
described as "distinguished philistinism. . .utterly remote from

what is most precious and vital in the soul of this nation," and hostile to talent, creativity, and originality.

626.   Dorfman, Ron. "Gelding Public TV." ChJR 6.4 (1973) 3-5.
A rapid history of public broadcasting with focus on why it will likely become "more politically cautious and aesthetically unimaginative."

627.   Dunham, Corydon. "Repeal of the Fairness Doctrine Held Vital to Free Speech in Era of Communications Explosion." TRA 29 (April 19, 1982) 36, 56.
"As government regulates news and information increasingly transmitted electronically over the air or by cable, the press and the public are denied much of the First Amendment's protection for news coverage. . . .Fairness Doctrine proceedings were used by them (watchdog groups) to try to stop the expression of views offensive to them. And so, the FCC becomes an agent under the Doctrine for the suppression of speech and press" (36).

628.   Ellul, Jacques. Propaganda: The Formation of Men's Attitudes. Trans. Konrad Kellen and Jean Lerner. New York: Knopf, 1965. 320.
Formerly, propagandists employed emotional appeals and saturation campaigns to control public opinion. Today, propaganda is more scientific, systematic, pervasive, and subtle in maintaining the national ideological viewpoint, because in contemporary technological society propaganda replaces the extended family, the neighborhood, and the church as the chief mechanism of social control. Technology has created new media methods that enable political leaders to indoctrinate an ideology: television, public opinion polls, etc.

629.   Gitlin, Todd. The Whole World Is Watching: Mass Media in the Making and Unmaking of the New Left. Berkeley: U of California P, 1980. 327.
The mass media are "a significant social force in the forming and delimiting of public assumptions, attitudes, and moods--of ideology, in short," central "to the continuation of the established order." The "command structures of this order are an oligopolized, privately controlled corporate economy and its intimate ally, the bureaucratic national security state, together embedded within a capitalist world complex of nation-states" (9). The mass media, which have become "core systems for the distribution" of the ideology of these structures protect and perpetuate the oligopoly by blacking out news "that effectively challenges" corporate and political elites and by "disparaging movements that radically oppose the system" (4-5).

630.   Glessing, Robert, and William White, eds. Mass Media: The Invisible Environment Revisited. Chicago: Science, 1976. 277.
Contains articles by many important critics of corporate

113

and government control of the media--Harry Skornia, Don Pember, Ben Bagdikian, Bob Woodward and Carl Bernstein, Dale Minor, Nicholas Johnson, and others.

631.   Gliserman, Marty. "Watch Out, Chicago." JC 5
         (Jan.-Feb. 1975) 7-8.
    Films like Death Wish, which portray crimes by lower social classes, reaffirm the hierarchy of power by diverting the populace away from crimes by higher social classes and by suggesting a common bond between the privileged and most people threatened by violent criminals.

632.   Goldsen, Rose. "The Great American Consciousness
         Machine: Engineering the Thought-Environment." JSR 1.2
         (1980) 87-102.
    Control of pervasively "mind-forming" television "rests largely in the hands of a small group of men and women dedicated to furthering the interests of the corporations they work for: networks, a coterie of satellite business, and the principal clients of both.

633.   Graber, Doris, ed. Media Power in Politics.
         Washington, DC: Cong. Quar., 1984. 348.
    Thirty-seven essays. Chs. 8 and 9 explore how media provide support for the established political regime. Essays in Section 2 deal with "Controlling Media Effects" (e.g., Bagdikian on the widespread propaganda of free news releases by corporations and other special interests.)

633a.   Graham, Fred. "1984 and All That." CJR 20.2 (1981)
         77-78.
    Review of Wicklein's Electronic Nightmare, a book about communications developments that endanger individual liberty.

634.   Hess, Judith. "Genre Films and the Status Quo." JC
         1 (1974) 1, 16.
    American genre films (the western, science fiction, horror, gangster) assist to maintain the "status quo" and "throw a sop to oppressed groups" who "accept the genre film's absurd solutions to economic and social conflicts."

635.   Jamieson, Kathleen, and Karlyn Campbell. The
         Interplay of Influence: Mass Media and Their Publics in
         News, Advertising, Politics. Belmont, CA: Wadsworth,
         1983. 287.
    "We assume that the tendency of any mass media system is to affirm establishment values. A system that failed to do so would not attract audiences or government or private sponsorship. News, advertising, and political communication in the United States reflect this ideological reality" (261). Ch. 5 deals with the audience, 6-8 on advertising, 9 on ways the public can influence the media, 10-11 on politics, news, and advertising.

636.   Kahane, Howard. Logic and Contemporary Rhetoric:
          The Use of Reason in Everyday Life. 2nd ed. Belmont,
          CA: Wadsworth, 1976. 259.
     A logic and language text but includes Ch. 7, "Advertising:
Selling the Product," Ch. 8, "Managing the News," and Ch. 9,
"Textbooks: Managing World Views." The author's purpose is to
"raise the level of political argument and reasoning by
acquainting students with the devices and ploys which drag that
level down."

637.   Lewis, Anthony. "Budget-Leadership Crisis Threatens
          Public Radio." AG (28 June 1983) 9A.
     Praises NPR's "All Things Considered" and "Morning Edition"
and regrets lack in US of British commitment to noncommercial
broadcasting, where public broadcasting is paid for by license
fees. "Public television and radio get from government what is
a pittance by world standards."

638.   Lippard, Lucy R. "Recycled Images Redeem Memory."
          ITT 10.8 (1986) 20.
     A review of a New York art exhibit which expresses how
"'the art of memory can prevent the loss of history'." For
example, Paper Tiger's Murray Bookchin reading "Time" and a
dissection of the "op-ed ads" of United Technologies (a defense
contractor with an interest in heroicizing war) are presented.

639.   Macy, John, Jr. To Irrigate a Wasteland: The
          Struggle to Shape a Public Television System in the
          United States. Berkeley: U of California P, 1974. 186.
     The author castigates the commercial television wasteland,
expresses the great potentiality for excellence in public
television, and offers concrete proposals for the achievement of
that potential.

640.   Mandel, Ernest. Delightful Murder: A Social History
          of the Crime Story. London: Pluto P, 1984. 152.
     The crime story has served to reinforce the ideas that
maintain the ruling class and state stability. The "common
ideology of the original and classical detective story in
Britain, the United States, and the countries of the European
continent remains quintessentially bourgeois." Individual
conflicts used as a generalized substitute for conflicts between
social groups and layers--"all this is bourgeois ideology par
excellence, a striking synthesis of human alienation in
bourgeois society" (47).

641.   Mattelart, Armand and Seth Siegelaub, eds.
          Communication and Class Struggle. Vol. I, Capitalism,
          Imperialism. New York: International General; Bagnolet,
          Fr.: IMMRC, 1979. 448.
     Sixty-two texts discuss bourgeois ideology and practice.
Mattelart gives an extensive introduction in "For a Class
Analysis of Communication."

COMPLEX

642.   McAnany, Emile, et al., eds. Communication and
Social Structure: Critical Studies in Mass Media
Research. New York: Praeger, 1981. 341.
     Twelve essays divided into three groups on communication
theory, US mass communication, and international mass
communication. One essay examines the context of children's
television, another the FCC's effort to increase minority
ownership of radio and television stations, another the effect
of subsidized information in enabling interest groups to
dominate policy. The editors call for universities to ensure
critical research on the "potentially dysfunctional social and
economic impacts of these institutions on society" (15).

643.   McAuliffe, Kevin. The Great American Newspaper: The
Rise and Fall of the "Village Voice." New York:
Scribner's, 1978. 486.
     When the Village Voice was sold in 1974, it "became not
something there because of the need for it, to give a voice to
voiceless people, but a prize of booty on the battlefield of
venture capitalism" (469).

644.   McDermott, John. "Knowledge is Power." Na 208
(April 14, 1969) 458-462.
     The maldistribution of knowledge in America, partly the
result of corporate and governmental power over information, is
producing increasingly unreal and even paranoid political
perceptions about politics.

645.   "Media, Political Access and Social Change." Win
19.15 & 16 (1983).
     Six essays explore "key questions concerning the flow of
information in the United States. Who controls the medium and
the message? How do we combat oppressive ideologies in the
currently existing media? What would a truly democratic,
egalitarian media look like? How does the government use the
media for its strategic purposes."

646.   Mooney, Michael. The Ministry of Culture:
Connections Among Art, Money and Politics. New York:
Wyndham, 1980. 427.
     The federal government in alliance with corporations is
using the arts to indoctrinate the public with a totalitarian
vision and repressing artistic freedom in the process.

647.   Moore, Ray. "Brave New Television World." TQ 2.4
(1963) 24-29.
     Television is seen as a "timid giant" which bows to
corporate and government supervision. Some exceptions are
lauded.

648.   Newcomb, Horace, ed. Television: The Critical View.
2nd ed. New York: Oxford U, 1979. 557.
     Twenty-nine essays confront numerous aspects of
television--soaps, news, ideology, etc., practical and

116

theoretical.

649.   Nimmo, Dan, and James Combs. <u>Mediated Political</u>
        <u>Realities</u>. New York: Longman, 1983. 240.
        "Few people learn about politics through direct experience;
for most persons political realities are mediated through mass
and group communication, a process resulting as much in the
creation, transmission, and adoption of political fantasies as
realistic views of what takes place." Various sections reveal
the great influence of the government and corporations in this
process. The book is divided into two parts, Part I on "mass-
mediated political realities": Ch. 1 fantasy themes, rhetorical
visions, and melodramas in televised news coverage of crises; 2
political campaigns, 3 popular culture, 4 political celebrities,
5 Hollywood, 6 sports. Part II deals with "group-mediated
political fantasies": Ch. 7 group-think, 8 pack journalism, 9
religion and politics, 10 conspiratorial fantasies, and a
conclusion on the fantasyland of America.

650.   Packard, Vance. <u>The Hidden Persuaders</u>. New York:
        McKay, 1957. 242.
        An analysis of the massive efforts by corporations and the
government "to channel our unthinking habits, our purchasing
decisions, and our thought processes by the use of insights
gleaned from psychiatry and the social sciences"--"depth"
psychology for engineering consent by motivational research.
Packard emphasizes the seriously anti-humanistic and anti-
democratic implications of behavioral research in the hands of
powerful institutions, since the assumption of both the
humanities and democracy is that the greatness of human beings
lies in their potential for self-guidance.

651.   Paletz, David, and Robert Entman. <u>Media, Power,</u>
        <u>Politics</u>. New York: Free, 1981. 308.
        A study of how diverse representatives of power
(presidents, members of Congress, et al.) manipulate the media,
"how media content (news and 'entertainment' alike) socializes
the majority of Americans into accepting the legitimacy of their
country's political, economic, and social system; how public
opinion on both domestic and foreign issues is strongly affected
by the media and their powerful manipulators; and how the media
often undermine the fitful attempts of ordinary citizens
to participate in politics" ("Preface"). The media "influence
the decisions and actions of politicians and officials," but
they also insulate them "from public accountability," they
reallocate power only "among the already powerful," they give
elites "predominant say over the content of the popular press,
thus over the media's effects on public opinion about such
governmental matters," they weaken public resistance to the
power structure, and they "help preserve the legitimacy of
America's political, economic, and social system." "The
consequence is quiescent mass loyalty" ("Conclusions").
[Excellent bibliography.]

652.   Prime Time Kids: An Analysis of Children and Families
         on Television. Washington, DC: National Commission on
         Working Women, 1985. 11.
     Families on prime time television do not reflect the
majority of American families. Issues such as racial
discrimination, financial worries, and child care availability
are largely ignored.

653.   "Public Television Constantly in Danger of Being
         Compromised by Sources of Its Money." AG (April 22,
         1976) 8A.
     Sometimes called the Petroleum Broadcasting System,
noncommercial TV is also subject to intense governmental
pressures to conform.

654.   "The Reality of Political Junk Mail." AG (April 20,
         1985) 17A.
     The corporate press release resembles the new presidential
news wire and the presidential television apparatus: all enjoy
direct access to the public unmediated by journalistic analysis.

655.   Salvaggio, Jerry, ed. Telecommunications: Issues
         and Choices for Society. New York: Longman, 1983. 182.
     Ten essays express varying degrees of apprehension
regarding central control of communication technologies,
invasion of privacy, corporate monopoly, violation of the First
Amendment, etc. Herbert Schiller, for example, asks, "How do we
deal with telecommunication systems that have been conceived,
designed, built, and installed with the primary objectives being
the maintenance of economic privilege and advantage and the
prevention of the kind of social change that would overturn and
eliminate this privilege?"

656.   Sarnoff, Irving. "The Campaign to Destroy the UN."
         SANE 25.5 (1986) 3.
     The right-wing "barrage" to "destroy the UN is complemented
by a propensity among the media to virtually ignore" its
accomplishments.

657.   Schwartz, Wendy. "The Politics of Prime Time TV." NA
         2 (Feb. 1985) 6-8.
     Television is homogenizing the people into conservatives
and right-wingers politically.

658.   Smith, Anthony. The Shadow in the Cave: The
         Broadcaster, His Audience and the State. Urbana, IL: U
         of Illinois P, 1973. 338.
     A study of the relationship between government, the
broadcast establishment and their shared constituencies, and a
series of case histories of several countries including the US.
The US system has become the handmaiden of the business
community.

659.   Solovitch, Sara. "NPR's Crisis Quarter." WJR 5.5

(1983) 16-17.
On NPR's $5.8 million deficit and President Frank
Mankiewicz' resignation.

660.   Steenland, Sally. Prime Time Kids: An Analysis of
    Children and Families on Television. Washington, DC:
    National Commission on Working Women, ca. 1985. 11.
The presentation of children and families on TV is unreal:
race and sex discrimination exist only mildly; bigotry "is
usually overcome at the end of the show by good-hearted people";
children "don't need child care, or it is provided automatically
by loving relatives or live-in help"; financial worries are
"virtually invisible"; the "intractable problems" poor people
particularly face are seldom shown.

661.   Vogel, Amos. "Independents: Smashing Myths About the
    Information Industry." FiC 18 (1982) 76-77.
An admiring account of a videotape project to analyze print
media, called Newspaper Tiger Television Production: Smashing
Myths About the Information Industry, produced by DeeDee Halleck
and several collaborators. In each half-hour segment, a
prominent scholar, artist or critic comments on one issue of a
particular publication.

662.   Weinberg, Meyer. TV in America: The Morality of
    Hard Cash. New York: Ballantine, 1962. 311.
Draws heavily on the quiz scandal and payola hearings to
show that sponsors, broadcasters, government and public have
behaved like Charles Van Doren. The press talked of reform, but
quickly forgot or gave up, as did the FCC. The author
particularly ridicules industry talk of self-regulation, which
has not been forthcoming.

663.   Winn, Marie. The Plug-In Drug. New York: Viking,
    1977. 231.
An argument against watching television because it is a
"pathogen," a source of modern ills: "alienation,
dehumanization, apathy, moral vacuum." Television also leads to
"poorer socialization" and makes "inroads" into "family life."

664.   Witty, Susan. "The Citizens Movement Takes a Turn."
    Ch 1.2 (1981) 68-73.
On the decline of the media reform movement (partly because
of the withdrawal of the Ford Foundation from public interest
funding) and the rise of right-wing groups, such as Accuracy in
Media (AIM), whose budget doubled in 1981 to more than $1
million. The FCC's decision to release broadcasters from
keeping program records is another setback to citizen groups.
Deregulation is another blow.

665.   Wood, Robin. Hollywood from Vietnam to Reagan. New
    York: Columbia UP, 1986. 328.
The book focuses mainly on sexual politics, but it is also
an examination of capitalism's "own methods of coercion and

119

suppression, so that is does not--yet--have to resort to direct state intervention" (although it repeatedly shows itself ready to do so). "The chief method is a complicated process of marginalization: the exclusion of radical positions from the popular media and their relegation to universities and generally short-lived counterculture periodicals," and the university challenge is "being systematically eroded both from without and within" (from Ch. 1). The films of Altman, De Palma, Scorsese, and others are appraised.

II. D. 2. News 666-787 (See IV. C.).

666.   Adams, William, ed. Television Coverage of
    International Affairs. Norwood, NJ: Ablex, 1982. 253.
Thirteen essays arranged into five sections: Global Coverage, Third World, The West and Presidential Diplomacy, Southeast Asia, and Audience. Chapters of special interest: 3 on three dominant motifs structuring Third World coverage; 5 on Latin American coverage, especially Chile and Nicaragua; 6 on Camp David Summit; 7 on the US boycott of the 1980 Moscow Olympics; 8 on terrorism; 10 on Vietnam; 11 on the battle of Khe Sanh; and 12 on the 1975-78 Cambodian holocaust.

667.   Adams, William, and Fay Schreibman, eds. Television
    Network News: Issues in Content Research. Washington,
    DC: School of Public and International Affairs, George
    Washington U, 1978. 231.
Ten essays focus particularly on methodology--a bibliographic essay, an essay on monitoring network news, a critique of television news criticism, a guide to TV news archives, content analysis of broadcast news, etc.

668.   Altheide, David. Creating Reality: How TV News
    Distorts Events. Beverly Hills: Sage, 1976. 220.
The author saw "in concrete detail how the interaction between politicians, businessmen, political activists, and the newsroom staff influenced the selection and treatment of news" (from Introduction).

669.   Altschull, J. Herbert. Agents of Power: The Role of
    the News Media in Human Affairs. New York: Longman,
    1984. 355.
The author's fundamental belief is that global understanding would be raised if we acknowledged "the similarities in the press everywhere" (281). His book leads to "seven laws" of similarity: "1. In all press systems, the news media are agents of those who exercise political and economic power," etc. Part 1, background; 2, three press models as foundation for the classification system of Part 4; 3, issues affecting the classification: social responsibility, the New World Information Order, news and finance; 4, the classification system: market, Marxist, and advancing.

670.   Anderson, Jack. "What You Don't Know Can Hurt You."

PM (Aug. 11, 1985) 8-9.
"Today and every day, Soviet officials and American
politicians alike are deceiving you and manipulating your
opinion."

671.   Arno, Andrew, and Wimal Dissanayake, eds. The News
    Media in National and International Conflict. Boulder,
    CO: Westview, 1984. 250.
One major theme of the collection is that media
organizations "operate within given technological limitations
and cultural conventions" (13). For example, Hamid Mowlana in
"The Role of the Media in the US-Iranian Conflict" complains
about the "radically biased stereotypes" of the Iranian
revolution shared by the US government and media, and the
failure of the media to go beyond official sources.

672.   Aronson, James. Deadline for the Media: Today's
    Challenges to Press, TV and Radio. Indianapolis:
    Bobbs, 1972. 327.
In general the communications media have been "a crucial
part of the power complex" of the Cold War. "The media
condition the citizen to think the thoughts that are preferred
by government, industry, the military and the educational
establishment--and by the media themselves." Fourteen essays
explore this interlocking relationship.

673.   Aronson, James. Packaging the News: A Critical
    Survey of Press, Radio, TV. New York: International,
    1971. 109.
Sixteen chs. on the reliability of news sources, the
control of the flow of news, the impact of the Nixon
administration on the news, government intimidation, etc.

674.   Babington, Charles. "Helms and Co.: Plotting to
    Unseat Dan Rather." CJR 24.2 (1985) 47-51.
Fairness in Media is seeking $2 billion to acquire CBS.

675.   Bad News. London: Routledge, 1976. 310.
[Although this book is about British television, the
assumptions of the authors, and the evidence which supports
those assumptions, are highly germane to US newsmaking.] News
"selects itself" by "filtering processes." "The fourth and most
important filter--since it partly contains the others--is the
cultural air we breathe, the whole ideological atmosphere of our
society, which tells us that some things can be said and others
had best not be said. It is that whole and almost unconscious
pressure towards implicitly affirming the status quo which is
"the context of the television news" (x). A second volume,
More Bad News (RKP, 1980), concentrates upon methods of
analysis, ways to analyze the language and visuals of
television, to reaffirm the thesis of volume one that television
news is based upon premises (inferential frames) sympathetic to
an industrial, corporate, government point of view rather than
worker perspectives.

676.   Bagdikian, Ben. <u>The Effete Conspiracy and Other</u>
    <u>Crimes By the Press</u>. New York: Harper, 1972. 159.
    Fifteen essays under three headings: "Secrecy and
Manipulation," "The Conglomerate Discovers Journalism," and "The
President and the Press." Essays on the Pentagon Papers,
presidential manipulation of television, Du Pont control of
newspapers, news from the news source, etc.

677.   Bardsley, Anne. "Boot-camps of the Press." <u>ChJR</u> 2.2
    (Feb. 1969) 11.
    "Most young journalists learn how to be obsequious flacks
for the Establishment" when they work for school newspapers
supervised by journalism professors.

678.   Barnouw, Erik. <u>Documentary: A History of the Non-</u>
    <u>Fiction Film</u>. New York: Oxford UP, 1974. 332.
    Laced with striking revelations, for example, that during
the 1950s "America's main surviving newsreels--Fox Movietone
News and the MGM-Hearst News of the Day--had become government-
subsidized under a highly secret arrangement with the code name
'Kingfish'" (272). The section on Vietnam (269-282) is
particularly revealing of manipulation of facts.

The next eight entries are a series and appear in chronological
order:

679.   Barrett, Marvin, ed. <u>Survey of Broadcast Journalism</u>
    <u>1968-1969</u>. Alfred I. duPont-Columbia Univ. Survey of
    Broadcast Journalism 1. New York: Grosset and Dunlap,
    1969. 132.
    The editor perceives the broadcast journalist struggling
idealistically against a tide of triviality and acquisitiveness.
Whatever it is called, "the inevitable result of this relentless
search for profits seems to be some form of pollution: from
broadcasting, of our minds, talents, and souls, our spiritual
environment." It is "under such cynical proprietorship, in an
atmosphere of measliness and deliberate distraction, that much
broadcast journalism is expected to function" (4-5). The book
contains the first annual survey of conditions with special
reports on investigative journalism and citizen protest.

680.   Barrett, Marvin, ed. <u>Survey of Broadcast Journalism</u>
    <u>1969-1970: Year of Challenge, Year of Crisis</u>. Alfred I.
    duPont-Columbia Univ. Survey of Broadcast Journalism 2.
    New York: Grosset, 1970. 156.
    The Annual Survey, with special attention to Vice-President
Agnew, television and the presidency, TV and political
campaigning, government regulation, the environment, the
consumer. Special Reports on "Newscasting on Earth Day--A
Monitoring Project," "The FCC and the Future of Broadcast
Journalism," and "Subpoenas: Should Reporters Be Forced to Tell
What They Know?"

681.   Barrett, Marvin, ed. <u>A State of Siege: Survey of</u>

Broadcast Journalism 1970-71. The Third duPont-
Columbia Univ. Survey of Broadcast Journalism. New York:
Grosset, 1971. 183.
The survey covers the selling of the Pentagon, government
and broadcasting, truth and PBS, advertising and the news,
cable, and other topics. Reports on bias in television,
fairness and access, and women.

682.   Barrett, Marvin, ed. The Politics of Broadcasting.
Alfred I. duPont-Columbia Univ. Survey of Broadcast
Journalism 4. New York: Crowell, 1973. 247.
Focuses upon the election of 1972 (as the first Survey
analyzed the 1968 presidential campaign). The editor sees the
broadcast journalist caught between a merchandising operation
and often hostile government. This annual Survey concentrates
on reporting the campaigning, with special reports on TV, radio
news, sports, and TV drama.

683.   Barrett, Marvin, ed. Moments of Truth? The Fifth
Alfred I. duPont-Columbia Univ. Survey of Broadcast
Journalism. New York: Crowell, 1975. 247.
The essay by Clay Whitehead, "Big Media--Free Press,"
describes the power of large media corporations wedded to their
advertisers and their profits.

684.   Barrett, Marvin, ed. Rich News, Poor News. The
Sixth Alfred I. duPont-Columbia Univ. Survey of Broadcast
Journalism. New York: Crowell, 1978. 244.
The Introduction, "Money, Money, Money": "The good news in
broadcasting in 1976-77 had to do with profits." The bad news
"had to do with the quality and nature of most of the fare with
which the profits were earned." The annual survey covered
Barbara Walters, efforts to expand news time, business and news,
terrorism, PBS, and other topics. Special reports on women and
cable.

685.   Barrett, Marvin and Zachary Sklar. The Eye of the
Storm. Alfred I. duPont-Columbia Univ. Survey of
Broadcast Journalism 7. New York: Lippincott, 1980.
240.
In addition to the annual Survey and awards there are
special reports on Three Mile Island, the Burger Court, and
foreign coverage. One section is about the coverage of the oil
crisis of 1979: a poll of news directors conveyed the feeling
that when they tried to "get below the surface of the oil
situation they invariably got stuck in a quagmire of lies,
cover-ups, inefficiency, ignorance, and contradictions--not the
least of which came from [the] Energy Department" (139).

686.   Barrett, Marvin, ed. Broadcast Journalism 1979-1981.
Alfred I. duPont-Columbia Univ. Survey of Broadcast
Journalism 8. New York: Everest, 1982. 256.
The annual survey covers the Carter-Reagan election
campaign, the credibility of broadcasting, the cable revolution,

religion in broadcasting, and other subjects. Special reports on the 1980 elections, new technology and the news, news consultants, government regulation of news, business and news (written by the Vice-President of Mobil Oil), investigative reporting, and other subjects.

687.   Barrett, Marvin. "TV Diplomacy and Other Broadcast
        Quandaries." CJR 18.1 (1979) 69-80.
    A duPont-Columbia Univ. interim report for 1977-78 includes a discussion of the difficulties documentary makers were having with both the networks and PBS, particularly when controversial.

688.   Barsamian, David. "NPR: All the Schmews That's Fit
        to Soothe." Audience 7 (July 4, 1985).
    "Most Americans find it difficult to accept that there is a quasi-state propaganda apparatus in this country. . . .CBS, Time, ABC, USA Today, National Public Radio and all the other mass media components closely identify with and adhere to certain fundamental dogmas of state ideology" which determine what can and cannot be said.

689.   Batscha, Robert M. Foreign Affairs News and the
        Broadcast Journalist. New York: Praeger, 1975. 254.
    A study of "the behavior of the individuals who control the composition of television news." The hypothesis of this study is that "in the area of foreign affairs coverage the television medium has both mechanical and structural characteristics that have caused members of the television press to define and perform their role in a manner that is distinctive to this medium." The focus of the study is on the foreign affairs correspondents and producers working for "the three major networks, CBS, NBC, and ABC" (xi-xiii).

690.   Beaubien, Michael. "Telling it Like it Isn't: U.S.
        Press Coverage of Zimbabwe." SA 13.6 (1980) 2-4, 21.
    As the new nation was taking shape, US reporters were still writing with a pro-Western, colonial bias, preoccupied with white, official opinion and giving short shrift to African nationalist/liberation leaders.

691.   Becker, Robert, et al. "The Charge of the Right
        Brigade: The New Right is Spreading its Message Through
        its Own Alternative Press." WJR 3.9 (1981) 21-25.
    A discussion of some of the major media instruments of the right which collectively "constitute a potent political force."

692.   Bennett, James R. "Page One Sensationalism and the
        Libyan 'Hit Team'." NRJ 4.1 (Fall 1982) 34-38.
    Because the charges against Gaddafi were so insubstantial, they should have been relegated to the back pages, or not reported at all.

693.   Bennett, James R., et al. "Reporting Poverty and
        Hunger in 1980." FS 54 (1982) 2-6.

A survey of the reporting of hunger in wire service reports, newspapers, magazines, and television broadcasts during 28 days in 1980. Journalists must bear much of the blame for the widespread ignorance about the causes of world poverty and hunger.

694.   Bennett, James R. and Christopher Gould. "Reporting the Embassy Hostage Crisis." IR 2.2 (1980) 6-16.
Examines the reporting of Iran and Iranians during late 1979 and early 1980 by the Arkansas Gazette, the Atlanta Constitution, and diverse magazines. The popular print media paid little attention to the abuses of the Shah's reign, while constantly attacking Iranians and their leader Khomeini as "madmen" and "fanatics." American officials and the public have been "uninformed or misinformed and even systematically inflamed against the Iranian revolution."

695.   Bennett, W. Lance. News: The Politics of Illusion. New York & London: Longman, 1983. 161.
The author locates the inadequacies of mass media news in the political system itself. "As long as the distribution of power is narrow and decision processes are closed, journalists will never be free of their dependence on the small group of public relations experts, official spokespersons, and powerful leaders whose self-serving pronouncements have become firmly established as the bulk of the daily news." As long as "the public has little political access and even less power, there will be little substance behind the familiar democratic rhetoric that somehow equates all decisions of state with the public interests." The news "provides little stimulus for enlightenment and few opportunities for expression should people attain their enlightenment elsewhere. In fact, the routine nature of news would seem to work against the elevation of civic consciousness by providing people with easy psychological escapes from the unpleasant reality of powerlessness" (Introduction, x-xi). "Politicians, journalists, and the public are locked into a set of power relations that reinforces political deception, promotes journalistic narrowness and deference to authority, and encourages public ignorance and retreat into a political fantasy world" (132).

696.   Bertrand, Claude-Jean. "French Scholar Both Loves and Hates U.S. Media." SLJR 13.84 (1986) 16-17.
"All American media sins derive" from three flaws: localism, commercialism, and consequent lack of full freedom of speech and press. But the "myth" of the First Amendment is a "powerful" force for freedom.

697.   Blyskal, Jeff, and Marie Blyskal. PR: How the Public Relations Industry Writes the News. New York: Morrow, 1985. 228.
An expose' of widespread corporate puffery disguised as news, of how public relations firms gain free advertising masquerading as news in complicity with news organizations too

understaffed, too lazy, or too uncritical to develop their own reports. The authors estimate that 40 to 50 percent of all news stories originate in public relations firms and conclude that "whole sections of the news are virtually owned by PR" by planting stories to sell wares under the flag of objectivity. Sections also on White House and Pentagon PR machinations.

698.   Boorstin, Daniel. The Image: Or, What Happened to the American Dream. New York: Atheneum, 1961. 315.
    In "From News Gathering to News Making: A Flood of Pseudo-Events," the author claims that "The power to make a reportable event is thus the power to make experience," and the modern public relations experts have "come close" to grasping that power (10-11).

698a.   Boot, William. "NASA and The Spellbound Press." CJR 25.2 (1986) 23-29.
    "Dazzled by the space agency's image of technological brilliance, space reporters spared NASA the thorough scrutiny that might have improved chances of averting tragedy." The shuttle seems to have been "one of the biggest con jobs in recent memory." The problems were not investigated because "most reporters covering the shuttle were popularizers of science rather than investigators." "One driving force in space reporting has long been a kind of techno-patriotism." "It is sad that it took the deaths of seven astronauts to goad journalists into assuming the thoroughly skeptical role they should have been playing all along."

699.   Boyd-Barret, Oliver. The International News Agencies. London, Beverly Hills: Sage, 1980. 284.
    A study of the "Big Four" in the news agency world: United Press International (UPI), Associated Press (AP), Reuters, and Agence France Presse (AFP). One part of the book analyzes the links between the information services sold to corporations (particularly important for AP and Reuters) which are regarded by news agencies as commercially more attractive than general news, which have become increasingly nonprofitable.

700.   Breen, Myles. "Australia on American Television News: Coverage of the Invisible Continent." Television Coverage of International Affairs. Ed. William Adams. Norwood, NJ: Ablex, 1982. 167-178.
    Australia is seldom reported on television news, possibly because commercial television panders to the nation's ethnocentricism.

701.   Breitbart, Eric. "From the People Who Brought You PBS." SD (March 16, 1979) 33-34.
    Generally in praise of the recommendations of the Carnegie Commission's 400-page report on the Future of Public Broadcasting, A Public Trust, which sets forth a new structure and long-range funding, including a spectrum-use fee on commercial broadcasters. But the Report is "hazy about

corporate control," and President Nixon's attacks are observed.

702.   Bunce, Dick. "The Crisis in Political Publishing."
     SocR 15.4-5 (1985) 7-12.
     "Right-wing money is multiplying and is fueling ambitious
media projects," including "the establishment of new journals of
conservative thought and the infusion of new capital to existing
ones."

703.   Chomsky, Noam. Radical Priorities. Ed. Carlos P.
     Otero. 2nd Rev. Ed. Montreal: Black Rose, 1981. 307.
     Chomsky's concern with deceptive language and propaganda is
central to his ethics and politics (58). Ch. 2, "Vietnam
Protests and the Media," discusses propaganda fabrications, etc.
Ch. 5 on East Timor includes discussion of US news management,
etc.

704.   Chomsky, Noam. "Visions of Righteousness." CulC 3
     (Spring 1986) 10-43.
     "A major theme of our history from the earliest days has
been a combination of hideous atrocities and protestations of
awesome benevolence."

705.   Cirino, Robert. Don't Blame the People. New York:
     Random, 1971. 339.
     This book is a plea for equal access to the technology
of persuasion. The author asks why Americans support a status
quo which condones racism, global intervention, unjust tax
distribution, pollution, and numerous other injurious
conditions. His answer is that the establishment has access to
the media. "Could America have ignored the hungry if the poor
had had their own ABC, NBC or CBS?" The establishment "has
prevented real public participation by not allowing all ideas to
compete fairly for public acceptance. They have allowed free
speech, but rendered it worthless by not allowing anti-
establishment voices to have equal access." The author's
inspiration is Supreme Court Justice Hugo Black, who stated the
importance of "the widest possible dissemination of information
from diverse and antagonistic sources," if the welfare of most
of the people is to be served. Cirino's twenty-two chs. cover
the reporting of hunger, auto safety, smoking, pollution, overpopulation, news bias, the power of corporations, the myths of
news media objectivity and fairness, etc.

706.   Cirino, Robert. Power to Persuade: Mass Media and
     the News. New York: Bantam, 1974. 246.
     The book provides "actual case studies in the production,
control, and dissemination of mass media products." The cases
focus especially upon who has communication power, whether the
entire political spectrum--from the radical left to the far
right--is represented, the complexities of "objectivity,"
government and corporate censorship, advertiser influence, the
Fairness Doctrine, and the Equal Time Provision. The author
also offers suggestions for improving the present communication

system to give more power to the consumer and to provide more diversity.

707.   Clarke, Peter, and Eric Fredin. "Newspapers, TV and
         Political Reasoning." POQ 42 (1978) 143-160.
An attempt to assess the relative contributions of newspapers and television in informing the public: television exposure diminishes information retention; more than one newspaper in a city enhances political awareness, etc.

708.   Cockburn, Alexander. "Perfect Executioners". ITT
         10.24 (1986) 12.
CBS News is nationalistic and militaristic.

709.   Cohen, Stanley, and Jock Young, eds. The
         Manufacturers of News: Social Problems, Deviance, and
         the Mass Media. Beverly Hills, CA: Sage, 1981. 506.
The mass media are "in the business of manufacturing and reproducing images. They provide the guiding myths which shape our conception of the world and serve as important instruments of social control" (12). This book explores the process of shaping and controlling by focusing upon "the conceptions of deviance and social problems revealed in the mass media and the implicit view of society behind such conceptions" (13). Throughout the authors weigh and compare the "mass manipulative" model with the "market" or "commercial" model of news manufacture. Most of the articles refer to America or Britain.

710.   Collum, Danny. "15 Seconds Over Manila." Soj 15.5
         (1986) 48-50.
"During their brief stay [preceding the fall of the Marcos regime], the networks reinvented the [Philippines'] geography" according to a a script written with help from "the U.S. Department of State." "This wasn't a story about colonialism, exploitation, and desperate poverty. It was a story about a nation's heartfelt yearning for a leader who would establish a 'friendly democracy'."

710a.   Cros, Michele, and David Nugent. "The Hunger
          Story: An Unbalanced Diet." CJR 20.5 (1985) 51-54.
"The nation's leading papers give us one side of a debate and only half the story." They present the "scarcity" perspective, when the "development" viewpoint is truer. A chief cause of hunger is the concentration of agricultural land in the hands of a few, which has drastically altered traditional farming methods by emphasizing a few cash crops. But journalists continue to perceive the problems in Malthusian rather than systemic economic terms.

711.   Dahlgren, Peter with Sumitra Chakrapani. "The Third
         World on TV News: Western Ways of Seeing the 'Other'"
         Television Coverage of International Affairs. Ed.
         William Adams. Norwood, NJ: Ablex, 1982. 45-66.
A study of "the ways TV news promotes seeing the Third

World" (47) by providing us with "culturally-rooted explanations
for interpreting" (61). TV news presents the Third World
mythically, in ways "congruent with the global relations which
characterize imperialism" and "in keeping with the needs and
interests of the social classes and groups who command economic
and political power" (62).

712.   Diamond, Edwin. "The Close-to-Home Syndrome." <u>WJR</u> 4
          (Jan/Feb 1982) 18.
     "What makes the newscasts different from country to country
is the story selection, which is culture bound and past bound."
"Close to Home has not meant closer to truth."

713.   Diamond, Edwin. <u>Sign Off: The Last Days of
          Television</u>. Cambridge, MA: MIT P, 1982. 273.
     The "last days" refer to the imminent replacement of the
old order of network television by the new cable-satellite
information order. The twenty chs. deal with a variety of
subjects, including chs. on coverage of labor, Three Mile
Island, political campaigns, and three chs. on the Iranian
Embassy hostages. His basic assumption is that "the so-called
objectivity of the news is inevitably shaped by perceived
national interests" (106), but he is critical of the "hegemonic
model" (243).

714.   Diamond, Edwin. <u>The Tin Kazoo: Politics,
          Television, and the News</u>. Cambridge, MA: MIT P, 1975.
          269.
     "But in the coverage of the daily concerns of our polity--
what I call the public news--television has been an uncertain
and weak instrument, a tin kazoo. Television journalism has, in
the main, hesitated to deliver that 'steady supply of
trustworthy and relevant news' that Walter Lippmann thought was
necessary to democracy" (xiv). Chs. deal with the Vietnam War,
the Pentagon Papers, Watergate, racism, and political campaigns.

715.   Dorman, William, and Mansour Farhang. <u>The U.S.
          Press and Iran: Foreign Policy and the Journalism of
          Deference</u>. Berkeley: California UP, 1987.

716.   Dorman, William, and Ehsan Omeed. "Reporting Iran
          the Shah's Way." <u>CJR</u> 17.5 (1979) 27-33.
     The "American news media routinely have characterized the
Iranian conflict as the work of turbaned religious zealots in
league with opportunistic Marxists, rather than--as they might
have--the reaction of people outraged by a repressive regime.
By doing so the press has helped to misinform American public
opinion and narrow the range of debate on this bellwether
foreign-policy crisis."

717.   Edgar, Patricia, ed. <u>The News in Focus: The
          Journalism of Exception</u>. London: MacMillan, 1980. 213.
     Twelve essays explore the manufacture of news and the
constraints "of time, news values, the medium itself and the

ideology of the society in which we live. Because of these
constraints, television news presents us with a view of the
world which the professional journalists believe is 'objective'
but which is in fact highly structured, very selective and
firmly supportive of the status quo. News is a form of
knowledge which has more to do with social control and social
cohesion than interest, diversity and impartiality (6).

718.   Ehrlich, Howard J. "The Politics of News Media
         Control." IS 4 (1974) 31-43.
    "The relationship between the news media and the two major
political forces in American society--government and business--
only appears to be contradictory. In some situations, the
connections seem to be conspiratorial, in others they may seem
to be in conflict, but in fact they are not" (31). This article
describes the corporate structure of media control and uses two
case studies to illustrate "how directly and openly the media
are controlled" (35).

719.   Epstein, Edward. Between Fact and Fiction: The
         Problem of Journalism. New York: Vintage, 1967. 232.
    Since journalists are "agents for others" who desire to
disclose information, they should clearly label "the
circumstances and interests behind the information" they report
so that it can be intelligently evaluated (17). The author has
chs. on Watergate, the Black Panthers, the Pentagon Papers,
financial reporting, etc.

720.   "Europe: Pieces of a Puzzle." CJR 20.1 (1981)
         27-29.
    "In the United States, reporting on the growth of this
[antinuclear] movement has been generally subordinated to
coverage of the activities and statements of NATO officialdom.
By and large, Americans have learned about the movement almost
purely from the viewpoint of NATO military planners.

721.   Fielding, Raymond. The March of Time, 1935-1951.
         New York: Oxford UP, 1978. 359.
    "Both in the United States and in Europe, newsreels were
compromised from the beginning by fakery, re-creation,
manipulation, and staging." The early years of the news-film
and newsreel "were the worst in this respect, with regular,
outright faking of scenes." "Many critics considered the
newsreel fundamentally flawed as a journalistic medium because
of its producers' reluctance to deal with controversial
subjects." In the end, "it proved a witless form and an
embarrassment to the journalistic family in which it claimed
membership."

722.   Fishman, Mark. Manufacturing the News. Austin: U
         of Texas P, 1980. 180.
    In this study I am concerned with the process by which a
very special and important reality is socially constructed: the
public reality of mass media news. I focus on the most

fundamental elements of newsmaking: the work routines with
which journalists approach the world, and "the methods by which
they transform that world into news stories." The final chapter
draws out the "political implications" of his findings, "the way
in which a free and uncensored press consisting of independent
news organizations winds up providing a uniform view of the
world which can only be characterized as ideological" (from ch.
1).

723.   Friendly, Fred. "The Campaign to Politicize
         Broadcasting." CJR 11.6 (1973) 9-18.
    Network and public television should not compromise
programming in order to receive federal funding.

724.   Gandy, Oscar H. "Information in Health: Subsidized
         News." MCS 2 (April 1980) 103-115.
    Explains and defends the "subsidy model" for understanding
government and corporate control of information. The news media
are dominated by purposive information supplied by "public
policy regulators."

725.   Gans, Herbert. "Are U.S. Journalists Dangerously
         Liberal?" CJR 24.4 (1985) 29-33.
    A skeptical analysis of the study of journalists by Stanley
Rothman, S. Robert Lichter, and Linda Lichter which claimed to
reveal a liberal and left bias on the part of journalists.

726.   Gans, Herbert. Deciding What's News: A Study of CBS
         Evening News, NBC Nightly News, Newsweek, and Time. New
         York: Pantheon, 1979. 393.
    On the rules that guide news judgment, the values and the
ideology behind the rules, and the "commercial, political, and
other forces that produce the rules and values." The author
concludes that American mass media news reportage is
conservative in content (ethnocentric, nationalistic,
capitalistic, centripetal) and in form (preferring dramatic
narrative, commercialistic). For example, coverage of the
Vietnam war was framed as a patriotic American war against an
evil communist enemy.

727.   Gans, Herbert. "How Well Does TV Present the News?"
         NYTM (11 January 1970) 31,32,35,38,40,43,46.
    "Like most other professionals," newsmen "are a part of the
middle-class culture that dominates America" and "often judge
other societies by these values." Thus, "they generally see
what goes wrong in Socialist countries more easily than what
goes right" and consider "protesters more militant than
insistent lobbyists." The professional criteria thus fit in
with the fact that newsmen are "employed by profit seeking
businesses" (35).

728.   Gervasi, Tom. Arsenal of Democracy, III: America's
         War Machine, The Pursuit of Global Dominance. New York:
         Grove, 1984. 344.

The US is the leading supplier of arms, more than double
the amount of the Soviet Union. The result of arms sales is the
further impoverishment of the world and the neglect of a vast
assortment of urgent human needs," including in the US itself.
Another result is the "staggering" increase of outright fraud
and"cost overruns." "$92 billion had been wasted" by 1981,
according to the Grace Commission. "This was a powerful
indictment. It was so powerful that it was announced only once
and not heard again." "Only Congress showed an inclination to
learn more. The media devoted only a minimum of attention to
its findings" (6).

729.   Gitlin, Todd. "Spotlights and Shadows: Television
          and the Culture of Politics." CE 38 (1977) 791-96.
How television news divides movements into legitimate main
acts and illegitimate sideshows as part of the networks' role in
sustaining the corporate-government-media complex.

730.   Griffith, Thomas. "Television, the Wealthy Eunuch."
          TQ 11.3 (1974) 5-12.
A discussion of some of the limitations of network news--
government regulation, a bias for action, a fondness for
novelty, a failure to mediate its coverage.

731.   Hartley, John. Understanding News. New York:
          Methuen, 1982. 203.
Wide-ranging chs. on how to critically examine the news.
The author's central argument is that the news is part of the
social relations it seeks to report, subject to the constraints,
pressures, and norms of larger and more fundamental agencies,
the two most important of which are commerce and government (47-
48). The news media's function is to reproduce these agencies
by "contributing to the process whereby people's submission to
the 'prevailing climate'. . . is secured" (56). [The British
focus of this book seems applicable to the situation in the US.]

732.   Herman, Edward. "The Fascist Network." CAIB 22
          (1984) 44, 41-2.
This review of Stuart Christie's Stefano Delle Chiaie,
Portrait of a Black Terrorist makes the point that US media give
much less attention to right-wing terror than to left-wing.

733.   Howell, Rex G. "Fairness . . . Fact or Fable?" JoB
          8 (1964) 321-330.
The "fairness doctrine" is unnecessary because it puts into
writing a concept already practiced by broadcasters. It is
dangerous because it may be misinterpreted by the FCC as a means
of control and by broadcasters as an excuse for avoiding
controversial issues.

733a.   Hoyt, Michael. "Downtime for Labor." CJR 22.6
          (1984) 36-40.
"Labor reporting is not uniformly bad," but while "business
coverage is on the rise, labor journalism is declining in

quantity and quality."

734.   "Iran and the Press in Retrospect." WJR 3.4 (1981)
         23-38.
     Four essays on the hostage crisis. David Altheide finds
uniformity, oversimplification, and underexplanation in network
news coverage of the experience, and a nationalistic bias, the
take-over having "no bias or justification," the Iranians
"fanatics," or "confused, insane, or just plain stupid."

735.   Karp, Walter. "Subliminal Politics in the Evening
         News." Ch 2.1 (1982) 23-37, 56.
     Coverage of the imposition of martial law by the Polish
army on December 12 reveals CBS and ABC more hawkish and
Sovietphobic than NBC, which was calmer and "skeptical of
rumors." ABC expressed pro-Reagan "right-wing" values.
Conservative, Republican NBC represented the President more
critically.

736.   Kemper, Vicki. "Fairness in Media?" Soj 14 (May
         1985) 6.
     Senator Helms' attempt to take over CBS because of its
alleged liberal bias is absurd because CBS expresses the vested
interests of the corporate state.

737.   Lang, Kurt and Gladys Lang. Politics and Television.
         Chicago: Quadrangle, 1968. 315.
     The way the world appears depends on the way the technology
is used, and media managers use it as members of an institution
which like all institutions reflects a point of view, "indeed, a
natural extension of the societal Establishment" (292). This
thesis is exemplified through a series of cases or events, for
example, MacArthur Day in Chicago, 1951.

738.   Lanouette, William. "The Atom and the U.S. Press."
         WQ 9.5 (1985) 106-7.
     "Television had long all but ignored the subject" of
nuclear power until the Three Mile Island disaster in 1979.
Before 1979 coverage was mostly positive or neutral in the
mainstream media; afterward it became more critical.

739.   Laqueur, Walter. "Foreign News Coverage: From Bad
         to Worse." WJR 5.5 (1983) 32-35.
     "The neglect of foreign news and the low quality of comment
has political consequences: American public opinion is by and
largeless well informed about world affairs than public opinion
elsewhere and this is also true for elite opinion." Most of the
article explains why US foreign coverage is so poor.

740.   Larson, James F. "International Affairs Coverage on
         U.S. Network Television." JoC 29.2 (1979) 136-147.
     Coverage of Third World countries lags behind that of more
developed nations. Most of what is covered is crisis-oriented
or presented according to US or other developed nations'

perspectives.

741.   LeRoy, David, and Christopher Sterling, ed. **Mass
     News: Practices, Controversies, and Alternatives**.
     Englewood Cliffs, NJ: Prentice, 1973. 334.
     An assessment of the wire services, newspapers, and
television as "mass news." Twenty-six essays are divided into
the three subjects of the title and then into eight sub-topics on
"News Media Bureaucracy," "Limitations in Mass News," "News:
The Ambiguous Tautology," "Conflict in Norms," "Reaction to
Study Commissions," "Change by the Government," "Change by the
Media," and "Change by the People." Part Four on
"Alternatives": "fifth-estate" journals playing watchdog on the
established media, further professionalism of the press corps,
ombudsmen, press councils, challenges to broadcast-license
renewals, an affirmative interpretation to the First Amendment,
etc.

742.   Lesher, Stephen. **Media Unbound: The Impact of
     Television Journalism on the Public**. Boston: Houghton,
     1982. 285.
     Journalism is notoriously inaccurate, and its inaccuracies,
magnified through television news, distort our perception of
reality. The quality of journalism has not declined, but its
faults are more glaring in television, as illustrated by the
reporting of the Iran hostage crisis, the Three Mile Island
nuclear disaster, and other events.

743.   Lewis, Roger. **Outlaws of America: The Underground
     Press and its Context**. Harmondsworth, Eng.: Penguin,
     1972. 204.
     The alternative press arose in protest against corporate
and government perceptions and values (commercialism, war) and
out of a recognition of the credibility gap between the people
and a press which functioned as a conduit for corporate and
government values.

743a.   Linsky, Martin, et al. **How the Press Affects Federal
     Policymaking: Six Case Studies**. New York: Norton,
     1986. 379.
     Revelations of often inept and deceitful officials
manipulating often subjective and under-informed journalists.
In the case of the neutron bomb, press coverage was incomplete
and unfair. In the Post Office case, the press helped Nixon's
postmaster move Congress to make the Post Office a semi-
independent corporation under the control of big business.

744.   Lynn, Joyce. "Filed and Forgotten: Why the Press
     Has Taken Up New Issues." <u>WJR</u> 2.4 (1980) 32-37.
     Even though "the problems of the 1960s--poverty, the
inability to pay medical bills"--are "worse," "no top national
newspaper or television network covers social services as a
beat."

134

745.   MacKenzie, Robert. "Ben Wattenberg's 1980." TVG
        (June 7, 1980) 45.
    A description of Wattenberg's ten PBS programs advocating
Republican Party ideology of less government and US anti-Soviet
ideology with its weapons gap tactic.

746.   MacKenzie, Robert. "Frontline." TVG (May 5, 1984)
        48.
    Although documentaries have virtually disappeared from
commercial TV, PBS's "Frontline" series offers a valuable
replacement. [The author does not observe what other critics
reveal--that documentaries have decreased in PBS also.]

747.   Manoff, Robert K., and Michael Schudson, eds.
        Reading the News. New York: Pantheon, 1987. 256.
    Examines how "the news," ostensibly "objective, factual,
reliable," is "in reality, a highly coded, ritualized narrative
in which the conventions of reporting and writing, as well as
the hidden pressures of the world journalists inhabit, shape and
even overwhelm the events being recorded" (from publisher's
advertising).

748.   Massing, Michael. "Is CBS Going Gee-Whiz?" CJR
        23.2 (1984) 47-49.
    The entertainment format of CBS's American Parade reflects
network dislike of hour-long documentaries, "a growing
preoccupation with ratings in the network news business," and a
belief that upbeat and patriotic human interest stories alone
attract Americans.

749.   Matusow, Barbara. "Sunday Best: The Race to Beat
        ABC's David Brinkley." WJR 7.6 (1985) 23-37.
    Reveals how important the Sunday morning television news
shows are to politicians for the Monday morning headlines they
offer. Short histories of the three network shows with emphasis
upon the stars and prestige.

750.   Mickiewicz, Ellen. "Soviet and American Television:
        A comparison of News Coverage." NmR 39 (1985) 7-11.
    A Comparison of ABC's World News Tonight, and Vremya
(Time), the SU's major prime-time newscast. A chief finding is
that the Soviet program devoted much more time to the US than
ABC devoted to the SU.

750a.   Morris, Roger. "Buffaloed by the Energy Boom." CJR
        20.4 (1981) 46-52.
    The mines and mills of the mountain states have produced
"only an occasional nugget of perceptive, sustained reporting."
Coverage of "the great western boom" is "largely a bust."

751.   Morris, Roger. "Mexico: the U.S. Press Takes a
        Siesta." CJR 23.5 (1985) 31-36.
    Coverage of Mexico "rarely captures the reality beneath the
surface" and sparsely covers even such stories as illegal

immigrants.

752.   Muwakkil, Salim. "Black Journalists Hit U.S. Media
       Distortions." ITT 10.20 (1986) 6.
     Black US journalists attending the Second World Mathaba
Conference Against Imperialism held in Tripoli, Libya, March 15-
18, discovered how much the US is "hated" by "the world's
oppressed people" and how much Khadafy is admired, contrary to
the images projected in US media.

753.   Newman, Robert, and Dale Newman. Evidence. Boston:
       Houghton, 1969. 246.
     "Ideologies are the most potent of the many factors which
distort perception. Whether Marxist-Leninist, Christian-
capitalist, racist, nationalist, or millennialist, the lenses
which direct the perceptions of the ideologue are usually
dangerously flawed" (60). The book contains numerous examples
of corporate and government ideological bias and lying. For
example, Jay Mallin's untruthful account of US intervention in
the Dominican Republic of 1965, Caribbean Crisis: Subversion
Fails in the Dominican Republic, commissioned by the USIA.
Evidence is divided into four parts: "The Uses of Evidence,"
"The Credibility of Evidence," "The Sources of Evidence"
(government, press, pressure groups, professional scholars), and
"Statistics."

754.   Nimmo, Dan, and James E. Combs. Nightly Horrors:
       Crisis Coverage by Television Network News. Knoxville,
       TN: U of Tennessee P, 1985. 216.
     Network news coverage determines the public's definition of
and relation to a crisis situation. Once a crisis is defined,
there are "three rhetorical visions" competing for the attention
of television news audiences: NBC's vision of affirmation, and
ABC's vision of subversion.

755.   Nimmo, Dan, ed. Watching American Politics:
       Articles and Commentaries About Citizens, Politicians,
       and the News Media. New York: Longman, 1981. 314.
     The authors of these essays hope to train the student how
to be more effective "watchers" of politics, so that "you need
not be a slave to any journalist's or scientist's version of the
political scene, but are liberated to create your own version."
Part 2, "Viewing the Powers That Be," contains essays on power
elites, the political parties, political advertising, etc. Part
3 deals with politics in the news and polls.

756.   "On the Record with Ted Koppel." Ch 6.1 (1986) 70-71.
     "What is sometimes referred to as media diplomacy is in
fact the diplomats using the media." Nightline "makes money for
the news division. We would not be able to do some of the
things we do if it were not a profitable program." But "by and
large, you are appealing to the lowest common denominator."

757.   Paletz, David, et al. "Terrorism on TV News: The

IRA, the FALN, and the Red Brigades." Television Coverage of International Affairs. Ed. William Adams. Norwood, NJ: Ablex, 1982. 143-165.
The authors stress the "notable omission" of right-wing terrorism in reporting by the networks. Left-wing terrorism enjoys attention, but it is "not endowed with legitimacy by television news." "With the occasional exception of the IRA, the justness of the terrorists' causes" is denied by silence as to underlying objectives.

758.   Parenti, Michael. Inventing Reality: The Politics of the Mass Media. New York: St. Martin's, 1986. 258.
"The media exert a subtle, persistent influence in defining the scope of respectable political discourse, channeling public attention in directions that are essentially supportive of the existing politico-economic system." The "major distortions" of social and political life are "systematic, and even systemic-- the product not only of deliberate manipulation but of the ideological and economic conditions under which the media operate" (ix). He explores "the way the press distorts and suppresses the news about major domestic and foreign events and policies, the hidden and not so hidden ideological values, the mechanisms of information control, the role of newspeople, publishers, advertisers, and government, the way patterns of ownership influence information output, and the instances of dissent and deviancy in the major media" (x).

759.   Petrusenko, Vitaly. The Monopoly Press, Or How American Journalism Found Itself in the Vicious Circle of the "Crisis of Credibility." Trans. Vladimir Leonov. Prague: International Organization of Journalists, 1976. 143.
The title comes from Ladd's Crisis in Credibility, which focused upon the federal government's secrecy, lying, and news management. The author assumes that "the news and propaganda media all see eyeball to eyeball as far as overall monopoly ideals and interests are concerned" (95) as the result of the alliance of "big business and state-monopoly power" (55).

759a.   "A Political Press." CJR 21.1 (1982) 20.
Analysis of The Wall Street Journal's attack on Raymond Bonner's reporting from El Salvador. The Journal claims that his stories were not objective--i.e., they did not sufficiently favor the US point of view.

760.   "Political Terrorism in the United States." Philadelphia, PA: American Friends Service Committee, Middle East Program, 1985.
A protest against media neglect of the political murder of the Arab Alex Odeh as compared to the saturation attention paid to the killing of Leon Klinghoffer by Arabs.

761.   Report of the Public's Right to Information Task Force. Staff Report to the President's Commission on

the Accident at Three Mile Island, 1979. 262.
The public information officials (Metropolitan Edison,
NRC, and White House) were completely--and the media partly--
unprepared for the disaster. The Report includes an analysis of
the coverage by the wires, the networks, and the Los Angeles
Times, New York Times, and the Washington Post.

762.   Rice, Michael, and James Cooney. Reporting U.S.-
         European Relations: Four Nations, Four Newspapers.
         New York: Pergamon, 1982. 120.
A comparison of reporting of US-European relations during
1980 in the Frankfurter Allgemeine Zeitung, The New York
Times, The Times of London, and Le Monde. In The New York
Times "European news often appears to be treated either as a
reflection of American interests or according to the 'spot
interest' of a particular editor in New York" (27).

763.   Robinson, Michael, and Maura Claney. "Network News,
         15 Years After Agnew." Ch 4 (Jan./Feb. 1985) 34-35,
         38-39.
"Most right-wing allegations [of liberal bias] about the
network news just don't hold up."

764.   Robinson, Michael, and Margaret Sheehan. Over the
         Wire and on TV: CBS and UPI in Campaign '80. New
         York: Sage, 1983. 332.
The authors make the case that the wire services and
traditional print media tend to report events, while TV news
tends to interpret. "Network news was more mediating, more
political, more personal, more critical, more thematic than old-
style print" (9). Their evidence qualifies hegemony theory--
that the media are handmaidens of the establishment. "Just as
the 'imperialist school' overstates the arrogance of the modern
news media, the 'hegemonist school' exaggerates their level of
diffidence" (296).

765.   Rosen, Jay. "What We Know About Arms Race Is More
         Than a Matter of Opinion." Dead 1.2 (1986) 1-2.
Because people are ignorant about war and peace issues,
news organizations should inform the public "far more than they
do." Fewer opinion polls should be given and more knowledge
tests, for knowledge is more newsworthy than opinion.

766.   Rubin, Barry. "International News and the American
         Media." International News: Freedom Under Attack.
         Ed. Dante B. Fascell. Beverly Hills: Sage, 1977. 181-
         245.
An indictment of the weak foreign coverage by US media, the
paucity of information, the "strong U.S. angle put on stories,"
and the "lack of reporting on totally foreign events and views."

767.   Rubin, Ronald. "The U.N. Information Officer." Gaz
         14.4 (1968) 253-269.
"Most information officers define U.N. news on the basis

of national interest rather than the broader goals of the U.N."

768.   Russett, Bruce, and Donald Deluca. "Don't Tread on
          Me: Public Opinion and Foreign Policy in the Eighties."
          PolSQ 96.3 (1981) 381-400.
Public opinion has shifted toward a more politically
hawkish posture partly because of press influence.

769.   Said, Edward. Covering Islam: How the Media and the
          Experts Determine How We See the Rest of the World.
          London: Routledge, 1981. 186.
Much of the book deals with the news coverage of Islam by
US media, compared to European coverage, which shows how
inaccurate, ethnocentric, stereotyped, and hostile is US media
in reporting Islam.

770.   Schneir, Walter, and Miriam Schneir. "The Right's
          Attack on the Press." Na 240 (March 30, 1985) 361-67.
The powerful effort by a coalition of jingoists,
Sovietphobes, and anti-abortionists to take control of the
"liberal" media.

771.   Schudson, Michael. Discovering the News: A Social
          History of American Newspapers. New York, Basic Books,
          1978. 228.
PP. 164-76 treat "Government and the Press: 'News
Management'." "The process of news gathering itself constructs
an image of reality which reinforces official viewpoints."

772.   Schwarzlose, Richard. "The American Wire Services:
          A Study of Their Development as a Social Institution."
          DAI 26 (1965) 2721-A.
"Development as a pivotal communication link among various
sectors of society is associated with five trends," two of which
are: "utilizing belief and action patterns which resemble those
of other mass communication industries and assume an operational
and perspective stance adjunctive to the business sector," and
"becoming increasingly subordinated to the political and
productive needs of news sources, particularly in government."

773.   Seldes, George. Freedom of the Press. Garden City,
          NY: Garden City, 1937. 380.
An analysis of why "from the the first day to the last" of
his reporter's life "there was censorship, there was suppression
of news, there was distortion and there was coloring of news,
there was always an attempt by someone to mislead the public"
(x). In particular was the controlling "oligarchy, dictatorial
big money and big business. . . always trying to destroy the
foundations upon which free government is built." But he also
acknowledges "the magnificent service of the press in exposing
and defeating these very same corrupting powers" (x-xiii).

774.   Seldes, George. Never Tire of Protesting. New York:
          Stuart, 1968. 288.

139

Ch. 30, "The People Don't Know": "There are hundreds of
subjects, not merely statistics or almanac or encyclopedia
facts--all related to the life, liberty, and pursuit of
happiness of the American people--about which the people know
little, about which they are misinformed, about which their
ignorance is a menace to the democratic form of government,
which they seem unable to define," and they are so ignorant and
consequently intolerant because of the failure of the so-called
"free press" to inform them adequately. In Part III,
"McCarthyism," the "same press which made Martin Dies powerful
and which to this day supports Un-American Activities
Committees, was largely responsible for Senator Joseph R.
McCarthy's success for many years."

775.   Sigal, Leon. Reporters and Officials: The
     Organization and Politics of Newsmaking. Lexington,
     MA: Heath, 1973. 221.
     Official sources dominate the news by the essentially
economic nature of the relations between news sources and
reporters in that routine channels are cheaper than interviews
or first-hand observation. These routine channels are heavily
subsidized by news sources who want to control the availability
and interpretation of information about issues.

776.   Skardon, James. "The Apollo Story: What the
     Watchdogs Missed." CJR 6.3 (1967) 11-15.
     The press was not prepared and had not prepared the public
for the Apollo fire of January 27, 1967, which killed three
astronauts. Coverage was "flawed" in not looking into the
performance of North American Aviation, the contractor, in not
examining the overall safety of the space program, and in not
giving the background of the fire itself. Following the fire
NASA withheld facts and issued misleading and wrong statements,
which were reported by the ill-prepared press.

777.   Skornia, Harry. Television and the News: A
     Critical Appraisal. Palo Alto: Pacific, 1968. 232.
     Americans are not receiving "from TV and radio the
diversity and depth of news, clarification and interpretation of
the right type, from the right places, that they need for
responsible decision-making." The causes are diverse--the
dependence of "news" reporting on advertising sponsors, the
replacement of dialogue between people and ruling institutions
with monologs and directives from government and corporations.
"A broadcast system operated largely by firms with huge defense
contracts which find the cold war, the space race, and high
preparedness and armament budgets profitable" can "hardly be
expected to be favorable to the promotion of peace" (5-6). Ch.
3 deals with corporate (sponsor) censorship, 4 with three cases,
including blacklisting.

778.   Thompson, David C. "The Coverage of Canada in the
     U.S. Media." CarlJR (Summer 1978) 1-24.
     American media avoid virtually all US-Canadian issues of

real importance or difficulty, focusing instead on crime, labor disputes, and other easy-to-cover subjects.

779.   Traska, Maria. "Health is Sick." ChJR 7.7 & 8 (1974) 12-14.
     Criticizes journalists for failing to report the efforts by the Nixon administration to undermine the mental-health profession and system.

780.   "Trouble at the Times." Prog. 49.11 (1985) 15.
     The New York Times "is not turning rightward: it has been there all along."

781.   Tuchman, Gaye. Making News: A Study in the Construction of Reality. New York: Free, 1978. 244.
     News "limits access and transforms dissent. It legitimates the contemporary state by eschewing analysis through ahistoricity, the logic of the concrete, and an emphasis on the contingency of events rather than on structural necessity." Such practices are ideological (177). "Viewing ideology as 'interested procedures people use as a means not to know' connotes that ideology prevents knowledge by limiting inquiry-- by closing off the possibilities of an analytic examination of social life" (179). Ch. 9, "News as a Constructed Reality," and 10, "News as Knowledge."

782.   Tuchman, Gaye. "News, the Newsman's Reality." DAI 30, 2644.
     "News is a picture of the newsman's conception of reality," what he takes for granted, his "notions about social and political reality," especially "a conscious emphasis upon stability, order and orderly progress, "reinforced by functional requirements of a news organization.

783.   Wald, Richard. "Possible Courses for News and Public Affairs." PTR 6.3 (1978) 50-57.
     A critique of what PTV should not and should be doing in public affairs programming. "PBS's main point," in contrast to commercial TV, "is reality." It should be explaining the US through live programming, a regular documentary series, a news of the week in review, a longer MacNeil/Lehrer, etc.

784.   Weaver, David, and G. Cleveland Wilhoit. The American Journalist: A Portrait of U.S. News People and Their Work. Bloomington: Indiana UP, 1986. 216.
     A report of a national telephone survey conducted in 1982 and 1983 of 1,001 American journalists working in television, radio, and print. Most claimed to be political moderates. The survey was modeled on a 1971 survey (John Johnstone, The News People, 1976) in order to chart changes. There has been "a decided rightward shift." The study counters claims by Robert Lichter and Stanley Rothman that most journalists are left-of-center. [The flaw in all of these studies is the polling of opinion rather than the establishment of definitions of center,

left, and right based upon global norms.]

785.   Weiss, Philip. "The Last, Best Hope for the TV
         Documentary." Ch 3 (Nov./Dec. 1983) 85-9.
"While commercial television has virtually abandoned the
documentary," the producer of the PBS Frontline documentary
series, David Fanning, is fighting to keep the form alive.

786.   Werden, Frieda. "Watchdogs Bay Over Bias of
         National Public Radio News." Current 4.14 (1985) 1,3.
An account of the right-wing Heritage Foundation's attacks
on NPR as a "'left-lib bureaucracy which has seemed to delight
in savaging the government that has so generously and
uncomplainingly paid its bills'."

787.   Zion, Sidney. Read All About It: The Collected
         Adventures of a Maverick Reporter. New York: Summit,
         1982. 362.
Many accounts of the nuts and bolts of the corporate-
government-media complex--e.g., of the "dirtiest secret of
journalism: Self-Censorship" (how the New York Post killed the
author's expose' of the financing of Robert Moses' World's Fair
because of advertising revenue) (20-25).

II. E. Education and Research 788-887

[See II. F. for items on direct repression.]

788.   Bennett, James R. "Corporate and Government
         Domination of Education in the United States: A
         Bibliography." RT 32 (1986).
Contains over 200 entries, an introduction, and subject
index. [A few of these items are repeated in the present
bibliography with shortened annotations.]

II. E. 1. Curriculum 789-858

789.   Allen, Henry. "Teaching Working-Class History." Ed
         27-28 (1974) 27-28.
"Essentially, working class students are taught to believe
that they have no history worth retelling; and they become
steeped in the myths which help to perpetuate and sustain the
status quo."

790.   Apple, Michael, ed. Cultural and Economic
         Reproduction in Education: Essays on Class, Ideology
         and the State. Boston: Routledge, 1982. 362.
Inequality is rooted in and reproduced by the economic,
political, and ideological forms which currently exist" (1 & 4).

791.   Apple, Michael. Education and Power: Reproduction
         and Contradiction in Education. Boston: Routledge,
         1982. 218.
A study of the pressures of economic, political, and

cultural organization both inside and outside the schools.

792.   Apple, Michael. Ideology and Curriculum. Boston:
          Routledge, 1979. 203.
     An examination of the relationship between economic power,
ideology, schools, and the reproduction and control of dominant
meanings and structures.

793.   Apple, Michael, and Lois Weis, eds. Ideology and
          Practice in Schooling. Philadelphia: Temple UP,
          1983. 286.
     Investigations into the process and production of ideology
in the schools.s

794.   Aptheker, Bettina. The Academic Rebellion in the
          United States: A Marxist Appraisal. Secaucus, NJ:
          Citadel, 1972. 218.
     Corporate ideology controls education. Ch. 10 sets for a
"reconstruction."

795.   Aronowitz, Stanley, and Henry Giroux. Education Under
          Siege: The Conservative, Liberal and Radical Debate Over
          Schooling. Hadley, MA: Bergin, 1985. 256.
     The authors desire a radical transformation of education
for the emancipation of all the students.

796.   Bennett, James R. "Corporate and Government Control
          of Education in the United States." Transforming the
          Present for the Future. Ed. James Van Patten.
          Fayetteville, AR: U of Arkansas, 1986. 121-27.
     Applies Katznelson and Kesselman's theory of hegemony in
the US to education.

797.   Bennett, James R. "Pre/face 9: Critical Pluralism
          and Democracy." Pre/Text 7.1-2 (1986).
     Former Supreme Court Justice Hugo Black's advocacy of the
maximum number of antagonistic points of view in a "free" press
should be fundamental practice in the classroom.

798.   Berlowitz, Marvin, and Frank Chapman, Jr., eds.
          The United States Educational System: Marxist
          Approaches. Minneapolis: Marxist Educ., 1980. 221.
     Fourteen essays. Of special interest are the four essays
on "Ideological Distortions of History."

799.   Bizzell, Patricia. "Cognition, Convention, and
          Certainty." Pre/Text 3.3 (1982) 213-43.
     "The kind of pedagogy that would foster responsible
inspection of the politically loaded hidden curriculum in
composition class is discourse analysis."

800.   Blackburn, Robin, ed. Ideology in Social Science:
          Readings in Critical Social Theory. New York: Vintage,
          1973. 382.

Sixteen critiques of "the less evident 'general' ideologies which conceal the real contradictions of capitalism and imperialism today" by "arresting social thought at inadequate and superficial concepts," particularly by fragmenting the various social sciences and by exalting empiricism or abstraction.

801.   Boffey, Philip. The Brain Bank of America: An Inquiry into the Politics of Science. New York: McGraw, 1975. 312.
An investigation of the National Academy of Sciences, and an indictment of the secrecy of the processes by which its reports and develop which hides the influence of special economic and governmental interests. "Corporations probably exert the most baleful influence on technological developments and government research programs" (from Ralph Nader's Introduction, xviii).

802.   Bowles, Samuel, and Herbert Gintis. Schooling in Capitalist America: Educational Reform and the Contradictions of Economic Life. New York: Basic, 1976. 340.
"Education in the United States plays a dual role in the social process whereby surplus value, i.e., profit, is created and expropriated.

803.   Camper, Natalie. "The Case of the Measurement Junkies." Ed 40-41 (1977) 4-8,46-47.
I.Q. testing is racially and culturally discriminatory social control for an elite class and the status quo.

804.   "Campus Cartels." Na 234.11 (1982) 325.
Pojaro Dunes Conference between five major universities and a score of corporations to develop principles to guide future industry-university relationships.

805.   Carnoy, Martin. Education as Cultural Imperialism. New York: McKay, 1974. 378.
"We argue that far from acting as a liberator, Western formal education came to most countries as part of imperialist domination."

806.   Carnoy, Martin, ed. Schooling in a Corporate Society: The Political Economy of Education in America. New York: McKay, 1975. 374.
The eighteen contributors challenge the widely held assumption that the goal of education in the US is to maximize everyone's potential.

807.   Clarkson, Fred. "New Right Money Finances New Student Papers." SLJR 12.74 (1985) 19.
Business-financed college publications are attacking "liberalism and leftism on campuses."

808.   Clements, Tim. "Ratepayers Finance Pro-Nuke Ads,
          Games--Nuclear Advertising in the Classroom: Captive
          Audience." CMJ 4.3 (1978) 8.
     Utility customers finance biased, pro-nuclear materials
distributed through local companies to schools. An example is
"The Energy-Environment Game."

809.   Cookson, Peter, Jr., and Caroline Persell. Preparing
          for Power: America's Elite Boarding Schools. New York:
          Basic, 1986. 288.
     A study of how elite schools prepare students to be leaders
in business, government, and the arts.

810.   Coons, John E., et al. Private Wealth and Public
          Education. Cambridge: Harvard UP, 1970. 520.
     A study of the discrimination by wealth inherent in local
school financing. The authors propose a solution, termed "power
equalizing," based upon application of state and local taxes.

811.   Davis, Jon K. "History: A Tale Told by Winners and
          Losers." Ed 39 (Nov.-Dec. 1976) 21-22.
     Current history lessons often legitimize actions performed
by ruling powers, such as Rockefeller or the United States.
Possible solutions are given.

812.   Dickson, David. The New Politics of Science. New
          York: Pantheon, 1984. 404.
     Policy decisions "are increasingly concentrated in the
hands of a class of corporate, banking, and military leaders,
assisted by those in other sectors, such as universities, whose
political allegiance lies with this class in practice."

813.   Dusek, Val. "Culture Boom in Science Museums."
          Guard 31.41 (July 18, 1979) 16.
     "Many of the new displays are pure propaganda for the
military, the oil and energy corporations, the electric power
companies and the junk food industry."

814.   Fitzgerald, Frances. America Revised: History
          Schoolbooks in the Twentieth Century. Boston: Little,
          Brown, 1979. 240.
     A book about the manipulation of the past to make the US
look better than it was and to portray it as changeless, for
commercial and ideological reasons.

815.   Franklin, Bruce. "The Teaching of Literature in the
          Highest Academies of the Empire." The Politics of
          Literature Ed. Louis Kampf and Paul Lauter. New
          York: Pantheon, 1972. 101-29.
     An autobiographical account of how the author became a
teacher of literature, in order to "remold our ideas so that we
can join the people and serve them" (107), followed by his reply
to the many attacks on the original article published in College
English.

145

816.   Giroux, Henry. <u>Ideology, Culture, and the Process</u>
      <u>of Schooling</u>. Philadelphia: Temple UP, 1981. 168.
"His project is to overcome the narrow ideological
objectives of contemporary education."

817.   Giroux, Henry. <u>Theory and Resistance in Education:</u>
      <u>A Pedagogy for the Opposition</u>. Hadley, MA: Bergin,
      1983. 304.
Giroux advocates resistance to the socialization model and
authoritarian curriculum geared to the labor market and based
upon the ideology of the corporate state.

818.   Giroux, Henry, and David Purpel, eds. <u>The Hidden</u>
      <u>Curriculum and Moral Education: Deception or Discovery</u>?
      Berkeley, CA: McCutchan, 1983. 425.
Twenty essays examine the schools as agencies of social,
moral, and economic reproduction of the existing society.

819.   "The Great American Dream Freeze." <u>Ed</u> 36 (1975)
      12-13.
The Carnegie Commission's report on the future of higher
education directs students from poor, working class, or non-
white families into vocational training in community colleges
rather than into four-year liberal arts programs.

820.   Green, Philip, and Sanford Levinson, eds. <u>Power and</u>
      <u>Community: Dissenting Essays in Political Science</u>. New
      York: Pantheon, 1970. 396.
Twelve essays share "a dual critique" of the discipline:
its pursuit of "petty methodological purity" and its support of
the "political status quo" and "false picture of political life
in western democracies." A central attack is upon the myth of
"democratic pluralism" (Preface).

821.   Greer, Colin. <u>The Great School Legend: A</u>
      <u>Revisionist Interpretation of American Public Education</u>.
      New York: Basic, 1972. 206.
He calls upon Americans to create an economy in which
autonomy and mobility are possible for all Americans, and an
education for literacy, critical thinking, democratic
participation, and humaneness, rather than the hostile
competitiveness and high drop-out rate which now degrades the
system.

822.   Grossman, Lawrence. "Let's Keep <u>All</u> Our Educational
      Channels." <u>TVG</u> (Aug. 13, 1983) 32-34.
An FCC plan to turn over part of the ITFS (Instructional
Television Fixed Service) frequencies to commercial TV is bad
policy.

823.   Harris, Kevin. <u>Teachers and Classes: A Marxist View</u>.
      London: Routledge, 1982. 190.
Analysis of the role of teachers in class struggle and an
attack on the myth of education as the "great equalizer." The

author urges teachers to promote class consciousness in the classroom, to encourage cooperative behavior, and to join in collective action with other teachers.

824.   Harty, Sheila. Hucksters in the Classroom: A Review of Industry Propaganda in Schools. Washington, DC: Center for Study of Responsive Law, 1979. 190.
"Corporations are inappropriate sponsors of educational materials precisely because they have something to sell."

825.   "Harvard, Yale Lead Colleges in Producing Executives." CHE 31.7 (1985) 2.
"Nearly a third of top U.S. business executives who hold college degrees are graduates of Ivy League or Big 10 universities," with Yale leading in undergraduate degrees and Harvard in graduate degrees.

826.   Helmer, John. The Deadly Simple Mechanics of Society. New York: Seabury, 1974. 313.
The prejudices of academic sociologists who function within an academic "cartel" in a "war" against the working class as part of the US system of economic, political, and social inequalities.

827.   Jungmeyer, Paul. "An Assessment of Sponsored Social Studies Curriculum Materials." Texas A & M U Diss., 1974. DAI 35 (1974) 4985-A.
Business sponsored materials "receive qualified recommendation for use in social studies classes."

828.   Kampf, Louis, and Paul Lauter, eds. The Politics of Literature: Dissenting Essays on the Teaching of English. New York: Pantheon, 1972. 429.
"These papers argue" that there are relationships between literary works, readers, and action, and that "in our culture-- white, Western, male, and bourgeois, for the most part--one primary effect of the processes of cultivation is to diminish people's desire or capacity to act for change" (50).

829.   Karabel, Jerome, and A. H. Halsey. Power and Ideology in Education. New York: Oxford UP, 1977. 670.
The authors focus on the relations of capitalism and class bias as the major determinants in shaping the US educational system and research.

830.   Kozol, Jonathan. The Night Is Dark and I Am Far From Home. Boston: Houghton, 1975. 208.
The school is expected "to develop, nurture and reward a series of well-broken, homogeneous generations": "proud of its country, unquestioning of its motives, antagonistic to all foreign ideologies, well-protected against ethical considerations other than those of an attractive and self-deprecating kind which serve to decorate its overall self-interest."

831.   Lemisch, Jesse. On Active Service in War and Peace.
         Toronto: New Hogtown, 1975. 150.
Historians have generally written history to support ruling
class interests, and radical exposure of that bias and working
class history have been suppressed.

832.   Lentricchia, Frank. Criticism and Social Change.
         Chicago: U of Chicago P, 1983. 173.
In the US the symbols and myths of liberty and justice have
been transformed into the conformity of desire for commodities
by commercial stimulation. Literary criticism has a role in
teaching how myth and symbols and language serve as normalizing
instruments for the class in power.

833.   Levy, Gerald. Ghetto School: Class Warfare in an
         Elementary School. New York: Pegasus, 1970. 178.
"American society would like to think of Midway as an
instrument of the American dream. In fact, Midway is an
instrument of the organizational control and perpetuation of the
lower class."

834.   Lichtman, Richard. "The University: Mask for
         Privilege?" CM (January 1968) 2-17.
"The University is at this moment an ideological
institution, a mask for systematic dominance and privilege."
The essay is followed by five responses and the author's
rejoinder.

835.   Moxley, Bob. "Enterprise. . . Is America."
         Washington, DC: Chamber of Commerce of the United
         States, 1985. 2.
A summary of "an all-new U.S. Chamber-sponsored education
program for high school students" for "helping students
understand the fundamentals" of how our economic and political
system works. This is the second economic education program
distributed by the Chamber.

836.   Nader, Ralph, "Law Schools and Law Firms," NR, 161
         (October 11, 1969) 20-23.
For over a half century Harvard Law School has enveloped
its students in the conceptual cocoons and expectations of the
corporate law firm.

837.   Nadler, Eric. "'Righting' the Balance." CJR 21.4
         (1982) 8.
The National Journalism Center, sponsored by the Education
and Research Institute, a spinoff of the American Conservative
Union, trains young journalists in "traditional" values. The
Center is supported by the Coors, Olin, and other corporate
foundations.

838.   Nicholas, Ralph. "Higher Education: A View of the
         Problem." NUT (1961) 38-42.
By subsidizing education, business interests control what

is taught and are the "major beneficiary."

839.   Noble, David. America By Design: Science,
          Technology, and the Rise of Corporate Capitalism. New
          York: Knopf, 1977. 384.
"This study traces the interwoven history of the twin
forces which together gave shape to modern America--scientific
technology and corporate capitalism--by focusing upon their
common medium, modern engineering." Capitalism has been
strengthened by technocrats and engineers who became the
conscious agents of corporate capital, for structuring the labor
force and fostering the social habits demanded by corporate
capitalism (Introduction).

840.   O'Connor, James. "The University and the Political
          Economy." Leviathan 1 (March 1969) 14-15.
The colleges and universities "constitute four great
overlapping departments of the U.S. ruling class"--production,
merchandizing, state bureaucratic social control, and
imperialist rule.

841.   Ohmann, Richard. English in America: A Radical View
          of the Profession . New York: Oxford UP, 1976. 344.
A study of "the teaching and study of language and
literature in America," "the way the modern American university
shapes our work" and "the way this technological society uses
universities and knowledge" (304-05).

842.   Ollman, Bertell, and Edward Vernoff. The Left
          Academy: Marxist Scholarship on American Campuses. New
          York: McGraw, 1982. 290.
The seven essays on seven major social science disciplines
amount to "a history of recent Marxist scholarship in the
Academy" and "critique of orthodox thinking in the academy."
The contributors "characterize the chief differences between
Marxist and non-Marxist work in their fields" and "explain how
Marxist work constitutes a criticism of prevailing modes of
scholarship."

843.   Penick, J. L., et al., eds. The Politics of American
          Science: 1939 to the Present. Rev. ed. Cambridge:
          MIT, 1972. 453.
The chief focus of the book is the "interrelated system of
government-supported university research."

844.   Pollock, Richard. "Energy Curricula: Valid Education
          Effort or Disguised Market Advertising?" CMJ 3.7 (1977)
          3,10.
Federal and industry sponsored educational materials on
energy stress nuclear power and often belittle people who oppose
nuclear development.

845.   Rossman, Michael. "The Authority Complex: The Other
          Side of the Coin Is Freedom." Ed 4 (1972) 8-13.

The university's current function is to train people in skills needed by corporate power. An alternative is a learning group situation in which students both teach and learn from one another.

846.   Roszak, Theodore, ed. The Dissenting Academy. New York: Pantheon, 1967. 304.
Eleven essays expressing hope that the universities will "cease functioning as the handmaidens of whatever political, military, paramilitary, or economic elite happens to be financing their operations, and [will] become an independent source of knowledge, value and criticism" (vi).

847.   Rothstein, Stanley W. "The University as People Processor." Cg 10.11 (1978) 8-9.
We should not accept "the state university as a people-processing plant devoted only to regimentation."

848.   Sexton, Patricia. Education and Income: Inequalities of Opportunity in Our Public Schools. New York: Viking, 1962. 298.
"Our public-school system has rejected its role of facilitating social mobility and has become in fact an instrument of social and economic class distinctions in American society" (Foreword by Kenneth B. Clark).

849.   Spring, Joel. Education and the Rise of the Corporate State. Boston: Beacon, 1972. 206.
The primary purpose of the school system is social control for a corporate state.

850.   "Standardization." RT 31 (June 1986) 1-30.
Eight essays on standardized testing and the "sorting function of schools, particularly of public schools," in which standardized testing is "playing an increasingly important role" in placing students to "their 'appropriate' place in the social structure."

851.   Surkin, Marvin, and Alan Wolfe, eds. An End to Political Science: The Caucus Papers. New York: Basic, 1970. 324.
Thirteen critiques of US politics and political science by members of the Caucus for a New Political Science. The Caucus was formed in 1967 to "challenge the complacency of American political science" and its commitment to "the dominant institutional and ideological interests of American society"--corporations, the CIA, and counterrevolution.

852.   Torney-Purta, Judith. "Political Socialization and Policy: The United States in a Cross-National Context," Child Development Research and Social Policy. Vol. 1. Ed. Harold Stevenson & Alberta Siegel. Chicago: Chicago UP, 1984. 471-523.
Excessive stress on patriotic ritual in classrooms will

harm democratic values. "State mandates pay little attention to
skills necessary for political participation or to tolerance of
diverse views."

853.   Wise, Arthur. Legislated Learning: The
        Bureaucratization of the American Classroom. Berkeley:
        U of California P, 1982. 238.
    "Bureaucracy appears to permit those in power to control
the school system" (88).

854.   Wolff, Robert. The Ideal of the University. Boston:
        Beacon, 1969. 161.
    Presents four models of an ideal university. The fourth is
"a radical critique of the university" as an instrument of
government, the military, and industry.

855.   Wolf-Wasserman, Miriam, comp. Demystifying School:
        Writings and Experiences. New York: Praeger, 1974.
        355.
    A series of essays about corporate and government control
of the schools. "One of the major functions of schools in any
society is to disseminate and inculcate the myths which that
society" tells about itself.

856.   Wolf-Wasserman, Miriam. "Schooling as Alienation
        Training." Ed 34 (April 1975) 4-5.
    "Education serves the corporate economy by training people
to be consumers."

857.   Wood, Barry. "American History Revisited: What They
        Didn't Tell Us." Ed 3 (May-June 1971) 3-7.
    Lists several events in the development of the American
labor movement that are not mentioned or are presented in
a biased manner in traditional history textbooks.

858.   Zinn, Howard. The Politics of History. Boston:
        Beacon, 1970.
    Advocates an activist writing of history dedicated to "the
urgent desire for a better world." Part II, "Essays in American
History," explores various falsifications of history regarding
class, race, and nationalism. For example, Ch. 12, "Aggressive
Liberalism," describes the generally suppressed "record of
imperialism, war, racism, and exploitation" abroad.

II. E. 2. Research 859-881

859.   Arditti, Rita, Pat Brennan, Steve Cavrak, eds.
        Science and Liberation. Boston: South End, 1980.
        398.
    Twenty-five essays grouped under four headings: The Myth
of the Neutrality of Science, Science and Social Control,
Working in Science, Towards a Liberating Science. Several of
the essays are listed separately.

860.   Baritz, Loren. The Servants of Power: A History of
the Use of Social Science in American Industry.
Middletown, CT: Wesleyan UP,1960. 273.
Corporations absorbed social scientists because "management
came to believe in the importance of understanding human
behavior" as a "sure way of improving its main weapon in the
struggle for power, the profit margin (191-2).

861.   Dickson, David. "Towards a Democratic Strategy for
Science." SciP 16.4 (1984) 6-11, 33.
Control of science is increasingly reposed in the hands of
fewer private decision-makers. A democratic science policy
would give access to research funds to groups lacking power.

862.   Du Boff, Richard, and Edward Herman. "The New
Economics: Handmaiden of Inspired Truth." RRPE
4 (1972) 54-84.
"Given their conservative and nationalistic premises, it is
understandable that the ["New" or Keynesian] Economists have
consistently looked upon the economic policies of Richard Nixon
as reasonable" (55). "For economists who do effectively service
the dominant forces of the system, the rewards are substantial--
money, influence, power, and ready access to the media" (83).

863.   Emerson, Steven. The American House of Saud: The
Secret Petrodollar Connection. Danbury, CT: Franklin,
1985. 450.
Aramco, a company formed by the Arabs with Texaco Inc.,
Standard Oil Co. of California, Mobil Corp., and Exxon has tried
to influence US policies in the Middle East. One chapter,
"Academia for Sale," describes the US colleges receiving
Saudi/Aramco funds and the price tag which accompanies the
money.

864.   Gilpin, Robert. American Scientists and Nuclear
Weapons Policy. Princeton: Princeton UP, 1962. 352.
A study of the conflict among scientists from 1945 to 1961
over a policy of disarmament or a policy of deterrence through
arms accelerations and the implications of this conflict for a
democracy. "Because scientists have become men of power and
because in a democracy power must be constantly and responsibly
evaluated, there is a need for both scientists and non-
scientists to understand the scientist as a political animal"
(341).

865.   Gilpin, Robert, and Christopher Wright, eds.
Scientists and National Policy Making. New York:
Columbia UP, 1964. 307.
The ten essays discuss the diverse relationships between
scientists and government. The essay by Wohlstetter focuses on
the many functions performed by scientists in military decision-
making and operations.

866.   Haberer, Joseph. Politics and the Community of

Science. New York: Van Nostrand Reinhold, 1969. 337.
Chs. 10 and 11 deal with the withdrawal of Dr.
Oppenheimer's security clearance and the weak response of his
fellow scientists. The final ch. contrasts the strong
"methodological ethic" of scientists (honesty and integrity) to
their weak "institutional ethic" ("political, social, and
interpersonal relations"). Modern states have encouraged the
use of scientists in government partly because they "perceived
no likely danger from the possible collective action of
scientists."

867.   Herman, Edward. "The Institutionalization of Bias
         in Economics." MCS 4 (1982) 275-291.
There has occurred a "sharp increase in the ideological
role of economists" by their attaching themselves to political
parties and by becoming paid consultants. Corporations are
increasingly co-opting the experts. And those expressing
opinions "favored by 'the market' (i.e., the business elite)
have been provided with disproportionate resources and access to
influence and power through the support of their sponsor in
grants, access to the mass media and influence in the political
arena. Money and a voice that can be heard have depended, more
than ever, on adherence to specific conclusions and ideological
service."

868.   Herzon, Mary.   "SIU-E Link to Big Business
         Excessive." SLJR 13.87 (1986) 12, 16.
On charges that Southern Illinois U has become too closely
involved with a business organization.

869.   Krimsky, Sheldon. "The Corporate Capture of Genetic
         Technologies." ScP 17.3 (1985) 32-37.
The "commercial applications of molecular genetics and cell
biology have resulted in a flurry of entrepreneurial activities
among academic biologists and universities eager to cash in on
the financial side of the biotechnology revolution."

870.   Krimsky, Sheldon. "Star Wars and Academic Freedom."
         ScP 18.1 (1986) 12.
The Star Wars research program is "incompatible with the
values and mission of universities," and "refusal of
universities to accept such research on behalf of its faculty
does not violate the principle of academic freedom."

871.   O'Leary, Brian. "R&D: The Thin Edge of the Wedge."
         BAS 31.8 (1975) 9-14.
Universities and private organizations must educate the
public as to what the government is currently researching and
developing, and they must urge the public to participate by
communicating with their congressmen.

872.   Reinhold, Robert. "In Academic Jet Set, Schedule is
         Hectic, Rewards High." NYT (June 18, 1969) 49, 95.
Government and industry use of academic research is

changing the priorities of professors away from school
priorities.

873.   Rips, Geoffrey. "Higher Education and the Cult of
     Technology." TO 77.25 (1985) 6-10.
     "In return for what amounts to an investment in a
university, the corporation receives researchers and research
technology, the credibility of a university imprimatur, a number
of tax incentives, and, in many cases, rights to the products of
the research."

874.   Said, Edward. The World, the Text, and the Critic.
     Cambridge, MA: Harvard UP, 1983. 327.
     In Ch. 8, "Reflections on American 'Left' Literary
Criticism," the author condemns the isolation of literature and
literary studies from the world, the result of the State's rule
over culture partly reflected in critics' pursuit of technical
brilliance divorced from the world's needs. If "we have
cooperated" in creating this condition, "it is because that is
where the money has been."

875.   Schuman, Pat. "Information Justice: A Review of the
     NCLIS Task Force Report: Public/Private Sector
     Interaction in Providing Information Services." LJ
     (June 1, 1982) 1060-1066.
     "Though lip-service is paid to the societal value of
information," the report "favors a free market system, with as
little government intervention as possible." The author sees a
decline in an informed citizenry as the result of treating
information as an economic commodity that would limit access.

876.   Singer, Michael. "Gene-Splicing for Profit and
     Prestige." SD 2.10 (1978) 24, 35.
     Dr. Boyer's relationship with Genetach, Inc. "undermines
the collaborative spirit of academic research."

877.   Torney-Purta, Judith. "Political Socialization and
     Policy: The United States in a Cross-National Context."
     Child Development Research and Social Policy. Vol. 1.
     Ed. Harold Stevenson and Alberta Siegel. Chicago:
     Chicago UP, 1984. 471-523.
     Excessive stress on patriotic ritual in classrooms will
harm democratic values because it distracts attention away from
skills necessary for political participation and from tolerance
of diverse views.

878.   Underhill, David. "Death at a Later Age: Political
     Science versus the Columbia Rebellion." An End to
     Political Science. Ed. Marvin Surkin and Alan Wolfe.
     New York: Basic, 1970. 245-87.
     Political science and political scientists dealt with the
major issues of the student rebellion at Columbia University "in
a highly arbitrary and biased manner that served status quo
interests." He then sets forth the six steps "necessary for

creating alternative approaches to the major issues."

879.   University Finances. Washington, DC: GAO, 1986.   59.
     A study of "how federal funding for research fits into the
total finances of research universities" by a sample of "28
institutions" for the years 1975 and 1980-84.   "Federal research
support has increased, but at a slower rate than most other
research revenue sources"--corporate and state/local.

880.   Williams, Cathleen, and Paul Barnett.   "Brave New
        Tomatoes."   PE 2.1 (1979) 2-3.
     Corporate research grants at the University of California
support development of dangerous or inferior products.

881.   "Writing About Corporations Challenges 'Public
        Historians'."   HS 59 (1984) 2-3.
     "Public historians who go to work for business must expect
some constraints on their work . . . . Even those who write
corporate histories from the safe confines of academia may have
trouble."

II. E. 3. Governing Boards and Officers 882-887

882.   Beck, Hubert.   Men Who Control Our Universities:
        The Economic and Social Composition of Governing Boards
        of Thirty Leading American Universities.   New York:
        King's Crown, 1947.   229.
     A study of power elite trustees of universities.   "The
biases apparent in the selection of trustees probably should be
thought of as reflecting the basic patterns of status, power,
and values that characterize contemporary American society"
(134).

883.   Hartnett, Rodney.   College and University Trustees:
        Their Backgrounds, Roles and Educational Attitudes.
        Princeton, NJ: Educ. Testing Serv., 1969.   71.
     Restrictive values of trustees--campus speakers should be
screened, etc.

884.   Piliawksy, Monte.   Exit 13:   Oppression & Racism in
        Academia.   Boston: South End, 1982.   252.
     The ruling elite dominates higher education through boards
of trustees.

885.   Rudolph, Frederick.   The American College and
        University: A History.   New York: Knopf, 1962.   516.
     "Conservative men of wealth" came to "dominate the college
governing boards."

886.   Smith, David N.   Who Rules the Universities? An
        Essay in Class Analysis.   New York: Monthly Review,
        1974.   295.
     The university system is "controlled by big businesmen and
war profiteers who use the universities for their private gain

155

and <u>our</u> shared loss."

887.   Veblen, Thorstein. <u>The Higher Learning in America:</u>
         <u>A Memorandum on the Conduct of Universities by Business</u>
         <u>Men</u>. New York: Hill, 1967 (orig. 1918). 209.
    The author describes the control over science, scholarship,
and theory by representatives of practical pecuniary interest,
and the replacement of "the personal equation" by "the
accountancy of modern business management, "proficiency in
matter-of-fact knowledge," and "use and wont."

II. F. Secrecy, Censorship, Disinformation, Deceit 888-1005

    (See III. F., IV. A. & E., V. D.)

888.   "An Appeal to Reason and Conscience in Defense of the
         Right of Freedom of Inquiry in the United States." <u>Na</u>
         167.16 (1948) 419-420, 447-449.
    A document containing 107 signatures which denounces the
censorship by the New York City public schools and the
Massachusetts state teachers' colleges of <u>The Nation</u>.

889.   Bagdikian, Ben H. "The Gentle Suppression." <u>CJR</u> 4.1
         (1965) 16-19.
    The press should publish all news, regardless of content,
in an unbiased manner.

890.   Bass, Carole, and Paul Bass. "More Than Censorship,
         Irrelevance Troubles U.S. Journalists." <u>SLJR</u> 11
         (January 1985) 17-18.
    An account of the New York writers' conference on
"Censorship and Culture."

891.   Bennett, Jonathan. "How Many Cover-Ups?" <u>Guard</u>
         38.28 (1986) 10.
    Speculates about "White House pressure" behind "NASA's
uncharacteristic eagerness to get the Challenger aloft despite
dire warnings of the danger." The possibility of a cover-up is
enhanced by the fact that the two formal investigations of the
loss of the Challenger are "being led by Reagan appointees."

892.   Bogart, Beth. "'Passive Censorship' of International
         News." <u>ITT</u> 4 (Aug. 13-26, 1980) 21.
    Station managers voted to eliminate PBS' <u>World</u> series, its
principal international programming, because the shows were too
controversial. PBS executives are so closely linked to the
White House, the State Department, and CIA-funded think tanks
that overt censorship is seldom needed to suppress films with
independent views.

893.   Bok, Sissela. <u>Secrets: On the Ethics of Concealment</u>
         <u>and Revelation</u>. New York: Pantheon, 1982. 332.
    Ch. 10, "Trade and Corporate Secrecy"; 11, "Secrets of
State"; 12, "Military Secrecy"; 14, "Whistleblowing and

Leaking"; 17, "Undercover Police Operations." "Control over
secrecy and openness gives power: it influences what others
know, and thus what they choose to do. Power, in turn, often
helps increase such control" (282).

894.   Bolinger, Dwight. Language--The Loaded Weapon: The
      Use and Abuse of Language Today. New York: Longman,
      1980. 214.
      Discusses the use of language by government agencies and
corporations to sway popular opinion.

895.   Brown, Ben. "Trouble in Paradise." AF 7.9 (1982)
      61-62.
      Computer data banks fed by cable television services could
be used by government or corporate powers to monitor and
influence citizens.

896.   Budiardjo, Carmel, and Liem Soei Liong. The War
      Against East Timor. London: Zed, 1984. 253.
      "One-third of East Timor's population--about 200,000
people--have been killed in the war that has raged since
Indonesian troops invaded in late 1975." Yet "the war against
East Timor is certainly the least known and the least
understood. The reason is not hard to find: the people of East
Timor are the victims of one of the West's most favoured Third
World dictatorships, the Suharto military regime."

897.   Burnham, David. The Rise of the Computer State. New
      York: Vintage, 1984. 273.
      One way the ruling class maintains hegemony over society is
through the vast, growing network of telecommunications systems
which provide a web of information and surveillance for the
centralization of power. There is an enormous potential that
the government and corporate data collectors will use the
information for control and repression, in the increasing
context of presidential directives, Supreme Court decisions,
and laws which facilitate the collection, use, and control of
information by the powerful, and of the growing acceptance by
the public of an image of themselves as merely part of a system
of efficient production.

898.   Burrow, Marian. You've Got It Made. New York:
      Morrow, 1984. 254.
      The author's introduction to this cookbook, "The Politics
of Dietary Guidelines," condemns the Reagan administration's
refusal to distribute nutritional guidelines in response to
agribusiness opposition.

899.   "Censorship on U.S. Television." NCTV News 7.3-4
      (1986) n.p.
      Sub-titles: "Censorship Growing at PBS; Big Business in
Control"; "Big Business Domination of News Grows Further";
"Political Censorship Misguided: White House & ABC."

900.   Commoner, Barry. The Politics of Energy. New York:
     Knopf, 1979. 101.
     "The people of the United States have been given only
scraps of contradictory information about the energy crisis and
are largely unaware of the facts that could explain what is
going on." The solution, solar energy, is being overlooked
through "the politics of evasion" because of the possible
economic losses which would be experienced by industry.

901.   Conway, Flo, and Jim Siegelman. Holy Terror: The
     Fundamentalist War on America's Freedoms in Religion,
     Politics, and our Private Lives. New York: Delta, 1984.
     496.
     The constitutionally-guaranteed separation of church and
state is today facing the most serious challenge in its history.
Fundamentalists and ultra-conservative politicians are using a
campaign of fear and intimidation to exploit religion in support
of the anti-communist corporate-Pentagon state.

902.   Davies, Peter. The Truth About Kent State: A
     Challenge to the American Conscience. New York: Farrar,
     1973. 242.
     There was "no excuse for the shooting" of the students at
Kent State; political expediency prevailed over law when former
Attorney General John Mitchell ordered the case closed in 1970.
The book exposes the lying, evasion, and doublethink that marked
the investigation of the case. The book was sponsored by the
United Methodist Church. [The case was reopened after the
publication of the book.]

903.   Dixon, Marlene. Things Which Are Done in Secret.
     Montreal: Black Rose, 1976. 290.
     A "documentary history of academic repression" practised at
McGill Univ., in the context of the Western university as
"necessary and central" to the "social order of mature
capitalism." Although in Canada, McGill Univ. is "to all
intents and purposes and American university" taught by a "large
proportion" of right-wing American professors and serving
"American corporate interests."

904.   Dorsen, Norman, ed. Our Endangered Rights: The ACLU
     Report on Civil Liberties Today. New York: Pantheon,
     1984. 333.
     Since the time of the book's predecessor, The Rights of
Americans (1971) "there have been some gains for civil
liberties, but more losses." For example, Morton Halperin shows
in his essay how "the deterioration of detente in the 1980s has
led to unjustified draft registration, interference with
peaceful demonstrations, widespread surveillance of Americans,
travel bans, visa denials, secrecy orders, and censorship of
former government officials. The peril is deepened by the
apparent lack of limits to what a government may define as
'national security'" (Introduction). The fifteen essays are
divided into three groups on "The Processes of Rights," "The

Rights of Groups," and "Changing Concepts in the Struggle for Rights."

905.   Emerson, Thomas I.   The System of Freedom of
          Expression. New York: Random, 1970. 754.
Twenty chs. elaborate and apply in concrete cases the basic ideas set forth in the author's Toward a General Theory of the First Amendment. The book's main concern is to "examine the legal foundations" of the system. After three introductory chapters the author treats 4, "External Security," 5-8 "Internal Security" (sedition, loyalty, etc.), 9-10 "Internal Order," etc.

906.   Ericson, Edward L. American Freedom and the Radical
          Right. New York: Ungar, 1982. 117.
Nine chs. on resurgent McCarthyism, evangelicals and the New Right, the politics of intolerance, abortion and homosexuality, controlling the classroom, anticommunism and the arms race, money and power, and America's democratic heritage.

907.   Ewing, David W. "Winning Freedom on the Job." CLR
          4.2 (1977) 8-22.
Both corporate and government employees are in the same ghetto of loss of personal freedom on the job.

908.   "The First Amendment in Second Place." CMJ 5.5 (1979)
          3,12.
The ACLU is campaigning against civil liberties violations by government and industry, such as loyalty checks and prior restraint of a publication.

909.   Freifeld, Karen. "Embargo: The Rule Not Made to be
          Broken." WJR 6 (Dec. 1984) 39-40.
An "embargo" is a "prohibition against the release of information until a designated time." It is "not uncommon for private enterprise and government officials to use embargoes to manipulate the media."

910.   Fried, Emanuel. "Union Life and the Arts." Ed 27-28
          (1974) 19-23.
Class-conscious sponsors and reviewers, along with FBI intimidation, have kept unions and working-class lifestyles out of the theater. Labor theater, made up of union factory employees, is an alternative which is slowly emerging.

911.   Friedman, Edward, and Mark Selden, eds. America's
          Asia: Dissenting Essays on Asian-American Relations.
          New York: Pantheon, 1971. 458.
"Asia is America's in three important ways": "we impose American categories" on Asian experience, we "channel, distort, and suppress" much that is Asia, and our Asian policy "strengthens the very repressive tendencies in our society most prone to crush aspirations for freedom, autonomy, and equality

in America." Individual essays examine the intellectual constructs which mask Asian realities, the high school textbooks which distort China's complexity "into a simple Manichean world," the foundations and government agencies which fueled US aggression and expansion, etc.

912.   Furgurson, Ernest B. "Fire On the Mountain." MORE 4.10 (1974) 14-18.
"Appalachia's Mountain Eagle crusades--against strip mining, secrecy in government, and police harassment of youths-- has drawn "boycotts, physical threats and now, perhaps, arson."

913.   Gofman, John. Radiation and Human Health. San Francisco: Sierra Books, 1981. 908.
The price we are likely to pay for exposure to radiation is much higher than either industry or the government has ever admitted--an increased risk of cancer, chromosome damage, and diseases. Corporate greed, irrational consuming, the nationalistic drive for global supremacy, and the worship of the nuclear idol are mortgaging the health of future generations.

914.   Greenberg, Daniel S. The Politics of Pure Science. New York: NAL, 1967. 303.
A history of the close relationship between government and basic or fundamental research from WWII to the 1960s includes the powerful impetus of the Cold War and anti-Sovietism. The author traces the gradual change from a huge, costly, growth-oriented, self-governing establishment to a governmental bureaucracy.

915.   Gregory, Richard. No More Lies: The Myth and the Reality of American History. Ed. James McGraw. New York: Harper, 1972. 372.
On the various myths created and perpetuated by white Americans and by which they maintain power: the myth of the savage, of Black content, of free enterprise, of emancipation, of free elections, etc.

916.   Grossman, Karl. Cover Up: What You Are Not Supposed to Know About Nuclear Power. Sagaponack, NY: Permanent, 1980. 293.
A description of the dangers of continued use and development of nuclear power--releases of radioactive by-products, nuclear accidents, uranium mining, and nuclear wastes. The author argues also that a powerful group of government and corporate officials have used deception and economic blackmail to sell nuclear power to the public. Chs. on "Accident Hazards," "Medical Consequences," "Radioactive Wastes," etc., the last two on "The Alternatives" and "What You Can Do About It."

917.   Haiman, Franklyn. Freedom of Speech: Issues and Cases. New York: Random, 1966. 207. Rev. ed. Skokie, IL: National Textbook, 1977. 221.

A study mainly of "the communication of ideas and feelings via public speaking, the theater, motion pictures, radio, and television" but also "with certain aspects of the press, and with handbills, picket signs, and silent demonstrations." These modes of communication are treated under three broad areas: "speech that inflames an audience and creates a danger of disorder; speech that is viewed as a threat to national survival; and speech that is regarded as corrupting to public morality."

918.   Harvey, Joan, dir. A Matter of Struggle. New York: Parallel Films, 1985. 90 min.
A documentary about the singer Richie Havens with two young children traveling the US to meet with people working against the current US build-up of nuclear weapons, foreign intervention, and domestic repression and hardship, and for peace and justice.

919.   Hatch, Richard. "The City Outside History." ITT 3 (May 23-29, 1979) 21.
Complains that PBS' original "accurate and ferocious" criticism of American life and culture, "Lewis Mumford: Toward Human Architecture," was severely diluted.

920.   Hawes, William. "TV Censorship: Myth or Menace?" TQ 4.3 (1965) 63-73.
Television censorship comes not from the general public but from specialty groups--corporate advertisers, government, and religious groups (who influence sponsors).

921.   Heller, Scott. "Watchdog Group Says Students at 110 Colleges Now Monitoring Classrooms for 'Liberal Bias'." CHE 31.7 (1985) 27-29.
Accuracy in Academia, a spin-off from Accuracy in Media is watching Marxists, radicals, and liberals on campuses with the help of student monitors.

922.   Henry, William III. "Apologies, PBS-Style." NR 182 (May 24, 1980) 6-8.
On the many pressures on PBS to censor the film "Death of a Princess," in order to avoid annoying oil-rich Saudi Arabia.

923.   Hilgartner, Stephen, et al. Nukespeak: Nuclear Language, Visions, and Mindset. San Francisco: Sierra Club, 1982. 282.
After World War II government and corporate developers mounted one of the most extraordinary public relations, information-management, and secrecy efforts in American history to sell nuclear development to the public. The nuclear industry developed a language to manage attitudes, in the manner of George Orwell's "newspeak," covered up damaging information, harassed and dismissed scientists who disagreed with official policy, generated false and misleading statistics, and repeatedly claimed there was no choice but to follow their

policies, when alternatives were always available. The book is dedicated to George Orwell.

924.   Hofstadter, Richard. <u>Anti-Intellectualism in American Life</u>. New York: Knopf, 1963. 432.
"The purpose of this book is to trace some of the social movements in our history in which intellect has been dissevered from its co-ordinate place among human virtues and assigned the position of a special kind of vice" (47). "One of the major virtues of liberal society in the past was that it made possible such a variety of styles of intellectual life." What matters is "the openness and generosity needed to comprehend the varieties of excellence that could be found even in a single and rather parochial society" (432).

925.   Huebner, Al. "The Myth of Overpopulation." <u>Ed</u> 36 (1975) 24-28.
Research sponsored by government and corporate foundations have blamed problems such as inadequate food and housing on overpopulation while ignoring more direct problems such as maldistribution.

926.   Hughes, Joseph. "CBP: Heat Shield or Crucible?" <u>Current</u> 4.15 (1985) 5-6.
An analysis of the Corporation for Public Broadcasting's failure to protect PBS from political interference.

927.   Hulser, Kathleen. "Bad Blood Flows at PBS." <u>ITT</u> 6 (August 11-24, 1982) 20.
About PBS's rejection of two documentaries recommended by peer panels. PBS claimed artistic reasons, but the author alleges dislike of the films' dissident politics.

928.   <u>The IRE Book</u>. Columbia, MO: Investigative Reporters and Editors, 1984. 98.
The best investigative stories of 1983 are summarized: toxic chemicals in the work place, radioactive waste, insurance fraud, etc.

929.   <u>The IRE Book II</u>. Columbia, MO: Investigative Reporters and Editors, 1985. 107.
Summaries of top investigations from 1984.

930.   Kaplan, Craig, and Ellen Schrecker, eds. <u>Regulating the Intellectuals: Perspectives on Academic Freedom in the 1980s</u>. New York: Praeger, 1983. 260.
Thirteen essays examine aspects of how US capitalism has perpetuated "democratic illusions to sustain and maintain itself" (1). One essay reveals how delusional is any belief that iconoclasts and dissenters have security in academia. Another analyzes how Princeton used academic freedom principles in defense of excluding certain ideas from its campus. A collection of studies on the limitations of the concept of academic freedom.

931.   Kelley, Kevin. "Flashpoint: PBS." Guard 38.29
          (1986) 2.
     The two biggest PBS outlets refused to transmit a two-hour
show entitled "Flashpoint: Israel and the Palestinians" because
one of the three films in the show presented the Palestinian
point of view regarding the West Bank, "Occupied Palestine."
The other two films were Israeli productions.

932.   Kelly, J. B. "Saudi Censors." NR 182 (May 18,
          1980) 14-16.
     Background to the attempted censorship of the film "Death
of a Princess" in the US (on PBS) and Britain.

933.   King, Jonathan. "PBS Preempts Controversy." MJ 7
          (July 1982) 11-12.
     On PBS rejection of non-orthodox films, e.g., a film about
a member of the Socialist Workers Party.

934.   Kirby, Laurie. "Non-Truth at the New York Times."
          CS 7 (June-Aug. 1983) 30-32.
     An analysis of one technique for making us misunderstand
events--the "non-truth," used by Ronald Reagan, advertisers, and
the Times. "This is a piece of information or analysis which
may itself be true, but which is surrounded by such a sea of
distortions that it loses its original meaning." The author
analyzes a one-page symposium on the state of the American left.

935.   Konecky, Eugene. The American Communications
          Conspiracy. New York: Peoples Radio Foundation, 1948.
          167.
     Written in response to the FCC's rejection of the Peoples
Radio Foundation's application for a license to operate a
station in New York City, and against "monopoly interests" that
have "seized hold of American communications."

936.   Krueger, Marlis, and Frieda Silvert. Dissent
          Denied: The Technocratic Response to Protest. New
          York: Elsevier, 1975. 194.
     "While the grumblings of dissent are now everywhere, one
former center of visible confrontation--the university--appears
quiet and accommodating. This book explores the sources of the
university's acquiescence to the economic necessity of limiting
its potential to create alternative modes of thought" (Preface).
That is, the book focuses upon "the effects of inequality and
the structural relationship of intellectuals to it," the
"interconnectedness of the university and the state" (5) during
the 1960s.

937.   Lacob, Miriam. "Reader's Digest: Who's in Charge?"
          CJR 23.2 (1984) 41-43.
     An account of the firing of the editor-in-chief of Reader's
Digest partly because he was "overly critical of the Reagan
administration."

163

938.   Lambro, Donald. <u>Washington, City of Scandals:</u>
<u>Investigating Congress and Other Big Spenders</u>. Boston:
Little, 1984. 299.
     Part 1 "Congress," 2 on "the Bureaucracy," and 3 "The
Reagan Administration." Chs. 8-12 set forth secrecy, waste, and
fraud in the Pentagon. Several chs. illustrate the privileges
enjoyed by the rich and corporations.

939.   "The Last Word: Censorship on Public Television."
     <u>JC</u> 27 (1982) 72.
     The National Endowment for the Humanities practices
censorship over independent film production by not funding
projects which oppose current political thought, and the
situation is worsening under the Reagan administration.

940.   "The Last Word: WNET Censorship." <u>JC</u> 22 (May 1980)
     39-40.
     Self-censorship by the PBS station in New York of four
"radical" films recommended by their own panel of independent
filmmakers.

941.   Leggett, John, and Janet Roach. "UConn Story:
     Rhetoric and Repression." <u>NP</u> 7.3 (1969) 68-83.
     An account of the firing of four faculty members which
exposes the myth of a free and democratic university to the
reality of establishment power exerted to repress criticism of
corporations and the military.

942.   LeMond, Alan, and Ron Fry. <u>No Place to Hide</u>. New
     York: St. Martin's, 1975. 278.
     "More people today are being bugged, tapped, tailed,
probed, watched, and investigated, without their consent, than
most of us would ever have thought possible." Surveillance and
computer data filing are being done by "almost every business or
government agency with whom you have done business or have been
in contact in any way."

943.   Levitch, Joel. "The Independent Producer and Public
     Broadcasting." <u>PTR</u> 5.6 (1977) 6-13.
     Because of the difficulty independent producers experience
in gaining access to the air waves, the author proposes a
National Independent Program Center to serve as a conduit for
funding independent projects. Because public TV has a mandate
to develop programs "of high quality, obtained from diverse
sources," documentaries by independents should be encouraged.

944.   Lewis, Lionel, and Michael Ryan. "In the Matter of
     University Governance During the 1960's." <u>SP</u> 19 (1971)
     255.
     "It would appear that the security of academics was greater
during the right-wing vigilanteism of the 1950s than today."

945.   Lingeman, Richard. "Muncie Protects Its Own." <u>Na</u> 234
     (June 12, 1982) 722-27.

In response to complaints from people in Muncie, Indiana, PBS asked the director of Seventeen, a cinema verite documentary of the lives of some teen-agers on the city's Southside, to re-edit the film and cut out some parts. The director refused and the film was not shown.

946.   Litwak, Leo, and Herbert Wilner. College Days in
          Earthquake Country. New York: Random, 1971. 235.
An account of the long and bloody student strike in 1968 at San Francisco State College.

947.   Lloyd, Frank. "Public TV: Will It Cover Media
          Issues Commercial TV Ignores?" PTR 4.2 (1976) 50.
An appeal for public TV to cover television itself, since commercial TV scants electronic media issues.

948.   Lloyd, Rees, and Peter Montague. "Ford and La Raza:
          'They Stole Our Land and Gave Us Powdered Milk.'" Ram
          9 (September 1970) 10-18.
The Ford Foundation has set up conservative political and social organizations in northern New Mexico in an attempt to help the government control the actions of militant inhabitants. "The colonial press in New Mexico, no stranger to suppression and manipulation, has done nothing to expose the federal/Ford axis and its antics."

949.   MacIver, Robert. Academic Freedom in Our Time. New
          York: Columbia UP, 1955. 329.
Part One, "The Climate of Opinion," discusses "The New Wave of Intolerance" and "The Champions of the New Orthodoxy." Part Two, deals with "Academic Government and Academic Freedom." Part Three, "The Lines of Attack on Academic Freedom," discusses the established lines (economic, religious, and social tradition) and anti-communism.

950.   MacKerron, Conrad. "Curbs on Hearings Process
          Proposed." CMJ 8.6 (1982) 16.
DOE's plans to speed up the licensing procedure for nuclear power plants includes curtailment of the hearing process.

951.   Magid, Larry. "Florida State University: A Lesson
          in Repression." Ed 3 (Nov. 1971) 14-15.
Florida State University's administration refused to allow two controversial non-credit courses to be held.

952.   Manoff, Robert. "He'd Rather Be Right." Prog 50.1
          (1986) 19.
The right-wing pressure group Accuracy in Media (AIM) "has accused Dan Rather of a succession of journalistic malefactions. It seems his incorrigible liberalism has led him to overemphasize the risks of Agent Orange, the dangers of NutraSweet, the extent of the Pentagon's censorship of the Grenada invasion, and the public relations aspects of Reagan's foreign travels."

953.   Marker, Dennis. "Under Attack." Soj 14 (March
    1985) 5-6.
    A reply to the distortions and misrepresentations of this
magazine's views by Accuracy in Media. AIM specializes in
attacking alleged liberal or leftist bias in the media, that is,
in supporting the government-corporate status quo.

954.   Marshall, Rachell. "The Bruce Franklin Affair."
    Prog 36 (May 1972) 27-29.
    Stanford University unfairly fired Marxist H. Bruce
Franklin on the unsubstantiated grounds that he incited illegal
acts of protest against the Vietnam War.

955.   McIntyre, Mark. "Muting Megaphone Mark." MORE 3.7
    (1973) 5-6.
    Some newspapers refused to run Gary Trudeau's Doonesbury
satire of Richard Nixon and John Mitchell.

956.   McWorter, Gerald. "Tragedy at Southern U: Accident--
    or Political Assassination?" Ed 22 (March 1973) 8-12.
    A student protest at Southern University in Louisiana
culminated in the killing of two students at a peaceful meeting.
The FBI and the local police of Baton Rouge investigated the
shootings and refused to release their findings.

957.   Means, Howard. "Keeping Watch on Media Watchdog."
    AG (Sept. 22, 1985) 3C.
    Accuracy in Academia, an offshoot of the conservative
Accuracy in Media, is "dedicated to uncovering and rooting out
Marxist bias in the faculties of America's colleges and
universities," a "campaign to intimidate the free exchange of
ideas."

958.   Meranto, Philip, et al. Guarding the Ivory Tower:
    Repression and Rebellion in Higher Education. Denver,
    CO: Lucha, 1985. 182.
    An examination of the "deep linkages between higher
education and the elitist corporate and political rulers of the
U.S. social system" (179) and the challenges to that system by
students, faculty, and community. Universities "portray
themselves as free and open educational institutions in which
all views are encouraged and protected." However, universities
"have historically been and currently are predominantly centers
of intellectual repression rather than freedom." Dissenting
scholars "more often than not, have been driven out of the halls
of the academy" (Introduction).

959.   Merwin, W. S. "Hawaii Wakes Up to Pesticides." Na
    240 (March 2, 1985) 235-37.
    The Department of Agriculture, Hawaiian pineapple industry,
and pesticide corporations' campaign against the tri-fly has
employed a variety of manipulation of information, but public
groups are fighting for the truth.

960.   Miles, Michael. "The Triumph of Reaction." Cg 4.10
         (1972-1973) 30-36.
     Some university administrations have infringed the civil
rights of students and faculty leftists and protesters through
restrictions on political activity and by press censorship.

961.   Miller, Arthur R. The Assault on Privacy: Computers,
         Data Banks, and Dossiers. Ann Arbor, MI: Michigan UP,
         1971. 333.
     An explanation of computer technology's inherent threat to
privacy and individual constitutional rights and of the
political and economic changes caused by private and government
data programs. The author makes several proposals for
reasserting control over information.

962.   Miller, Arthur S. Democratic Dictatorship: The
         Emergent Constitution of Control. Westport, CT:
         Greenwood, 1981. 268.
     "My main theme may be simply stated: governmental powers
are increasing to the extent that repression will become
routine. We are, indeed, already well down the road toward a
regimented society, one governed by a newly emergent
Constitution of Control" (Prologue), the Corporate State already
in control.

963.   Mitchell, Greg. "Puncturing the Air-Bag Rule." Na
         240 (1985) 171-2.
     Contrary to their claims of being pro-safety, the Ford
Motor Company and Lee Iacocca impeded significant safety
advances.

964.   Nelson, Jack. Captive Voices. The Report of the
         Commission of Inquiry into High School Journalism. New
         York: Schocken, 1974. 264.
     The "repressive conditions we found ought to be the
exception rather than the rule." "Any censorship of journalism
is a dangerous thing" (from the Introduction by Franklin
Patterson, Chairman).

965.   Packard, Vance. The Naked Society. New York: McKay,
         1964. 369.
     "Today, with the onslaughts of new technologies, ever
mounting surveillance, ever widening bureaucratic controls, and
other forces we've examined, the guarantees of the 'Bill of
Rights' are being both diluted and often ignored."

966.   Payne, Les. "For 20 Minutes, Apartheid Vanished."
         C&C 45 (February 4, 1985) 40-44.
     An expose' of a segment of 60 Minutes by Morley Safer which
whitewashed South Africa's "penal colony" and made a hero of its
President, Pieter Botha, who contrary to Safer's portrait has
"continued to oversee South Africa's brutal crackdown against 83
percent" of its people.

967.   "PBS Drops Film." NT 4.5 (1986) 5.
The film Dark Circle, "which profiles individuals whose
lives have been destroyed or disrupted by the nuclear weapons
industry," has been rejected by PBS for nationwide showing.

968.   Pell, Eve. The Big Chill: How the Reagan
          Administration, Corporate America, and Religious
          Conservatives Are Subverting Free Speech and the
          Public's Right to Know. Boston: Beacon, 1984. 269.
A compendium of recent transgressions against the First
Amendment--against free speech, free expression, and the
public's right to know--by the Reagan-corporate-religious right
complex, and a warning of a deep freeze coming. Recent Reagan
administration restrictions on government information and on
public and press disclosure, book bannings in schools and
libraries, the increase in libel and slander lawsuits and the
general hostility toward the press and dissenters will increase
intolerance, censorship, fear of new or foreign ideas, and other
attitudes incompatible with free expression and open government.

969.   Phelan, John, ed. Communications Control: Readings
          in the Motives and Structures of Censorship. New York:
          Sheed, 1969. 238.
Parts I and III of interest: I: "Censorship and Social
Structures," "shows how communication, as the cognitive net that
enables societies to function coherently, is inevitably
institutionalized in such a way as to automatically shape the
content of all communications to meet the needs of the society
and culture it serves," III: "Censorship and Conflict,"
examines the "exercise of censorship in concrete laws and actual
cases," one essay on "Anglo-Saxon Law Against Seditious Libel,"
another on "The Espionage Act and the Abrams Case."

970.   Powers, Ron. "For Public Television: Hard News =
          Hard Times." TVG (March 24, 1979) 2-6.
Significant public-affairs programming by PBS is often
opposed by corporate and government enemies of hard-hitting
documentaries. For example, "The Banks and the Poor," which
exposed practices by savings and loan institutions prejudicial
to the poor, "horrified" the Establishment.

971.   Powledge, Fred. Public Television: A Question of
          Survival. Washington, DC: Public Affairs, 1972. 46.
A study of the need for "long-range insulated financing" of
PBS. A brief history of public broadcasting includes a
discussion of problems over documentaries critical of power--
"Banks and the Poor" and a segment on the FBI cut from NET's
"Great American Dream Machine"--and analysis of the Nixon
Administration's use of financial pressure "to force the system
to change its direction."

972.   Preston, William, Jr. "The Real Candidates for 'The
          Crime of the Century'" ORK (Spring 1984) 1-4.
The media have paid enormous attention to the alleged

treason of the Rosenbergs, but have neglected or suppressed the
tremendously more important conspiratorial alliance between
American corporations and the Nazis before and during WWII.

973.   Price, Sean. "View from the Right at UT." TO 79.7
        (1986) 13-14.
There is not much to attack on the UT campus, since it is
"hardly a liberal institution," but the Texas Review "flails"
professors with left-leaning views and even tried to prevent one
professor from receiving tenure because of his anti-
administration class on nuclear war.

974.   Project Censored. Rohnert Park, CA: Department of
        Sociology, Sonoma State U.
An ongoing effort to identify and publicize suppression and
avoidance of information in our society, believing that the
public must know about the major issues in society as
a prerequisite to making informed decisions.

975.   Randal, Judith. "Government and Industry in An Affair
        to Remember." Cg 10.4 (1978) 8-9.
A researcher of radiation danger at the Hanford Nuclear
Plant was relieved of his duties when he found a high rate of
certain types of cancer in Hanford employees.

976.   Randall, Willard. "Cancer Country: Where Newspapers
        Fear to Tread." CJR 18.3 (1979) 67-71.
A review of three books on pollutants and cancer:
Whiteside's The Pendulum and the Toxic Cloud, Boyle's
Malignant Neglect, and Epstein's The Politics of Cancer. "The
fact that these three books on various aspects of the
preventable plague of our synthetic society are needed is a mark
of the failure of many American newspapers to fulfill the
promise of their environmental coverage."

977.   Rapoport, Roger. "Catch 24,400 (or, Plutonium Is My
        Favorite Element)." Ram 8 (May 1970) 16-21.
The Atomic Energy Commission "covers up mistakes with
national security blankets, and suppresses reports, scientists,
and employees critical of its failures."

978.   "Repression at Univ. of Wash." Ed (June/July 1970)
        6.
Physical education professor Jack Scott's contract was
cancelled because his department feared opposition by Regents
who opposed Scott's political viewpoints.

979.   Retboll, Torben, ed. East Timor, Indonesia and the
        Western Democracies: A Collection of Documents.
        Copenhagen: International Secretariat of the
        International Work Group for Indigenous Affairs, 1980.
        138.
One purpose of the book is to demonstrate the cover-up in
the Western mass media of the Indonesian atrocities in East

Timor. In his Introduction, Noam Chomsky reviews "the basic historical facts and their systematic distortion by the major Western powers and the compliant press," particularly in the US.

980.   Robbins, William. The American Food Scandal: Why You Can't Eat Well on What You Earn. New York: Morrow, 1974. 280.
"Abetted by government agencies, the businesses that form the nation's food-supply chain are the authors and beneficiaries" of "a hoax of mammoth proportions."

981.   Rosenweig, Roy. "Marketing the Past: American Heritage and Popular History in the United States, 1954-1984." RHR 32 (1985) 7-29.
During the 1950s and 1960s, the magazine popularized establishment historiography against economic interpretations of the Constitution and Radical Reconstruction and in favor of big business, while it omitted "serious treatments of Afro-Americans, women, workers, strikes, and social conflict."

982.   Roth, Jeffrey, and Kathy Riley. "The Bill of Rights and the Student Press." ChJR 6.1 (1973) 3-6.
A discussion of court rulings on student press and student action freedom since the landmark US Supreme Court ruling in Tinker v. Des Moines School District.

983.   Ryan, Geoffrey. "USA--Ten Best Censored Stories." IC 8.1 (1979) 18-21.
An account of Dr. Carl Jensen's "Operation Censored," a media research center "to explore and publicize the extent of censorship" in the US. The first report covered 1976. Jensen places primary responsibility for the neglect or suppression of significant stories on the media themselves. The author points out how little Jensen's reports are covered by the media and nominates as "the best censored story of 1978--'The Ten Best Censored Stories of 1977.'"

984.   Sale, Kirkpatrick. "Myth as Eternal Truths." MORE 3.6 (1973) 3-5.
In covering Students for a Democratic Society and the New Left in the 'sixties, the media were guilty of "inaccurate and remarkably hysterical reporting" and of "performing as the meliorator for and protector of the powers-that-be in this country."

985.   Schiller, Anita, and Herbert Schiller. "Commercializing Information." Na 243.10 (1986) 306-09.
The powerful private information sector and their advocates in government oppose the fundamental mission of American libraries to insure free access to information for all citizens.

986.   Schiller, Herbert. "Information--A Shrinking Resource." Na 241.22 (1986) 708-710.

"Corporate control, which allows access only to those who can afford to pay for it, is being promoted," while former advocates of full availability of information--the Federal government and the universities--are being demoted. And the Reagan administration's and the Pentagon's "secrecy mania" is further reducing the information citizens need for self governance. The press "has been of little help" in examining these developments and alerting the public.

987.   Schechter, Daniel. "Media Myopia." MORE 7.12
          (1977) 26-31.
Most US journalists have failed to grasp and to report the economic underpinnings of aparthaid and the "crucial U.S. economic relationship with South Africa." "The American press has been reluctant to explore these ties or to explain U.S. policy as an outgrowth of this economic relationship."

988.   Schrag, Peter. Mind Control. New York: Pantheon,
          1978. 327.
"In the past generation, there has been a fundamental shift in the way government and other organizations control the lives and behavior of individuals." More specifically, "it is reflected in the replacement of overt and sometimes crude techniques--threat, punishment, or incarceration--with relatively 'smooth' methods: psychotropic drugs; Skinnerian behavior modification; aversive conditioning; electronic surveillance; and the collection, processing, and use of personal information to institutionalize people outside the walls of institutions." Ch. 7, "The Benevolent Eye": pervasive surveillance, not only by the intelligence agencies but by"private organizations and the 'benign' branches of government."

989.   Schumach, Murray. The Face on the Cutting Room
          Floor: The Story of Movie and Television Censorship.
          New York: Da Capo, 1964. 305.
Ch. 4, "Aftermath of Cowardice," and ch. 7, Sect. 2, "Madison Avenue's Blacklist Tremens," denounce "censorship by blacklisting" people thought to be radical in belief.

990.   Shaheen, Jack. "Media Coverage of the Middle East:
          Perception and Foreign Policy." Annals 482 (November
          1985) 160-175.
"A distorted media image of the Arab people is becoming ingrained in American culture."

991.   Sichel, Berta. "Disinformation Lumps." ITT 9.27
          (1985) 20-21.
An account of the exhibit held at New York's Alternative Museum called "Disinformation: The Management of Consent," disinformation defined as a process of deliberately altering information, "not merely a lie to be challenged." Disinformation has become "an integral part" of US domestic and particularly of foreign policy. Noam Chomsky wrote the catalog

171

essay.

992.   Smith, Robert E. <u>Privacy: How to Protect What's</u>
        <u>Left of It</u>. Garden City, NY: Doubleday, 1979. 346.
    A study of the huge government and business record keeping
organizations. The desire for information by government and
business brought about the methods, particularly computers and
electronic surveillance, lie detectors, fingerprinting, etc.

993.   "Smokeless Cancer." <u>HL</u> 1.1 (1985) 5-7.
    Users and potential users of snuff and chewing tobacco are
"not being told" about the risks.

994.   Steger, Tina. "Freedom of the Press." <u>Q&S</u> 59.1
        (1984) 14-16.
    One student newspaper advisor's experiences in reconciling
First Amendment rights with a hostile administration.

995.   Swaim, J. Carter. "Censorship in a Free Society."
        <u>Chm</u> 199 (March 1985) 9.
    A rapid survey of US domination of information: wire
services, bullying UNESCO, Grenada invasion secrecy and future
control of military operations reporting by the Pentagon, the
White House news and television service.

996.   Tajima, Renee, and Debra Goldman. "Dark Cycle: Film
        Dropped in PBS Balancing Act." <u>Independent</u> 9.7 (1986)
        2-4.
    PBS reneged on its offer to air Independent Documentary
Group's film <u>Dark Circle</u>, which portrays those who have worked
in and against the atomic industry.

997.   "Ten Lost Stories of News Reporting. <u>Pr</u> 6.10 (1978)
        4-6.
    An account of Project Censored's "Ten Best Censored Stories
of 1977," stories of great importance which did not make even
the top twenty of a wire service's poll of American editors.

998.   Udell, Richard. "DOE Suppresses Distribution of
        Consumer Pamphlet." <u>CMJ</u> 7.1 (1981) 4.
    Reagan's Secretary of Energy, James Edwards, impounded the
last issue of his department's monthly consumer publication
because of its "alleged 'anti-nuclear bias.'"

999.   Udell, Richard, and Sarah Rosenson. "Study Reveals a
        Dangerous and Deeply Flawed Technology." <u>CMJ</u> 7.3 (1981)
        6-7.
    Licensee Event Reports (LERs), occurrences which exceed
"technical design specifications," "do not tell the whole
nuclear safety story. Many mishaps go unreported or are
reported elsewhere."

1000.   "Universities Urged to Join in Fighting AIA Threat."
        <u>SLJR</u> 13.84 (1986) 12.

A report of the letter sent by the American Civil Liberties Union to 123 major universities and 36 educational organizations denouncing the efforts by Accuracy in Academia to monitor the ideological "errors" of instructors.

1001.   "USA: TV Doctoring." IC 8.6 (1979) 62-63.
On the heavy editing by PBS of a television documentary, "Blacks Britannica," about racism in Britain. The doctoring of the film resulted from "the fact that it dealt with racism in a way that was applicable not just to Britain, but as well to the United States."

1002.   Van Houten, Margaret. "The Politics and Proliferation of Data Banks." CS 2.3 (1975) 21-26.
"The technical capability now exists in modern society to collect, store, and retrieve information on every aspect of our society via computers and data banks." The author makes several recommendations to head off the growing centralization of information collection.

1003.   Wasserman, Harvey, et al. Killing Our Own: The Disaster of America's Experience with Atomic Radiation. New York: Dell, 1982. 368.
"Our government is so deeply committed to nuclear weapons and nuclear power that it will ignore damning evidence, deny the truth, mislead our people, jeopardize health and even life itself, and try to blacken the reputation of scientists who disagree with its policies" (from the Introduction by Dr. Benjamin Spock).

1004.   Weir, David, and Dan Noyes. Raising Hell: How the Center for Investigative Reporting Gets the Story. Reading, MA: Addison, 1983. 340.
Eight cases with "Behind the Story" commentary, including investigations of the Bechtel Construction Company and the US Navy's atomic testing in the Pacific in 1955.

1005.   Wicklein, John. "The Assault on Public Television." CJR 24.5 (1986) 27-34.
Examines efforts by government, Congress, and corporations, to undermine "the independence of public broadcasting." Offers suggestions for how "the system's integrity could be saved" by the establishment of an Independent Public Broadcasting Authority.

III. CORPORATIONS 1006-1473

Introduction

A. Concentration of Ownership   1006-1095

B. Lobbying and Campaigning   1096-1146

C. Sponsors, Product Advertising, Consumer Culture 1147-1320

D. Public Relations, Image and Advocacy Advertising 1321-1418

E. Foundations   1419-1429

F. Secrecy, Censorship, Intelligence Activities   1430-1473

Concentration

Benjamin Compaigne in <u>Who Owns the Media?</u> minimized the
dangers to democracy of media concentration, but the reviews in
<u>CJR</u>, <u>NmR</u>, and <u>MCS</u> demurred, one declaring that Compaigne's "own
data belie his assertion" that there is "media ownership diver-
sity." The issue of media monopoly and its impact on the kind of
communications needed for a democracy is disputed, but the books
and articles gathered together here significantly increase the
"significant detail" needed to make the case that monopoly is an
increasing threat to political choice and participation.
According to Herman Schwartz, writing in 1981, "business now
dominates America to a degree not seen since Andrew Mellon gave
away the Treasury." Edward Herman in <u>Corporate Control, Corpo-</u>
<u>rate Power</u> describes the accelerated concentration of economic
power through mergers, takeovers, interlocked directorates, trade
associations, joint ventures, and government advisory committees.
He is particularly concerned with how business uses government
for protection and subsidy, while avoiding significant control.
On the one-hand, business has mounted a massive campaign to persuade Americans it is in their interest to contain government,
i.e., to reduce the helping institutions of government--social
welfare and health and safety regulation. In 1976 both Jimmy
Carter and Gerald Ford ran on a pro-big business platform of
deregulation, and Ronald Reagan has intensified what amounts to a
concerted bipartisan attack on the social services philosophy so
successfully embraced by countries like Denmark. On the other
hand, business "clamors for government protection" for itself. A
book or two would be needed to catalog all the ways the millions
of dollars and thousands of employees have been used to discredit
non-business needs and to exalt corporate demands. The EPA,
OSHA, and the Clean Air Act, for example, remain, though disas-
trously attenuated, but business now generally has its way.
Ben Bagdikian in <u>The Media Monopoly</u> reaches similar conclusions about media corporations, a book repleat with details about
media corporate interlocks, control of subsidiaries, and other
techniques of "this American economic aristocracy, acquired in
morganatic mergers in the manner of forteenth-century monarchs"
(20). The "most powerful influence" of the parent company (Westinghouse, etc.) over its subsidiaries is "the power to appoint
media leaders" sympathetic to corporate desires. The corporations "from which Americans get most of their news and ideas" are
part of "the endless chain" of corporate directorate interlocks
and conflicts of interests. For example, media coporations are
interlocked with oil companies and defense contractors whose news
they report. Gannett, "the largest seller of newspapers in the
country," shared directors with numerous large corporations. And
Bagdikian does not merely expose the financial connections of
media and corporate power, he also demonstrates direct corporate
influence over the "reality" reported by the media. For example,
when Sears, Roebuck was accused by the FTC of "dishonest adver-

CORPORATIONS

tisement," the Chicago Tribune, whose board of directors included
an executive from Sears, "failed to carry a word of it, although
Sears's national headquarters are in Chicago" (24). Bagdikian
gives numerous examples of the close relationships between the
structure of power in the U.S. and the reality projected or
avoided by the media, yet one reviewer said he was "light on convincing detail." The contributors to this section of the bibliography (and in many other sections) provide more evidence that
the "'summits of American business' now control or powerfully
influence the major media that create American public opinion"
(28). And scholars like Hamelink (1983) find global parallels in
the increasing convergence of interests between the "highly oligopolised transnational information industry" and the "highly
oligopolised transnational banking system."

Lobbying

The enormous expense of campaigns is driving members of
Congress to seek more and more money from wealthy individuals and
corporations. At the same time corporations are increasing their
lobbying efforts. Lewis describes six ways corporations can
systematically influence "the policy-making process." 1) monitor
legislation in Congress likely to affect business, 2) maintain a
Washington office, 3) build a coalition with groups holding similar views, 4) obtain grass roots support by using all means of
communication, influencing news columns and editorials, sending
representatives to speak before organizations, and focusing on
key emotional issues and symbols, 5) form a political action
committee within the company, and 6) formally lobby legislators.
These efforts combine to skew the system to favor the wealthy.
Etzione sees a deepening corruption in the capitol. But Ralph
Nader and Common Cause continue their struggle to reform campaign
financing, to open meetings, to disclose lobbyists and their contributions, to make review of government agencies mandatory, to
expose and reduce conflicts of interest, to require full financial disclosure, and in general to check the growing power of
concentrated wealth and organization.

Sponsors

That the US is a promotional and consuming culture and the
corporations wield great power as the sponsor of advertisements
and programs are propositions hardly in dispute. But the process
is complex. The best-planned ads and programs fail. The actual
impact of ads and programs on audiences is often not known. Does
advertising promote consumption as a way of life? And what are
the effects of an acquisitive way of life? Some of the arguments
against advertising and the programs designed to bring the
audience to them are that a goods-intensive economy produces
social irresponsibility (smoking and lung cancer), plundering of
natural resources (denuded forests), selfishness, narcissism,
valuing commodities more than people, allowing commodities to
replace love and friendship, a politically passive and uncritical
citizenry, producer rather than consumer sovereignty, exploitation of women, and pervasive fraudulence.

Schudson believes that national advertising of consumer goods, which he calls "capitalist realism," promotes acquisition and consumption at the expense of other values. Capitalist "realism" presents people as social categories or stereotypes, pictures life as it should be, focuses on the new, "always assumes there is progress," and is "thoroughly optimistic," all problems solved via a product or life style (215). It is like socialist realism in subordinating "everything to a message that romanticizes the present or the potential in the present" and in advancing a national way of life--the "American" or "capitalist" way glorifying "the pleasure and freedoms of consumer choice in defense of the virtues of private life and material ambitions" (218). This is not to say that advertising is an official, state art, but "all ideals and values are called into the service of and subordinated to the purchase of goods and the attainment of a materially satisfying way of life" (220).

The power over television by the marketplace and global corporations is further elaborated by Erik Barnouw in The Sponsor, a book about not only business but government, education, religion, and political sponsors. Barnouw depicts an arrangement based upon the needs and wishes of sponsors "so essential, so crucial to the whole scheme of things" as to seem inevitable to most people. Commercial television has become a huge selling machine. The sponsor is "the potentate of our time." Page after page exposes the social consequences of the selling/consuming system: some $20 billion a year spent on personal care (sleeping pills, deodorants, headache tablets); 5 percent of the world's population "consuming the globe's resources at a rate approximating that of the rest of the world combined"; and so on. In consequence, a "basic revision of economic arrangements" is needed, and "the communication system interlocked with them."

Public Relations

This is a well-researched area of corporate behavior perhaps because unlike corporate surveillance practices, for example, it is accessible to study. Because what America is and what it should be are contested, and control depends significantly upon persuasion, corporations spend billions of dollars to ensure a favorable perception and to divert blame for society's problems away from themselves.

Still the best book on the subject, biased though it is in favor of corporate perspectives, Sethi's Advocacy Advertising and Large Corporations argues persuasively that corporations and media corporations should afford greater opportunities for the airing of opposing viewpoints, media should require disclaimers on advocacy ads to make a clear distinction between ad copy and media editorials, media should require clear identification of an ad's real sponsor, corporations should be accurate and fair and not present personal viewpoint as fact, and corporations should be willing to submit their claims to public scrutiny (278-281). And he recognizes that corporate advocacy campaigns can overwhelm public and alternative views (292).

Foundations

Ferdinand Lundberg (1968) describes the foundation as a device by which capitalists can avoid regulation and taxes. During House of Representative hearings, foundations were epitomized as "the base of the network of organizations through which the nerve centers of wealth impress their will on Washington" (10). Nielsen describes them historically as "orthodox, timid, and anchored in the status quo," but he also believes they have been at times autonomously creative and critical and can offer some alternatives to orthodoxy.

Secrecy

Corporate secrecy, although sometimes necessary, is used also to cover up questionable behavior, as Brodeur's studies, the books on the Dalkon Shield,and many other studies show. Instances of direct censorship are rare, since self-censorship usually exerts sufficient control over dissidents and whistle-blowers. Gitlin's Inside Prime Time, for example, intimately reveals how television's self-regulating system of conformity works. The growing intrusion by business not only by surveillance of employees but of a wide range of people and activities has barely begun to receive the attention it deserves.

Works Cited

Bennett, James R. Review of S. P. Sethi, Advocacy Advertising and Large Corporations, in RSQ 9.1 (1979) 37-42.

Hearings Before the Committee on Ways and Means on the Subject of Tax Reform. 91st Cong., 1st Sess., Pt. I. Washington, DC: GPO, December 5, 1969.

Lewis, Karen. The Business Lobby: A Case Analysis. U Texas Thesis, 1984. 70.

Schwartz, Herman. "Business Networking." Na 233.8 (1981) 248-49.

III. CORPORATIONS 1006-1473

III. A. Concentration of Ownership 1006-1095

1006.   Abel, Elie, ed. What's News: The Media in American
         Society. San Francisco: Inst. for Contemporary
         Studies, 1981. 296.
    Some of the essays: "The Media Baronies: Bigger, Fewer,
More Powerful," "News as Entertainment," "The News Business and
Business News." The essayists discuss the role of the
marketplace in shaping our media, how they came to depend so
heavily upon advertising revenues, their obligations toward the
community, the effects of chain ownership, etc.

1007.   Archer, Gleason. Big Business and Radio. New York:
         American Hist. Soc., 1939. 503.
    This and his earlier volume, History of Radio to 1926,
offers an account of how radio became controlled by a few
corporations.

1008.   Bagdikian, Ben. "Case History: Wilmington's
         'Independent' Newspapers." CJR 3.2 (1964) 13-17.
    The DuPont Company owns and determines the content of both
newspapers in Wilmington, Delaware.

1009.   Bagdikian, Ben. The Media Monopoly. Boston: Beacon,
         1983. 282.
    "By the 1980s, the majority of all major American media--
newspapers, magazines, radio, television, books, and movies--
were controlled by fifty giant corporations. These corporations
were interlocked in common financial interest with other massive
industries with a few dominant international banks. . . .They
constitute a new Private Ministry of Information and Culture."
"For the first time in the history of American journalism, news
and public information have been integrated formally into the
highest levels of financial and nonjournalistic corporate
control. Conflicts of interest between the public's need for
information and corporate desires for 'positive' information
have vastly increased (xiv-xviii).

1010.   Bagdikian, Ben. "News as a Byproduct." CJR 6.1
         (1967) 5-10.
    News and its interpretation should not be merely a
byproduct of huge corporations "whose primary concern must be
conventional gain."

1011.   Bagdikian, Ben. "The U.S. Media: Supermarket or
         Assembly Line." JC 35.3 (1985) 97-109.
    "Despite the vast number of local media outlets, the actual
range of available ideas and serious information is relatively
narrow, due to the nature of ownership and media economics, with
a resulting homogenization of content."

1012.   Barber, Benjamin. "The Second American Revolution."

Ch 1.6 (1982) 21-25, 62.
The author wonders "whether Big Brother may prove to be the more apt metaphor for television's second age," since the abundant new channels and services seem to be "rapidly falling under conglomerate control."

1013.   Barber, Benjamin. Strong Democracy. Berkeley: U of
          California P, 1984. 320.
Wealthy corporate interests exercise disproportionate influence in the political process, and liberal values of individualism and privatism undermine efforts to build citizen communities. Institutions as civic communications cooperatives to promote democratic uses of new telecommunications technologies, and civic videotex services to provide equal access to information will help create a "strong democratic program."

1014.   Barnett, Stephen R. "Monopoly Games--Where Failures
          Win Big." CJR 19.1 (1980) 40-47.
The Newspaper Preservation Act was intended to rescue failing local papers, but in practice it has raised the profits of owners and stifled competition.

1015.   Bazelon, David. "The First Amendment's Second
          Chance." Ch 1.6 (1982) 16-17.
On the basis of the ideal of diversity as expressed in the First Amendment, the author weighs the problems caused by concentration in communications technology. The author recommends the vigorous use of antitrust laws to increase diversity of programming.

1016.   Brush, Judith M. and Douglas. Private Television
          Communications: An Awakening Giant. Boston:
          Herman, 1977. 160.
A report on the rapidly growing field of corporate and institutional video, a revolution resulting from the increasing availability of the videocassette recorder and the video camera.

1017.   Bunce, Richard. Television in the Corporate Interest.
          New York: Praeger, 1976. 150.
"What we see in the case of diversified conglomerates is a few mammoth organizations actively shaping military policies and implementing them; actively shaping social welfare, health and education programs and implementing them; producing a multitude of consumer items and shaping consumer interest in them; and controlling the substance and shape of the communications flow to the public on all these matters of public interest" (125).

1018.   Colby, Gerard. Du Pont Dynasty. Seacaucus, NJ:
          Lyle Stuart, 1984. 968. (Expanded from Du Pont:
          Behind the Nylon Curtain, 1974).
A book about "the richest family on earth, a family with a corporate empire that stretches over six continents of the

world." A sample ch. is 12, "Cold Warriors From Wilmington,"
which describes du Pont political power under the Truman and
Eisenhower administrations and its two chief corporate aims:
labor repression and international expansion, and the use of
anticommunism to effect both aims. Scattered throughout are
revelations of the family's power through media ownership and
influence, secrecy, and intimidation. The Foreword describes
the semi-censorship of the first version of the book and the
federal court suit instituted by Colby (then named Zilg) against
du Pont and Prentice-Hall.

1019.   Coleman, James S. The Asymmetric Society. New York:
     Syracuse UP, 1982. 191.
     Corporations enjoy a plethora of information via marketing
research, credit bureaus, etc., in contrast to little or no
information for individual persons (ch. 5).

1020.   Collum, Danny. "The Way America Does Business: A
     Look at the Economic Need for Community and Democracy."
     Soj 14.10 (1985) 12-17.
     "Corporate centralization reaches into the very fabric of
daily life" yet the people have "no access at all to the
decision-making power. No one except corporate board members
gets to vote on questions like the shutdown of a factory" or
"the location of a toxic waste site."

1021.   Common Sense II: The Case Against Corporate
     Tyranny. New York: Bantam, 1975. 111.
     Partly about the ways corporations control public
understanding by secrecy, duplicity, lobbying, and public
relations--what they tell us versus what they do.

1022.   Compaine, Benjamin, et al. Who Owns the Media?
     Concentration of Ownership in the Mass Communications
     Industry. 2nd ed. White Plains, NY: Knowledge, 1982.
     529.
     A "substantially rewritten and expanded" new edition which
includes a new chapter that identifies the companies,
individuals and financial institutions who actually own the
media. Separate chs. cover newspapers, book publishing,
magazines, theatrical film, television and radio broadcasting,
cable and pay television. The purpose of the book is to provide
perspective to the term "media concentration" by bringing
together a host of data on the nature and degree of ownership
and competition.

1023.   "Conglomerates and Press Freedom: A Canadian View."
     CJR 20.4 (1981) 55-57.
     "The structure of the newspaper industry . . . is clearly
and directly contrary to the public interest."

1024.   Danielson, Michael. The Politics of Exclusion. New
     York: Columbia UP, 1976. 443.
     "To a greater degree than in other modern societies, the

United States has separated people spatially along economic and social lines" in which "blacks are separated from whites, the poor from the more affluent, the disadvantaged from economic and educational opportunity, and local jurisdictions with the greatest public needs from communities which possess the greatest share of the public resources."

1025.   Davis, Bill. "Book Publishing: No Big Deal." Pr 9.3 (1981) 14-16.
The increasing conglomerate ownership and concentration of the industry.

1026.   de Leseps, Suzanne. "Who Controls the News You Receive?" Pr 5.9 (1977) 16-18.
A report on media monopolies and the possible "abridgement of expression that the Founding Fathers feared from the government."

1027.   Diamond, Edwin. "Who, What, Why? Managers, Monopoly & Money." WJR 1.3 (1978) 36.
Newspapers and broadcast outlets, owned by large corporations, are run as businesses, with an emphasis upon profit.

1028.   Doudna, Christine. "When Wall Street Talks." Ch 1.2 (1981) 58-61.
The Wall Street brokerage house Entertainment Analysis Group has a powerful influence with investors and in the business press in their quest for profit.

1029.   Dreier, Peter, and Steve Weinberg. "Interlocking Directorates." CJR 18.4 (1979) 51-68.
"Most of the 290 directors of the 25 largest newspaper companies are tied to institutions the paper cover" or "fail to cover." "Overall, the directors are linked with powerful business organizations, not with public interest groups; with management, not labor; with well-established think tanks and charities, not their grassroots counterparts."

1030.   Edsall, Thomas. The New Politics of Inequality. New York: Norton, 1985. 288.
The shift to the Right in favor of those with economic power began in the mid-1970s. By then both the Republicans and the Democrats had largely deserted the poor and the working class, increasingly favoring Big Business and the affluent. Under the Reagan administration the process speeded up.

1031.   Edwards, Richard C., et al., eds. The Capitalist System: A Radical Analysis of American Society. 2nd ed. Englewood Cliffs, NJ: Prentice, 1978. 546.
Fourteen chs. divided into six parts: 3, "Monopoly Capitalism in the United States," 4 "Class Structure and Exploitation," 6 "Toward an Alternative to the Capitalist System."

1032.   Ernst, Morris L. The First Freedom. New York:
          Macmillan, 1946. 316.
     A critique of concentrated corporate power, censorship, and
manipulation. "Concentrated economic power" is reducing press
competition and diversity, and increasing public passivity
because "the people of our nation have been kept in ignorance"
of the growing monopoly. The book is divided into three parts:
"an exploration of the philosophy of freedom on which we as a
people have staked our all; a detailed factual exposition of the
trends, practices and control of press, radio and movies;" and
the "means of reversing the monopoly trend and upsetting the
present cartelization of press, radio and movies" (Foreword).

1033.   Eversole, Pam. "Concentration of Ownership in the
          Communications Industry." JQ 48 (1971) 251-60.
     "Mass media concentration and control of communications
networks by electronic conglomerates intimately linked to
military activities pose a potential threat to a free flow of
creative ideas so necessary in society."

1034.   Flippo, Chet. "Time Inc.'s Sticky Wicket." MORE
          4.4 (1974) 20-21.
     East Texas stockholders in Time, Inc. have influenced its
magazines to ignore a major conservation story in the area.

1035.   Foley, Joseph. "The Information Society: A New
          Threat to Freedom of Speech." FSY 1984. Ed. Henry
          Ewbank. Annandale, VA: Speech Communication Assoc.
          51-57.
     Expression of concern over the increasing "economic value"
of information. "As the generation and sale of information
comes to be the dominant activity in the US economy, the very
foundations of the ideal of a free flow of information are
challenged. . . . If information is expensive, it may be
impossible for speech to be free."

1036.   Ghiglione, Loren, ed. Chain Reactions: The
          Buying and Selling of America's Newspapers.
          Indianapolis: Berg, 1984. 200.
     Asorption of local newspapers by media chains has varying
effects upon quality, but more often than not the newspaper
degenerates.

1037.   Graber, Doris. "Media Giants." SLJR 8 (1982) 13-14.
     "If present trends are allowed to continue, 10 large
corporations will own nearly every daily paper in the U.S.
before the turn of the century. Fewer than 10 corporate giants
will dominate the production and airing of the television
programs. . . . What is at stake here is the quality of
political life in the U.S. Diversity of knowledge and opinion
is essential in a vigorous democracy."

1037a.   Green, Mark, et al., eds. The Big Business Reader
          On Corporate America. New York: Pilgrim, 1983. 514.

"Instead of thousands of sellers, we now see huge oligopolies and conglomerates dividing up the market in very non-competitive ways. Instead of full and honest information, we have been flooded with advertising that stresses the least important characteristics of a product while often deliberately obscuring the things we most need to know." Forty-eight essays examine the ways the corporations function as the dominant institution in the US, grouped by such topics as "The Corporation and the Consumer," "The Corporations and Labor," "The Corporation and National Resources."

1038. Guma, Greg, and Jeffrey Polman. "The News Magazines: A License to Interpret." Pr 8 (1980) 10-11.
Time and Newsweek project the mainstream ideology of two corporate empires, Time, Inc. and the Washington Post Company.

1039. Hamelink, Cees. Finance and Information: A Study of Converging Interests. Norwood, NJ: Ablex, 1983. 170.
A follow up of the author's The Corporate Village, which dealt with control of international communications by transnational corporations. The present volume focuses upon an aspect of the control, the relationships between the "information-industrial complex and its financiers." The increasing integration of the information industry (mass media, computer services, hardware and software manufacturers, enterprises buying and selling information, etc.) and the transnational financial system, all requiring enormous capital, is increasing the concentration of "allocative" control over global information resources and the privatization of information.

1040. Harker, Dave. One for the Money: Politics and Popular Song. London: Hutchinson, 1980. 301.
Popular music represents "a significant sector of the USA's economic base" (90), and it is usually co-opted by the profit system, but innovative and especially political music survives in spite of the structures of commercial ownership and control.

1041. Herman, Edward. Corporate Control, Corporate Power. New York: Cambridge UP, 1981. 432.
Corporations "have remained faithful to their basic objective, which is to maximize profits," and "they continue to be relatively impervious to the demands that they have a responsibility for the public welfare" (from the Foreword by M. J. Rossant). The first four chs. concern corporate control--the concept of control, the evolution of control, etc. Ch. 5 deals with the government and the large corporation, 6 with centralization of corporate power and 7 with corporate accountability and responsibility to the public, with proposals for making the corporation more responsive to the general welfare.

1042. Hertsgaard, Mark. Nuclear Inc.: The Men and Money Behind Nuclear Energy. New York: Pantheon, 1983. 339.

The story of the struggle over nuclear power told from the viewpoint of the industry via interviews. The financial-corporate-government complex of monopoly capitalism receives considerable attention, as do their strategies for a victory for atomic power.

1043.   Jess, Paul. "Antitrust Law: A New Approach to Access to the Media." PhD Diss., U of Minnesota, 1972. DAI 33 (1972) 2964A.
A study of ownership concentration for the year 1970. "Only 64 of the nation's 1,500 plus daily newspaper cities . . . were served by competitive newspapers." The author recommends antitrust case law to eliminate the "barrier created by captive printing plants."

1044.   Joffe, Phyllis. "How Much Media Clout for One Company?" Ch 4 (1985) 14-15.
On the dangers of information domination when a community's single newspaper and cable television are jointly owned, as in the case of the Hartford, Conn. Courant, the city's only daily, which owns the cable franchise.

1045.   Johnson, Nicholas. How to Talk Back to Your Television Set. Boston: Little, 1970. 228.
Ch. 2, "The Media Barons and the Public Interest," discuses the implications that concentrated control may have on the content of televised information and opinion." Ch. 3, "The Silent Screen," deals with "the problem of corporate censorship." The last two chs. propose specific remedies for the problems of television.

1046.   Johnson, Nicholas. "The Media Barons and the Public Interest: An FCC Commissioner's Warning." AM 221:6 (1968) 43-51.
Opposes agglomerative ownership of mass-media because of its ability to control the flow of ideas.

1047.   Kefauver, Estes. In a Few Hands: Monopoly Power in America. New York: Pantheon, 1965. 239.
"Monopoly permeates the society" in diverse ways and "takes its toll": excessive prices, a rigid price structure, crushing of small business, fixed prices, waste, pursuit of government subsidies, etc.

1048.   Kinsley, Michael. Outer Space and Inner Sanctums: Government, Business, and Satellite Communication. New York: Wiley, 1976. 280.
An analysis of the claim that satellite communication is a triumph of capitalism and government working together, since government provided very little oversight of the cooperating "free market competitors." The book demonstrates how AT&T and ITT and other corporations used Comsat for their own profit rather than for the public good. PBS, that is, the public, should have had free service, since tax money made Westar

possible.

1049.   Kopkind, Andrew. "Tools of Power." MORE 8.2 (1978)
          30-34.
     Review of books on The Los Angeles Times and The
Washington Post, which explore the newspapers as evolving
structures of power bound to specific economic and political
conditions.

1050.   Kotz, David. Bank Control of Large Corporations in
          the United States. Berkeley: U of California P, 1978.
          217.
     Giant corporations are the central economic institution in
the US, and a small number of giant banks are the major group
that controls the corporations, principally in New York City.
"The power held by the leading bankers should be of concern
. . . to anyone else interested in the concentration of economic
power in present-day capitalism."

1051.   Lindstrom, Duane. "Concentration Is the Name of the
          Media's Game." ChJR 4.12 (1971) 3-6, 15.
     On media monopoly in Chicago.

1052.   Lord, Benjamin. America's Wealthiest People: Their
          Philanthropic and Nonprofit Affiliations. Washington,
          DC: Taft, 1984. 78.
     "Profiles over 500 of America's wealthiest families and
individuals."

1053.   "Lords of the Air." Na 240.12 (1985) 355-6.
     The purchase of ABC by Capital Cities Communications is
another instance of the increasing concentration of
communications power "to manipulate mass culture." PBS offers
no significant alternative.

1054.   Lundberg, Ferdinand. America's 60 Families. New
          York: Vanguard, 1937. 544.
     A study of who owns and thereby controls the large fortunes
of the day, and how these fortunes are used. Ch. VII, "The Press
and the Plutocracy," shows the connections between wealth and
journalism.

1054a.   Lundberg, Ferdinand. The Rich and the Super-Rich:
          A Study in the Power of Money Today. New York: Stuart,
          1968. 1009.
     The US is ruled by an oligarchy of a "handful" of
"extravagantly endowed" people who have "limitless resources of
casuistry" and whose "agents deafen a baffled world with a never-
ceasing chant about the occult merits of private-property
ownership." Some chs.: "The New Rich," "Crime and Wealth," "The
Inheritors," "The Great Tax Swindle," "Oligarchy by Default."

1055.   Massing, Michael. "Should Public Affairs Be the
          Networks' Private Domain?" CJR 19.1 (1980) 34-37.
     "Twenty-six leading [independent] producers have brought a

lawsuit against the three networks and their owned-and-operated
stations in New York, claiming that their exclusion of outside
news and public affairs represents monopolization in violation
of anti-trust laws."

1056.   McGovern, James. The Oil Game. New York: Viking,
         1981. 239.
Secrecy, kick-backs, lobbying, public relations, and
advertising are some of the weapons employed by the oil
companies to direct attitudes and dominate policies in the US
(121-47).

1057.   Meehan, Eileen R. "Towards a Third Vision of an
         Information Society." MCS 6 (1984) 257-271.
Instead of the utopian democratic vision of the
information/communication revolution, or the dystopian military-
industrial fascist vision, the author offers a third vision:
"more of the same for fewer people," access to information
increasingly limited by the ability to pay and by "costing
arrangements between providers and cable operators." The future
will continue "concentration, integration, and commoditization in
the long run" (270).

1058.   Mirow, Kurt, and Harry Maurer. Webs of Power:
         International Cartels and the World Economy. Boston:
         Houghton, 1982. 324.
Markets in crucial industries such as oil, electrical
machinery, chemicals, uranium, steel, synthetic fibers, and
shipping are now under the control of the cartel giants which
set the prices of products we use every day. "Cartels, of
course, are not the problem. They are a symptom of an
underlying malady: the progressive takeover of the capitalist
world's economy by corporations for whom oligopolistic practices
are a second nature" (241).

1059.   Morano, Roy W. The Protestant Challenge to Corporate
         America: Issues of Social Responsibility. Ann Arbor,
         MI: UMI Research P, 1984. 244.
The Protestant church challenged corporations during 1970-
1979 through the filing of shareholder resolutions. "In almost
every case, corporations opposed the proposals that were being
made by the churches, and the stockholders consistently followed
the recommendations of corporate executives and overwhelmingly
defeated church proposals" (166).

1060.   Noah, Timothy. "The Washington Post: Monopoly
         Profits and Broken Promises." WM 15 (1984) 14-33.
The Post gives precedent to the bottom line over ideals.
When its only competitor the Washington Star ceased publication,
the Post expressed noble sentiments regarding its "new
obligations" as a monopoly newspaper. Two years later the Post
seems more interested in how "to divide up the newspaper's
impressive new profits" than in being responsive to the community.

1061.   Packard, Frank. "Literature as Big Business." BT
          (Fall 1980) 8-12.
     The balance between profit and art in the publishing
industry "began to change when the booming economic climate of
the 1960s brought the sights of expansion-minded conglomerates
upon the education industry."

1062.   Phillips, Kevin. "Busting the Media Trusts." Har
          255 (July 1977) 23-34.
     A case against monopoly of news and information. The
author would employ anti-trust remedies to anticompetitive
tendencies and would promote increased competition by all means
available--e.g., a fourth network, divestiture. Two pages offer
a sample of conglomerates in the communications industry showing
what the goliaths own.

1063.   Pollak, Richard. "A Case Against Press Councils."
          MORE 3.2 (1973) 3.
     The proposed Press Council will fail because it fails to
cope with the basic problem of exclusive control of a news
organization by the owners. Now "money decides."

1064.   Powell, Walter. "The Blockbuster Decade: The Media
          as Big Business." WP 7.2 (1979) 26-36.
     A few giant multi-media corporations control most of
America's information and entertainment outlets. Due to this
concentration, diversity of available books, records, films, and
news has become second to the desire for huge profit.

1065.   Powledge, Fred. Fat of the Land. New York: Simon,
          1984. 287.
     Attributes the widespread ignorance of Americans about
nutrition and the food industry to the practices of concentrated
ownership in the industry, deceptive advertising, corporate
greed, and weak government regulation.

1066.   Proceedings of the Symposium on Media Concentration,
          December 14 and 15, 1978. 2 vols. Bureau of
          Competition, Federal Trade Commission. Washington, DC:
          GPO, n.d. 761.
     The symposium is divided into three sections. "The first
section, an overview section, addresses three topics: the
effect of concentration on the flow of information; the policy
implications of the First Amendment; and the economic
characteristics of the media. The second section addresses four
discrete topics--the role of competition in the electronic
media; local cross-ownership of media properties; the newspaper
industry; and concentration and conglomeration in book
publishing. The third and final section addresses the role of
antitrust policy in the media."

1067.   Putney, Bryant. "The Republicans and the First
          Freedom." Na 164.3 (1947) 67-68.
     "Republican leaders in the Senate have managed to head off

a Congressional inquiry into [monopoly] economic forces limiting a truly free press in America."

1068.   Reel, Frank A. The Networks: How They Stole the Show. New York: Scribner's, 1980. 208.
An attack on the networks as "the most powerful, most effective, and most impregnable monopoly in the history of the United States." Their economic monopoly is rendered impregnable by the reluctance or powerlessness of the FCC to regulate it. The author sees one solution in switching the nation from the VHF spectrum (twelve channels) to the UHF (seventy channels). One ch. explains how the networks exert control over the program process.

1069.   Reidy, John S. "The Players: Powers That Be." Ch 2.4 (1982) 64-68 field guide.
An overview of the companies which more than likely will play a major role "in the emerging new age of television."

1070.   Rewiring Your World. Communications Workers of America, 1984.
Three TV programs on the dislocations for workers caused by the new communications technology and its monopoly control by corporations.

1071.   Rickover, Hyman G. "The Moral Responsibility of Business." TR 85 (May/June 1982) 12-14.
Admiral Rickover discusses the increasing power of corporations and the government's reluctance to regulate them. "Through their control of vast resources, these large corporations have become, in effect, another branch of government. They often exercise the power of government, but without the checks and balances inherent in our democratic system."

1072.   Ridder, Pamela. "Good Question." CJR 18.6 (1980) 68.
Rev. of Compaine's Who Owns the Media? The "mass of information in the book compels the conclusion that a handful of companies controls a staggeringly high percentage of the media industry."

1073.   Role of Giant Corporations. Hearings Before the Subcommittee on Monopoly of the Select Committee on Small Business, U.S. Senate, 91st Cong., 1st Sess. 4 vols. Washington: GPO, 1969-1972.
Vol. 1: "Automobile Industry"; 2 "Corporate Secrecy: Overviews"; 3 "Corporate Secrecy: Agribusiness"; 4 "Corporate Secrecy: Ownership and Control of Industrial and Natural Resources." From the opening statement by Senator Gaylord Nelson, Subcommittee Chairman: "The basic problem is ever greater power in ever fewer hands." The "share of assets held by the 100 largest corporations of today is about equal to the share held by the 200 largest of 1948." This trend "does not

leave much room for small business." From Vol. 2: Since the issue is power, the hearings also deal with "the importance of corporate secrecy in the building and maintaining" of corporate power. "Francis Bacon insisted that 'knowledge is power.' Corporate secrecy may be viewed as monopolization of knowledge, and thereby of power." Senator Nelson provides a list of "seven different aspects of corporate secrecy" and "sixteen major questions" to be considered regarding that secrecy.

1074.   Rose, Ernest. "Moral and Ethical Dilemmas Inherent in an Information Society." Telecommunications: Issues and Choices for Society. Ed. Jerry Salvaggio. New York: Longman, 1983. 78-84.
The information society may increase the advantages of the corporate world while reducing protection of the individual. Decontrolling of telecommunications favors corporate property rights and ignores individual rights.

1075.   Rosenau, Neal B. "On Covering the Revolution." ChJR 3.9 (1970) 3-4.
The Left view of the American press "as hopelessly establishmentarian in its ownership and operation" and "as counter-revolutionary in its effect" is "frightfully accurate."

1076.   Rowe, James. "Ralph Nader Reconsidered." WM 17 (March 1985) 12-21.
In praise of Nader's efforts to make democracy work, against the corporate drive for monopoly.

1077.   Rucker, Bryce. The First Freedom. Carbondale, IL: Southern Illinois U P, 1968. 322.
In general about the turn from competition of ideas in the marketplace of thought toward monopoly. Fifteen chs. discuss the daily newspaper (1-5), broadcasting (6-13), and magazines (14). The final ch. presents "A Blueprint for Action." The problem of the conflict between media owners and the public interest "is compounded when individuals or groups amass large chains, thereby dangerously extending their power to persuade. The nearer we approach communications monopoly in any given area, the more restricted our freedom" (222).

1078.   Schiller, Herbert. "Behind the Media Merger Movement." Na 240.22 (1985) 696-98.
"There is a growing concentration of capital and resources in the United States, the dominant center of the world communications network." The situation has deteriorated to such an extent that the FCC, "historically a defender of the quality of the nation's information, has abandoned all considerations of the public interest."

1079.   Schiller, Herbert I. Who Knows: Information in the Age of the Fortune 500. Norwood, NJ: Ablex, 1981. 187.
"The elevation of private, corporate over public, social interest is especially transparent in the dynamic communication-

information sector. Here the institutional processes are being
arranged to enable the already powerful to seize control and
direct the new technologies to corporate ends, while the few
public structures with potential countervailing influences are
progressively weakened." In spite of this growing power, the
author urges his readers not to be overcome by what may appear
to be an "unassailable information apparatus, at the disposition
of a system of concentrated, corporate capital" (xii-xviii).
Ch. 4, all aspects of corporate appropriation of new
communications technologies; ch. 5, corporate domination of the
international flow of information; etc.

1080.   Schorr, Daniel. "A Point of Privilege." _WJR_ 1.6
         (1979) 26-27.
    The press rates low in polls because "once
characteristically anti-establishment," the press is now
perceived as having become a vast establishment in its own
right--often allied with the governing establishment."

1081.   Schwartz, Robert. "Public Access to Cable
         Television." _HLT_ 33 (March 1982) 1009-1044.
    "A high concentration of ownership in the communications
industry and a lack of public access to the media" have
"discouraged individual participation in mass media." The
Supreme Court's ruling in _Midwest II_ was wrong. Public access
to cable systems "should be constitutionally protected and
affirmatively promoted."

1082.   Schwoch, James. "The Information Age: The AT&T
         Settlement--Corporatism-in-the-Making." _MCS_ 6 (1984)
         273-288.
    "The AT&T and IBM settlements mark the abandonment of
antitrust suits as an instrument of American policy," one of the
"most powerful weapons of justice" in our system. But the
author hopes that American consumers will resist corporate power
and control by insisting upon "ownership of information to be an
unalienable right."

1083.   Sterling, Christopher, and Timothy Haight. _The Mass
         Media: Aspen Institute Guide to Communication Industry
         Trends_. New York: Praeger, 1978. 457.
    Data on concentration of ownership, with the warning that
"ownership is not the only question relevant to a study of
information control."

1084.   Swerdlow, Joel. "Why Is Everyone Afraid of Ma Bell?"
         _Ch_ 1.4 (1981) 29-33.
    "The cable, computer, and publishing industries are
battling to keep the world's largest corporation from growing
still bigger--and seizing their turf."

1085.   Tate, Cassandra. "Gannett in Salem: Protecting the
         Franchise." _CJR_ 20.2 (1981) 51-56.
    In spite of its record for defending the First Amendment,

the Gannett Co., Inc., the nation's biggest newspaper chain, secretly set forth in "Operation Demolition" to force the closure of a Salem, Oregon, competitor in violation of state and federal antitrust laws, and the litigation over the case has been kept secret.

1086.   Trillin, Calvin. "U.S. Journal: Kentucky." New Yorker 45 (December 27, 1969) 33-36.
Very few weeklies published in the US "ever print anything that might cause discomfort to anyone with any economic power" (33).

1087.   "Trustbusting: Too Little, Too Late." Prog 46.4 (1982) 10-11.
The "need for significant restraints on corporate power is greater than ever."

1088.   Tunstall, Jeremy, and David Walker. Media Made in California: Hollywood, Politics, and the News. Oxford UP, 1981. 204.
A study of Californian media as a paradigm for an understanding of American media. The concentration of film, television, and music industries reveal the extent of interlocking ownership across media which provides US-based multinational corporations with enormous cultural reach.

1089.   Van Allen, Judith. "Eating It! From Here to 2001." Ram 10 (May 1972) 26-33.
The American food industry is a set of oligopolies which exerts control over foundations, government agencies, congressional committees, university research, and training centers, through their vast advertising expenditures and an army of paid and unpaid propagandists.

1090.   Villarejo, Don. "Stock Ownership and the Control of Corporations: Part III." NUT 2 (1962) 47-65.
"The great mass of the populace neither owns nor controls corporate stock but rather a relatively small group of persons, the propertied rich, both own and, substantially, control the giant enterprises of the nation."

1091.   Wasko, Janet. "The Political Economy of the American Film Industry." MCS 3 (1981) 135-153.
Bankers support the film industry primarily for economic reasons, and exert control over film corporations (management purges, choice of producer, budget restrictions) primarily for business reasons, but bankers also understand films as offering "a means of reinforcing dominant ideology, or selling a specific way of life."

1092.   Wasserman, Harvey. Energy Wars: Reports from the Front. Westport, CT: Lawrence Hill, 1979. 253.
A "running documentary account" of the "energy war"--the struggle between "the multinational cartels that dominate the

193

world energy market," the "monopolization of energy by a financial and scientific priesthood beyond our control," and citizens "demanding a full-scale alternative."

1093.   Weinstein, James. The Corporate Ideal in the Liberal
         State 1900-1918. Boston: Beacon, 1968. 263.
   "The ideal of a liberal corporate social order" (known later by such names as the New Freedom, the New Deal, the New Frontier, and the Great Society) was developed under the supervision of "those who then, as now, enjoyed ideological and political hegemony": the more sophisticated leaders of America's largest corporations and financial institutions.

1094.   Whiteside, Thomas. The Blockbuster Complex:
         Conglomerates, Show Business and Book Publishing.
         Middletown, CT: Wesleyan UP, 1981. 207.
   Since the early nineteen-sixties "trade-book publishing has been subjected to some startling changes." There has been "a seemingly relentless trend toward concentrating the ownership of individual publishing houses into ever-larger corporate organizations.

1095.   Wicklein, John. "Technology Untamed." C&C 44 (1984)
         335.
   Review of new TV series, "Rewiring Your World," produced for the Communications Workers of America and showing increasing monopoly control of technology by corporations.

III. B. Lobbying & Campaigning 1096-1146

1096.   Arieff, Irwin. "Violent Reaction." MORE 7.11 (1977)
         8-9.
   The networks successfully pressured the House Communications Subcommittee to water-down its report on televised violence.

1097.   Buell, John. "The Nuclear Congress." CMJ 7.11 (1982)
         7-9.
   Nuclear corporations' political action committees have influenced several members of Congress who are involved in nuclear-related legislation.

1098.   Clevett, John. "Nuclear Industry Lobbies for
         Licensing Reform." CMJ 8.12 (1983) 10.
   Congress is considering a bill promoted by the nuclear industry which would put strong limits on the amount of public access to information about nuclear power plants being constructed.

1099.   Cobb, Jean. "What, Me Lobby?" CC 9.6 (1983) 38.
   The insurance lobby is not required to report a lot of money it spends on lobbying.

1100.   "A Congressional Rising Star Calls It Quits." CC

8.3 (1982) 24-26.
Senator William Brodhead speaks about the tax loopholes and subsidies created because of PAC pressure.

1101.   Curry, Beth Ann. "Dirty Money May Mean Dirty Air."
         CC 7.3 (1981) 12.
Corporate interests seek to undermine the Clean Air Act by influencing congressmen by means of PAC money.

1102.   "'Dirty Dozen' Cleans Up in PAC Money." CC 8.2
         (1982) 14.
Members of the House Health and Environment Subcommittee who voted to weaken the Clean Air Act received monies from the PACs of affected industries.

1103.   Drew, Elizabeth. Politics and Money: The New Road to
         Corruption. New York: Macmillan, 1983. 165.
A fuller and updated account of articles originally published in The New Yorker. The pressure to raise money to pay for campaigns "is driving the politicians into a new form of political corruption."

1104.   Dwyer, Paula. "How Corporate Lobbying Stalled Two
         Defense Fraud Bills." BW 2954 (July 7, 1986) 48-9.
Legislation that would make it easier to prosecute corporations that cheat the government was derailed by the Harris Corp. and other large military contractors, partly through generous campaign contributions to key senators.

1105.   Easterbrook, Gregg. "They Don't Get No Respect."
         CC 7.6 (1981) 22-24.
Corporate lobbyists join together to improve their public image and fight disclosure laws.

1106.   Easton, Nina. "Boys Will Be Boys." CC 9.6 (1983) 7.
Corporations influence Congress even in their off hours.

1107.   Etzioni, Amitai. Capital Corruption: The New
         Attack on American Democracy. New York: Harcourt,
         1984. 337.
This is a book about the "pervasive and endemic" political corruption in the nation's capital brought about by the "whole set of laws" that "opened the floodgates to special interests, undermining the representative system." Part I deals with the source of the corruption, the "new plutocracy" of concentrated economic power, not one ruling class but a variety of power wielders. "In the interest-group state, the government works overtime only for the strongest groups." Part IV sets forth changes necessary to return the US to a more representative system.

1108.   "FCC Needs Disclosure Rule for Lobbyists." CC 8.3
         (1982) 32.
Companies whose lobbying rates are set by the FCC are not

required to disclose their lobbying expenses.

1109.   Ferguson, Thomas, and Joel Rogers, eds. The Hidden
         Election: Politics and Economics in the 1980
         Presidential Campaign. New York: Pantheon, 1981. 342.
    The eight essays attempt to explain the election in terms
of the structure of power in America--the economic interests
which define American public life, the candidates' links to the
business community, source of money, etc. Elections are really
two campaigns, one public, the other the "complex process by
which pivotal interest groups like oil companies, international
banks, weapons producers, labor unions, and even foreign
countries coalesce behind particular candidates to advance their
own ends."

1110.   "Firm Big Contributor to Lawmakers in FHLB Fight." AG
         (Nov. 3, 1986) 12A.
    Congressmen who helped a savings and loan company fight the
Federal Home Loan Bank Board's attempts to regulate risky
investment were rewarded with $150,000 in campaign
contributions.

1111.   Frendreis, John, and Richard Waterman. "PAC
         Contributions and Legislative Behavior: Senate Voting
         on Trucking Deregulation." SSQ 66.2 (1985) 401-12.
    The American Trucking Association's million dollar campaign
"to convince Congress and the American people that deregulation
was not in the public interest" did influence congressional
recipients of PAC money, particularly those closest to a
reelection bid. There were "clear and strong statistical
associations between contributions and voting" in this case.

1112.   Garcia, Elise D. "When It Comes to PACs, Business
         Means Business." CC 7.2 (1981) 12.
    The amount of financial support congressmen receive from
business action committees is rapidly increasing.

1113.   "A Government of, by and for the PACs." CC 8.4
         (1982) 16.
    "Republican Rep. Jim Leach of Iowa says that Political
Action Committee contributions are threatening the
democratic process."

1114.   Graves, Florence. "Taxpayers Foot B-1 Lobby Costs."
         CC 7.5 (1981) 7.
    The Rockwell Corporation added the cost of selling the US
government the B-1 bomber into the overall price of the bomber.

1115.   Graves, Florence, and Lee Norrgard. "Money to Burn."
         CC 11.1 (1985) 20-31.
    A relatively small group of commodity traders exert big
influence in Congress via political action committees.

1116.   Hanson, C. T. "Skinner-box Journalists." CJR 20.6

(March-April 1982) 17-18.
News coverage of the Alaska natural gas pipeline bill (to shift the financial risk of funding the $40-to-$50 billion pipeline "from industry to the consumer") went virtually unreported by the media, partly as the result of skillful lobbying.

1117.   "The Hill is Alive With the Sound of Money." CC 7.2
         (1981) 10.
Senators receive large sums of money from special interest groups in the form of speaking fees.

1118.   "Inside the Great Campaign Finances Case of 1976."
         CLR 4.3 (1977) 8-19.
Those who favored the Federal Election Campaign Act of 1971 hoped that it would reduce the corruption caused by large campaign contributions, and that it would place candidates on a more equal footing, but those hopes were not realized.

1119.   Kaplan, Joel, and James Pratt. "From Rags to Riches."
         CCd 12.1 (1986) 14-21.
Examines the "wheeling and dealing" of Congressman William Boner (D-Tenn) with James Wellham, owner of American Specialty Metals, who sold metal to the federal government "that did not meet the quality requirements specified in his contracts."

1120.   Kaplan, Sheila. "Join Congress--See the World." CC
         12.5 (1986) 17-23.
Special interests exert influence by providing congressmen with free vacations in the guise of "fact-finding tours."

1121.   Kaplan, Sheila. "A Sweet Deal." CC 12.3 (1986)
         24-29.
US consumers are paying more for sugar than they should have to because of government price supports and import restrictions designed to protect sugar growers. These growers are mainly "wealthy corporations and families" who use their money to influence congressmen.

1122.   "Keeping the Party Lines Open." CC 8.2 (1982) 14.
Certain PAC's give money to leaders of both Republican and Democratic parties.

1123.   Kosterlitz, Julie. "At the Mercy of the Highest
         Bidder." CC 8.4 (1982) 8-15.
"PAC dollars are rapidly becoming more powerful than your vote," and the dollars come increasingly from corporations.

1124.   Kosterlitz, Julie. "The Money Behind the MX." CC
         11.2 (1985) 15-17.
Some of the impetus behind a costly and dangerous weapons system has little to do with national security or arms control" and much to do with "campaign contributions, honoraria, high-priced lobbyists and the kind of pork barrel politicking

designed to appeal" to Members of Congress.

1125.   Kosterlitz, Julie. "'Safe Harbor'--Troubled Water
          for Democrats." CC 8.3 (1982) 12.
     The Democratic Business Council gave money to the
Democratic Party in return for consideration of their thoughts
on the Economic Recovery Tax Act.

1126.   Kosterlitz, Julie. "Take $2,000 and Call Me in the
          Morning." CC 8.2 (1982) 12-15.
     The AMA's powerful lobbying groups in Washington and in the
state governments.

1127.   Kosterlitz, Julie, and Patricia Theiler. "Money on
          Their Minds." CC 10.4 (1984) 16-23.
     Congressional candidates are courting special interests as
never before.

1128.   "Lobbying Lockheed Style." CC 12.5 (1986) 8.
     Lockheed employees were recently pressured by company
officials to sign prepared letters and send them to their
congressmen.

1129.   Looking to Purchase or Rent. Washington, DC:
          Common Cause, 1984.
     A study of the National Association of Realtors Political
Action Committee, one of the biggest contributors to
congressional candidates.

1130.   Matusow, Barbara. "When Push Comes to Shove." Ch 1
          (1981) 33-39.
     The "extremely powerful" broadcast lobby in Washington
seeks "to free broadcasters from as many government restraints
as possible, while simultaneously securing government protection
from the competition." For example, by "one of the most
ferocious lobbying drives ever waged on Capitol Hill," the
broadcasters killed the FTC's effort to restrict advertisements
for heavily sugared cereals aimed at children.

1131.   McQuaid, Kim. "Back-Door Policymaking." WP 7.2
          (1979) 50-54.
     The Business Council and Business Roundtable, organizations
composed of top executives of major corporations, meet in
secret, often with government officials, to lobby for or present
political policy.

1132.   "Nuclear PACs: Three Million Dollar Votes."
          Washington, DC: Public Citizen, 1984. 28.
     Contributions by the nuclear industry to members of
Congress and corresponding voting records.

1133.   "Paper Reports Nofziger Got Defense Firm Stock." AG
          (Nov. 3, 1986) 6A.
     Wedtech, a defense construction firm, gave one million

dollars worth of stock to a former Reagan aide in return for his getting them business.

1134.   "Preparing for a Petroleum Bailout." AG (Nov. 16, 1986) 2C.
     Domestic petroleum producers are beginning a massive lobbying effort aimed at persuading the administration to raise the price of oil.

1135.   Reitz, Sara. "Oblivion for the Closest Thing to Consumer Protection." Pr 8 (March 1980) 4.
     Corporate resistance to FTC regulation. "The number of corporations with public affairs offices here [Wash.] has grown to more than 500."

1136.   Sabato, Larry. PAC Power: Inside the World of Political Action Committees. New York: Norton, 1984. 251.
     "PACs are not the chaste and innocent political cheerleaders or selfless civic boosters that their proponents often contend they are. Neither are they cesspools of corruption and greed, modern-day versions of Tammany Hall." Ch. on their growth, organizing and fundraising, their candidates and contributions, etc.

1137.   Safire, William. "Access-Peddling Is Shaky Business." AG (February 20, 1986) 15A.
     "'Access' is today's euphemism for 'influence'. . . . access-peddling has mushroomed wildly in the second Reagan term."

1138.   "Superfund$: Chemical Producers Contribute Over $2 Million to the U.S. Congress." Washington, DC: Public Citizen, 1984. 55.
     Manufacturers' contributions and legislators' corresponding voting records.

1139.   Talbot, David, and Richard Morgan. Power and Light Political Strategies for the Solar Transition. New York: Pilgrim, 1981. 262.
     In spite of public support for solar energy, policies are determined "by a handful of people--people who head companies like Exxon, Mobil, and American Electric." Through "millions of dollars in political contributions, industry has effectively bought control over the nation's energy policy" (Foreword by George McGovern)

1140.   Theiler, Patricia. "Let's Get Ethical, Ethical." CC 9.1 (1983) 10.
     The American League of Lobbyists' new code of ethics, which committed the members to defend the public interest, barely passed at its annual conference and only after the motion included the phrase, "with opportunity to amend."

1141.   Theiler, Patricia.   "Wheelers and Dealers."   CC 7.5
          (1981) 15-21.
Car dealers lobby in Washington to ward off pending
regulation of used-car sales.

1142.   Theiler, Patricia.   "The Twelve Months of CHRISTMAS."
          CC 9.6 (1983) 30-31.
Corporate gift giving to possibly helpful congressmen.

1143.   The Washington Lobby. 3rd ed. Washington, DC:
          CQ, 1979. 225.
Following an Introduction on aspects of lobbying,
individual chs. treat "The Presidential Lobby," "The Politics
of Lobbying" (law, PACs, etc.), "Business and Labor Lobby," "The
Foreign Interest Lobby," "Public Interest Lobbying," and
"Lobbies at Work." Bibliog. 215-217.

1144.   Weinberg, Steve.   "The Press' Last Uncovered Story."
          WJR 3.4 (1981) 45-6.
On the power of lobbyists in Washington and the importance
of press scrutiny of their behavior. The author suggests ways
to investigate them.

1145.   Weiss, Kenneth.   "PAC Journalism: Cash, Candidates
          and Conflict of Interest." WJR 6 (1984) 49-53.
Expresses concern about the damage to press objectivity as
the result of involvement of media companies in political action
committees.

1146.   Wertheimer, Fred.   "What Mobil Didn't Tell You." CC
          10.6 (1984) 46.
Mobil Oil's defense of political action committees as
good for democracy suppresses "the fundamental difference
between spending money to express ideas publicly and giving
money to elected officials to buy access and influence."

III. C. Sponsors, Product Advertising, Consumer Culture 1147-
          1320

1147.   Adler, Richard P., et al. The Effects of Television
          Advertising on Children. Lexington, MA: Lexington,
          1980. 367.
Children pay attention to commercials and are influenced by
them. Some of the conclusions: food advertising is
significantly effective, etc.

1148.   Agnew, Jean-Christopher. "The Consuming Vision of
          Henry James." The Culture of Consumption. Ed. Richard
          Fox and T. J. Jackson Lears. New York: Pantheon, 1983.
          65-100.
James embodied and described a nascent consumer mentality
of "acquisitive cognition" in which the public seeks commodities
both as things and as symbols.

1148a.   Allen, Margaret. <u>Selling Dreams: Inside the Beauty
        Business</u>. New York: Simon and Schuster, 1981. 286.
How the cosmetics industry packages and sells the illusions
of beauty. Traces the careers of the entrepreneurs starting in
the early 1900s--Helena Rubinstein, Elizabeth Arden, Charles
Revson, Max Factor, et al.

1149.   Anderson, Kent, ed. <u>Television Fraud: The History and
        Implications of the Quiz Show Scandals</u>. Westport, CT:
        Greenwood, 1978. 226.
The fixed quizzes occurred chiefly because they increased
the ratings of the programs and thereby made money for
producers, the networks, and the sponsors, and because the
contestants followed materialistic American success values.

1150.   Aronson, Steven. <u>Hype</u>. New York: Morrow, 1983.
        399.
A study of celebrities and their creators, chs. on Cheryl
Tiegs, film stars, hairdressers, plastic surgeons, publicists,
Barbara Cartland, and others.

1151.   Aufderheide, Pat. "Commercialization and Its
        Discontents." <u>ITT</u> 7 (May 11-17, 1983) 8-9.
Discusses the ways public TV is becoming increasingly
dominated by corporations.

1152.   Aufderheide, Pat. "'This Program Was Not Made
        Possible. . .'" <u>ITT</u> 4 (March 5-18, 1980) 13.
"PBS has decided that labor unions, at least in one
instance, are unacceptable public TV sponsors. The instance is
a planned TV series on labor history called <u>Made in USA</u>."

1153.   Auster, Albert. "In Defense of the Working Class:
        Hollywood and Its New Labor Films, 'Blue Collar' and
        'F.I.S.T.'" <u>RHR</u> 18 (1978) 136-141.
"Hollywood's treatment of the working class and labor
unions has never been noted for its realism," and recent films
offer no improvement.

1154.   Badhwar, Inderjit. "What Do Doctors Recommend."
        <u>ChJR</u> 4.9 (1971) 9-10.
On the failure of the National Association of Broadcasters
to control lying advertisements.

1155.   Bagdikian, Ben. "Public Broadcasting: The Invisible
        Vision." <u>PTR</u> 3.6 (1975) 17-21.
The "cultural and political malnutrition" of commercial TV
("the acquisition of fashionable material goods. . . shooting,
knifing or judo chops") was "not our choice." Public television
can be alternative, but it will require "a new coalition of
people to campaign" for it. "Democracy will not survive without
an informed and thoughtful citizenry or without a rich and
diverse reservoir of public ideas and activities. Instead of
"the narrow goals of sales and profits," public TV supports "the

beleaguered human spirit."

1156.   Baker, Samm. The Permissible Lie. Cleveland: World,
         1968. 236.
    Abuses in advertising--puffery, deception (the "permissible
lie" of the title)--must be corrected by an aroused and
organized public, since the FTC is slow, understaffed, and
virtually powerless. [This extremely mild critique was
cancelled by its original publisher, Funk & Wagnalls, by the
intercession of its owner, Reader's Digest.]

1157.   Barnouw, Erik. The Sponsor: Notes on a Modern
         Potentate. New York: Oxford U P, 1978. 220.
    The communication system is "in trouble" because the
sponsor, "the merchant," has been in control (182). The first
part sketches the rise of the sponsor in radio and then
television; the second examines the impact of this power on
programming; and the final section assesses what this dominance
means and may mean for our society.

1158.   Barrett, Edward W. "TV Overview." CJR 17.5 (1979)
         20.
    Locally produced television documentaries are increasing
"in both quantity and quality," but "on networks the full-scale
documentary seems to be moving toward extinction."

1159.   Battaglia, Frank. "Federal Bread." QRD 7.3 (1981)
         3, 6.
    "Daily bread," in the US, "cannot be judged by its label."

1160.   Bedell, Sally. Up the Tube: Prime Time TV and the
         Silverman Years. New York: Viking, 1981. 313.
    "Unalloyed greed gripped executives at all three networks"
during the 1970s "as they scrambled for rating points." Fred
Silverman became "the central player" in the "battle for profits
and corporate prestige," as commercials doubled in quantity and
programs declined in quality.

1161.   Behrens, Steven, and Brooke Gladstone. "Public
         Broadcasting: The High Cost of Going Private." Ch 1
         (1982) 41-43.
    The use of advertising by PBS means increased control by
corporations, decreased diversity of thought, and attention to
Nielsen ratings rather than investigation and analysis.

1162.   Bell, Clark. "Some Doctors Terminate a Smoking
         Relationship." Pr 10.1 (1982) 5.
    The advertising firm of Ruder & Finn broke its relationship
with the American Academy of Family Physicians because the
Academy wished to attack cigarette companies by name. Ruder &
Finn also represented Philip Morris.

1163.   Bennett, James R. "American Literature and the
         Acquisitive Society, Background and Criticism: A

ography." <u>BoB</u> 30 (1973) 175-184; 37 (1980)
1-15, 53-71.
US imaginative writers have provided traditionally a
searching critique of the business ethos.

1164.   Bennett, James R. "Newspaper Reporting of U.S.
Business Crime in 1980." <u>NRJ</u> (1981) 45-52.
Twelve case studies of corporate misdeeds show papers
generally pro-business.

1165.   Bensman, David. "The Downside of the G.M. Contract."
<u>Na</u> 239 (Nov. 3, 1984) 440-442.
"<u>Business Week</u> called it 'The Right Kind of Auto Contract,'
and the rest of the media concurred." But the contract "has a
darker side, which the media largely ignored."

1166.   Blakely, Robert. <u>The People's Instrument: A
Philosophy of Programming for Public Television</u>.
Washington, DC: Public Affairs, 1971. 179.
A critique of the limitations of commercial television and
an attempt to set forth a systematic statement of basic
principles for a system that would enrich and enlighten the
lives of Americans of all ages.

1167.   Blakely, Robert. "Rethinking the Dream: A
'Copernican' View of Public Television." <u>PTR</u> 3.5
(1975) 30-39.
The purpose of the commercial media in the US is to
manipulate the public "to do what the advertisers want them to
do, to the neglect of other social purposes and at the expense
of weakening organic ties of community." In contrast, a public
system should offer a genuine alternative to profit and
consumerism by promoting "public understanding" as "the basis
for decision-making at the highest levels."

1168.   Boot, William. "Star-spangled News Package." <u>CJR</u>
25.3 (1986) 18-21.
The "Liberty Weekend" Fourth of July extravaganza
celebrating the Statue of Liberty's facelift "displayed the news
media at their worst," promoting "national narcissism" for
"profits and p.r."

1169.   Boot, William. "Time Inc.'s 'Unbiased' Satellite."
<u>CJR</u> 20.1 (1981) 43-48.
"The <u>Star</u> has joined its corporate parent in an 'American
Renewal' campaign," particularly to "show more respect for our
major corporations."

1170.   Bordewich, Fergus. "Supermarketing the Newspaper."
<u>CJR</u> 16.3 (1977) 24-30.
An analysis of the increasing attention to market rather
than news values, to excitement, the personal, and the simple.
"Editors are not talking about attracting and educating readers
with more investigative reporting, more correspondents," more

CONTROL OF INFORMATION

203

"in-depth coverage," but are cutting back on public-affairs coverage.

1171.   Bowlby, Rachel. Just Looking: Consumer Culture in Dreiser, Gissing and Zola. New York: Methuen, 1985. 160.
The novels of the three authors reflect the penetration of culture by commerce, particularly with the rise of the department store and advertising. Women were drawn into this glamorous new commercial culture and exploited by men as both consumers and commodities.

1172.   Bray, Howard. The Pillars of the Post: The Making of a News Empire in Washington. New York: Norton, 1980. 308.
An account of the mixed record of the Post as a critic of established power. E.g., it published the Pentagon Papers, but (154-7) it supported the government's seven month prior restraint violation of First Amendment rights of The Progressive magazine. [Bray seldom offers sustained analysis of such issues.]

1173.   Brennan, Timothy. "Masterpiece Theatre and the Uses of Tradition." ST 4.3 (1985) 102-112.
Masterpiece Theatre's snobbery (the popularization of classic novels) "is only an instrument of a larger, sometimes very conscious, corporate strategy," an "attempt to fuse together the apparently incompatible national myths of England and the United States, in order to strengthen imperial attitudes."

1174.   Broadcast Advertising and Children. Hearings Before the Subcommittee on Communications of the Committee on Interstate and Foreign Commerce, HR, 94th Cong. Washington, DC: GPO, 1976. 495.
The problems associated with broadcast advertising directed toward children, the amount and content of such advertising, and the regulatory functions of the FCC and FTC. Children's advocates and broadcasters presented arguments but advertisers refused to participate.

1175.   Broughton, Diane. "Thumper." NMA (1985) 4.
The "effects of eating petrochemically grown food seldom make the news."

1176.   Brown, Les. "Broadcasting's Vanishing Species." Ch 5.3 (1985) 15-16.
The increasing commercialization of public broadcasting is resulting in decreasing controversial programming.

1177.   Brown, Les. "Living in a Nielsen Republic." Ch 2.1 (1982) 20-21.
Government corporate heads "think of us today not as citizens but as consumers" demanding not rights but things and

conveniences, not as active participants in a community but "as components of an economic system."

1178.   Brown, Les. "A Question of Involvement." TQ 11.1
         (1973) 72-78.
The TV industry "is in the hands of generally good men who operate in the amoral climate of big business. Profits matter more than social responsibility." One solution would be for groups to sponsor endorsements for programs of high moral stature.

1179.   Brown, Les. Television: The Business Behind the
         Box. New York: Harcourt, 1971. 374.
"In day-to-day commerce, television is not so much interested in the business of communication as in the business of delivering people to advertisers" (15-16). In this business the networks are much alike: "They initiate each other feverishly, buy their programs from the same sources, interchange their personnel, and operate from the same city but from the same neighborhood" (4). Programming "is not a critic's schedule but a salesman's--one that will sell rapidly at the prices asked" (62).

1180.   Brenkman, John. "Mass Media: From Collective
         Experience to the Culture of Privatization." ST 1
         (Winter 1979) 95-108.
"Capital cannot speak, but it can accumulate and concentrate itself in communications media," whereby corporations dominate cultural forms and practices, breaking collective experience into the "isolation of the private experiences of individuals," and other techniques. The important role of the critic today is to resist.

1181.   Buxton, Edward. Promise Them Anything: The Inside
         Story of the Madison Avenue Power Struggle. New York:
         Stein, 1972. 302.
This book is about the nuts and bolts of the advertising business. Ch. 1 sets forth the main types of advertising malpractice--spurious demonstration, false authority, etc.

1182.   Carter, Bill. "Whatever Happened to TV
         Documentaries?" WJR 5.5 (1983) 43-46.
The networks' commitment to documentaries is shrinking because of their low Nielsen ratings.

1183.   Chaplan, Debra. "Multinationals: New Blacklisters
         of the 80s." ORK (Summer 1982) 9.
Corporate sponsorship controls program content, e.g., Kimberly-Clark's withdrawal of sponsorship of the Lou Grant TV program because the show's star, Ed Asner, raised funds for medical aid for refugees from the war in El Salvador. Kimberly-Clark is a major investor in El Salvador.

1184.   "Children's Television Education Act of 1985," H.R.

205

3216. Subcommittee on Telecommunications, Consumer Protection, and Finance of the Committee on Energy and Commerce, HR.
A bill to increase the diversity of programming for children by using the broadcast license renewal process to enforce the bill's provisions. The bill also directs the FCC to investigate programs created to promote products. The bill is in response to the FCC's abdication of regulatory responsibility in this area.

1185.   Christenson, Reo. "Report on the Reader's Digest. CJR 3.4 (1965) 30-36.
The Reader's Digest generally supports corporate values.

1186.   Comanor, William, and Thomas Wilson. Advertising and Market Power. Cambridge: Harvard UP, 1974. 257.
Those firms which advertise most heavily reap monopoly returns; that is, "heavy advertising outlays primarily permit established sellers in certain industries to put new entrants at a hopeless disadvantage and thus create market power for themselves." These dominant advertisers also provide "an inefficient supply of information to the public" (Foreword).

1187.   Conrad, Peter, ed. Television: The Medium and Its Manners. London: Routledge, 1982. 180.
"The original technological revolution was about saving time, shortcutting labor; the consumerism which is the latest installment of that revolution is about wasting time we've saved, and the intitution it deputes to serve that purpose is television." While the hero of capitalism was the saver, the hero of consumerism is the spender, and television serves to persuade us to spend. Separate chs. on talk shows, soap operas, game shows, ads, news programs, and drama.

1188.   Cook, David A. "Your Money and Your Life." CJR 18.2 (1979) 64-66.
Americans think of television as free entertainment, but the real cost, in terms of wasted time and higher prices due to advertising, is quite high.

1189.   Cornelius, Kay. "'This Won't Last Long': Famous Phrases from Your Friendly Real Estate Agent." QRD 8.1 (1981) 6.7.
Language which the real estate industry uses to promote its product.

1190.   Croft, Jack. "Du Pont's Curtain to be Opened in Court." PI (24 May 1981) 1B.
"The author of an unflattering history of the Du Pont clan is suing the Delaware chemical company and his publisher, Prentice-Hall," which "caved in to Du Pont pressure" to drastically curtail promotion and distribution of Du Pont: Behind the Nylon Curtain.

1191.   Dahlgren, Peter. "Network TV News and the Corporate
          State: The Subordinate Consciousnes of the Viewer-
          Citizen." Ph.D. diss. The Grad. Center, City of New
          York, 1977. 199. DAI 38 4426.
     "To facilitate its activities, and to separate the populace
from the centers of economic and political command, the
corporate state has developed a strategy of responses which seek
to elicit a quiescent mass loyalty," by "the deployment of
instrumental rationality. The logic of instrumental
rationality, when applied to news media output, tends to
suppress and constrict normative, reflective discourse." TV
news assumes and helps create non-reflective, subordinate,
dependent consciousness.

1192.   Dahlgren, Peter. "TV News as a Social Relation."
          MCS 3 (1981) 291-302.
     TV news "generally contributes to the hegemony of the
corporate state," not only by its content but by its program
format neither of which is neutral.

1193.   D'Ari, Paul. "The Selling of the Airwaves." ITT 4
          (June 4-17, 1980) 18-19.
     An account of the pro-corporate, free market programming at
WQLN in Erie, PA, which is increasingly funded by corporations.

1194.   Deeb, Gary. "ABC's Censors Remove 'Barney Miller'
          References to Dow, Dupont." AG (Dec. 22, 1978) 10B.
     References to corporate crime were excised from one
program of the series.

1195.   Deibel, Mary. "Mr. Zip Takes the Measure of America."
          Pr 10.4 (Aug. 1982) 14.
     A marketing company uses ZIP Codes to categorize people by
class and affluence to pinpoint TV audiences for advertisers.
The owners hope to apply their methods to politics.

1196.   Dorfman, Ariel. The Empire's Old Clothes: What the
          Lone Ranger, Babar, and Other Innocent-Heroes Do To Our
          Minds. New York: Pantheon, 1983. 223.
     The Lone Ranger, Babar, Donald Duck, Reader's Digest, and
Mampato (a Chilean children's magazine) help create a self-
censoring "subservient and passive consumer" (200) by
transforming "reality's unsettling questions into docile,
comforting, bland answers" (7).

1197.   Dreier, Peter. "Capitalists vs. the Media: An
          Analysis of an Ideological Mobilization Among Business
          Leaders." MCS 4 (1982) 111-132.
     This article explains "business's perception of the media
as hostile to corporate interests" and "why business has felt
the necessity to mobilize, and to spend large sums of money, to
defend itself and try to pull in the reins on the news media.

1198.   Eckert, Charles. "Shirley Temple and the House of

Rockefeller."   JC 2 (July-Aug. 1974) 1, 17-20.
By 1936 the controlling Morgan or Rockefeller interests
increasingly introduced formulas, propaganda, and especially
"suppression and obfuscation" into films.

1199.   Edmundson, Mark. "TV's Celebration of Itself." Ch
    5.3 (1985) 67-8.
Entertainment Tonight (ET) "draws out the tendencies of the
evening news to the point of caricature" by dividing us "from
the burdens (and the dignities) of anxiety and care, putting
itself in the place of the world."

1200.   Eisler, Benita. Class Acts: America's Last Dirty
    Secret. New York: Franklin Watts, 1983. 352.
"From commercials to family sitcoms to the 'style' of
anchorpersons, the prevailing picture on the screen is America
as a one-class society," in spite of the fact of wide
divergencies of income and mobility. Not until the 1960s did
the government tabulate the "great wealth and poverty" which is
systematically suppressed on television. Ch. 4 treats media
dissemination of corporate consumerism values.

1201.   Elliott, Philip. "Intellectuals, the 'Information
    Society' and the Disappearance of the Public Sphere."
    MCS 4 (1982) 243-253.
"What we are seing and what we face is a continuation of
the shift away from involving people in society as political
citizens of nation states towards involving them as consumption
units in a corporate world." A mass society has developed
founded on "an acceptable level of comfort, pleasure and control
in which people participate as members of the market."

1202.   "Enhanced Underwriting: Where Do We Draw the Line?"
    Current 4.19 (Nov. 5, 1985) 5-8.
A forum of six brief essays on corporate advertising for
public broadcasting.

1203.   Ewen, Stuart and Elizabeth Ewen. "Americanization and
    Consumption." Telos 37 (Fall 1978) 42-51.
An appraisal of the basic premises of the consciousness
industries that "in a corporate industrial world, it is the
agencies of communication which provide the mechanism for social
order," defined by "the retail (individualized) consumption of
goods and services; a world in which social relations are
disciplined by the exchange of money."

1204.   Ewen, Stuart. Captains of Consciousness: Advertising
    and the Social Roots of the Consumer Culture. New York:
    McGraw-Hill, 1976. 261.
In the nineteenth century industrial leaders brought about
the proletarianization of the industrial work force. They
understood the necessity of integrating religion, education,
legislation, the military, and the power "to insure the
perpetuation of bourgeois and, later, corporate power within the

industrial structure." In the twentieth century, the economic
leaders realized they must become not only captains of industry
but captains of consciousness in order to secure productive
process and to blunt anti-corporate feeling. Thus advertising
and mass consumption developed as an additional tool of social
control.

1205.   Ewen, Stuart. Channels of Desire: Mass Images and
         the Shaping of American Consciousness. New York:
         McGraw-Hill, 1982. 312.
A critique of the contradictions resulting from the
Industrial Revolution, the spread of mass-produced goods, and
the rise of the mass media, particularly the rise of mass
imagery in the US and the role these images have played in the
development of a commercial culture. For example, films
Americanized immigrants with images and ideas of clothes,
politics, sexuality, and a climate for war.

1206.   Feldman, Orna. "The Case of the Cancerous Cowboys."
         CJR 22.1 (1983) 42-44.
The British film Death in the West debunks the Western
macho image Philip Morris has created for its Marlboro cigarette
by undercutting the company's denial of conclusive evidence
linking cancer with smoking.

1207.   Fielding, Raymond. The American Newsreel, 1911-1967.
         Norman, OK: U of Oklahoma P, 1972. 392.
"The known instances of content manufacture, re-creation,
personality impersonation, and blatant fraud were so great in
number, so common in nature, and so continuous in occurrence
throughout the history of the American newsreel that its overall veracity and fidelity as a medium of public information is
rendered suspect" (310). This situation developed because the
producers of newsreels held "show business" values and profit
motives almost exclusively.

1208.   Flippo, Chet. "Gushing Over Oil in Houston." MORE
         4.1 (1974) 10-11, 14-15.
"In this company town, the two local newspapers--the Post
and the Chronicle--are so busy flacking for the oil industry
that house organs may become obsolete."

1209.   Fox, Richard Wightman and T. J. Jackson Lears, eds.
         The Culture of Consumption: Critical Essays in American
         History 1880-1980. New York: Pantheon, 1983. 236.
An effort "to discover how consumption became a cultural
ideal, a hegemonic 'way of seeing' in twentieth-century
America," as the result of "powerful individuals and
institutions who conceived, formulated, and preached that ideal
or way of seeing." The consumer culture is "not only the value-
system that underlies a society saturated by mass-produced and
mass-marketed goods, but also a new set of sanctions for the
elite control of that society. While nineteenth-century elites
ruled through ethical precepts that they encouraged people to
internalize, twentieth-century elites rule through subtler

promises of personal fulfillment. The older idiom was
individualistic and moralistic; the newer one is corporate and
therapeutic" (x, xii). The six essays range from a history of
advertising and the "therapeutic roots of the consumer culture"
to "selling the moon."

1210.   Gaventa, John. Power and Powerlessness: Quiescence
         and Rebellion in an Appalachian Valley. Urbana:
         Illinois UP, 1981. 267.
Includes study of how absentee mine owners dominated an
impoverished Appalachian valley, including control over the
media, which never questioned the policies of the coal company.

1211.   Geis, Michael. The Language of Television
         Advertising. New York: Academic, 1982. 257.
Advertisers "should be held responsible not only for what
their advertisements assert and entail but also for what they
imply," but the "National Association of Broadcasters and the
three major television networks, evidence a considerable
disregard for what advertisers say to children." The chs. on
adults (1-6) discuss comparatives, descriptive terms, use of
conversational language, etc. The chs. on children (7-9) focus
on the ability of children to cope with advertising and then on
advertisements for fruit-flavored products and for cold
breakfast cereals.

1212.   Gitlin, Todd. Inside Prime Time. New York:
         Pantheon, 1983. 369.
If "we are serious about living in a democracy, the
fundamental responsibility of the media should be to help people
better pursue their rights and obligations as citizens, not to
sell goods, or serve as an amplification system for politicians,
or shore up the prestige of the privileged, or sprinkle flakes
of celebrity and blips of disconnected fact upon the daily life
of a society otherwise dedicated to private gain" (334). Part I
is about the calculations the networks make in pursuit of the
maximum audience"; II about the "small, revolving world of
major suppliers and agents"; III "the everyday and extraordinary
ways in which network decisions about prime-time series are
affected by politics: national political trends," the "crusade
of the fundamentalist right," and the "normal political weight
of the advertisers," including analysis of Hill Street Blues
(14-15).

1213.   Gitlin, Todd. "Prime Time Ideology: The Hegemonic
         Process in Television Entertainment." SP 26 (1979) 251-
         64.
The conventions of US television entertainment support the
dominant commercial system, but the system does allow some
aspects of alternative ideology.

1214.   Goldsen, Rose. The Show and Tell Machine: How TV
         Works and Works You Over. New York: Dial, 1977. 427.
Corporate executives "make the policy decisions" required

"to fulfill obligations to stockholders" who invest for profit. The job of network, public-relations, and advertising executives is to provide the advertising and programs which will bring the greatest profit to the corporate executives and their stockholders.

1215.   Gossage, Howard. "The Fictitious Freedom of the
          Press." Ram 4.4 (1965) 31-36.
"Our press by committing the overwhelming portion of its financial well-being to the discretion of advertisers, has done its readers, itself, and even advertising, irremedial harm."

1216.   Goulart, Ron. The Assault on Childhood. Los
          Angeles: Sherbourne, 1969. 278.
An attack upon those who exploit children--"the television producers, the toymakers, the cereal manufacturers, the comic book publishers, and the army of others who make a living by selling things to youngsters." "For many of the manufacturers of mass products, the word consumer is synonymous with childlike. It is not an exaggeration. . . that many of these manufacturers would like the worst characteristics of children-- selfishness, impulsiveness, delight in the simple-minded, uncontrolled aggressiveness, and prejudice--to survive into adult life" (3), because the "only important universally shared aim of the entire kid business is to turn children into consumers" (6).

1217.   Grant, Mark. "I Got My Swimming Pool by Choosing
          Prell Over Brand X." MORE 6.11 (1976) 24-28.
"The typical testimonial commerial is designed on a kind of 'Jeopardy' principle: the advertising agency lays out a finished storyboard (script) and then back-pedals 'to find people to fit it.'"

1218.   Green, Timothy. The Universal Eye: The World of
          Television. New York: Stein, 1972. 276.
Ch. 2 "The United States: The Commercial Colossus": "Although television in the United States is unequaled anywhere in wealth and output, the Americans remain a remarkably underprivileged nation in what they are actually offered on the screen." The US "has been imprisoned in a narrow world, whose confines are defined by the advertisers rather than by the broadcaster or the viewer." American television "is chiefly in the business of selling goods" (17-18).

1219.   Gwyn, Robert J. "Education for Consumption: A
          Perspective on Commercial Broadcasting." TS 18.2
          (1970) 23-26.
The broadcast media gear their news programming toward attracting listeners to corporate advertising by avoiding controversial issues and emphasizing the pictorial and dramatic.

1220.   Hall, Bob. "The Brown-Lung Controversy." CJR 16.6
          (1978) 27-35.

The textile industry has a history of denying the existence of byssinosis, of blocking attempts to study it, and of paying few claims. Partly because a mill ower was the principal employer in a town and "a paper's largest advertiser," the disease and its ramifications have gone under-investigated and under-reported.

1221.   Hall, Ross Hume. <u>Food for Nought: The Decline in Nutrition</u>. New York: Harper, 1974. 292.
Marketing food is a gigantic system in which the object is to force an ever-increasing consumption of fabricated products. Consequently, the book is also a study of science and technology and the corporations which employ them for their "own mechanistic and economic goals." Ch. 4, "Consumerism," gives an account of the consumer movement's efforts to control big business for the public good. Ch. 11, "The Fabrication of Technologic Man," examines how two parts of the educational system--children's TV and agricultural training institutes-- "educate young people for a role conceived for them by the sociotechnologic system," when what is needed is training in "social context."

1222.   Haug, Wolfgang. <u>Critique of Commodity Aesthetics: Appearance, Sexuality, and Advertising in Capitalist Society</u>. Minneapolis: U of Minnesota P, 1986. 224.
Analysis of the ways in which human sensuality is molded and exploited by the advertising system.

1223.   Havig, Alan. "Frederic Wakeman's <u>The Hucksters</u> and the Postwar Debate Over Commercial Radio." <u>JB</u> 28 (1984) 187-99.
Wakeman's book and the film made from it briefly stirred some controversy about the commercialization of radio, the domination of the sponsor, and the subservience of the networks.

1224.   Hennessee, Judith. "Can Television Save Detroit?" <u>Ch</u> 1.1 (1981) 76-80.
"For thirty years commercials sold cars on their size and power. In a desperate shift of gears, big advertising dollars now go to make Americans think small."

1225.   Hess, John. "The Taking of PBS 1-2-3." <u>Ch</u> 1 (April/ May 1981) 62-67.
An expose' of Robert Chitester's campaign "to use public television [WQLN-TV, Erie, Pa.] as a vehicle for flat-out ultraconservative propaganda," to sell the free-market system and attack socialism. "The weakness built into the public television system--detected by Chitester and the keystone of his success--is its great dependency" on corporate donors.

1226.   Holder, Dennis. "Mixing Public Radio With Private Enterprise." <u>WJR</u> 6.5 (1984) 43-47.
Minnesota Public Radio, the country's largest regional public radio network, depends upon "a host of entrepreneurial

enterprises" and "massive support" from corporations.

1227.   Horowitz, Andrew. "Playing Monopoly with the News."
         MORE 5 (1975) 16-17, 23.
    Independent film makers find little acceptance from the
networks.

1228.   Horowitz, Daniel. The Morality of Spending:
         Attitudes Toward the Consumer Society in America,
         1875-1940. Baltimore: Johns Hopkins UP, 1985. 254.
    Intellectuals have warned generally that the growing
consumption of material goods endangered the moral fiber of
society. Nineteenth-century writers emphasized the
possible increase of profligacy among workers. Twentieth-
century writers feared the middle class would turn into a nation
of passive conformists.

1229.   Howard, John, and James Hulbert. Advertising and the
         Public Interest: A Staff Report to the Federal Trade
         Commission. New York: 1973. (Pagination by sections).
    "The exercise of theoretical sovereignty by the consumer is
limited," because "the seller has a strong informational
advantage." The report suggests ways the consumers' power might
be strengthened within the free enterprise system.

1230.   Johnson, Flora. "Stampede on Page One." CJR 18.5
         (1980) 8,12.
    The 1979 front page exposes of Ford Motor Co. culpability
for Pinto fires in the Chicago Sun Times and Tribune were two
years too late. Mother Jones published Mark Dowie's expose' in
1977.

1231.   Johnson, Nicholas. "The Corporate Censor." Language
         Awareness. Ed. Paul Eschholz, et al. New York: St.
         Martin's, 1974. 173-182.
    Large corporations in the pursuit of profits withhold
important information from the public.

1232.   Johnson, Nicholas. Test Pattern for Living. New
         York: Bantam, 1972. 154.
    About the "pressures in our lives generated by Big Business,
Big Broadcasting, and Big Government." Ch. 1 deals with "the
corporate state whose cancerous growth [television, Ch. 2]
fertilizes." "Of all the corporate influences of our lives, the
corporate control of television is perhaps our nation's greatest
tragedy" (i.e., the aggrandizement of corporate values of greed,
consuming, and obedience). Over half the book presents
alternatives to the corporate control of life in the US:
personal simplification, decrease in consumption, equal tax
laws, etc.

1233.   Kaufman, Joel, et al. Over the Counter Pills That
         Don't Work. New York: Pantheon, 1983. 302.
    Hundreds of products for treating multiple symptoms and

containing expensive multiple ingredients "are rarely all safe
and effective" (ix). This situation is the result of
"successful and expensive advertising" and lax enforcement of
the laws by the FDA.

1234.   Kopkind, Andrew. "The Unwritten Watergate Story."
     MORE 4.11 (1974) 5-6,26.
     The media focus on the stars of Watergate "while virtually
ignoring the corporate villains," the "corporate corrupters of
the political and bureaucratic corruptees."

1235.   Koughan, Martin. "The Fall and Rise of Public
     Television." Ch 3 (1983) 23-24, 26-29, 40.
     Corporate advertising is questioned as a funding
alternative because of the types of programs corporations "will
not support."

1236.   Langer, John. "Television's 'Personality System.'"
     MCS 3 (1981) 351-365.
     "The locus and structure of action in the world is
significantly shifted out of the public domain and into the
region of the private" (363). The personality system "operates
to mask the gap between the powerful and the powerless, ensuring
that the real unities of power, class, prestige, and interest
can continue relatively intact and unexamined" (364).

1237.   Lasch, Christopher. Haven in a Heartless World:
     The Family Beseiged. New York: Basic, 1977. 230.
     A commentary on the ways in which academic and clinical
social theorists have reinforced the institutional structures of
corporate capitalism and have helped render the family
vulnerable to the full power of hucksterism and market
manipulation.

1238.   Lasch, Christopher. The Minimal Self: Psychic
     Survival in Troubled Times. New York: Norton, 1984.
     317.
     A critique of the consequences of division of labor
(meaningless work) and its cure (consumption, advertising, and
public relations). Lasch calls for political protest,
meaningful work, a sane treatment of the environment, and a
holistic self to produce a radical democracy.

1239.   Lears, T.J. Jackson. "From Salvation to Self-
     Realization: Advertising and the Therapeutic Roots of
     the Consumer Culture, 1880-1930." The Culture of
     Consumption. Ed. Richard Fox and T.J. Jackson Lears.
     New York: Pantheon, 1983. 1-38.
     An ethos of fragmentation and unreality produced by the
corrosive impact of the market, technology, and secularization,
promoted the spread of advertising as a therapeutic agency of
self-realization. But the "real life" projected by advertising
was always just out of reach of the consumer.

1240.   Leiss, William.   The Limits to Satisfaction: An
         Essay on the Problem of Needs and Commodities.   Buffalo,
         NY: U of Toronto P, 1976.   159.
         The advertising and mass-consumption apparatus does not
simply shape needs but confuses needs.   "Consumerism" has "now
reached the point where state power is largely legitimated by
its ability to increase the number of commodities: this has
created a unique social culture in which marketing is the main
social bond.   Values no longer shape and condition needs, wants,
drives, or preferences."

1241.   Levenstein, Alan.   "Can This 48 1/2-inch Kid Make You
         Eat Cake for Breakfast?"   MORE 6.9 (1976) 22-28.
         On how ITT-Continental uses children to sell non-nutritious
food identical to competing brands.

1242.   MacDougall, Allan Kent.   Ninety Seconds to Tell It
         All: Big Business and the News Media.   Homewood, IL:
         Dow Jones, 1981.   154.
         "Not only do editorial writers generally endorse business
positions, but newspapers publish a considerable amount of fluff
supplied by businesses to promote food, fashions, travel, real
estate, sports, and stocks.   And many smaller papers and TV and
radio stations use, often without attribution to the source,
business-supplied canned editorials, columns, and features that
grind industry's ax and polish its image" (p. 10).   Furthermore,
business security and secretiveness make it difficult to uncover
corporate crimes, while the complexity of the issues and the
threat of libel suit turn most business reporters to easily
covered stories "that reflect favorably or neutrally on
business" (12-13).

1243.   Madsen, Axel.   60 Minutes: The Power and the
         Politics of America's Most Popular TV Show.   New York:
         Dodd, 1984.   255.
         The purpose of 60 Minutes is to raise ratings and make
enormous profits.   Unlike classical muckrakers, it does not seek
to change the system, but rather typically exposes peanut vices.
Thus the implicit purpose of its random, disconnected approach
to mainly petty crime, interlaced with celebrity profiles and
inconsequential travelogues, is to leave things as they are,
just as the sponsors wish.

1244.   Mander, Jerry.   Four Arguments for the Elimination
         of Television.   New York: Morrow, 1978.   371.
         "Television technology is inherently antidemocratic.
Because of its cost, the limited kind of information it can
disseminate, the way it transforms the people who use it, and
the fact that a few speak while millions absorb, television is
suitable for use only by the most powerful corporate interests
in the country.   They inevitably use it to redesign human minds
into a channeled, artificial, commercial form, that nicely fits
the artificial environment.   Television freewayizes,
suburbanizes and commoditizes human beings, who are then easier

to control. Meanwhile, those who control television consolidate their power. Television aids the creation of societal conditions which produce autocracy; it also creates the appropriate mental patterns for it and simultaneously dulls all awareness that this is happening."

1245.   Mankiewicz, Frank, and Joel Swerdlow. Remote
         Control: TV and the Manipulation of American Life.
         New York: Times, 1978. 308.
    At the time of this study, 97% of all American households had at least one television set, the nightly audience was around 60 million. "The purpose of nearly every television program, including a disturbing percentage of those presented on the so-called public broadcasting channels, is to deliver the maximum possible audience for advertisements. These advertisements accomplish more than just the sale of deodorants, cars, and floor waxes; they sell a set of values." The people "who control the Age of Television are animated by little more than a simple search for profits" (12).

1246.   Mankin, Eric. "Mobil and the Masterclass." ITT 8
         (Feb. 22-28, 1984) 20.
    It is no coincidence that Mobil Oil supports Masterpiece Theater, which provides series about the picturesque past, people with money and position, and traditional British institutions.

1247.   Margolius, Sidney. The Innocent Consumer vs. The
         Exploiters. New York: Trident, 1967. 240.
    A compendium of business deceptions and businessmen who consider the consumer as little more than a consuming machine to be exploited to the maximum.

1248.   Marquis, Donald, and Thomas Allen. "Communication
         Patterns in Applied Technology." AP 21 (1966) 1052-
         1062.
    Because the professional journals are virtually incomprehensible to the average technologist, they turn to heavily advertised commercial magazines. "The net result is that the most widely used formal written channels of communication are no longer under the control of the professionals who use them. Control has passed to a group of businessmen (publishers and advertisers) who exercise power over the journal's contents" (1057).

1249.   Massing, Michael. "The Missouri Compromise." CJR
         20.4 (1981) 35-41.
    "To survive," the once-pugnacious Post-Dispatch is pulling its punches to avoid boycotts by business.

1250.   Medsger, Betty. "Asbestos: The California Story."
         CJR 16.3 (1977) 41-50.
    An indictment of the major newspapers in California for failing to do original research and writing on the effects of

asbestos. "At worst, the major papers have failed to report that asbestos is a serious problem today among California workers" and that "hundreds of lawsuits have been filed" by workers who were "lied to by company doctors."

1251.   Melody, William. Children's Television: The Economics of Exploitation. New Haven: Yale UP, 1973. 164.
"As a special television audience," children "need protection from pinpoint advertiser exploitation. In addition, they may require special programming directed to their needs and interests. Under the existing institutional arrangements for the supply of commercial children's television, the presently operative economic forces in the industry will tend to make today's problems in commercial children's television worse" (139).

1252.   Mintz, Morton. By Prescription Only: A Report on the Roles of the United States Food and Drug Administration, the American Medical Association, Pharmaceutical Manufacturers, and Others in Connection with the Irrational and Massive Use of Prescription Drugs that May Be Worthless, Injurious or Even Lethal. 2nd ed., rev. Boston: Houghton, 1967. 446. (Rev. The Therapeutic Nightmare, Houghton, 1964).
Describes among other matters the dangerous involvement of news media in the uncontrolled publicity about unproved drugs. One ch. describes the sensational cover-story of a new "wonder" cancer cure which turned out to be without substance.

1253.   Morris, Julie. "Auto Ads Billed as 'Public Service.'" ChJr 3.5 (1970) 10-11.
A nationwide campaign of free broadcast and print media ads urged people to buy a new car. In contrast, Detroit public service organizations rarely enjoy free advertising.

1254.   Navasky, Victor. "Substantiating the 'Permissible Lie.'" MORE 2.12 (1972) 5-7.
On an FTC staff report on deceptive advertising and an appeal to journalists to spend more time evaluating false ads.

1255.   Nelson, Jill. "N-E-S-T-L-E-S Makes the Very Best?" SD 2.7 (1978) 28.
"Multinational Corporations' infant formula exports to the Third World prove deadly," contrary to advertisements.

1256.   Nelson, Madeline. "Money Makes the Press Go 'Round." MORE 4.3 (1974) 1,10-11,14-17.
"Few cows are as sacred as David Rockefeller and his Chase Manhattan Bank." The press "fawns over the man and his money," and "hard questions are almost never asked." A survey of The New York Times, The Wall Street Journal, Business Week, Newsweek, and Time in 1973.

217

1257.   Nicholas, Jeff. "Nuclear Friction." <u>Pr</u> 8 (Jan. 1978) 8-9.
An account of PBS rejection of Don Widener's film <u>Plutonium, Element of Risk</u>, because of pressure from corporate sponsors.

1258.   Noah, Timothy. "Upscale, Downscale." <u>NR</u> 185.8&9 (1981) 12-14.
The public broadcasting system's increasing dependence upon corporations betrays its noncommercial mandate.

1259.   O'Connor, John. "Grunts and Groans." <u>CJR</u> 21.1 (1982) 62-63.
Review of Teague's <u>Live and Off-Color: News Biz</u>, which decries "triviality, banality, and gimmickry." Teague would remove newscasts from the traditional ratings system in order to distance them from sponsor control, but the reviewer considers this remedy hopeless, given the profits involved in ratings for advertising.

1260.   Ohanian, Susan. "On Labels." <u>QRD</u> 8.1 (1981) 10.
Critical of product packaging.

1261.   O'Reilly, William. "The King of Endorsement." <u>MORE</u> 6.9 (1976) 52-3.
Endorsements of <u>House Beautiful</u> by famous people are a "sham."

1262.   Owen, David. "The Cigarette Companies: How They Get Away With Murder." <u>WM</u> 17 (1985) 48-54.
<u>The New Republic</u> commissioned this article but killed it in fear of tobacco company reprisals. The author indicts the tobacco companies for advertising a lethal product, and criticizes media for self-censorship because of fear of the tobacco industry (an absence of articles on the hazards of smoking in supposedly health-conscious magazines such as <u>Ms.</u> and <u>Mademoiselle</u>, <u>Time's</u> deletion of information about the dangers of smoking in a section on a healthier life, etc.).

1263.   Panitt, Merrill. "A New Vehicle for Television." <u>TQ</u> 1.3 (1962) 55-60.
Networks should sell advertising time as a unit and assign the time to specific programs as needed, thereby stopping corporate control of programming.

1264.   "PBS Bites Corporate Bait." <u>MJ</u> 5 (August 1980) 9.
Mainly about WQLN in Erie, Pa. and its increasing pro-corporate alliances.

1265.   "PBS Turns Down Unions." <u>MJ</u> 5 (May 1980) 10.
The president of PBS rejected money from labor unions in support of a program, yet accepted (and accepts) money from corporations for programs.

1266.   Perl, Peter. "Asbestos: The Connecticut Story."
    CJR 16.3 (1977) 50-54.
"Considering the seriousness of the diseases and the
number of workers and families involved, the asbestos story at
E. B. [Electric Boat submarine shipyard] was generally
underlayed by four daily newspapers that covered 'the Boat
Beat.'"

1267.   Phelan, John. Mediaworld: Programming the Public.
    New York: Seabury, 1977. 169.
Both public issues and celebrities are "functionally
identical instances of the star system, and "the star system is
a corollary to capital-intensive production for mass markets."
The author sees popular culture "as a centrally manufactured and
globally distributed substitute for local community and as a
subversion of tradition." The book offers a "systematic context
for understanding the cultural and cognitive counter-ecology
that increasingly permeates our mental and moral environment"
(Preface).

1268.   "The Pinto Story: The Press in Low Gear." CJR 17.1
    (1978) 24-25.
The British press offered a better account of Ford's
negligence in producing the Pinto than did most American news
sources.

1269.   Pollan, Michael. "The Season of the Reagan Rich."
    Ch 2.4 (1982) 14-15, 86.
Prime time television's portrayal of society's wealthy
projects the imagery of Reaganism--the self-made man, etc.

1270.   Pollock, Francis. "The Common Cents Approach to
    Consumer Reporting." CJR 16.3 (1977) 37-38.
The new newspaper supplement Common Cents labels itself as
"consumer reporting" but its articles will offend no advertiser.
"Increasingly, newspapers seem to be turning to editorial matter
prepared and-or placed solely by the advertising department."

1271.   Pollock, Richard. "Atom Firms Block TV Program:
    Show on Radiation Perils Blacked Out by Industry
    Pressure." CMJ 4.12 (1979) 7.
Nuclear industries pressured several PBS member stations to
refuse to broadcast "Paul Jacobs and the Nuclear Gang." The
documentary depicts the effects of radiation exposure on nuclear
plant workers.

1272.   Pollock, Richard. "Is the Nuclear Industry Silencing
    the Press?" CMJ 3.4 (1977) 1,8.
The Atomic Industry Forum's "Infowire" pressures networks
and news agencies to suppress news and documentaries which
portray nuclear power negatively.

1273.   Pollock, Richard. "The Nuclear Industry...Silencing
    the Media." CMJ 3.10 (1978) 3,10.

The nuclear industry has banded together to convince the media to cease production and airing of critical programs.

1274.   Pool, Gail, and Michael Comendul. "The Computer
         Magazines' Puffery Problem." CJR 24.3 (1985) 49-51.
   "If companies seek to use magazines for their own marketing plans, magazines, often with an eye on future ads, frequently appear to cooperate."

1275.   Powers, Ron. The Newscasters: The News Business as
         Show Business. New York: St. Martin's, 1977. 243.
   Misguided commercialism is turning local and national broadcast news into entertainment.

1276.   Preston, Ivan. The Great American Blow-Up: Puffery
         in Advertising and Selling. Madison: U of Wisconsin P,
         1975. 422.
   Makes a case for government regulation not only of hard-core but of soft-core deception, that is, of claims which are not literally true and/or are not subject to proof, because not only is it unfair to consumers but like Watergate it undermines confidence in our institutions.

1277.   Rank, Hugh. The Pitch. Park Forest, IL: Counter-
         Propaganda P, 1982. 207.
   A grammar of advertising as a structure of "attention-getting," confidence-building," "desire-stimulating," "urgency-stressing," and "response-seeking." Contains a taxonomy of the merits claimed for products and a forty-page "Reference Guide" itemizing the kinds of intensification and downplaying in ads for thirty-nine genres of products and services.

1278.   Raymond, Chris. "Whose Health and Welfare?" SciP
         16.2 (1984) 24-29.
   "The mass media image of occupational hazards denies the structural reasons which make it both necessary and profitable for industry to ignore health safety."

1279.   Roe, Yale. The Television Dilemma: Search for a
         Solution. New York: Hastings, 1962. 184.
   A network sales executive appeals for greater responsibility on the part of sponsors, broadcasters, government, and public. Among other recommendations, he calls on the networks to present hour-long cultural programs one evening a week.

1280.   Roman, James. "The Underwritten Rule of Public TV."
         QRD 8.2 (1982) 7-8.
   "Most of the programming presented by corporations can be defined as 'cultural,' [and] culture has also become synonymous with safe programming."

1281.   Roshco, Bernard. "No Business Like News Business."
         CJR 7.4 (1968-69) 27-28.

News departments stress "the entertainment values of show business and the socioeconomic values of big business." News judgments are "indirectly but fundamentally shaped not in the newsroom but in the boardroom, which is dominated by the social and economic values to be expected in a corporate enterprise."

1282.   Rowland, Willard, Jr. "Public Involvement: The
      Anatomy of a Myth." PTR 3.3 (1975) 6-22.
"In place of real 'public involvement,' we have domination of public broadcasting at all levels by a handful of the wealthy and well-connected."

1283.   Rubin, David. "Surprise! TV Guide Is No Longer a
      Toothless Wonder." MORE 6.10 (1976) 32-6.
The magazine "ducks serious and lengthy reviews of television's major programming efforts" and is "conservative, favoring a privately owned system of commercial broadcasting."

1284.   Sahin, H. and J. P. Robinsin. "Beyond the Realm of
      Necessity: Television and the Colonization of Leisure."
      MCS 3 (1980) 85-95.
The "colonization of free time by television in the United States can be seen as another manifestation of the historical process in which free time has been turned into a commodity and re-expropriated by the forces in control of the realm of necessity," i.e., by corporations.

1285.   Sampson, Anthony. The Sovereign State of ITT.d
      Greenwich, CT: Fawcett, 1974. 335.
"Throughout its five decades," ITT "has remained irresponsible and uncontrollable" (65). "The nation is the only institution strong enough to stand up to the multinationals, and to instill comparable loyalties." The "recent history of ITT shows very clearly, I believe, that they cannot be allowed to be the custodians" (311-12). The author reveals ITT's manipulations of governments, political parties, and media on an international scale.

1286.   Schwichtenberg, Cathy. "The Love Boat: the
      Packaging and Selling of Love, Heterosexual Romance, and
      Family." MCS 6 (1984) 301-311.
The essay examines the ideology of love "transformed into a commodity as the central motivation for the 'love boat' cruise" (303). "Within the commodity-structure of capitalism, money floats out and what floats back is a packaged experience that reaffirms the correctness of existing social institutions." "The Love Boat is representative of commercial television par excellence" (310).

1287.   Schrag, Peter. "The Powers That Be." MORE 6.1 (1976)
      26,28.
Since he produced a critical documentary on nuclear power, Powers That Be, Don Widener has not been employed by network television. He won a $7.75 million libel suit against Pacific

221

Gas & Electric Co., which was assisted by KNBC, the NBC-owned outlet in Los Angeles.

1288.   Schrank, Jeffrey. Snap, Crackle, and Popular Taste: The Illusion of Free Choice in America. New York: Dell, 1977. 192.
"Freedom exists only in the presence of choices, but it does not follow that the presence of choices creates freedom. Some choices contribute only to the illusion of freedom . . . . Pseudo-choice is a selection guided by invisible limitations and structures. It is the invisibility of the decision-shaping factors that contributes to pseudo-choice." Chs. on television, food, autos, advertising, etc.

1289.   Schudson, Michael. Advertising, The Uneasy Persuasion: Its Dubious Impact on American Society. New York: Basic, 1984. 288.
A study not of advertisements but of advertising--the marketing of commodities, the manufacture of commercials, the system of symbols--and its role in shaping US values and life patterns. The author omits industrial product, corporate image, and political advertising to focus upon the process of national consumer goods advertising. Chs. 1-3 examine the agency/symbol makers, their business clients, and the consumers; chs. 4-6 examine the basic sources of the consumer culture in addition to advertising; and chs. 7-8 look at advertising as a system of symbols.

1290.   Selig, Michael. "Conflict and Contradiction in the Mass Media." JC 30 (March 1985) 19-20.
A potentially significant film about nuclear power was diluted by conventional narrative appeals and by "ignoring the problem's ongoing existence in an advanced industrial social order."

1291.   Seltzer, Curtis. "The Pits: Press Coverage of the Coal Strike." CJR 20.2 (1981) 67-70.
Press predictions of no strike reveal how closely journalists had become aligned with the companies and union leadership and how ignorant of and prejudiced against the rank-and-file perspective.

1292.   Shayon, Robert L. The Crowd-Catchers: Introducing Television. New York: Saturday Review, 1973. 175.
"It is incontrovertible that television is used overwhelmingly for advertiser-supported escapist entertainment, and only minimally, as an exercise in tokenism, for the informing of the electorate" (109). Ch. 4, "Citizen Forum or Circus--Does TV Serve the Public Interest?"

1293.   Sibbison, Jim. "Pushing New Drugs--Can the Press Kick the Habit?" CJR 24.2 (1985) 52-54.
Pharmaceutical companies manipulate both the media and the government regulatory agencies through product evaluations and

press releases.

1294.   Siepmann, Charles. <u>Radio's Second Chance</u>. Boston: Little, 1946. 282.
Denounces the many ways radio programmers had failed the public interest by their passion for profits.

1295.   Silverman, Milton and Philip Lee. <u>Pills, Profits, and Politics</u>. Berkeley: U of California P, 1974. 403.
Includes analysis of the methods used by the pharmaceutical industry to generate favorable news and public relations such as industry sponsorship of conferences which are attended by journalists and science writers as much or more than by physicians or research scientists. "Too often, the drugs are misrepresented, misprescribed and misused," and "much of the blame must be placed on the multibillion-dollar-a-year prescription drug industry and its incredibly effective promotional campaigns." Ch. 3, "Drug Promotion: 'The Truth, the Whole Truth, and Nothing but the Truth.'"

1296.   Silverstein, Brett. <u>Fed Up! The Food Forces That Make You Fat, Sick, and Poor</u>. Boston: South End, 1984. 200.
TV commercials and food industry fronts lie to the public. The book presents ways to resist and eat healthily.

1297.   Simon, Roger. "What's Red, White and Blue--and Makes Madison Avenue See Green?" <u>TVG</u> (July 13, 1985) 36-7.
More and more advertisers feel that patriotic themes will sell their products.

1298.   Sklar, Robert. <u>Prime Time America: Life On and Behind the Television Screen</u>. New York: Oxford UP, 1980. 200.
A negative analysis of sitcoms with many examples of their basic principle of playing it safe under the control of the networks which have their eye always on the ratings.

1299.   Skornia, Harry. "Has Public Broadcasting Lost Its Nerve?" <u>PTR</u> 2 (October 1974) 34-38.
An indictment of PBS for evading controversial issues and a discussion of "some of the national problem areas" that "public broadcasting must attack."

1300.   Skornia, Harry. <u>Television and the News</u>. Palo Alto, CA: Pacific, 1968. 232.
Cites numerous examples of interference by sponsors in the content of broadcasting and TV policy as a whole, the considerable constraint upon the coverage of poverty, racial unrest, anti-war movements, etc. "Business applied to programs and information the same practices it applied. . . to goods." Is it "any wonder, then, that industry should find it reasonable to hold off the market <u>facts</u> or <u>ideas</u> also, which might similarly jeopardize their profit or monopoly position?" (71).

1301.   Skornia, Harry. Television and Society: An Inquest
          and Agenda for Improvement. New York: McGraw, 1965.
          268.
     The present broadcast system "is neither accidental nor
natural." It is what it is now "because this form of
broadcasting is most profitable to those who control it, not
because it serves the public interest better than, or even as
well as, any of a number of alternatives might" (10). Ch. 2
deals with "The Business Corporation as a Controller in
Broadcasting": "The favorable position of the United States
corporation in the minds of most citizens has been achieved as a
result of industry's control of the electronic mass media" (30).
Ch. 5 treats "The Hidden Economics of Broadcasting": it is not
free but is paid for by the public. The final ch. offers an
"agenda for change."

1302.   Skornia, Harry. "TV Debases Everything It Touches
          . . . and TV Touches Everything." ChJR 7.12 (1974)
          16-27.
     "TV has produced the gospel of Consumerism, fanned the
flames of the revolution of rising expectations, dulled our
senses with repetition, turned a nation of viewers into zombies
who expect to be entertained in everything, who see force and
violence exalted over reason as the means of resolving conflict,
whose capacity to believe and trust has been impaired by
disingenuous commerciality." "Money, power, and products are
everything."

1303.   Smith, Eleanor. "If At First You Don't Succeed. . .
          Play Dirty." NMA 8 (1978) 4-5, 10.
     Focuses upon the opposition of the nuclear industry to
films made for PBS by Don Widener, an Emmy Award-winning
California filmmaker.

1304.   Smith, R. C. "The Magazine's Smoking Habit." CJR
          16.5 (1978) 29-31.
     Magazines "that have accepted growing amounts of cigarette
advertising have failed to cover tobacco's threat to health."

1305.   Sussmann, Leila A. "Labor in the Radio News." Mass
          Media and Mass Man. Ed. Alan Casty. New York: Holt,
          1968. 241-242.
     The image of labor over the radio "is sometimes strong,
sometimes weak, but what it does is nearly always morally wrong:
no one approves of labor except the labor leaders themselves."

1306.   Tate, Cassandra. "Letter From 'The Atomic Capital of
          the Nation.'" CJR 21.1 (1982) 31-35.
     The Tri-City Herald of Richland, Washington, near a nuclear
power plant, pulls for nuclear power like a newsletter of the
chamber of commerce.

1307.   "Toothpaste Wars." QRD 8.2 (1982) 8.
     Huge amounts of advertising dollars are spent "to promote

products that are essentially the same."

1308.   Torre, Marie. "Labor Looks at Television--and Vice
          Versa." TQ 21 (1984) 25-31.
     On the AFL-CIO's efforts to present labor's side in a
television dominated by corporations and by anti-labor content
and images.

1309.   Truse, Kenneth. "The Children Are Dying--But, First,
          Here's a Commercial." TQ 11.1 (1973) 53-57.
     Serious documentaries about agonizing problems are vitiated
by trivial commercials. Commercial television "insists on
fragmenting relationships and destroying concentration."

1310.   Tuchman, Gaye. "Assembling a Network Talk-Show."
          The TV Establishment. Ed. Gaye Tuchman. Englewood
          Cliffs, NJ: Prentice, 1974. 119-135.
     A study of the television talk-show as the culture
industry's "gatekeeper whose cooptation facilitates the economic
success of a cultural product, such as a new movie."

1311.   Tuchman, Gaye, ed. The TV Establishment: Programming
          for Power and Profit. Englewood Cliffs, NJ: Prentice,
          1974. 186.
     Ten essays and a lengthy Introduction by the editor focus
on the ways the networks use their enormous power to interpret
reality, to disseminate the values of the establishment, and to
tailor programs as "lead-ins" to the commercials. Television is
increasingly mainly a propaganda agency for consumerism, the
status quo, and vested political and economic interests
(Introduction).

1312.   Turner, Richard. "Changes Made in Toxic-leak Film
          by ABC." TVG (February 22, 1986) A-2.
     "ABC censors demanded two total rewrites and a host of
other changes" in "Acceptable Risks" about a Bhopal-like toxic
chemical leak, because the film "portrayed the chemical company
as negligent" and ABC wanted to "'spread the blame around.'"

1313.   Valdez, Armando. "The Economic Context of U.S.
          Children's Television: Parameters of Reform?"
          Communication and Social Structure: Critical Studies
          in Mass Media Research. Ed. Emile McAnany, et al. New
          York: Praeger, 1981. 145-180.
     The author rejects the "deep-rooted, capitalist orientation
among communication scholars in the United States" which results
in studies of "content and audience effects" based upon "the
caveat emptor attitude characteristic of our capitalist
marketplace." He focuses upon the "economic infrastructure of
children's television programming."

1314.   Voran, Marilyn. Add Justice to Your Shopping List:
          A Guide for Reshaping Food Buying Habits. Scottdale, PA:
          Herald, 1986. 64.

Analysis of the ways supermarket chains, food processors, and multinationals attempt to manipulate consumers and make it difficult to shop for economy, nutrition, and justice. The author also explains how to work for change in the production, distribution, and marketing of food.

1315.   Weisman, John. "How Creeping Commercialism Is
         Sneaking Up on Public TV." TVG (June 27, 1981) 42-46.
      Corporate sponsors are pressing for more control--and besieged PTV might have to give in.

1316.   Weiss, Ann. The School on Madison Avenue:
         Advertising and What It Teaches. New York: Dutton,
         1980. 131.
      "The needs of business come first. And their primary need, in the opinion of businesses and advertising people, is unceasing growth. Unceasing growth means making more money year after year after year. And that is possible only if people buy more goods every year. That's why advertising is vital to American business."

1317.   Weiss, Philip. "Muzzled in Minneapolis." CJR 23.1
         (1984) 10,12.
      A sports columnist was reassigned because of his criticism of the sports establishment and lack of boosterism.

1318.   Welles, Chris. "Business Journalism's Glittering
         Prizes." CJR 17.6 (1979) 43-45.
      Some of the awards sponsored by corporations or business associations are objective and professional, but others are designed to support business and capitalism.

1319.   Whelan, Elizabeth, et al. "Analysis of Coverage of
         Tobacco Hazards in Women's Magazines." JPHP 2.1 (1981)
         28-35.
      On the weak reporting of the connection between tobacco and cancer in women's magazines which accept tobacco ads.

1320.   Wilson, Christopher P. "The Rhetoric of Consumption:
         Mass-Market Magazines and the Demise of the Gentle Reader,
         1880-1920." The Culture of Consumption. Ed. Richard
         Fox and T.J. Jackson Lears. New York: Pantheon, 1983.
         39-64.
      Along with advertising and therapy, new magazines emerged around the turn of the century to provide the sense of intense "real life" an increasing number of the public sought. The result of these mass circulation magazines was the subversion of the autonomy of their readers, e.g., the transformation of the ideal of self-made manhood into salaried employment and the generation of needs only the magazines and their advertisers could fill.

III. D. Public Relations, Image and Advocacy Advertising
          1321-1418

1321.   "Alert."   Safe Energy Communication Council pamphlet,
         1984.
The pamphlet exposes the annual $25 million national PR
campaign by the corporate-sponsored Committee for Energy
Awareness (CEA) and the $10 million campaign by Edison Electric
Institute (EEI) to generate popular support for nuclear power.

1322.   Ambrosio, Angela. "It's in the Journal. But This Is
         Reporting?" CJR 18.6 (1980) 34-35.
The Wall Street Journal often puts its byline above
corporate press releases.

1323.   Asher, Thomas. "Smoking Out Smokey the Bear." MORE
         2.3 (1972) 12-13.
The Advertising Council's "public service ads are, for the
most part, carefully structured to protect the image and
interests of the nation's industrial and governmental power
brokers."

1324.   Astor, Gerald. "The Gospel According to Mobil." MORE
         6.4 (1976) 12-15.
Mobil Oil is attempting to influence the energy debate for
its own interests, as in its "collision" with New York's WNBC-
TV.

1325.   Aufderheide, Pat. "Free Speech for Broadcasters
         Only." Na 239 (Sept. 1, 1984) 140-42.
Senator Robert Packwood's efforts to end government
regulation of broadcasters (the fairness doctrine, regular
license renewal) is welcomed and funded by media conglomerates.
The removal of the fairness doctrine will mean free speech for
media monopolies, not diversity and balance for the public.

1326.   Beck, Joan. "Outlook Shifts in Cigarette Lawsuits."
         AG (Sept. 5, 1985) 15A.
Tobacco companies are spending millions of dollars on
advertising aimed at creating doubts about the scientific
evidence linking cigarettes with disease.

1327.   Bennett, James R. "An Analysis of Corporate Ideology
         Advertising." JACR 7 (1979) 23-29.
Offers "a method of examining the arguments and the
language of ideology ads as one defense against the growing
monopoly of access and advocacy by corporations" and applies the
method to an ad by the Chromalloy American Corporation published
in The Atlantic Monthly.

1328.   Bennett, James R. "Corporate Sponsored Image Films:
         Are They Better Than Ever?" JBE 2.1 (1983) 35-41.
The vast number of high quality corporate image and
advocacy films, combined with the many other instruments of
persuasion controlled by corporations, direct popular attitudes.
The article analyzes one of the films (distributed free to the
public schools)--Chesebrough-Pond's Family.

227

1329.   Bennett, James R. "A Lesson in Doublespeak." FM 13
          (1979) 14-16.
     Mobil Oil Company's advocacy advertising entitled
"Observations" and published in newspaper Sunday supplements
(costing $2.5 million in 1977 alone) persuades us to esteem
Mobil and the oil industry and big business, and to condemn
regulatory government.

1330.   Bennett, James R., et al. "Mobil Oil in the Land of
          King Sam the Avuncular." Etc. 37 (1980) 6-16.
     As part of the "corporate media blitz" against government
regulation, Mobil Oil's Sunday supplement series,
"Observations," teaches "Mobil-our-benefactor, government-our-
enemy."

1331.   Bennett, James R. "Saturday Review's Annual
          Advertising Awards." JBE 2.2 (1983) 73-78.
     In 1977 Saturday Review damaged its annual advertising
awards by blurring the distinction between "public-service" and
"public relations" advertising into the single category of
"public spirited ads."

1332.   Bennett, James R. "The Westinghouse Broadcasting
          Company's 'Corita' Advertising Campaign." FSN 51
          (June 1981) 3-8.
     Group W's two-page, color ads illustrated by Corita Kent
and apparently praising free speech and broadcasting's
contribution to pluralism of all points of view mask the
actually narrow access to media. Analysis of one ad reveals
major discrepancies between what the ad claims and what
Westinghouse does.

1333.   Bernstein, Dennis, and Connie Blitt. "Lethal Dose."
          Prog 50.3 (1986) 22-25.
     The questionable ways that the Kerr-McGee company tried to
explain away its responsibility for an accident.

1334.   "Big Mac Is Watching You." Prog 46.4 (1982) 11.
     The American Council on Science and Health (ACSH) is an
instrument of the food industry, according to a report from the
Center for Science in the Public Interest, Voodoo Science,
Twisted Consumerism.

1335.   "Bloat." CJR 17.5 (1979) 25.
     Newspapers are too dependent upon the food industry news
releases.

1336.   Bonafede, Dom. "We're the Good, Rich Guys." WJR
          1.5 (1979) 26.
     US business is relying increasingly upon image and advocacy
advertising to promote its own version of society--"and not
uncoincidentally to assure profits."

1337.   Brown, William, and Richard Crable. "Industry, Mass

Magazines, and the Ecology Issue." QJS 59.3 (1973) 259-272.
Industry's massive mass media campaign of 1970-72 to divert blame for pollution away from itself. In 1970 alone, 27 companies spent $6 million to advocate industry's side and to deny capitalistic cupidity, most of the advertising paid for by the five industries with the worst records. The ads often identified corporations with the Edenic myth as a crusade to retain and regain innocence.

1338.   Caplan, Lincoln. "Freer Political Speech for Corporations." CJR 17.2 (1978) 18-19.
The Supreme Court ruled that corporations have the same First Amendment rights as individuals.

1339.   Cassidy, Robert. "Stripping Out the Facts." MORE 2.4 (1972) 3-5.
Coal strip mining companies' deceptive media campaigns are "designed to make the public believe the environment is being scrupulously protected." Environmentalists lack money, and laws related to deceptive ads are nonexistent or weak.

1340.   Cerra, Frances. "Countering the Oil Slick." MORE 4.8 (1974) 12-15.
"Once the gas lines abated last spring, the energy crisis all but disappeared. But the oil companies are still busily propagandizing," and almost no one in the media is challenging the messages.

1341.   Charlton, Linda. "Upwardly Mobil." Ch 1 (1981) 28-32.
An appraisal of Herb Schmertz, Vice-President for Public Relations for the Mobil Oil Company, and his public-relations budget of $20 million.

1342.   "A Citizen's Guide to Countering the Nuclear Industry's Media Blitz." CMJ 5.10 (1980) n.p.
How to counter false or misleading statements in schools and media.

1343.   Clark, Jeff. "The Media Control the Democratic Process." Pr 10 (1982) 10-11.
Attacks on the Fairness Doctrine and the Equal Time Provision by well-financed corporations and their supporters.

1344.   Cloherty, Jack. "Seven Flacks for Seven Sisters." WJR 1.2 (1978) 29-35.
Oil companies' efficiency in "selling its point of view." Seven oil industry public relations officers are highlighted.

1345.   Cowan, Paul. "Slicking Over the Oil Industry." MORE 1.1 (1971) 7.
"Little that appears in newspapers, magazines, or on television convey the sense of the huge scale of the oil

industry."

1346.   Crespi, Irving. "Polls as Journalism." POQ 4 (1980)
         462-476.
    Public opinion polls are controlled, both financially and
institutionally, by the major media corporations, and their
contents reflect the interests and bias of those corporations.

1347.   Dodge, Charlie. "Masterpiece P.R." Ch 1 (Aug./Sept.
         1981) 31.
    Since corporate profit today depends upon freedom from
government interference and public disfavor, control of PBS is
one important instrument of Mobil Oil's propaganda program
against regulation (e.g., Wattenberg's In Search of the Real
America) and to attract favor (e.g., Masterpiece Theatre). The
result is success for the oil industry's political agenda.

1348.   Dodge, Charlie. "Should Corporate Advertisers Be
         Allowed to Sell Ideas?" Ch 1.6 (1982) 52-4.
    Presents arguments pro and con regarding corporate advocacy
advertisements. Those in opposition fear that "the corporate
points of view on critical issues. . . will come to dominate
the media if giant companies are allowed to buy all the air-time
they want."

1349.   Dos Passos, John. The 42nd Parallel. 1st ed. New
         York: Harper, 1930. 426.
    A novel about J. Ward Moorehouse, public relations expert.

1350.   Dujack, Stephen. "Smoking Out the Truth." CC 12.3
         (1986) 8-9.
    Reynolds Tobacco Company deceptively used out-of-date
opinion to deny the American Lung Association's claim that
second-hand smoke is a health hazard.

1351.   Egan, Jack. "Press Encounters." MORE 8.1 (1978)
         38-40.
    How the publicists of the film Close Encounters of the
Third Kind spent $7 million to con the press into promoting the
film.

1352.   "Empirical Uses of Rewritten History." AG (June 4,
         1983) 12A.
    "One of the most effective marketing jobs ever executed in
this country" is the "Revitalize America" advertising campaign
by the Chamber of Commerce and various corporations to elect
Ronald Reagan and reduce taxes for corporations under the
camouflage of doing good by stimulating economic growth.

1353.   Fair, Elizabeth. "AP&L Pledges $500,000 for PR Push."
         AG (May 27, 1983) 1A.
    Arkansas Power and Light Company is "one of 50 utilities
supporting the Washington-based United States Committee for
Energy Awareness, an electricity industry-sponsored group that

is planning to run $25 million in television advertisements,"
passing the costs on to ratepayers.

1354.   Fausy, Verna. <u>Lifting the Secrecy Veil: A Guide to
    the Tennessee Business Roundtable</u>. Nashville, TN:
    Southern Neighborhood Network, 1984. 45.
An account of how one business lobbying and advocacy
organization influences the public, including the use of
duplicity.

1355.   Fisher, June, et al. "The Role of Popular Media in
    Defining Sickness and Health." <u>Communication and Social
    Structure: Critical Studies in Mass Media Research</u>.
    Ed. Emile McAnany, et. al. New York: Praeger, 1981.
    240-262.
The <u>Ladies Home Journal</u>, <u>Reader's Digest</u>, and <u>Time</u> between
1959 and 1974 "reveal the underlying social messages" of
"capitalist medicine," i.e., support of the status quo and
expensive technology.

1356.   "Free Enterprise Kits a Hit in High School." <u>IW</u> 198.6
    (1978) 48-52.
The US Chamber of Commerce sponsors a pro-free-enterprise
program in the public schools made up of films, worksheets, and
teachers' manuals. The materials are paid for by companies.

1357.   Friedman, Robert. "Try American Capitalism Today!"
    <u>MORE</u> 6.5 (1976) 12-14.
"Funded and directed by the country's largest corporations,
advertising agencies and media conglomerates, the Advertising
Council is the vehicle by which big business and the executive
branch of the federal government speak 'in the public
interest.'"

1358.   Gofman, John, and Arthur Tamplin. <u>Poisoned Power:
    The Case Against Nuclear Power Plants</u>. Emmaus, PA:
    Rodale, 1971. 368.
"The public has been and <u>is being</u> deceived by a clever,
well-financed propaganda campaign of delusions concerning
'clean, cheap, safe nuclear power'" (21).

1359.   Goodell, Rae. "The Gene Craze." <u>CJR</u> 19.4 (1980)
    41-45.
The press is now "pushing" genetic engineering partly as
the result of "carefully timed and orchestrated" industry
"promotion." The "immediate and long-range political and
ethical issues raised in the 1970s remain largely unreported and
unresolved."

1360.   Green, Mark. "The Faked Case Against Regulation."
    <u>PC</u> (Spring 1975) 5.
Business propaganda against "big government" and regulation
is designed to increase corporate power.

1361.   Griffee, Carol. "Dark Days Await U.S. Without More
          Plants, Power Spokesman Says." AG (April 7, 1985) 7C.
A representative of the Electric Power Research Institute
(EPRI), an arm of the electric utility industry, advocates
building more power plants.

1362.   Gruening, Ernest. The Public Pays: A Study of Power
          Propaganda. New York: Vanguard, 1931. 273.
A study of "the most highly organized peace-time effort to
shape public opinion" by the public utilities.

1363.   Guerra, Joe. "Nuclear Industry May Need $42 Million
          to 'Set the Record Straight.'" CMJ 8.2 (1982) 11.
The Committee for Energy Awareness, an industry based, pro-
nuclear organization, has developed a series of television
commercials designed to present only the positive aspects of
nuclear energy.

1364.   Guerra, Joe. "Selling Nuclear Power: A Look at the
          Industry's 'Foolish' Ad." CMJ 7.4 (1981) 6-7.
The ad, entitled "Maybe the World Won't Go to War Over Oil
three teenagers going off to war because their country foolishly
failed to build enough nuclear reactors, is a "melodramatic
attempt to drape the flag over nuclear power" and "plays upon
some of our deepest fears" and "our cheapest emotions."

1365.   Harnik, Peter. Voodoo Science, Twisted Consumerism.
          Washington, DC: Center for Science in the Public
          Interest, January 1982. 67.
Analysis of the American Council on Science and Health, a
pro-corporate research organizations that favors relaxing clean-
air standards, defends junk foods in schools, exonerates the
herbicide 2,4,5-T, etc. Its reports are widely accepted by
print media as reliable scientific data. But it is deeply
involved with corporations. Eight of the council's reports were
studied by other experts, who found errors, omissions, and
misrepresentations of fact and conclusions.

1366.   Henry, J. S. "From Soap to Soapbox: The Corporate
          Merchandising of Ideas." WP 7.3 (1980) 55-57.
Corporate political advocacy ads have become widespread
throughout the mass media. Their careful construction and
presentation of "pseudo-facts" influence the public to share the
political opinions which benefit the rich and powerful.

1367.   Hirsch, Glenn. "Only You Can Prevent Ideological
          Hegemony: The Advertising Council and Its Place in the
          American Power Structure." IS 5 (1975) 64-82.
"The Ad Council will continue to shore up ruling class
ideological hegemony through the continued domination of 'free'
public service broadcast time," unless its domination of Public
Service Announcements (PSA's) is broken.

1368.   Hoffman, Nicholas Von. "The Advertising World:

Questions About Noncommercial TV." <u>PR</u> 9 (1981) 38-9.
Individual and government contributions to PBS allow "Exxon
and Allied Chemical and Mobil to piggy-back on by making a small
payment that doesn't begin to cover the real costs, but which
lets them put their names on the air."

1369.   Joseph, Nadine. "Water, Water Everywhere." <u>CJR</u> 19.5
        (1981) 8-9.
The coverage by the <u>Los Angeles Times</u> of a proposal to
expand the state's water system is colored by the economic self-
interest of the <u>Times</u> owners. The Chandler family owns 270,000
acres seventy miles north of Los Angeles and would benefit
directly from the expansion, which the newspaper advocates.

1370.   Jungk, Robert. <u>The New Tyranny: How Nuclear Power</u>
        <u>Enslaves Us</u>. Christopher Trump, trans. New York:
        Grosset, 1979. 204.
"Public protest, previously dismissed by experts, now looms
as one of the principal worries of the nuclear industry. This,
despite the vigorous propaganda undertaken by all nations with
nuclear energy programs to 'enlighten' their citizens." Power
companies "grind out their own propaganda" which "say nothing
about the risks and dangers of nuclear energy. People who raise
questions and call for a public debate all too often are
smeared." "The American Nuclear society spends millions of
dollars on television spots made by top advertising agencies.
To influence referendums on nuclear power plants in eight
states, the United States power lobby spent some $8,000,000 in
1976" (76-78).

1371.   Karp, Walter. "Big Business and the Little Minister."
        <u>Ch</u> 1.4 (1981) 12-14.
On the religious and conservative forces behind the
"Reaganites' anti-democratic creed, their belief that the very
rich are <u>entitled</u> to rule over the rest of us." One of the
instruments of persuasion is the Rev. Donald Wildmon and the
Coalition for Better Television, a group of right-wing
organizations seeking to force the networks to support "the rule
of unshackled capitalists."

1372.   Keegan, Paul. "Press Misinterprets TMI Report." <u>WJR</u>
        2.1 (1980) 7.
The report by the President's Commission on the Accident at
Three Mile Island "is actually an indictment of the nuclear
power industry and its regulators," yet the national news media
made it seem as though the Commission had "given nuclear power
its blessing."

1373.   Kazis, Richard, and Richard Grossman. <u>Fear At Work:</u>
        <u>Job Blackmail, Labor and the Environment</u>. New York:
        Pilgrim, 1982. 306.
Corporations, supported by the Reagan administration, by
actions and propaganda have split environmentalists and labor
and have weakened rights and protections.

1374.   Ladd, Anthony. "Corporate Energy Futures: A Dumbo
        Ride Through Epcot Center." SciP 18.2 (1986) 21-26.
    Epcot Center (Experimental Prototype Community of Tomorrow)
"is a $900-million, 260-acre addition" to Walt Disney
Productions containing a Future World of multinational corporate
pavilions--Exxon, General Electric, General Motors, etc. It is
"a marketplace of corporate entities selling themselves as the
white knights of technology, scientific progress, and the
future."

1375.   Levin, Jack. Power Ethics: An Analysis of the
        Activities of the Public Utilities in the United States,
        Based on a Study of the U.S. Federal Trade Commission
        Records. New York: Knopf, 1931. 191.
    A digest of the FTC investigation of the electrical
utilities, the first twenty volumes of which and parts of the
remaining six "are concerned exclusively with propaganda, or the
attempts of this industry to control every aspect of American
public opinion in the private interests of this industry" (xv).
Chs. 9 and 10 focus upon propaganda in the schools and colleges.

1376.   Lutz, William. "'The American Economic System': The
        Gospel According to the Advertising Council." CE 38
        (1977) 860-65.
    The Advertising Council, whose Board of Directors is drawn
from among advertisers, advertising agencies, and the media,
controls public service advertising. Corporations thus sell
their ideas as public service announcements, exclude opposing
views, and avoid structural and systemic problems.

1377.   Lutz, William. "Doublespeak, Accounting, and the
        Annual Report." QRD 9.4 (1983) 1-2.
    The deception of corporate accounting in annual reports.

1378.   Lyon, Matthew. "And Now the Word from Our Sponsor:
        Buying Into the Public Schools." TO (Nov. 3, 1978) 2-9.
    Companies like Exxon and Gulf Oil are investing millions of
tax-deductible dollars in the form of product, image, and
advocacy advertising materials in the nation's public schools.
The US Chamber of Commerce is spearheading this effort, and has
placed filmstrips in 15,000 secondary schools. The Institute
for Constructive Capitalism (U of Texas) estimated the Fortune
500 companies spent $55 million in 1976 "to explain or promote
the private enterprise system."

1379.   MacDougall, A. Kent. "A Business Problem: Bull
        Market in Bad News." WJR 2.6 (1980) 32-3.
    Businessmen's efforts to force the media to present a more
favorable picture of business and businessmen.

1380.   MacDougall, A. Kent. "The Credibility Gap." WJR
        3.6 (1981) 20-25.
    Led by the US Chamber of Commerce and Mobil Oil, business
is increasing its efforts "to influence public opinion and

government legislation," with pro-business editorials, columns, cartoons, recorded interviews, free teaching materials for schools, professorships and fellowships at universities, etc.

1381.   MacDougall, A. Kent.   "Taking Stock of Dow Jones."
    CJR 21.4 (1982) 59-63.
    A review of two books on The Wall Street Journal: Lloyd Wendt's The Wall Street Journal and Jerry Rosenberg's Inside the Wall Street Journal. "Neither book ever quite gets a handle on the newspaper's news product" because "both books are based mainly on the records and recollections of Dow Jones management and are practically devoid of independent appraisals of the Journal". Wendt's book "is a company history commissioned by Dow Jones."

1382.   MacKenzie, James.   "A Critical Review of the Printed
    Ads of the U.S. Committee for Energy Awareness."   CMB
    1.12 (1984) 3-6.
    The Committee for Energy Awareness (CEA) was created by the nuclear industry for the purpose of pushing electricity and nuclear power. Its ads are "decidedly lopsided, and often distorted" in exalting nuclear power over alternative energy sources.

1383.   MacKenzie, James.   "Critique of Committee for Energy
    Awareness Ads: Waste and Radiation Issues."   Washington,
    DC: Union of Concerned Scientists, 1984.   4.
    Shows how misleading are five ads.

1384.   MacKenzie, James.   "Critique of U.S. Committee for
    Energy Awareness TV Ad: 'Tomorrow'."   Washington, DC:
    Union of Concerned Scientists, 1984.   9.
    The ad makes two "arguably false" statements. "The first is that electricity from solar technologies is not available today. The second is that nuclear energy is an energy source America can count on today."

1385.   Mander, Jerry.   "$30 Billion Questions."   CJR 16.5
    (1978) 57-59.
    A review of Controversy Advertising, Sethi's Advocacy Advertising and Large Corporations, and Paletz, et al.'s Politics in Public Service Advertising on Television. "All advertising" is "advocacy advertising," and corporations are spending billions of dollars to dominate politics and society in what has become a grossly "one-sided information environment."

1386.   Mastro, Randy M., et al.   Taking the Initiative:
    Corporate Control of the Referendum Process Through Media
    Spending and What to do About it.   Washington, DC: Media
    Access Project, 1980.   71.
    Three cases demonstrate the ability of corporate money and advocacy advertising to change voters' minds in local referendums.

235

1387.   Mayer, Allan, and Pamela Simons. "Advertising:
        Selling Free Enterprise." Newsweek (Sept. 20, 1976) 74.
     The Commerce Department and the Advertising Council's pro-
big business booklet, The American Economic System, covers up
unemployment, corporate crime, and alternatives to the corporate
state. A consumer group, the People's Business Commission, has
prepared a counter-argument in Common Sense II: The Case
Against Corporate Tyranny.

1388.   McCartney, Laton. "How IBM Spindles the Media."
        MORE 3.9 (1973) 1, 19-21.
     "The private sector today is a citadel ringed by a multi-
million dollar public relations moat of obfuscation at best and
lies at worst."

1389.   "Mobil Gets Maximum Media Mileage." QRD 8.3 (1982)
        11-12.
     Through image and advocacy advertising Mobil effectively
promotes itself as a public interest company.

1390.   Morris, Roger. "A Bullish Pulpit: The NYT's Business
        Desk." CJR 20.1 (1981) 31-37.
     "To read the Times's financial coverage through 1979 and
into early 1981 is to pass" through "a business looking glass
into an unreal world of almost universally benign commercial
forces. . . What most troubles concerned intramural critics of
the business section is that, in a field in which the
opportunities for investigative reporting are vast, there should
be so little of it."

1391.   Munson, Richard. "Harold Finger's Greatest Game." AJ
        7.3 (1986) 24-27.
     Analysis of the US Committee for Energy Awareness (CEA), "a
combine made up of electric utilities and nuclear-plant
producers" formed in 1979 "to counteract the negative publicity
following the Three Mile Island nuclear accident," with "an
annual budget of approximately $25 million." Harold Finger is
its director.

1392.   Munson, Richard. The Power Makers. Emmaus, PA:
        Rodale, 1985. 260.
     A history of the electric industry in the US. "Utilities
burn subsidized fuels, pay few taxes, and enjoy guaranteed
profits." Scattered throughout but particularly in Ch. 7 is
discussion of industry public relations and advertising
encouraging consumers to use more electricity, to oppose public
or government-owned power systems, etc.

1393.   Nelson, Lin. "Nuclear Industry Gives Women the Hard
        Sell." CMJ 8.14 (1983) 4-5. Rpt. from The Progressive.
     The industry-sponsored Nuclear Energy Women, an affiliate
of the Atomic Industrial Forum, has developed a mass program to
convince women that nuclear energy is essential.

1394.   Nemeth, Louis. "Mendacity in Michigan." MM 7.6
           (1986) 3-7, 12.
     General Motors represents itself as "Mr. Nice Guy" in its
efforts to gain property tax reductions, buts its tactics in
closed meetings are "pernicious" and full of "double talk."

1395.   Ohmann, Richard. "Language, Power, and the Teaching
           of English." CEAF 6 (October 1975) 1-9.
     An analysis of the pro-business ideology and the semantics
of the messages purveyed by the Advertising Council. Business
not only dominates paid advertising but free advertising too.

1396.   Paletz, David, et al. Politics in Public Service
           Advertising on Television. New York: Praeger, 1977.
           123.
     This book is about PSA's as propaganda for corporations.
PSA's derive largely from the Advertising Council, which is made
up of corporations, particularly those in the advertising and
communications industries. From 1942, the time of the Council's
inception, "$8 billion worth of time and space have been donated
to its campaign materials." PSA's espouse capitalism,
nationalism, obedience, etc., propose solutions to problems
favorable to corporations, exclude dissident groups, and cover-
up systemic flaws.

1397.   Penelope, Julia. "The Dress of Thoughts." QRD 9
           (1982) 6-7.
     The SOHIO booklet, "What Makes America Run?" by Herbert
Stein, was purportedly published "in the interest of improving
economic understanding," but it is shoddy in logic and uses "the
kind of language we call 'doublespeak'."

1398.   Reece, Ray. The Sun Betrayed: A Report on the
           Corporate Seizure of U.S. Solar Energy Development.
           Boston: South End, 1979. 234.
     Ch. 7, "By Any Means Necessary: Selling the Corporate
Point of View," exposes "a series of distortions, deceits, and
manipulations ranging from the pathetic to the socially
dangerous and punishable by law."

1399.   Ridgeway, James. "Exploits of 'The New Adventurers'."
           MORE 2.7 (1972) 1,18-19.
     On image advertising by Standard Oil of New Jersey:
"Esso's eight-page bit of four-color trickery" to convince the
public that off-shore drilling is not only perfectly benign and
necessary but downright heroic.

1400.   Ridgeway, James. "Trying to Catch the Energy Crisis."
           MORE 4.1 (1974) 1,15-17.
     An analysis of the energy companies' successful but
questionable advertising campaign to persuade the media and the
public that there is a shortage of oil and gas and the shortage
was created by government pricing policies.

1401.   Rosenthal, Herma. "Beware of News Clips Massaging
         Your Opinions." TVG (April 12, 1984) 4-9.
Companies now pitch their products and viewpoints through
cleverly disguised video press releases, the electronic
counterpart to the printed press release.

1402.   Rowse, Arthur. "1. A Warning from the Mailman." CRJ
         6.4 (1967) 24-26.
Criticism of Reader's Digest publication of misleading
advertising from the Pharmaceutical Manufacturers Association
without clearly marking it as advertising.

1403.   Rubin, David. "Anatomy of a Snow Job." MORE 4.3
         (1974) 18-22.
The widespread reporting of the Chase Manhattan Bank and
its president, David Rockefeller, is partly the result of a well
organized public relations operation.

1404.   "Say It Ain't So, Annie." ITT 8.36 (1984) 4.
On disinformative ads by the US Committee for Energy
Awareness, funded by electrical utilities, construction
companies, and equipment manufacturers.

1405.   Schwab, Priscilla. "Introducing Johnny and Mary to
         the World of Business." NB 66.1 (1978) 57-59.
An upbeat account of the US Chamber of Commerce's
"Economics for Young Americans" Program designed to dispel
negative attitudes toward business and the American economic
system.

1406.   Sethi, S. Prakash. Advocacy Advertising and Large
         Corporations: Social Conflict, Big Business Image, the
         News Media, and Public Policy. Lexington: Lexington,
         1977. 355.
"To the extent that such advertising becomes widespread and
is used by a significant number of large corporations and
industry groups, there is a danger of their squeezing out
alternative viewpoints from the public comunication space and
thereby impairing public access to information from all sources"
(4). Part I, "Dimension and Scope of Advocacy Advertising,"
Part II, "Advocacy Advertising in Action" (a study of two
campaigns), Part III, "Economic, Sociopolitical, and Legal
Implications of Advocacy Advertising."

1407.   Shute, Nancy. "The Selling of Waste Management." AJ
         7 (1985) 8-17.
An account of Waste Management Inc.'s multi-million dollar
image advertising campaign to counteract its mismanagement of
hazardous waste disposal sites ranging from sloppy paperwork to
criminal violations of federal environmental statutes.

1408.   Sourcebook on Corporate Image and Corporate Advocacy
         Advertising. Subcommittee on Administrative Practice and
Procedure, Committee on the Judiciary, US Senate, 95th

Congress, 1978. 2133.
The basic documents, mainly in chronological order,
relating to the Subcommittee's inquiry into FTC, FCC and IRS
jurisdiction over corporate image and advocacy advertising, and
the First Amendment status of commercial speech. Part 1 gives
expenditures of such advertising, 2 case studies, 3 organization
and purpose, publications (all but one from Fortune Magazine and
Public Relations Journal), 4 First Amendment, and the rest on
the regulatory agencies.

1409.   Sternberg, Steve. "The Drug Companies' Media Campaign
    to Extend the Patent Monopolies." Pr 9.4 (1981) 50.
The Pharmaceutical Manufacturers Assoc. "is so committed to
obtaining the bill's passage that the association has dispatched
public relations executives across the country to try to win
newspaper editors and science writers over to the industry point
of view."

1410.   "Utilities Can't Be Forced to Include Messages in
    Bills, Court Decides." AG (February 26, 1986) 2C.
The Supreme Court ruled that utility companies have First
Amendment rights like individual persons and cannot be required
to give equal space to views opposing their own, even though
they are regulated for the public welfare and routinely include
their own political messages in billing envelopes.

1411.   Wallace, Mike. "Mickey Mouse History: Portraying
    the Past at Disney World." RHR 32 (1985) 33-57.
Disney's EPCOT--the Experimental Prototype Community of
Tomorrow--is "an extraordinary effort by corporate America" to
reconstitute the past as Progress through commodities and
mastery of the environment. Corporations are working to create
a Future free of problems: they serve the public and support
the ecology movement; Exxon champions alternative energy, and GM
promotes mass transit. Unfortunately, "Corporate Walt's history
is bad history."

1412.   Weinstein, Henry. ". . .And Selling Truth." Ram 13
    (1974-1975) 27, 64-65.
Opposes the monopoly held by the Advertising Council over
public service ads and advocates time and space for public
interest groups seeking social alternatives and change.

1413.   Weisman, John. "Why Big Oil Loves Public TV." TVG
    (June 20, 1981) 4-10.
Huge grants from energy companies go far in creating public
and government favor.

1414.   Wertheimer, Fred. "What Mobil Didn't Tell You." CC
    10 (1984) 46.
A critique of advertisements run by the Mobil Oil Corp.
attacking Common Cause and trying to make the case that special
interest political action committees (PACs) are good for
democracy.

1415.   West Glen Films.

A service for the free loan, rental, and sale of corporate films.

1416.   Winsten, Jay. "Science and the Media: The Boundaries
        of Truth." HA 4.1 (Spring 1985) 5-23.
Competitive journalism and particularly competitive scientific centers produce distorted science news, as illustrated by the coverage of a single study on Alzheimer's disease.

1417.   Zachar, George R. "Press Swallows Atom Industry Bait:
        Industry-Sponsored Tour of Soviet Union Nets Pro-Nuclear
        Coverage." CMJ 4.9 (1978) 8.
The Atomic Industrial Forum, a US public-relations group which promotes nuclear energy, sponsored a trip to the Soviet Union for reporters.

1418.   Zeidner, M. A. "Medical Research and the Language of
        Nospeak." QRD 11.1 (1984) 8-9.
"Our diet of research into new drugs consists largely of placebo-coated doublespeak."

III. E. Foundations 1419-1429

1419.   Anderson, James D. "Philanthropic Control Over
        Private Black Higher Education." Philanthropy and
        Cultural Imperialism. Ed. Robert Arnove. Boston:
        Hall, 1980. 147-178.
Black higher education after World War I "survived mainly within the limits imposed by industrial philanthropy," and that philanthropy is still "a controlling force in the power structure of black higher education."

1420.   Curti, Merle, and Roderick Nash. Philanthropy in the
        Shaping of American Higher Education. New Brunswick:
        Rutgers UP, 1965. 340.
Not only did rich capitalists create institutions, as with John D. Rockefeller's University of Chicago, but their positions on boards of trustees and as contributors gave them substantial say in the development of the modern university, not in day-to-day control but in the determination of long-range goals.

1421.   Darknell, Frank. "The Carnegie Corporation:
        Directing Higher Education." Ed 36 (1975) 14-17, 32.
The Carnegie Commissions on Education reflect corporate attitudes.

1422.   Horowitz, David. "Billion Dollar Brains: How Wealth
        Puts Knowledge in Its Pocket." Ram 7.12 (1969) 36-44.
The "development of the modern American university was not left to the natural bent of those within its ivory towers; it was shared by the ubiquitous charity of the foundations and the guiding mastery of wealth."

1423.   Horowitz, David, and David Kolodney. "The
          Foundations: Charity Begins at Home." <u>Ram</u> 7.11 (1969)
          38-48.
     Foundations "sustain the complex nerve centers and guidance
mechanisms for a whole system of institutional power. To a
remarkable and not accidental degree, this power has both
characterized and defined American society and its relations
with the rest of the world in the 20th century."

1424.   Howe, Barbara. "The Emergence of Scientific
          Philanthropy, 1900-1920: Origins, Issues, and
          Outcomes." <u>Philanthropy and Cultural Imperialism</u>. Ed.
          Robert Arnove. Boston: Hall, 1980. 25-54.
     Focuses upon the Walsh Commission hearings of 1915 about
the role of foundations in American society, including the
"dangers inherent in their concentration of wealth and power
closely tied to corporate capitalism." The "millionaires" won
the debate, and it was not until the 1950s that "any further
congressional investigation" of foundations occurred.

1425.   Lagemann, Ellen. <u>Private Power for the Public Good:
          A History of the Carnegie Foundation for the Advancement
          of Teaching</u>. Middletown, CT: Wesleyan UP, 1984. 246.
     The growth of industrial capitalism which produced the
foundations to defend capitalism by preempting socialist
alternatives also produced managers somewhat independent from
the commercial sponsors. And all elements of foundations were
constrained by that aspect of democratic ideology which
distrusted power.

1426.   Marks, Russell. "Legitimating Industrial Capitalism:
          Philanthropy and Individual Differences." <u>Philanthropy
          and Cultural Imperialism</u>. Ed. Robert Arnove. Boston:
          Hall, 1980. 87-122.
     Foundation dollars and leadership taught individual
differences and "promoted a consciousness of reality based on
the limitations rather than the possibilities of human nature."

1427.   Nielsen, Waldemar. <u>The Big Foundations</u>. New York:
          Columbia UP, 1972. 475.
     Of the 25,000 foundations, 33 of them control $11 billion
in assets, half the resources of the entire group. These
foundations are headed by leaders of the financial and
industrial community who often are "in conflict of interest,"
the intimate financial links often serving private interests of
the donor families as much as the interests of charity. The
author hopes to show "trustees and officers the urgent need to
initiate procedures for self-reform and self-renewal," for he
remains "a strong believer" in the "potential importance" of
foundations as "independent centers of initiative to challenge,
criticize and provide a creative spark for the massive
governmental, economic, social and religious institutions which
increasingly dominate our nation's life" (Preface).

1428.   Rothmyer, Karen. "Citizen Scaife." CJR 20.2 (1981)
         41-50.
    Perhaps "more than any other individual in the past five or
six years" Richard Mellon Scaife has shaped the country's right-
wing direction through use of his immense fortune in support of
Sovietphobic, pro-military, pro-corporation foundations, think
tanks, lobbying groups, and publications, yet the press "has
generally overlooked" him. All of the groups receiving
substantial money from Scaife foundations are listed p. 47. "By
multiplying the authorities to whom the media are prepared to
give a friendly hearing, Scaife has helped to create an illusion
of diversity where none exists."

1429.   Scardino, Albert. "A Look at the Conservative
         Alternative." CJR 25.3 (1986) 35-39.
    The rise of campus right-wing journalism is funded by
corporations like GE and P&G and by the Scaife and Coors
foundations as part of a campaign to enhance the corporate-
national security-education complex.

III. F. Secrecy, Censorship, Intelligence Activities 1430-
          1473

1430.   Bagdikian, Ben. "The Self-Protective Press." CLR
         2.1 (1975) 162-66.
    A review of seven books which reveal how much "the press
has contributed to its own vulnerability by keeping the general
public largely in the dark about its own inner workings."

1431.   Baldwin, Deborah. "The Loneliness of the Government
         Whistleblower." CC 11 (1985) 32-34.
    Employees face great difficulties in exposing waste,
fraud, and abuse.

1432.   Boot, William. "The Empire Strikes Back." CJR 20.1
         (1981) 44-45.
    The Washington Star's Tom Dowling's attack on the film The
Empire Strikes Back and on the film industry's preference for
profit over art cost him his job.

1433.   Brenton, Myron. The Privacy Invaders. New York:
         Coward, 1964. 240.
    A book on "our disappearing privacy," our lives "secretly
bought, sold, manipulated and exploited by an ever-growing army
of private inquirers," those "whose main consideration is
personal gain, financial or otherwise," in some instances "so
excessive they would be considered intolerable were they
emanating from governmental circles." "Big Brother" is "in the
marketplace, on the job, and around the community" through
secret files, computer systems, lie detector tests,
evesdropping, wiretaps, two-way mirrors, etc.

1434.   Brodeur, Paul. Outrageous Misconduct. New York:
         Pantheon, 1985. 357.

An account of the fifty years (beginning in 1933) that Johns-Manville Corporation knew how fatal to its employees was asbestos. Throughout the 1950s, the company stifled disclosure of the danger. By the 1960s the hundreds of suits against the company not only by its own workers but by those who had installed the final product made the company's criminality clear.

1435.   Brodeur, Paul. The Zapping of America: Microwaves, Their Deadly Risk, and the Cover-Up. New York: Norton, 1978. 343.
The danger of microwave radiation has been steadily denied by the Pentagon and industry and largely ignored by the press.

1436.   Brown, Les. "Whose First Amendment Is It, Anyway?" Ch 2.3 (1982) 24-25.
Cable "is doing its utmost to be spared having to provide outlets for free speech--and doing it shamelessly in the name of the First Amendment."

1437.   Chobanian, Peter. "The Mooney Case: A Bibliography." BoB 43.2 (1986) 82-99.
Because of their efforts to organize unions and strikes, Thomas Mooney and Warren Billings were sent to prison on perjured evidence. Even after their innocence had been "clearly and undeniably established" the prosecutors were supported in opposing their release from prison by powerful California political, business, and newspaper interests.

1438.   Clewett, John. "'Flash in the Pan' Now a Major Blaze." CMJ 8.11 (1983)4.
Employees of the Three Mile Island power plant who have publicly admitted to illegal and/or dangerous downgrading of safety have suffered some type of retaliation.

1439.   Engelmayer, Sheldon, and Robert Wagman. Lord's Justice: One Judge's War Against the Infamous Dalkon Shield. New York: Anchor, Doubleday, 1985. 300.
A. H. Robins officials knew its uterine device Dalkon Shield was flawed but covered up the truth. The title refers to US District Judge Miles Lord of Minnesota who took an active part in probing the truth.

1440.   Ewing, David. "Employees Rights: Taking the Gag Off." CLR 1.4 (1974) 54-61.
"For employees, civil liberties are not greatly advanced from what they were in the Middle Ages." Two remedies for company dictatorship is the informal company "court" for hearing employee complaints, and the ombudsperson.

1441.   Freund, Charles. "License Hunters." CJR 20.5 (1985) 7-8.
An account of attacks on the Pacifica radio group by right-wing publications and foundations--Accuracy in Media, the

American Legal Foundation, etc. The ALF (funded by Richard Mellon Scaife) has challenged Pacifica's Washington, DC, outlet's license.

1442.   Gold, Michael. "Journalists on Cancer." CJR 16.3
         (1977) 54-55.
Review of three books on the corporate/industrial causes of cancer and, indirectly, on the failure of the media to expose "the story of cancer in the depth with which it needs to be told": Agran's The Cancer Connection and What We Can Do About It, Brody's You Can Fight Cancer and Win, and Randall and Solomon's Building 6: The Tragedy at Bridesburg.

1443.   Hayden, Trudy. "How Much Does the Boss Need to Know?"
         CLR 3.3 (1976) 23-43.
It is "in connection with employment--and especially the search for employment--that people most commonly experience the conflict between what they feel to be their right of privacy and what some other person believes to be a justified demand for information."

1444.   Healy, Tim, and Peter Marshall. "Big Business Is
         Watching You." ITT 10.14 (1986) 12-13.
The methods that corporations use to spy on employees "in order to control them."

1445.   Hickey, Neil. "The Man Who Set the Standard." CJR
         24.6 (1986) 54-57.
A review of Ann Sperber's biography of Edward R. Murrow, Murrow: His Life and Times. His speech in 1958 attacking corporate greed at the expense of public interest "effectively ended his career."

1446.   Hochberg, Lee. "Environmental Reporting in Boomtown
         Houston." CJR 19.1 (1980) 71-74.
The Houston press consistently see industry's side of environmental issues, refusing to probe deeply into any problem or crime which might endanger the city's economic boom.

1447.   Hogan, Bill. "Corporations and the Press Are Now in
         Business." WJR 5.6 (1983) 35-37.
On corporate privacy, secrecy, and avoidance of the press.

1448.   Hogan, Bill. "Nobody's Business." WJR 6.6 (1984)
         41-44.
Corporations are increasingly going private in order to avoid public and government scrutiny. Private companies are "'woefully undercovered.'"

1449.   "How the Phone Company Interrupted Our Service." Ram
         11 (1972) 10-11, 16-17.
AT&T forced Ramparts magazine to recall and suppress an entire issue of the magazine because it printed a 4-page article that AT&T didn't like.

1450.   Howell, Leon.   "CBS, Westy, and Us."   C&C 45.7 (1985)
        152-4.
Shows connections between conservative corporations,
foundations, and libel suits and their chilling effect on
investigative reporting.

1451.   Hoyt, Michael. "Publish and Perish in Ohio." CJR
        23.6 (1985) 14-16.
On the suppression of the union newspaper, Educational
Informer, by the Wheeling-Pittsburgh Steel Co. in Yorkville,
Ohio, "largely because it didn't like what the newspaper had to
say," by firing the paper's editor, the union president who
supervised him, and another union official who was an active
writer.

1452.   Katel, Peter. "Plugging In to the Power Company."
        CJR 19.3 (1980) 13,15.
Following a series by the Albuquerque Journal critical of
some of its practices, the electric utility launched a powerful
attack on the newspaper.

1453.   Kotelchuch, David. "Asbestos, Science for Sale."
        in Arditti, 128-144.
Industry has consistently obscured and controlled
scientific evidence regarding asbestos and its relation to
respiratory diseases, and industrial scientists have manipulated
data to place the asbestos industry in a non-culpable light.

1454.   Kupferberg, Seth. "Union Monitors Static in Labor's
        TV Image." CJR 19.1 (1980) 13-14.
Union members who monitored television programs in a
nationwide project found a consistent bias against labor.

1455.   Mintz, Morton. At Any Cost: Corporate Greed, Women,
        and the Dalkon Shield. New York: Pantheon, 1985. 308.
An indictment of the A. H. Robins Company for selling the
Dalkon Shield. "The Salkon Shield created a disaster of global
proportions because a few men with little on their minds but
megabucks made decisions, in the interest of profit, that
exposed millions of women to serious infection, sterility, and
even death." Some ch. titles: "Deceiving Doctors," "Deceiving
Women," "Dodging the FDA," "Insidious Infections, Insidious
Cover-Ups."

1456.   Moore, Michael. "How to Keep 'Em Happy in Flint."
        CJR 24.3 (1985) 40-43.
For many years The Flint Journal was a General Motors
booster, but in 1978 a new editor tried to add investigative
reporting of General Motors and Flint business. The editor was
fired and replaced by a booster.

1457.   Mysak, Joseph. "Air Attack." MORE 7.1 (1977) 7.
McDonnell Douglas Corporation's libel suit against Robert
Sherrill and The New York Times is a matter both of intimidation

and the taxpayers' money, "because McDonnell Douglas is
federally subsidized for its Army aircraft."

1458.   Parker, Richard. "Press Fiddles While Drivers Burn."
           CJR 18.2 (1979) 8, 13-14.
Press coverage of an oil shortage in California was
hampered by general ignorance of the subject and dependence on
the oil companies for vital statistics.

1459.   Perry, Susan, and Jim Dawson. Nightmare: Women and
           the Dalkon Shield. New York: Macmillan, 1985. 261.
The story of A. H. Robins Company's dangerous uterine
device which was promoted as "the safest and most satisfying
form of contraception" but which was dangerous and killed at
least twenty women. The company marketed the device for four
years to 2.2 million women even though its officials knew it was
flawed.

1460.   Picard, Robert. "The Might of the Media: Media Self-
           censorship." Pr 9.2 (1981) 16-18.
"American publishers and broadcasters are increasingly
exercising self-censorship to avoid costly litigation" over
libel, privacy suits, and confrontations with government
attorneys. The "result is a decline in press freedom."

1461.   Pollock, Francis. "Knight-Ridder Wants to Know the
           Real You." CJR 16.5 (1978) 25-28.
Knight-Ridder, a large newspaper chain, uses personality
tests to insure that their employees suit their purposes.

1462.   Rashke, Richard. The Killing of Karen Silkwood (The
           Story Behind the Kerr-McGee Plutonium Case). New York:
           Houghton, 1981. 407.
An attempt to cut through the confusion of the murder of
Silkwood caused by the police, the FBI, the AEC, and the Kerr-
McGee Corporation.

1463.   Rosenthal, Bruce. "Va. Utility Guilty of Cover-Up."
           CMB 1.4 (1975) 2, 11.
The Virginia Electric and Power company concealed
geologists' reports and built a nuclear power plant over a
geological fault.

1464.   Scharff, Ned. "Vepco Made False Statements on
           Atomic Site, Panel Finds." CMJ 1.1 (1975) 8.
The Virginia Electric and Power Co. denied the existence of
a geological fault at their proposed atomic power plant site and
left it off of their topographic maps. The Nuclear Regulatory
Commission also found that the company had not reported collapse
of a construction wall near the area.

1465.   Shaikh, Salim, et al. Bhopal: Beyond Genocide.
           Montreal, Can., 1985.
16mm. and video film placing the killing of 2,500 Indian

people by toxic poisoning from a Union Carbide pesticide in the context of the devastation which multinationals can bring to third world countries. One of the major points in the film is the concealment of information by Union Carbide both before and after the disaster.

1466.   "Shutting Up Schanberg." CJR 24.4 (1985) 24.
     Pulitzer Prize winner Sidney Schanberg was ordered to end his "New York" column with the New York Times by the publisher, Arthur O. Sulzberger, forcing him to resign.

1467.   Snel, Alan. "A Manager Who Blew the Whistle." Prog
     49.5 (1985) 17.
     A manufacturer fired its plant manager for complaining about poor safety conditions and dumping caustic chemicals.

1468.   Sorensen, Jeff, and Jon Swan. "VDTs: The Overlooked
     Story Right In the Newsroom." CJR 19.5 (1981) 32-38.
     Newspapers are neglecting or suppressing the health and safety controversy affecting thousands of journalists and milions of other US workers--the video display terminal.

1469.   Sperber, Ann. Murrow: His Life and Times. New York:
     Freundlich, 1986. 608.
     At the height of his fame, Edward R. Murrow gave a speech criticizing television for not living up to its potential. From that time forward he was cut off from influence in CBS and elsewhere by the establishment executives.

1470.   Stein, Loren and Diana Hembree. "VDT Regulation: The
     Publishers Counterattack." CJR 23.4 (1984) 42-44.
     Newspaper publishers are fighting pending legislation which would set health standards for the use of video display terminals in the workplace.

1471.   Stevenson, Russell, Jr. Corporations and
     Information: Secrecy, Access, and Disclosure.
     Baltimore: Johns Hopkins U P, 1980. 226.
     An analysis of the many aspects of secrecy in corporations and an effort to suggest ways of expanding access to and disclosure of corporate information as part of their responsiveness to the needs of society. The author advocates changes in rules governing access and disclosure rather than direct government regulation.

1472.   Swan, Jon. "Uncovering Love Canal." CJR 17.5
     (1979) 46-51.
     The Gannett newspaper the Niagara Gazette revealed the Hooker Chemical Company dumped dangerous chemicals near a school and residential area in full awareness of their danger and then lied about their knowledge.

1473.   Tobias, Andrew. The Invisible Bankers: Everything
     the Insurance Industry Never Wanted You to Know. New

York: Linden, 1982. 336.

The insurance industry uses secrecy and manipulation of data to obtain inordinate profits, and it is inefficient. One "prime cause" is "lack of adequate disclosure, which prevents us from shopping intelligently" (94). Yet its power is so great that it persuaded the Senate to pass a bill banning the FTC from investigating or even reporting on the industry.

IV. GOVERNMENT 1474-2187

Introduction

A. The Presidency 1474-1641
    1.   Public Relations, News Management, Media Access 1475-1542
    2.   Secrecy, Censorship, Cover-Up, Surveillance, Repression 1543-1585
    3.   Presidential Disinformation 1586-1621
    4.   Presidential Elections, Campaigning 1622-1641

B. Watergate 1642-1652

C. Bureaucracy 1653-1876
    1.   Secrecy, Classification, Censorship, Self-Censorship, Cover-Up 1653-1805
    2.   Bureaucratic Disinformation 1806-1834
    3.   Bureaucratic Surveillance, Repression 1835-1876

D. Congress 1877-1888

E. Think Tanks 1889-1905

F. Washington Press Corps 1906-1928

G. Wars 1929-2033
    1.   Post-World War II 1929-1945
    2.   Vietnam War 1946-2033
        a.   Government Disinformation, Secrecy, and Censorship 1946-1979
        b.   Media and Education 1980-2033

H. Latin America 2034-2187
    1.   Central and South America 2034-2040
    2.   Central America and the Caribbean 2041-2117
        a.   Nicaragua 2118-2161
        b.   El Salvador 2162-2179
    3.   South America 2180-2187

INTRODUCTION

The Presidency

Clinton Rossiter in The American Presidency identifies the
many roles by which the president exerts power: chief executive,
commander-in-chief of the armed forces, chief diplomat, chief
legislator, and voice of the people. Katznelson and Kesselman
focus on "the three broad purposes on behalf of which contemporary presidents exercise power: to assist corporate production
at home, defend corporate capitalism abroad, and maintain social
control" (264). These roles and purposes are furthered through
domination of information. If it is true that "manipulation is
one of the chief instruments of control at the disposition of a
small governing group of corporate and governmental decision-
makers," as Herbert Schiller argues in The Mind Managers, then
the president possesses a privileged position for the exercise of
power through numerous avenues of communication. This power is
effective particularly through television, whose "newscasts and
public affairs programs unquestionably constitute the major
source of political reality for most Americans" (Ranney, 16), and
which gives the president premier access for the construction of
that reality.

In 1960 in Presidential Power Richard Neustadt probed the
weaknesses of personal presidential influence. But in his 1980
revision he acknowledges the growing power of any president able
to master television, because of the increasing importance of
prestige or of the image of reputation (238). Even in this revision, however, which has the lessons of presidents Johnson and
Nixon as evidence of presidential power, he still neglects numerous sources of power and bases of persuasion considered significant in this bibliography--anticommunism (the outside threat) as
a rallying cry, alliance with financial and industrial interests,
agenda setting, definition of "responsible" debate, initiation of
laws, news management, secrecy, disinformation, war power, covert
operations, intelligence agencies, etc.

As Francis Rourke argues, "the possibility of controlling
communications has now opened up an avenue through which the gap
between totalitarian and democratic government can progressively
be narrowed, as modern dictators gradually substitute persuasion
for coercion, and as democratic leaders acquire the ability to
manufacture the consent upon which their authority is supposed to
rest" (vii).

Watergate

Too many of the books on President Nixon's illegal grab for
power provide merely a factual narrative of his "brazen falsehoods" and "obstructing justice" (Jaworski, 334-5). Two books
which place that episode in a meaningful context are Rasberry's
The "Technique" of Political Lying and Evans and Myers's Watergate. The "technique" of Rasberry's title derives from Jacques
Ellul"s explanation of a way of life which gives primacy to effi-

cient problem solving at the expense of "values like truth and justice" (251). Watergate is seen as only an extreme manifestation of the "basic public relations tactics employed by Nixon's staff during political campaigns," the purpose of which was to triumph over opponents. Nixon hired the best problem solving, former advertising executive technocrats he could find, and they functioned identically in campaign and cover-up (253).

Evans and Myers place Watergate in the context of 1) US monopoly capitalism and its extension throughout the world, 2) the acceleration of Third World anti-colonialism, 3) competition with other developed nations, and 4) the revival of domestic radicalism (12). All the machinations and illegalities now loosely identified by the label "Watergate" were only a dramatic manifestation of established policies: continuing the war in Vietnam as part of continued economic and military expansion abroad, and suppression of radical, anti-establishment beliefs at home. Nixon, his Democratic opponent, Hubert Humphrey (the peace candidacy of Eugene McCarthy was rejected), and the third party candidate, George Wallace, ran on virtually the same "law and order" platform.

The scandal inspired several reform proposals and some legislation from 1974 to 1978--tightening election laws (1974), limiting the FBI Director's term to 10 years (1976), making presidential records public property (1976), the Ethics Act (1978), and others ("Watergate Revisited" 684). Some of these do help check abuse, but the contributors to this bibliography find them insufficient.

The Bureaucracy

Thomas Dye reports a great similarity among people appointed to "top executive posts"; whether Democrat or Republican there are "few discernible differences in the class backgrounds, educational levels, occupational experience, or previous service" among the appointees (94-5). These high level bureaucrats, beginning especially with the president, protect and enlarge the secrecy system that is the present "national security state." Secrecy, including the classification system and executive privilege, censorship (prior restraint), misinformation, lying, record keeping, wire-taps, subpoenas, grand juries, imprisonment, and various interventions and impositions (Schrag) signal closed government. Halperin and Hoffman and others show how the constant "threat" to "national security" has been used to intrude illegally or inappropriately in the private lives of citizens. The inherent tendency of bureaucrats to avoid disclosure has been hardened by new pre-publication and non-disclosure regulations (NSDD 84). Gilson and others throughout this bibliography reveal how a covert bureaucracy and economic power nourish each other (see II.A.-C.). Demaris, for example, complains of the lack of FBI statistics of corporate crimes compared to street crimes (15). Hilgartner, et al., remind us how "awesome" is the Department of Energy's power "to restrict the flow of information" (57) and how aggressive the public relations of the nuclear industry (80-81). What is less known perhaps because less obvious is the decline of information available to the public as the direct result of budget cuts. As Donna Demac shows, attacks on "big government" (always excluding the Pentagon and the intelligence agencies) and the Gramm-Rudman-Hollings budget reduction bill mean reduction of the information the public must have for informed thought and action. Critics of these trends advocate increased budgets for public information, an activist interpretation of the First Amendment, and the abolition of subversion and sedition laws, and they defend the FOIA, whistleblowers, and the public's right to know what their government is doing, and urge the press to increase investigative reporting.

Congress

Mark Green perceives a Congress dominated by corporate lobbyists and PACs and by pro-corporate bureaucrats led by the president. Thomas Dye observes how little Congress participates in foreign policy decisions. Consequently, many of the contributors to this bibliography would have Congress more resistant to concentrated power and more responsive to public needs.

At least, many congressmen maintain (Frantzich), Congress should possess information as rapidly and completely as the White House and the large corporations. Some critics believe more viable parties would invigorate Congress. Probably all would return power to declare war and to initiate foreign intervention to Congress (now virtually ceded to the president) and would ensure its participation in all important government decisions. Some are hopeful that televizing proceedings will enlarge public awareness and interest in its elected representatives. If power in a democracy is supposed to be founded in the people, and if public alienation is to be challenged (marked by low voter turnout), then ways must be forged to increase the connection between the public and their representatives, as Marcus Raskin argues. James MacGregor Burns believes revival can result from a return to "our over-arching values" of defense of civil liberties and civil rights, abolition of poverty, and protection of the environment--a positive equality of condition and distributive justice, instead of the narrow and negative equality of opportunity now ideologically in the saddle (and then often only in word and not in deed).

Think Tanks

According to Ralph Nader in his Introduction to The Shadow Government, "Social Security and veterans' benefits aside, the predominate activity of government is letting contracts, grants, and subsidies to corporations for the purpose of performing governmental missions." The "drive to merge Government and business power to the advantage of the latter has been unceasing in recent decades." Think tanks contribute to this symbiosis. Washington is "littered with Hoover [Institute] alumni." Many are privately funded by corporations or wealthy individuals or families to influence government policy. The best financed and most influential are conservative to right-wing. The Heritage Foundation, for example, advocates paramilitary force against pro-Soviet countries, urges renunciation of the ABM Treaty, and campaigns tirelessly for "Star Wars." (See III. E. on Foundations.)

GOVERNMENT

Washington Press Corps

Helen Thomas and a few others excepted, opinion of these prestigious reporters is not high. The constant danger to the correspondent is co-optation, for the representatives of government
naturawant a favorable press. Many critics like Von Hoffman consider them mere conduits for official propaganda, "buttressing
faith" in the Establishment. According to Hess, most of the
reporters are conservative, capitalist of course, and too many
avoid necessary research, and prefer to cover bull sessions
instead of probing into the institutions. (See V. B. Pentagon
and the Media.)

Wars

In general, with notable exceptions like I. F. Stone, these
studies reveal a chauvinistic press and education in the reporting of the nation's wars since 1945. There was some sharply
critical reporting, for example, of the bombing of the Hanoi-
Haiphong area of North Vietnam in December 1972. But correspondents and textbook writers tended in all the wars to report
events from the official point of view, complicit by generally
accepting Washington's interpretation of history, the wars, their
causes and their purposes. The public heard little about torture
in Saigon jails, for example, or violations of the Peace Agreement by the South, but it did receive "a plethora of stories
about 'Vietcong' or `North Vietnamese" violations" (Rosenau).
"Television helped generate public support" for Kennedy's and
Johnson"s war against Vietnam and "then served to mute opposition
to the pace of Nixon's four-year policy of extrication" (Entman
and Paletz).

In extenuation, many contributors partly blame government
secrecy, distortion, manipulation, and coverup for correspondents' nationalistic bias. 500,000 US soldiers would not have
died in an invasion of Japan in 1945 as President Truman claimed
in rationalization of the destruction of Hiroshima and Nagasaki
(Bernstein). The US destroyers Maddox and Turner were not
attacked by North Vietnamese torpedo boats as alleged by military
and government officials to justify the escalation of the war in
Vietnam (Austin). Inhabited Laotian villages were illegally and
atrociously bombed for over five years contrary to the denials by
generals, ambassadors, and Pentagon secretaries (Branfman).

Latin America

Control of information has two targets: the American public
and the people of Latin America. Information about Latin America
is distorted not merely because it is so minimal. That is, misinformation has more than organizational causes (the number and
location of camera crews, for example). It is also highly ideological. As Herman says, "the mass media follow a patriotic
agenda." Juan Arevalo spells communism with a "k" in order to
distinguish between real communism and the "kommunism" fabricated
by the US in order to control Latin America through "national
security" client states. Anticommunism is said to mask U.S.
geopolitical interests in Latin America. The contributors to

253

this section of the bibliography examine the methods of information control which serve US political, military, and economic
strategies. (Also see I on Sovietphobia, VI on the CIA, and VII
on global reach.)
Critics mainly concentrate on government misinformation and
press failure sufficiently to expose official distortion and
lying and its neglect of the human toll of US intervention. In
Contempt of Congress documents the half truths and deceptions
told by administration officials to Congress about Central America by juxtaposing official White House statements with contradicting internal government documents and cables and congressional reports. The US has systematically denied "the authenticity
of revolutionary movements in Central America" and explained them
as Soviet subversion of "our" hemisphere (Persky). Too often
official rationales and "facts" have been reported uncritically.
US-backed terror receives less attention than rebel terror.
Cockburn, for example, asks for attention to the Honduran raid on
the Colomancagua refugee camp and the increase of U.S. gunships
to El Salvador and the devastation of the air war there. The
press is guilty of "ignoring the people's voices in favor of the
politicians," says Oakes.
The manipulation of reality to persuade the US population to
support intervention in Latin America for US economic and military interests turns also outward. The Spanish-language services
of AP and UPI "are the major source of international news for
Hispanic media in the Western Hemisphere" (Massing). US economic expansion via television has significant warping effects on
the countries south of the border. What is good for ABC and CBS
and NBC and their sponsors is not necessarily good for Guatemala
(Wells).

Works Cited

Bennett, James R. Rev. of Eve Pell, The Big Chill: How the
Reagan Administration, Corporate America, and Religious Conserva-
tives Are Subverting Free Speech and the Public's Right to Know
in FSY 24 (1985) 166-170.
Burns, James M. Uncommon Sense. New York: Harper, 1971.
Jaworski, Leon. The Right and the Power: The Prosecution of
Watergate. New York: Pocket, 1977.
Myerson, Michael. Watergate: Crime in the Suites. New York:
International, 1973.
Neustadt, Richard. Presidential Power: The Politics of Lead-
ership from FDR to Carter. New York: Wiley, 1980.
Olsen, Marvin. Participatory Pluralism: Political Participa-
tion and Influence in the United States and Sweden. Chicago:
Nelson-Hall, 1982.
Ranney, Austin. Channels of Power: The Impact of TV on Amer-
ican Politics. New York: Basic, 1983.
Raskin, Marcus. Notes on the Old System: To Transform Ameri-
can Politics. New York: McKay, 1974.
Rossiter, Clinton. The American Presidency. New York:
Harcourt, 1960.
Schrag, Peter. Mind Control. New York: Pantheon, 1978.
"Watergate Revisited." Congress and the Nation. Vol. V.
Washington, DC: Congressional Quarterly, 1984.

Introduction

IV. A. The Presidency 1474-1641 (See I. & II. A. and B.)

1474.   Bennett, James R. "Presidential Control of
    Information: A Bibliography." ORK (1986-87).
Almost 200 entries on President Reagan published serially
in four parts beginning with the Spring 1986 issue. Part I,
"Access to Media": the White House press, the press conference,
News Service, etc.; II, "Doublespeak, Disinformation, and
Deceit" (Fall 1986); III, "Anti-Sovietism" (Winter 1986-87); IV,
"Secrecy and Censorship" (Spring 1987). [These items are not
repeated in this book, except for significant books, annotations
shortened.]

IV. A. 1. Public Relations, News Management, Media Access
    1474-1542 (See II. D.)

1475.   Adams, William, ed. Television Coverage of the Middle
    East. Norwood, NJ: Ablex, 1981. 167.
In a conflict between the US and a foreign antagonist, as
in the case of the Soviet invasion of Afghanistan, the president
has a tremendous advantage in the political and media process.
Opponents have little access, and the administration can control
the release of information. Commercialism plays a role also,
since the populace prefers stories of simple conflict, familiar
values, and nationalism, and the media are only too ready to
provide them (124-5). Network correspondents, as in the Iranian
hostage events, tend to be spokespersons for the government in
foreign affairs coverage, providing virtually "a unified
'policy' of selection, interpretation, and presentation of
information" (154).

1476.   Appleman, Daniel. "The OTP and Reorganizational
    Alternatives." PTR 5.1 (1977) 44-51.
An assessment of the White House Office of
Telecommunications Policy. "Because of the great potential for
authoritarian control over the media in the hands of the
Executive, regulatory activities in the nongovernmental sector
must remain with the FCC." But an agency under the president is
needed for comprehensive telecommunications policy.

1477.   Bagdikian, Ben. "Press Independence and the Cuban
    Crisis." CJR 1.4 (1962) 5-11.
Analysis of news management by the Kennedy Administration
during the Cuban missile crisis. "The Kennedy Administration
demonstrated the most sophisticated, skillful, and precisely
planned control of news in peacetime history."

1478.   Bagdikian, Ben. "Television--'the President's
    Medium'?" CJR 1.2 (1962) 34-38.
The author answers his question with a resounding yes. The
president has the "awesome power" to "transmit himself into the
living room" "verbatim and without filtration by reporters and

editors."

1479.   Barger, Harold M.   The Impossible Presidency:
          Illusions and Realities of Executive Power.   Glenview,
          IL: Scott, 1984.   450.
An effort "to reduce our present dependency on symbols,
myths, and illusions" through "a better understanding of the
real condition of the presidency." Ch. 1 the "importance of the
presidency as a popularized leadership role," 2 the "myths and
illusions surrounding the political leadership role of the
president," 3 the "role of the president as legislative
leader," etc. (ten chs. in all).

1480.   Bennett, James R. "Out of Disaster a Pep Talk." QRD
          12.1 (1985) 10-12.
President Reagan's speeches and press conferences following
the bombing of the Marine barracks at the Beirut Airport on
October 23, 1983, follow a pattern of threat, bonding, cause,
and response.

1481.   Berman, Larry.   The Office of Management and Budget
          and the Presidency, 1921-1979.   Princeton, NJ: Princeton
          UP, 1979.   180.
This chronological study of the Bureau of the Budget/OMB
reveals a qualitative change between 1921-1960 and 1961-1979.
After 1960 partisan presidential demands "undermined BOB's and
later OMB's credibility as a presidential agent" (Preface).
This is a part of the history of the growing centralization of
power in the White House.

1482.   Bonafede, Dom. "The New Political Power of the
          Press." WJR 2.7 (1980) 25-27.
"Just as the party conventions are programmed media events,
the new breed of politicians are essentially performers" for
news stories.

1483.   Bonafede, Dom. "The President's Publicity Machine."
          WJR 2.4 (1980) 42-44.
Criticism of President Carter's "news extravaganzas" and
the secret complicity of the press.

1484.   Bonafede, Dom. "Uncle Sam: The Flimflam Man?"   WJR
          1.3 (1978) 65-71.
The federal government under Nixon and subsequently Carter
employed a huge public relations staff to sell government
policies, programs, and personalities, and "to withhold
information when it is believed to be against the
administration's interest."

1485.   Boot, William. "Capital Letter." CJR 24.4 (1986)
          11-18.
The "White House press conference has been converted by
Ronald Reagan into a forum for inaccuracy, distortion, and
falsehood--and the press, for all its alleged might and

skepticism, has been unable to do anything about it."

1486.   Cannon, Lou. <u>Reagan</u>. New York: Putnam's, 1982.
    464.
    In the ch. "The Worlds of Ronald Reagan" the author
stresses Reagan's "world of heroes," a "world defined" by heroic
stories, "a make-believe world in which heroic deeds had the
capacity to transform reality," the world of Harold Bell Wright,
Horatio Alger, and Edgar Rice Burroughs. "The capital of
Reagan's make-believe world became Hollywood."

1487.   Clift, Eleanor. "How the White House Keeps Reporters
    in Their Place." <u>WJR</u> 8.6 (1986) 9.
    In an administration "where little of a theatrical nature
is left to chance," the behind-the-scenes choreography of a
presidential press conference is both extensive and effective.

1488.   Cockburn, Alexander. "Beat the Devil." <u>Na</u> 242.4
    (1986) 102-3.
    The "important members of the opinion-forming elite,
notably <u>The New York Times</u> and <u>The Washington Post</u>, have fallen
in step with the Reagan Administration in belittling the
importance of [nuclear] test bans."

1489.   Cockburn, Alexander. "Silence is Golden." <u>Na</u> 242.18
    (1986) 638.
    "The success of the Reagan Administration so far as news
management is concerned--news management being its central
preoccupation--is its conditioning of the media to 'see' and not
to see."

1490.   Cohen, Bernard. <u>The Press and Foreign Policy</u>.
    Princeton, NJ: Princeton UP, 1963.   288.
    A study mainly of newspapers and the large news agencies,
"the people working for them who are responsible for gathering
and interpreting foreign policy news in the United States." The
author is trying to explore the "map-making" function of the
press, for the press "is stunningly successful in telling its
readers what to think <u>about</u>." A study therefore of the
"constraints" over the presentation of "reality" by the press.

1491.   Coney, Cargill. "Reagan Snake Oil Not Selling Well on
    Campus." <u>Guard</u> 38.32 (1986) 5.
    President Reagan continues to promote Star Wars
successfully with Congress and the public even though opposed by
hundreds of university scientists.

1492.   Cornwell, Elmer E., Jr. <u>Presidential Leadership of
    Public Opinion</u>. Bloomington, IN: Indiana UP, 1965.
    370.
    The President "finds in the populace not only his base of
electoral support, but the very essence of his power to
influence the process of governance." Since his power derives
from the popular support he can mobilize, his ability to

persuade is of utmost importance. Chs. 2-6 provide a historical
survey; chs. 7-8 discuss the press conference; 9 the White House
staff and public relations; and 10 the electronic media.

1493.   David, Michael and Pat Aufderheide. "All the
      President's Media." Ch 5.3 (1985) 20-24.
      "The TV President is using satellites to pitch his policies
directly to the masses here and abroad, sidestepping the
Washington press corps." The new technologies "give the Chief
Executive a sales apparatus for his policies that no previous
President has ever had."

1494.   Dowie, Mark. "How ABC Spikes the News." MJ 10.9
      (1985) 33-39,53.
      In 1984 ABC's World News Tonight suppressed three important
Reagan administration scandals involving important Republicans:
USIA Director Charles Wick, Nevada Senator Paul Laxalt, then
Secretary of Labor Raymond Donovan.

1495.   Dugger, Ronnie.   "The Administration's Long Knives
      and the Hazards of Nationalism." Dead 1.4 (1986) 1-4.
      Dugger reports on the Reagan administration's Cold War
attempts to control the press via threats of prosecution (prior
restraint) and appeals to patriotism.

1496.   Dugger, Ronnie. The Politician: The Life and Times
      of Lyndon Johnson. New York: Norton, 1982. 514.
      "In Johnson's career and period we can plainly see that
conventional politics is just the puppet show of economic
power." After WWII "we lived through a twenty-year scramble of
incorporated commercialism, maldistributed prosperity,
anticommunism as a shield for rapacious corporate power at home
and abroad, and an increasingly bristling and independent
militarism." And Johnson worked the "levers" of this politics
(13-15).

1497.   Dugger, Ronnie. On Reagan: The Man & His
      Presidency. New York: McGraw, 1983. 616.
      In contrast to the image he was projecting during the 1980
campaign, Reagan's radio broadcasts between 1975 and 1979 reveal
him to be "a hard-line right-wing ideologue with fully formed
and recently expressed prejudices on all of the outstanding
issues of the times."

1498.   Erickson, Paul. Reagan Speaks: The Making of an
      American Myth. New York: New York UP, 1985. 172.
      The book "examines President Reagan's technique as a teller
of tales." Ch. 2 considers his style and persona, including his
various "more or less imaginary personalities." Ch. 3 examines
how Reagan alternates between rhetoric and reality, and how his
audience becomes characters in his parables. Ch. 4 deals with
the stock characterizations he employs for his good and bad
people. Ch. 5 places his rhetoric in the wide context of the
battle between ultimate good and evil, and his frequent use of

crisis rhetoric. The 6th ch. focuses on the 1984 presidential campaign. The final ch. comments on contemporary political rhetoric.

1499.   Firestone, O. J. The Public Persuader: Government Advertising. Toronto: Methuen, 1970. 258.
An exposition and denunciation of partisan political use of the channels of information available to government, particularly in the use of paid advertising by the Executive. The author advocates a central Board to supervise expenditures of public funds for the communication of information to the public. The book is about Canada, but the problem applies to the US as well.

1500.   Frankel, Max. "The 'State Secrets' Myth." CJR 10.3 (1971) 22-26.
Frankel claims that the Pentagon Papers provide direct evidence of "the uses of top secret information by our government in deliberate leaks to the press for the purposes of influencing public opinion."

1501.   Gelb, Leslie, and Anthony Lake. "Kissinger's 'Peace at Hand.'" MORE 3.2 (1973) 1,14-16.
As part of the White House negotiating strategy, Kissinger "sucked" the press into optimism by his announcement in October 1972 that "peace is at hand," only to be followed in December by massive B-52 bombings.

1502.   Grossman, Michael, and Martha Kumar. "It is Inevitable, Say Two Scholars on the White House. The Institution, not the Men, Make it So." WJR 2.4 (1980) 52-56.
The White House inevitably involves "managing the flow of news, wooing reporters with ingratiating approaches, using their control over access to avoid reporters and attacking the credibility of the media."

1503.   Grossman, Michael, and Martha Kumar. Portraying the President: The White House and the News Media. Baltimore: Johns Hopkins UP, 1981. 358.
"What we found . . . was that almost every important White House official--and a large proportion of the not so important-- was involved in presidential publicity. The White House contains a vast array of presidential strategists who share responsibility for portraying the President to his public throughout the media" (Preface). A study of twenty-five years of presidential news in The New York Times and Time and in ten years of CBS broadcasts reveal a "consistent pattern of favorable coverage of the President" (253), yet all presidents complain about unfair coverage.

1504.   Grossman, Michael, and Francis Rourke. "The Media and the Presidency: An Exchange Analysis." PolSQ 91.3 (1976) 455-470.

Press and government are often not adversaries in service
of the public, but rather act as partners seeking their own best
interests. "The adversary concept provides no mechanism for
understanding the enormous amount of cooperation and even
collaboration that takes place in the interaction" between press
and government. The "exchange system" has been "very
profitable" to presidents.

1505.   Haig, Alexander M., Jr. Caveat: Realism, Reagan,
     and Foreign Policy. New York: Macmillan, 1984. 367.
     Includes an analysis of how under the Reagan administration
"the Times and the Post and the networks and the news magazines
have let themselves be converted into White House bulletin
boards" (18).

1506.   Hallin, Daniel, and Paolo Mancini. "Political
     Structure and Representational Form in U.S. and Italian
     Television News." T&S (1984) 829-850.
     The "narrative conventions of American TV news not only
make it hard to deal with abstract political ideas," but also
"encourage the search for heroes and bolster the centralized
authority of the American presidency."

1507.   Hart, Roderick P. Verbal Style and the Presidency:
     A Computer-Based Analysis. Orlando, FL: Academic, 1984.
     322.
     Chs. on "The Chief Executive as Chief Persuader," "The
Presidency Speaks," "The Case of Truman and Eisenhower," "JFK,
LBJ, and the Politics of Discourse," "Richard Nixon: Prisoner
of Rhetoric," "Ford and Carter," "Jimmy Carter's Rhetorical
Odyssey," "The Great Communicator and Beyond." A study of "over
400 speeches by presidents Truman through Reagan" by a computer
program "written expressly for this purpose." A rhetorical
model for the presidency is necessary because "the nation's
media and the presidency have, especially since 1945, developed
an intensively symbiotic relationship" and because "the power of
the presidency [is] the power to persuade its various rival
constituencies."

1508.   Haskell, Anne. "Live From Capitol Hill: Where
     Politicians Use High Tech to Bypass the Press." WJR
     4.9 (1982) 48-50.
     Politicians are sending their own programs directly to
local newspapers and television stations rather than
communicating with the traditional press.

1509.   Hertsgaard, Mark. "What Became of the Freeze?" MJ
     10.5 (1985) 44-47.
     "The freeze movement has virtually dropped off the media
map in this country," and the dream of stopping the arms race,
so compelling just two years ago, gets edged out of our
collective consciousness by the tranquilizing drone of news
reports about the latest superpower chess moves in Geneva."

1510.   Hoekstra, Douglas. "Presidential Power and
     Presidential Purpose." <u>RP</u> 47.4 (1985) 566-87.
A critique of "the ways in which Richard Neustadt's
<u>Presidential Power</u> attempts to connect the activities of power-
seeking presidents to the public ends their actions presumably
further."

1511.   Hogan, J. Michael. <u>The Panama Canal in American
     Politics: Domestic Advocacy and the Evolution of Policy</u>.
     Carbondale, IL: Southern Illinois UP, 1986. 291.
"With Americans increasingly dependent upon the media of
mass communications for their political information, those
political elites with the greatest access to the media exercise
more and more influence over public opinion on matters of
American foreign policy. The debate over the Panama Canal
illustrates the power of the president to set the agenda and to
define the terms of debate over American foreign policy."

1512.   Hohenberg, John. "The Great Press Put-On." <u>SR</u>
     52.10 (March 8, 1969) 120-21.
The news conference is "the lowest form of journalism in a
free society" because the reporter is "helpless."

1513.   Johansen, Robert. <u>The National Interest and the
     Human Interest: An Analysis of U.S. Foreign Policy</u>.
     Princeton, NJ: Princeton UP, 1980. 517.
Contrasts the "professed values" used to deceive the public
with the real values in US policies: on the one hand to
"sustain democratic parties and maintain pluralism," on the
other to "undermine and prevent the exercise of the right of
self-determination and democratic government." Arms control
policies, aid to India, human rights in Chile, and marine
pollution are used to illustrate the author's thesis. "Witness
the tension between the rhetorical respect given by U.S. leaders
to nonintervention, self-determination, and sovereign equality
as guiding principles of foreign policy and the actualities of
an interventionary, even a counterrevolutionary diplomacy" (from
the Foreword by Richard Falk).

1514.   Kelly, Kevin. "Newsmen Bite 'Mad Dog.'" <u>Guard</u> 38.30
     (1986) 2.
"Corporate journalism in the U.S., always prone to cartoon-
like simplification of international events, is now portraying
the undeclared war on Libya as a one-on-one shootout pitting The
Avenger v. Dr. Death."

1515.   Kern, Montague, et al. <u>The Kennedy Crises: The
     Press, the Presidency, and Foreign Policy</u>. Chapel Hill,
     NC: North Carolina UP, 1983. 290.
Analysis of the Kennedy administration's relationship with
the press during the Laotian, Berlin, Cuban missile, and Vietnam
crises, studying coverage by the <u>New York Times</u>, <u>Washington
Post</u>, <u>Chicago Tribune</u>, <u>St. Louis Post-Dispatch</u>, and
<u>San Francisco Examiner</u>, with interviews of more than sixty media

and government officials. Despite the strong impact of presidential leadership on press treatment of crisis issues, the overall generalization emerges that "the president dominates press coverage primarily in situations where competing interpretations of events are not being espoused by others whom journalists consider important" (195). [The author does not confront the anti-Soviet unity of the press and the government in these crises and perceives diversity and freedom in a debate over limited alternatives.]

1516.   Leubsdorf, Carl P. "Winging it with Jimmy." CJR 17.2
         (1978) 42-43.
    President Carter was able to use the press to present the idea that he was expanding funding for solar energy research, when in fact his administration spent less on such research than the previous one.

1517.   Manoff, Robert K. "State-Sponsored Journalism."
         Prog 50.6 (1986) 36.
    Following the bombing of the Libyan cities of Tripoli and Benghazi on April 14, the strike timed "for the evening television news," the press "allowed the Administration to dominate the news with the official version of events and the official rationale for its own decisions."

1518.   McCartney, James. "Must the Media be 'Used'?" CJR
         8.4 (1969-70) 36-41.
    In the age of public relations, "managed news," and pseudo-events, the media must revise coverage procedures or continue to be exploited.

1519.   Mickelson, Sig. The Electric Mirror: Politics in an
         Age of Television. New York: Dodd, 1972. 304.
    Ch. 7, "Government and Television," focuses especially upon the power of the presidency in the media.

1520.   Minow, Newton, et al. Presidential Television. New
         York: Basic, 1973. 232.
    Television has created a new, potent, and dangerous instrument of Presidential power which has helped disrupt the Constitutional balance between government and the responsible opposition. Also, the prevailing rules of fairness, equal time, and party access are altogether inadequate.

1521.   Moffett, Toby. The Participation Put-On: Reflections
         of a Disenchanted Washington Youth Expert. New York:
         Delacorte, 1971. 267.
    An account of the author's tenure as Director of the Department of Health, Education, and Welfare's Office of Students and Youth, 1969-1970. He was appointed with a mandate to serve as "an advocate for youth," but he discovered that the Nixon administration "wanted to use his office to co-opt legitimate dissent and save face for political appointees." He calls this process of creating an illusion of action "the participation

put-on." Moffett resigned in May 1970 in protest against the
illegal bombing of Cambodia and the killing of students at Kent
State.

1522.   Morris, Scott.   "SDI Violates Lone US-USSR Arms
          Treaty, Jackson Says." AT (Nov. 1, 1985) 1.
     The Reagan administration has reinterpreted the 1972 Anti-
Ballistic Missile Treaty, which "patently" outlaws any space-
based missile defense system, to allow the Strategic Defense
Initiative (SDI). The administration has launched a television
ad campaign to persuade the public to embrace the illegal
program.

1523.   Nix, Mindy.   "Meet the Press Game." MORE 3.2 (1973)
          12-14.
     NBC's "Meet the Press," CBS' "Face the Nation," and ABC's
"Issues and Answers" are promotional exercises "aimed at landing
on page one." These Sunday programs "have always served
primarily as conduits for communicating Administration
positions." Their "very intentions contain powerful, unspoken
assumptions about how society works. The most obvious is, of
course, that Washington is the mover and everywhere else the
moved."

1524.   Novak, Michael. Choosing Our King: Powerful Symbols
          in Presidential Politics. New York: Macmillan, 1974.
          324.
     Drawing evidence mainly from the 1972 presidential contest
between Nixon and McGovern, the author argues that "the
presidency is the nation's most central religious symbol"
against whose immense symbolic powers the Constitution "provides
too little countervailing balance."

1525.   Perry, Roland. Hidden Power: The Programming of the
          President. Beaufort, 1985. 232.
     An appraisal of some of the high-tech methods politicians
in general and presidents in particular use to enhance their
image with the voters, especially the use of targeted opinion
polls such as the Political Information System (PINS) of Reagan
pollster Richard Wirthlin.

1526.   Pollard, James E. The Presidents and the Press,
          Truman to Johnson. New York: Macmillan, 1947. 866.
     A president-by-president survey from Washington to Truman,
with special attention to the press conference, which gained
truly national and even international importance beginning with
Theodore Roosevelt. The press conference is "an effective
medium in the necessary and increasingly important development
of American and world public opinion" and "of deep importance to
every American who has a genuine belief in the democratic
processes."

1527.   "Reagan Recovers the High Ground." Turnabout.
          Arlington, MA: WAND Education Fund Report, 1986. 26-29.

Reagan has successfully transformed his image from that of a "mad bomber" to "a man of reason" while continuing military escalation.

1528.   Relyea, Harold, et al. The Presidency and Information Policy. New York: Center for the Study of the Presidency, 1981. 216.
Essays on the people's right to know, information management, executive privilege, national security, presidential libraries and papers, and the president's media image.

1529.   Reston, James. "The Hucksters Are Getting Out of Hand and Into Government." AG (April 14, 1986) 9A.
Ronald Reagan "is better than any" other president at the "popularity business" and "using television to argue that Nicaragua and Libya are major threats to our security and that a permanent ban on the testing of nuclear weapons" is "just another Soviet trap."

1530.   Riencourt, Amaury de. The Coming Caesars. New York: Capricorn, 1957. 384.
"Political power in the Western world has become increasingly concentrated in the United States of America, and in the office of the President within America." It is in Washington that "the Caesars of the future will arise." "The prime element in this situation is neither political nor strategic--it is essentially psychological. It is the growing 'father complex' that is increasingly evident in America, the willingness to follow in any emergency, economic or military, the leadership of one man."

1531.   Spear, Joseph. Presidents and the Press: The Nixon Legacy. Cambridge, MA: MIT P, 1984. 349.
Analysis of the presidential media organization--spokesmen, pollsters, image-makers, speech writers, television experts, media monitors--which increasingly attempts to manipulate the press and manage the news.

1532.   "State of Siege." CJR 19.1 (1980) 25-26.
The press is supporting the government's new hard-line foreign policy and its devaluation of human rights.

1533.   Stockman, David. The Triumph of Politics: How the Reagan Revolution Failed. New York: Harper, 1986. 422.
In spite of the subject's absence from the Index, the book gives instances of White House preoccupation with managing the news.

1534.   Tebbel, John, and Sarah Watts. The Press and the Presidency: From George Washington to Ronald Reagan. New York: Oxford UP, 1985. 583.
The "ambition to manage the news" among presidents involves a crucial failure to understand the First Amendment regarding prior restraint which is fatal to democracy. Especially since

the time of Theodore Roosevelt the media have been vulnerable to manipulation by the White House, but the recent growth of presidential power combined with a willingness to disseminate lies and disinformation has greatly increased that vulnerability. Now anywhere from 150 to 500 of Reagan's staff are engaged in "staging" the presidential news. The authors warn that the "imperial presidency" may "well be capable of nullifying the First Amendment, in a relatively short time and with public support."

1535.   Thomas, Helen. "Ronald Reagan and the Management of the News." The White House Press on the Presidency. Ed. Kenneth Thompson. Lanham, MD: UP of America, 1983. 34-59.
"Access to Reagan is very limited and under the most controlled of circumstances." The "term 'managed news' coined in the Kennedy era has been developed to a fine art. . . .Many of the reforms that grew out of the nightmare that was Watergate have been eliminated or will be if Reagan has his way. The drive has been systematic to cut down legitimate access to news in the foreign policy field. New regulations have been devised to tighten the circle of those with access to top secret documents. The Freedom of Information Act is under siege, and Reagan's forces seek to legitimatize domestic spying by the CIA" (36-38).

1536.   Thompson, Kenneth, ed. The White House Press on the Presidency: News Management and Co-option. Lanham, MD: UP of America, 1983. 81.
Speeches presented by Frank Cormier, James Deakin, and Helen Thomas followed by questions and answers. The three reporters "are united in opposition to what they consider news management or co-option of reporters by particular presidents." They are "impatient" with the view that certain issues should be "shielded from public disclosure." They are critical of the typical press briefing by the press officer and resent being herded together for what they contemptuously refer to as press or 'photo opportunities.'"

1537.   Turnabout: The Emerging New Realism in the Nuclear Age. Washington, DC: Women's Action for Nuclear Disarmament Education Fund, 1986. 48.
Interviews with 100 reporters and editors who have covered the nuclear weapons debate revealed 1) sympathetic coverage of the nuclear weapons freeze campaign as a popular call for serious negotiations, but dismissal of the actual Freeze proposal as naive on technical and political grounds (22-25); 2) Reagan White House communications skills and resources for deflection of criticism of its nuclear policies and portrayal of the President as a peacemaker confronted with a hostile Soviet adversary (26-27); 3) public support of the Freeze by many arms control experts, but private rejection (28-9).

1538.   Weisman, Steven. "The President and the Press: The

Art of Controlled Access." NYTM (14 Oct. 1984) 34-37, 71-74, 80, 82-83.

President Reagan has gained the power "to decide when, where and how he will engage" the press. He "has tended to operate in a kind of cocoon, sheltered from the press. Compared with his predecessor, he has held few formal news conferences. In public appearances, he strictly limits opportunities for questions. . . .More significantly, even when he entertains questions from the press "he controls access by evading the question or denying its premise or answering another question."

1539. "What If He Gave a News Conference and Nobody Came?" CJR 23.3 (1984) 22.

"The infrequency" of President Reagan's news conferences "means that there can hardly be any continuity in the questioning," and they "leave the impression that they have become little more than another item in the repertory of presidential theater."

1540. Whittemore, L. H. "The Plugging of the President." MORE 2.2 (1972) 4-6.

President Nixon's manipulation of television and the press conference "to his own advantage." He has "learned how to reduce the White House press corps to a condition bordering on impotence."

1541. Windt, Theodore, ed., with Beth Ingold. Essays in Presidential Rhetoric. Dubuque, IA: Kendall, 1983. 323.

Two essays discuss the "rise of the rhetorical presidency"; eighteen analyze the rhetorical performances of US presidents from Kennedy to Reagan. Johnson's rhetoric is the subject of five essays. Presidential rhetoric, his ability to persuade the bureaucracy, Congress, and the public, is a "major source" of his power. Presidential rhetoric is also "a means of legitimation of his authority," and "the center of democratic politics."

1542. Yudof, Mark G. When Government Speaks: Politics, Law, and Government Expression in America. Berkeley: U of California P, 1983. 323.

Government propaganda, advertising, and disinformation are as important a First Amendment issue as government secrecy because of the size and power of government access versus alternative versions of reality.

IV. A. 2. Presidential Secrecy, Censorship, Cover-Up, Surveillance, Repression 1543-1585

1543. Anderson, Jack, and Carl Kalvelage. American Government . . .Like It Is. Morristown, NJ: General Learning, 1972. 117.

The ch. on "News Media and the Public" describes a generally ignorant public, a government manipulating public opinion, and a press failing to perform its job of informing the people, the people's "sleeping watchdog."

1544.   Anderson, Jack, with George Clifford. The Anderson Papers. New York: Random, 1973. 275.
Accounts of a few of Anderson's investigative coups: Nixon's cancellation of an anti-trust decree against AT&T, government concealment of its true position in the Bangladesh revolution. "All too many who write about government have been seduced by those who govern."

1545.   Beschloss, Michael. Mayday: Eisenhower, Kruschev, and the U-2 Affair. New York: Harper, 1986. 544.
President Eisenhower personally approved the flights over Soviet territory, often viewing photos taken by the planes, but he and other officials denied his knowledge of the flights when the plane piloted by CIA employee Francis Gary Powers was downed and Powers was captured. Then he took responsibility defiantly, causing Kruschev to cancel the approaching summit. Eisenhower liked covert operations (CIA overthrow of Iran and Guatemala).

1546.   Breckenridge, Adam. The Executive Privilege: Presidential Control Over Information. Lincoln, NE: U of Nebraska P, 1974. 188.
A study of the rise of executive privilege.

1547.   Claybrook, Joan, et al. Reagan on the Road: The Crash of the U.S. Auto Safety Program. Washington, DC: Public Citizen, 1982. 92.
National Highway Safety Administration secrecy under Reagan.

1548.   Claybrook, Joan, et al. Retreat From Safety: Reagan's Attack on America's Health. New York: Pantheon, 1984. 270.
Suppression of information by health and safety regulatory agencies under Reagan.

1549.   Commager, Henry S. The Defeat of America: Presidential Power and the National Character. New York: Simon, 1974. 163.
US anticommunism and anti-Sovietism caused the US to oppose "the revolution of two-thirds of the human race striving to emerge from five centuries of poverty and misery" and to expand our power throughout the world. Much of this was done covertly and "never debated or specifically authorized by Congress." "What was new was the presumptuous claim that the President was above the law." The "defeat of America which this book recounts was primarily moral." We "may emerge from defeat stronger in our understanding of the Constitution and in our devotion to it" (Introduction).

1550.   "Congress Wrestles with Privacy Issues." CLA 9.1-2 (1986) 11.

"The Reagan Administration fired the opening shot in the privacy debate by proposing a new FBI computer surveillance program and legislation to grant the government wider access to computerized bank records."

1551.   Cook, Blanche. The Declassified Eisenhower. Garden City, NY: Doubleday, 1981. 432.
"Although Eisenhower sincerely deplored the military-industrial complex, it was empowered as never before during his presidency" (vii). This legacy is now understood through the aid of the Freedom of Information Act, which revealed how much Eisenhower worked undercover.

1552.   Cronkite, Walter. "The Rebirth of Mistrust." Ch 2.2 (1982) 54-56.
Reagan's attempts to restrict the FOIA and other actions seem to question the idea that "an informed people can intelligently govern itself."

1553.   Dahl, Robert. Controlling Nuclear Weapons: Democracy Versus Guardianship. Syracuse, NY: Syracuse UP, 1985. 128.
The American people do not possess enough information necessary for us to delegate the authority to our elected officials to make decisions regarding the control and use of nuclear weapons. The author also wrote Pluralist Democracy in the United States.

1554.   Demac, Donna. Keeping America Uninformed: Government Secrecy in the 1980's. New York: Pilgrim, 1984. 192.
An overview of the Reagan administration's effort to control information and to subvert the public's right to know by concealment, lying, distortion, misinformation, media access denial, tightening of the functions of the regulatory agencies, cutbacks in access to federal statistics, etc.

1555.   Denniston, Lyle. "New Curbs on Information?" WJR 8.6 (1986) 48.
Efforts by the Reagan administration since 1981 to narrow access to government documents through FOIA are moving forward.

1556.   "Eclipse in Baltimore." MORE 4.3 (1974) 8-9.
Spiro Agnew persuaded the Baltimore Sun to kill an article about the sale of his Maryland home.

1557.   Ellison, Harlan. The Glass Teat: Essays of Opinion on the Subject of Television. New York: Jove/HBJ, 1975. 319. 1st ed. Ace, 1970.
A collection of some of the author's essays on television written for the Los Angeles Free Press in late 1960s, attacking President Nixon and Vice-President Agnew and the increasingly "frightened and restrictive" networks. The Introduction gives an account of how the Nixon administration managed to restrict the sale of the book and to intimidate the publisher into

withdrawing from its contract to publish another collection of
the author's essays. This second collection was finally
published in 1975 as The Other Glass Teat.

1558.   Epstein, Edward Jay. "Peddling A Drug Scare." CJR
          16.4 (1977) 51-56.
     "How Nixon and his aides sold a heroin horror story to the
national media" as a first step in reorganizing drug enforcement
agencies into a superagency responsible to the executive branch,
which amounted to the establishment of a "presidential police
force with almost unlimited powers."

1559.   "50 Secret Missions Allegedly Approved by Reagan in
          Term." AG (Nov. 16, 1986) 3A.
     The Reagan administration has relied heavily on covert
operations to achieve its objectives.

1560.   Guilfoy, Christine. "Reagan Will Get You If You Don't
          Watch Out!" Guard 38.30 (1986) 8.
     A forum on repression sponsored by the National Lawyers
Guild and entitled "The Right to Resist: Government Repression
in the 80s" presented evidence of harassment against the
Sanctuary, Black, Puerto Rican independence, and other movements
and warned that "the Reagan administration is undertaking
statutory changes to facilitate repression."

1561.   Halperin, Morton. "Secrecy and National Security."
          BAS 41 (Aug. 1985) 114-117.
     "The public's right to debate national security issues is
severely threatened by the judiciary's increased willingness--
since the Pentagon Papers case--to let the executive branch
decide what may or may not be published."

1562.   Halperin, Morton, and Daniel N. Hoffman. Top
          Secret: National Security and the Right to Know.
          Washington: New Republic, 1977. 158.
     "In the aftermath of Vietnam and of Watergate it appears
that secrecy has been neither a rare nor a benign phenomenon.
On the contrary, the executive branch has made secrecy an
essential part of its modus operandi." Not only has "secrecy
undermined the constitutional prerogatives of Congress and the
electorate, it has also led directly to substantial
infringements of civil liberties." Ch. 2 tells the stories of
the Pentagon Papers, the bombing of Cambodia, and the secret
intervention in Angola to illustrate "how the secrecy system
works" (Ch. 3). Ch. 4 discusses "Recent Efforts at Reform."
Ch. 5 makes recommendations for a more open system. Ch. 6
explains the constitutional foundation for an open government.

1563.   Hersh, Seymour. The Price of Power: Kissinger in
          the Nixon White House. New York: Summit, 1983. 698.
     "As both the memoirs [by Nixon and Kissinger] showed,
neither man ever came to grips with the basic vulnerability of
their policy: They were operating in a democracy, guided by a

constitution, and among a citizenry who held their leaders to a reasonable standard of morality and integrity." Both had resorted to "illegal wiretapping and spying" and "secret threats and secret military activities." "In the end, it was Henry Kissinger who survived."

1564.   Hunter, Jane. Undercutting Sanctions: Israel, the U.S., and South Africa. Washington, DC: Washington Midle East Assoc., 1986. 68.
The US has made every effort to cover up the Israeli-South African relationship: South African products enter the US labeled "Made in Israel," military secrets and technology pass through Israel to South Africa.

1565.   Karp, Walter. "Liberty Under Siege." Har 271.1626 (1985) 53-67.
Subtitled "The Reagan Administration's Taste for Autocracy," concerned with "a systematic assault on the concept of government accountability and deterrence of illegal government conduct." The Reagan administration "has been engaged in an unflagging campaign to exalt the power of the presidency and to undermine the power of the law, the courts, the Congress, and the people." A year-by-year chronicle of campaign against freedom and democracy.

1566.   Karpatkin, Marvin M. "En Route to 'A Gross Conforming Stupidity': Lamentations on the Systematic Suffocation of Civil Liberties in the Declining Days of the Nixon Administration, as Aided and Abetted by the Supreme Court." TS 22 (Winter 1974) 7-14.
The General Counsel of the ACLU cites specific court cases to underscore eight categories of civil rights violations performed under the Nixon Administration, violations over which the ACLU calls for the impeachment of Nixon.

1567.   Lash, Jonathan, et al. A Season of Spoils: The Reagan Administration's Attack on the Environment. New York: Pantheon, 1984. 385.
The attack includes secrecy, cover-up, perjury, and obstruction of Congressional investigation, in addition to command of the PR resources of the EPA and the White House.

1568.   "Less Access to Less Information By and About the U.S. Government: A 1981-1984 Chronology." Chicago: Association of College and Research Libraries, American Library Assoc., 1984 (with updates).
"What was first seen as an emerging trend in April 1981" has "by December 1984 become a continuing pattern of the federal government to restrict government publications and information dissemination activities."

1569.   Levine, Robert F. and Thomas W. Sarnoff. "Letter to the President. 6 February 1973." TQ 10.3 (1973) 54-55.
The President and Chairman of the Board of the National

Academy of Television Arts and Sciences asked President Nixon to
retract threats by the government to control television news.

1570.   Mathias, Charles, Jr. "State of Emergency." CLR 1.2
         (1974) 75-81.
The development of the US toward a national-security state
is the result of four proclamations of national emergency going
back to 1933. The author urges Congress to exercise its
constitutional responsibility to make the law; if not, "the
unmistakable drift toward one-man government will continue."

1571.   Morris, Roger. Uncertain Greatness: Henry Kissinger
         and American Foreign Policy. New York: Harper, 1977.
         312.
"That figurative gun in foreign policy is always in the
hands of those in power, whatever their politics," loaded with
"ignorance, incompetence, hypocrisy and deceit."

1572.   Oppenheim, Jerrold. "White House Media Czar
         Threatens Fairness Public TV." ChJR 5.6 (1972) 11-13.
The head of the White House Office of Telecommunications
Policy, Clay T. Whitehead, would abolish the fairness doctrine,
destroy public television and in general drastically diminish
the diversity of news sources.

1573.   Orman, John M. Presidential Secrecy and Deception.
         Westport, CT: Greenwood, 1980. 239.
A study of "presidential uses of secrecy and deception from
the Kennedy through the Ford administrations": Kennedy's
program to eliminate the Castro regime, Johnson's secret war in
Laos, Nixon's subversion of the Allende government, and Ford's
response to the Church and Pike Committee investigations during
1975-76.

1574.   "Papers Reveal Threat by Nixon to Cut PBS Aid." AG
         (February 25, 1979) 20A.
Nixon reacted to the appointment of certain newsmen with a
memo by an aide directing the cutting of PBS's budget. He also
attempted to control public broadcasting by his five
appointments to the Board of the Corporation for Public
Broadcasting.

1575.   Porter, William. Assault on the Media: The Nixon
         Years. Ann Arbor: U of Michigan P, 1976. 320.
The "wide-ranging efforts of governmental authority, over a
period of five and one-half years, to intimidate, harass,
regulate, and in other ways damage the news media in their
functioning as part of the American political system.

1576.   Powe, Scot. "Espionage, Leaks, and the First
         Amendment." BAS 42.6 (1986) 8-10.
"The Reagan Administration's prosecution of Samuel L.
Morison for leaking U.S. satellite photos to a British
publication presages development of an official secrets policy

271

and will constrict debate on U.S. defense policy."

1577.   Ryan, Geoffrey. "Inside the CBS." IC 7.2
         (1978) 72-78.
     A review of Daniel Schorr's Clearing the Air, which is
especially an account of President Nixon's manipulation and
"cold war" against television, which he perceived to be "the key
to the American people." A second main subject is the way CBS
caved in to pressure from the White House.

1578.   Schorr, Daniel. "Spy Article Squelched by '50 Law."
         AG (May 25, 1986) 6A.
     Even though "Moscow must have known about" US submarines
patrolling the Soviet coastline and entering its harbors for
communications intelligence "for a long time," pressure from the
CIA and President Reagan forced The Washington Post to postpone
and to suppress information in an article on the subject.

1579.   Thomas, Helen. Dateline: White House. New York:
         Macmillan, 1975. 298.
     A collection of the author's experience as the UPI reporter
covering the White House. "Too often in my years at the White
House there has been a lack of candor and a misjudgment of the
character of our people in this democratic society. Secrecy in
matters of public interest can be destructive."

1580.   "Unfinished Business." Prog 46.4 (1982) 4.
     US embargo against the organ of the Communist Party of
Cuba, Granma, is a violation of the First Amendment, an act
identical to what the Reagan administration had denounced the
Polish government for doing.

1581.   Weinberg, Steve. "Creeping Secrecy." CJR 22.4 (1983)
         31-32.
     President Reagan's Executive Order 12356 is a "radical"
change toward increased secrecy. It throws out all of President
Carter's public-access requirements, instructs officials "to
classify material at the highest level of secrecy in doubtful
cases," etc. Now Reagan has issued another directive requiring
all "present and former federal employees" who have been given
access to secret information "to sign a pledge to obtain
clearance before publishing material that even if not presently
classified, might be classified." The author urges the press to
"speak up."

1582.   Weinberg, Steve. "Trashing the FOIA." CJR 23.5
         (1985) 21-28.
     Under the Reagan administration officials are increasingly
undermining the FOIA through delays, costs, "excessive and absurd
deletions," EO 12356, and other hardening of secrecy.

1583.   "Winston Smith Goes to Washington." CJR 22.6 (1984)
         20.
     Examples of government secrecy and censorship, the worst of

all being National Security Decision Directive 84, which requires all who handle sensitive information to "sign contracts binding them for life" to clear "what they write and say in public with their one-time employer, the government," a la Orwell's 1984.

1584.   Wise, David. The Politics of Lying: Government Deception, Secrecy, and Power. New York: Vintage, 1973. 614.
"Because of official secrecy on a scale unprecedented in our history, the government's capacity to distort information in order to preserve its own political power is almost limitless" (500-01). Part I deals with lying by government officials; Part II with secrecy, particularly the classification system; Part III with President Nixon's public relations management; Part IV with manipulation of the press; Part V the author's recommendations.

1585.   Yoakum, Robert. "The Great Smut Hunt." CJR 25.3 (1986) 24.
Attorney General Edwin Meese's Commission on Pornography is engaged in censorship of ideas. The press "overlooked" the "crucial fact" that Playboy and Penthouse contain political articles with "messages that are anathema to the Reagan administration." Sexual and political "censorship go hand in hand," as the communist bloc countries and South Africa show.

IV. A. 3. Presidential Disinformation 1586-1621

1586.   Anderson, William, and Sterling J. Kernek. "How Realistic is Reagan's Diplomacy?" PolSQ 100 (1985) 389-409.
Reagan has an "unrealistic vision of the world, a taste for hard-line gestures of power politics and a talent for developing versatile rationalizations." He is unrealistic also because he is uninformed, for example, "his obtuseness about local conflicts in the Middle East."

1587.   Baker, Russell. "Messages to Convey to the Numbing Masses." AG (March 17, 1985) 4C.
Examples of the increase of exaggeration and disinformation by government leaders like Rusk, Nixon, and Reagan.

1588.   Bennett, James R. "Doublethink and the Rhetoric of Crisis: President Reagan's October 22, 1983 Speech on Arms 'Reduction'" Oldspeak/Newspeak: Rhetorical Transformations. Ed. Charles Kneupper. Arlington, TX: Rhetoric Soc. of Am., 1985. 54-66.
In his October 22, 1983, speech on arms "reduction," President Reagan combines techniques of the traditional international crisis genre with distortion of information to place the United States in an entirely benign role and to depict the Soviet Union as utterly malign.

1589.   Block, Herbert. Herblock Through the Looking Glass.
          New York: Norton, 1984. 287.
     Block's cartoons accompanied by commentary about the "world
according to Ronald Reagan." Ch. 1, "Looking-Glass Land,"
describes Reagan's falsehoods and exaggerations; 2, "Staying
Alive," on tobacco and handguns; 3, "The Money Tree," on
Reaganomics and deficits; etc.

1590.   Buchwald, Art. "Disinformed by Best Washington
          Offers." AG (Oct. 28, 1986) 11A.
     An imagined conversation with Reagan's "White House
Official of Disinformation."

1591.   Buchwald, Art. While Reagan Slept. New York:
          Putnam's, 1983. 334.
     Over 100 of the humorist's columns arranged into eight
groups.

1592.   Crowell, George H. "Still a Chance for CTB." C&C
          45.21 (1985) 510-11.
     The Reagan administration has diverted attention from the
Comprehensive Test Ban undertaken by the USSR. "The media have
done little to correct the resulting distortion."

1593.   Delgado, Richard. "The Language of the Arms Race:
          Should the People Limit Government Speech?" BULR 64
          (1984) 961-1001.
     The executive branch of the government "engages in
systematic dissembling" in the area of nuclear armaments and
strategy, and "the one-sided views that the government
propagates are unlikely to be corrected in the marketplace of
ideas because of widely shared human response mechanisms and
official secrecy. This situation has profound implications for
democratic decision theory and suggests that various remedies
may be in order."

1594.   Detzer, David. The Brink: Cuban Missile Crisis,
          1962. New York: Crowell, 1979. 352.
     A day-by-day account. Kennedy misrepresented the truth to
the public more for political reasons than for military or
national security considerations.

1595.   Eskey, Kenneth. "Government Statistics Change During
          an Election Year." Pr 8 (Nov. 1980) 9-10.
     How statistics can be manipulated to increase government
power.

1596.   Flynt, Larry, and Donald Freed. The Secret Life of
          Ronald Reagan. n.p.: Hustler, 1984. 210.
     The book is divided into three "Acts"--The Actor, The
Governor, The President--each of which contrasts the facts of
Reagan's covert actions, psychological warfare, and lying since
1946 with the official propaganda of the public man.

1597.   Frye, Jerry K. "American Newspapers vs. Agnew's 1970
         Political Campaign." JACR 4 (1976) 25-39.
     Contrary to Agnew's accusations of unfairness, the reporting
of his speeches was accurate, he was given considerable front-
page coverage, and Democratic newspapers provided more thorough
reports of Agnew's campaign speeches than Republican
newspapers."

1598.   Gartner, Alan, et al. What Reagan Is Doing To Us.
         New York: Harper, 1982. 307.
     "The Reagan approach is the more mean-spirited for its
hypocrisy. While espousing conservative rhetoric, it seeks to
strip the courts of their traditional functions. While denying
the farmer use of the tax code for redistributive effects, it
now uses it to redistribute benefits to the rich. While
appealing to the spirit of volunteerism, it attacks neighborhood
and self-help activities. While attacking government
intervention, it extends governmental authority into the most
intimate of matters, the decision to have an abortion. While
acclaiming the value of work, its budget cuts hit hardest the
so-called 'working poor.'"

1599.   Gonchar, Ruth, and Dan Hahn. "Richard Nixon and
         Presidential Mythology." JACR 1.1 (1973) 25-48.
     President Nixon utilized "three specific Presidential
myths": all problems are caused by outgroups, leaders are
benevolent heroes who will lead us out of danger, and the
function of the citizen is to sacrifice and work hard to do the
bidding of the leadership. These are "Presidential myths"
because "each of them supports the status quo and thus
strengthens the power of an incumbent President."

1600.   Grady, Sandy. "Hustling Big Bucks in D.C.: The
         Return of David Stockman." AG (April 29, 1986) 11A.
     In his recent book, David Stockman reveals the "lying,
deception, betrayal" during his tenure in the Reagan
administration. "Like other reporters, I heard Stockman
passionately preaching the Reaganomics gospel on Capitol Hill.
Now we know he was flat lying," because he knew "big Pentagon
budgets and tax cuts" were a "sham."

1601.   Green, Mark, and Gail MacColl. There He Goes Again:
         Ronald Reagan's Reign of Error. New York: Pantheon,
         1983. 127.
     The authors compare a quarter century of Ronald Reagan's
remarks with authoritative sources and conclude that "No modern
president has engaged in so consistent a pattern of misspeaking
on such a wide range of subjects."

1602.   Greene, Bob. "Campaign '80: It's Empty--But It's
         Got Style." QRD 7.4 (1981) 11.
     Discusses the misuse of information by presidents.

1603.   Halperin, David. "Reel Security." NT 4.5 (1986) 11.

Another example of President Reagan's "proclivity for borrowing movie dialogue for his public statements, and passing them off as historical facts." In this case, Reagan quoted from his 1940 film <u>Murder in the Air</u> to defend his Star Wars Program.

1604.   Kahn, Albert E., comp. <u>The Unholy Hymnal</u>. New York:
         Simon, 1971. 159.
A compendium of falsities and delusions uttered by US officials during the Johnson and Nixon administrations. "It is likely that most Americans, wishing to respect their nation's leaders, are reluctant to think of them as liars. This perhaps accounts for the politely euphemistic tone of the phrase, 'Credibility Gap,' which was coined in the mid-1960s and has since become indispensible to our vocabulary" (11).

1605.   Kelly, John. "CIA In Iran." <u>CS</u> 3.4 (1979) 24-36.
    Carter Administration deception and sometimes lying in regard to US intervention in Iran.

1606.   Kneupper, Charles W., ed. <u>Oldspeak/Newspeak:
         Rhetorical Transformations</u>. Arlington, TX: Rhetoric
         Soc. of Am., 1985. 267.
A selection of twenty-one of the papers presented at the Rhetoric Society of America 1984 national conference based on the theme of Orwell's <u>1984</u>: analysis of misleading explanations of reality by the government, Reagan's October 22, 1983, speech on arms "reduction," etc.

1607.   Krepon, Michael. "The PR Administration." <u>BAS</u> 42.9
         (1986) 6-7.
    "Public relations is the Reagan Administration's preeminent product line," and in a context of "rampant consumerism" abuses at home are "routinely cast aside." On arms control, Reagan's arguments have been so "unreal," "far-fetched," and "patently absurd" for so long that the media have given up refuting them.

1608.   Lens, Sidney. "Civil Defense: Carter's Idiot
         Arithmetic." <u>Inq</u> 2.3 (1979) 6-9.
    About misinformation on a civil defense plan that a nuclear war with Russia is winnable and with relatively few casualties.

1609.   Lewis, Anthony. "Blundering Lies Put Reagan in Bad
         Light." <u>AG</u> (Nov. 2, 1986) 3C.
    The White House version of what Reagan had agreed to at the Rykjavik summit kept changing, undermining the president's credibility and calling into question any hope for arms control progress.

1610.   Lewis, Anthony. "The White House Runs on Ideology."
         <u>AG</u> (April 8, 1986) 11A.
    "Ideology is king in the White House today." The Reagan Doctrine is a "crusade against left-wing governments in the Third World" regardless "of realities."

1611.   Loeb, Paul. "The Right Chord of Patriotism for
     America." SJMN (July 2, 1985).
     Compares Waylon Jennings' and Lee Greenwood's songs about
the US. Greenwood's "God Bless the USA" is about America
walking tall; Jennings' "America" raises unsettling questions
and praises dissenters. Ronald Reagan used Greenwood's song as
a frame for his 1984 campaign film.

1612.   McMahan, Jeff. Reagan and the World: Imperial Policy
     in the New Cold War. New York: Monthly Review, 1985.
     320.
     President Reagan has made a consistent effort to shape the
world in a certain way. It is only the manipulated divergence
between stated aims and actual behavior that has given rise to
the impression that his policy is confused. The author
attempts to pierce the screen of official propaganda to expose
the forces that drive the administration's policies. Chs.: 1
"The Quest for Global Control," 2 "Nuclear Weapons As
Instruments of Political Coercion," and 3 "Arms Control as an
Exercise in Public Relations" are the most relevant of the eight
chapters.

1613.   Musil, Robert. "On Calling a Bomb a Bomb." NT 1
     (March 1983) 26-8.
     "Part of the real power of any society is in the act of
defining reality through symbols and language." The US
government has controlled the arms race through classification
of information, public relations, technocratic jargon, myth,
mystery, and virtual sacred worship. These activities are
designed to "mold the minds of the public through the
suppression and distortion of language."

1614.   Pike, Otis. "Stockman's Book: A Tale of Politics
     and Power." AG (April 16, 1986) 15A.
     A review of former Budget Director David Stockman's book,
The Triumph of Politics: Why the Reagan Revolution Failed.
Pike stresses Stockman's participation in deceptions "designed
to placate Congress and the populace." "Stockman helped make
irresponsibility popular."

1615.   Rips, Geoffrey. "The President's Nose." TO 77.18
     (1985) 2-3.
     "There is a loose cannon in the White House. It is a
propaganda machine with little concern for the truth . . . .How
many more lies must the President tell before the press regards
his every word with skepticism?"

1616.   Robreno, Gustavo. "Manipulation of Information."
     ORK (Spring 1986) 16.
     "One characteristic of the Reagan administration from its
very beginning has been the way in which the manipulation of
information has reached the level of state-policy making."

1617.   Szulc, Tad. The Illusion of Peace: Foreign Policy

in the Nixon Years. New York: Viking, 1978. 822.
Of particular interest is the contradiction between the
public statements and policies of Nixon, Kissinger, and their
administration, and the real, private and secret beliefs and
behavior.

1618.   "Terrorism." CAIB 26 (Summer 1986).
Several articles on the Reagan administration's "perversion
of the language" with its "campaign against 'terrorism.' It has
managed to convince much of the public, and a large part of the
media, that terrorism is simply the actions of our enemies"
(Editorial).

1619.   Terrorism: A Closer Look. Oakland, CA: Data Center,
         1985. 62.
Reprints of articles from magazines and newspapers which
reveal that the US is guilty of "international terrorism" by the
CIA's 1980 definition. The Reagan administration's actions
regarding terrorism are simply one aspect of its "rightist
ideology" and propaganda campaign to distract public attention
"from its own involvement in supporting terrorism."

1620.   Wicker, Tom. On Press. New York: Viking, 1978.
         271.
A main focus of these essays is on the nature of "objective
journalism." "Objective journalism almost always favors
Establishment positions and exists not least to avoid offense to
them" (36-7). For example, former President Eisenhower's speech
at the Republican convention of 1964 was reported in "the most
obvious terms" and missed "the meaning of that moment."
"Objective journalism" reports "mostly the contents of official
documents, of statements delivered by official spokesmen" (3).

1621.   Weapons In Space. Volume I: Concepts and
         Technologies. Daedalus 114.2 (1985). 192. Vol. II:
         Implications for Security. Daedalus 114.3 (1985).
         205.
The collection of essays includes both supporters and
critics of the Reagan administration's Strategic Defense
Initiative (SDI, "Star Wars"), but in general the writings
confront the problems in the plan. The essayists agree that an
impermeable defense of the US population is technically
infeasible, contrary to the president's "defense shield"
deception.

IV. A. 4. Presidential Elections, Campaigning 1622-1641

1622.   Auletta, Ken. "Covering Carter Is Like Playing Chess
         with Bobby Fischer." MORE 6.10 (1976) 12-22.
An account of Jimmy Carter on the campaign trail, how the
candidate tries to use the press, and how they respond.

1623.   Blume, Keith. The Presidential Election Show:

Campaign '84 and Beyond on the Nightly News. South
Hadley, MA: Bergin, 1986. 352.
Television and the print media have unwittingly transformed
participatory democracy into a spectator sport. Interweaving
newscast transcripts with commentary, the author illustrates the
tendency of television news to report on image, poll results,
and campaign strategy rather than on the important issues.

1624.   Commoner, Barry. "Talking to a Mule." CJR 19.5
         (1981) 30-31.
The press neglects third parties even though they confront
the central issues largely ignored by the Republican and
Democratic candidates. [Commoner was the Citizens Party
candidate for president.]

1625.   Diamond, Edwin, and Stephen Bates. The Spot: The
         Rise of Political Advertising on Television. Amherst:
         MIT P, 1984. 416.
A history of the use of TV 30- and 60-second ads from the
1948 campaign through 1984 and a defense of their use, in spite
of the ample evidence provided that the commercials often
deceive.

1625a.   Ferguson, Thomas, and Joel Rogers, ed. The Hidden
         Election: Politics and Economics in the 1980
         Presidential Campaign. New York: Pantheon, 1981. 342.
Eight essays provide a study of the "hidden campaign," the
process by which basic power structures dominate politics--"the
candidates' links to the business community, sources of money,
prominent (if unpublicized) supporters," etc.

1626.   Ginsberg, Benjamin. The Consequences of Consent:
         Elections, Citizen Control and Popular Acquiescence.
         Reading, MA: Addison, 1982. 271.
A study not of voting behavior but of elections as
institutions of social control. "For elections are among the
principal mechanisms through which contemporary governments
regulate mass political action and maintain their own power and
authority" (Preface). Modern democratic governments "tend to
increase their control over the public's putative means of
controlling their actions" by reconciling citizens to the
desirability of state control and intervention--taxation,
military service, global expansion, arms production, etc.

1627.   Graber, Doris. "The Press as Opinion Resource During
         the 1968 Presidential Campaign." POQ 35 (1971) 168-
         182.
The public received "an image of the ideal president based
primarily on personal qualities, with little information
provided on candidates' political philosophy or executive
ability."

1628.   Graber, Doris. "Press and TV as Opinion Resources
         in Presidential Campaigns." POQ 40 (Fall 1976) 285-303.

Coverage remained "narrowly focused on a small array of presidential qualities and issues."

1629.   Hiebert, Ray, et al., eds. The Political Image
          Merchants: Strategies in the New Politics. Washington,
          DC: Acropolis, 1971. 311.
Twenty-nine essays explore the new political approaches and techniques "that had gained both widespread use and considerable notoriety in the decade of the 1960s." Section I, "The New Politics and the Old Parties," II, "A Look at the New Techniques," III, "Television and Image Making," IV, "The Science of Polling and Survey Research," V, "The Application of Data Processing and Computers to Politics," VI, "New Managers for the New Techniques," VII, "Ethics of the New Politics," and VIII, "What the Future Holds." One of the repeated concerns running throughout the essays is the danger to democracy of the expensiveness of campaigning, which places control in the hands of a few wealthy interest groups.

1630.   Jamieson, Kathleen. Packaging the Presidency: A
          History of Criticism of Presidential Campaign
          Advertising. New York: Oxford UP, 1984. 505.
Political advertising "legitimizes our political institutions by affirming that change is possible within the political system, that the president can effect change, that votes can make a difference. As a result, advertising channels discontent into the avenues provided by the government and acts as a safety valve for pressures that might otherwise turn against the system to demand its substantial modification or overthrow."

1631.   Kaiser, Robert G. "The Powers That Weren't." CJR
          21.1 (1982) 59-61.
Favorable review of Greenfield's The Real Campaign, which argues that "television and the media made almost no difference in the outcome of the 1980 Presidential campaign." But Greenfield pays too little attention to TV's power "to change the nature of our elections" by destroying traditional political parties. This change brought about the election of "a retired movie actor who had no personal experience dealing with the great national issues of the day." We now have rhetoric and symbolism instead of statesmanship.

1632.   Kraus, Sidney, ed. The Great Debates: Carter vs.
          Ford, 1976. Bloomington, IN: Indiana UP, 1980. 553.
These twelve essayists and fourteen reports applaud the bi-partisan consensus revealed and encouraged by the debates.

1633.   Lowenstein, Douglas. "Covering the Primaries." WJR
          2.7 (1980) 38-42.
A study of the primary campaign reporting of the Washington Post, the New York Times, and the Chicago Tribune reveals the same abuses and weaknesses of the past--neglect and manufacture of issues, hyping events, etc.

1634.   McGinniss, Joe. The Selling of the President 1968.
        New York: Trident, 1969. 253.
        Richard Nixon used television advertising to create an
image and secure election. The book is also about the alliance
between politicians and advertising executives, who "recognized
that the citizen did not so much vote for a candidate as make a
psychological purchase of him."

1635.   McGovern, George. "George McGovern: The Target
        Talks Back." CJR 23.2 (1984) 27-31.
        Presidential hopeful McGovern describes himself as running
on issues and blames the press for neglecting his candidacy and
the issues. The press is too fascinated with "who is winning or
losing" to attend properly to ideas and problems. But he cites
exceptions.

1636.   Sears, John. "The Press Elects the President." WJR
        2.7 (1980) 32,36.
        "The news media control the nomination and election of the
president today." Sears is opposed by Edwin Diamond, "Not
Really" (33,37).

1637.   Shaw, Donald L., and Maxwell E. McCombs. The
        Emergence of American Political Issues: The Agenda-
        Setting Function of the Press. St. Paul: West, 1977.
        211.
        The editors and reporters of the news media "not only guide
and direct, they actually supply the building blocks we use in
constructing our mental mosaics of the political arena. The
mass media both focus attention and structure our cognitions."
Focuses upon the 1972 presidential campaign.

1638.   Swerdlow, Joel. "The Decline of the Boys on the Bus."
        WJR 3.1 (1981) 15-19.
        "Television dominates the stage," with "little substance"
in its "disregard of the real issues." It's a "sham, like all
show business gimmickry."

1639.   Westbrook, Robert. "Politics As Consumption:
        Managing the Modern American Election." The Culture of
        Consumption. Ed. Richard Fox and T.J. Jackson Lears.
        New York: Pantheon, 1983. 143-174.
        Political consultants shared the assumption of advertising
and professional-managerial elites that people were irrational
and manipulable. Since the 1960s, however, political
merchandisers have focused less upon changing voters than upon
packaging candidates like products to suit voters.

1640.   Wright, J. S. Kelly. "Politics and the Constitution:
        Is Money Speech?" YLJ 85.8 (1976) 1001-1021.
        The Supreme Court's decision in Buckley v. Valeo, which
struck down campaign spending ceilings, erroneously treated the
regulation of campaign monies as the regulation of political
expression, which in effect said that "money is speech."

1641.   Wyckoff, Gene. The Image Candidates: American Politics in the Age of Television. New York: Macmillan, 1968. 274.
On the power of television to exploit irrational responses in viewers, to make "face" value more important than issues.

IV. B. Watergate 1642-1652

1642.   Bernstein, Carl, and Bob Woodward. All the President's Men. New York: Simon, 1974. 349.
The story of how these two Washington Post reporters helped expose the Watergate cover-up.

1643.   Bird, Kai, and Max Holland. "Historians' Footnote: Nixon Archives." Na 240.4 (1985) 359.
The attempt by Richard Nixon and his aides to restrict access to about 1.5 million pages of Nixon's papers.

1644.   Dean, John. Blind Ambition: The White House Years. New York: Simon, 1976. 415.
A confession and account of the Watergate conspiracy by Nixon's counsel, who provided essential testimony for the conviction of Mitchell, Ehrlichman, Haldeman, and others, and leading to the resignation of Nixon.

1645.   "A Secretive Security." CM 11.4 (1978) 8-11,13-6.
Using the Pentagon Papers case as a touchstone, discussants elaborate on the relative dangers of judicial, legislative, and executive authority in matters of intelligence; the definition of national security in applications of prior restraint; etc.

1646.   Drew, Elizabeth. Washington Journal: The Events of 1973-1974. New York: Random, 1975. 428.
Drew's journal of Watergate events.

1647.   The Final Report of the Select Committee on Presidential Campaign Activities, U.S. Senate. Washington: GPO, 1974. 1250.
An investigation of the "illegal, improper, or unethical activities" during the 1972 presidential campaign and election to determine the need for new legislation. In the opinion of Frank Donner, "No one who seeks an understanding of the world of intelligence--data collection, 'dirty tricks,' infiltration, provocation, wire-tapping and related matters--can fully understand the subject without a study of the hearings" of the Watergate Committee.

1648.   Greeley, Bill. "Nixon--'Out of Sync' and (At Last) Off the Tube." TQ 12.1 (1974) 51-55.
The "elaborate and complex schemes of the Nixon administration to exercise control over television came very near capturing the medium." But CBS's record in reporting Watergate is admirable.

1649.   Kurland, Philip. <u>Watergate and the Constitution</u>.
Chicago: U of Chicago P, 1978. 261.
"The constitutional limitations on power have been eaten
away slowly but surely. There is no longer a division of
sovereignty between the nation and the states." "There are only
tenuous remnants of the concepts of separation of powers and
checks and balances within the national government. Power has
accumulated in the executive branch and, at least through the
Watergate period and probably beyond, in the White House Office"
(4). Ch. 3 examines "Executive Privilege to Deny Information to
Congress."

1650.   Lang, Gladys, and Kurt Lang. <u>The Battle for Public
Opinion: The President, the Press, and the Polls During
Watergate</u>. New York: Columbia UP, 1983. 353.
The press did not create Watergate, the hearings did not
change many minds, and the public was only a bystander. But a
group of political insiders (Sirica, Ervin, Cox, Rodino, and
others) challenged the president on open television, public
reaction emboldened the insiders, and press exposure helped
convince the insiders and the public that the outcome was just.

1651.   Weissman, Steve, ed. <u>Big Brother and the Holding
Company: The World Behind Watergate</u>. Palo Alto, CA:
Ramparts, 1974. 350.
The authors in seventeen essays plus documents make a case
for further investigation into the wealthy individuals and
corporations behind Watergate. That is, Watergate is not an
aberration but "a generally rational--if wholly rotten--effort
to build the 'emerging Republican majority.'" Essays on the
Huston Plan, the Vietnam Veterans Against the War, United Flight
553, Charles Colson, etc.

1652.   Woodward, Bob, and Carl Bernstein. <u>The Final Days</u>.
New York: Simon, 1976. 529.
An account of President Nixon's and his White House staff's
lying, cover-up, illegal wiretapping, bribery, perjury,
obstruction of justice and other crimes.

IV. C. Bureaucracy   1653-1876 (See II. D. 2. & F.)

IV. C. 1. Secrecy, Classification, Censorship, Self-
Censorship, Cover-Up 1653-1805

1653.   Abrams, Floyd. "<u>Progressive</u> Education." <u>CJR</u> 18.4
(1979) 28-29.
The government in applying prior restraint against the
publication of an article on the H-bomb in <u>The Progressive</u>
magazine acted "as if <u>no</u> First Amendment rights were at risk at
all."

1654.   Anderson, Jack, and James Boyd. <u>Confessions of a
Muckraker: The Inside Story of Life in Washington During
the Truman, Eisenhower, Kennedy and Johnson Years</u>. New

283

York: Random, 1979. 354.
A book about Drew Pearson, the "inexhaustible cornucopia of evils to fight," and the "moral objectives of the newspaper column and the just society" at a time when the establishment press failed "to live up to its watchdog responsibilities."

1655.   "Atomic Censorship." Na 170.14 (April 8, 1950) 313.
The Atomic Energy Committee stopped publication of a portion of a Scientific American article because the information, none of it secret, was being given by H. A. Bethe of Cornell University, an author the committee disliked.

1656.   Aufderheide, Pat. "Film Clips." ITT 7 (Nov. 10-16, 1982) 14.
Sharon Sopher's film on the Polisario guerrilas at war with Morocco, Blood and Sand, made for PBS, was bumped from its planned prime-time to a later time slot, apparently for political reasons (it was scheduled to run at the same time the Moroccan King Hassan was to visit the US). As a result the film was carried in only a few cities and without advance notice.

1657.   Aufderheide, Pat. "Hear No Evil." ITT 10.24 (1986) 14.
"Gramm-Rudman-Hollings [budget reduction bill] has given government agencies an excuse to further reduce public information."

1658.   Aufderheide, Pat. "The Sounds of Silence," ITT 5 (April 29-May 5, 1981) 13,15.
Current pressures to reduce PBS's budget involve, as in the past, pressures for content control.

1659.   Bagdikian, Ben. "What Did We Learn?" CJR 10.3 (1971) 45-50.
We learned from the Pentagon Papers that freedom to report government activities is essential to democracy.

1660.   Baldwin, Hanson W. "Managed News: Our Peacetime Censorship." AM 211.4 (1963) 53-59.
Federal agencies during the Kennedy administration monitored and controlled information. The press is encouraged to "break through the wall of secrecy and government."

1661.   Bario, Joanne. Fatal Dreams. New York: Dial, 1985. 301.
A biography of the author's husband, a Drug Enforcement Agency agent who was allegedly poisoned. The book reveals the intricate workings of the DEA and how difficult it is to obtain information from that agency.

1662.   Barker, Carol, and Matthew Fox. Classified Files: The Yellowing Pages. A Report on Scholars' Access to Government Documents. New York: Twentieth Century

Fund, 1972. 115.
An attempt to "demonstrate how, why, and when the
government maintains security over state papers and other
records of its business and how its practices and procedures
affect access to archives by those intent on scholarly
research." An appeal for greater public disclosure and less
secrecy.

1663.   Begun, Jay. "The State Department's Patsy Picker."
     CJR 25.3 (1986) 10.
Assistant secretary of state for inter-American affairs,
Elliott Abrams, refuses to face a number of journalists in
public because he dislikes their criticism.

1664.   Benjamin, Gerald, ed. The Communications Revolution
     in Politics. New York: The Acad. of Political Science.
     1982. 205.
Of the seventeen essays, some of those in
"Communications in Government" and "National Defense and
International Relations" relate to the subject of information
control by government. For example, "Technology and the Federal
System" reveals that "the new technologies have reinforced the
ascendance of professional managers and information elites";
"Media Diplomacy" that "the marriage of the media and diplomacy
may be an unholy alliance"; and "Strategic Intelligence" that
since "national security, strategic intelligence, arms reduction
agreements, and technology are intertwined," more information
should be shared internationally.

1665.   Bennett, Jonathan. "Publicity is the Biggest Hazard
     for OSHA Bosses." Guard 38.20 (1986) 5.
A scandal involves OSHA's failure "for five years to
enforce job safety laws at two New York City thermometer
factories."

1666.   Bossong, Ken. "Drawing the Lead Curtain at the NRC."
     PC 6.5 (1986) 6-7.
Increasing secrecy at the Nuclear Regulatory Commission by
more discussions in private.

1667.   Brown, Robert McAfee. "The Debasement of Language."
     QRD 11.1 (1984) 9-12.
Examines varieties of government doublespeak and offers
solutions: "The only cures for the debasement of language are
valiant attempts to expose this debasement wherever it occurs,
and equally valiant attempts to use language responsibly
oneself."

1668.   Burger, Robert, ed. "Privacy, Secrecy, and National
     Information Policy." Library Trends 35.1 (1986) 182.
Eight essays on information policy, the political control
of information, which question both laissez-faire and
regulation.

1669.   Caldicott, Helen.   "Helen Caldicott on Tactics."   <u>BAS</u>
          42.5 (1986) 45-6.
     Women's Action for Nuclear Disarmament's <u>Turnabout</u> study of
the present state of the antinuclear movement shows that many
media representatives "failed to accept the freeze as sane arms
control or as valid legislation" because "they said
they consulted only with well-known arms control experts (many
of whom are architects of the arms race)."   "Not once did an
objective analysis of the freeze appear in a major publication."

1670.   Cameron, Juan.   "Whose Authority?"   <u>AM</u> 204 (1959) 38-
          42.
     Authorities (business-type agencies developed to construct
public works such as bridges, parks, and apartments) conceal
information on revenue use and operational procedures from both
legislature and the general public.

1671.   Chittick, William.   <u>The State Department, Press, and
          Pressure Groups: A Role Analysis</u>. New York: Wiley,
          1970. 373.
     This study of tensions among four groups involved in making
foreign policy in a democracy--State Department policy officers,
information officers, reporters, and leaders of nongovernmental
organizations--show that the governmental representatives
mmanipulate, delay, and suppress information.

1672.   Chomsky, Noam.   "East Timor: The Press Cover-Up."
          <u>Inq</u> 2.5 (1979) 9-15.
     Indonesian government is slaughtering thousands of people
in East Timor.   The US press looks the other way while the US
government supplies the Indonesian government.

1673.   Cockburn, Alexander.   "Haiti, Before and After."   <u>ITT</u>
          10.24 (1986) 12.
     US media have failed to report direct US support of Haitian
police brutality past and present, for the Tonton Macoutes have
been replaced by the Leopards, and the US supplied and is
supplying weapons.

1674.   Cole, John N.   "NASA's Little Secret."   <u>Pr</u> 8 (Aug.
          1980) 32.
     NASA reported finding a way to provide all major electrical
needs with sunlight in a process that could be competitively
priced within six years.   The information was suppressed because
the country was involved in a so-called energy crisis.

1675.   Cook, Richard.   "The Challenger Report: A Critical
          Analysis of the Report to the President of the
          Presidential Commission on the Space Shuttle Challenger
          Accident."   King George, VA, 1986.   137.
     The Rogers commission report on the shuttle Challenger
disaster is either incompetent or a cover-up.   The military
establishment used a public relations extravaganza as a
smokescreen for speeding up the militarization of the shuttle

program.

1676.   Corn, David. "Fear and Obstruction on the K.A.L.
          Trail." Na 241.4 (1985) 110-113.
A report on the intimidation and array of official
obstacles used to discourage research into the Soviet downing of
the K.A.L. Flight 007. The author questions why Congress has
held back from a full and formal inquiry into this tragic
episode in the Cold War.

1677.   Cranberg, Gilbert. "Warren Berger's Flimsy Case."
          CJR 25.2 (1986) 19-20.
The Supreme Court's objections to recording and
broadcasting proceedings "is no service to the Constitution and
brings no credit to the court."

1678.   Day, Samuel H., Jr. "Hot Cargo." Prog 50.2 (1986)
          29-33.
"The Government's fixation--secrecy as its first line of
defense against nuclear terrorists--puts the public at risk of
contact with radioactive, explosive matter."

1679.   "DES: Government Keeps Secret Its New Recommendations
          for DES Mothers and Daughters." HL 1.3 (1985) 6-7.
Despite the well-proven danger of diethylsilbestrol, the
Secretary of Health and Human Services has kept secret for over
four months the recommendations of its DES Task Force.

1680.   Devol, Kenneth. Mass Media and the Supreme Court:
          The Legacy of the Warren Years. New York: Hastings,
          1971. 369.
Case studies regarding the protection of minority rights
and the media arranged by twelve categories: "Prior Restraint,"
"Postal Censorship," "Control of Broadcasting," etc.

1681.   DeVolpi, Alexander, et al. Born Secret: The H-Bomb,
          the "Progressive" Case and National Security. Elmsford,
          NY: Pergammon, 1981. 320.
In 1979 the US government moved to stop publication in The
Progressive magazine of an H-bomb design outline culled from
unclassified material. It was the first case of extended prior
restraint of the press in American history. This book
examines the implications of the case for national security,
civil liberties, and nuclear nonproliferation.

1682.   Divine, Robert A. Blowing on the Wind: The Nuclear
          Test Ban Debate, 1954-1960. New York: Oxford UP, 1978.
          393.
The public was never made aware of how dangerous atomic
testing was before the late 1950s or early 1960s when
Eisenhower started trying to get a test ban with the USSR. The
government suppressed this information starting with the Truman
administration.

1683.   _Docket Report 1984-85_. New York: Center for
         Constitutionall Rights, 1984.   32.
     Summaries of the court cases undertaken by the Center,
including several FOIA, secrecy, surveillance, and censorship
cases.

1684.   "Does 'The Progressive' Have a Case?"   _CJR_ 18.1 (1979)
         25-27.
     Criticism of the government's effort to impose prior
restraint on an article on the H-bomb to be published in _The
Progressive_ magazine, and denunciation of the many newspapers
which supported the government.

1685.   Dorsen, Norman and Stephen Gillers, eds.   _None of Your
         Business: Government Secrecy in America_.   New York:
         Viking, 1974.   362.
     Twelve papers and a discussion presented at a conference on
the dangers of government secrecy, dealing with executive
privilege, classification, covert intelligence, legislative
secrecy, local government, the Freedom of Information Act,
pressures on the press, whistle blowing, the Pentagon Papers,
and the technology of secrecy.

1686.   "Doublespeak at the EPA."   _QRD_ 8.1 (1981) 11.
     The Environmental Protection Agency is "busy cleaning up
the dictionary."   "One EPA press aide put it, 'Health hazards
aren't going to be mentioned.'"

1687.   "Dr. Thomas Mancuso: The Health Researcher the U.S.
         Tried to Silence Speaks Out."   _CMJ_ 4.2 (1978) 6-7.
     The federal government attempted to halt research by Dr.
Thomas Mancuso when results indicated harmful effects of
radiation even at a very low level.

1688.   Dorsen, Norman, Paul Bender, and Burt Neuborne.
         _Emerson, Haber, and Dorsen's Political and Civil Rights
         in the United States_.   4th ed., Vol. 1.   Boston: Little,
         1976.   1695.
     Part One, "Freedom of Expression," deals with national
security, government secrecy and the public's right to know,
access to media, etc.   See Halperin and Hoffman (1977).

1689.   Falbaum, Berl.   "The Secret Branch of Government."
         CJR 16.5 (1978) 14-16.
     The media have given the judiciary "privileged news
coverage" in not probing "into judicial decisions."

1690.   Feinberg, Lotte.   "FOIA: Your Window of Opportunity."
         IREJ 8 (Spring 1985) 16-19.
     An account of the Freedom of Information Act, its value to
a democracy, and an explanation of how to use it and of the many
limitations and difficulties involved.

1691.   Finn, Chester, Jr.   _Education and the Presidency_.

Lexington, MA: Lexington, 1977. 167.
"Where the early months of the Nixon administration were
characterized by a number of imaginative domestic policy
proposals, in its later days only the authoritarianism and self-
righteousness, still cloaked in secrecy, would remain" (102).
"The White House working groups as developed under Nixon bore
some characteristics of what Schlesinger branded the 'Imperial
Presidency'" (119).

1692.   "FOI News." SLJR.
Every issue of the Review contains a page on recent Freedom
of Information Act happenings.

1693.   Franck, Thomas, and Edward Weisband, eds. Secrecy
     and Foreign Policy. New York: Oxford UP, 1974. 453.
A comparison of the US, the United Kingdom, and Canada "in
the area of secrecy and the law." "Secrecy is itself a prime
factor in any power system; and the more authoritarian the
system the greater the need for and use of secrecy. Conversely,
the greater use of secrecy, the greater the likelihood of
approaching authoritarian models." Chs. on "Executive Secrecy
in Three Democracies," "The Classification System in the U.S.,"
"Conflict Between Press and Government," "American Espionage
Statutes," etc.

1694.   Franklin, Marc, and Ruth Franklin. The First
     Amendment and the Fourth Estate: Communication Law for
     Undergraduates. Mineola, NY: Foundation, 1977. 727.
A study of the language of Supreme Court decisions, the
reasoning of the majority, dissenting, and concurring justices.
Ch. 1 sets forth the philosophy of freedom of expression, 2 the
judicial system and Court views of the First Amendment, 3 legal
problems journalists may encounter in gathering information, 4
problems in publishing information; the last three chs. focus on
broadcasting.

1695.   Freedom of Information: 1984-85 Report of the Society
     of Professional Journalists, Sigma Delta Chi. Chicago:
     SPJ, SDX, 1984. 80.
The annual report of the SPJ, SDX National Freedom of
Information Committee. Contains a 28-page state-by-state survey
of open meeting and record laws.

1696.   The Freedom of Information Reform Act. Hearings
     Before a Subcommittee of the Committee on Government
     Operations, House of Representatives, 98th Congress, May
     24, 30; June 20; and August 9, 1984. Washington: GPO,
     1985. 1153.
Opinions pro and con the FOIA, particularly in support of
the FOIA.

1697.   Freund, Charles. "Regulating the Electronic Eye."
     CJR 22.5 (1984) 8-9.
The FDA imposes restrictions on media coverage of drug

approval hearings.

1698.   Friedman, Robert. "The United States v. The
    Progressive." CJR 18.2 (1978) 27-35.
    In squelching the publication of the Progressive's H-bomb
story, the government did not keep atomic secrets out of the
hands of our enemies (all the writer's sources were
nonclassified), but rather stifled the flow of information to
the American people. And some newspapers supported the government,
including the NYT and the WP. The suppression is "causing
irreparable damage to the First Amendment."

1699.   Fuller, John. The Day We Bombed Utah: America's
    Most Letal Secret. New York: NAL, 1984. 268.
    The story of the Atomic Energy Commission's atomic bomb
tests in Southwestern Utah and Eastern Nevada during the 1950s,
the deadly consequences of the fallout, and the government's
secrecy, lies, cover-up, and eventual denial of responsibility
for the ensuing deaths.

1700.   Gabis, Stanley. "Political Secrecy and Cultural
    Conflict: A Plea for Formalism." Administration and
    Society 10 (1978) 139-75.
    Perceives an increase of governmental secrecy and covert
action, and argues for secrecy to "justify itself."

1701.   Galnoor, Itzhak, ed. Government Secrecy in
    Democracies. New York: Harper, 1977. 317.
    Part I presents six essays on "The Context of Government
Secrecy," Part II nine essays on "Government Secrecy in Ten
Democracies," two of the essays on the US, one general, the
other focusing on executive privilege.

1702.   Gilson, Lawrence. Money and Secrecy: A Citizen's
    Guide to Reforming State and Federal Practices. New
    York: Praeger, 1972. 293.
    "Citizens do not have access to their own government. They
cannot hold it accountable. It is not responsive to their
needs. Behind a veil of secrecy, money dictates political
outcomes."

1703.   Goldman, Neal M. "Tests of Media's 1st Amendment
    Rights Increasing." TRA 31 (1984) 48, 88-89.
    "Media organizations are subject to indirect censorship via
lawsuits for damages for libel, via restrictions on access to
information and via subpoena to them and their personnel to
require disclosure of confidential sources" (89).

1704.   Goodman, David. "Countdown to 1984: Big Brother May
    Be Right on Schedule." Fu 12 (1978) 345-55.
    Orwell's 1984 is proving to be an accurate forecast of what
has happened and might happen regarding the control of
information.

CONTROL OF INFORMATION

1705.   Goodman, Julian. "Network News: Running Shackled?"
         TQ 15.3 (1978) 41-44.
Some instances in which the court system has controlled the
press.

1706.   Granato, Leonard. "Prior Restraint: Resurgent Enemy
         of Freedom of Expression." PhD Diss., Southern
         Illinois U, 1973. 538. DAI 34 (1974) 5895-A.
A history of prior restraint in Britain and the US and an
effort to call attention to the erosion by the Supreme Court of
the absolute freedom of speech and press guaranteed by the First
Amendment.

1707.   Grossman, Karl. "Of Space Shuttles and Plutonium."
         ORK (Spring 1986) 1-4.
The dangers of a plutonium-fueled space probe aboard the
Shuttle have been covered up, and the mainstream media have
cooperated by not raising questions and not exposing the
possible consequences of using "the most toxic substance in the
universe which, if it fell back on earth, could cause mass
catastrophe."

1708.   Grossman, Zoltan. "Nuclear Power's Credibility
         Meltdown." ITT 10.23 (1986) 3.
Secrecy and cover-up have accompanied nuclear power
development in both the US and the SU. Both countries also
revere technology and technocracy for solving problems.

1709.   Halperin, Morton. "Increasing Government Secrecy:
         Revising the Classification Order." FP 7.2 (1981) 1,
         8-10.
New legislation increases secrecy.

1710.   Halperin, Morton, and Daniel Hoffman. Freedom vs.
         National Security: Secrecy and Surveillance. New York
         and London: Chelsea, 1977. 594.
The courts "have attempted to balance the requirements of
national security, as determined by the President and Congress,
against the constitutional rights of Americans." The authors
would "help alert a new generation to the danger [of illegal
governmental intrusion in the private lives of citizens] which
too many of us ignored for too long" (ix and xi).

1711.   Hansen, George. To Harass Our People: The IRS and
         Government Abuse of Power. Washington, DC: Positive,
         1984. 222.
An exposé of force, harassment, lies, and cover-up by the
IRS.

1712.   Harris, Amanda. "Prying Out the Truth." MORE 6.1
         (1976) 6-8.
High praise for the FOI Act and exhortations to the press
to use it. The Rosenbergs' case illustrates the value of the
Act.

291

1713.   Hentoff, Nat. "Making the First Amendment as Real as
        Sex." CLR 4.6 (1978) 51-54.
The poor teaching in high schools about the first ten
amendments to the constitution "create passivity among students
and make them 'cynical about the guarantees of a free press
under the First Amendment.'"

1714.   Hentoff, Nat. "The Perils of S. 1437." MORE 8 (1978)
        38-40.
The new Criminal Code Reform Act of 1978 threatens press
freedom and whistleblowers and in many ways diminishes the First
Amendment.

1715.   Holderness, Mike. "Here's a Nuke Foul-up News
        Blackout Made in U.S.A." Guard 38.32 (1986) 3.
The April 10 Mighty Oak test at the Nevada desert nuclear
weapons test site malfunctioned, and DOE repeatedly denied it.

1716.   Horton, Forest and Donald Marchand, eds.
        Information Management in Public Administration: An
        Introduction and Resource Guide to Government in the
        Information Age. Arlington, VA: Information Resources,
        1982. 588.
Most of the essays in this collection deal with managing
paperwork, but the essay by Itzhak Galnoor, "Government Secrecy:
Exchanges, Intermediaries and Middlemen," examines the role of
secrecy as part of the political and administrative culture of
the governing process, a process which encourages secrecy over
the public's right to know.

1717.   Hunt, Linda. "U.S. Coverup of Nazi Scientists." BAS
        41.4 (1985) 16-24.
US officials in charge of the program to exploit German and
Austrian specialists concealed incriminating information about
Nazis so they could legally immigrate.

1718.   Hynds, Ernest. American Newspapers in the 1970s. New
        York: Hastings, 1975. 349.
Ch. 6, "Right to Know--Right to Publish," focuses on
government limitations on access to information about government
(prior restraint, delaying tactics) and use of subpoenas to
force reporters to reveal confidential sources.

1719.   Isbell, Florence. "Dissidents in the Federal
        Government." CLR 4.3 (1977) 72-75.
"Don't Make Waves is what is enshrined in the hearts and
minds of every right-thinking civil servant." She advocates
"new realistic legislation, strongly backed by a White House
directive, that reprisals against whistle blowers will no longer
be tolerated."

1720.   Johnson, Giff. "Micronesia: America's 'Strategic'
        Trust." BAS 35.2 (1979) 10-15.
After relocating inhabitants of the islands of Micronesia

and conducting several atomic and hydrogen bomb tests, the federal government returned the natives to their homeland without explaining to them the effects of radiation exposure. The inhabitants still suffer physical and psychological damage.

1721.   Johnson, M. B. The Government Secrecy Controversy: A Dispute Involving the Government and the Press in the Eisenhower, Kennedy, and Johnson Administrations. New York: Vantage, 1967. 136.
A history of the conflict from 1952 to 1966.

1722.   Karmen, Andrew. "FOIA in the News." ORK (Winter 1984) 9-12.
A number of shorter articles noting the rampant manipulation of information and control by the government. [A regular feature in ORK as in SLJR.]

1723.   Karmen, Andrew. "Secrecy and Privacy in the News." ORK (Spring 1986) 12-13.
Excerpts from newspapers and magazines. [A regular feature in the magazine.]

1724.   "Keeping Government Honest." CJR 21.6 (1983) 24-25.
A rapid summary of the history of the FOIA and of presidential opposition to it, particularly the Reagan administration's intense attacks.

1725.   Kennedy, Pam. "Fine-Tuning the FOIA." CJR 23.3 (1984) 8-9.
Congress circumvents the FOIA by attaching exemptions to "package bills."

1726.   Knoll, Erwin. "The Masses." Prog 50.2 (1986) 35-38.
"The Masses was the first well-known publication to fall victim to the Government's new censorship powers" in 1917.

1727.   Knoll, Erwin. "Through the Looking Glass." Prog 49 (February 1985) 4.
The contradictory behavior of The Washington Post regarding government censorship.

1728.   Laitner, Skip. "NRC Continues Censorship of Data." CMJ 1.2 (1975) 3.
Information provided by the Advisory Committee on Reactor Safeguards is incomplete due to censorship of major portions of the minutes of its meetings.

1729.   Lancaster, John. "Red Alert at CNN." CJR 25.1 (1986) 14.
Ted Turner's Cable News Network's plan to tap Soviet television news fed directly from a Russian satellite has gained a temporary license from the FCC, but the State Department "has reserved the right to revoke permission if it determines the exchange is 'inconsistent with the national interest.'"

1730.   Landau, Jack C. "The State of the First Amendment."
   NmR 23.10 (1979) 24.
   Landau criticizes assaults by the government upon the
freedom of the press.

1731.   Leamer, Laurence. The Paper Revolutionaries: The
   Rise of the Underground Press. New York: Simon, 1972.
   220.
   An account of "common and frequent harassment" and abuses
"a thousandfold worse." Ch. 9, "Repression."

1732.   Lederer, William. A Nation of Sheep. New York:
   Norton, 1961. 192.
   The author criticizes the US for its "government by
misinformation," "publicity," and secrecy, and he blames the
press for its complicity in the process.

1733.   Le Duc, Don R. "Television Coverage of NATO Affairs."
   JoB 24 (1980) 449-465.
   Television news broadcasting of NATO decisions is
discouraged by the NATO Press Service. Networks are not given
advance notice of important policy decisions, and must rely upon
English or French news crews on account of the lack of a US
network office in Brussels.

1734.   Lindsay, Sue. "Atomic Publicist: Thomas Saffer."
   Pr 10.5 (1982) 41-2.
   On the struggles to break through government secrecy
surrounding atomic testing and the exposure of soldiers to
radiation.

1735.   Lopez, Alfredo. "A Crack in the Cover-Up." SD 2.2
   (1978) 10-11.
   The government covered-up the Cosmos 954 incident, which
"could have amounted to a major urban disaster" involving
fallout of satellite debris.

1736.   Lyford, Joseph. "The Pacification of the Press." TQ
   10.3 (1973) 15-22.
   News given on the broadcast media is determined or tempered
by government; he calls for a more global view of news.

1737.   Mackenzie, Angus. "Bandaid Solution." NaR 9 (Winter
   1986) 10-13.
   "The Reagan administration is trying to muzzle five million
federal employees" by requiring publication review and
nondisclosure agreements. The aim of these measures is not to
stop espionage "but to stop leaks to the press."

1738.   Mackenzie, Angus. "When Auditors Turn Editors." CJR
   20.4 (1981) 29-34.
   The IRS attack on the nonprofit press: Mother Jones,
Report on the Americas, Harper's, and the Catholic Press
Association.

1739.   MacKerron, Conrad. "Stripping Away Intervenors'
          Rights." CMJ 8.4 (1982) 7.
     Actions by the Nuclear Regulatory Commission and pending
Congressional proposals will limit public hearings before the
licensing of nuclear power plants.

1740.   Manoff, Robert K. "The Media: Nuclear Secrecy vs.
          Democracy." BAS 40.1 (1984) 26-29.
     Ever since World War II the media have been willing to
accept the government's press releases in regard to nuclear
weaponry.

1741.   Manoff, Robert K. "The Silencer." The Quill
          (February 1984) 5-11.
     Not only Japanese but US journalism was among "the first
casualties of the bombing of Hiroshima," for in the US the bomb
was conceived and developed in secrecy and censorship, the
bombing itself and information about it were "managed as a
modern media event" by the War Department, and long afterward
details of the bomb and the bombing and its radiation after-
effects were suppressed.

1742.   Marnell, William. The Right to Know: Media and
          the Common Good. New York: Seabury, 1973. 221.
     Part I deals with instances and issues of prior restraint.

1743.   Marwick, Christine. "The Freedom of Information
          Act and National Security Secrecy: How It's Working
          After Two Years." FP 2.4 (1976) 1-12.
     A progress report on the success of the FOIA in dealing
with government "national security" restrictions.

1744.   Marwick, Christine. "The Growing Power to Censor."
          FP 4.10 (1979) 1-5.
     Controls on secrecy are "now being reversed."

1745.   Mathews, Anthony S. The Darker Reaches of
          Government: Access to Information about Public
          Administration in the US, Britain, and South Africa.
          Berkeley: U of California P, 1978. 245.
     The vast superiority of the US over South Africa in regard
to open government should not obscure weaknesses in the US,
where the information flow "tends to be unreliable, halting and
irregular. By contrast the Swedish system appears to produce a
regular, routinized flow of information." Information in Sweden
"also seems to be got more cheaply and with less expenditure of
forensic or political effort" (211).

1746.   Mathewson, Judith. "The Unkindest Cuts." CC 12.3
          (1986) 11.
     Gramm-Rudman budget cut of the Federal Election Commission
will make it more difficult for reporters and the public to
detect donor-PAC-candidate connections.

1747.   McCartney, James. "What Should Be Secret." CJR 10.3
         (1971) 40-44.
   Classification reform is necessary so only necessarily
secret documents are kept secret.

1748.   McFeatters, Ann. "The State Department Accelerates
         Secrecy, Slows History." Pr 9.4 (1981) 13.
   "The State Department has begun to suppress foreign affairs
documents once released routinely."

1749.   McGaffin, William, and Erwin Knoll. Anything But the
         Truth: The Credibility Gap--How the News Is Managed in
         Washington. New York: Putnam, 1968. 250.
   Government "secrecy, deception, and distortion of the news"
are "grave and growing."

1750.   McGehee, Fielding, III. "Exemption 1: F.O.I.A.'s
         Catch-22." CJR 16.6 (1978) 18-19.
   Exemption 1 makes the Pentagon and the intelligence
agencies virtually immune to FOIA suits.

1751.   McGrory, Mary. "Why They Hide Truth in Official
         Washington." AG (February 14, 1985) 21A.
   Examples of officials who told the truth as they were
leaving office or after they had resigned. "Once they have
spoken the truth, they have nowhere to go but out."

1752.   Meiklejohn, Alexander. Free Speech and Its Relation
         to Self-Government. New York: Harper, 1948. 107.
   The First Amendment forbids the government to make any law
abridging the freedom of speech.   Yet in recent years, the
government "has in many ways limited the freedom of public
discussion." The author argues in defense of the First
Amendment as an absolute shield against the suppression of ideas
and speech.

1753.   Mills, Kay. "This Broadcast Will Be Delayed." MORE
         4.4 (1974)5-7.
   The Pacifica Foundation, operator of FM stations in New
York, Houston, Los Angeles, and Berkeley, has for six years been
denied a license for Washington, D.C., by the FCC whose
commissioners feared its counterculture politics.

1754.   "The Missing Tape." Na 240.10 (1985) 292-3.
   Consistent pattern by the US government of suppressing
information regarding the downing of Korean Air Lines Flight 007
by a Soviet pilot.

1755.   Mollenhoff, Clark. Washington Cover-Up. New York:
         Doubleday, 1962. 239.
   Most of the book is an account of how the Truman and
Eisenhower administrations covered up information that was
unfavorable to them--Truman "ducking and dodging," Eisenhower
employing executive privilege increasingly.   The author

recommends laws defining and regulating executive privilege.

1756.   Morgan, Richard E. _Domestic Intelligence: Monitoring Dissent in America_. Austin: U of Texas P, 1980. 194.
An analysis not of counterintelligence, counterespionage or foreign intelligence gathering, but of "information gathering and record keeping by law enforcement agencies which is unrelated to a particular, known crime and is directed at persons and groups engaged in political activity" (9). He would abolish all subversion and sedition laws which restrict speech and dissent, but would allow intelligence gathering for the prevention of felonies.

1757.   Moritz, Owen. "FHA Blackout." _MORE_ 3.2 (1973) 10.
The enormous FHA scandal has been little reported because of the Federal Judge's news blackout. The "stakes are too high for anything but public exposure."

1758.   Morland, Howard. _The Secret That Exploded_. New York: Random, 1981. 288.
The story of the author's quest for the H-bomb secret, an exposure of the secrecy of the nuclear establishment, an account of the article he wrote on the H-bomb for _The Progressive_ magazine, and the government's attempt to censor both him and the magazine in an attempt to protect a "secret" that was already in the public domain. A persistent theme is that the curtain of secrecy surrounding the nuclear weapons industry was erected in an effort to keep us ignorant of the danger of nuclear war. The passivity of the public "in the face of a situation which cannot possibly benefit them is due in part to their faith in military secrecy, and in the exclusive brotherhoods it creates of those who know and those who do not" (232).

1759.   Neier, Aryeh. "USA: 'Born Classified.'" _IC_ 9.1 (1980) 51-54.
An account of the government's attempt to censor Howard Morland's article planned for publication in _The Progressive_ magazine.

1760.   O'Neill, Terry, and Bruno Leone, eds. _Censorship: Opposing Views_. St. Paul, MN: Greenhaven, 1985. 234.
A collection of opposing arguments divided into 5 sections: "Should There Be Limits to Free Speech?" "Should the News Media Be Regulated?" "Does National Security Justify Censorship?" "Is School and Library Censorship Justified?" "Should Pornography Be Censored?"

1761.   _Paul Jacobs and the Nuclear Gang_. New York: Time Films, 1979.
A film on "the U.S. government's attempts to suppress information about the health hazards of radiation."

1762.   Peters, Charles, and Taylor Branch. _Blowing the Whistle: Dissent in the Public Interest_. New York:

Praeger, 1972. 305.
Cases of individual courage in breaking through secrecy to reveal official corruption, including Christopher Pyle on Army Intelligence abuses and Daniel Ellsberg on the Pentagon Papers.

1763.   Peterson, Trev. "National Security Exception to the Doctrine of Prior Restraint." NLR 60.2 (1981) 400-415.
The Progressive case represents "a severe inroad on First Amendment rights."

1764.   Pilpel, Harriet, and Marjorie Parsons. "Dirty Business in Court." CLR 1.4 (1974) 30-41.
An appraisal of the 1973-74 Supreme Court obscenity decisions "with grave implications for First Amendment freedoms." "The real target is not obscenity at all, but unpopular, dissident, irreverent, or satirical expression unsettling to current complacencies."

1765.   Pollock, Richard. "The Case of ERDA's Missing Materials Caper." CMJ 2.6 (1976) 5.
The Energy Research and Development Agency invoked a national security classification to suppress a report by the General Accounting Office that it cannot account for great quantities of weapons-grade uranium and plutonium.

1766.   Pollock, Richard. "The Rains of October." CMJ 2.8 (1976) 9-10.
The federal government did not report the atmospheric nuclear test of the People's Republic of China in October 1976 or the radioactive particles which fell on America's Atlantic coastline.

1767.   Pope, James. "The Suppression of News." AM 188 (1951) 50-54.
"Only recently have most editors begun to realize" a "broad-scale offensive" by government "against freedom of information."

1768.   Powledge, Fred. The Engineering of Restraint: The Nixon Administration and the Press. Washington: Public Affairs, 1971. 53.
"Attacks on the press by the officers of government have become so widespread and all-pervasive that they constitute a massive federal-level attempt to subvert the letter and the spirit of the First Amendment" (6). "It could, and should, be argued that the threat would not be nearly so great if the press itself had fought harder for its own freedom" (41).

1769.   Preston, William, Jr. "'Balanced' News: A View from the U.S. Post Office." ORK (Fall Winter 1984-85) 1-3.
Looks at various injustices that the Post Office participated in, including "the alleged interception and opening of mail itself," and "censorship in a sweeping and arbitrary manner largely without judicial intervention."

1770.   "Punish Leakers: Stump Introduces Surveillance Bill."
     SLJR 12.73 (1985) 14.
On legislation to make it easier to prosecute federal
workers for leaking classified information to the press.

1771.   The Public's Right to Know. Washington, DC:
     Editorial Res. Rpts., Cong. Quart., 1980. 196.
A handbook on a wide range of topics from the Supreme Court
to the FOIA.

1772.   "Regulate Chemicals, Three Urge." AG (May 23, 1985)
     8C.
The legislation "would require the EPA to collect--and make
public--information about chemical leaks" as well as other
measures.

1773.   Ripmaster, Terence. "The United States Thought
     Police." QRD 9.4 (1983) 2.
The Justice Department labeled three informative Canadian
films as "propaganda" and prohibited their showing in the US.

1774.   Rivers, William, and Michael Nyhan, eds. Aspen
     Notebook on Government and the Media. New York:
     Praeger, 1973. 192.
"I am not overly disturbed by open battles between
government and the media. More threatening than these
confrontations are the subtle pressures that affect the flow of
communications without the public's knowledge" (Prologue). Ch.
on press rights and responsibilities regarding the First
Amendment, the public's right to know, regulation, access, etc.

1775.   Roisen, Jill, and Michele B. Galen. "FOIA in the
     Courts." ORK (Winter 1984) 13-15.
Another number of shorter articles concerning a variety of
reasons the FOIA Inc. has been involved with court cases around
the country.

1776.   Rourke, Francis. Secrecy and Publicity: Dilemmas of
     Democracy. Baltimore, MD: Johns Hopkins UP, 1961. 236.
     New ed. 1966.
A study of "the power that has come to rest in the hands of
government officials to control" the "flow of information to the
public." Its impact is "sharpest" in the areas of the military
and foreign affairs, "where public officials come closest to
having monopoly power in the field of information."

1777.   Rowan, Carl. "A Warning to Americans." AG (May 5,
     1986) 11A.
Soviet secrecy following the Chernobyl nuclear power plant
disaster should alert US citizens to the drift toward secrecy in
the US through new censorship laws and secrecy regulations.

1778.   Rubin, Barry. Secrets of State: The State
     Department and the Struggle Over U.S. Foreign Policy.

New York: Oxford UP, 1985. 335.
A history from 1933 of the process of decision making: "the greatest secrets of state are the techniques and failures of the policymaking process" (ix). There is "a growing danger that those on top will react more and more on the basis of instinct and internal struggle and less and less in response to facts. More than once, American leaders have created a world of illusion--the Bay of Pigs invasion, Vietnam, and Iran--in which ignorance led to choices remote from reality" (264).

1779. Rubin, David. "Consider the Source: A Survey of National Security Reporters." Deadline (March-April 1986) 4-6.
Arms control journalists "ought to place more emphasis on testimony, reports, books, articles and other pieces of documentary evidence, with names attached."

1780. Ruby, Robert. "Withholding Nuclear Plant Accident Information 'Knowingly' Is OK." Pr 10.2 (1982) 15-16.
Engineers at Three Mile Island withheld information "knowingly," not a criminal offense, but did not withhold it "willfully," a criminal offense.

1781. Saffer, Thomas, and Orville Kelly. Countdown Zero. New York: Putnam, 1982. 351.
Used the FOIA to uncover the effects of radiation on American servicemen exposed to atomic testing during the 1950s and 1960s. "This book is an indictment, an accusation lodged against the rash scientists and macho military men who ignored common-sense precautions in their headlong pursuit of nuclear superiority. It is also an exposé of a systematic thirty-year cover-up by high officials in the U.S. government of the plague of cancer and other illnesses they needlessly inflicted on the soldiers and civilians who were unwitting participants in their experiments" (Introduction by Steward Udall, Former Secretary of Interior).

1782. Safire, William. "Marching in the Vanguard of the Media-haters." AG (May 2, 1985) 15A.
Criticism of Court of Appeals Judge [now Supreme Court Judge] Antonin Scalia, "who has shown himself to be the worst enemy of free speech in America today."

1783. "The Saga of Lucky Seven." CJR 17.2 (1978) 22-23.
The FCC threatens operators of an underground television station.

1784. Sandman, Peter M., and Mary Paden. "At Three Mile Island." CJR 18.2 (1979) 43-58.
The press either ignored or barely touched on the most important facet of the Three Mile Island nuclear accident, that the NCR didn't know what it was doing.

1785. "Secrecy and the Public's Need to Know." CM 18.3

(1985) 15-29.
A dialogue mainly among journalists critical both of the government and themselves.

1786.   "The Secret Life of NSDD 84." CJR 23.2 (1984) 22-23.
Eleven of the thirteen provisions of National Security Decision Directive 84 have been in effect "since March 11, 1983, when the president issued it. And although section 1(b)-- requiring some 127,000 officials to submit to lifelong censorship"--was temporarily suspended, section 1(a) "remains intact" requiring "the signing of nondisclosure agreements that constitute an almost equally restrictive form of censorship" for four million federal workers. It is a "damnable directive."

1787.   "Secret Memo Calls for New FBI Unit to Investigate
          Leaks, Paper Reports." AG (May 26, 1986) 3A.
"An administration working group has recommended . . . a special FBI strike force to investigate leaks of classified information," to include "punitive action against those responsible for the disclosures as well as pressure on news organizations not to publish government secrets" and "more widespread use of polygraph tests."

1788.   Security Classification Policy and Executive Order
          12356. HR, Committee on Gov. Ops. Report. 97th Cong.,
          2nd sess., Aug. 12, 1982. 49.
"Abuse of classification authority and over-classification of government information continues to be a serious problem."

1789.   Shattuck, John H. F. "You Can't Depend On It: The
          Carter Administration and Civil Liberties." CLR 4.5
          (1978) 10-27.
Asks "whether Carter will defend a strong civil rights or civil liberties position against popular criticism."

1790.   Shils, Edward. The Torment of Secrecy: The
          Background and Consequences of American Security
          Policies. Glencoe, IL: Free, 1956. 238.
An attack on the sources of extremism which lead to an obsession with secrecy in America--hyperpatriotism, xenophobia, isolationism, fundamentalism, etc.

1791.   "Silencing Federal Employees." CJR 17.1 (1978) 24-25.
The Justice Department sued, Frank Snepp, a former CIA employee, for revealing information about that agency without its approval.

1792.   Skardon, James. "The Apollo Story: The Concealed
          Patterns." CJR 6.4 (1967) 34-39.
"If there was one aspect of the space program in which it was incumbent on the press to serve as watchdog, it was in the matter of safety. Yet the record shows a superficial and incomplete performance--despite the frightening precedent of the Mercury project." Analysis of coverage of the Apollo program

leading up to the deaths of Grissom, White, and Chaffee. [See Index, Challenger shuttle.]

1793.   Smith, Fred L. "The Selling of the First Amendment: An Analysis of Congressional Investigation of Four CBS Television Documentary Projects." PhD Diss., Florida SU, 1972. DAI 33 (1972) 2964-A.
Congressional committees investigating possible bias of CBS documentaries paradoxically aligned government and people against the press. "If the press values its protection from government interference under the First Amendment, it has an affirmative duty to defend that protection."

1794.   "Sorry, Pat, Sorry, Ron." CJR 25.1 (1986) 23.
Vladimir Posner of Radio Moscow attacked President Reagan's Feb. 26 speech on national defense on ABC News. The White House complained, and the president of ABC News, Roone Arledge, apologized. "First Amendment scholar Thomas I. Emerson has written that such communication from government 'becomes for all practical purposes an informal sanction against private dissenting expression, often equivalent in its effect to a formal sanction.'"

1795.   Stanford, Phil. "Watergate Revisited." CJR 24.6 (1986) 46-49.
A discussion of Jim Hougan's book on Watergate, Secret Agenda, which argues that information was withheld concerning Watergate. "Hougan makes a convincing argument that at least some of what we think we know about Watergate is wrong. It is high time the press started facing up to that possibility."

1796.   Stein, Robert. "'Telling It Like It Is.'" TQ 10.2 (1973) 48-52.
Television news broadcasts derive their content in a large part from the current politicians' demands. "In all the media, power still determines the news."

1797.   Stone, I. F. The "I. F. Stone's Weekly" Reader. Ed. Neil Middleton. New York: Random, 1973. 321.
From 1953 to 1971, Stone spoke out against government secrecy and censorship and the Cold War used to justify limiting a free press. Many of these essays deal with information control--e.g., "The Crisis Coming for a Free Press," "Another Way to Elude the Censor and See the Fate in Store for that 'Peace Dividend,'" "The Price We Pay for Empire," "Withholding the Truth on Weapon Losses," "U.S. Public Not Informed of Guevara's Olive Branch at Punta del Este."

1798.   Stone, I. F. In a Time of Torment. New York: Random. 1967. 463.
One of Stone's chief objects of attack in all of its manifestations was the government's efforts to use information to instill unity: "the blacklist and the House Committee on Un-American Activities had the effect, designed or not, of

reminding the rest of us that we were employees and had best get in line with the firm" (from the Introduction by Murray Kempton). The almost 100 essays are divided into nineteen sections, including "Our Less Than Free Press."

1799.   Sturges, Gerald D. "Arresting Ideas." Prog 46.4
           (1982) 21.
Secrecy in the US Patent Office affects the amount of time it takes for a patent to be issued on an invention.

1800.   Swan, Jon. "The Rush To Write a Law." CJR 17.3
           (1978) 26.
Laws protecting journalists' sources have repeatedly been swept aside by judges when it served their purposes; the best protection for newsmen is the First Amendment.

1801.   "Terrorism: Further Restricts FOI Act; Favors Private
           Access to FBI Records." SLJR 12.73 (1985) 14.
On legislation to further weaken the FOIA and to give nuclear power plant operators access to FBI criminal history files.

1802.   "Terrorism in Miami: Suppressing Free Speech." CS
           8.3 (1984) 26-30.
Revelations of "direct and indirect support Miami's leading politicians, the police department, the Republican Party in Florida, and the White House have given [right-wing Cuban and Nicaraguan exile organizations] terrorism."

1803.   Unger, Stephen. "The Growing Threat of Government
           Secrecy." TR 85 (Feb.-March 1982) 30-33,35-36,38-39,
           84-85.
"Under the guise of national security, barriers are being erected to the free flow of scientific information. This trend endangers fundamental freedoms and, ironically, may damage US technological development."

1804.   Weiss, Andrea. "FOIA in the Courts." ORK (Spring
           1985) 12.
A regular column in this magazine.

1805.   "X-ray Laser and Secrecy." BAS 42.1 (1986) 2.
"Flaws in the X-ray laser tests were well hidden by the government's secrecy system."

IV. C. 2. Bureaucratic Disinformation 1806-1834

1806.   Adams, Robert M. Bad Mouth: Fugitive Papers on the
           Dark Side. Berkeley: U of California P, 1977. 138.
One ch. deals with "The New Arts of Political Lying": "Twenty Encyclopedia Britannica's would not suffice, nowadays, for a prolegomenon to a systematic treatise of political lying" (43).

1807.   Anderson, Jack. Washington Exposé. Washington, DC:
        Public Affairs, 1967. 487.
    In domestic and international issues, federal government
"officials have . . . played loose with the truth to cover up
blunders, hide corruption and make bad policies look good."

1808.   Bird, Kai, and Max Holland. "Star Wars Fiction." Na
        242.18 (1986) 640.
    Department of Energy Secretary John Herrington misled a
Congressional panel several times recently in his testimony on
Star Wars.

1809.   Brown, Harrison. "Fallout and Falsehoods." BAS
        41.4 (1985) 3.
    Prior to the 1963 banning of nuclear tests on the ground,
in the water, and in space, government officials "failed to warn
the public about the potential dangers of fallout and even
engaged in misrepresentation and distortion bordering upon
lies."

1810.   Crosby, Ned. "Public Opinion and the Lessons of War."
        WP 7 (May-June 1980) 10-11, 63-64.
    "Presidents can defy public opinion on foreign policy
because of their power to structure the way issues are
presented," especially their "enormous power to structure
options."

1811.   De Zutter, Henry. "The Media's Mythical Scenario."
        ChJR 2.4 (1969) 4-5.
    Police are claiming and the media are reporting
unsubstantiated reports about conspiracy behind riots and police
as targets of revolt.

1812.   "Disinformation." CS 7.4 (1983).
    Eight pieces (pp. 7-32) on diverse distortions of the truth
by the US government and its officials and supporters.

1813.   Ecenbarger, William. "State Needs a Euphemism Dept."
        QRD 8.4 (1982) 5-6.
    Although "euphemisms are a legitimate adjunct of language,"
officials of the US government use "words and phrases that
attempt to soften and often distort reality."

1814.   Empty Promise: The Growing Case Against Star Wars.
        Boston: Beacon, 1986. 192.
    Money, politics, science, and the manipulation of the
public are linked in President Reagan's "Star Wars fantasy."
The Strategic Defense Initiative cannot provide a remedy to the
nuclear danger.

1815.   Farrell, James J. The Nuclear Devil's Dictionary.
        Minneapolis, MN: Usonia, 1985. 125.
    An expose' of the doublespeak of nuclear policy, much of it
created or perpetrated by the Reagan administration, that has

made the unthinkable thinkable and that prevents people from penetrating the duplicity of the policymakers--"limited nuclear war," "peacekeeper," etc.

1816.   Friedrich, Otto. "Of Words That Ravage, Pillage, Spoil." QRD 10.3 (1984) 10-12.
Government officials use euphemisms in order to "implicitly deny" their actions.

1817.   Gilbert, James. "Memorializing the Bomb." RHR 34 (1986) 101-104.
A critique of the display, "Building the Bomb: Forty Years after Hiroshima," at the National Museum of American History in Washington, DC. The exhibit and accompanying brochure suppress many questions.

1818.   Hahn, Daniel F. "Political Lies." QRD 9.2 (1983) 9-10.
Looks at the term "lie" and how a "lie" is expressed in politics.

1819.   Johnson, David, and Gene La Rocque. "The Mythology of National Defense." BAS 30.7(1974) 21-26.
The government is attempting to justify funding for unneeded new weapons by using misleading statistics combined with the threat of a possible limited nuclear war.

1820.   Judis, John. "The U.S. and Libya: Heirs to Terror." ITT 10.21 (1986) 3, 10.
The "American response to the new wave of terror in the Mideast has been shaped by a group of conservative academics and journalists who have become self-styled experts in terrorism": Ray Cline, Michael Ledeen, Yonah Alexander, and Claire Sterling. Cline and Alexander "define terrorism" as "identical to communism."

1821.   "KAL 007 and U.S. Intelligence." CS 8.4 (1984).
Several articles attacking the US version of the Korean Air Liner downed by Soviet fighters.

1822.   "The Last Word: Finding and Using the Truth." JC 29 (1984) 71-72.
Mass media information about the Third World comes from government news releases that are often untrue or outdated.

1823.   Marro, Anthony. "When the Government Tells Lies." CJR 23 (March/April 1985) 29-41.
"Official deceptions, half-truths, and outright lies impose a heavy burden on the press." A former Washington correspondent surveys the scope of the problem and suggests ways reporters can cope with it.

1824.   Massing, Michael. "America's Top Messenger Boy." NR 193.12 & 13 (1985) 21-25.

305

The new ambassador to the United Nations, Vernon A. Walters, exemplifies the contradictory nature of US foreign policy. "In the name of freedom, this America makes common cause with dictators and despots."

1825.   Mechling, Thomas B.   "PR Firms Who Work for
          Dictators." BSR 29 (Spring 1979) 15-21.
Many of the top PR firms perform work for some of the "most repressive, regressive dictatorial regimes" (15).

1826.   Morgan, Paul, and Sue Scott. The D.C. Dialect: How
          to Master the New Language of Washington in Ten Easy
          Lessons. New York: Washington Mews, 1975. 128.
A humorous approach to the language of power, focusing especially upon Watergate (hearings, transcripts, trials), legal, military, business, and sports language.

1827.   Rasberry, Robert. The "Technique" of Political Lying.
          Washington, DC: UP of America, 1981. 289.
Part I offers a theory of technology, politics, and human values for the study of lying in the political realm based upon the works of Jacques Ellul. For Ellul, technology brings about "human subversion" through the "supremacy of 'techniques,' or means over ends." Ellul enables one to understand "why and how lying is an active political process." In Part II "the theories are applied to the Watergate crisis as a case in modern political lying."

1828.   Radecki, Thomas. "Is the Word Terrorism a Way to
          Dehumanize Your Enemy?" NCTVN 7.5-6 (1986) 12.
Yes it is, the author declares and urges readers to avoid using the word.

1829.   Roshco, Bernard. "Making the Incredible Credible."
          CJR 7.2 (1968) 41-45.
Individuals and organizations "process various forms of data and opinion into policy and then offer it to the press for publication as news."

1830.   Silverstein, Brett. "Statistical Propaganda and the
          Nuclear Arms Race." SciP 16.4 (1984) 12-16.
"Some types of mathematical chicanery are used more frequently than others, and it is not difficult to learn to recognize the most common statistical tricks." Both government and media sources are violators in this "numbers game."

1831.   Sloman, Larry. Reefer Madness: The History of
          Marijuana in America. Indianapolis: Bobbs, 1979.   404.
Little information was available about marijuana before the 1960s. The literature mainly available was propaganda distributed by the Bureau of Narcotics under the direction of Henry Anslinger, who completely distorted the truth about the drug.

1832.   Smith, Doug. "'Washingtonspeak' Often Means the
          Opposite of Stated Message." AG (March 17, 1985) 9C.
     The euphemisms, circumlocutions, doubletalk, and newspeak
government officials use to hoodwink the public.

1833.   "Swept Away." CJR 19.6 (1981) 21.
     On nationalistic reporting of the Iranian Embassy hostages,
their release and return.

1834.   Thompson, Thomas. "The Real Taiwan Issue." Inq 28
          (April 2, 1979) 8-10.
     The American public has been misled until recently that
Taiwan was a "free" country. In fact it is a police state.

IV. C. 3. Bureaucratic Surveillance, Repression 1835-1876
          (See VI, Intelligence)

1835.   Ackroyd, Carol, et al. The Technology of Political
          Control. Rev. London: Pluto, 1980. 336.
     A study mainly of Great Britain but applicable to the US.
The book aims "to relate the whole range of political control
technologies [monitoring, controlling demonstrations,
interrogation methods, etc.] to the need of states to reduce
internal dissent and to silence particular critics at different
times in different ways. There is a chilling familiarity about
the concepts underlying these techniques: they stem from the
historic process, interrupted only by revolutions, whereby the
small minority of rulers of societies have always tried to
neutralize or destroy opposition." Yet "despite this
similarity, the technology of political control we describe" is
"specific to the latter half of the twentieth century," and, in
particular, to advanced capitalist states, "with a liberal
democratic political structure" (Introduction to Second
Edition).

1836.   "Another Turn of the Screw." CJR 17.2 (1978) 22.
     A recent Supreme Court ruling opens the door for government
harassment of the press.

1837.   Bennett, James R. "McCarran Goodthinkful." FS 60
          (Fall 1986) 8-11.
     The government's plan to deport Margaret Randall under the
flawed McCarran-Walter Act of 1952 makes urgently clear how
needed is the "Free Trade in Ideas" legislation (S. 2263 and
H.R. 2361, 3825, and 3827).

1838.   Biskind, Peter. "U.S.A. Political Prisoners, By any
          Other Name." SD 1.8(1977) 23-25.
     A look at the "130 [or more] political prisoners in
American jails" and Amnesty International's efforts at justice.

1839.   Belair, Robert R. "Less Government Secrecy and More
          Personal Privacy?" CLR 4.1 (1977) 10-18.
     The FOIA and Privacy Acts "have had little, if any,

positive impact on the way government handles personal data."

1840.   Bird, Kai, and Max Holland. "The Tapping of 'Tommy
         the Cork.'" Na 242.5 (1986) 129, 142-45.
The story "of the most extensive partisan political wiretap
instigated by any postwar President," Truman's tapping of Thomas
Corcoran.

1841.   Boyer, Brian. "Reporter Threatened by Subpoena
         Actions." ChJR 3.3 (1970) 13-15.
On the growing abuse of the subpoena power to acquire a
reporter's confidential information, and an appeal to the media
to resist.

1842.   Butz, Tim. "Counter-Insurgency Comes Home." CS 2.1
         (Fall, 1974) 19-25.
The Nixon Presidency militarized the police community in
general and formed a private army within the Justice Department
in particular. "The most grim example of this particular abuse
of power is the Siege of Wounded Knee, a 71-day standoff between
the private army of the Justice Department and several hundred
members of the Independent Oglala Sioux Nation and the American
Indian Movement."

1843.   "The Caldwell Decision." CJR 11.3 (1972) supplement
         1-12.
A complete text of the Supreme Court's decision that Earl
Caldwell et al. had acted illegally when they refused to provide
source information to grand juries.

1844.   Christensen, Jack. "The Study of Meaning." M&M 10
         (Sept. 1973) 35-37, 53-58.
"In the realm of politics and 'objective' news reporting,
the American public has been controlled, manipulated and 'hood-
winked' in a blatant attempt at Orwellian thought-control." The
author suggests ways teachers can make their students more aware
of the problem.

1845.   Christgau, John. "Enemies": World War II Alien
         Internment. Ames, IO: Iowa State UP, 1985. 187.
The "dreadfully wrong" Enemy Alien Internment Program,
1941-1946, confined more than 31,000 persons. Christgau
concentrates on individual experiences in one of these camps,
Fort Lincoln, North Dakota. He warns it could happen again
since the Enemy Alien Act (1941) remains unchanged.

1846.   Civil Liberties Alert. Washington, DC: American
         Civil Liberties Union.
Almost every issue of this legislative newsletter contains
something on governmental secrecy, censorship, or illegal
surveillance.

1847.   Colhoun, Jack. "Truong: A Spy or a Political
         Hostage?" Guard 37.45 (1985) 8.

David Truong was sent to prison in 1978 as a spy, but the founder of the Vietnamese-American Reconciliation Center still maintains he was "an activist working for normalization of diplomatic relations between the U.S. and his native Vietnam."

1848.   Copelon, Rhonda. "Reconstitutionalizing the Grand
          Jury." FP 2.8 (1977) 1-8.
Discusses the illegality of certain grand jury activities and suggests "urgent reforms."

1849.   Elsworth, Peter C. T. "The Menace of the Machine."
          Ch 3 (Sept./Oct. 1983) 68-72.
"Government access to detailed computer files on individuals may permit easy identification of dissidents and racial or religious minorities for the purposes of surveillance, harassment, or worse."

1850.   "The Executive Order on Intelligence Activities." FP
          7.3 (1982) 7-10.
"Reagan's order represents an exercise in Orwellian doublespeak and goes beyond the Carter and Ford executive orders and expands the already expansive executive assertion of authority to conduct intelligence activities."

1851.   Goodell, Charles. Political Prisoners in America.
          New York: Random, 1973. 400.
Part I provides a history of political prisoners in the United States; Part II explores the mechanisms of repression in America; Part III explains the value of civil disobedience. A protest against the continuing urge by members of the government to twist statutes and the Constitution in order to repress dissent.

1852.   Graham, Fred. "Will Earl Caldwell Go to Jail?" MORE
          2.6 (1972) 1,14.
Caldwell's refusal to give a grand jury his inside reporter's information about the Black Panther Party.

1853.   Grodzins, Morton. Americans Betrayed: Politics and
          the Japanese Evacuation. Chicago: U of Chicago P, 1949.
          444.
The decision in favor of evacuating Japanese Americans from the Pacific Coast during the early months of WWII "was in error, fundamentally at odds with the spirit of democracy and unnecessary as a war measure." Press response supported the hysteria: of 269 editorials, 163.5 were for evacuation and 105.5 against.

1854.   Halperin, Morton. "Further Adventures of a Tappee."
          CLR 1.2 (1974) 131-33.
The author's phone was illegally tapped by the National Security Council while he was employed by the NSC and for 16 months afterward. He explains why he is suing Kissinger and other officials and the telephone company.

1855.   Hentoff, Nat. "After Farber: The Illusions of the
        Press." Inq 2.3 (1979) 4-6.
        This article is about M. A. Farber going to jail because he
would not reveal his sources or his notes to the court.

1856.   Hentoff, Nat. "Privacy for Writers and Doctors Only."
        Inq 2.5 (1979) 5-7.
        Investigative journalists are not protected under the law.

1857.   Horowitz, Irving. "Can Democracy Cope with
        Terrorism?" CLR 4.1 (1977) 29-37.
        Focuses on "the dangers to civil liberties when the state
invokes counterterror to quell disturbances." He notes that
increases in terrorism invite increases in counter measures,
from "increased security checks, greater police surveillance,
and improved search and seizure measures to changes in the basic
legal code, such as the restoration of capital punishment."

1858.   "Human Rights in the USA." IC 9.5 (1980) 4-16.
        Three articles on violations of the Helsinki Accords in the
US. The first article, by Dorothy Connell, gives a report of
"major areas of concern," e.g., visa policy (McCarran-Walter
Act). The second article by Geoffrey Rips and Kathy Silberthau,
concentrates on visa policy and the exclusion of "undesirable"
aliens like Mexican novelist Carlos Fuentes. The third article
is by Amiri Baraka, black author, about his trial for resisting
arrest.

1859.   Jackson, Nancy. "The Politics of Revenge." MORE
        4.2 (1974) 5-8.
        President Nixon is behind some of the challenges to the
licenses of two television stations in Florida owned by The
Washington Post Co.

1860.   Justice, William. "Judicial Retreat: Federal Judges
        Are Failing To Protect Individual Rights." TO 78.1
        (1986) 11-13.
        "Condoning illegal searches by federal agents, endorsing
wholesale sweeps on factories to catch a few illegal aliens, and
requiring incriminating information as the basis for awarding
government benefits seems to condemn the people."

1861.   Koch, Lewis. "The Conspiracy Trial: a Reading List."
        ChJR 2.8 (1969) 10.
        A reading list to understand the background of the trial of
the "Chicago 8" (Abbie Hoffman, et al.), who denounce the trial
as an act of political suppression.

1862.   Landau, Jack C. "Harassing the Press." MORE 2.12
        (1972) 8-9.
        A case-by-case rundown on reporters facing government
harassment.

1863.   Lindorff, Dave. "A Special 'Party Line.'" SD 2.5

(1978) 11.
The government has access to all kinds of information by use of individuals' phone numbers.

1864.   Lowi, Theodore.   The Politics of Disorder. New York: Basic, 1971. 193.
Includes an analysis of the "agencies of systematic repression" on three levels: national, state-local, and nongovernmental (104ff.), in a ch. entitled "Postwar Panic and the Chilling of Dissent," which traces the decline of tolerance in America beginning in the late 1940s, combined with an increase of federal and state investigations and surveillance.

1865.   Marwick, Christine M. "The Espionage Laws: In Need of Reform." FP 1.9 (1976) 3-9.
The public and Congress should participate in decisions affecting the First Amendment protection of a free press.

1866.   McClellan, Grant S., ed. The Right to Privacy. New York: Wilson, 1976. 240.
Reprints of articles are divided into philosophical issues, role of the federal government, FBI and CIA, computerized records, and the Privacy Act of 1974.

1867.   Mead, Judy. "The Grand Juries: An American Inquisition." FP 2.1 (1976) 3-8.
The grand jury is "one of the most powerful instruments for intelligence gathering and political disruption in use today."

1868.   Millman, Joel. "Paper Raid." WJR 7 (January 1985) 10-11.
Immigration and Naturalization Service harassment of New York's Spanish-language newspaper El Diario-La Prensa, which had been critical of the INS.

1869.   Peck, Keenen. "The Take-Charge Gang." Prog 49.5 (1985) 1, 18-24.
An analysis of the Federal Emergency Management Agency (FEMA), which is intended to "take charge in case of a national emergency"--to monitor political dissent, maintain secrets, censor communications, imprison terrorists, etc. It is a "growing cloak-and-dagger operation" which represents "a dangerous threat to our rights."

1870.   Peterzell, Jay. "Surveillance and Disruption of Anti-Nuclear Protest." FP 6.3 (1980) 1-7.
The anti-nuclear movement has become the object of disruption by government and private agencies.

1871.   "Press Freedom in the USA." IC 2.2 (1973) 91-92.
A resolution of the Inter-American Press Association deploring jailing of reporters in the USA for refusing to disclose sources.

1872.   Preston, William. "How We Became Addicted to Drug
          Control." CLR 4.2 (1977) 68-71.
     The "history of legislative control over 'dangerous drugs'
is a case study in the damage a prohibition reflex by lawmakers
can inflict to civil liberties."

1873.   Ridgeway, James. "Of Meese and His Men." TO 77.6
          (1985) 11-13.
     An inquiry into Edwin Meese's "20-year obsession with law
and order at the expense of civil liberties and freedom."

1874.   Rodgers, Raymond S. "Movement on the Periphery:
          Foreign Travel as a First Amendment Right." FSY 21
          (1982) 50-69.
     Recent court rulings have supported government restrictions
of the right to travel.

1875.   Schwartz, Herman. Taps, Bugs, and Fooling the People.
          New York: Field Foundation, 1977. 48.
     "The largest impact of wiretapping and bugging in this
country in the last three decades has not been on crime, but on
the growth of lawlessness and the corruption of law enforcement
at the police, the prosecutorial and the judicial levels."

1876.   Taylor, Terri. "U.S. Customs Seizes Iran Books." ORK
          (Summer 1982) 18-19.
     Intelligence files found by Moslem students in the US
Embassy in November 1979 were printed in 12 volumes and sold
throughout the Mideast and Europe. The author and another
reporter bought two sets of these documents. The FBI
confiscated one set at Boston's Logan Airport and interrogated
the author.

IV. D. Congress 1877-1888 (See II. B.)

1877.   Bagdikian, Ben. "Congress and the Media: Partners
          in Propaganda." CJR 12.5 (1974) 3-10.
     The media often quote press releases and display film
provided by members of Congress rather than cover the stories
themselves.

1878.   Blanchard, Robert O. ed. Congress and the News Media.
          New York: Hastings, 1974. 506.
     A collection mainly of previously published essays, a few
original essays, and transcripts of some congressional
proceedings not widely available. The contents present Congress
as a political communicator, relations with correspondents, and
media-congressional interdependence. Other issues treated:
First Amendment, FOIA, shield law, Watergate, due process,
access of media.

1879.   Corning, Steve. "How Public Broadcasting Could Bring
          Congress to the American People: A Modest Proposal."
          PTR 2 (June 1974) 40-43.

Criticism of the media for failing to report Congress better. Congress "has been emasculated," while the power of the executive and judicial branches has grown. The media has been an "'accomplice after the fact'" by neglecting the legislative for the other branches "where the action is." [Televised House proceedings began in 1979, Senate in 1986.]

1880.   Ferguson, LeRoy C., and Ralph H. Smuckler. Politics in the Press: An Analysis of Press Content in 1952 Senatorial Campaigns. East Lansing: Michigan State UP, Gov. Res. Bur., 1954. 100.
Press coverage of the reelection campaigns of Senators Joseph McCarthy of Wisconsin and William Benton of Connecticut emphasized the candidates' personalities more than their policies. The public "may not have had adequate opportunity to choose between alternative views on policy questions, party programs, or characteristics of the candidates."

1881.   Frantzich, Stephen. Computers in Congress: The Politics of Information. Beverly Hills: Sage, 1982. 285.
"Information stands out as a key factor in determining who has power both within Congress and in government in general." One of "the primary motivations of computer promoters in Congress stemmed from the desire to regain some of the power lost to the executive branch and outside interest groups due to an imbalance of relevant information" (234 and 242).

1882.   Green, Mark, and Michael Waldman. Who Runs Congress? 4th ed. New York: Dell, 1984. 432.
In his introduction, Ralph Nader perceives Congress aiding corporations in countless ways. "This conduct is in a long tradition of shielding corporate misbehavior from the rule of law and turning Congress and the executive branch into a bustling bazaar of bonanzas" for corporations. A rising source of corporate power over Congress is the political action committee. Congress should be dealing with the urgent, large problems facing the nation, but they are largely paralyzed by the power of the corporations and the presidential agent of that power.

1883.   Hardee, Patty. "Politicos Toot Horn: Papers Print Music." WJR 1.1 (1977) 8-9.
Congressional press releases are generally printed verbatim as news stories, particularly in the weeklies and smaller dailies.

1884.   Hayden, Tom. Rebellion and Repression. New York and Cleveland: World, 1969. 186.
Testimony by the author before the National Commission on the Causes and Prevention of Violence and the House Un-American Activities Committee. He believes that the hearings by both were intended to "put radicalism on trial" as the response by the "power elite" to their failures at home and abroad. HUAC and

NCV "are two sides of the same coin of political persecution."

1885.   McClellan, Jimmie. "Two Party Monopoly Institutional
          Barriers to Third Party Participation in American
          Politics." PhD Diss., Union for Experimenting Colleges
          and Universities, 1984. DAI 45 (1985) 3199-A.
     "The claim of the United States to be a model of democratic
virtue is contradicted by its treatment of third parties."
Hostility to third parties "is an active effort to promote the
major parties while discouraging the emergence of opposition to
them."

1886.   Schneiders, Greg. "The 90-Second Handicap: Why TV
          Coverage of Legislation Falls Short." WJR 7.6 (1985)
          44-46.
     On the decline of TV coverage of Congress--"the number of
network nightly news stories cut 50 percent in ten years" and
those mainly negative. Observers "worry about the effect . . .
on the balance of power between the executive and the
legislative branches."

1887.   Tyler, Suzanne. "Former Congressman Faults the
          Imperial Presidency for Ignoring the U.S. Congress."
          SLJR 11 (February 1985) 19.
     An account of former Missouri Representative Thomas Curtis'
campaign to draw attention to White House, media, and scholarly
disregard of the War Powers Resolution and Title 18, Section
1913, a criminal statute barring the executive branch from
lobbying Congress with federal funds.

1888.   Veenstra, Charles. "The House Un-American Activities
          Committee's Restriction of Free Speech." TS 22 (Winter
          1974) 15-22.
     The Un-American Activities Committee is shown to have
denied witnesses at its hearings the right of free speech.
Notes following the essay contain much supplementary reading
material. [See I., Anti-Sovietism.]

IV. E. Think Tanks 1889-1905 (See III. E.)

1889.   Critchlow, Donald T. The Brookings Institution,
          1916-1952: Expertise and the Public Interest in a
          Democratic Society. DeKalb, IL: Northern Illinois UP,
          1985. 247.
     On the positive side, Brookings "contributed to the
establishment of a modern budget system in the United States,
the reorganization of the Bureau of Indian Affairs in the
1920s, the drafting of the National Industrial Recovery Act, and
the founding of the United Nations." Yet Brookings "took a
stand against the National Recovery Administration, Keynesian
economics, and Truman's proposals for national health insurance
and for the extension of Social Security benefit payments. This
study presents the history of the Brookings Institution in a
broad interpretive framework that emphasizes the relationship of

elite groups to the American political environment and economic order" (Preface).

1890.   Domhoff, G. William, ed. Power Structure Research.
          Beverly Hills: Sage, 1980. 270.
     Ch. 7, "Think Tanks and Capitalist Policy," by Irvine Alpert and Ann Markusen: an analysis of Brookings and Resources for the Future public policy institutions. "It is our view that these organizations perform a brokerage function between private capital and the state. We characterize their operations as a production process in which the product is policy, ideology, and plans."

1891.   Eisenberg, Carolyn. "Two Cheers for Reagan from Old
          Establishment." ITT 7.41 (1983) 18-19.
     The Council on Foreign Relations and its journal, Foreign Affairs, are "loyal to an imperial vision."

1892.   Elias, Thomas. "President Reagan's Think Tanks Have a
          Plan for the Media." Pr 9.3 (1981) 4.
     San Francisco's Institute for Contemporary Studies has produced a report on how to tame White House reporters. The Claremont Economic Institute supports David Stockman's economic budget-trimming policies.

1893.   Gavshon, Arthur. "The Power and Influence Behind
          America's Right." MGW (Dec. 1, 1985) 9.
     The Heritage Foundation, with its $10 million headquarters in Washington and a $11-12 million annual budget, and its "stunning" influence on President Reagan, Margaret Thatcher, and like-minded leaders, is pulling together conservative and right-wing elements "to ensure the permanence of the American shift to the Right."

1894.   Green, Philip. "Science, Government and the Case of
          RAND: A Singular Pluralism." WoP 22 (1968) 301-326.
     An account of how scientists are acculturated into powerful corporate and governmental organizations.

1895.   Guttman, Daniel, and Barry Willner. The Shadow
          Government. New York: Pantheon, 1976. 354.
     Subtitled: The Government's Multi-Billion-Dollar Giveaway of Its Decision-Making Powers to Private Management Consultants, "Experts," and Think Tanks. Hidden by considerable camouflage, this consultants' game is designed "to ratify, certify, or initiate what the Federal bureaucracies and their corporate beneficiaries--a well-fused duo--are doing or would like to do." To "appreciate the significance of The Shadow Government, one must understand the extent and function of delegation of governmental responsibilities to private special interests by the Executive Branch in a society where government power so consistently derives from the generic power of corporations."

1896.   Hall, Earl. "Mein Kampf Translated? The Ultra-Right

Parallels Pre-Hitler Days in Germany." <u>Chm</u> 199
(January 1985) 6-7.
A critique of the Heritage Foundation and the second volume
of its <u>Mandate for Leadership</u>, II. The right-wing Heritage
Foundation has great influence with the Reagan administration.

1897.   Kidder, Rushworth. "Ideas Rain from Brainstorms in
     Think Tanks." <u>RMN</u> (October 21, 1984) 83 (from the <u>CSM</u>).
Most of the research and publishing organizations, all the
most wealthy and influential, are center to right in ideology.

1898.   Kiester, Sally. "New Influence for Stanford's Hoover
     Institution." <u>Cg</u> 13.7 (1981) 46-50.
On the increasing influence of the Institution as the
result of the rise of conservative thought in the US and its
direct ties to Ronald Reagan, one of three honorary Hoover
fellows (with Alexander Solzhenitsyn and the conservative
economist Friedrich Hayek). The Hoover has taken "a staunch
anti-communist stance," after its founder's stated purpose "to
demonstrate the evils of the doctrines of Karl Marx." The
institution's endowment has reached $40 million mostly
contributed by businessmen.

1899.   Lawrence, Ken. "The Academic Subversive Today." <u>CAIB</u>
     4 (1979) 23-26.
Focuses partly on the staunch anticommunism of Stanford
University's Hoover Institute's African publications.

1900.   Merbaum, Richard. "RAND: Technocrats and Power."
     <u>NUT</u> 3 (Dec.-Jan. 1963-64) 45-57.
The Rand Corp. was formed to do research for the US Air
Force. "[T]he RAND specialists never challenge any" of the Air
Force's assumptions about the Cold War, and their assumptions
about a hot war are quite unrealistic" (46). RAND probably will
not change significantly, partly because of "the absence of an
adequate alternative theoretical position accepted by a large
number of intellectuals" (56).

1901.   Muro, Mark. "Heritage Redefines Think Tanks." <u>AG</u>
     (Feb. 23, 1986) 1C.
A description of the Reaganite Heritage Foundation founded
in 1973 by Adolph Coors.

1902.   Smith, Philip. "Who Is Who at the Think Tanks." <u>Pr</u>
     10.3 (June 1982) 22-25.
Discusses RAND, the Heritage Foundation, the Brookings
Institution, the Hoover Institution, the American Enterprise
Institute, all conservative, representing various factions of
the Establishment. "There is no liberal equivalent to Heritage"
except for the very small Institute for Policy Studies.

1903.   Stern, Sol. "The Defense Intellectuals." <u>Ram</u> 5.8
     (1967) 31-37.
Concerns RAND corporation activities involving the Cold War

and Vietnam, and documents some of McNamara's activities with the RAND corporation both in and out of Vietnam.

1904.   Russo, Anthony. "Inside the RAND Corporation and Out: My Story." Ram 10 (April 1972) 45-55.
Russo relates his experiences with the RAND Corporation and the background of his involvement in the publication of the Pentagon Papers.

1905.   Schulzinger, Robert. The Wise Men of Foreign Affairs The History of the Council on Foreign Affairs. New York: Columbia UP, 1984. 326.
A history of a private policy organization interlocked with the US "national security" apparatus and the wealthy and powerful.

IV. F. Washington Press Corps 1906-1928 (See II. D. 2. & V. B.)

1906.   Bethell, Thomas. "The Myth of an Adversary Press." Har 254 (Jan. 1977) 33-40.
The media bureaucracy is a department of government. Media power is "indistinguishable" from government, their personnel "increasingly interchangeable."

1907.   Bonafede, Dom. ". . . The Press." WJR 2.4 (1980) 48-50.
A description of the White House press corps, by whom "conformity is more prized than unorthodoxy" and whose "rituals and customs" remind one of the "Court of St. James." They tend to "passively record day-to-day events, minus any historical framework."

1908.   Broder, David. "Political Reporters in Presidential Politics." WM 1 (February 1969) 20-33.
An account of the close relationship between Robert Kennedy's speech writers and reporters flying with the candidate, the reporters routinely filing the story provided by the writers.

1909.   "The Company They Keep." CJR 19.6 (1981) 22.
On the close connection between the government and the NYT through its correspondent Richard Burt. "The dangers to Washington reporters who get too close to their sources grow clearer year by year."

1910.   Cook, Faye, et al. "Media and Agenda Setting: Effects on the Public, Interest Group Leaders, Policy Makers, and Policy." POQ 47 (1983) 16-35.
The media "influenced views about issue importance among the general public and government policy makers." But "policy change resulted from collaboration between journalists and government staff members."

1911.   Cormier, Frank. "Co-option of the Press." The White
          House Press on the Presidency. Ed. Kenneth Thompson.
          Lanham, MD: UP of America, 1983. 60-80.
     "Every president, I'm convinced, does his best to co-opt the
press or, at the very least, to keep us docile and friendly"
(65).

1912.   Deakin, James. "The Problem of Presidential-Press
          Relations." The White House Press on the Presidency:
          News Management and Co-option. Ed. Kenneth Thompson.
          Lanham, MD: UP of America, 1983. 7-33.
     "The government wishes to manipulate the press. It spends
at least a billion dollars annually and employs an estimated
19,000 publicity agents in a tireless effort to use the news
media advantageously. The press does not wish to be exploited
by the government" (7-8). The speech focuses especially upon
presidents Johnson and Nixon.

1913.   Deakin, James. Straight Stuff: The Reporters, the
          White House, and the Truth. New York: Morrow, 1984.
          378.
     Revelations about the Washington news process, life with
the "imperial" presidency (Democratic and Republican), Reagan's
falsehoods and errors, the uncritical reporting of the Reagan
administration, etc., by the St. Louis Post-Dispatach's White
House correspondent.

1914.   Hess, Stephen. The Government-Press Connection.
          Washington, DC: Brookings, 1984. 160.
     A generally approving study of the government press
officer, the "flack," in the State Department, the Pentagon, the
White House, the Department of Transportation, and the Food and
Drug Administration.

1915.   Hess, Stephen. "The Golden Triangle: The Press at
          the White House, State, and Defense." BR 1.4 (1983) 14-
          19.
     This follow-up of the author's The Washington Reporters
makes close comparisons of the three press corps.

1916.   Hess, Stephen. The Washington Reporters. Washington,
          DC: Brookings, 1981. 174.
     A study of the domestic press corps in Washington based
upon interviews and questionnaires. The author's intention is
to "explain how the press fits into the web of governance," by
examining its political bias, pack journalism, etc. The author
claims to have found no ideology. "The slant of Washington news
is more a product of the angle from which it is observed than
from ideology" (115), but most of the press corps are
conservative, few want to criticize corporations, and they
neglect important beats like the Pentagon and the regulatory
agencies.

1917.   Hoffman, Nicholas Von. "Dining Out in Medialand."

MORE 8.2 (1978) 24-5.
On the close relationship between top news people and
government officials. "The occasional adversary role of the
news business has been so exaggerated that little effort has
been expended in noting the normal and ordinary role of news
executives, which is to facilitate the running of the country."

1918.   Hume, Brit. "The Invisible Bestseller." MORE 2.8
          (1972) 3-4.
Questions why the Washington press corps has suppressed
discussion of Robert Winter-Berger's The Washington Pay-Off:
A Lobbyist's Own Story of Corruption in Government.

1919.   Klugman, Craig. "Evans-Novak and Nixon-Laird." ChJR
          3.7 (1970) 11.
Rowland Evans and Robert Novak, authors of the syndicated
column, Inside Report, "have recently decided to serve the Nixon
administration."

1920.   Mathews, Jay. "All the President's Men." CJR 20.4
          (1981) 5-7.
Because of the President's "gracious" treatment of the
press "the White House Reporters genuinely like and respect
Reagan."

1921.   Nimmo, Dan. Newsgathering in Washington. New York:
          Atherton, 1964. 282.
"News" results for the interaction of two processes: the
information-dispensing process by governmental officials and the
newsgathering process by members of the media. Officials
seek to influence the public through media. The media provides
this channel for promotional messages but ideally not merely as
a conduit but as a defining and interpreting filter, in order to
provide the public with sufficient accurate information for
choice. The author focuses upon government public relations
officers and the news organizations and individuals in
Washington.

1922.   Powell, Jody. The Other Side of the Story. New York:
          Morrow, 1984. 322.
A critique of the media's coverage of the Carter
Administration and an appeal for more media self-criticism,
because reporting the White House is too superficial. "The fact
is that news has to sell," and that "creates a bias to make news
reports interesting." Thus, "members of the press wrestle with
the most basic and pervasive of human motivations: greed and
ambition."

1923.   Rivers, William. The Opinion Makers. Boston:
          Beacon, 1965. 207.
Explore the interplay of politics and the mass media,
government officials and reporters, as the foundation of
democracy, since the struggle over political information has "as
its end the making of public opinion." The "elite of the

Washington press corps" and "officialdom, bossdom" shape what the people "hear, see, and read." Chs. on power, the elite, Walter Lippman, news managers, etc.

1924.   Shannon, William. "The Newlywed Game." MORE 4.9
          (1974) 1, 19-20.
     "Despite the lessons of Watergate, President Ford and the press are now embarked on a cozy honeymoon--a Washington tradition long in need of overhaul, like White House coverage in general."

1925.   Sherrill, Robert. "The Arrangement." CJR 20.2 (1981)
          72-75.
     Favorable review of Grossman and Kumar's Portraying the President. The White House "spends a great deal of our money and its time on propaganda" and the press "spends a great deal of its own money and time cooperating with the White House."

1926.   Watters, Susan. "The Seduction of Hildy Johnson."
          WJR 2.3 (1980) 26-29.
     An analysis of and expression of anxiety about "the symbiotic relationship between the media and government policymakers" as manifested in socializing--entertaining, parties, dinners, etc.

1927.   "What the Readers See: How a Sample of Newspapers
          Treats Washington News." CJR 1.1 (1962) 21-23.
     Selected days in 1961 reveal a "ragged" reporting of Washington.

1928.   Wolfson, Lewis W. The Untapped Power of the Press:
          Explaining Government to the People. New York: Praeger,
          1986. 202.
     His thesis is that the press fails to explain government adequately because it depicts it "not as a process, but as a succession of events, many of them in fact staged for the media." Instead of breaking news, personalities, and confrontations, the press should tell people more about the inner workings of government, how it affects them, "and how they can influence it." One of his remedies is a proposal for a Center on the Media and Government in Washington to train journalists how to examine government critically and to inform the public of what they know.

IV. G. Wars 1929-2033

IV. G. 1. Post-World War II 1929-1945

1929.   Abrams, Pamela. "Local Coverage of Peace Issues
          Outshines the National Press." Dead 1.4 (1986) 10-12.
     The "major national news organizations do tend to regard the peace movement as about as important as a Sunday-school picnic. But coverage at the grassroots level" is "a good deal better."

CONTROL OF INFORMATION

1930.   Bernstein, Barton. "A Postwar Myth: 500,000 U.S.
    Lives Saved." BAS 42.6 (1986) 38-40.
    President Truman claimed half a million US lives were saved
by the atomic bombing of Hiroshima and Nagasaki, but "military
planners before Hiroshima had placed the number at 46,000 and
sometimes as low as 20,000 American lives."

1931.   Burchett, Wilfred. Again Korea. New York:
    International, 1968. 188.
    "Suppression of News" (61-64): "lies of Ridgeway's press
officers," "the dishonest behavior of the American delegates,"
etc.

1932.   Clark, Ramsey. "Libya, Grenada and Reagan." Na
    242.17 (1986) 605.
    Clark calls for "the impeachment and trial of Ronald
Reagan."

1933.   Cockburn, Alexander. "Superfiend." Na 242.16 (1986)
    576-77.
    Press coverage of Qaddafi is "appalling." The known cases
of Libyan political killings or attempted killings are a
"miniscule total when set beside the killings wrought by U.S.-
trained and -funded murderers in Central America alone, which
number in the tens of thousands." But the media overwhelmingly
report the administration's point of view.

1934.   Fehrenbach, T. R. This Kind of War. New York:
    Macmillan, 1963. 688.
    On the poor reporting of the Korean War, which the author
attributes to ethnocentricism, nationalism, and patriotism (149-
51, for example).

1935.   Gruber, Carol S. Mars and Minerva: World War I and
    the Uses of the Higher Learning in America. Baton Rouge:
    Louisiana State UP, 1975. 293.
    A study of the academics "who were most vocal and visible
in devoting their talents and energy to the prosecution of the
war" (7).

1936.   Knightley, Phillip. The First Casualty: From the
    Crimea to Vietnam: The War Correspondent as Hero,
    Propagandist, and Myth Maker. New York: Harcourt, 1975.
    465.
    Ch. 14, Korean War military censorship reached "ridiculous
lengths," supported by rabid anticommunism in the press back
home. Chs. 16 and 17 deal with the Vietnam War: "In the end,
the Vietnam War was better reported than any of the other wars
examined here. But this is not saying a lot."

1937.   Krepon, Michael. "Neoconservative War of the Worlds."
    BAS 42.3 (1986) 6-7.
    Neoconservatives have made it "intellectually respectable
to engage in covert or unilateral military action," partly

through their numerous media outlets.

1938.   "The Media Go to War--From Vietnam to Central
          America." Spec. no. of RA 17 (July-August 1983).
     Six articles focus especially on the administration's
domination of news.

1939.   Minor, Dale. The Information War. New York:
          Hawthorn, 1970. 212.
     A study of the "forces and tendencies which act to
constrict, control, and manipulate the information the public
gets." Chs. on the Korean War, the Vietnam War, the Dominican
intervention, etc.

1940.   Said, Edward. "Iran." CJR 18.6 (1980) 23-33.
     During the embassy hostage crisis, journalists joined the
government in presenting Iran and Islam as "forces of darkness
in a Manichean clash between good and evil." Most journalists
"blindly" served a highly biased administration policy instead
of seeking the truth and informing the public.

1941.   "Showing the Flag." CJR 18.6 (1980) 19-20.
     In response to the hostages in Tehran, the press joined the
government in rallying the people in patriotic nationalism,
instead of fulfilling their "mandate to inform."

1942.   Singleton, Kathy. "A Survey of the Historiography of
          the Korean War." MA Thesis, U of Arkansas, 1985. 157.
     The writers of the 1950s, "with the exception of I.F.
Stone," were "biased toward the actions taken by the Truman
Administration, for to disapprove would almost be tantamount to
treason." Beginning with Stone, "soft revisionists" placed
responsibility for the Cold War and therefore for the Korean War
on Truman and the failure of American statesmanship. The
"hard" or "New Left" revisionists, typified by the Kolkos,
placed responsibility for the Cold and Korean wars upon the US
system of "continuous economic expansion" by corporations. The
war "could be viewed as being the product of two clashing
imperialisms."

1943.   Stone, I. F. The Hidden History of the Korean War.
          Monthly Review. 1952. (2nd ed. 1969) 364.
     After noticing how different were the reports of the war by
British and French correspondents compared to US
correspondents, Stone set out to assess the coverage of the war.
The book is both a study in the Cold War and "a study in war
propaganda." "Emphasis, omission, and distortion rather than
outright lying are the tools of the war propagandists."

1944.   Ward, Larry. The Motion Picture Goes to War: The
          U.S. Government Film Effort during World War I. Ann
          Arbor, MI: UMI Research, 1985. 176.
     An examination of "the use of motion pictures by the
Committee on Public Information (CPI), the US government's

official wartime propaganda agency" under George Creel, and the "inextricably linked" relations between the government's program and the private film industry.

1945.   "We are Teaching Barbaric War Ethics, Dressed in 20th Century Clothing." SLJR 13.84 (1986) 19.
An account of efforts by the National Coalition on Television Violence to educate the public about the negative effects of "war toys and violent cartoons on young viewers."

IV. G. 2. Vietnam War 1946-2033

IV. G. 2. a. Government Disinformation, Secrecy, and Censorship 1946-1979

1946.   Austin, Anthony. The President's War: The Story of the Tonkin Gulf Resolution and How the Nation was Trapped in Vietnam. Philadelphia: Lippincott, 1971. 368.
No attack ever occurred against the US destroyers in the Gulf of Tonkin, but the managers of the national security establishment "deliberately misled Congress and the American people" in the belief that "preventing the spread of Communism justified the means employed" and "through that deception were able to obtain Congressional authorization for a war they had secretly decided on months before, while promising the voters peace" (345-6).

1947.   Branch, Taylor. "The Scandal That Got Away." MORE 3.10 (1973) 1,17-20.
"By any yardstick, the secret bombing of Cambodia in 1969 is at least as grave an issue as Watergate. But once the facts were revealed, few in the press found them nearly as intriguing as Howard Hunt's red wig." The 3,630 secret B-52 raids on a neutral country were illegal by both national and international law; and the President conspired with the military to keep a new war hidden from Congress, which alone has the power to enter into a war, but the press did not discover the bombing until after they ended, and allowed the story to die quickly.

1948.   Branfman, Fred. Voices from the Plain of Jars: Life Under an Air War. New York: Harper, 1972. 160.
An account of the destruction of a rural Laotian society of some fifty thousand people by secret, illegal bombings by the US from 1964 to 1969. Over 25,000 attacks were flown against the Plain of Jars and from 75,000 to 150,000 tons of bombs were dropped, yet "one searches in vain through the newspapers and magazines of the western world for a single word about the bombing of the Plain." The secrecy was maintained for 5 1/2 years by denial, by prohibiting newsmen from going out on bombing raids, and by refusing them the right to interview the pilots. Finally, when in October 1969, the US admitted to the bombing, officials lied to Congress that they had not bombed villages.

1949.   Browne, Malcolm W. "Vietnam Reporting: Three Years
     of Crisis." CJR 3.3 (1964) 4-9.
     This Associated Press correspondent relates his
difficulties in relating negative factual information because of
opposition from Vietnamese and American authorities.

1950.   Epstein, Jason. The Great Conspiracy Trial: An
     Essay on Law, Liberty, and the Constitution. New York:
     Random, 1970. 433.
     An account of the trial of the Chicago 8, another effort by
the state to repress free speech during the Vietnam era.

1951.   Eshenaur, Ruth. "Censorship of the Alternative Press:
     A Descriptive Study of the Social and Political Control
     of Radical Periodicals (1964-1973)." PhD Diss., Southern
     Illinois U, 1975. 371. DAI 36 (1976) 7705.
     "Public officials had censored 68% of the respondents with
660 formal actions one or more times; civilians had censored 51%
with 317 informal actions one or more times; and public
officials and civilians had censored 21% with 88 illegal actions
one or more times." The fact that "periodicals had to expend
considerable effort and resources in self defense constituted a
form of harassment."

1952.   Goulden, Joseph. Truth Is the First Casualty: The
     Gulf of Tonkin Affair--Illusion and Reality. Chicago:
     McNally, 1969. 285.
     Contrasts the account given by the Johnson Administration
with the truth, and the process through which the Senate learned
of the difference.

1953.   Gravel, Michael. The Senator Gravel Edition--The
     Pentagon Papers. Boston: Beacon, 1971. 100.
     Officials in Washington refused to acknowledge the true
state of affairs in Vietnam and brought America into a war under
false pretenses.

1954.   Halberstam, David. The Best and the Brightest. New
     York: Random, 1972. 688.
     As the Vietnam conflict escalated during the Kennedy and
Johnson administrations, the press tried to find out what was
really going on at home and abroad.

1955.   Hovsepian, Nubar, and Stuart Schaar. "Who Wanted David
     Truong Put Away?" Na 240 (March 2, 1985) 240-41.
     The prosecution and severe sentencing of Truong for
espionage derived from his opposition to US policies in Vietnam.

1956.   Knightly, Phillip. "'Vietnam 1954-1975' [and] 'War
     is Fun 1954-1975.'" First Casualty: From the Crimea to
     Vietnam--The War Correspondent as Hero, Propagandist, and
     Myth Maker. New York: Harcourt, 1975. 373-426.
     Accounts of atrocities committed by American soldiers in
Vietnam and the correspondents' difficulties in getting their

accounts of these actions published by American publications.

1957.   Marks, John D. "The Story that Never Was?" MORE
          4.6 (1974) 20-22.
     Tad Sulc claims that his story revealing the planned US and
South Vietnam invasion of Cambodia was canceled by the editor of
the NYT at the request of Henry Kissinger. The editor denies
it.

1958.   Mitford, Jessica. The Trial of Dr. Spock, the Rev.
          William Sloane Coffin, Jr., Michael Ferber, Mitchell
          Goodman, and Marcus Raskin. New York: Knopf, 1969.
          272.
     The trial of Dr. Benjamin Spock and others was a political
trial intended by the government to silence opponents of the
Vietnam War. The remedy is an end to political trials.

1959.   News Policies in Vietnam. Senate Committee on
          Foreign Relations, 8th Congress. 2nd Sess. Washington,
          DC: GPO, 1966. 161.
     Senate hearings to confirm the level of news management and
censorship in news reports from Vietnam. "News management is a
fact. Knowing about it, we can evaluate the news more
accurately."

1960.   Oberdorfer, Don. Tet! Garden City, NY: Doubleday,
          1971. 385.
     The Tet Offensive in 1968 marked the end of American
confidence as to victory in Vietnam. The press "became more
pessimistic, with inevitable impact on the public."

1961.   Oppenheim, Jerrold. "Good News and Bad News: Anti-
          Trust Suit Against Networks." ChJR 5.9 (1972) 13.
     The suit has had the effect of intimidating the networks
"in their response to the bombing" of Hanoi and Haiphong by the
Nixon administration.

1962.   Rothmyer, Karen. "Westmoreland v. CBS." CJR 24.1
          (1985) 25-30.
     Concerning the charge by Westmoreland that CBS had libeled
him. The trial was financed largely by right-wing organizations
and individuals, particularly by Richard Mellon Scaife. "What
seemed to emerge from the testimony was a picture of widespread
agreement on the part of top political, intelligence, and
military officials to deceive not each other but the press and
the American people" (29).

1963.   Rubin, Trudy. "Stalking Beacon Press." MORE 2.9
          (1972) 5-7.
     Government investigation of Beacon and its owner, the
Unitarian Universalist Association, for publishing the Gravel
edition of the Pentagon Papers.

1964.   Rustin, Richard. "Censorship and Cam Ne." CJR 4.3

(1965) 22-23.
An account of press censorship in Vietnam.

1965.   Schandler, Herbert Y. The Unmaking of a President:
          Lyndon B. Johnson and Vietnam. Princeton, NJ: Princeton
          UP, 1977. 419.
Johnson's decisions on Vietnam were made privately and
secretly, "a method of policy making whose grave defects were
demonstrated throughout the Vietnam war." After the Tet
Offensive in 1968, Vietnam became an issue which devastated his
authority as president.

1966.   Scheer, Robert, and Warren Hinckle. "The 'Vietnam
          Lobby.'" Ram 4.3 (1965) 16-44.
Concerned with "the history of a small and enthusiastic
group of people--including a Cardinal, an ex-Austrian Socialist
leader, and a CIA agent--who maneuvered the Eisenhower
administration and the American press into supporting the
rootless, unpopular and hopeless regime of a despot and believed
it actually was all an exercise in democracy."

1967.   Schrag, Peter. Test of Loyalty: Daniel Ellsberg
          and the Rituals of Secret Government. New York: Simon,
          1974. 414.
An account of the trial of Ellsberg and Anthony Russo, Jr.,
the so-called Pentagon Papers trial, for conspiracy,
misappropriation of government property, and violations of the
Espionage Act, "perhaps the most important case of its time" on
the relation between government power and individual liberty.

1968.   Shawcross, William. Sideshow: Kissinger, Nixon and
          the Destruction of Cambodia. New York: Simon, 1979.
          467.
An account of the secret, illegal, and unconstitutional
bombings of Cambodia by the US during the Vietnam War. "None of
the Congressional committees, whose duty it is to recommend
appropriations and thus enable Congress to fulfill its
constitutional function of authorizing and funding war, was
notified that the President had decided to carry war into a
third country, whose neutrality the United States professed to
respect." Furthermore, the bombing records were falsified by
the Strategic Air Command.

1969.   Sheinbaum, Stanley, and Robert Scheer. "Addenda:
          Special Report from Cambodia and Saigon." Ram 4.12
          (1966) insert 10,50.
The two journalists' observations of activities in
Southeast Asia differ substantially from a government report
issued concerning US military actions in the two areas of the
war.

1970.   Small, William. Political Power and the Press. New
          York: Norton, 1972. 423.
A study of government "meddling" with the news. Four of

the eleven chapters deal with the Pentagon Papers.

1971.   Sonn, Bill. "H. Bruce Franklin: Another First."
    Prog 38 (1974) 36-37.
    On Marxist Professor H. Bruce Franklin's difficulties
obtaining employment after being fired from Stanford University
for allegedly inciting student violence against the Vietnam War.

1972.   Stein, Meyer. _Under Fire: The Story of American War_
    Correspondents. New York: Messner, 1968. 256.
    Ch. 9, "Vietnam: Terror of the Jungle," recounts the
experiences of the war correspondents and their frustration with
Pentagon and South Vietnamese government "news manipulation--
withholding of certain facts and unnecessary delay in feeding
information to the press."

1973.   Stone, I. F. _The Killings at Kent State: How Murder_
    Went Unpunished. New York: Review/Random, 1971. 158.
    An exposé of the conspiracy by Ohio officials and National
Guard officers and men to obstruct justice and fabricate
testimony and evidence regarding the killing of the students by
guardsmen at Kent State, May 4, 1970, and the failure of the
President's Commission on Campus Unrest (Scranton Commission) to
spotlight those responsible for the killings.

1974.   Turner, Kathleen. _Lyndon Johnson's Dual War: Vietnam_
    and the Press. Chicago: U of Chicago P, 1985. 358.
    On Johnson's elaborate efforts to make the American people
and the press believe and even love him, but his passions for
secrecy and manipulation often created opposition by the press.
The chs. follow a chronological order and show the increasing
intertwining of Johnson's handling of Vietnam and his relations
with the press, until "they are virtually inseparable." Ch. 5
concentrates on Johnson's address of April 7, 1965, at Johns
Hopkins University "to provide a detailed examination of the
role of media-government interaction in the development and
delivery of a major presidential message" (Preface).

1975.   Warsh, David. "The Stars & Stripes Flap." _ChJR_ 2.10
    (1969) 3-4.
    On efforts by the Army to censor the _Pacific Stars and_
Stripes during the Vietnam War. The military brass "see the war
as constantly coming up roses." The enlisted reporters "often
disagree."

1976.   Witcover, Jules. "Two Weeks That Shook the Press."
    The _New York Times_ and several other newspapers were
involved in a Supreme Court battle with the Justice Department
over the right to publish information from the classified
documents about Vietnam now called the Pentagon Papers.

1977.   Witcover, Jules, et al. "The First Amendment on
    Trial." _CJR_ 10.3 (1971) 7-15.
    Seven separate articles consider legal freedoms of the

press as related to the Pentagon Papers incident. Authors include Max Frankel and Ben Bagdikian.

1978.　　Woode, Allen. "How the Pentagon Stopped Worrying and Learned To Love Peace Marchers." Ram 6.7 (1968) 46-51.
The author, a Pentagon intelligence officer assigned to report on anti-Vietnam war protesters, was "appalled to see how neatly the government had the peace movement pegged."

1979.　　Zinn, Howard, and Noam Chomsky, eds. The Pentagon Papers: Critical Essays. Vol. 5. Boston: Beacon, 1972. 341.
Contains also an index to Vols. 1-4 of the Senator Gravel ed.

IV. G. 2. b. Media & Education　1980-2033

1980.　　Allman, T. D. "PBS's Vietnam: How TV Caught the Unprintable Truth." Ch 3 (1983) 10-11, 82-83.
The PBS series on the Vietnam War was "biased" not ideologically but by showing the concrete facts of US destructiveness.

1981.　　Arnett, Peter. "Tet Coverage: A Debate Renewed." CJR 16.5 (1978) 44-48.
A critique of Braestrup's Big Story which concludes that Braestrup "fails to clinch the argument."

1982.　　Bailey, George. "Interpretive Reporting of the Vietnam War by Anchormen." JQ 53.2 (1976) 319-324.
"The network anchormen, in their daily summaries of the war, read short stories of events without much interpretation, certainly without challenging, adversary interpretation."

1983.　　Bailey, George. "The Vietnam War According to Chet, David, Walter, Harry, Peter, Bob, Howard, and Frank: A Content Analysis of Journalistic Performance by the Network Television Evening News Anchormen, 1965-1970." U of Wisconsin Diss., 1973. 451. DAI 34 (1974) 4182-A.
"The anchormen generally covered the war by the uncritical relaying of press releases from the American military and government," though in later years criticism grew.

1984.　　Biskind, Peter. "A Balance of Error?" Na 237 (Dec. 3, 1983) 570-73.
PBS's Vietnam: A Television History offers a smokescreen of bogus impartiality in the eleven segments on the US role. In numerous ways the film is slanted toward the US side. [In 1985 Accuracy in Media (AIM) persuaded PBS to present their film arguing that Vietnam favored the enemy.]

1985.　　Braestrup, Peter. Big Story: How the American Press and Television Reported and Interpreted the Crisis of Tet

CONTROL OF INFORMATION

1968 in Vietnam and Washington. Boulder, Col.:
Westview, 1977. Vol. I, 740.
"In overall terms, the performance by the major American
television and print news organizations during February and
March 1968 constitutes an extreme case. Rarely has contemporary
crisis-journalism turned out. . . to have veered so widely from
reality" in reporting a defeat for the allies during the Tet
offensive. The cause for such reporting was only slightly
ideological; the main causes were suspicion of the Johnson
administration's credibility, impatience with the war's length,
revulsion at its horrors, and other personal and professional
grounds.

1986.   Chomsky, Noam. "American Media and Foreign Policy."
    IR (February 1980) 10-19.
    The author distinguishes between the explicit controls by
totalitarian governments and the methods of democracies by which
"the indoctrination system tries to capture the entire system of
thinkable thought," though within the framework of assumptions
"debate can rage." This thesis is illustrated by examples of
media treatments of the Vietnam War, especially of Peter
Braestrup's book on the coverage of the Tet offensive.

1987.   Chomsky, Noam. "Reporting Indochina: The News Media
    and the Legitimation of Lies." SocP 4.2 (1973) 4-19.
    "The press, serving as a faithful instrument of state
propaganda, has adopted the Washington version of the substance
of the [Paris] agreements and the course of events that led to
them. Thus it is helping to lay the basis in public opinion for
renewed support for American aggression in Indochina in
violation of the agreements. The "official state doctrine" both
"legitimizes the continued use of force" and stifles dissent;
the press is complicit by generally accepting Washington's
interpretation of events "in one of the most effective exercises
in political indoctrination in recent memory."

1988.   Chomsky, Noam. "The Secular Priesthood:
    Intellectuals and American Power." WP 6.3 (1978) 25-33.
    Technocratic and policy-oriented intellectuals make up a
"secular priesthood" which, "relying on the method of feigned
dissent characteristic of democratic propaganda systems, has
very largely succeeded, within only a few years, in destroying
the historical record [of the Vietnam War] and supplanting it
with a more comfortable story, transferring the moral onus of
American aggression to its victims."

1989.   Chomsky, Noam. "10 Years After Tet: The Big Story
    That Got Away." MORE 8.6 (June 1978) 16-23.
    Review of Peter Braestrup's Big Story. The author argues
that Braestrup asked the wrong questions and got the wrong
answers. Instead of examining the US justification of
intervention in Vietnam, studies like Braestrup's focus on the
minor issue of whether the media were too pessimistic in their
assessment of one incident.

329

1990.   Chomsky, Noam, and Edward Herman.   "Operation
      Whitewash." Inq 2.7 (1979) 23-27.
    A book review of America in Vietnam by Guenther Lewy, who
defends America's intervention in Vietnam.

1991.   Chomsky, Noam and Edward Herman. The Political
      Economy of Human Rights, Vol. II: After the Cataclysm:
      Postwar Indochina and the Reconstruction of Imperial
      Ideology. Boston: South End, 1979. 392.
    A "major emphasis will be on the ways in which these facts
have been interpreted, filtered, distorted or modified by the
ideological institutions of the West" (vii). "The Free Press
has fulfilled its primary obligations to the state by averting
Western eyes from the carnage of the war and effacing U.S.
responsibility. As noted, all problems are attributed to the
evils of Communism. The propaganda barrage has not only been
highly selective, but has also involved substantial
falsification. All in all, the performance of the Free Press in
helping to reconstruct a badly mauled imperial ideology has been
eminently satisfactory. The only casualties have been truth,
decency and the prospects for a more humane world" (x).

1992.   Clark, Michael. "Remembering Vietnam." CulC 3
      (Spring 1986) 46-78.
    About war films. The "memory of Vietnam has ceased to be a
point of resistance to imperialist ambition and is now invoked
as a vivid warning to do it right next time." Some of the films
discussed: Born Losers, Rolling Thunder, The Choirboys, Blue
Thunder, Year of the Dragon, etc.

1993.   Donovan, Kevin. "A Textbook View of Vietnam." Ed 39
      (Nov.-Dec. 1976) 8-10.
    Several high school history textbooks present the US
involvement in Vietnam as honorable and justified, ignoring or
barely mentioning contrary opinion or even information from the
Pentagon Papers.

1994.   Dorfman, Ron. "Bringing the War Home." ChJR 4.8
      (1971) 10-11.
    Rev. of Aronson, The Press and the Cold War, and Sheehan,
et al., The Pentagon Papers. "A reading of The Pentagon Papers
and The Press and the Cold War should convince any reasonably
sensitive journalist and, more importantly, any patriotic
citizen, that the real enemy" is "the American government and
its foreign policy and defense establishments." There seems "to
be growing up in the country the idea that the government has to
lie and mislead and carry on secret warfare and secret
diplomacy."

1995.   Entman, Robert, and David Paletz. "The War in
      Southeast Asia: Tunnel Vision on Television."
      Television Coverage of International Affairs. Ed.
      William Adams. Norwood, NJ: Ablex, 1982. 181-201.
    "Our hypothesis is that, dovish reputation notwithstanding,

television news did more to contain than to spread opposition to
the policies of Presidents Johnson, Nixon, and Ford" (181).

1996.   Faulkner, Francis. "Bao Chi: The American News Media
         in Vietnam, 1960-1975." Phd Diss., U of Massachusetts,
         1981. 823. DAI 41 (1981) 4875-A.
Journalists "covered the action and generally ignored
analysis, interpretation or investigative reporting. Vietnam
was covered most as a sports event or a police beat, with many
brave, but few intellectually aggressive reporters challenging
the basic premise of the war or receiving any encouragement to
do so from editors in the United States."

1997.   Gibson, William. "Apocalypse Then." ITT 7.37 (1983)
         12-13, 23.
PBS's Vietnam: A Television History makes "two vitally
important ideological 'breaks' with the network treatments of
the war, although the vast majority of material simply
reiterates lies and excuses made by U.S. officials." First, the
film presents "the previously hidden faces of the other side."
Second, it shows "just what dead and dying people look like."

1998.   Goldstein, Jonathan. "Vietnam Research on Campus:
         The Summit/Spicerack Controversy at the University of
         Pennsylvania, 1965-67." P&C 11.2 (1986) 27-49.
The University of Pennsylvania became "a center for Cold
War-oriented" chemical and biological research and development
in 1951. This article gives an account of the twenty-month-long
campus conflict over the propriety of CBW at Penn. which
resulted in the termination of all CBW contracts with the
Pentagon in 1967, the only US university "to make such a clear
break with classified war research" during the Indochina war.
The university accepted such contracts for national defense and
for money, but by 1967 enough faculty and students opposed the
program to force the president and trustees to end it.

1999.   Griffen, William. "Vietnam History in the Schools."
         Ed 29 (1974) 10-11.
Corporate or government sponsored educational materials
often present America's role in Vietnam in an inaccurate and
glorified manner.

2000.   Griffen, William, and John Marciano. Teaching the
         Vietnam War: A Critical Examination of School Texts and
         an Interpretative Comparative History Utilizing the
         Pentagon Papers and Other Documents. Montclair, NJ:
         Allanheld, Osmun, 1979. 183.
A study of 28 high school textbooks to show "how the
Vietnam War was explained to American students" as part of "an
ideological function: to pass on an uncritical acceptance of
the official view" of the war, "in particular, to view the war
either as an honorable policy or as a mistake, but not as part
of a deliberate policy of imperialism and aggression" (Preface).
The authors "show with compelling evidence that the educational

system, far from being 'objective,' fulfills the aims of the Establishment" (Foreword by Howard Zinn).

2001.   Hallin, Daniel. The "Uncensored War": The Media and Vietnam. New York: Oxford UP, 1986. 285.
In general, the media presented the war "within official perspectives," particularly during the early years. Part I, "Escalation and News Management, 1961-1965," "is an analysis of New York Times coverage from 1961 through mid-1965." Tapes of network coverage began to be available in 1965. Thus, Part II, "The War on Television, 1965-1973," deals with "a sample of network evening news from August 1965 through the cease-fire in January 1973." "Both parts also draw on a set of interviews with journalists (and with a more limited number of officials) involved in the war." Chs. 2 and 3 "are concerned with the nature of the constraints" during the Kennedy administration and the 1964-65 escalation under Johnson. Ch. 3 deals with the "ideology of the Cold War" shared by both officials and journalists. Ch. 4 treats the ways in which the routines of "objective journalism" make it "possible for officials to manage the news." Chs. 4 and 5 deal with television coverage "before and after the Tet offensive and the political changes of 1968." It was "particularly patriotic in its early coverage and then, like other media, changed as the political climate shifted at home and among American soldiers in the field."

2002.   Harris, Richard. "The Strange Love of Dr. Kissinger." MORE 2.3 (1972) 1, 14-16.
"A compliant and unwitting press" helped the Nixon administration conceal what its peace proposal to North Vietnam really meant.

2003.   Hellman, John. American Myth and the Legacy of Vietnam. New York: Columbia UP, 1986. 241.
The myth of an America projecting "freedom" throughout the frontier of the world created the Green Berets, the Vietnam War, President Kennedy as hero, and the global struggle with the evil Soviet Union.

2004.   Holk, Richard. "Print Coverage of Military Conflict: The Los Angeles Times and the Vietnam War (A Content Analysis, 1964-1972)." MA Thesis, California SU, Fullerton, 1979. 88. MA 18.1 (1980) 41.
Anti-war movement and military spending received "the least" coverage, but anti-war protest coverage increased during the nine years.

2005.   Hotaling, Edward. "Does Editors' War in Words Affect Opinions on Vietnam?" EP 102.15 (1969) 11,52.
Editors discuss what to call the forces opposing the US in Vietnam--communists, Viet Cong, North Vietnamese, NLF, or what? And what difference the label might make.

2006.   Hung, N. M. "Vietnam: A Television History: A Case

Study in Perceptual Conflict Between the American Media and the Vietnamese Expatriates." World Affairs 147.2 (1984) 71-84.
The series is not a "Vietnamese history," but is "utterly unfair to America's fallen allies, to the Vietnamese soldiers, to the Vietnamese refugees."

2007.   Johnson, Paul. "Creator of 13-hour History of Vietnam Sets 'Hearings.'" AG (Oct. 2, 1983) 1C,9C.
Many potential corporate sponsors found the series "too controversial."

2008.   Lesage, Julia. "Talkin' to Us." JC 5 (1975) 3-4.
Analysis of the film Speaking Directly: Some American Notes, which makes us question "the media representation" of Vietnam, "American economics and imperialism," Nixon, and Kissinger, by exploring "epistemological questions in a political way."

2009.   MacDonald, J. Fred. Television and the Red Menace: The Video Road to Vietnam. New York: Praeger, 1985. 256.
Television helped prepare the American public to accept US military involvement in Vietnam by systematically and uncritically affirming the superiority of US attitudes and fantasies, presenting action as superior to thought, and reducing the world's complexities to a contest between a good US and an evil SU.

2010.   Marciano, John. "The Ideological Lessons of the Vietnam War." The United States Educational System: Marxist Approaches. Ed. Marvin Berlowitz and Frank Chapman, Jr. Minneapolis: Marxist Educational P, 1980. 213-221.
"The treatment of the Vietnam War in American history textbooks is a glaring example" of how groups in power interpret history in order to legitimate their power. The essay is a summary of the author's (with William Griffen) Teaching the Vietnam War, a study of twenty-eight high school textbooks.

2011.   Marin, Peter. "Rerunning the War." MJ 8.9 (1983) 11-16.
The PBS series Vietnam: A Television History failed "to examine the war in relation to our economic and political aims and strategies as a nation"; for example, French occupation of Vietnam is treated as colonialism, but "when the United States takes center stage, there is no more talk of colonialism." Nor does the series explain the relationship between the "perfidy and cupidity of our leaders" and the popular support of the war.

2012.   Mastroberardino, Joy. "PBS Will Give AIM Air to Blast At Vietnam Series." Current 4.6 (1985) 1,4.
An account of how the right-wing Accuracy in Media

organization won money and time to reply to the 13-part series
Vietnam: A Television History. The program, tentatively titled
Inside Story Special: Vietnam a Public Inquiry, claims that PBS
criticized the US too severely in the series. [No mention is
made of complaints that the series was too lenient on the US.]

2013.   Mathurin, Victor. "A Content Analysis of Vietnam War
         News in The Times of London, Using The New York Times
         Content as a Basis for Comparison." MA Thesis, American
         U, 1967. 63. MA 5 (1967) 12.
    "The two newspapers were in substantial disagreement." The
London Times "showed the U.S. to be militarily and morally
inferior; New York gave the opposite impression."

2014.   McNulty, Thomas. "Network Television Documentary
         Treatment of the Vietnam War, 1965 to 1969." PhD Diss.,
         Indiana U, 1974. DAI 35 (1974) 2210-A.
    In 1966 both ABC and CBS "displayed very positive attitudes
toward American policy," afterwards more "balanced in their
evaluative statements" but in general supportive. ABC relied on
experts more than CBS. From 1965 to 1967, CBS "relied heavily
on Administration spokesmen and U.S. Senators," but during 1968-
69 turned dramatically to its own correspondents.

2015.   Mohr, Charles. "Once Again--Did the Press Lose
         Vietnam?" CJR 22.4 (1983) 51-56.
    A refutation of right-wing claims that the press lost the
Vietnam War and that the press willfully misrepresented the Tet
offensive. "For practical reasons, journalists always reported
the claims, appraisals, and statements of the senior officials
who asserted that 'progress' was being made. These stories
almost always got prominent play."

2016.   Moore, Robin. The Green Berets. New York:
         Ballantine, 1983. 339.
    A fictionalized account of the "marvelous undercover work
of our Special Forces in Vietnam and countries around the
world."

2017.   Parham, Paul. "Vietnam 1958-1961: U.S. Newsmagazine
         Coverage." MA Thesis, U of Missouri, 1971. MA 10.1
         (1972) 65.
    Coverage by Time, Newsweek, and U.S. News & World Report
was "minimal" and "superficial" and did not provide sufficient
information for an "accurate public opinion."

2018.   Patterson, Oscar. "An Analysis of Television Coverage
         of the Vietnam War." JoB 28.4 (1984) 397-404.
    Between 1965 and 1975 no other single event so dominated
television news programs as did the war in Vietnam. Yet
analysis of the content of actual news broadcasts does not
support the contention that nightly news programs were filled
with pictures of battle, or the dead, dying and wounded.

2019.   Patterson, Oscar. "The Vietnam Veteran and the Media:
A Comparative Content Analysis of Media Coverage of the
War and the Veteran 1968-1973." PhD Diss., U of
Tennessee, 1982. 254. DAI 43 (1983) 2822-A.
Vietnam was the dominant topic on network news but not in
the weekly news magazines studied. "Anti-war news reports
received more coverage on a per-item basis on television and in
news magazines than did combat."

2020.   Peck, Abe. Uncovering the Sixties: The Life and
Times of the Underground Press. New York: Pantheon,
1985. 365.
A history of the New Left and underground newspapers
against the Vietnam War (1964-1973) and a critique of the
relationship between propaganda and truth. Peck was the editor
of the underground newspaper the Chicago Seed. Coverage of the
1965 Watts riot by the Los Angeles Times and the Los Angeles
Free Press, and the 1968 student rebellion at Columbia
University in Rat and in The New York Times reveal how the
protest press probed the causes of conflicts while the
establishment press reported the stories as crime news. The
book includes accounts of government repression against the
underground press, from grand juries to FBI subversion.

2021.   Pfeiffer, Richard. "The Popular Periodical Press and
the Vietnam War: 1954-1968." MA Thesis, U of
Louisville, 1978. 106. MA 17.1 (1979) 56.
"No distinct opinion" in Time, Newsweek, and U.S. News and
World Report from 1954 to 1964, but from 1965 to 1968 Newsweek
"criticized the war" while Time and U.S. News "appeared to
support American involvement."

2022.   Pollak, Richard. "Trying to Remember Vietnam." MORE
3.3 (1973) 8-9.
The Washington Post was reluctant to print advertisements
opposing the Vietnam War and criticizing President Nixon.

2023.   "The RAND Papers." Ram 11 (Nov. 1972) 25-42, 52-62.
On the importance of the RAND Corporation to US Vietnam
policies through three administrations. Articles "Behind the
Policy Makers: RAND and the Vietnam War" by David Landau and
"Looking Backward: RAND and Vietnam in Retrospect" by Anthony
Russo. The Introduction pinpoints RAND as a major source for
the government's optimism in the intervention.

2024.   Rollins, Peter. "TV's Battle of Khe Sanh: Selective
Images of Defeat." Television Coverage of International
Affairs. Ed. William Adams. Norwood, NJ: Ablex, 1982.
203-16.
The Dien Bien Phu analogy and microcosm "drew attention to
the worst news" and "told a misleading story of Dien Bien Phu
revisited," which contributed to popular doubts about success in
the war.

2025.   Rosenau, Neal. "No Cease-Fire in Chicago Press."
        ChJR 6.5 (1973) 3-8.
The Chicago press offers "a sadly unbalanced picture of
what's happening in Vietnam and the rest of Indochina" by
depending excessively on US and South Vietnam official sources.

2026.   Rosenau, Neal. "The Secret Plan to End the War."
        ChJR 5.9 (1972) 3-5, 16-18.
Condemns the failure of the media to expose the Nixon
administration's acceleration of technological warfare in
Vietnam of immense destruction. Information about the war which
the public needs if it is to make judgements is available, but
in general the media have not sought it.

2027.   Showalter, Stuart. "Coverage of Conscientious
        Objectors to the Vietnam War: An Analysis of the
        Editorial Content of American Magazines, 1964-1972."
        PhD Diss., U of Texas at Austin, 1975. 173. DAI 36
        (1976) 6351-A.
The nation's "most widely read and respected popular
magazines took their responsibility to defend individual rights
seriously, for they usually projected positive images of
objectors."

2028.   Singer, Benjamin. "Violence, Protest and War in
        Television News: The U.S. and Canada Compared." POQ
        34.4 (1970-1971) 611-616.
"The American television news show exceeds the Canadian
program in aggression items for every one of the 21 consecutive
days monitored."

2029.   Springer, Claudia. "Military Propaganda: Defense
        Department Films from World War II and Vietnam." CulC 3
        (Spring 1986) 151-67.
A comparison of Frank Capra's Why We Fight WW II films to
films about the Vietnam War--Why Vietnam? (1965), The Unique War
(1966), Vietnamese Village Reborn (1967), etc. The films about
Vietnam replaced Hollywood dramatic techniques with
"ethnographic imagery and pseudo-scientific approach."
Underlying their supposed objectivity, however, are
"significant omissions and assumptions" that make them "more
insidious than Capra's Why We Fight."

2030.   Strouse, Jean. "The Battle Over 'Hearts and Minds.'"
        MORE 4.12 (Dec. 1974) 5-8, 19.
The highly acclaimed documentary about the Vietnam War,
"Hearts and Minds," is being withheld by its producer, Columbia
Pictures.

2031.   Suid, Lawrence. "The Film Industry and the Vietnam
        War." PhD Diss., Case Western Reserve U, 1980. 296.
        DAI 41 (1981) 3164-A.
The movies "about Vietnam that went into release beginning
in 1977 have portrayed the military and the war in negative

terms." First traces the history of military/Hollywood
cooperation up to the Vietnam War, then the history of films
about the war from The Green Berets to Apocalypse Now.

2032.   Turnbull, George, Jr. "Reporting of the War in Indo-
     China: A Critique." JQ 34.1 (1957) 87-89.
     The San Francisco Chronicle, the Palo Alto Times, and Time
magazine did not provide their readers with enough information
about the war from 1946 to 1954 "to enable them to think
adequately about it," even though by 1952 the US was
contributing "one-third the cost." The New York Times was
better.

2033.   Welch, Susan. "The American Press and Indochina,
     1950-1956." Communication in International Politics.
     Ed. R. L. Merritt. Urbana: U of Illinois P, 1972. 207-
     31.
     The press generally "reinforced the preconceptions of the
Administration" and "insured that the reading public would view
the war as a struggle between Communism and the Free World."
Whenever the press did criticize the government it focused upon
means "not the goal itself."

IV. H. Latin America 2034-2187 (See VI. C. CIA and VII.
     Global)

IV. H. 1. Central and South America 2034-2040

2034.   Arevalo, Juan J. Anti-Kommunism in Latin America:
     An X-Ray of the Process Leading to a New Colonialism.
     New York: Stuart, 1963. 244.
     In his final ch., "The Geese of the Capitol," the author
denounces Madison Avenue, "news moguls," and lesser journalists
for following the official US line in a betrayal of freedom of
the press in both North and South America.

2035.   Brown, Cynthia, ed. With Friends Like These: The
     Americas Watch Report on Human Rights and U.S. Policy in
     Latin America. New York: Pantheon, 1985. 281.
     The Reagan administration consistently distorts facts and
employs a double standard. Ch. 1, "A Rhetoric of Convenience,"
exposes the chicanery of the administration in its human rights
policy, which is routinely reported by the press as facts.

2036.   Massing, Michael. "Inside the Wires' Banana
     Republics." CJR 18.4 (1979) 45-49.
     The Spanish-language desks at both the AP and the UPI are
biased in favor of the status quo in Latin America in order to
avoid problems "with Latin American embassies and governments--
especially those of dictatorships."

2037.   "The News from Latin America: Excerpts from a Report
     to the Center for the Study of Democratic Institutions."
     CJR 1.3 (1962) 49-60.

A study of the news coverage by US wire services and The New York Times during February 1962, concentrating upon five countries: Argentina, Brazil, Chile, Mexico, and Venezuela. The AP file is "pitifully short in quantity and far from representative of events" (50). The UPI "never really entered the race" (51). The Times gave "very frequent attention to Latin America" but it was "geographically uneven and restricted in subject matter" (54).

2038.   "Science as Cultural Imperialism." Por Que? Science and Technology in Latin America. Jamaica Plain, MA: Science for the People, 1972. 19-23.
    The role of science in US cultural imperialist policy in Latin America.

2039.   Tarasov, Konstantin and Vyacheslav Zubenko. The CIA in Latin America. Moscow: Progress, 1984. 280.
    A study of the CIA as a "powerful tool of U.S. foreign policy," particularly against socialism in Latin America, which amounts to a "secret war." Two general chs. are followed by chs. on Chile, Bolivia, Cuba, El Salvador, and Nicaragua.

2040.   Wells, Alan. Picture-Tube Imperialism? The Impact of U.S. Television on Latin America. Maryknoll, NY: Orbis, 1972. 197.
    A study of the destructive effect of US government and corporations on Latin American television and thereby on the people and the economy. The author finds a deleterious effect from US consumerist (sales and entertainment) television: "Advertisements [and programming] encourage the consumption of foreign-made or imitated products; they do not encourage asceticism and personal savings habits, nor are they likely to stimulate the production and sale of indigenous mass products in the 'traditional' sector." Television does not educate or help the populations become producers. The US should encourage indigenous educational television as a corrective to US commercial television. But the author does not hold out much hope that it will.

IV. H. 2. Central America and the Caribbean 2041-2117

2041.   Barry, Tom, and Deb Preusch. The Central America Fact Book. New York: Grove. 1985. 288.
    US government and corporate dollars control events in Central America.

2042.   Bennett, James R. "Doublespeak, Disinformation, and Deceit." ORK (Fall 1986) 17-21.
    Many of the entries in this bibliography about the Reagan administration pertain to Central America.

2043.   Bennett, James R. "The 'Kissinger Report' on Central America: President Reagan Seeks Consensus." NPS 16 (1986).

A study of the process of the commission report from the
Executive order establishing the commission, the report itself,
the commissioners, the senior counsellors, and the consultants,
to Henry Kissinger's letter of transmittal. At no step in the
process was the inquiry impartial. The commission was
established to affirm US Cold War and economic doctrines toward
Central America.

2044.   Bennett, James R., and Jimmie Thomas. "Reporting Tio
          Sam's 'Free World' Dictatorships in the Caribbean Basin."
          CRPV 5 (1982) 218-239.
          "U.S. media give tremendous preference to communist terror
over terror in U.S. client states, while U.S.-sponsored terror
is systematically evaded." U.S. News and World Report, Time,
Newsweek, the Arkansas Gazette, and the Washington Post are
examined.

2045.   Berryman, Phillip. What's Wrong in Central
          America and What to Do About It. 4th ed., rev. American
          Friends Service Committee, 1984. 58.
          Media treatment of US involvement in Central America tends
to "focus on specific questions" which "fail to recognize that
the United States is orchestrating an overall military,
economic, political, and diplomatic strategy whose central
purpose is the defeat of the insurgencies in El Salvador and
Guatemala, and (if possible) the overthrow of the Nicaraguan
government" (6).

2046.   Bonpane, Blase. Guerillas of Peace: Liberation
          Theology and the Central American Revolution. Boston:
          South End, 1985. 119.
          "The people of Nicaragua, El Salvador, and Guatemala have
made it possible for us to study scripture outside of the realm
of empire, outside of a controlled press which describes both
sides in the conflict as 'two extremes'" (79). "I would like to
review how El Salvador has been covered in recent years by the
press and to identify the lies that have been perpetrated on the
people of the United States" (98)--i.e., six myths promulgated
by the US government and retailed by the press as true.

2047.   Brenner, Philip. "U.S. Crusade in Central America."
          C&C a45 (July 22, 1985) 288-292.
          An examination of the "current anticommunist crusade," a
crusade of "good vs. evil" in which rationality, reality, and
morality are rejected for demagoguery. "The Reagan
administration has propped up the campaign with a sustained
barrage of lies and distortions."

2048.   Burbach, Roger, and Patricia Flynn, eds. The
          Politics of Intervention: The United States in Central
          America. New York: Monthly Review, 1984. 255.
          Seven essays examine "a modern empire determined to defend
the status quo and the social and political forces struggling
to build a new society." The US "is committed to sustaining

governments and political systems that maintain capitalist
relations in the economic, political, and social spheres."

2049.   Burns, E. Bradford. "The Kissinger Report: Visions
          of History Through Alice's Looking Glass." LASAF 15
          (Spring 1984) 13-15.
          The Report mistreats history.

2050.   Catto, Jessica. "Publisher's Note." WJR 5.10 (1983)
          4.
          "The refusal of the United States government to allow
newsmen into Grenada as independent keepers of the record of the
military action was a stunning and unprecedented act of
censorship."

2051.   Chace, James. Endless War: How We Got Involved in
          Central America and What Can Be Done. New York:
          Vintage, 1984. 144.
          The Kissinger Report is full of "contradictions" and lacks
"careful analysis" (80-93).

2052.   Chomsky, Noam. Turning the Tide: U.S. Intervention
          in Central America and the Struggle for Peace. Boston:
          South End, 1985. 298.
          Considers "some aspects of the reality that is often
concealed or deformed by the reigning doctrinal system, which
pervades the media, journals of opinion, and much of
scholarship. An honest inquiry will reveal that striking and
systematic features of our international behavior are
suppressed, ignored or denied." Ch. 1 concerns the realities of
normal life in Central America; 2 turns to the backgrounds for
US policy; 3 places these matters in the context of US history;
4 examines US national security policy and the Cold War system
and the structure of power in the US; 5 surveys the attacks by
dominant elites on the democratic revival in the US during the
1960s, and the opportunities now "to enlarge the sphere of
freedom and justice" (Introduction). [Winner of the Gustavus
Myers Award for 1985.]

2053.   Cockburn, Alexander. "The Secret Refugees." Na
          241.8 (1985) 230.
          The US press neglects US intervention in Central America.

2054.   Cohen, Joshua, and Joel Rogers. Inequality and
          Intervention: The Federal Budget and Central America.
          Boston: South End, 1986. 66.
          The Reagan program enriches the wealthy, oppresses the
poor, and eliminates by violence if necessary any threat to this
arrangement.

2055.   Cohen, Joshua, and Joel Rogers. The Rules of the
          Game: Constraints and Opportunities for the Central
          America Movement. Boston: South End, 1986. 40.
          Analysis of the US two-party and electoral system and

possibilities of initiatives on nonintervention in Central
America.

2056.   "Contra Kissinger." Na 238.3 (1984) 66-7.
     The Kissinger Report's deliberate obfuscations of history.

2057.   "Deporting Dissent." Na 242.15 (1986) 539-40.
     The Reagan administration's interventions in Central
America "have a domestic correlative in the campaign to
criminalize dissent and repress solidarity in the growing
'antiwar movement' of the 1980s," as illustrated by the
sanctuary trial in Tucson and the attempt to deport Margaret
Randall.

2058.   Diskin, Martin, ed. Trouble in Our Backyard: Central
     America and the United States in the Eighties. New York:
     Pantheon, 1984. 264.
     In the Foreword John Womack, Jr., says that prolongation of
the present "U.S.-subsidized rightist survival" would mean
"ever-deepening American delusion, shame, and decadence, and
Central American torment as gruesome as perdition." Of the ten
articles, "Reagan and Central America: Strategy Through a
Fractured Lens" by Luis Maira is perhaps most closely related to
this compilation. He argues against "forcing the struggles of
Central American people onto an East-West axis." Gunter Grass
in "America's Backyard" compares the Polish trade-union movement
Solidarity and the Nicaraguan Sandinistas, and the US and SU.

2059.   Draper, Theodore. "Contaminated News of the
     Dominican Republic." Mass Media and Mass Man. Ed. Alan
     Casty. New York: Holt, 1968. 212-214.
     Details about the lies our ambassador to the Dominican
Republic and President Lyndon Johnson told reporters and the
American people to whitewash the US illegal invasion of that
country in 1965 in order to install its choice as head of the
government.

2060.   Dugger, Ronnie. "The State as Terrorist." TO 77.22
     (1985) 6-7.
     Reagan "would have us condemn only the tortures and murders
that are committed by the leftist states" and denies that the
invasion of Grenada or the mining of Nicaragua's harbors are
state terrorism.

2061.   Flora, Jan. "Human Rights in El Salvador and
     Nicaragua." LASAF 15 (1984) 24-27.
     The atrocities committed by the government of El Salvador
cannot be compared with the minor political violations in
Nicaragua, contrary to official US statements.

2062.   Gerdeman, Alice. "U.S. State Department and Central
     America." Breakthrough 6 (Fall 1984) 4-5.
     In presenting its policies toward Central America, the US
State Department ignores information given by protesting

organizations and citizens of the area. Its biased views
arc then given much greater access than the opposed
perspectives.

2063.   "Goodbye, Grenada." CJR 23.2 (1984) 8-9.
     Award-winning journalist Donald Foster was expelled from
Grenada by the US-sponsored government because he had been
"saying things that were not in the best interests of Grenada,"
i.e., for reasons of "national security."

2064.   Gould, Andrew. "Chief of the Contra Crusaders."
     Guard 37.45 (Sept. 18, 1985) 7.
     Retired Gen. John Singlaub, a leading rightist (on the
board of Soldier of Fortune magazine, founder of the Institute
for Regional and International Studies to train Contras and
Salvadoran police) has received assistance from the Pentagon for
his anticommunist programs in Central America.

2065.   "The Government Runs the Death Squads Behind an Anti-
     Communist Smokescreen But Wealth & Power is the Name of
     the Game." Guatemala: The Terrible Repression and Its
     Roots in the U.S. National Security State, spec. no. GR
     37 (1981) 13-15.
     "'Communists' are defined by the wealthy as anyone who
rebels, protests, or organizes against one of the most unjust,
repressive social structures in the world."

2066.   Grenada: Background and Analyses. Oakland, CA: Data
     Center, 1983. 150.
     A collection of articles from magazines and newspapers
gathered from sources "over the past five years" to provide
background information for understanding the US invasion of the
nation of Grenada. The collection was prepared two days after
the launching of the invasion.

2067.   Guatemala! Spec. no. of Green Revolution 37 (Winter
     1981). 71.
     One article indicts the US press for failing to report the
terrible massacres of the people by the army and death squads,
while another calls upon the transnational news-services to
report the slaughters and blames UPI and AP for underreporting
them.

2068.   Guatemala! The Horror and the Hope. Ed.
     Rarihokwats. York, PA: Four Arrows, 1982. 288.
     Pt. 3 deals with attacks on media, legal profession,
and church, the rightist network, US government and media
support of the repression, etc. Pages 201-205 focus upon
US media collusion with the US government in the repression and
violence: "The Willing Collaboration of the Media in
Brainwashing Under Freedom," "Slanting the News: The Semantics
of Terror," and "Understanding How We Are Made Confused: A
Guide to Media." The interest of the US government and US
corporations in Guatemalan oil and the rabid Sovietphobia of the

US are exposed as partial motives for US support of Guatemalan
state terrorism.

2069.   Guatemala Revised: How the Reagan Administration
         Finds "Improvements" in Human Rights in Guatemala. New
         York: Americas Watch, 1985. 20.

2070.   Halloran, Richard. "How the Pentagon and the Press
         Can Call a Truce." WJR 6.1 (1984) 22-23.
     The Grenada experience need not be repeated if agreements
between the Pentagon and individual news organizations are made
in advance providing for military security and the public's
right to know.

2071.   Hans, Dennis. "This Week With David Brinkley: ABC-
         TV." C&C (Feb. 20, 1984) 45-6.
     Brinkley's program on Central America and the Kissinger
Report was extremely prejudiced in favor of US official policies
and the Report.

2072.   Herman, Edward. "Diversity of News: 'Marginalizing'
         the Opposition." JoC 35.3 (1985) 135-46.
     Analysis of coverage of the strife in Cambodia and
East Timor and the elections in El Salvador and Nicaragua
reveals "selective use of criteria and attention in line with
national political agendas." Criticized by William Adams with
reply by Herman, JoC 36.1 (1986) 189-92.

2073.   Herman, Edward. "The New York Times on the 1984
         Salvadoran and Nicaraguan Elections." CAIB 21 (Spring
         1984) 7-13.
     The favorable media treatment of the Salvadoran election
and the unfavorable treatment of the Nicaraguan by The New York
Times.

2074.   Hoffman, Mike. "Kissinger Strikes Again." LS 8
         (1984) 10-12.
     The purpose of the Kissinger Commission Report is to gain
support for Pentagon intervention abroad.

2075.   Hollyday, Joyce, ed. Crucible of Hope. Washington,
         DC: Sojourners, 1984. 146.
     Includes appraisals of US propaganda and misinformation
about Central American countries.

2076.   Immerman, Richard. The CIA in Guatemala: The Foreign
         Policy of Intervention. Austin: U of Texas P, 1982.
         291.
     The ignorance of US leaders regarding Guatemala and
Guatemalans and their baseless fear of SU operations in that
country led to the disastrous policy of intervention, covert
operations, and finally to the overthrow of the legal government
of Jacobo Arbenz Guzman.

2077.   In Contempt of Congress: The Reagan Record of Deceit
          and Illegality on Central America.   Washington, DC:
          Institute for Policy Studies, 1985.   60.
     "Reagan Administration officials have misled Congress about
the nature of its activities and goals in Central America.   The
disturbingly systematic record of such deceit has prompted this
report."

2078.   "Invasion: A Guide to the U.S. Military Presence in
          Central America." Philadelphia: American Friends
          Service Committee, 1986.   24.
     Documents "the vast web of roads, bases, airstrips,
communication links, and training exercises that have made
Central America an extension of the US military network" and
that have been little reported by the media.

2079.   "Is Our Government Telling Us the Truth About the
          Military Operation in Grenada?" New York: Fund for
          Open Information and Accountability, n.d.   4.
     Accuses the US of lying about an imminent takeover of
Grenada by the Soviets and Cubans and about the number of Cuban
military in Grenada.

2080.   Jetter, Alexis. "Screen Test for the Left." MJ 10
          (Aug./Sept. 1985) 10-11.
     Filmic opposition to US foreign policy is "small-fry
compared with right-wing videotanks" like the American Security
Council Foundation (Only the Strong, The SALT Syndrome, Attack
on the Americas).   But the film Faces of War by the one-room
Central America Television Organization Project/Neighbor to
Neighbor is an important criticism of US policy in Central
America.

2081.   Jonas, Susanne, and David Tobis, eds. Guatemala.   New
          York: NACLA, 1974.   264.
     "The Best Lobby in Washington" describes the Guatemalan
"interventionist" organization representing diverse ideological
and economic groups.

2082.   Kelly, John. "Launching the U.S.S. Honduras." NaR
          9.1 (1985) 36-39.
     "A secret General Accounting Office (GAO) report lays bare
the Pentagon's massive preparations for war in Central America.
The report details the escalation in U.S. military policy
and build-up in the region under the guise of conducting
exercises and maneuvers in the region."

2083.   Kenworthy, Eldon. "Grenada as Theater." WPJ 1
          (Spring 1984) 635-51.
     Critical analysis of official US justifications for
invading Grenada, October 25, 1983, which were widely retailed
by the press.

2084.   Kilian, Michael. "In Memory of a Glorious Victory in

Battle of Grenada." AG (Oct. 26, 1984) 19A.
"The White House is asking us all to join in National Joy on
the occasion of the first anniversary of the Glorious Victory
over the Communist Fiends of Grenada."

2085.   Kinzer, Stephen, and Stephen Schlesinger. Bitter
         Fruit: The Untold Story of the American Coup in
         Guatemala. Garden City, NY: Doubleday, 1982. 320.
How the CIA at the request of the United Fruit Company
overthrew the legal government of Guatemala, using all the
methods of covert action, secrecy, and disinformation within the
power of the CIA. The influence of United Fruit's propaganda in
the US, including the media, preceding the overthrow of Arbenz
is also revealed.

2086.   Klare, Michael T. "Grenada Syndrome." Na 237.15
         (1983) 453-54.
The Reagan administration's "clear and consistent military
doctrine" of worldwide intervention to counter alleged Soviet-
inspired insurgency is illustrated by the invasion of Grenada.

2087.   "KLRT-TV Will Show Film Opposing U.S. Policies in
         Central America." AG (March 8, 1986) 3A.
Only one of four TV stations in Little Rock will show the
film Faces of War sponsored by Neighbor to Neighbor, a private
organization. The film criticizes Reagan administration
policies in Central America and interviews US citizens living
there who condemn US actions in the region.

2088.   Krehm, William. Democracies and Tyrannies of the
         Caribbean. Westport, CT: Hill, 1984. 352.
Krehm was a correspondent for Time magazine in the 1940s in
the Caribbean and Central America. "Very little of what he
wrote ever appeared in Time, due to the unwillingness of the
magazine's editors at the time to offend the large corporations
which had investments in the region, but Krehm's research
eventually became a book that vividly describes the tyrannical
and corrupt forces that controlled most of the Central American
countries, with American support. At the time, no US publisher
was willing to issue such a controversial book, but it was
translated into Spanish and widely distributed throughout
Central and South America. Now it is being published for the
first time in English" (from the publisher's advertisement).

2089.   Kwitny, Jonathan. "Oh, What a Lovely War!" MJ 9.5
         (1984) 27-33, 46.
As the invasion of Grenada demonstrates yet again, the
first casualty of war is the truth.

2090.   LaFeber, Walter. "Covering the Canal or, How the
         Press Missed the Boat." MORE 8.6 (1978) 26-31.
The media "neither shaped nor fully informed public
opinion" regarding the Panama Canal treaties because they did
not explain "why the Panamanians had pushed for years to obtain

these treaties--and with them their de jure independence from
U.S. colonial control."

2091.   LaFeber, Walter. Inevitable Revolutions: The U.S.
          in Central America. New York: Norton, 1984. 377.
     A history of Central America seldom seen in the media and
little known among the American people: How US military and
commercial interests combined to create a system of dependency
in Central America for American investments and markets, a
system that spawned enormous concentrations of land in a few
oligarchic families and the military force to maintain that
concentration. [Winner of the Gustavus Myers Award for 1984.]

2092.   LaFeber, Walter. "Lest We Forget the Bay of Pigs."
          Na 242.15 (1986) 537, 549-50.
     A reminder of the disastrous consequences of secrecy and
other factors which brought about the failed invasion of Cuba in
1961.

2093.   Lagnado, Lucette. "Anti-Castro PAC in Washington."
          Na 237.11 (1983) 332-33.
     The National Coalition for a Free Cuba is lobbying Congress
and giving campaign contributions. One of their causes has been
Radio Marti.

2094.   LeoGrande, William. "Through the Looking Glass: The
          Kissinger Report on Central America." WPJ (Winter 1984)
          252-84.
     Why the Report, widely reported by the press, over-
simplifies the situation in the area to suit US aims.

2095.   Matthews, Herbert L. A World in Revolution: A
          Newspaperman's Memoir. New York: Scribner's, 1971.
          462.
     The author praises the intention of The New York Times to
publish all the news, yet he does not "believe it lived up to
those slogans in the case of Cuba."

2096.   McAnany, Emile. "Television and Crisis: Ten Years of
          Network News Coverage of Central America, 1972-1981."
          MCS 5 (1983) 199-212.
     "The focus is almost entirely on the day to day military
actions or on the official positions as defined by the
governments involved through their spokesmen and news sources
and little is heard from dissidents, guerilas or nonofficial
groups (such as the Catholic Church)." The "wars and
especially the US foreign policy position regarding the origin
and solution of the civil wars seem to take the spotlight,
keeping the public focused on official positions and
explanations rather than on important historic shifts in social
and political relationships in the region."

2097.   Nation, Fitzroy. "Banned from Barbados." CJR 22.5
          (1984) 7-8.

Caribbean Contact editor Rickey Singh was ordered to leave Barbados after denouncing the Grenada invasion.

2098.   Nelson-Pallmeyer, Jack.   The Politics of Compassion: A Biblical Perspective on Hunger, the Arms Race, and U.S. Policy in Central America. Maryknoll, NY: Orbis, 1986. 128.
The author examines three interconnected social problems: mass hunger, US supported aggression in Central America, and the threat of nuclear holocaust.

2099.   Norton, Chris. "Political Killings Rise as Economy Worsens." ITT 9(Aug. 7-20, 1985) 11.
The Reagan administration and the government of Guatemala have claimed improvement in human rights enough to justify increased US aid, but the violence and terror continue.

2100.   Oakes, John. "The Human Dimensions of Government Policy." TO 77 (July 12, 1985) 13-14.
"American newspapers have not provided the Central America feature articles--the human interest story that gets to the basics."

2101.   O'Shaughnessy, Hugh.   Grenada: An Eyewitness Account of the U.S. Invasion and the Caribbean History That Provoked It. New York: Dodd, 1984. 261.
Ch. 7, "The First Casualty of War": "In the war of words that the US and Grenadian governments waged on each other the first casualty was the truth." "The absence of the media from the invasion gave the US government full opportunity to manage the news to its own best advantage. It allowed it to distort in specific areas"--that the bulk of the resistance was Cuban, that the US forces were smaller than in fact they were, that the invasion was necessitated to save US medical students, etc.

2102.   "Other Voices--On Grenada." CJR 22.5 (1984) 20-21.
Journalists give their views on the news blackout in Grenada.

2103.   Payne, Anthony, et al. Grenada: Revolution and Invasion. New York: St. Martin's, 1984. 233.
Ch. 7, "The US Invasion," contains details of US disinformation to justify the invasion. "Reagan's reasoning was disingenuous in the extreme," etc.

2104.   Persky, Stan. America, the Last Domino: U.S. Foreign Policy in Central America Under Reagan. Vancouver: New Star, 1984. 284.
The lack of logic and evidence which the Reagan administration uses to justify "the ferocity" of its "domino theory" rhetoric.

2105.   Preston, William, Jr. "The Devil and Ronald Reagan: A History of Repression from Salem to Grenada." ORK

(Winter 1984) 1-4.
"Ronald Reagan and the Grenada invasion must be evaluated, therefore, not as weird aberrations in an otherwise open and rational democratic system, but as the full flowering of the Salem mentality in modern America."

2106.   Pruessen, Ronald W. "Revisionism 2." RHR 33 (1985) 155-164.
A review of five books that locate the rise of the Cold War partly or mainly in the aggressive US search for economic and political advantages: Cook, The Declassified Eisenhower; Kaufman, Eisenhower's Foreign Economic Policy; Immerman, The CIA in Guatemala; Schlesinger and Kinzer, The Untold Story of the American Coup in Guatemala; Wittner, American Intervention in Greece.

2107.   Ruether, Rosemary. "Christians and Cubans: A Renewal of Faith." C&C 45.13 (1985) 329-333.
The recent US embargo, which makes it difficult to visit Cuba, "has as one of its primary effects disinforming the U.S. public about Cuba."

2108.   Sanders, Jerry. "Terminators." MJ 10 (Aug./Sept. 1985) 36-40.
A tour of Washington right-wing think-tanks which promulgate and propel current US foreign policy against wars of national liberation: the Council for Inter-American Security, the Committee on the Present Danger, the Center for Strategic and International Studies, the American Security Council, the Heritage Foundation, and others.

2109.   Schaap, William. "Combat Coverage." ORK (Fall/ Winter 1984-85) 11-12.
On the Reagan administration's desire to limit reporting of military activities, as illustrated by the invasion of Grenada. The Pentagon's Sidle Panel established to examine the Grenada media ban basically expressed the belief that reporters should trust the military and not be adversarial.

2110.   Searle, Chris. Grenada: The Struggle Against Destabilization. London: Writers and Readers Publ. Coop. Soc., 1983. 164.
The book has "two main objectives": "The first is to seek to itemise, categorise and describe the various approaches and strategies of destabilization used primarily by the U.S. government agencies against Grenada." The other is to describe how the country is defending itself from the onslaught. "Propaganda Destabilization" (60-68) describes the "campaign of lies and slander" by the "imperialist press" and its "caribbean regional press." [The US invaded Grenada in October 1983 and overthrew its government.]

2111.   Shear, Marie. "Double-Standard Reporting: Nicaragua and the Networks." CJR 13.5 (1985) 17-18.

The networks gave the impression that the election in El Salvador was more pluralistic and democratic than the one in Nicaragua, when the truth is the opposite.

2112.   Survey of Press Freedom in Latin America 1983/1984. The Council on Hemispheric Affairs and the Newspaper Guild, June 1984. 42.
Includes revelations of US censorship of the press during the invasion of Grenada and expulsion of a Canadian correspondent for a Cuban news agency.

2113.   Szulc, Tad. Dominican Diary. NY: Dell, 1966. 319.
Includes a close look at governmental deception during the US intervention in the Dominican Republic in 1965. The American people were given a snow job by their government via deliberate, systematic lying.

2114.   Vinas, Angel. "History's Role in the Kissinger Report." CSM 76 (March 19, 1984) 16.
Report not scholarly research but a policy-oriented undertaking. US direct interventions in Central America are "conveniently explained away."

2115.   Wattenmaker, Steve. "Central America: Report Paves Way for Wider U.S. War." IP 22 (Feb. 6, 1984) 36-8.
Kissinger Commission purveys lie about "Cuban-Soviet threat."

2116.   Welch, Richard, Jr. Response to Revolution: The United States and the Cuban Revolution, 1959-1961. Chapel Hill, NC: U of North Carolina P, 1985. 244.
US response to Cuba was a mirror of our Cold War assumptions and frustrations and of our apprehensions about revolutionary movements abroad. Four sections: Castro's revolution, responses of the Eisenhower and Kennedy administrations, US public opinion, and the larger context of the Cold War.

2117.   White, Richard A. The Morass: United States Intervention in Central America. New York: Harper, 1984. 319.
"Because of the strong political constraints imposed upon U.S.-sponsored counterinsurgency operations, it is imperative to confer international legitimacy upon client governments, while at the same time discrediting the insurgent forces. This is necessary to gain the support of, or at least to neutralize the criticism from, the international community as well as the U.S. public, news media, and Congress" (35-6).

IV. H. 2. a. Nicaragua 2118-2161

2118.   "Abusing Human Rights Abuse." Har 271.1626 (1985) 21-24.
From a report issued by Americas Watch, Human Rights in

Nicaragua, "the administration disregards the norms of impartial reporting on human rights when it deals with Nicaragua."

2119.   Bennett, James R., and Jimmie Thomas. "Nicaragua in Our Back Yard and on Our Doorstep: Madison, the First Amendment, and a Free Press." FS 55 (December 1982) 6-15.
The reporting of Nicaragua "demonstrates the preponderant presence of the Administration's ideology and opinion in the news." A study of U.S. News and World Report, Time, Newsweek, the St. Louis Post-Dispatch, the Arkansas Gazette, and The New York Times.

2120.   Bermann, Karl. Under the Big Stick: Nicaragua and the U.S. Since 1848. Boston: South End, 1986. 300.
In the final chs., Bermann attacks the myth of a friendly Carter administration support for the Sandinistas and analyzes the propaganda of the Reagan administration toward the Nicaraguan government. After examining the dominant perceptions of the US stake in Nicaragua, the author offers a reinterpretation of the US "national interest" in the region.

2121.   Berryman, Phillip. "Central America: A Commitment to Intervention." C&C 45.8(1985) 171-172.
"No one in the political and journalistic mainstream can really find anything positive to say about the Sandinista revolution."

2122.   Berryman, Phillip. "Illusions of Villainy: The U.S. Government's Propaganda Campaign Against Nicaragua." Crucible of Hope. Ed. Joyce Hollyday. Washington, DC: Sojourners, 1984. 33-7.
"In order to win public opinion to its policies, the Reagan administration has sought to give a heroes-and-villains account of what is happening in Central America."

2123.   Bitter Witness: Nicaraguans and the "Covert" War, A Chronology and Several Narratives. Santa Cruz, CA: Witness for Peace Documentation Project, 1984. 172.
A selection of acts of war carried out by US-sponsored Nicaraguan counterrevolutionary groups against Nicaraguan communities and individuals since January 1981. The purpose is "to provide the most accurate information" available about the human costs of the undeclared war, "as a contribution to an informed public discussion of U.S. foreign policy in Central America" (4).

2124.   Brody, Reed. Contra Terror in Nicaragua: Report of a Fact-Finding Mission, September 1984-January 1985. Boston: South End, 1985. 206.
In complete reversal of the truth, Ronald Reagan has accused the Sandinistas of creating a totalitarian state and has praised the Contras as "freedom fighters" and the "moral equals of our Founding Fathers." "In short, no epithet, however lurid

or fantastic, has been spared in an effort to convince the
American public to support the campaign against Nicaragua" (from
the Introduction).

2125.   Brumberg, Abraham.   "'Sham' and 'Farce' in Nicaragua?"
          Dis 32 (1985) 226-236.
     Ronald Reagan dismissed the Nov. 4, 1984 election in
Nicaragua as sham and farce, but "parties opposed to the FSLN
(on both the right and the left) obtained 35 out of the 96 seats
in the National Assembly" because the FSLN "pulled only
67 percent of the total vote." The statements by the Reagan
administration regarding Nicaragua "recall some Soviet modi
operandi." The US press poorly reported the election.

2126.   Burns, E. Bradford. "Guest Commentary." NicP 11
          (Fall 1985) 3-4.
     "Most of the world recognizes the current struggle in
Nicaragua for what it is: A once privileged minority is trying
to reimpose its domination over the long-suffering majority."
The "avalanche" of US newspaper coverage "hostile to the
Sandinistas" cannot hide the opposition's "lack of any political
program for the future to develop Nicaragua."

2127.   Cabestrero, Teofilo. Blood of the Innocent: Victims
          of the Contras' War in Nicaragua. Maryknoll, NY: Orbis,
          1985. 112.
     Interviews in February 1985 of some 60 civilians in
northern Nicaragua who were victims of Contra kidnappings,
ambushes, rapes, and other kinds of brutality. These atrocities
are held up to President Reagan's praise of the Contras as
"freedom fighters."

2128.   "A Case of Deliberate Deception." CAA 2.7 (1984) 1.
     Reagan administration claims that Nicaragua is a threat to
its neighbors are examples of psychological warfare and perception
management--creating negative images, disseminating false and
misleading data, etc. The US government is using the Big Lie
against Nicaragua.

2129.   Chamorro, Edgar, with Jefferson Morley. "Confessions
          of a 'Contra.'" NR 193.6 (1985) 18-23.
     Edgar Chamorro served as a director of the anti-Sandinista
organization, the Nicaraguan Democratic Force, from 1982 to
1984. He tells how the CIA masterminds the Nicaraguan
insurgency.

2130.   Cockburn, Alexander. "The Captive Press." Na 240.11
          (1985) 328-9.
     President of Nicaragua Daniel Ortega's recent peace
proposals presented to a delegation of US Catholic bishops was
either ignored or distorted by the media.

2131.   Coffin, Tristram. "The Emperor's Tattered Clothes."
          WS 12.9 (1986) 1-3.

351

Organized public resistance is growing, including a statement by more than 100 religious leaders denouncing Reagan's "exaggeration, misinformation and outright falsehoods" about Nicaragua.

2132.   "Debating Rules." NR 194.14 (1986) 4.
The charge by the Reagan administration that "opponents of aid to the contras are 'objectively' serving the interests of the Sandinistas, whatever their professed or actual motives, strikes me as an authentic McCarthyite smear."

2133.   Dickey, Christopher. With the Contras: A Reporter
    in the Wilds of Nicaragua. New York: Simon, 1986. 327.
A study of how officers and soldiers of Somoza's National Guard formed the Nicaraguan Democratic Force (FDN), who trained them, the repeated efforts of the CIA to repackage their discredited leadership, etc.

2134.   Freedom of Expression in Nicaragua. New York:
    National Lawyers Guild, 1986. 52.
Denies President Reagan's claims that Nicaragua is a totalitarian country. A Guild delegation found to the contrary that "the draconian picture painted by the extremist opposition and the Reagan Administration is largely exaggerated for political reasons." The restrictions which do exist result from the US sponsored invasion of the country. The US itself has always imposed constraints on reporting and opinion in time of war, including recently our invasion of Grenada and the bombing of Libya.

2135.   Griffin-Nolan, Edward. "The Web of Deceit and
    Brutality." Soj 15.5 (1986) 44-5.
Review of Christopher Dickey's With the Contras: A Reporter in the Wilds of Nicaragua (1986). "Dickey tells the tale of the web of deceit, treachery, brutality, and betrayal that gave birth to the sorry but vicious forces which Nicaraguans refer to simply as the contras" and Ronald Reagan refers to as "freedom fighters."

2136.   Gunn, Herb. "Contra Blast Kills Thirty-Two, Kinzered
    by the Press." Voice 7.5 (1986) 2.
An account of media neglect of the killing of thirty-two civilian Nicaraguans by the US organized and supported contras. "Kinzered" is coined from the name of New York Times correspondent Stephen Kinzer, who buried and mangled the story and diverted the reader from the essential issues.

2137.   Hellinger, Dan. "Interviewing Western Reporters in
    Nicaragua." SLJR 11.65 (1984) 19-22.
The inadequacy and bias of US media coverage of Nicaragua.

2138.   Hitchens, Christopher. "Minority Report." Na 242.15
    (1986) 542.
Contrary to administration and right-wing claims that

opposition to the Sandinistas arose from their excesses and
betrayal of their revolution, the historical record shows that
Reagan was sympathetic to Somoza and hostile to the Sandinistas
prior to overthrowing the dictator.

2139.   Holland, Max. "Nicaragua: A Despot Falls, the Press
          Stumbles." CJR 18.3 (1979) 46-7.
"How well does the American press report a popular
revolution that challenges United States policy? In Iran,
badly. In Nicaragua, better--although still too much the way
the falling leader and the State Department see it."

2140.   Kemper, Vicki. "'Stop the Lies, Stop the Killing.'"
          Soj 15.5 (1986) 8-10.
An account of the March 4 protest in Washington, DC by
religious leaders against the "14 specific administration. . .
'myths' and lies" about Nicaragua.

2141.   Lappe, Frances, and Joseph Collins. Now We Can Speak:
          A Journey Through the New Nicaragua. San Francisco:
          Institute for Food and Development Policy, 1983. 120.
First hand experiences "reveal why Nicaragua's revolution
defies stereotypes and shatters the myths created in
Washington."

2142.   Millman, Joel. "The Managua Twist." CJR 23.2 (1984)
          9-10.
A segment of ABC World News Tonight by Peter Collins
falsely reported that Nicaragua's annual Good Friday procession
in the capital was a demonstration against the government.

2143.   Millman, Joel. "Narco-Terrorism: A Tale of Two
          Stories." CJR 25.3 (1986) 48-51.
The government's unsubstantiated charges that Nicaragua has
been involved in smuggling cocaine was eagerly reported, but the
substantiated evidence of contra drug trafficking was
"lackadaisical."

2144.   Millman, Joel. "Whodunit: The Pastora Bombing." CJR
          24.6 (1986) 20.
Two free-lancers investigated the attempt to kill Contra
leader Eden Pastora in his jungle headquarters near the Costa
Rican border in 1984. They describe "a sophisticated
disinformation campaign" by Washington "to shift the blame onto
Basque terrorists allegedly in the hire of the Sandinista
government."

2145.   Morales, Waltraud. "Revolutions, Earthquakes and
          Latin America: The Networks Look at Allende's Chile
          and Somoza's Nicaragua." Television Coverage of
          International Affairs. Ed. William Adams. Norwood, NJ:
          Ablex, 1982. 79-116.
When they are reported, they are treated via stereotypes,
ethnocentrism, and crisis. "Half of the Latin American

countries have been ignored almost entirely" by ABC, CBS, and NBC. Some countries, "such as Chile under Allende and Cuba under Castro, were consistently reported from the single perspective of US national security" (79), but treatment of the Sandinista revolution against Somoza was "highly sympathetic to the rebels" (102).

2146. Morley, Morris, and James Petras. The Reagan Administration and Nicaragua: How Washington Constructs Its Case For Counterrevolution in Central America. New York: Institute for Media Analysis, 1986. 120.
"State Department White Papers on Nicaragua" are used "to paint what the authors describe as a totally distorted picture of the realities in Central America and U.S. policy towards the region" (from publisher's description).

2147. Mutnick, Deborah. "Congress Blusters, Gets Set To Cave In." Guard 38.25 (1986) 5.
Another instance of the Republican-Democrat-anti-Soviet, anticommunist crusade in their hostility to Nicaragua.

2148. Nicaragua: What They Say--What We Saw. Tuscon, AZ: Action for Peace in Nicaragua (Tucson), ca. 1983. 30.
A report of a visit to Nicaragua by a group of citizens from Tucson contradicting official US perceptions and statements from that country which enjoy such great access to the media.

2149. Norsworthy, Kent, and William Robinson. David and Goliath: The U.S. War Against Nicaragua. New York: Monthly Review, 1987. 320.
Includes analysis of US low intensity war doctrine as a reaction to the defeat in Vietnam and as applied to Nicaragua.

2150. Peinado, Jaime. "Discrediting Nicaragua: U.S. Takes Aim at Religion." NicP 5 (Winter 1983) 20-22, 32.
Assistant Secretary of State for Human Rights Elliot Abrams falsely accused Nicaragua of repression of religion in regard to some incidents in the summer.

2151. "Reagan's Old Devil Won't Wash." ITT 10.17 (1986) 14.
Behind Reagan's lies against Nicaragua was "the idea of the Evil Empire."

2152. Reding, Andrew. "Under Construction: Nicaragua's New Polity." C&C 45 (July 22, 1985) 269-77.
"Whatever the underlying reasons for the frequent failures of foreign coverage, the fact is that an assignment to cover the Nicaraguan legislature currently has low priority or none at all. In contrast, "an event like Daniel Ortega's mission to Moscow qualifies as instant prime-time and front-page news: it confirms the prevailing consensus (shared by Democrats as well as Republicans) and justifies the policy that flows from it" (277).

354

2153.   "Resource: Contra Film." NaR 9 (Winter 1986) 9.
    The Contras: Serving Our Interests? a video documentary
reveals "that the contras are not the 'freedom fighters' of
President Reagan, but rather are confirmed right-wing
terrorists."

2154.   Rosset, Peter, and John Vandermeer, eds. The
    Nicaragua Reader: Documents of a Revolution Under Fire.
    New York: Grove, 1983. 359.
    Part 3 covers "US Intervention," Ch. 1 "America's Secret
War." The final ch. is entitled "The US War for Tyranny in
Central America: Reaganism Unchallenged": the US "can organize
the overthrow of a popular revolutionary government and the
destruction of a third world economy without a murmur of protest
from congress or the media" (359).

2155.   Sharkey, Jacqueline. "Disturbing the Peace." CC 11.5
    (1985) 20-22, 24-34.
    An analysis of the anti-Sandinista "Contras." The author
questions this "new way for our government to use private
citizens as surrogates in a military conflict in total disregard
of Congress' constitutional responsibilities to declare war."

2156.   Siegel, Daniel, et al. Outcast Among Allies: The
    International Costs of Reagan's War Against Nicaragua.
    Washington, DC: Institute for Policy Studies, 1985. 21.
    "Ronald Reagan argues that his policy of aggression against
Nicaragua is necessary to maintain America's strategic alliances
and enhance U.S. credibility abroad," but he is "perceived
throughout the world as an international outlaw," "despite
enormous diplomatic and propaganda efforts to convince them
otherwise."

2157.   Sklar, Holly. "Reading Nicaragua." Na 241.6 (1985)
    185-189.
    Rev. of about three dozen books which refute Reagan
administration allegations that Nicaragua is a communist
totalitarian state and which reveal the atrocities of the US
Contra mercenaries.

2158.   Smith, Norma. "Mystery MiGs Fly into the U.S. Press."
    NicP 10 (Spring-Summer 1985) 18-20.
    President Reagan on prime time TV accused the Soviet Union
of sending a cargo of MiGs to Nicaragua and threatened a
preemptive air strike against the ship. When the falsehood was
made absolutely clear to the world, the Reagan administration
shifted to accusations that Nicaragua was amassing an arsenal
to invade other Central American countries, also a fabrication.

2159.   "U.S. Media Distort Relocation Story." NicP 11
    (Fall 1985) 16-17.
    Independent video producers Mary Churchill and Peter White
went to Nicaragua in March 1985 to do stories for a San
Francisco TV station. Their observations were the opposite of

those by CBS, ABC, the Washington Post, and the Voice of
America. CBS refused to buy footage of what Churchill and White
saw, preferring anti-Sandinista footage. And "ABC really went
out of their way to get a negative story."

2160.   Wallis, Jim. "Lives at Stake." Soj 15.6 (1986) 4.
     What "the great East-West confrontation," "our great
crusade against communism," comes down to is young men killing
each other in Nicaragua. But more than 200 US religious leaders
"told the truth about Nicaragua"--that "the Reagan
administration is simply lying."

2161.   Workman, John. "'Thou Art the Administration.'" AG
         (March 15, 1986) 15A.
     An account of a demonstration in Washington by religious
leaders denouncing Ronald Reagan's misinformation and lies about
Nicaragua. Among the statement's 200 signers were 22 Catholic
and Protestant bishops.

IV. H. 2. b. El Salvador 2162-2179

2162.   "Air War Targets Salvadoran Civilians: U.S. Media
         Keep Silent." NicP 11 (Fall 1985) 34-35.
     Even though Napoleon Duarte is a rightist, "the U.S. press
continues to portray" him "as a moderate."

2163.   Anderson, Jon. "The Other War in El Salvador." CJR
         25.2 (1986) 8-10.
     The obstacles and dangers the El Salvadoran army places in
the path of journalists trying to cover the civil war there.

2164.   Bennett, James R. "Reporting the El Salvador Civil
         War." FSN 8 (December 1981) 11-15.
     A study of the Washington Post, The New York Times, the
Tulsa World, the Arkansas Gazette, and the Christian Science
Monitor, Time, Newsweek, and U.S. News and World Report, during
January and February, 1981. All gave one-sided access to the
US/El Salvadoran government's perspectives.

2165.   Bonner, Raymond. Weakness and Deceit: U.S. Policy
         and El Salvador. New York: Times, 1984. 408.
     "It wasn't just the military that had tightened its grip on
the tiny country during the Reagan administration, but the most
conservative elements, officers with 'fascist' ideology," in
contrast to Reagan's public assertions of support for human
rights and democracy there.

2166.   Brodhead, Frank, and Edward Herman. Demonstration
         Elections: U.S.-Staged Elections in the Dominican
         Republic, Vietnam and El Salvador. Boston: South End,
         1984. 270.
     The book focuses on the use of fraudulent "free" elections
in US client dictatorships as tools of US foreign policy.
Ch. 5, "The Role of the Mass Media in a Demonstration Election,"

reveals for example, how "Giving dominant place to U.S. and Salvadoran government press releases, and addressing questions only to officials of these governments, allow the agenda to be set by the holocaust managers" (154).

2167.   Brown, Cynthia. "Friendly Fire in San Salvador." <u>CJR</u>
         21.3 (1982) 9.
US embassy and military hostility to correspondents John Dinges and Ray Bonner for their revelations of US military activities in El Salvador.

2168.   Brown, Cynthia. "How UPI Spells Relief." <u>CJR</u> 20.3
         (1981) 6-7, 9.
The UPI reported stories falsely claiming that humanitarian agencies (OXFAM, Catholic Relief, World Council of Churches) were funneling weapons to El Salvadoran guerillas. The fabrications were probably another manifestation of the US disinformation campaign against the rebels, like the State Department's White Paper, "Communist Interference in El Salvador."

2169.   Ege, Konrad. "El Salvador White Paper?" <u>CS</u> 5.3
         (1981) 3-9.
The media uncritically accepted the Reagan administration's dubious White Paper entitled "Communist Interference in El Salvador."

2170.   "El Salvador White Paper (Cont.)." <u>CS</u> 5.4 (1981)
         11-12.
On the failure of the State Department to answer the evaluations of its report "Communist Interference in El Salvador" by the <u>Wall Street Journal</u> and the <u>Washington Post</u>.

2171.   Gettleman, Marvin E., et al., eds. <u>El Salvador:</u>
         <u>Central America in the New Cold War</u>. New York: Grove,
         1981. 397.
Part one is entitled "Seeing Red: the Reagan Administration Looks at the World," dealing with Reagan's revival of "the old fundamentalist mood and language." Ch. 2 of Part Four examines the "flimsy assumptions and fabricated data" of the White Paper on El Salvador (230). Part Five, "The 'Dominoes' of Central America" exposes the "political misconceptions that find expression in irrelevant metaphors" (298).

2172.   Gusmao, Ivna, and Alan Benjamin. <u>"The New York Times'</u>
         Coverage of El Salvador." New York: El Salvador
         Information Office, 1981.
Compares the <u>Times</u>' coverage to that of France's <u>Le Monde</u>, Mexico's <u>Excelsior</u> and <u>Uno Mas Uno</u>, Britain's <u>Latin America</u> <u>Weekly Report</u>, and "many documents published by church, human rights and United Nations organizations." The authors conclude that the <u>Times</u> "subscribed to the official U.S. policy in El Salvador" (the government was centrist, the opposition extremist) and that "many important events were often not

reported while many others were misrepresented, leaving the
readership misinformed, with a one-sided view of the situation
in that country and a misleading impression of the U.S. role in
El Salvador."

2173.   Loeb, Paul. "The Vietnamization of Language." <u>SLMN</u>
         (June 5, 1985) 1C.
         Navy Lt. Cmdr. Albert Schaufelberger, deputy head of US
military advisers in El Salvador, was killed by Salvadoran
guerrillas May 25. His death was called "a shocking, cowardly
murder" by US Ambassador Deane Hinton, and this judgment was
"echoed throughout the news media." But Schaufelberger was on
an American military mission in support of one side in a civil
war. Underlying the Ambassador's distortion of language is the
wholesale erosion of language which occurred during the Vietnam
war.

2174.   Maslow, Jonathan Evan, and Ana Arana. "Operation El
         Salvador." <u>CJR</u> 20.1 (1981) 52-58.
         "The administration dusted off the domino theory. The
pushover press fell into Line." "The goal of the publicity
blitz carried out by the military-intelligence bureaucracy was
to prove that El Salvador represented 'a textbook case of
indirect armed aggression by Communist powers' through Cuba....
Luckily for the administration, if not for the public,
the press that it engaged was functionally illiterate on
Central America."

2175.   Massing, Michael. "About-Face on El Salvador." <u>CJR</u>
         22.4 (1983) 42-49.
         "The about-face in the coverage out of El Salvador in
recent months has been little short of remarkable. In a word,
the news media have gone soft." Several causes are involved
(reporters threatened with death, etc.) but nothing "has had
quite the same impact as the expert news management by the
Reagan administration."

2176.   Nairn, Allan. "Confessions of a Death Squad Officer."
         <u>Prog</u> 50.3 (1986) 26-30.
         Contrary to Reagan administration denials of involvement in
death squad activity in El Salvador, the CIA assisted El
Salvador officials in carrying out their murders.

2177.   Norton, Chris. "Build and Destroy." <u>RA</u> 19.6 (1985)
         26-36.
         An analysis of the chicanery and manipulation by the
American Institute for Free Labor (AIFLD) in El Salvador. AIFLD
is an instrument of US Cold War policy designed to build a trade
unionism around the world favorable to the US. "Over 90% of
AIFLD's budget comes from the Agency for International
Development (AID)."

2178.   Russell, Philip. <u>El Salvador in Crisis</u>. Austin, TX:
         Colorado River, 1984. 168.

A review in TO declares that the "fine book cuts
through the disinformation of U.S. administrations and the
shallowness of jet-set journalism." For example, Russell's
"badly needed critical evaluation of the 1982 and 1984
Salvadoran elections" describe how, "for the gullible back in
the United States, an appearance of democracy was manufactured."

2179.   Spence, Jack. "Second Time Around: How to Cover an
         Election." CJR 22.6 (1984) 41-43.
US media presented the Salvadoran election of a constituent
assembly, held on March 28, 1982, "as an overwhelming defeat for
the left," but they omitted analysis of how "a civil war skews
the election process in the direction of those who control the
polling places."

IV. H. 3. South America 2180-2187

2180.   Allende', Hortensia. "Chile: Made in USA." CS 2.3
         (1975) 42-47.
An attack on US intervention abroad, particularly in Chile,
and the CIA and the secrecy which enables it. "It is necessary
that the mysteries that envelop the monstrous maneuvers
executed by the great economic interests and hidden from the...
people of the United States, be revealed."

2181.   Corry, Steve. "Now we Know." IC 7.2 (1978) 74-75.
A review of Genocide in Paraguay, an edited version in
English of The Ache Indians: Genocide in Paraguay by Mark
Munzel. "Munzel's report was given some media coverage in
Europe but practically none in North America," perhaps because
the militia killers are trained and armed by US technicians
and there is heavy private American investment in Paraguay and
substantial aid to the government.

2182.   Kelley, Kevin J. "Allende' Breaks McCarran Act
         Blacklist." Guard 38.12 (1985) 16.
The Reagan administration's "politically motivated visa
denials" are generated by the idea that Hortensia Allende's
"presence would adversely affect U.S. foreign policy." The
administration did grant her a visa after all, however.

2183.   Leggett, John, et al. Allende, His Exit and Our
         "Times". New Brunswick, NJ: New Brunswick Cooperative,
         1978.
A study of The New York Times treatment mainly of the
overthrow of Salvador Allende's government in 1973, with lesser
study of the abortive Portugese revolution and the SLA-Hearst
coverage. "It is our contention that major newspapers
legitimate overseas and successful fascist assaults on left-wing
democratic governments in large measure because conservative and
moderate metromedia owners privately prefer capitalist-saving
fascism to expropriating left-democracy" (viii). The New York
Times illustrates the "seven stages" of a "counter-revolutionary
news story."

2184.   Moraes, Maria, and George Lawton.   "Images of Chile in
       the U.S. Press."   <u>BS</u> 4 (1974) 1-57.
       The image of Chile in pre-coup and post-coup periods as
presented in four major US and two European newspapers shows
that the US press coverage of the 1973 Chilean coup followed the
official US line and underplayed the torture and murder.

2185.   Pearson, Ted.   "Coverage of Chile: 'Preconceived,
       Wishful View.'"   <u>ChJR</u> 6.10 (1973) 3-5.
       On the pro-US distortions about Chile in the Chicago press.
"This willful distortion makes Chicago's establishment press
partners in the crimes of the junta."

2186.   Pollock, John, and David Eisenhower.   "The New Cold
       War in Latin America: The U.S. Press and Chile."   <u>The
       Chilean Road to Socialism</u>.   Ed. Dale L. Johnson.   Garden
       City, NY: Anchor, 1973.   71-86.
       The hostile US press coverage of Allende's Popular Unity
government as expressed by six daily newspapers during 1970-72.

2187.   Pollock, John, and Michele Pollock.   "The U.S. Press
       and Chile."   <u>DJ</u> 4 (1975) 4-8.
       The ideology, language, and omissions in US reporting on
Chile.

V. PENTAGON 2188-2381

Introduction

A. Militarism   2188-2238

B. Public Relations, Media, Recruiting   2239-2303a

C. Education and Research   2304-2317

D. Secrecy, Censorship, Disinformation, Cover-Up
    2318-2381

INTRODUCTION

Militarism

George Washington warned the new nation of the danger of an overgrown military establishment--"under any form of government inauspicious to liberty" and "to be regarded as particularly hostile to republican liberty." On the evening of January 17, 1961, in his Farewell Address, President Dwight D. Eisenhower, who admired Washington enormously, repeated the warning: "In the councils of Government, we must guard against the acquisition of unwarranted influence. . .by the military-industrial complex. The potential for the disastrous rise of misplaced power exists and will persist." Today the "economy of death," as Richard Barnet refers to the MIC, may be suggested by its budget--the $163 billion for past military expenditures (veterans benefits, interest on national debt created by military spending) and the $310 billion for Fiscal Year 1986 (includes the military portion of NASA, CIA, etc.; the Congressional Budget Office's An Analysis of the President's Budgetary Proposals for Fiscal Year 1986 gives $323 billion, February 1985). According to the War Resisters League, whose estimates I have just quoted, past and current expenditures total 64% of the total budget for 1986. A part of the budget is $34.8 million in FY 1984 for Pentagon public information and community relations, the latest figure my Senator was able to acquire from a reluctant Pentagon.

During December of 1969, J. William Fulbright, Chairman of the Senate Foreign Relations Committee, spoke repeatedly on the Senate floor to "make the Senate and the public at large aware of the multi-faceted and quietly pervasive nature of the Defense Department's public relations activity." These speeches he expanded into his book warning of the dangers of militarism in the United States, The Pentagon Propaganda Machine. "It is my generation who must halt, then turn back the incursions the military have made in our civilian system. These incursions have subverted or muffled civilian voices within the Executive branch, weakened the constitutional role and responsibility of the Congress, and laid an economic and psychological burden on the public that could be disastrous" (157). The purpose of Fulbright's speeches and his book was to alert the public to one mode of the increase of military and the decrease of civilian control--the ability of the military to sell the public its point of view.

Public Relations

Other prescient voices preceded Fulbright's, but his prestige as the father of the Fulbright Exchange Program and as Chairman of the Foreign Relations Committee for the first time brought national attention to the growth of the "warfare state's" propaganda apparatus. Unfortunate it is that his impetus failed to inspire more research from other scholars than it has. Swomley (1953), Cook (1962), and Fulbright were virtually Cassandra

voices. Though several writers have provided substantial studies
since then--books by Boyer, Dickson, Heise, Ladd, Raymond, Ridgeway, and Yarmolinsky, articles by Adler, Arkin, Burkholder, Ehrlich, Hedemann, Kaplan, and others, and a small-circulation magazine, Recon, watches the Pentagon--total scholarship on the
millions of dollars spent annually by the Pentagon to persuade
the public to believe its reality and its values is sparse, considering the significance of the subject.

Education and Research

Military influence also operates through schools and
research. Ellen Edelman helped inaugurate the Akron Free School
because she felt public schools taught war and militarism. Steve
Burkholder believes the Pentagon is "on campus in a big way, and
most universities" are doing what they can to make it "feel at
home." He fears that because large contracts will enable military values to play the tune, universities as institutions
devoted to the unfettered pursuit of knowledge will be damaged.

Secrecy

We can largely blame Pentagon secrecy for the inadequacy of
research, as everyone who has tried to acquire information from
it knows. One of the Pentagon's "Principles of Information"
states: "Information will only be withheld when disclosure would
adversely affect national security or threaten the safety or privacy of the men and women of the Armed Forces." But information
pertaining neither to security nor safety nor privacy is systematically withheld, information that should be readily available
not only to our elected representatives but to the public
directly. Even Senators of the United States must struggle to
elicit pitifully tiny bits of information about military public
relations expenditures.

Remedies

Over thirty years ago John Swomley expressed his anxiety
regarding the advance of militarism into all aspects of American
life. That power has continued to deepen and spread, the contributors to this bibliography contend, until it includes even
the public trust, respect for the military now higher than for
religion (Gallup Poll, July 1986). The Pentagon Propaganda
Machine's true danger--surpassing anything Eisenhower or Fulbright could imagine--derives from its force as part of the power
system set forth in this bibliography: Sovietphobia specifically
and anti-socialism generally, interlocking monopoly capital, the
military industrial complex, the military in education, in
science, and in technology, ideological repression, the con-
sumer/mass consumption ideology and global expansion, think
tanks, the classification/secrecy system, covert operations by
the FBI and CIA abroad and at home, and all of the institutions
and processes which threaten what Bertram Gross calls "friendly
fascism."
Thus Fulbright's proposed but never achieved solutions to

the danger of military propaganda power possess even more urgency
today: 1) a ceiling on public relations spending; 2) regular,
detailed reports to the Congress and to the public on its "information" budget and activities; 3) elimination of all activities
outside the military's proper role in a democracy (to inform, not
promote or deceive); and 4) strict clearance of all films,
speeches, and other materials involving foreign policy (150-51).
He also urged the public and the press to examine more carefully
attempts by the military to sell them its point of view, and the
media to look more critically on the military's attempts to
influence or use them. Others urge a halt and a reversal of military indoctrination in the schools and universities.

Works Cited

Barnet, Richard. <u>The Economy of Death</u>. New York: Atheneum,
1970.
    Note: Such books as Robert Coulam's <u>Illusions of Choice: The
F-111 and the Problems of Weapons Acquisition Reform</u> and John
Kenneth Galbraith's <u>How to Control the Military</u> are not listed,
since they offer nothing or very little about information control.

V. Pentagon

V. A. Militarism 2188-2238 (see II.B.)

2188.   Ackley, Charles. <u>The Modern Military in American</u>
      <u>Society: A Study in the Nature of Military Power</u>.
      Philadelphia: Westminster, 1972. 400.
      A study of "the thoughts of military thinkers and writers,
especially American and modern, respecting the nature of
military power," and the "impact of its values in a free
society." The author, a former Navy chaplain, explores the
challenge of My Lai, the militarization of the country through
"deepening patterns of rationalized violence," the effects of a
large standing army, the dangers of acceptance of a "garrison
state" mentality as normal, etc. For "much of the world and
many of our own people, especially the youth, we have already
arrived at a position of militarism. Some even of the military
establishment itself have adopted this conclusion. Certainly
the danger seems real if we stay, unthinkingly, on our present
course" (26).

2189.   Ambrose, Stephen, and James Barber, Jr. <u>The Military</u>
      <u>and American Society: Essays and Readings</u>. New York:
      Free, 1972. 322.
      "The United States has created the most powerful Armed
Forces the world has ever known. The military has reached a
size and has an influence on American society far beyond
anything anyone dreamed of before 1938. It has a direct and
deep impact on all Americans and it is apparently here to stay."
Twenty-two essays divided into eight groups and a Conclusion on
the military-industrial complex, the draft, ecology, etc.

2190.   Baral, Jaya. <u>The Pentagon and the Making of US</u>
      <u>Foreign Policy: A Case Study of Vietnam, 1960-1968</u>.
      New Delhi: Radiant, 1978. 333.
      "The military neither controls foreign policy-making, nor
does it play simply the role of an instrument or a conduit for
serving the interests of civilians. The truth lies somewhere
between the two" (308).

2191.   Betts, Richard. <u>Soldiers, Statesmen, and Cold War</u>
      <u>Crises</u>. Cambridge, MA: Harvard UP, 1977. 292.
      An analysis of "one element in American cold war decision
making: military advice and influence on the use of force,"
especially "how the proportion of military influence, relative
to that of civilian advisers, has varied since World War II."
The author concludes that "with few exceptions, the military
have had neither more nor less influence than they should have,
and that they have erred--albeit in different ways--neither more
nor less than their civilian colleagues" (Preface). "No one who
seeks to fix responsibility for disasters in cold war crises by
blaming only the military or only the civilians will find
comfort in the evidence taken as a whole. There is enough blame
to go around for both camps" (Introduction).

2192.   Boyer, William. <u>Education for Annihilation</u>. Honolulu:
     Hogarth, 1972. 162.
     "This book is an analysis and critique of the way in which
most Americans are educated, formally and informally, to
consider war as a necessity in dealing with human problems.
Such war education is received through schools, government,
churches, businesses, the mass media, and of course the military
establishments. In fact, it pervades our entire thought pattern
and value system." Such militaristic thinking is outmoded, "pre-
atomic", and will result in annihilation unless changed. Part I,
"Teaching for War Through Military Institutions," II, "Teaching
for War Through Civilian Institutions," III "Reconstructing
American Society." Ch. 2, "Indoctrinating Military Ideology,"
examines the black-white thinking about communists and the
Soviet Union, they totally evil, the US good, "free," in mortal
combat with the Enemy.

2193.   Clotfelter, James. <u>The Military in American
     Politics</u>. New York: Harper, 1973. 244.
     Too little attention has been given "to the leading
competitor for national priorities, the military" in spite of
its "central role in political decision-making," not only "in
regard to foreign policy but also to the distribution of
economic and political resources within the country." Ch. 4,
"The 'Complex': The Military, Business, and the Economy," 5,
"The Military, the Media, Politics, and Public Opinion," 7, "The
Military and Congress," etc.

2194.   Coffin, Tristram. <u>The Passion of the Hawks:
     Militarism in Modern America</u>. New York: MacMillan,
     1964. 280.
     A survey of diverse aspects of the Warfare State with the
Pentagon at the center: Sovietphobia, violence, aggression,
expansionism, standing army, arms race, science, etc.

2195.   Cook, Fred. <u>The Warfare State</u>. New York:
     Macmillan, 1962. 376.
     Examines the inversion of the constitutional and
traditional role of the military as the servant to civilian
authority, and the historical, political, econmic,
technological, and psychological reasons for the military's
ascendancy. Having put the country on a permanent war economy,
the military-industrial complex must keep the public mood
truculent to justify the need for militarism and the war
economy. Ch. 4, "Madison Avenue in Uniform," focuses upon the
Pentagon propaganda system.

2196.   Courrier, Kathleen. "Militarizing Energy." <u>Prog</u>
     44.5 (1980) 9-10.
     The Department of Energy's largest expenditure--$3.2
billion of its $8.4 billion budget in fiscal 1980--goes to
nuclear weapons development.

2197.   Croteau, David. "Militarizing Space: NASA's Space
     Shuffle." <u>NA</u> 3.3 (1986) 8-9.

"Despite all of the media attention, a central fact about the space shuttle is often overlooked: the space shuttle is a military vehicle," its design dictated by Air Force needs and half of its future missions planned as secret military ventures. Many of NASA's stated nonmilitary goals--landing an astronaut on the moon, for example--"provided cover for military space activities."

2198.   Dibble, Vernon K. "The Garrison Society." NUT
         5.1 and 2 (1967) 106-115.
Corporate executives, politicians, and the military have become interdependent. As a result, military control has penetrated into business, labor unions, and the economy due to lucrative defense contracts, and into research and scholarship through student loans and through university grants for the study of chemical and biological warfare.

2199.   Donovan, James A., Col. Militarism, U.S.A. New York:
         Scribner's, 1970. 265.
An analysis of the "socio-economic-political influence of our immense military establishment, its civilian and uniformed leaders, and the vast complex of money, people, industry and vested interests, who make up America's 'defense-industry team.'" This complex has become "vast and complicated--with its own terminology, secrets, technology, and propaganda." This book is "an effort to inform readers by explaining the whats, hows, and whys of the current militaristic trend which has become such a dominant aspect in our culture and by describing some of the forces at work in the new American militarism" (Preface). Much of the book is about the "highly sophisticated public relations efforts" of the armed services: "flim-flam about the conduct and progress of the Vietnam War" (171ff.), influencing Congress (190ff.), etc.

2200.   Falk, Richard. Normative Initiatives and
         Demilitarization: A Third System Approach. New York:
         Institute for World Order, 1982. 18.
Individual citizens "need to monitor developments in the world from a demilitarizing perspective."

2201.   Getlein, Frank. "Gentlemen First." Prog 44.10
         (1980) 12.
Carter's Presidential Directive 58 is part of US WW III plans by its aim to ensure the survival of national leaders in the event of enemy attack.

2202.   Hoffman, Lyla. "Feminist Education--A Key to Peace."
         IBCB 13.6-7 (1982) 6-8.
The interrelationships between sex role socialization and militaristic values and behaviors. "Militarism directly contradicts a number of feminist goals."

2203.   Kaku, Michio, and Daniel Axelrod. To Win a Nuclear
         War: The Pentagon's Secret Strategy. Boston: South

End, 1986. 350.
A survey of US plans to wage nuclear war from 1945 through
the present. "The authors demonstrate how US policymakers, in
over a dozen episodes, brought the world to the brink of nuclear
war. In contrast to the popular belief that deterrence has been
the policy of the US since the dawn of the nuclear age, the
authors convincingly prove the opposite: US planning--from
Operation 'Broiler' to SIOP 6--has always aimed To Win a
Nuclear War (publisher's description). Introduction by Daniel
Ellsberg.

2204.   Klare, Michael. "Come to the Arms Bazaar." Prog
          42.10 (1978) 44-45.
The "lavish displays at the various arms bazaars" by the
"many arms firms." One at the Army Association convention is
described.

2205.   Klare, Michael. "Is Exxon Worth Dying For?" Prog
          44.7 (1980) 21-26.
President Carter and the Pentagon plan "for energy wars."
Instead of military solutions, the US should restructure the
energy industry.

2206.   Lapp, Ralph. Arms Beyond Doubt. New York: Cowles,
          1970. 210.
The author fears a missile technology which increasingly
dominates defense policy (173-78).

2207.   Lens, Sidney. "Ban the Bomb." Prog 46.8 (1982)
          24-25.
Pentagon and Administration strategy to defeat the peace
movement by outlasting "public concern."

2208.   Loory, Stuart. Defeated: Inside America's
          Military Machine. New York: Random, 1973. 405.
The author examines "the pervasiveness of the American
military machine" in US society, the decline of civilian
control, the priority of the machine to the society "it
protected." The Vietnam War is seen "not as an aberration" but
"as an inevitable result of a militaristic policy that had been
pursued" (Introduction). The defeat of the title refers not to
battlefields but to "the huge bureaucracy" the military built.

2209.   MacCann, Donnarae. "Militarism in Juvenile Fiction."
          IBCB 13.6-7 (1982) 18-20.
A survey of scholarship and novels.

2210.   "Mad, Mad, Mad." Prog 44.10 (1908) 10-11.
President Carter's Presidential Directive 59 expresses a
first strike doctrine.

2211.   Manno, Jack. Arming the Heavens: The Hidden
          Military Agenda for Space, 1945-1995. New York: Dodd,
          1984. 245.

An analysis of the ideologies and myths that lie behind the
military space program. Behind the high tech mystique and the
myths of space adventure "lie familiar, old-fashioned power
grabs," and the "goal is global military superiority." "The
rise to power of a right-wing president in the United States and
the growing confidence among the American military in advanced
technology have brought about the latest round in the
militarization of space" (3). "Billions will have been spent
building the military space hardware and designing the systems
before any public debate takes place. By the time the
American people become aware of what the Pentagon has planned,
the momentum of the space arms race may have already become
unstoppable" (187). The 18 chs. are organized chronologically--
ch. 1, "The Nazi Legacy," ch. 6, "The Forming of NASA," ch. 14,
"The Mid-Seventies: Militarization Completed," etc. In ch. 18,
"Disarming the Heavens," the author urges the citizenry to
oppose the militarization of space and support as a first step
"an international treaty banning weapons in space" (191).

2212.   Manno, Jack. "The Military History of the Space
         Shuttle." ScP 15.5 (1983) 6-10, 30-32.
    "Although it has masqueraded as many things," the shuttle
"has been one of the two top priorities of the military space
program for twenty years."

2213.   Markusen, Ann. "The Militarized Economy." WPJ 3.3
         (1986) 495-516.
    "One major cause" of the "poor performance" within "certain
industries and regions" is "the dramatic shift in federal
expenditures toward military hardware and away from other types
of public spending." The US now has an industrial policy that
"favors aerospace, communications, and related high-tech
industries" over other kinds of basic manufacturing. I.e., the
Pentagon has assumed a major role in industrial policy, and
this policy cannot enable the US "to maintain a healthy,
diversified economy."

2214.   McGaffin, William, and Erwin Knoll. Scandal in the
         Pentagon: A Challenge to Democracy. Greenwich, CT:
         Fawcett, 1969. 192.
    "The military-industrial complex is no longer a potential
threat to America but a deeply entrenched reality. It had
already acquired a dangerous degree of influence in the dozen
Cold War years preceding Eisenhower's [1961 Farewell] speech.
Its power has grown and multiplied at a colossal rate in the
decade of the 1960s" (8). "The Pentagon spends massive sums to
make friends and influence people in behalf of its policies and
programs" (147). Ch. 4, "Contracts and Congressmemn," focuses
on Pentagon control of Congress; ch. 5, "Where the Brass Goes,"
deals with the corporate-Pentagon "revolving door"; 7, "the
Military-Academic Complex"; 8, "the Propaganda Factory."

2215.   Melman, Seymour. "American Needs and Limits on
         Resources: The Priorities Problem." NUT 5.1 and 2

369

(1967) 3-8.
Federal officials ignore social welfare and urban improvement programs and instead allocate funds to military and space programs. Priorities must be changed to emphasize "productive growth."

2216.   Moore, Taylor, III. "The Navy's Number-cruncher."
         Prog 44.11 (1980) 32-33.
The Navy's computerized program to destroy the Soviet submarine and nuclear deterrent fleet by targeting the sounds of the subs through a worldwide network of hydrophonic and electromagnetic sensing devices.

2217.   Musil, Robert. "The Marine Corps Builds Myths (and
         Breaks Men). Prog 40.10 (1976) 31-34.
Despite Marine Corps public relations and promises of reform, mistreatment and death in the Marine Corps will continue because the Corps is predicated upon brutality, racism, and injustice. It is time "to put an end at last to the whole bloody tradition."

2218.   Naiman, Adeline. "Video Games: Mindless, Macho,
         Militaristic." IBCB 13.6-7 (1982) 26-27.
An appeal for games which exclude militaristic and sexist content.

2219.   New Evidence of the Militarization of America.
         Washington, DC: National Council Against Conscription,
         1949. 64.
"Illustrations of the still-expanding influence of the military." It is "the basic pattern that is dangerous. It is the trend that is wrong and must be reversed." Chs. on "Military Control of American Life," "The National Security Act--Militarism Becomes Law," "Military Publicity and Propaganda," etc.

2220.   Parenti, Michael. "More Bucks from the Bang." Prog
         44.7 (1980) 27-30.
The increasing Pentagon budgets "are less a response to international crises (real or fabricated) than to imperatives built into the U.S. corporate market economy."

2221.   Raymond, Jack. Power at the Pentagon. New York:
         Harper, 1964. 363.
In the process of creating "the most powerful armed forces in history," we altered our traditions and "placed tremendous peacetime authority in the hands of our defenders, military and civilian" (Preface). Ch. 8, "Research and the Federal Government," is inspired by President Eisenhower's statement in his farewell address that "the prospect of domination of the nation's scholars by Federal employment. . . and the power of money is ever present and is gravely to be regarded"; ch. 11, "The Military Lobbies"; ch. 18, "From a Reporter's Notebook," pp. 322-28 on how the government manages the news--background

briefings, lying, etc.

2222.   Reardon, Betty. Sexism and the War System. New York:
    World Policy Institute, 1985. 136.
    On the relationship between sexism and militarism and the
need to integrate feminist scholarship with peace research.

2223.   Rodberg, Leonard, and Derek Shearer, eds. The
    Pentagon Watchers: Students Report on the National
    Security State. Garden City, NY: Doubleday, 1970.
    416.
    The ten essays are divided into three groups on "State
Power," "Intervention," and the "Arms Industry," plus appendixes
on researching the military, a course outline, and a
bibliography. Ch. 3 by Derek Shearer, "The Pentagon Propaganda
Machine," discusses the various operations of military public
relations: "film making, speakers' bureaus, traveling art
shows, civilian 'orientation' tours, and numerous publications,
all aimed at convincing the American public that the road to
true national security lies in more sophisticated weapons
systems, a worldwide counterrevolutionary military force, and
patriotism that supports any and all military adventures in the
name of anti-communism" (100).

2224.   Scott, John V. Athletics for Athletes. Oakland, CA:
    Other Ways, 1969. 111.
    "Professionalized" sports contribute to authoritarianism,
conformity, obedience, and military precision at the expense of
self-expression.

2225.   Siegel, Lenny. "Space Wars." Prog 46.6 (1982) 27-29.
    A summary of US military spacecraft in orbit and military
communications satellite programs, and the "Blue Cube," the
Sunnyvale Air Force Station, which controls them for a future
"nuclear war in space." These are the Command, Control,
Communications, and Intelligence technology, known to nuclear
strategists as C^3I--or "see-cubed-eye."

2226.   Stares, Paul. The Militarization of Space: U.S.
    Policy, 1945-1984. Ithaca, NY: Cornell U P, 1985. 352.
    A book on antisatellite (ASAT) weapons. Under Reagan "the
chance for a significant antisatellite arms control agreement
was lost--possibly forever."

2227.   "Star Wars Doomed Shuttle." EIJ (March 1986) 3.
    Shuttle safety was reduced "to accommodate the shuttle's
hidden military mission . . . .The school children who sent in
quarters to build a new challenger should realize the growing
dominance of NASA's military role."

2228.   Stringfellow, William. "An Assault Upon Conscience:
    Violence in the Technocratic Society." Soj 13.9 (1984)
    22-25.
    "The Pentagon is archetypical of the principalities and

powers of the technocratic state and is representative in the operation of how any of the great public or private corporate powers act and of how they victimize human beings."

2229.   Swomley, John, Jr. The Military Establishment.
        Boston: Beacon, 1964. 266.
An "attempt to trace the story of the growth of military influence over civilian American government" through examination of "the current military role in foreign policy, publicity, media, education, and other areas of national life." Efforts "to warn the American people" of the expansion of military power "have received little space in the nation's newspapers and magazines, many of which either cooperate with the well-developed military public relations program or for other reasons believe it is not in their best interest to question or impede the growth." Ch. 10, "A Propaganda Machine Second to None," gives particulars about the machine: seminars, cultivating the press, making films, etc.

2230.   Thompson, E. P. The Heavy Dancers. New York:
        Pantheon, 1985. 361.
"The 'heavy dancers' are the image-conscious public persons who crowd the media of the world, summoning up the ancient spirits of the tribe as they prepare us for the ultimate war": Caspar Weinberger, Margaret Thatcher, Georgi Arbatov, et al.

2231.   Tirman, John, ed. The Militarization of High
        Technology. Cambridge, MA: Ballinger, 1984. 247.
The ten essays argue in general "that military procurement has a profound, perhaps damaging, effect on the vitality of commercial high technology" and that the "current rearmament" is "excessive" because it jeopardizes "the nations's economic competitiveness" (xiii). Ch. 8 "explores the role of the scientist in defense work, the specific ways a scientist may become ensnared in the industry."

2232.   Tolley, Howard, Jr. Children and War: Political
        Socialization to International Conflict. New York:
        Teachers College P, 1973. 177.
Generally, "children reflect contemporary public opinion."

2233.   Wieseltier, Leon. Nuclear War, Nuclear Peace.
        New York: New Republic, Holt, 1983. 109.
A repudiation of Ronald Reagan and his nuclear hawks, their Sovietphobia, their "Defense Guidance" strategy, and their belief in a winnable nuclear war, a limited nuclear war, and nuclear superiority.

2234.   Wiesner, Jerome. "The United States: A Militarized
        Society." BAS 41.7 (1985) 102-105.
US citizens must free themselves from Cold War dogmas that have stifled common sense and initiative. Sovietphobic pressures from the military, industry, Congress, journalists, veterans' organizations, and other groups have pushed

administration after administration into unneeded arms
acquirements. "Such pressure groups no longer need to operate on
the president. President Ronald Reagan not only accepts the
ideas of the groups Eisenhower warned against, he has become
their most articulate spokesman. . . .Reagan's reelection is an
indication that the militarization of U.S. society is proceeding
with the complicity, if not the overt support, of ordinary
citizens. . . .It is no longer a question of controlling a
military-industrial complex, but rather, of keeping the United
States from becoming a totally military culture."

2235.   Williams, Greg. "Racism and Militarism: Exploring
          the Links." IBCB 13.6-7 (1982) 9-12.
     How racism and militarism support and reinforce each other.

2236.   Wolf, Charles, Jr., et al. Is America Becoming
          Militarized? New York: Council on Religion and
          International Affairs, 1971. 68.
     The contributors fear the US is becoming captive to
military rather than diplomatic thinking and to military
technology rather than alternatives to violence.

2237.   Yarmolinsky, Adam. The Military Establishment:
          Its Impacts on American Society. New York: Harper,
          1971. 434.
     An attempt to increase public understanding of the military
establishment to enable the people to better control it ("we
cannot expect this or any other major institution in our society
to control itself"). Part II deals with the power of the
military in government and business. Part III includes chapters
on the military's public relations network, its handling of
news, and its ideological "education of the military and the
public." The military establishment is "the single most powerful
and pervasive establishment in our society."

2238.   Zillman, Donald N. and Edward Imwinkelried. "The
          Legacy of Greer V. Spock: The Public Forum Doctrine
          and the Principle of the Military's Political
          Neutrality." GLJ 65.3 (1977) 773-806.
     The Supreme Court "unnecessarily contracted first amendment
rights in resolving the public forum issue" and "failed to
announce the outright ban of partisan political activities on
military posts that constitutional law and contemporary
realities require."

V. B. Public Relations, Media, Recruiting 2239-2303a

2239.   Aufderheide, Pat. "And Don't Forget, We're Paying
          for It." ITT 10.24 (1986) 14.
     A Government Accounting Office survey estimated that the
cabinet and federal agencies spend a minimum of $437 million
annually in public relations. But "the big money is, of course,
in the military," which runs "'the largest media conglomerate in
the world'" with a budget of at least $100 million annually.

2240. Caldwell, Terry. "Air Force Takes the Media to Europe."
AG (August 6, 1982) 13A.
A personal account of how the USAF pumps up its image by
flying media representatives and community leaders around Europe
for "dog and pony" shows in which "we couldn't get a straight
answer" for the hard questions.

2241. Cockburn, Andrew. "Pictures from the Pentagon." Ch 2
(June/July 1982) 15-16.
About the dependence of television news upon the Pentagon
or weapons manufacturers for film or videotape of weaponry.
This favorable coverage provided by the "Pentagon's [and
corporate] legion of public-relations cadres" is surpassed in
deception only by the public relations cadres of the Soviet
Ministry of Defense.

2242. Cockburn, Andrew. "Threat Inflation." Inq 6
(June 1983) 19-21.
The military pitchmen of the Pentagon and the Kremlin
wildly exaggerate their foes' capabilities for their own gain.

2243. Congressional Record. Washington, DC: GPO,
December 1, 2, 4, and 5, 1969.
Documents and newspaper articles placed by Senator J.
William Fulbright giving details about the Pentagon propaganda
machine.

2244. Conrad, Thomas. "Winning Hearts and Minds for the
All-Volunteer Military Force." Prog 41.9 (1977) 28-31.
"The new, intensified [recruiting] program masquerades as
'career counseling' and entails a wholesale penetration by the
Pentagon of the nation's educational system."

2245. "Disingenuous Defense." NR 192.11 (1985) 8-9.
Four examples of Pentagon "misleading and untenable
arguments" regarding arms spending.

2246. DOD Legislative Activities. Washington, DC: GAO,
1986. 22.
The services "have done little to address past
congressional, GAO, and DOD IG reports" on "the need for
improvement in overall control, accountability, and reporting of
all legislative activities costs to the Congress." Cost of
legislative activities reported by DOD organizations in 1985 was
almost $28 million.

2247. Epstein, Joshua. The 1987 Defense Budget.
Washington, DC: Brookings Inst., 1986. 61.
Because the annual military budget is partly ideological
advocacy and always geopolitically and technically disputable,
the Brookings Institution publishes an annual analysis. The
author argues the government could spend $117 billion less than
the Reagan administration proposes over the next four years and
get more for the public's money in terms of real security.

2248.   Everett, Robert R. "Yesterday, Today, and Tomorrow in
          Command, Control, and Communications." TR 85 (1982)
          66-68.
     This article discusses the 3 major components of the
military's information system--command, control and
communications--and focuses on the two major changes in the
communications area that affect the military's operations.
These major changes were the development of the satellite and
the computer.

2249.   Fain, Jim. "Incest Is Press Problem." AG
          (13 March 1985) 15A.
     Fain's focus is upon the "government/media revolving door"
(Gelb had held Chain's position as Pentagon director of the
Bureau of Politico-Military Affairs). "There are platoons of
revolving door veterans in journalism," and this "fuzzes a
necessarily adversarial relationship." Also see "Chain of
Fools," Na 240 (March 16, 1985) 293 and "Beyond Redemption,"
Prog 49 (April 1985) 12.

2250.   Feld, Bernard T. "On 'Soviet Military Power.'" TR
          85 (Jan. 1982) 63.
     "All of the arguments" in the Pentagon's Soviet Military
Power are "one-sided."

2251.   Ferber, Michael. "A Citizen's Guide to Arms Control
          Euphemisms." C&C 45.17 (1985) 421-424.
     Analysis of the Reagan administration's use of the words
"modernization," "accuracy," "hard targets," "counter-force,"
"first-strike capability," and "other words politicians tell
lies with."

2252.   Frank, Robert. "The IAS [Institute for American
          Strategy] Case Against CBS." JoC 25.4 (1975) 188-189.
     A negative review of Lefever's study of CBS news coverage
of national defense, TV and National Defense.

2253.   Friendly, Jonathan. "Media-Military Cease-Fire."
          WJR 6.3 (1984) 9-10.
     On the preparation of guidelines for press coverage of
combat actions.

2254.   Fulbright, J. William. The Pentagon Propaganda
          Machine. New York: Vintage/Random House, 1970. 166.
     "This book represents an expansion of a series of speeches
given on the Senate floor in December of 1969. My aim at that
time, as it is now, was to make the Senate and the public at
large aware of the multi-faceted and quietly pervasive nature of
the Defense Department's public relations activity." "In use is
every device and technique of the commercial public relations
man and even some that he cannot afford such as cruises on
aircraft carriers and 'firepower' demonstrations by battalions
of artillery and squadrons of aircraft all designed to shape
public opinion and build an impression that militarism is good

for you" (11). A corrolary to these revelations is the author's
warning throughout the book that "the constitutional
responsibilities of the Congress have been eroded in dangerous
measure by the diversion of power to the President and the
Joint Chiefs and the Department of State" (4). Ch. 9 sets
forth "The Dangers of the Military Sell": acceptance of a
professional army and militarism, adoption of a military outlook
by civilian leaders, possible military take-over of the
government, etc.

2255.   Gay, Lance. "The Pentagon Favors Public Relations
         Over Money for Bullets." Pr 10.5 (1982) 4.
Pentagon officials "say the added demand for congressional
public relations and lobbying is so great it will cost $2.1
million more than the $7.5 million limit put on the Pentagon's
lobbying expense account this year."

2256.   Gervasi, Tom. "The Doomsday Beat." CJR 18.1 (1979)
         34-40.
Aviation Week serves as a "mouthpiece" for the Pentagon
and defense contractors, not only looking out for their
interests within its own pages, but also serving as a source of
aviation information for much of the news media.

2257.   Getlein, Frank. "The Word from Washington." Prog
         42.3 (1978) 14-15.
Various rhetorical ploys used by the Pentagon to increase
its budget.

2258.   Hairston, Marc. "The Price of Truth and Beauty."
         TO 79.7 (1986) 22-23.
President Reagan's Strategic Defense Initiative (SDI) or
Star Wars is defended by "the large aerospace and electronics
industries" and opposed by "independent scientists in the
nation's colleges and universities." The Pentagon "has begun a
campaign to win the hearts and minds of the skeptics."

2259.   Halverson, Richard. "Air Follies Topple General."
         MORE 7.4 (1977) 8-9.
Major General Harry Meir Jr. lost his post as commanding
general of the Pennsylvania National Guard because he used
military aircraft for personal pleasure. The city editor of the
Harrisburg Patriot blacked out the story, because the editor is
an honorary civilian aide to the Secretary of the Army, and the
General helped obtain the editor's appointment.

2260.   Hartman, Thomas. "Reporting for Service: The Big
         Guns of the Military Press." WJR 6.6 (1984) 29-32.
A small group of independent publications that cover
military issues "have become must reading for Pentagon
officials, Pentagon customers and Pentagon-watchers." The most
prestigious of the magazines is Aviation Week & Space
Technology, which its editor describes as "industry oriented,"--
for example, it supports the government's "star wars" program.

2261.   Heise, Juergen. Minimum Disclosure: How the
Pentagon Manipulates the News. New York: Norton,
1979. 221.
[Along with Fulbright's The Pentagon Progaganda Machine one
of the best revelations of Pentagon control of information.]
Ch. 1 on the failure of the Pentagon to live up to the principle
"so piously" preached by the Defense Information School about
the handling of news: "maximum disclosure with minimum delay";
2 the rise of public relations in the armed forces, and the
evolution of restrictive information practices; 3 control over
bad news (the main focus of the book); 4 centralized review
leading to censorship; 5 the use of "national security" as an
excuse for pervasive secrecy; 6 an overview of the military
public relations system; 7 FOIA, the public's right to know, and
the insufficient sense of public responsibility in the military;
8 the weakness of the regular Pentagon correspondents, their
tendency to report what is told them rather than digging for the
truth; 9 summary and recommendations (e.g. increase the number
of journalists watching the Pentagon).

2262.   Hersh, Seymour. Chemical and Biological Warfare:
America's Hidden Arsenal. Indianapolis: Bobbs, 1968.
354.
Evidence of Army promotional campaigns, suppression of
information, and lying, in relation to their CBW plans and
programs.

2263.   Hersh, Seymour. "From the Pentagon (But Don't
Tell Anyone I Told You)." NR 157.24 (1967) 13-14.
Private briefings of the Pentagon press corps, even at the
homes of correspondents, are a "commonplace" aspect of the
corps' service as a propaganda conduit.

2264.   Hersh, Seymour. "Germ Warfare: for Alma Mater, God
and Country." Ram 8 (December 1969) 21-28.
The Army is secretly developing new means of biological
warfare and is determining their effectiveness through unknowing
volunteers and open-air testing.

2265.   Hume, Brit and Mark McIntyre. "Polishing Up the
Brass." MORE 3.5 (1973) 6-8.
"Of the 155 stories written by the Pentagon Press corps
during one month recently--122 were based on public
pronouncements or the say-so of anonymous military officials."
"Most of the reporters regularly assigned to the Department of
Defense consistently pass up stories embarrassing to the military
in favor of the information the brass wants written." [See IV.
F.]

2266.   "Humpty Dumptian Semantics." Prog 42.2 (1978) 6-7.
The Pentagon's "Office of Humpty Dumptian Semantics (OHDS)"
is charged with making us love the Neutron Bomb, or the
"Blast/Enhanced Radiation Warhead."

2267.   Kaplan, Fred. "Going Native Without A Field Map."
        CJR 19.5 (1981) 23-29.
    The Pentagon reporter falls prey to the "Going Native
Syndrome"--losing objectivity and skepticism and perceiving
reality "measured on a scale established by Pentagon analysts."
This explains "the quite miserable job done by most of the
national-security press corps in covering the latest episode in
the saga of limited-nuclear-war doctrine--President Jimmy
Carter's July 25 [1980] signing of Presidential Directive (PD)
No. 59." [See IV. F.]

2268.   Kaplan, Sheila. "Take Me Along." CC 12.3 (1986) 8.
    One of the Pentagon's taxpayer-subsidized public relations
activities is known as "Tiger Cruises": male relatives of
crewmen returning home from overseas on Navy vessels get to come
aboard for the last seven to ten days. The Navy has no record
of how much the program costs.

2269.   Keisling, Phillip. "Mis-led and Under-worked: Life
        in Today's Air Force." WM 16.1 (1984) 28-37.
    Air Force recruiting ads are misleading, like commercial
"bait and switch" ads. Most recruits do routine jobs, in spite
of their high-sounding titles.

2270.   Kelley, Joseph. "Behind the Push to Revive the
        Draft." Prog 44.5 (1980) 23-24.
    The Army wants to select soldiers to guarantee "a supply of
men for the managerial class that runs today's Army."

2271.   Kelly, John. "CBS Aids Pentagon Cover Up." CS
        3.2 (1976) 55-62.
    An account of Col. Anthony Herbert, author of Soldier, an
account of Vietnam war crimes committed by US soldiers. Herbert
is suing CBS and "60 Minutes" for $22 million for their program
"The Selling of Col. Herbert," which Herbert claims was a
hatchet job designed to discredit him and the war crimes issue.
Several atrocities are narrated following the story about
Herbert.

2272.   Klare, Michael. "Building a Fortress America." Na
        240. (1985) 321, 337-9.
    The Pentagon's 1986 budget request is as much ideological
propaganda as it is budget. It is mainly intended to expand
America's capacity to intervene abroad (though the Star Wars
program captured the press's attention); its tone is
"unadulterated alarmism."

2273.   Koger, Daniel. "The Liberal Opinion Press and the
        Kennedy Years in Vietnam: A Study of Four Journals
        (The New Leader, The Reporter, The New Republic,
        and The Nation)." PhD Diss., Michigan SU, 1983.
        DAI 44 (1984) 2612A.
    The New Leader and The Reporter were "strongly in favor of
U.S. military intervention to stop the spread of communism in

Southeast Asia." During 1960-63 The New Republic supported
intervention, but late in 1963 began advocating military
withdrawal. The Nation consistently opposed US support of
autocratic Asian leaders.

2274.   Kosterlitz, Julie and Lee Norrgard. "The Selling of
    the Pentagon." CC 10 (Nov./Dec. 1984) 14-19.
An account of "an elaborate public relations campaign by
the Pentagon designed to counter charges of Defense Department
(DOD) mismanagement." The campaign began in early Sept., 1984
and ended on Nov. 3--that is, it was timed to coincide with the
peak election campaign period, and it was intended to deflect
Democratic criticism away from the Republican Party.

2275.   Lefever, Ernest. TV and National Defense: An
    Analysis of CBS News, 1972-73. Boston, MA: Institute
    for American Strategy, 1974. 209.
CBS-TV "presented the U.S. military establishment in an
unfavorable light most of the time" and downplayed skeptical
views regarding "detente, the SALT arms control agreements, or
increased U.S. trade with Moscow and Peking" (46); it under-
reported Soviet military and missile developments (Ch.3); etc.
[See No. 2252.]

2276.   Loving, Bill. "NORAD Visits Called Lobbying." RMN
    (31 March 1985) 34.
The Air Force flew 40 Fort Worth citizens to the North
American Air Defense Command near Colorado Springs for two days
as part of selling the Air Force's and the Pentagon's point of
view.

2277.   Lutz, William. "Politics and the English Language."
    QRD 7.4 (1981) 1-3.
A critique of Robert Mitchell, who attacks the NCTE and
QRD, and "picks up nice fees making regular talks for the Air
Force."

2278.   Mark, Norman. "A Reporter's Guide to Military PR."
    ChR 2.9 (Sept. 1969) 5.
An incident of prevarication by a Pentagon press team
causes the author to assert a general skepticism about military
honesty.

2279.   Massing, Michael. The Invisible Story." CJR 19.4
    (1980) 51-54.
"Busy chasing leaks, the press seldom asked if Stealth
[aircraft] was all it was cracked up to be."

2280.   Mayer, Milton. "Hell, No." Prog 44.6 (1980) 44-46.
Possible Army efforts to limit conscientious objection
status.

2281.   Mollenhoff, Clark. The Pentagon: Politics, Profit
    and Plunder. New York: Putnam's, 1967. 450.

On the danger of unchecked power in the office of the Secretary of Defense. "The daily press is reluctant to take on the job of criticizing those who control the major sources of news at the Pentagon."

2282.   Morris, Roger. "Reporting for Duty: The Pentagon and the Press." CJR 19.2 (1980) 27-33.
"Between Vietnam and Afghanistan, the press forgot a lesson: beware of Pentagon sources. Recent national security coverage reveals a militant press--and few conscientious objectors." The author focuses upon the Iranian hostage crisis and Soviet troops entering Afghanistan. "For most of the media, the Iranian and Afghan crises seemed plain enough: the United States had become ominously weak, and its Soviet enemy defiantly, perhaps decisively, stronger," which was the Pentagon line for increasing its budget.

2283.   Morrissette, Walt. "Recruiters Hit the Road in Cinema Vans." ArT (Sept. 30, 1985) 22,32.
Eight $350,000 tractor trailers that expand into theaters travel to high schools to recruit for the Army, as part of its Total Army Involvement in Recruiting program, which includes the Fife and Drum Corps and the Army Band.

2284.   Noah, Timothy. "The Pentagon Press: Prisoners of Respectability." WM 15 (Sept. 1983) 40-45.
The failure of the media to report the important story of a Pentagon whistleblower named George Spanton--another example of the "dismaying shortcomings" in Pentagon coverage. [See IV. F.]

2285.   Ott, George. "Now It's a 'Naval Gap.'" Prog 42.9 (1978) 22-24.
"To make this gap believable, armed forces handouts follow the familiar pattern of overselling the Soviet threat." "The U.S. taxpayer has less to fear from the firepower of the Soviet navy than from the propaganda of the U.S. Navy."

2286.   "Pentagon Hucksterism." Na 209 (Dec.22, 1969) 685.
"An important aspect of Pentagon PR activity is speechmaking by general officers."

2287.   "The Pentagon's Army Within an Army." USNW 87 (Aug. 27, 1979) 46.
Military bands, Army parachutists, Air Force and Navy fliers--"these displays are only the visible tips of the Pentagon's far-flung and many-sided publicity operation."

2288.   "The Pentagon Vs. The Press." Har 271.1626 (1985) 37-52.
A forum entitled "The Military and the News Media," held at Princeton University.

2289.   Picard, Robert. "Pentagon Manipulated Satellite Story." SLJR 11 (February 1985) 9.

"In the midst of the charges and countercharges surrounding the disclosure of the satellite [for monitoring Soviet communications], the press missed the real issues and played into the hands of the military."

2290.   Pike, John.   "Soviet Military Power, 1983.
         Illustrated Disinformation."   CS 7 (June-Aug. 1983)
         21-22.
This 107-page centerpiece of the Reagan administration's military propaganda campaign contains numerous mistakes and inconsistencies, exaggerates the Soviet threat, does not mention that the US has a clear technological lead, and repeatedly claims without substantiation that the US is defending freedom against an offensive Soviet Union.

2291.   Prendergast, Alan.   "The Boys in the Bush."   CJR
         22.4 (1983) 59-63.
Soldier of Fortune's "network of military contacts--not to mention its staunchly conservative, pro-military politics--gives its writers a definite edge" with the Pentagon, as illustrated by SOF's "recent involvement in El Salvador."

2292.   "The Press's Own War Games."   CJR 19.5 (1981) 19-21.
Many Pentagon reporters become "explicators of Pentagon strategy" and forget about the consequences.

2293.   Pringle, Peter.   "The Army Wages Propaganda for
         Chemical Warfare."   Pr 10.2 (1982) 14.
"The army has been secretly running a massive propaganda campaign to support its new chemical warfare production plan. American journalists, academics and key members of the Reagan Administration have been 'targeted' by a special army task force charged with promoting positive public CW (chemical warfare) awareness."

2294.   Pringle, Peter.   "How the Pentagon Tried to Stifle
         Missile Debate."   Ob 16 (Oct. 3, 1983) 14.
The Pentagon's public relations campaign to justify deployment of the cruise and Pershing missiles in Europe included passing on selected facts to well-placed journalists, academics, and politicians.

2295.   Richman, Sheldon.   "Bathtub Navy."   Inq 6
         (July 1983) 48.
How the Bath Iron Works (which builds ships for the Navy) helps the Navy in its $100 billion quest for a 600-ship battle force by advocacy ads in newspapers. The author challenges the corporation/Navy claims that the Navy had been allowed to decay.

2296.   Roane, Stephen.   "Ringknocking: A Guide to the
         Folkways of the United States Navy."   Prog 44.6 (1980)
         48-49.
The "new Naval world" is "designed to lure both recruits and Congressional appropriations."

2297.   Scheinin, Richard. "Harry Zubkoff and His Pentagon
        Papers." WJR 7.3 (1985) 33-38.
    An account of the chief of the news Clipping and Analysis
Service at the Pentagon and its magazine Current News.

2298.   Schoenberger, Erica, and Amy Glasmeier. "Selling the
        MX: The Air Force Asks Nevada to Move Over." Prog
        44.5 (1980) 16-21.
    Teams of high-level Air Force officials are visiting Nevada
towns to advocate its proposed mobile MX missile system.

2299.   Schreiber, Mark E. "Civil Liberties in the Green
        Machine." CLR 3.2 (1976) 34-47.
    "There should be a ban on false or misleading recruitment
advertising."

2300.   Sedacca, Sandra and Robert DeGrasse. Star Wars:
        Questions and Answers on the Space Weapons Debate.
        Washington, D.C.: Common Cause, 1985. 36.
    The SDI television commercial is countered in this
presentation of the views of scientists who believe deployment
of a fully effective defense against nuclear weapons is
impossible, and efforts to build such a defense will only
accelerate the arms race.

2301.   The Shelter Hoax and Foreign Policy. New York:
        Marzani, 1961. 96.
    The essay by Carl Marzani, "The Shelter Hoax," denounces
the Pentagon's pamphlet "Fallout Protection, What to Know and Do
About Nuclear Attack," of which twenty-five million copies were
printed. The shelter program is part of the Pentagon's plan to
fight a nuclear war and a diversion from the achievement of
disarmament.

2302.   Smith, Myron, Jr., comp. "The Selling of the
        Pentagon." U.S. Television Network News. Jefferson,
        NC: McFarland, 1984. 32-35.
    Twenty-eight items on the CBS program based upon
Fulbright's The Pentagon Propaganda Machine.

2303.   Swomley, John. Press Agents of the Pentagon.
        Washington, D.C.: National Council Against
        Conscription, 1953. 55.
    "The growth of military influence and control over American
life and institutions which has developed since the Second World
War is in large part the result of an effective military 'public
relations' program." Separate chapters treat the growth, the
extent, the purpose (prepare public psychologically for war,
promote legislation, etc.), the techniques, and the content of
military publicity, and UMT as a case study in military
propaganda.

2303a.   Wolfe, Alan. "Defense Crisis at 'The Times.'" Na
        231.16 (1980) 503-06.

The New York Times front-page, seven-part series on military
"unpreparedness" was "a nonstory filled with Pentagon
propaganda."

V. C. Education and Research 2304-2317 (see II.E.3)

2304.   Bennett, James R. "Corporate and Government
          Domination of Education in the United States: A
          Bibliography." RT (forthcoming).
     Some forty items deal with education and the Pentagon.
Some of the books but none of the articles are repeated here.

2305.   Brick, Allan. The Campus Protest Against R.O.T.C.
          Philadelphia, PA: American Friends Service Committee,
          1960. 24.
     An attack upon compulsory ROTC, a critique of voluntary
ROTC, and a recommendation of alternative service instead of
ROTC for those who choose.

2306.   Butts, Nina. "Texas Universities Become Star Wars
          Boomtowns." TO 77.22 (1985) 11-12.
     Under the leadership of Hans Mark, Chancellor of the
University of Texas System, former secretary of the Air Force
and former deputy administrator of NASA, the University of
Texas is amassing "millions of dollars in Star Wars contracts."
"Outside the Reagan administration and the Pentagon, the main
defenders of Star Wars are the researchers who benefit from
SDI."

2307.   Fallows, James. "On Political Books." WM 15
          (Sept. 1983) 52-4.
     The author perceives an improvement in the explanation of
the military by journalists, and praises two new books--Andrew
Cockburn's The Threat and Fred Kaplan's The Wizards of
Armageddon.

2308.   Klare, Michael. The University-Military-Police-
          Complex: A Directory and Related Documents. New York:
          NACLA, 1970. 88.
     Klare calls the "nexus of university laboratories and
research institutes which constitute the military research
network" the "fourth armed service." Klare's Introduction
explains this fourth service. Part I gives a directory of
military research organizations. II a directory to chemical and
biological warfare research, III foreign affairs, and IV police
training. Klare summarizes the conflicts between "research and
education" 6-8.

2309.   Lane, Winthrop D. Military Training in Schools and
          Colleges of the United States. New York: Committee on
          Military Training, 1925. 31.
     A warning to Americans "to be on their guard against"
R.O.T.C. "becoming a means of militarizing America" and an
appeal for schools to provide "a positive education for peace."

Objects to military training in high schools and recommends voluntary military training in colleges.

2310.   Lepkowski, Wil. "The Chancellor Goes to Washington."
         Prog 45 (June 1981) 30.
    The issue is "whether the academic science community should mutely allow the military culture to seep further and further into the general social system."

2311.   Levine, Bruce. "Universities in the War Games."
         NP 6.3 (1967) 16-19.
    Decries the power of the Pentagon over universities through "purchasing power." "The university thus becomes an agent of the military not through conspiracy or cabal, but simply through the 'free play of the free market.'"

2312.   Long, Franklin A. "Government Dollars for University
         Reaserch." BAS 42.3 (1986) 45-49.
    A look at the escalation under the Reagan administration of government money for military research and development.

2313.   Nelkin, Dorothy. The University and Military
         Research: Moral Politics at M.I.T. Ithaca and
         London: Cornell U P, 1972. 195.
    An account of the student and faculty protest in 1969 against M.I.T.'s Instrumentation Laboratory, which in that year received $54.6 million from the Pentagon and NASA for design and development of enertial guidance systems. The protesters demanded the conversion of university technological resources to social rather than military objectives.

2314.   Rosenau, William. "The Warriors of Academe." Inq 5
         (Feb. 15, 1982) 13-15.
    American college presidents "turned into military camp whores every time the Pentagon announced a budget increase." "Unbiased analysis cannot be expected from the government or those who are hired by the government to perform research."

2315.   Swomley, John, Jr., ed. Militarism in Education.
         Washington, DC: National Council Against Conscription,
         1950. 80.
    "In recent months the nation's press has reported an increase in military activity and influence in our American educational institutions. This activity, represented by military subsidy of science departments, expanded military training units, increased use of schools and colleges as recruiting grounds and military propaganda directed toward students and faculty has serious implications both for the future of our nation and for world peace."

2316.   "The U/California Operation of the Lawrence Livermore
         and Los Alamos Scientific Laboratories." Science and
         Liberation. Ed. Rita Arditti, et al. Boston: South
         End, 1980. 93-112.

The supposed neutral and humane academic laboratories are responsible for the conception, design, and testing of every nuclear warhead in the U.S. arsenal.

2317.   "War Research Returns to Campus." D&S 79
         (September 1982) 12-13.
Government-sponsored grants to universities for military research have increased greatly, as have other aspects of on-campus military spending, such as ROTC scholarships. This military emphasis has limited university research on more domestic problems, such as solar energy.

V. D. Secrecy, Censorship, Disinformation, Cover-Up 2318-2381

2318.   Adler, Allan. "Unclassified Secrets." BAS 41.3
         (1985) 26-8.
"Two laws which blur the line between classified and unclassified information have been enacted with little public debate. The statutes could severely limit public information about problems" in the Pentagon and the Department of Energy.

2319.   Alderman, Jeffrey. "The Army Way: News Management
         at Fort Hood." CJR 7.4 (1968-69) 22-24.
The burning of 12,000 copies of the post newspaper at Fort Hood, Texas, is "symptomatic of the kind of unhealthy news management carried on, not only by the Army, but by cooperative community publishers." A remedy for the censorship is a strict application of the 1967 Freedom of Information law.

2320.   Aldridge, Robert. "First Strike: The Pentagon's
         Secret Strategy." Prog 42.5 (1978) 16-19.
US nuclear policy is not deterrence, as is claimed by the Pentagon and the government, but "counterforce" against military sites such as missile silos. "Concealment of this first-strike strategy may be the greatest hoax ever perpetrated against the American people."

2321.   "America's Secret Soldiers: The Buildup of U.S.
         Special Operations Forces." DM 14.2 (1985) 1-16.
"Unlike the CIA's covert operations, the Pentagon is not required to report details of SOF activities to Congress. Special Operations Forces could be used in clandestine activities to evade Congressional oversight and circumvent law." "A Uniformed CIA? 'There's a real danger these Special Forces could be used by CIA programs and thus skirt Congressional review.'"

2322.   Anderson, Marion. Neither Jobs Nor Security:
         Women's Unemployment and the Pentagon Budget.
         Lansing, MI: Employment Research Associates, 1982.
The Pentagon and the Reagan administration claimed employment advantages, but the 1980 military budget cost the jobs of more than 1,280,000 women nationwide. Jobs for men were lost too, but not as severely.

2323.   Arkin, William.   "Waging Secrecy."   BAS 41.3
         (1985) 5-6.
    The Pentagon's information "warfighters" "hide their own
secrets to buttress or protect their policies and forestall
embarrassments."

2324.   Bennett, John.   "Good and Bad News About
         Whistleblowers."   Pr 10.4 (Aug. 1982) 5-6.
    The good news is the return of Pentagon whistleblower A.
Ernest Fitzgerald, who was fired 13 years ago. The bad news is
that the President's Council on Integrity and Efficiency "is
something of a fraud itself."

2325.   Bennett, Jonathan.   "Shuttle Cover-Up Explodes."
         Guard 39.7 (1986) 1,5.
    The shuttle program is being increasingly militarized.

2326.   "Bombs, Bunkers, and Blind Justice."   Prog 46.2
         (1982) 10-11.
    The US Supreme Court supports a presidential executive
order requiring secrecy of locations of nuclear weapons, against
Hawaiians who sued the US Navy to require it to draw up an
environmental impact statement on its weapons storage depot.

2327.   Bradley Vehicle: Concerns About the Army's
         Vulnerability Testing. Washington, DC: GAO,
         February 1986.   1-10.
    A report to the Committee on Governmental Affairs, U.S.
Senate, disclosing the Army's cover-up of the vehicle's
battlefield vulnerability. For example, "the Army avoided, in
almost all cases, shots that could have directly penetrated
stowed ammunition which it knew" could cause "catastrophic
losses" (2).

2328. Bram, Steven.   "Cruise Missile Crashes in Canada,
         A Crashing Bore to U.S. Press."   Dead 1.2 (1986) 6-7.
    US media neglected the important story of the
malfunctioning of a US cruise missile in Canada.

2329.   Burchett, Wilfred.   Shadows of Hiroshima.   London:
         Verso, 1983.   123.
    One of the first Westerners to enter the city after the
atomic blast, Burchett reveals details of the attempts by the
US army and government to suppress the effects of the blast,
the pressure to silence him through deportation from Japan,
McArthur's censorship and destruction of a 100-page report on
Nagasaki. He found "a pattern of news suppression on a vast
scale and in a monstrous cause" (45).

2330.   "Concern Expressed Over Leak."   AG (April 23, 1985)
         6A.
    After Grenada the Pentagon agreed to allow a preselected
pool of newsmen to accompany them in future activities. The
secret maneuvers in Honduras, "Universal Trek, '85," was revealed

by the Washington Post, not part of the pool.

2331.   The Costs and Consequence of Reagan's Military
          Buildup. New York: The Council on Economic Priorities.
          1982.
     The militarization of the economy will slow growth, damage
civilian industries, fail to improve employment, etc., contrary
to reassuring administration claims.

2332.   Diamond, Edwin. "The Atrocity Papers." ChJR 3.8
          (1970) 3-4, 12-14.
     Pressure upon CBS by the Pentagon illustrated by copies of
correspondence.

2333.   Dillon, Jay. "The 'Underwater Satellite' Comes
          Ashore." Prog 44.3 (1980) 41-45.
     Secret breeder reactor research by Westinghouse Corporation
under the supervision of Admiral Hyman Rickover and his Naval
Reactors Branch.

2334.   Drogin, Bob. "Deaths at Fort Jackson." Prog 42.10
          (1978) 51.
     The Army's response to the outcry over the deaths of two
recruits involved "conflicting stories and a lid of secrecy."

2335.   Fuller, John. The Day We Bombed Utah: America's
          Most Lethal Secret. New York: NAL, 1984. 183.
     An account of atomic bomb tests conducted by the Atomic
Energy Commission in Southwestern Utah and Eastern Nevada, of
test errors, death of thousands of sheep, rise in cancer victims
throughout the area, and government cover-up.

2336.   Gollon, Peter J. "SDI Funds Costly for Scientists."
          BAS 42.1 (1986) 24-27.
     Part of the price to be paid by institutions accepting Star
Wars research money will be "an increase in secrecy and
dissimulation--hardly what we have come to expect at our best
scientific institutions, and not the qualities which have
contributed to their present excellence."

2337.   Goulding, Phil. Confirm or Deny: Informing the
          People on National Security. New York: Harper, 1970.
          369.
     This ex-Assistant Secretary of Defense for Public Affairs
recounts several crises of "misadventures in national security"
and asserts the need for improvement of internal reporting and
investigation in the Pentagon, and praises an "agressive press"
as "the most effective single checkrein on an arrogant
government."

2338.   Grambart, James. "The Stealth 'Secret.'" Prog 44.12
          (1980) 34-36.
     "The program is being kept under wraps not to protect
national security but to protect what promises to be a multi-

billion-dollar windfall for the aerospace industry.

2339.   Hersh, Seymour. _Cover-Up_. New York: Random, 1972.
         305.
    An examination of the army's secret investigation of the
massacre at My Lai 4 during the Vietnam War, called the Peers
Report. Not only the abuses which occurred in the process of
the cover-up of the massacre are the subject of this book, but
also the army system which made them possible.

2340.   Hersh, Seymour. _My Lai 4: A Report on the Massacre_
         and its Aftermath. New York: Random House, 1970.   210.
    Ch. 7 gives an account of "The Cover-Up," Chs. 8 and 9
"The Uncovering," and Ch. 10 offers an illuminating account of
how and why the story broke so slowly in "the Press."

2341.   _Internal Controls: Defense's Use of Emergency and_
         Extraordinary Funds. Washington, DC: GAO, 1986.   11.
    E&E funds, $25 million in 1985, are for entertaining guests
or for confidential intelligence activities. "The Office of the
Secretary of Defense (OSD) lacks a vital control over E&E funds
used for confidential expenditures," regarding "how such funds
may be used" and whether they may be used "in violation of law."

2342.   Irons, Peter. _Justice at War_. New York: Oxford
         U P, 1984.   407.
    On the relocation of 110,000 Americans of Japanese descent
from the West Coast in 1942. Government officials withheld from
the Supreme Court the fact that the FBI and the FCC had found no
evidence to support the War Department claims of widespread
Japanese-American espionage and sabotage.

2343.   Kaplan, Fred. "Weinberger Paints the Defense Budget
         With an Expressionist's Brush." _AG_ (February 11, 1986)
         11A.
    Weinberger lied when he claimed that his defense budget for
fiscal year 1987 "provides 3 percent real growth." The real
growth is 8.5 percent. The author gives other examples of the
Secretary's distortion of reality.

2344.   Kowet, Don. _A Matter of Honor: General William C._
         Westmoreland versus CBS. New York: Macmillan, 1984.
         317.
    An attack on the CBS television exposé of an alleged
conspiracy by the US military in 1968 to underestimate the
numbers of enemy troops in Vietnam, entitled _The Uncounted_
Enemy: A Vietnam Deception. [The film did not substantiate the
suggestion that the army tried to deceive the President and the
public deliberately, but it did show lying by the military.]
Rev. _CJR_ (July-Aug. 1984) 50-52: Kowet committed "the same
journalistic misdemeanors for which he faulted the producer" of
the film.

2345.   Ladd, Bruce. _Crisis in Credibility_. New York:

NAL, 1968. 247.
"This book grew out of a concern for the people's right to
know about their national government. . . .It deals exclusively
with three practices of the executive branch--secrecy, lying,
and news management." Ch. 7, "The Pentagon," discusses mainly
the secrecy and news management perpetrated by Secretary
McNamara and his information chief, Arthur Sylvester. "The
military must never be taken for granted and never be considered
too complicated for public inspection."

2346.   Landau, Fred. "Nuclear Nevada." Prog 44.2 (1980)
         28-30.
Secrecy and lethality in bomb testing.

2347.   Lapp, Ralph. Kill and Overkill--The Strategy of
         Annihilation. New York: Basic, 1962. 197.
The arms race is also fueled by excessive secrecy, which
denies citizens the information it needs for participation in
decision-making.

2348.   Lech, Raymond B. All the Drowned Sailors.
         Briarcliff Manor, NY: Stein, 1982. 309.
The U.S.S. Indianapolis was sunk on July 30, 1945, with
great loss of life. This is an account of the sinking, the
search, the inquiry, and the court martial, and "a massive
cover-up that lasted for over thirty years."

2349.   Lemann, Nicholas. "Defense Budget Games." NR
         192.5 (1985) 16-18.
How the Pentagon successfully defends its budget through
distortion of information and outright fabrications. The
"defense" budget is "best understood" as "a self-referential
document."

2350.   Lens, Sidney. "But Can We Trust the Russians?"
         Prog 44.7 (1980) 19-20.
Each year the Pentagon uses an alleged Soviet "threat" to
boost its budget.

2351.   Lens, Sidney. The Day Before Doomsday. An Anatomy
         of the Nuclear Arms Race. New York: Doubleday, 1977.
         274.
The arms race derives from technology, vested interests,
anticommunism, etc., and myths which have been promoted by the
Pentagon and government. One of the myths is that the US
would never strike first, yet the Pentagon has for many years
been planning the first-strike destruction of Soviet weapons.
The book confronts this and other myths employed to sustain and
enlarge US power.

2352.   Lytle, Stewart. "Did the "Titanic" Sink Government
         Movie Censors?" Pr 8.8 (1980) 6.
How a British film company circumvented State
Department/Navy requests for a different ending to the film

"Raise the Titanic."

2353.   Lytle, Stewart. "The Military Cultivates Its
         Hollywood Connection." Pr 8.6 (1980) 9.
    "When it comes to making war movies, the Pentagon is in the
catbird seat"--refusing scripts it does not like, refusing use
of ships, airplanes or men, and demanding rewriting of scripts.

2354.   Marchino, Michael. "No Place to Hide." Prog 42.4
         (1978) 27.
    Military-industrial complex propaganda regarding surviving
a nuclear war through civil defense is completely misleading.

2355.   McGrory, Mary. "Pentagon Lacking in Smarts,
         Subtlety." AG (August 8, 1985) 19A.
    Criticism of the Pentagon's treatment of its critics--
Representative John Dingell and A. Ernest Fitzgerald, "the most
famous whistleblower in government."

2356.   Nelson, Lars-Erik. "Critics of Gun Smeared." AG
         (Sept. 5, 1985) 15A.
    Testing of the $1.5 billion Sgt. York antiaircraft gun was
faked to make the weapon look good on film. The whistleblowers
in the Pentagon are likely to be purged.

2357.   Norris, Robert, Thomas Cochran, and William Arkin.
         "History of the Nuclear Stockpile." BAS 41
         (Aug. 1985) 106-109.
    "The largely secret history of nuclear warhead production"
reveals "that an astounding array of weapons has been created
for every conceivable purpose by a gigantic, self-perpetuation
system."

2358.   Park, Robert. "Intimidation Leads to Self-censorship
         in Science." BAS 41 (March 1985) 22-25.
    "Bowing to pressure from federal authorities and individual
scientists" under contract to the Pentagon, "universities and
scientific groups are beginning to close the doors to their own
conferences."

2359.   Parnas, David. "Why I Quit Star Wars." CC 12.3
         (1986) 32-35.
    After joining the Strategic Defense Initiative program, the
author concluded that a shield against missiles was impossible
and that the program would only speed up the arms race. He also
disapproves of the way Star Wars is being sold to the public:
"some of the statements made by SDI supporters seem designed to
mislead the public."

2360.   "Pentagon Links Change in Script, Eastwood Aid."
         AG (May 26, 1986) 6A.
    "Filmmakers rely on Pentagon approval for movies about the
military, mostly because it owns the props that add to realism."

390

2361.   Peterson, Ted and Jay W. Jensen. "The Case of General
    Yamashita: A Study of Suppression." JQ 28 (Spring 1951)
    196-204.
    In 1946, Tomoyuki Yamashita, the "conqueror of Singapore"
and "Tiger of Malaya," was hanged by the US Army. One of the men
who had defended Yamashita, Capt. A. Frank Reel, believed the
Japanese general had been unjustly accused and executed and wrote
a book about the case. This article describes how Capt. Reel's
book was suppressed by the military in both the US and in Japan.

2362.   Piller, Charles. "Test Site for Germ Warfare?"
    Na 240 (March 9, 1985) 270-73.
    The Army's past and present secret experiments with
biological warfare at the Dugway Proving Ground, now pushed
forward by the Reagan administration's exaggeration of Soviet
threats.

2363.   Proceeding Against Frank Stanton and the Columbia
    Broadcasting System, Inc.: Report. 92nd Congress,
    1st Session, Washington, DC: GPO, 1971. 272.
    The refusal of CBS to produce materials relating to its
Pentagon documentary, "The Selling of the Pentagon," places it
and its president in contempt of Congress.

2364.   Rhea, John. "Big, BIG Ideas at the Pentagon." Prog
    41.4 (1977) 13-18.
    The military's Selected Acquisition Report (SAR) intended
to keep Congress informed of the Pentagon's future spending
plans fails to include many projects under way. People and
contractors are already working on the details of weapons not
approved by Congress.

2365.   Rosenberg, Howard. "The Guinea Pigs of Camp Desert
    Rock." Prog 43.6 (1979) 37-43.
    A history of the exposure of military personnel and
civilians to radiation during 192 nuclear bomb tests between
1946 and the atmospheric test ban treaty of 1963. Some of these
people have died or are ill from cancer, yet the Pentagon and
the government have obstructed investigation and assistance to
the ill.

2366.   Sanders, Jerry. "Aloha: Surf and Turf Maneuvers."
    Prog 46.8 (1982) 44-46.
    Military "community relations" tactics in Hawaii, backed by
the courts, are designed to check the anti-nuclear movement by
repressing dissent. "People are coming to see that, in the name
of defense and security, they are being held hostage by their
own militarized governments."

2367.   Schwartz, Berl. "The Military Quietly Abandoned an
    Independent Assessment." Pr 7 (July 27, 1979) 5.
    The Pentagon closed the office it had established to
provide independent assessments of proposed weapons systems
reportedly because it gave negative assessments to proposed

weapons systems developed by the military.

2368.   "Science and Secrecy." BAS 41 (March 1985).
Four articles on the muzzling of military scientific
information, by William Arkin, Robert Park, Allan Adler, and
Melvyn Nathanson.

2369.   "Secrets in Space." Prog 49 (February 1985) 10.
The attempt by the Pentagon to restrict news coverage of
the military space shuttle mission in December, 1984. "Most
ominous of all is the new thrust toward secrecy in the space
program--part of a persistent effort to persuade the mass media
and the American people that more and more Government
information ought to be placed off limits on grounds of 'national
security.'"

2370.   Smith, F. Leslie. "CBS Reports: The Selling of the
         Pentagon." Mass News. Ed. David Leroy and
         Christopher Sterling. Englewood Cliffs, NJ:
         Prentice, 1973. 200-210.
An account of unsuccessful congressional efforts to punish
CBS with a contempt citation for its program on the "massive
public relations and promotional activities" of the Pentagon.

2371.   Steinert, Sylvia. "AP Carrier Pigeon." Dead
         (March-April 1986) 6.
Pentagon Secretary Weinberger's "alarms" over the new
Soviet aircraft carrier were "swallowed whole" by the military
writer for the Associated Press.

2372.   Stone, Peter. "The Special Forces in 'Covert
         Action.'" Na 239.1 (1984) 8-12.
Increasing Pentagon/CIA cooperation in counterinsurgency
operations.

2373.   Subpoenaed Material RE Certain TV News Documentary
         Programs. Committee on Interstate and Foreign Commerce,
HR, 92nd Cong., First Session. Washington, DC. 373.
On April 7, 1971, this subcommittee ordered that certain
subpoenas be served on the CBS and NBC networks and Wolper
Productions Inc. in regard to the CBS program The Selling of
the Pentagon. The purpose of this meeting was to receive the
materials subpoenaed.

2374.   Suid, Larry. "Carter Nixes Coppola Aid." MORE
         7.7 & 8 (1977) 6.
The Pentagon refused assistance to Francis Ford Coppola for
his film Apocalypse Now because they disliked the plot.

2375.   "Thar She Blows." Prog 46.3 (1982) 10-11.
Navy secrecy surrounding use of LX09, the explosive
Poseidon warhead trigger, until three workers were accidentally
killed by one.

2376.   "Verification: Data Used to Scare Can Serve to
          Protect." NMPN (Spring 1985) n.p.
The Pentagon reports a Soviet arms buildup based upon
apparently thorough inside knowledge of their weapons
development, but the Pentagon also resists arms control or
disarmament on the basis of lack of assurance about Soviet
compliance.

2377.   Wagman, Robert J. "The Navy's Call For The Draft Is
          Based On False Figures." Pr 7.6 (1980) 12.
"The various branches of the U.S. Armed Services have been
substantially overstating the problems they have been having
recruiting . . . and no where is this more true than in the
Navy."

2378.   "Whopper: Here or to Go?" NT 4.5 (1986) 6-7.
The Pentagon "has apparently decided to make
misrepresentation official policy" by its disinformation
campaign purportedly designed not to mislead Congress "but
rather to stop the flow of technical data to the Soviet Union."

2379.   Witcover, Jules. "Surliest Crew in Washington."
          CJR 4.1 (1965) 11-15.
Pentagon news reporters must dodge secrecy and suppression of
information by public information officers.

2380.   Wood, David. "Pentagon Newspeak: Future War with Bit
          of Jabberwocky." QRD 8.3 (1982) 7-8.
The Pentagon uses euphemisms "to mask from the public, and
from the military itself, the unimaginable destructive power of
missiles."

2381.   Zuckerman, Solly, Sir. Scientists and War: The
          Impact of Science on Military and Civil Affairs.
          New York: Harper, 1967. 177.
Scientific studies of more socially beneficial impact take
place primarily in laboratories in which information is freely
shared and "work is exposed to the full blaze of scientific
criticism." "If basic science must be pursued in government
laboratories" leading to weapons, it should become "part of the
open world of science."

VI. INTELLIGENCE AGENCIES 2382-2768

Introduction

A. The Apparatuses 2382-2512

B. Federal Bureau of Investigation 2513-2596

C. CIA 2597-2761

D. National Security Agency 2762-2768

INTELLIGENCE AGENCIES

INTRODUCTION

The Apparatuses

William Shannon believes that "when it comes to plotting
assassinations, subverting governments, and spreading propaganda,
Americans are not at their best." The Soviet Union, he says, is
better at it, more efficient. That is, some of the covert
behavior by our intelligence agencies becomes public.

We must begin with the history of secrecy in the US since
1945, for secrecy is the necessary condition of deceit and violence. "Secrecy," states a 1971 report by the Library of Congress, "has been a factor in making foreign policy since the
first days of the nation's history," but "since World War II" it
has increased tremendously: nuclear testing from July 16, 1945,
to the present, the Atomic Energy Act of 1946, National Security
Council 68 (the Cold War manifesto kept secret from 1950 to
1975), Eisenhower's Executive Order 10501 authorizing thirty
agencies and departments to classify documents (Lens), etc. And
most of all the secret illegalities of the intelligence agencies
"beyond the law and the constitution" (Berman and Halperin): the
FBI harassing Martin Luther King, Jr., spying on thousands of
dissidents at home, breaking into homes and offices, the CIA subverting Italian electoral affairs and supporting the overthrow of
the governments of Iran, Guatemala, the Dominican Republic, and
Chile, the secret wars in Lao and Cambodia and invasion of Grenada. In 1976 the U.S. House of Representatives Pike Committee
and the Senate Church Committee revealed that the CIA and the FBI
engaged in subversion, terror, violence, and disruption of democratic processes at home and abroad, and that these activities
were systematically organized at the highest levels of state.
And the reports were partly censored and did not deal with "the
most sordid programmes" (Chomsky). "It is now clear that the
same lawlessness that has characterized America's foreign policy
has come home and threatens the country's political process"
(Halperin, et al.).

What was the purpose of these covert operations? In the
opinion of the contributors to this section of the bibliography,
the purpose was less national security and protection from the
Soviets, and more to hide "illegal or immoral acts" by the
national security state--the CIA, FBI, NSA, NSC, DIA, LEAA, military intelligence, etc. (there were about seventy agencies with
intelligence functions in 1976). These acts are being kept
secret from the public, "who might be outraged if they knew about
them" (Lens).

Have intelligence abuses been restrained since the Pike and
Church reports? "Despite the shock of the revelations, the
machinery continues to grind on," and the people are unaware
(Cowan, et al.). I have concentrated my selections on recent
years, 1979 to the present, to indicate the persistence and even
worsening of the old problems.

Remedies

Halperin et al. spend all of Ch. 12 on "Designing Effective Reforms": 1) end clandestine government, 2) legislate to make abuses clearly illegal and laws definitely enforcable, 3) establish legislative charters, 4) enforce the laws. Castelli and many others urge the curbing of presidential Executive Orders (which created so much of the secrecy system). Burnham would prohibit absolutely surveillance and data-keeping on people for political purposes; Seattle has already placed strict controls over political information gathering. Morgan would revoke all sedition laws. Contributors to this section of the bibliography feel a special urgency over the need to restrain the ever-growing machinery for repressing dissent at home and for advancing US interests abroad regardless of Constitution or laws. Halperin et al. observe (1976) that "a few patchwork elements of reform have been put into effect." In 1979 the process of removing the patches began and continues today.

A glance at Athan Theoharis' notes and bibliography in Spying on Americans reveals how much more evidence of intelligence illegalities and usurpations is available than may be found in this bibliography. Yet it should not be forgotten that all of the published evidence still represents only the tip of the iceberg of abuse.

Works Cited

Chomsky, Noam. "The Secret Terror Organizations of the U.S. Government." Radical Priorities. 2nd rev. ed. Montreal: Black Rose, 1981. 169-172.

Lens, Sidney. "The Secrecy Mill." Inq 6.12 (1983) 14-16.

Shannon, William. "U.S. Isn't Suited for Disinformation Game." AG (October 13, 1986) 13A.

NATIONAL SECURITY INTELLIGENCE BUREAUCRACY

Presidential
A. White House and Executive Agencies
    1. National Security Council
    2. Central Intelligence Agency
    3. Foreign Intelligence Advisory Board
    4. Intelligence Oversight Board
B. Departments
    1. State
       Intelligence and Research
    2. Pentagon
       a. National Security Agency
       b. Defense Intelligence Agency
       c. Intelligence Oversight
       d. Command, Control, Communications and Intelligence
    3. Army Intelligence
    4. Naval Intelligence
    5. Air Force Intelligence
    6. Justice Department
       Federal Bureau of Investigation

Congressional
A. Senate
    1. Governmental Affairs Committee (NSC)
    2. Armed Services Committee (military intelligence)
    3. Select Committee on Intelligence (NSA, CIA, DIA, etc.)
B. House of Representatives
    1. Armed Services Committee (military)
    2. Foreign Affairs Committee (foreign military intelli-
       gence)
    3. Government Operations Committee (Pentagon, CIA, FEMA)
    4. Permanent Select Committee on Intelligence (NSA, CIA,
       DIA, etc.)

"The clandestine bureaus are the true progeny of the postwar presidency, tracing their legal birthright not to legislation but to presidential assertions of 'inherent power'" (Halperin, et al. 220).

VI.   Intelligence Agencies

VI.   A.   The Apparatuses   2382-2512

2382.   Bennett, James R.   "The Agencies of Secrecy." NaR
        9.3-4 (1986) 41-47.
     One hundred and forty-three books and articles. Most of
these items are not included in the following list. [Also see
I.]

2383.   Arisian, Khoren.   "Inside Look at American History."
        Chm 199 (February 1985) 6-8.
     "The administration's drive to wrap an ever larger cloak of
secrecy around the activities of our several intelligence
agencies is part and parcel of its itch for military showdowns
wherever possible. . . .What the Reaganites want is an
uninformed, gullible, politically inert citizenry."

2384.   Berman, Jerry J., and Morton H. Halperin, eds.
        The Abuses of the Intelligence Agencies. Washington,
        DC: Center for National Security Studies, 1975. 185.
     "This report is an effort to inform the public about the
abuses of power committed by the Intelligence Agencies of the
United States Government in the name of national security. It
brings together the facts about the intelligence and
counterintelligence activities of the CIA, FBI, IRS, NSA,
Secret Service, and Military Intelligence directed against
American citizens and covert actions against foreign
governments."

2385.   Bird, Kai, and Max Holland.   "Secret Computer Czar."
        Na 241.17 (1985) 544.
     President Reagan's National Security Decision Directive
145 is a "step closer to the Official Secrets Act" his
administration "has always lusted after."

2386.   Blitt, Connie, and Dennis Bernstein.   "Sanctuary
        Churches Sue U.S. for Bugging Worship Services."
        ITT 10.10 (1986) 9.
     INS infiltration of churches in opposition to sanctuary for
Guatemalan and El Salvadoran refugees.

2387.   Blum, Richard H., ed.   Surveillance and Espionage
        in a Free Society: A Report by the Planning Group on
        Intelligence and Security to the Policy Council of the
        Democratic National Committee. New York: Praeger,
        1972. 319.
     "There are features of our present security and
intelligence system which are quite evidently ill-used,
misdirected, or otherwise mal-developing." Ch. 11, "Friend or
Foe: The Fourth Estate and the Intellignece Community,"
summarizes encroachments of intelligence agencies over the press
and makes several recommendations for a stronger free press:
strengthening the Freedom of Information Act; cancellation of

injunction power of courts to forbid publication except where
clear and present danger to the national security exists;
absolute prohibition of agents to masquerade as journalists;
national legislation guaranteeing a reporter's right to refuse to
disclose confidences.

2388.   Cancelled.

2389.   Borosage, Robert L. "What to Do with the
         Intelligence Agencies." WP 4.4 (Winter 1977) 38-45.
    "In varying degrees, all of the military and civilian
organizations that make up [America'a national security]
apparatus cloak their operations in secrecy, obscure their
purposes with rhetoric, and are controlled only by executive
order or bureaucratic inertia rather than by legislation."

2390.   Brandt, Daniel. "Everyone You Need To Know." NaR 9
         (Winter 1986) 27-40.
    A cumulative name index to all of the past volumes of The
National Reporter/Counterspy.

2391.   Brooks, Julie. "The Name Might Be Changed, But Only
         to Protect the Guilty." SD 4.1 (1977) 21.
    Congressman MacDonald has "shared files on liberals and
radicals with police, the FBI, IRS, and CIA officials for the
past seven years."

2392.   Burkholder, Steve.   "The War on Open Government."
         Prog 44.4 (1980) 10.
    Further attacks on the FOIA.

2393.   Burnham, David. "Tales of a Computer State."
         Na 236.17 (1983) 527, 537-541.
    "Computerized surveillance" by government and industry "is
a largely unacknowledged reality of American life." During the
1960s the Army collected data on about 100,000 potentially
"subversive" citizens and created "blacklists of organizations
and personalities." The FBI has easy access to industry
records, such as those collected by car rental and credit
companies. "Can the United States continue to flourish when the
physical movements, the buyings habits and the conversations of
most citizens are under surveillance"?

2394.   Callen, Earl. "A Freedom-of-Information-Act Fable:
         What's In a Name File?" CLR 3.2 (1976) 58-66.
    Callen comes out of the closet and discusses his work for
the NSA and his attempt to obtain information amassed by
intelligence agencies on his work.

2395.   Castelli, Jim. "Protecting Civil Liberties."
         Prog 42.4 (1978) 11-12.
    President Carter's recent Executive Order regarding
surveillance of US citizens by intelligence agencies grants
"sweeping authority" to the agencies and only "amorphous

checks." "The broad discretion enjoyed by the Executive in
these matters must be curbed."

2396.   Churchill, Mae. "LEAA: Mission Accomplished."
         Prog 44.11 (1980) 20.
The ending of the Law Enforcement Assistance Administration
was desirable because it was "militarizing" the police.

2397.   "The C.I.A., the F.B.I., and the Media: Excerpts
         from the Senate Report on Intelligence Activities."
         CJR 15.2 (1976) 37-42.
Specific instances are provided of the intelligence
agencies using the media to influence public opinion.

2398.   Cockburn, Alexander. "The Second Time As Tragedy."
         Na 240.23 (1985) 726.
The CIA engineered the overthrow of the Guatemalan
government and now with the NSA and the Pentagon has made plans
for the overthrow of the Nicaraguan government.

2399.   "The Core of the Crisis." Na 243.20 (1986) 658-61.
    The Reagan Administration has developed a "system of covert
operations" and "shady deals." There are at least fifty CIA
covert-ops around the world.

2400.   "Covert Actions in an Open Society - the Persistent
         Issue." CM 18.4 (1985) 10-24.
    A dialogue among journalists, scholars, and government
officials.

2401.   Cowan, Paul, Nick Egleson, and Nat Hentoff. State
         Secrets: Police Surveillance in America. New York:
         Holt, 1974. 333.
Federal and local police are invading the privacy of
citizens and eroding First Amendment rights.

2402.   "Curbing Police Spies." Prog 44.1 (1980) 8.
    Local police in various cities have instituted intelligence
units. Seattle is the first city to pass legislation placing
strict controls on police powers to gather political
information.

2403.   Davis, William J. "Schemes and Devices:
         Surveillance." Soj 15.2 (1986) 16-19.
Discusses wide variety of surveillance techniques.

2404.   "Defend Your Political Rights: Stop FBI Crimes."
         Political Rights Defense Fund, 1981.
    A pamphlet sponsored by many prominent citizens and groups
in support of a suit against the FBI, CIA, Immigration and
Naturalization Service, and other government agencies for
violating the rights of the Socialist Workers Party and Young
Socialist Alliance and their members.

2405.   Dennis, Elissa. "Are the Plumbers Back?: Cambridge,
     Massachusetts." Prog 50.9 (1986) 17.
     Offices of groups opposing Reagan administration policies
in Central America have been broken into since 1984.   The groups
suspect intimidation as the motive.

2406.   Dobrin, Arthur. "An American Prisoner of Conscience:
     the Saga of Martin Sostre." Prog 44.5 (1980) 35-39.
     Sostre is a "political prisoner," an "American prisoner of
conscience."

2407.   Donner, Frank J. The Age of Surveillance: The Aims
     and Methods of America's Political Intelligence System.
     New York: Knopf, 1980. 554.
     "None of the manifold excesses of the past can compare in
scope and intensity with the secret war waged continuously for
over fifty years against all shades of dissenting politics by
the domestic intelligence community, a virtually autonomous
network of executive agencies dominated by the Federal Bureau
of Investigation and supported and protected by a powerful
congressional constituency."

2408.   Donner, Frank. "Electronic Surveillance: The
     National Security Game." CLR 2.3 (1975) 15-47.
     "It is the very pervasiveness of the fear of electronic
surveillance that makes it such an efficient instrument of
intimidation." "For more than three decades, dissenting and
radical political groups in this country have been monitored not
only by informers from within, but by tappers and buggers from
without."   A history of the conflict between officials who wish
to monitor citizens and those who wish to preserve rights
protected by the Fourth Amendment.

2409.   Donner, Frank. The Legacy of Haymarket: A History of
     Political Repression by Police in Urban America.
     (forthcoming).

2410.   Donner, Frank. "Travelers' Warning for Nicaragua."
     Na 241 (July 6/13, 1985) 13-17.
     "The Reagan Administration is using domestic surveillance
techniques to intimidate dissenters against its Central America
policies and to collect intelligence that would be useful in a
military intervention in Nicaragua."

2411.   Dorfman, Ron. "Watching the Watchers." ChJR 4.1
     (1971) 3-6.
     An argument for ending "political surveillance by police
forces" and "the imposture of newsmen by undercover cops."

2412.   Epstein, Edward Jay. Agency of Fear: Opiates and
     Political Power in America. New York: Putnam's, 1977.
     261.
     A study of former President Nixon's installation of "a
series of new offices" such as the Office of Drug Abuse Law

Enforcement and the Office of National Narcotics Intelligence
which he hoped "would provide him with investigative agencies
having the potential and the wherewithal and personnel to assume
the functions of 'the Plumbers' on a far grander scale." Nixon
"methodically moved" through these agencies "to destroy the
informal system of leaks and independent [government agency]
fiefdoms" in what amounted to an attempt to achieve a coup
d'etat. In his "war on heroin" Nixon tried "to gain control
over all the levers of real power in the government, then
legitimize the new configuration under the name of eliminating
some great evil in society." Ch. 20 deals with "The
Manipulation of the Media."

2413.   "Equal Protection." Na 232.19 (1981) 588.
     INS plans to deport noncitizen members of the Socialist
Workers Party during the trial of SWP's $40 million suit against
the government is "a dangerous and cynical attempt to justify
forty years of illegal harassment and surveillance of a lawful
political organization."

2414.   Flaherty, Francis. "Open Season on Privacy."
     Prog 48.4 (1984) 22-25.
     Electronic surveillance endangers civil liberties.

2415.   Foreign and Military Intelligence: Final Report,
     Book I. United States Senate, Select Committee to Study
     Governmental Operations with Respect to Intellignence
     Activities. 94th Congress, 2nd Session. Washington:
     U.S. GPO, 1976. 651. [See No. 2438.]
     "Intended to provide . . . the basic information about the
intelligence agencies of the United States required to make the
necessary judgments concerning the role such agencies should
play in the future." Also see Book IV, Supplementary Detailed
Staff Reports on Foreign And Military Intelligence.

2416.   French, Scott R. The Big Bother Game. San Francisco:
     Gnu, 1975. 237.
     "Some days I tend to view the whole government, FBI, CIA,
police included, as no better than a huge block to keep the
people in power IN POWER, and on other days I feel like rushing
to help any of the above villains shoot some son-of-a-bitch that
has ripped me off." Ch. on "electronic surveillance,"
"telephone surveillance," "locks," "optics," "files," etc.

2417.   Garrison, Omar V. Spy Government: The Emerging
     Police State in America. New York: Stuart, 1967. 277.
     "A host" of "federal, state and local agencies are engaged
in a massive intrusion into the privacy of the individual
citizen." The instances of "clandestine surveillance,
intimidation and entrapment recounted in the following pages
happen to people like you and me every day of every year. The
fact of innocence is no safeguard."

2418.   Gelbspan, Ross. "Computers Bring '1984' Closer."

AG (Dec. 15, 1985) 1c,7c.
Record systems used for law enforcement, investigative or
intelligence purposes "currently contain 288 million records on
114 million people. That represents half the population of the
United States. And the figure does not include data held by the
Central Intelligence, Defense Intelligence and National Security
Agencies."

2419.   Goodman, James. "A Politician Called Smith."
         Na 234.14 (1982) 429-31.
Attorney General William French Smith is doing everything
he can to further President Reagan's desire to deny information
to the public, to increase censorship, and to enlarge the
imperial presidency.

2420.   "Gumshoes, Inc." Prog 43.9 (1979) 9-10.
Police threats to political liberty "are even more
widespread" than "in 1976."

2421.   Halperin, Morton, et al. The Lawless State:
         The Crimes of the U. S. Intelligence Agencies.
         Harmondsworth, Eng.: Penguin, 1976. 328.
"For the past four years, the crimes and abuses of the
secret realm of government [CIA, FBI, military intelligence
agencies, NSA, IRS] have been unearthed, in fascinating and
finally numbing detail." They operate "in secrecy at home and
abroad, beyond the normal view of citizen, judge, or public
official" (1). Twelve chs. divided into four parts: "The CIA
Abroad," "The FBI at Home," "The Other Agencies at Home," and
"Controlling the Intelligence Agencies."

2422.   Halperin, Morton. "We Need New Intelligence
         Charters." CM 18.3 (1985) 51-54.
"Almost always" abuse of power and violations of civil
liberties "come from Presidents seeking to use intelligence
agencies and police forces." It is therefore necessary to
design laws to restrain electronic surveillance, illegal
searches and seizure, denial of visas, etc.

2423.   Harger, Richard. The Scourge of Secrecy: A Personal
         Testimony and Appeal. Jackson, MS: Gordy, 1980. 218.
This former Air Force Intelligence officer analyzes
attempts to stifle dissent, disrupt the anti-war movement, etc.

2424.   Harris, Richard. Freedom Spent: Tales of Tyranny
         in America. Boston: Little, 1976. 450.
Three stories about people who struggled against social and
governmental harassment to preserve what they believed were
their constitutional rights, each case focusing upon a specific
provision of the Bill of Rights--freedom of speech, prohibition
of unreasonable search and seizure, and privilege against self-
incrimination.

2425.   Hentoff, Nat. "Snoops in the Pews." Prog 49.8

(1985) 24-26.
INS harassment and prosecution of religious people who gave
sanctuary to refugees from Central American civil wars and death
squads.

2426.   Homer, Frederick. "Government Terror in the United
         States." The State as Terrorist: The Dynamics of
         Governmental Violence and Repression. Ed. Michael Stohl
         and George Lopez. Westport, CT: Greenwood, 1984.
         167-182.
By its own standards of justice and fairness the US fails
because it operates mainly on a containment/crime control model
of social order instead of a due process model.

2427.   Homer, Frederic. "Terror in the United States: Three
         Perspectives." The Politics of Terrorism.
         Ed. Michael Stohl. 2nd ed., rev. New York and Basel:
         Dekker, 1983. 145-178.
One of the author's concerns is the existence of "permanent
antiterror troops" which may "create an enemy to fight." "It is
easy to convince the American public of a conspiracy and then
operate against the 'conspiracy' in a rough and clandestine
fashion."

2428.   Houlding, Andrew. "Tap City USA: the Wiring of New
         Haven." Na 230.22 (1980) 685-688.
A civil suit has been instituted against the FBI and the
police department of New Haven for eavesdropping on thousands of
conversations from 1964 through 1971, in "what was probably the
most sweeping illegal wiretapping operation yet exposed."

2429.   "I.N.S. on Trial." Na 242.3 (1986) 68.
INS Operation Sojourner against the Sanctuary Movement
involves "tactics against political organizations that are
more invasive than any that have been seen in this country since
the F.B.I.'s Cointelpro and the C.I.A.'s Chaos."

2430.   Intelligence Activities. Hearings Before the Select
         Committee to Study Governmental Operations with Respect
         to Intelligence Activities of the U.S. Senate, 94th
         Cong., 1st Session. 7 vols. Washington: GPO, 1975.
The Church Committee Hearings. Vol. 1: "Unauthorized
Storage of Toxic Agents," 2: "Huston Plan," 3: "Internal
Revenue Service," 4: "Mail Opening," 5: "The National Security
Agency and Fourth Amendment Rights," 6: "Federal Bureau of
Investigation," 7: "Covert Action."

2431.   Intelligence Activities. Hearings Before the Select
         Committee to Study Governmental Operations with Respect
         to Intelligence Activities of the U.S. Senate, 94th
         Congress, 1st Sess. Vol. 1: "Unauthorized Storage
         of Toxic Agents." Washington: GPO, 1975. 245.
The first of many hearings to establish "to what degree"
the intelligence agencies "have turned their techniques inward

to spy on the American people" instead of foreign governments. The case under examination "involves the illegal possession of deadly biological poisons which were retained within the CIA for 5 years after their destruction was ordered by the President" after an international agreement not to maintain them.

2432.   Intelligence Activities. Hearings Before the Select Committee to Study Governmental Operations with Respect to Intelligence Activities of the U.S. Senate, 94th Cong., 1st Sess. Vol. 2: "Huston Plan." Washington: GPO, 1975. 403.
An investigation of the plan developed by the intelligence agencies and White House aide Tome Charles Huston, approved by President Nixon, and implemented by the FBI, the CIA, and the military intelligence agencies. "Some provisions of the plan were clearly unconstitutional; others violated Federal statutes."

2433.   Intelligence Activities. Hearings Before the Select Committee to Study Governmental Operations with Respect to Intelligence Activities of the U.S. Senate, 94th Cong., 1st Sess. Vol. 3: "Internal Revenue Service." Washington: GPO, 1975. 124.
Examination of the IRS as an intelligence agency, in particular the ways in which other intelligence services have used the IRS for data on citizens, sometimes illegally, e.g., to disrupt political activists.

2434.   Intelligence Activities. Hearings Before the Select Committee to Study Governmental Operations with Respect to Intelligence Activities of the U.S. Senate, 94th Cong., 1st Sess. Vol. 4: "Mail Opening." Washington: GPO, 1975. 260.
Investigation of "why the Federal Government has been opening the mail of American citizens for over two decades," a "policy fundamentally at odds with freedom of expression and contrary to the laws of the land."

2435.   Intelligence Activities. Hearings Before the Select Committee to Study Governmental Operations with Respect to Intelligence Activities of the U.S. Senate, 94th Cong., 1st Sess. Vol. 5: "The National Security Agency and Fourth Amendment Rights." Washington: GPO, 1975. 165.
The NSA has "tremendous potential for abuse." As the hearings on the Huston Plan revealed, the NSA "favored using this potential against certain U.S. citizens for domestic intelligence purposes," and in fact had been "intentionally monitoring the overseas communications of certain U.S. citizens long before the Huston plan was proposed--and continued to do so after it was revoked. This incident illustrates how the NSA could be turned inward and used against our own people."

2436.   Intelligence Activities. Hearings Before the Select Committee to Study Governmental Operations With Respect

to Intelligence Activities of the U.S. Senate, 94th
Cong., 1st Sess. Vol. 6: "Federal Bureau of
Investigation." Washington: GPO, 1975. 1000.
Hearings on whether the FBI's domestic surveillance
programs operated according to the standards of the Constitution
and the statutes. FBI harassment of the VVAW, the Communist
Party, the Socialist Workers Party, the Black Panther Party,
the New Left, and other organizations by the COINTELPRO is
examined.

2437. Intelligence Activities. Hearings Before the Select
Committee to Study Governmental Operations with Respect
to Intelligence Activities of the U.S. Senate, 94th
Cong., 1st Sess. Vol. 7: "Covert Action." Washington:
GPO, 1975. 230.
On the propriety of covert action as an instrument of US
foreign policy and specifically the involvement of the US in
covert activities in Chile from 1963 through 1973. "The nature
and extent of the American role in the overthrow of a
democratically-elected Chilean Government are matters for deep
and continuing public concern."

2438. Intelligence Activities and the Rights of Americans.
Final Report, Book II, United States Senate, Select
Committee to Study Governmental Operations with Respect
to Intelligence Activities. 94th Congress, 2nd Session.
Washington: W. S. GPO, 1976. 396. [See No. 2415.]
A study of Federal domestic intelligence activities
concerning "abuses in intelligence activity and weaknesses in
the system of accountability and control" which "make a
compelling case for substantial reform" necessary "to protect
the rights of Americans." Also see Book III, Supplementary
Detailed Staff Reports on Intelligence Activities and the Rights
of Americans. [Few reforms were instituted and secrecy has
deepened under the Reagan administration.]

2439. The International Journal of Intelligence and Counterintelligence (IJIC)
A quarterly journal for the analysis of intelligence
activities and their relationship to political intrigue. Began
in 1985.

2440. Jacobs, Jim and Richard Soble. A Blow Against the Red Squads."
Na 232.6 (1981) 168-170.
The Michigan State Police Intelligence Unit was
established in 1948 to root out "subversives." As the result
of a lawsuit, Benkert v. State of Michigan, the court ordered
the police to notify the 38,000 who had a file they could
acquire their file. "This mass notification, the first ever
ordered by American courts," is "a major stride toward ending
intelligence abuses in the 1980s." But intelligence agencies on
all levels are "stalling."

2441. James, Peter. The Air Force Mafia. New Rochelle, NY:

Arlington, 1975. 347.
An account of the troubles the author experienced (fired
from his Pratt & Whitney Aircraft job, etc.) when he tried to
expose "the incompetence and Mafia-like tactics of espionage
agents affiliated with the Air Force Foreign Technology
Division." "The Air Force Mafia story is another mosaic of the
Watergate saga, when men almost stole a nation under the guise
of national security" (Prologue).

2442. Johnson, Loch K. A Season of Inquiry: The Senate
      Intelligence Investigation. Lexington: UP of
      Kentucky, 1985. 317.
A study of the 1975 Senate probe of abuses by the
intelligence community, which is a story "about rulers at
work," the "difficulty of achieving any change," and "the
enormously frustrating task, always faced by Congress, of prying
information loose from the executive bureaucracy." Yet the
investigation "succeeded" (2) in that it exposed "unlawful mail
openings, break-ins, wiretaps, assassination plots," the
"interception of cables and telegrams, dubious covert actions,
buggings, intelligence failures, and inefficiencies," and
"'indifference to constitutional restraints'" (266). But the
legislative charter which Senate reformers and civil
libertarians hoped for never emerged, though the 1980
Intelligence Oversight Act was "a long step in law." However,
President Reagan's Executive Order 12333 in 1981 returned
"considerable discretion in surveillance operations to the CIA."

2443.   Judis, John B. It Didn't Start With Watergate."
     ITT 11.5 (1986) 7, 22.
Beginning with Nixon and Kissinger, the NSC became "a
surrogate State and Defense Department within the White House"
not subject "to congressional advise and consent and scrutiny,"
to carry out private, unpopular activities in secret.

2444. Jussim, Daniel. "The Privacy Invaders: Lies, Damn
      Lies--And Polygraphs." Na 241.21 (1985) 665, 682-84.
The polygraph is becoming "as familiar as the time clock
in more and more American workplaces."

2445.   Kahn, David. "The Public's Secrets: How a Federal
     Agency Laid Claim to a Branch of Higher Mathematics."
     Prog 44.11 (1980) 27-31.
Government efforts to control cryptology--making of codes,
codebreaking, encryption, cryptosystems, etc.--are intensifying.
Suppression of technological information has more harm than
benefit to science and liberty.

2446.   "Keep the Leash." Prog 44.6 (1980) 13.
A defense of the FOIA against those who would weaken it.

2447.   Kellermann, Bill. "Wise As Serpents, Gentle As
     Doves." Soj 15.2 (1986) 24-29.
Offers a biblical perspective on surveillance and how Jesus

faced this problem.

2448.   Kohn, Alfie. "The Return of Cointelpro?" Na 242.3
(1986) 74-76.
Break-ins and thefts have occurred all across the country in
offices and homes of people opposing the government's Central
American policies. The pattern resembles activities of
intelligence agencies during the Vietnam War.

2449. Lehman, Bruce, and Timothy A. Boggs. "How Uncle Sam
Covers the Mails." CLR 4.1 (1977) 20-28.
Documents the kinds of surveillance techinques carried out
by local, state and federal officials under the cover of the
postal service.

2450.   Lens, Sidney. "On the Uses and Abuses of Secrecy."
Prog 44.3 (1980) 46-47.
This general indictment of governmental secrecy includes
illegal FBI and CIA operations.

2451.   Lewis, Anthony. "What Country Is This, Russia or the
USA?" AG (March 3, 1985) 3C.
Customs and FBI officials behaved like thought police when
they confiscated the address book and diary and other documents
belonging to a free-lance journalist just back from a two-month
stay in Nicaragua.

2452.   Lewis, Phyllis. "Government Secrecy: Signs of the
Times." ORK (Spring 1983) 11-13.
Propaganda, lie detection, electronic surveillance, etc.

2453.   Lindorff, Dave. "Policing the Press in Los Angeles."
CJR 22.1 (1983) 7-8.
Revelations about the Los Angeles police Public Disorder
Intelligence Division, which for several years and on an annual
budget of at least $2.2 million spied on the ACLU, NOW, other
organizations, public officials, and the press.

2454.   "Love of Liberty." Na 234.13 (1982) 387-8.
The Senate's 90 to 6 vote for the Intelligence Identities
Protection Act is the "biggest 'incursion' into the First
Amendment since the Smith Act."

2455.   Mackenzie, Angus. "Sabotaging the Dissident Press."
CJR 19.6 (1981) 57-63.
The story of "the secret offensive waged by the U.S.
government against antiwar publications," the "systematic and
sustained violation of the First Amendment during the late 1960s
and early 1970s," primarily by the CIA, the FBI, and the Army.

2456.   Mann, James. "Resurrecting the National Security
State." WP 8 (March-April 1981) 27-33.
Investigations into activities of the CIA and the FBI have
ceased, and the agencies have been given renewed power.

2457.   Marwick, Christine. "The Government's Attitude Toward
        Political Surveillance: No Change." FP 3.8 (1978) 1-5.
    Three targets of government surveillance and disruption are
suing, and the Justice Department is defending "discredited
intelligence programs."

2458.   Marwick, Christine. "A Law to Control the
        Intelligence Agencies: H.R. 6051, The Legislation
        Supported by the American Civil Liberties Union."
        FP 2.9 (1977) 1-6.
    Examines seven titles of the Federal Intelligence Agencies
Control Act of 1977 which seek to prohibit "political
intelligence outright by all Federal agencies--CIA, FBI, IRS,
NSA, military Intelligence."

2459.   Marx, Gary. "I'll Be Watching You: Reflections on
        The New Surveillance." Dissent 32.1 (Winter 1985)
        26-34.
    "Surveillance has become penetrating and intrusive in ways
that previously were imagined only in fiction. The information-
gathering powers of the state and private organizations are
extending ever deeper into the social fabric. The ethos of
social control has expanded from focused and direct coercion
used after the fact and against a particular target to
anticipatory actions entailing deception, manipulation,
planning, and a diffuse panoptic vision."

2460.   Marx, Gary. "Undercover Cops: Creative Policing or
        Constitutional Threat?" CLR 4.2 (1977) 34-44.
    "Police departments themselves must scrutinize undercover
work more closely."

2461.   Military Surveillance of Civilian Politics.
        A Report of the Committee on the Judiciary,
        Subcommittee on Constitutional Rights. Washington:
        U.S. GPO, 1973. 150.
    "Army surveillance of civilians engaging in political
activities in the 1960's was both massive and unrestrained."
Military surveillance "was both unauthorized and in violation of
the first amendment."

2462.   Miller, Judith. "A New Threat to Freedom." Prog
        40.10 (1976) 7-8.
    S.3197, the "Foreign Surveillance Intelligence Act," expands
wiretapping.

2463.   Morgan, Richard E. Domestic Intelligence:
        Monitoring Dissent in America. Austin and London:
        U of Texas P, 1980. 194.
    The book has "four objectives: 1. To trace the way in
which government agencies became involved with domestic
intelligence gathering. 2. To review the record of
intelligence abuses revealed in the mid-1970s. 3. To examine
critically intelligence reforms adopted thus far. 4. To

suggest what additional reforms are necessary." The author believes that general and routine information gathering about individuals or groups by law enforcement agencies for political and not criminal activities is "illegitimate."

2464. "The Mysterious Supplement B; Sticking it to the 'Host Country.'" CAIB 3 (1979) 9-18.
U. S. Army Field Manual FM 30-31 deals with US intelligence liaison with intelligence in host countries for the purpose of suppressing insurgencies. Supplement B to the Manual, however, explains how to infiltrate the host country intelligence agencies.

2465. Nairn, Allan. "Assault on Sanctuary." Prog 49.8 (1985) 20-23.
The Immigration and Naturalization Service (INS) is harassing Central Americans escaping from death squads, as in the case of El Salvadoran Rene Hurtado.

2466. Navasky, Victor. "McCarthy Time? Security and Terrorism." Na 232.6 (1981) 167-68.
Cautions against allowing the new Senate Security and Terrorism Subcommittee of Senator Strom Thurmond's Judiciary committee to become another anticommunist witch-hunter like the old Senate Internal Security Subcommittee.

2467. "On the Trail of a Secret War." CJR 19.6 (1981) 22-23.
Police in Beloit, Wis., harassed the staff of the antiwar People's Dreadnaught. The editor then found "irrefutable evidence that agencies of the federal government had indeed done their best to put hundreds of other [antiwar] publications out of business."

2468. Oseth, John M. Regulating United States Intelligence Operations: A Study in Definition of the National Interest. Lexington: U of Kentucky P, 1985. 236.
Chs. 4-6 examine the Ford, Carter, and Reagan administrations. The Reagan Administration "worked consciously and conspicuously to strengthen intelligence operations" against civil liberty.

2469. "'Patricia Daniloff.'" Na 243.14 (1986) 428.
INS refusal to permit Columbian journalist Patricia Lara to enter the country for a conference without a hearing in spite of her valid visa.

2470. Pearson, David. "K.A.L. 007: What the U.S. Knew and When We Knew It." Na 239.4 (1984) 105-124.
Official administration, military, and intelligence accounts of the incident "are neither complete nor credible."

2471. Peck, Keenen. "Silent Intruders: A Court That Never Says No." Prog 48.4 (1984) 18-21.

411

The Foreign Intelligence Surveillance Court has approved
every surveillance request brought before it. "The subversion of
constitutional rights often takes on a benevolent face."

2472.   Pennington, Francis. "First Amendment Suits Against
         Governmental Surveillance: Getting Beyond the
         Justiciability Threshold." SLULJ 20 (1976) 692-721.
The "justiciability standard applied in surveillance cases
must be . . . modified to afford persons a reasonable
opportunity to gain access to the courts to protect precious
first amendment rights."

2473.   Peterzell, Jay. "Can You Name That Agent?" CJR 23.4
         (1984) 46-47.
The Intelligence Identities Protection Act prohibits anyone
from revealing the names of U.S. intelligence agents, but
magazines and newspapers that have done so have not yet been
prosecuted.

2474.   Peterzell, Jay. Nuclear Power and Political
         Surveillance. Washington, DC: Center for National
         Security Studies, 1980. 110.
A study of police and industry harassment of the anti-
nuclear movement.

2475.   Peterzell, Jay. "Unleashing the Dogs of McCarthyism."
         Na 232.2 (1981) 33, 51-2.
The Heritage Foundation Report section on intelligence
warns of great threats to US security and calls for
strengthening of intelligence agencies.

2476.   "Power to Destroy." Na 237.16 (1983) 485.
IRS efforts to cancel the anti-corporation and anti-Reagan
Mother Jones's educational status appear to be political
harassment, since other magazines similar to MJ, such as
National Geographic, have not experienced a challenge to their
tax status.

2477.   Presidential Campaign Activities of 1972. Hearings
         Before the Select Committee on Presidential Campaign
         Activities of the U.S. Senate, 93rd Cong., 1st Sess.
         26 vols. Washington: GPO, 1973-74.
The Watergate Hearings.

2478.   Preston, William, Jr. "Cops and Bosses: The Origins
         of American Police Work." CLR 5.1 (1978) 23-26.
Looks at the "historical entrails" of police activity in
the US, and notes "the notorious absence of accurate
statistics and reliable historical data in the study of urban
due process."

2479.   Pritt, Denis N. Spies and Informers in the Witness
         Box. London: Hanison, 1958. 96.
"The subject of this book is the evils attendant on the

employment of informers and spies [and accomplices and agents provocateurs] as witnesses in prosecutions on criminal charges." These evils are worldwide, but the author confines himself "to cases within the Anglo-Saxon legal systems, indeed within Great Britain, the United States of America and the British colonies."

2480.   Pyle, Christopher. "Military Surveillance of Civilian Politics, 1967-1970." DAI 38 (1978) 4364-A.
"A study of the Army's massive surveillance" of civilians during the late 1960s, based upon "interviews with more than 100 former intelligence agents, Congressional hearings, court cases, and thousands of formerly classified intelligence documents." In order to answer the question, Why was the illegal surveillance not stopped earlier? the author also investigates "the culture of secrecy and deceit" and the "weakness of civilian control."

2481.   "The Red Squad Settlements Controversy: Checks on Police Spies." Na 233.2 (1981) 43-46.
The settlement of the suit against the New York City "Red Squad" charging illegal surveillance, infiltration, and intimidation of political activity has created "considerable controversy among civil libertarians and political activists." Two essays present opposing sides.

2482.   Reisig, Robin. "The Trials of Kathy Boudin: Punishment First, Sentencing Later." Na 239.20 (1984) 644-647.
The harsh treatment by the police of political defendents and prisoners.

2483.   Richelson, Jeffrey. The U.S. Intelligence Community. Hagerstown, MD: Ballinger, 1985. 392.
An attempt to provide in one volume "a comprehensive and detailed order of battle of the US intelligence community--to describe its organizations, activities, and management structure." Ch. 16 considers such issues as the "acceptability, morality, or wisdom of the activities described"--such as "covert action, secrecy, and the ethics of intelligence collection operations" (Preface).

2484.   Ridgeway, James. "Spying On Dissidents." TO 77.10 (1985) 8-9.
Gives a series of examples of growing FBI, state and local police, and private security company harassment of "subversive" opponents of various government policies (travelers to Nicaragua, the Sanctuary movement, White Train protesters, etc.). These are evidence of counterinsurgency in the US.

2485.   Rips, Geoffrey, ed. The Campaign Against the Underground Press. San Francisco: City Lights, 1981. 176.
The FBI and CIA attempted to sabotage the alternative press during the 1960s and 1970s. Essays on the war against

dissidence by the editor, Aryeh Neier, Todd Gitlin, Angus Mackenzie, and Allen Ginsberg.

2486.   Roos, Joe. "Listening In on the Church." Soj 15.2
          (1986) 4.
     Publisher Roos speaks of one person's experience with
government surveillance--the magazine's editor, Jim Wallis.

2487.   Rushford, Gregory G. "Making Enemies: The Pike
          Committee's Struggle to Get the Facts." WM 8.5-6
          (1976) 42-52.
     The House Select Committee on Intelligence encountered
great resistance from Ford, Kissinger, and the intelligence agencies
while gathering material to produce its report.

2488.   Schonberg, Edward. "Search Warrants and Journalists'
          Confidential Information." AULR 25.4 (1976) 938-970.
     Law enforcement officials "should only be allowed to use
search warrants to seize information from the press when there
is no other method available," and "the police should be
required to show clearly that a substantial likelihood exists
that the evidence will be destroyed unless a search warrant is
issued."

2489.   Schwartz, Herman. "Bugging Binge: The Intrusive Ears
          of the Law." Na 238.23 (1984) 721, 725.
     The Omnibus Crime Control and Safe Streets Act of 1968,
which legitimized wiretapping and bugging, facilitated the Nixon
Administration "binge in the early 1970s." Now "electronic
eavesdropping by Federal law enforcement agencies" is "rampant."

2490.   Schwartz, Herman. "How Do We Know FISA Is Working?"
          Na 237.13 (1983) 397-399.
     Congress passed the Foreign Intelligence Surveillance Act
of 1978 to curb presidential use of electronic surveillance in
national security matters, but "judicial scrutiny and
legislative oversight of the administration of FISA are
essential if the act is to achieve its purposes."

2491.   Schwartz, Herman. "Reagan's Bullish on Bugging."
          Na 236.22 (1983) 697-699.
     Wiretapping and bugging by Federal law enforcement agencies
is increasing because of the Reagan administration's war on
drugs and racketeering. A minimum of $18 million was spent in
1982 on electronic surveillance. But the expenditure is largely
a waste.

2492.   Schwartz, Herman. "Time to Get the Bugs Out." Na
          231.13 (1980) 401-403.
     Room bugging is increasing, and "the harm from bugging far
outweighs its minimal value."

2493.   Schwartz, Herman and Ira Glasser. "Your Phone Is a
          Party Line." Har 245 (Oct. 1972) 106-114.

Government wiretapping of private homes and businesses is widespread. The people undergoing surveillance have generally not committed crimes but are suspected for political views and activities.

2494.   "Search Warrants and the Effects of the Stanford Daily Decision." House Committee on Government Operations. Washington, DC: U.S. GPO, August 21, 1978.
A study by the Information and Individual Rights Sub-committee explains the case and stresses the threat of the decision to a free press and privacy. It recommends that a search warrant not be issued without probable cause against the property of a third party unless it is shown that a request or subpoena would result in a destruction or removal of the evidence.

2495.   Shattuck, John. "Cutting Back on Freedom By Fiat." Na 236.23 (1983) 719, 734.
President Reagan's many executive orders include several which strike at individual liberties--granting the CIA authority to conduct surveillance in the US, classifying more information, and "most sweeping" of all, the March 11 Presidential Directive on Safeguarding National Security Information, "which establishes the broadest secrecy system in U.S. history." "Institutionalized secrecy and surveillance are the centerpieces of Ronald Reagan's government by executive order."

2496.   Sheinfeld, Lois P. "Washington vs. The Right To Know." Na 240.14 (1985) 426-428.
A compendium of instances of the Reagan administration's use of secrecy and censorship "to protect itself from public scrutiny and criticism." The intelligence agencies are central to this policy.

2497.   Sherrill, Robert. "Opening Day at the Subcommittee." Na 232.18 (1981) 553, 572.
CIA and other Sovietphobes like Claire Sterling "helped launch the new Senate Subcommittee on Security and Terrorism."

2498.   Sherrill, Robert. "The Powers of Darkness." Na 230.23 (1980) 725-27.
Review of Frank Donner's The Age of Surveillance, the "best book on the subject" of "the disease of political spying."

2499.   Sobel, David L. and Greg Levine. "Wreaking Mischief On Political Activities." ON 6.8 (1982) 6-7.
An account of a seminar on government informers, undercover agents, agents provocateurs, electronic surveillance and the serious First and Fourth Amendment issues these practices involve.

2500.   Surveillance, Dataveillance, and Personal Freedoms: Use and Abuse of Information Technology. Fair Lawn, NJ: Burdick, 1973. 247. (Orig. pp. 1-235 of Columbia

Human Rights Law Review 4.1 [1972]).
Shows "chillingly" how we "are allowing ourselves to be
trapped by our own technology of surveillance and repression."
Eight essays on privacy, computers, data banks, the First
Amendment, police surveillance of political dissidents, etc.

2501.   Tackwood, Louis. The Glass House Tapes. New York:
         Avon, 1973. 284.
Tapes of confessions by Louis Tackwood, former agent
provocateur for the Los Angeles Police Department, compiled with
commentary by the Citizens Research and Investigation Committee,
Donald Freed, editor. The Glass House was part of "a network of
local, federal, military and credit intelligence systems." "The
Glass Houses of the nation, like so many domestic Pentagons,
are, ultimately, symbols of concentrated power and control."

2502.   Theoharis, Athan. Spying on Americans: Political
         Surveillance from Hoover to the Huston Plan.
         Philadelphia: Temple UP, 1978. 331.
A comprehensive history of the abuses of the American
domestic intelligence system from 1936 until May 1978,
especially the step-by-step expansion of the authority of the
FBI and other agencies to investigate the loyalty of American
citizens: illegal wiretaps, mail openings, break-ins, security
indexes, emergency detention plans, loyalty programs, infiltration,
harassment, slander, disinformation, cover-up techniques, all
rationalized in terms of Cold War prejudices regarding loyalty
and orthodoxy. In spite of Watergate substantive safeguards for
the civil liberties of citizens have not been insured.

2503.   Turner, William W. "Some Disturbing Parallels."
         Ram 6 (June 29, 1968) 33-36.
Article reexamines connections between the Kennedy and
King assassinations, contending that an "investigation should be
undertaken by a joint staff un-beholden to the FBI, the Secret
Service and the CIA."

2504.   "Under the Thumb." Win.
A regular feature on current cases of political repression.
The March 1, 1982, number, for example, reported awards to peace
activists by a federal court jury for damages from the FBI and
DC police, and attempts by the FBI to censor David Garrow's
book, The FBI and Martin Luther King, Jr.

2505.   Valentino, Linda. "The LEIU: Part of the Political
         Intelligence Network." FP 4.5 (1979) 1-7.
The Law Enforcement Intelligence Unit "has probably been
the chief mechanism through which derogatory, inaccurate, and
irrelevant information about political activists was spread from
one police agency to another."

2506.   Van Atta, Dale. "Soviet Intentions: the C.I.A.'s
         Great Debate." Na 230.13 (1980) 397-399.
An analysis of disagreement over Soviet policies and powers

within the intelligence community.

2507.   Wallace, Bill. "LEIU's Political Police." Inq 2.1
         (1978) 5-6.
The Law Enforcement Intelligence Unit, a confederation of
various levels of police and intelligence units supposed to be
investigating Mafia-type organized crime, were involved with
the surveillance of such groups as the Black Panthers, SDS,
Radical Student Union, and the Progressive Labor party.

2508.   Wise, David. The American Police State: The
         Government Against the People. New York: Random,
         1976. 437.
Chs. 1-3 on illegal wiretaps, 4 on President Nixon's
secret police operating against political opponents, 5 break-ins,
6-7 the CIA, etc.

2509.   Wise, David and Thomas Ross. The Invisible
         Government. New York: Random, 1964. 375.
The power and secrecy of the intelligence agencies
virtually uncontrolled by Congress or any public scrutiny.

2510.   Wylie, Jeanie. "Cat-and-Mouse Games: Surveillance."
         Soj 15.2 (1986) 20-21.
One woman's personal record of government surveillance in
Detroit.

2511.   Young, Peter L. "America's Mysterious 'Space Base'
         Down Under: The Aussies Are Looking the Other Way."
         Prog 44.7 (1980) 31-33.
The "Pine Gap" base in Australia, "run by the CIA and the
NSA, is the U.S. command center in the Southern Hemisphere for
reconnaissance and early warning satellites" to grab foreign
military communications and for "espionage."

2512.   Zuckerman, Laurence. "COINTELPRO Redux?" CJR 25.1
         (1986) 14-16.
The Reagan administration has "stepped up domestic
surveillance of political dissidents," as illustrated by the
surveillance of Sojoiurners magazine by agents of the National
Security Agency or some other intelligence agency.

VI. B. Federal Bureau of Investigation 2513-2596

2513.   "The ACLU and the FBI: Over 50 Years of Constant
         Surveillance." CLR 4.4 (1977) 17.
The ACLU obtained "over 10,000 pages" of surveillance
documents from the FBI under the Freedom of Information Act.

2514.   Aronson, James. "On Assignment with WFBI." MORE
         2.2 (1972) 1.
Police and FBI use of press credentials for surveillance of
peace, black, and other dissenting groups.

417

2515.   Arvidson, Cheryl. "The FBI Bears Down." <u>CJR</u> 22.3
          (1983) 5-6.
A Canadian reporter finds himself in trouble with the FBI
after reporting on proposed cruise-missile tests.

2516.   Baker, Beth. "Is Someone Watching You?" <u>CC</u> 12.1
          (1986) 28-29.
"Thousands of Americans [were] spied on by the FBI over the
past 60 years," including the International Physicians for the
Prevention of Nuclear War.

2517.   Blackstock, Nelson. <u>COINTELPRO: The FBI's Secret</u>
          <u>War on Political Freedom</u>. New York: Vintage, 1976.
          216.
The FBI's counterintelligence program (Co-Intel-Pro) against
Socialists and protesters of the Vietnam War was illegal and
unconstitutional.

2518.   Blank, Susan. "FBI Ruled Responsible for Klan
          Violence It Could Have Stopped." <u>CL</u> 347
          (Fall 1983) 6.
The beating of Walter Bergman could have been prevented by
the FBI, who had advance warning.

2519.   Blinken, Anthony. "Ray Donovan's Lucky Break." <u>NR</u>
          191.26 (1984) 13-17.
The FBI withheld information from and even lied to the
Senate regarding the Donovan nomination.

2520.   Boudin, Leonard B. "Significant Case." <u>Na</u> 239.21
          (Dec. 22, 1984) 666.
The Judith Coplon case revealed FBI misconduct.

2521.   Bowart, Walter. "The FBI vs. Scientology." <u>Inq</u> 2.5
          (1979) 7-8.
The FBI and other agencies for years have been harassing
the Church of Scientology.

2522.   Blum, Bill, and Gina Lobaco. "The Assassination
          Bureau." <u>Prog</u> 48.9 (1984) 15.
FBI harassment of Frank Wilkinson and the National
Committee Against Repressive Legislation.

2523.   Chaberski, Stephen. "Inside the New York Panther
          Trial." <u>CLR</u> 1.1 (1973) 111-155.
An account by one of the jurors of the trial of Panthers
for alleged bombings and plans to bomb and to murder policemen.
The Panthers were unanimously acquitted by the jury. "What was
even clearer [than the innocence of the accused] after the
verdict was that this trial had bared some terribly unjust
practices in the American criminal justice system that had been
allowed to go unchecked largely because of the combination of
antiblack and antiradical sentiment generated among public
officials, the press, and much of public opinion in reaction to

the 'Panther threat'" (140-41). The article ends with an attack on police surveillance of radical political activity and on the press for having "made the defendants' guilt virtually a foregone conclusion" (145).

2524.   Clark, Blair.   "'The File.'" <u>Na</u> 237.20 (1983)
          620-621.
Denunciation of police state invasion of the privacy of Penn Kimball by the FBI, CIA, and State Department.

2525.   Colhoun, Jack.   "Anti-Espionage Overkill." <u>Prog</u> 42.8
          (1978) 10.
The conviction of Ronald Humphrey and David Truong of espionage and conspiracy is political.

2526.   Cook, Fred.   "Alger Hiss - a New Ball Game." <u>Na</u>
          231.11 (1980) 340-343.
Documents obtained through the FOIA reveal that "Hiss was victimized by a prosecutorial vendetta" and "wholesale violation of his rights" so bad that "his conviction should be expunged from the record."

2527.   Cook, Fred.   "The F.B.I. and Organized Crime." <u>Ram</u>
          4.1 (1965) 16-26.
"Local and state law officers cannot control national mob crime rings; the Federal Bureau of Investigation won't even try."

2528.   Cook, Fred.   <u>The FBI Nobody Knows</u>. New York:
          Macmillan, 1964. 436.
By a "monumental propaganda effort," Hoover and the FBI have made themselves sacrosanct. Consequently, the "police state looms on the horizon" (414).

2529.   Cook, Fred.   "On Being an Enemy of the F.B.I."
          <u>Na</u> 242.11 (1986) 426-29.
The Bureau's "rage and frustration" over Cook's criticisms and its inability to detect any conspiracy or communist plot on his part.

2530.   "The Corruptors." <u>Na</u> 230.8 (1980) 227-228.
The Abscam operation illustrates again how antithetical is "the informer system, endemic to all secret police organizations," to an open society.

2531.   Diamond, Sigmund.   "Hoover Goes to Harvard." <u>Na</u>
          233.13 (1981) 393, 405-411.
Like Yale, Harvard cooperated with the FBI in probes of alleged Communists on campus, and Harvard maintains strict secrecy over the relevant records.

2532.   Diamond, Sigmund.   "The Lessons of Collaboration:
          A Study of the FBI and Academia." <u>ORK</u> (Spring 1985) 6-8.
A study of the history of the collaboration during the 1950s. The cases of City College of New York and Harvard provide

illustrations.

2533.   DiBernardo, Gail. "FBI Subjects U.S. Journalist
        To Political Harassment." SLJR 12.73 (1985) 7.
    On his return from Nicaragua, free-lance journalist Ed
Hasse's personal papers were seized by FBI and Customs agents
who said they were looking for "subversive materials."

2534.   Dolan, Thomas, and Bill Nigut, Sr. "Public Enemies
        and the FBI." ChJR 7.6 (1974) 4-7.
    Dolan criticizes the FBI's "using the press against
Panthers and other groups." Nigut challenges the FBI's annual
summary of crime in the US, which omits "crimes committed by
politicians, the police, public officials, and businessmen
against the people."

2535.   Donner, Frank. "How J. Edgar Hoover Created His
        Intelligence Powers." CLR 3.6 (1977) 34-51.
    The bureau's intelligence powers are "themselves the result
of an intelligence coup." Documentation of Hoover's
machinations for over thirty years.

2536.   Donner, Frank. "Oedipus Cowed." Na 229.12
        (1979) 373-76.
    Rev. of The Bureau: My Thirty Years in Hoover's FBI, by
William Sullivan and Bill Brown. Sullivan, former head of the
FBI's Domestic Intelligence Division, presents "a plea for
absolution for sins" he claims "he committed under duress."

2537.   Donner, Frank. "Rounding Up the Usual Suspects."
        Na 235.4 (1982) 97, 110-116.
    The FBI is driving to "legitimize the Bureau's discredited
internal security operations," backed by Senators Strom
Thurmond, Jeremiah Denton, and John East of the Senate
Subcommitte on Security and Terrorism. "Congressional
reluctance to enact F.B.I. charter legislation and to confront
the abuses disclosed by a chain of investigations dramatizes the
grip of the subversive myth on our political life."

2538.   Elliff, John T. The Reform of FBI Intelligence
        Operations. Princeton: Princeton UP, 1979. 248.
    A study of FBI internal security intelligence operations,
how reforms of abuses emerged during the 1970s, and "what their
impact was." "The first principle was that the Constitution and
the law applied to intelligence activities," as set forth in the
Supreme Court Keith decision in 1972. "The principal conclusion
of this study is that FBI intelligence programs are necessary to
achieve compelling law enforcement and national security
objectives, and that they can do so without violating
constitutional rights" (189).

2539.   "The FBI." Prog 43.2 (1979) 9.
    "Our national thought police spied on Senator Paul H.
Douglas for more than two decades."

2540.   FBI Annual Report. Washington, DC: United States
          Department of Justice.
     In spite of the significant omissions, Victor Navasky in
his review of the 1972 Report recommends it for the insights it
provides into FBI priorities, practices, style, and purposes
(CLR 1.1 [Fall 1973] 101-103).

2541.   "FBI Index." Na 170.19 (1950) 449.
     The FBI keeps a list of people who sign petitions or write
critical comments to government offices.

2542.   Freeman, Joshua. "'Gee, Man! I Wanna Be a G-Man.'"
          Na 238.1 (1984) 25-27.
     Rev. of Richard Powers' G-Men and Penn Kimball's
The File. Powers charts the process of FBI image-making and the
development of Hoover as an authority figure. Kimball reveals
how the investigatory process can distort the truth.

2543.   Garrow, David. The FBI and Martin Luther King, Jr.:
          From "Solo" to Memphis. New York: Norton, 1981. 320.
     The book reveals the systematic abuse of power by the head
of the FBI, two presidents, and their subordinates to silence
this dissident leader.

2544.   Getlein, Frank. "The Word from Washington." Prog
          42.6 (1978) 12-13.
     Criminal indictments of L. Patrick Grey III, Richard Helms,
and other high officials have been so reduced by Attorney
General Bell that none will go to prison and fines will be
light.

2545.   Gordon, Diana, and Mae Churchill. "Interstate I.D.
          Index: 'Triple I' Will Be Tracking Us." Na 238.16
          (1984) 497, 513-515.
     The FBI's national computerized arrest data bank is too
indiscriminate and contains incomplete and erroneous
information, and is therefore "potentially damaging" to "law-
abiding citizens."

2546.   Graves, Florence. "Anatomy of a Secret File."
          CC 12.1 (1986) 22-27.
     Interview with Penn Kimball, who for thirty years was under
secret and baseless investigation as a national security risk.
His efforts to gain access to his file are recounted.

2547.   Hitchens, Christopher. "Minority Report." Na 238.25
          (1984) 792.
     The FBI and CIA repeatedly harassed Greek journalist Elias
Demetracopoulos because he opposed the Greek dictatorship, which
had "links to the Nixon gang."

2548.   Hoch, Paul, and Jonathan Marshall. "JFK: The Unsolved
          Murder." Inq 2.2 (1978) 10-12.
     The FBI manipulated the Warren Commission to produce its

conclusion.

2549.   "House Probes FBI." NT 4.5 (1986) 7.
    The FBI has a classified file on Samantha Smith.

2550.   "Inside the FBI." SD 2.6 (1978) 15-17.
    Overview of abuses by FBI and how "top executives of the
FBI falsified their testimony before the Senate Select Committee
on Intelligence in 1976."

2551.   Kanter, Elliot. "The FBI takes Aim at A.I.M." SD 1.5
    (1977) 7-10, 34-35.
    Discusses the abuse of the American Indian Movement by the
FBI.

2552.   Kelly, John. "Amnesty Faults FBI." CS 6.2 (1982)
    4-6.
    A discussion of Amnesty International's report on FBI
practices, Proposal for a Commission of Inquiry into the Effect
of Domestic Intelligence Activities on Criminal Trials in the
United States of America. "The report maintains that the FBI
has violated the legal and political rights of U.S. citizens."

2553.   Kimball, Penn. The File. New York: Harcourt, 1984.
    356.
    An account of how the author failed a government security
check on the basis of hearsay, innuendo, and speculation and how
that judgment affected his life.

2554.   Kimball, Penn. "The History of The Nation According
    to the F.B.I." Na 242.11 (1986) 399-426.
    Through the FOIA the Nation acquired a part of its FBI
file, which began in 1918 because the magazine was thought to be
"radical." "The F.B.I. launched special field investigations of
Nation contributors, pressured teachers who used the magazine in
the classes, and cooperated with government agencies seeking to
discredit opponents of their policies--all in the name of
Americanism."

2555.   Knoll, Erwin. "Do We Want to Trust the FBI?" Prog
    41.9 (1977) 11.
    No matter who is Director, the Agency will still be a
"secret police."

2556.   Knoll, Erwin. "Filed But Not Forgotten: the F.B.I.
    and The Progressive." Prog 50.10 (1986) 24-25.
    The FBI's files on the magazine (about half of which have
been released under a FOIA request) reveal "the national police
force preoccupied itself for almost four decades with the most
detailed scrutiny" of the magazine.

2557.   Knoll, Erwin. "Under Surveillance." Prog 50.1
    (1986) 4.
    Chicago Red Squad surveillance in the 1970s.

2558.   Kunstler, William.   "The Sting F.B.I. Style: Crime in
     the Name of the Law." Na 238.25 (1984) 796-798.
     Sting operations raise serious legal and moral issues.

2559.   Kunstler, William, and Stewart Albert.   "Tales of Judge
     Hoffman: The Great Conspiracy Trial of '69." Na 229.9
     (1979) 257, 273-276.
     FBI and government misconduct in the Chicago Conspiracy
Trial - illegal wiretaps, mail openings, suppression of
exonerating evidence, etc.

2560.   "Late, But Not Better." Prog 49.3 (1985) 12.
     The American Bar Association endorsed the government's
"domestic security" guidelines, which allow the FBI to spy on
political organizations.

2561.   Lingeman, Richard.   "Papa and the Feds." Na 236.12
     (1983) 355.
     A parody of an FBI report on Ernest Hemingway.   The FBI
kept a file on Hemingway from the 1940s to his death and "sought
to discredit him at every opportunity."

2562.   Lowenthal, Max. The Federal Bureau Of Investigation.
     New York: Sloane, 1950.   559.
     A study of the development of the FBI from its original
purpose to investigate criminal activity to its present
investigation of noncriminal activities and opinions
accompanied by the extensive collection of files and
surveillance of noncriminal citizens, "habitual to political
police systems in Europe but abhorrent to a democracy."

2563.   Mackenzie, Angus.   "Peace Doctors Examined by FBI."
     NaR 9 (Winter 1986) 5-6.
     "In violation of FBI guidelines that limit political
investigations, the Bureau from 1982 through 1984 conducted
nationwide probes of moderate peace organizations," including
Physicians for Social Responsibility.   The probe of the
physicians actually began in 1967 in an attempt to link the
group with the communists, became dormant in the mid-70s, until
resumed in 1982.

2564.   Markowitz, Gerald E.   "Secrecy, Duplicity, Dirty
     Tricks: The Incomplete Record of the Rosenberg Case."
     ORK (Fall 1983) 2-5.
     The FBI has "succeeded in partially frustrating researchers
hoping to get their hands on primary source material on the
Rosenberg-Sobell case."

2565.   Matthiessen, Peter. In the Spirit of Crazy Horse.
     New York: Viking, 1983.   628.
     An analysis of the shoot-out near Oglala, South Dakota, in
which two FBI agents and one Indian were killed, and the
subsequent "ruthless persecution" of Leonard Peltier, accused
murderer, in terms of "underlying issues of history, racism, and

economics, in particular Indian sovereignty claims and growing opposition to massive energy development on treaty lands and the dwindling reservations."

2566.   McWilliams, Carey. "Second Thoughts." Na 229.72
         (1979) 678-79.
    Elmer (Geronimo) Pratt was "a target of Cointelpro's program to 'neutralize' certain Black Panther Party leaders." He "did not have a fair trial."

2567.   National News Council Report. "Statement on Jean
         Seberg Case." CJR 18.4 (1979) 101-104.
    Seberg "was deliberately and outrageously maligned by the FBI in 1970."

2568.   Neier, Aryeh. "Adhering to Principle: Lessons from
         the 1950s." CLR 4.4 (1977) 26-32.
    Examines the 1950s' relationship between the FBI and ACLU and concludes "that the ACLU staff members in the 1950s who fed information about their colleagues to the FBI persuaded themselves that they were defending the cause of liberty," albeit this was certainly a false assumption; "with the advantage of hindsight, we can call what they were doing betrayal."

2569.   Ola, Akinshiju. "No End in Sight for 15-year FBI
         Frame Up." Guard 38.32 (1986) 8.
    Black activists David Rice and Edward Poindexter, jailed in 1970 for allegedly murdering a policeman, are described as victims of the FBI Cointelpro project of disruption of radical groups. A chapter of Ammnesty International in Bremen, West Germany, "has taken up" the case.

2570.   O'Reilly, Kenneth. "The F.B.I.--HUAC's Big Brother."
         Na 230.2 (1980) 42-45.
    Cooperation between the FBI, Senator Joseph McCarthy, and the House Committee on Un-American Activities is further illustrated by FBI Cointelpro and Cominfil programs directed against the National Committee to Abolish HUAC. The FBI is "the principal threat" to the civil liberties of "thinking Americans," yet Congress has failed to restrict FBI investigations to non-political activities.

2571.   O'Reilly, Kenneth. Hoover and the Un-Americans:
         the FBI, HUAC, and the Red Menace. Philadelphia:
         Temple UP, 1983. 411.
    "Both Senator McCarthy and HUAC belong on center stage, but they must share it with FBI Director J. Edgar Hoover and FBI Assistant Directors Louis B. Nichols and Cartha DeLoach," who "sought to gain acceptance for their own political belief that radical political and economic reforms were 'subversive,' as were those who questioned the emerging anticommunist consensus and those who condemned the cultural pollution and blacklists of the so-called McCarthy era."

2572.   Payne, Cril. Deep Cover: An FBI Agent Infiltrates
the Radical Underground. New York: Newsweek, 1979.
348.
An account of the author's six-year attempt to infiltrate
the peace movement and the Weathermen, using bribes, illegal
entries, illegal taps, breaking and entering, and other illegal
practices.

2573.   Pell, Eve. "FOIAbles of the New Drug Law." Na
243.20 (1986) 666-668.
Senator Orrin Hatch's amendment to the Anti-Drug Abuse Act
of 1986 by restricting access to information under the FOIA will
"inhibit disclosure of the F.B.I.'s disruption of legal
political groups."

2574.   Powers, Richard. G-Men: Hoover's FBI in American
Popular Culture. Carbondale: Southern Illinois UP,
1983. 356.
An account of how Hollywood glorified the FBI and its
Director, J. Edgar Hoover, and the FBI public relations machine
which encouraged the image-making.

2575.   "Restraining the FBI." Prog 44.1 (1980) 8.
The proposed FBI charter proclaims civil liberties for
political dissenters but actually "legitimizes even more
dangerous intrusions."

2576.   Reuben, William. "New Development." Na 239.15
(1984) 469.
New revelations of FBI ability to commit forgery by
typewriter may affect the key evidence against Alger Hiss.

2577.   Ross, Caroline, and Ken Lawrence. The Politics of
Repression in the United States, 1939-1976.
Jackson, MS: American Friends Service Committee, 1978.
23.
A "survey of the U.S. strategy for repression from 1939 to
1976" through "a careful study of the Emergency Detention
Plan," whose purpose was "to identify individuals considered
most dangerous to the government so that in the event of
'national emergency' they could be rounded up by the FBI and
placed in designated concentration camps."

2578.   Ryter, Mark. "COINTELPRO: Corrupting American
Institutions." FP 3.9 (1978) 1-5.
Discusses COINTELPRO and the FBI, and how "the Bureau's
covert operations spread propaganda, exploited and manipulated
American institutions--the press, the political process, the
universities, the churches, and even other agencies of
government."

2579.   Ryter, Mark. "COINTELPRO: FBI Lawbreaking and
Violence." FP 3.10 (1978) 1-6.
The "FBI ran a propaganda mill which fed into the U.S.

INTELLIGENCE

media, it undermined American elections, it violated principles
of academic freedom, and it made cynical use of the courts of
law."

2580.   Salisbury, Harrison. "The Strange Correspondence of
        Morris Ernst and John Edgar Hoover, 1939-1964." Na
        239.18 (1984) 575-589.
    "The significance of the correspondence lies in what it
reveals about the state of civil liberties and its flawed
defenders during a critical time for the Bill of Rights--the
McCarthy period" of 1948-1952. Hoover "mouthed cliches of
freedom while slipping documents into the hands of its enemies";
Ernst, "a champion of civil liberties. . . succumbed to the
conviction that Hoover with his F.B.I. stood as a bastion
against the threat of Soviet communism."

2581.   Schneir, Walter, and Miriam Schneir. "The Story the
        'Red Spy Queen' Didn't Tell." Na 236.25 (1983) 790-794.
    "Exculpatory information" about the Rosenberg case,
suppressed at the time by the FBI, has come to light. "All the
files relating to the Rosenberg-Sobell case, without exception,
should be released."

2582.   Schwartz, Richard Alan. "What the File Tells: The
        F.B.I. and Dr. Einstein." Na 237.6 (1983) 168-173.
    The some 1,500 pages that the FBI accumulated on Albert
Einstein between 1932 and 1955 contain "a litany of horrors"
that suggest the Bureau's suspicion of Einstein's Communist
ties. Most of the material "concerns Einstein's exercise of his
rights of free speech," which "should have little place in an
espionage investigation."

2583.   Shattuck, John, Jerry J. Berman, and Morton H.
        Halperin. "Chartering the F.B.I." Na 229.10
        (1979) 294-301.
    Ten statements regarding the need for reform of the FBI to
prevent the FBI from continuing as a political police.

2584.   "Slack Guidelines." Na 236.12 (1983) 353-4.
    The new FBI guidelines on surveillance and the strictures
on government employees' exercise of free speech are "screws
tightening on the First Amendment."

2585.   Sorkin, Michael. "The FBI's Big Brother Computer."
        WM 4.7 (1972) 24-30.
    The FBI is assembling a nationwide computer network which
contains information on anyone who has been arrested for any
charge, whether found innocent or guilty.

2586.   "Stanley Levison." Na 229.9 (1979) 261.
    FBI lies about Martin Luther King, Jr.'s friend in order to
undermine King.

2587.   Stuart, Lyle. "The FBI and Me." SD 2.11

(1978) 22.
One man's horror at what he found in his FBI file.

2588.   "S.W.P.'s Day in Court." Na 243.6 (1986) 161.
The Socialist Workers Party was awarded $264,000 in damages
for what amounted to an FBI domestic contra operation against a
lawful and peaceful political oganization for 18 years costing
$1.7 million.

2589.   Tasini, Jonathan. "J. Edgar Hoover's Dress
          Rehearsal." Prog 48.6 (1984) 14.
FBI surveillance of Marcus Garvey from 1918 to 1927.

2590.   Theoharis, Athan, ed. Beyond the Hiss Case: The
          F.B.I., Congress and the Cold War. Philadelphia:
          Temple UP, 1982. 423.
The 10 essays "examine the critical issues involved in the
abuse of power, particularly the methods FBI officials, HUAC,
and conservative reporters and congressmen employed to effect
Hiss's indictment and conviction and to harass and discredit
other dissident activists and organizations," focusing on
"representative" FBI techniques and priorities, especially
break-ins and filing procedures. The essays reveal "the
Bureau's disdain for the law" in amassing information on
dissidents and disseminating derogatory information to
"friendly" reporters and congressmen (5-6).

2591.   Turner, William W. "I Was a Burglar, Wiretapper,
          Bugger, and Spy for the F.B.I." Ram 5.5 (1966) 51-55.
Wide-spread wiretapping and other illegal activities during
1951 to 1961, when he served as a special agent for the FBI.

2592.   Ungar, Sanford. FBI: An Uncensored Look Behind
          the Walls. Boston, Toronto: Little, 1975. 682.
Chs. on "How It Began," "How the Bureau Works" (criminal,
civil, counterintelligence, internal security), "Three Different
Worlds" (headquarters, field offices, overseas), "The People"
("The King," "The Dukes," agents and G-women), "What the Bureau
Does And Doesn't Do," etc. Ch. 15, "Winning Friends and
Influencing People on Capitol Hill," Ch. 16, "Building a Public
Image."

2593.   Walsh, Joan. "The New Communism." Prog 44.6
          (1980) 11.
The proposed FBI charter will not stop domestic political
counterintelligence programs.

2594.   "Watch This Space." Na 229.21 (1979) 645.
Henry Kissinger's links to the FBI.

2595.   "The Word from Washington." Prog 42.9 (1978) 14-15.
FBI rituals to gain budget approval.

2596.   Zimroth, Peter. Perversions of Justice: The

Prosecution and Acquittal of the Panther 21. New
York: Viking, 1974. 423.
Ch. 3, "The Government Strikes: Tappanoia and Other
Diseases of the Spirit," places the trial in the context of
illegal police repression at the time--wire tapping, bugging
rooms, secret informers, computerized files on dissidents, etc.--
intended not only to control actions but to control thought.

VI. C. CIA 2597-2761

[For related works see the Anti-Soviet, Latin America, and
Global sections, and my "Corporate and Government Domination of
Education in the United States: A Bibliography," RT (1986).]

2597.   Agee, Philip. Inside the Company: CIA Diary.
New York: Stonehill, 1975. 639.
Revelations of "the kinds of secret activities that the US
government undertakes through the CIA in Third World countries
in the name of US national security."

2598.   Agee, Philip. "On Naming C.I.A. Agents." Na 232.10
(1981) 295-98.
This former CIA agent explains why he names his quondam
colleagues and what is wrong with the Intelligence Identities
Protection bill. Seven responses follow.

2599.   Agee, Philip. "Where Myths Lead to Murder."
CAIB 1 (1978) 4-7.
A modified version of the introduction to Agee's and Wolf's
Dirty Work: The CIA in Western Europe; it "expresses much of
the philosophy" of the CAIB, whose purpose is to expose the
CIA/US government/US corporation secret interventions in
countries throughout the world.

2600.   Agee, Philip, and Louis Wolf, eds. Dirty Work:
The CIA in Western Europe. Secaucus, NJ: Stuart, 1978.
734.
Thirty-one essays and 415 pp. of details on CIA agents as
part of "the effort to unmask the CIA's personnel and the
operations" for use by all who "oppose secret intervention by the
CIA."

2601.   Alleged Assassination Plots Involving Foreign Leaders:
Interim Report. Senate Select Committee to Study
Governmental Operations with Respect to Intelligence
Activities. Washington, DC: GPO, November, 1975. 349.
The US government is alleged to have been involved in death
plots against five foreign leaders.

2602.   Alter, Jonathan. "Slaying the Message: How the Frank
Snepp Case Hurts Us All." WM 13.7 (1981) 43-50.
The government prosecuted Frank Snepp for his book
criticizing the CIA, Decent Interval, even though he had
revealed no secrets.

428

2603.   Ambrose, Stephen E., with Richard Immerman. Ike's
          Spies: Eisenhower and the Espionage Establishment.
          New York: Doubleday, 1981. 368.
     "When Eisenhower became President, he encouraged the growth
of the CIA."

2604.   Anawalt, H.C. "A Critical Appraisal of Snepp v.
          United States: Are There Alternatives to Government
          Censorship?" SCLR 21 (1981) 697-726.
     "The order to submit writing for prepublication review
should have been considered an invalid prior restraint."

2605.   Anderson, Dave. "In Boulder, the CIA Gets the Cold
          Shoulder." Guard 38.13 (Dec. 1985) 7.
     A Boulder, Colorado group, Community in Action, "wants to
bring the issue of CIA criminality to the courts."

2606.   Andres, Monica. "The Quality of Censorship: What
          the CIA Defines as Damaging to the National Security."
          FP 5.7 (1980) 6-7.
     Once again, "the CIA has gained the power to censor its
critics as well as its friends."

2607.   Autin, Dianna M.T.K. "FOIA in the Courts." ORK
          (Spring 1983) 14.
     A look at how loopholes have allowed the CIA to "withhold
the information requested by Nassar Afshar, an Iranian-born U.S.
citizen and longtime critic of the former Shah of Iran."

2608.   Beck, Melvin. Secret Contenders: The Myth of Cold
          War Counterintelligence. New York: Sheridan, 1984.
          158.
     The author criticizes covert operations for "often"
straying "into activities that were not its job or in its
charter" at "the urging of shortsighted, irrational people in
power who defied reform." "The same centers of entrenched power
were responsible for implanting an unreasoning Cold War attitude
and almost fanatical anti-communist stance that undermined the
purposes for which the Agency was created."

2609.   Bennett, James R. and Christopher Gould. "Reporting
          the CIA: National Security or Civil Liberties?" FSN
          7 (June 1981) 3-12.
     The authors found insufficient coherence, substantiation,
and diverse perspectives in the newspapers studied for well-
informed judgment on the part of readers.

2610.   Bernstein, Carl. "The CIA and the Media." RS
          (Oct. 20, 1977) 55-67.
     More than 400 American journalists had worked with the CIA
because of the Cold War and such media as the Washington Post,
UPI, AP, ABC, NBC, CBS, the Hearst Chain, and Newsweek. The
CIA's most valuable link among news organizations has been the
New York Times, CBS, and Time. The final report of the Senate

429

Intelligence Committee, chaired by Senator Frank Church, understated the scope of CIA activities.

2611.   "Better No Law." Na 230.19 (1980) 579.
The CIA is "a national disgrace" but legislation will probably only worsen its behavior.

2612.   "Between (and under) Covers." Prog 46.12 (1982)
          13-14.
The CIA is "one of the world's largest [book] publishers," and perhaps the most secretive.

2613.   "Bigger Than Us." Na 236.18 (1983) 562.
The Nation's suit against the CIA for censoring an article it published by Ralph McGehee.

2614.   Bird, Kai, and Max Holland. "C.I.A. Methods--Plus
          ça Change." Na 240.4 (1985) 104.
Intelligence officials arranged for Klaus ("Butcher of Lyon") Barbie to flee Germany in the late 1940s, and in 1979 the CIA helped the director general of Iran's bloody secret police, SAVAK, escape to Turkey.

2615.   Bird, Kai, and Max Holland. "C.I.A. Police Training."
          Na 242.22 (1986) 783.
The CIA and AID's Office of Public Safety trains state terrorist police.

2616.   Biskind, Peter. "How the CIA Manages the Media."
          SD 2.1 (1978) 26-27.
"Publishers and high-level management not only welcome CIA overtures but often volunteer their services."

2617.   Black, George, and Anne Nelson. "The U.S. in Honduras:
          Mysterious Death of Fr. Carney." Na 239.3 (1984)
          65, 81-84.
There are "strong suggestions that U.S. intelligence and military personnel took part in the Honduran combat operations" which resulted in the death of Father James Francis Carney in 1983.

2618.   Borosage, Robert L., and John Marks, eds. The CIA
          File. New York: Grossman, 1976. 236.
Eleven papers on covert action. "Covert action violates some of the basic principles of our constitutional order, of international law, and of values generally shared by American citizens" (Preface).

2619.   "Broad Discretion to Keep Its Sources Secret Given to
          CIA." AG (April 17, 1985) 1A.
"The Court, by a 7 to 2 vote, gave the CIA unlimited power to protect not only secret agents but all other sources of information--classified and unclassified."

2620.   Caldeira, Mark, and Rebecca Thatcher. "U. Mass. Calls
     in Cops to Break Sit-in." Guard 39.10 (1986) 3.
     Students (including Amy Carter from Brown U) protested CIA
recruiting on campus because of the agency's violations of laws
globally.

2621.   Carson, Hank. "Harvard Mideast Scholar Sacked."
     Guard 38.15 (1986) 4.
     Concerns the "CIA funding scandal that rocked Harvard's
Center for Middle Eastern Studies in October," but questions why
investigators failed to address "the fundamental political and
moral issue, which is why Harvard and other U.S. universities
tolerate policy-related intelligence gathering under the guise
of purportedly scholarly research."

2622.   Chavkin, Samuel. The Murder of Chile: Eyewitness
     Accounts of the Coup, the Terror, and the Resistance
     Today. New York: Everest, 1982. 286.
     The CIA and the Nixon-Kissinger team were chief causes of
the destabilization of Chile and the murder of its president,
Salvador Allende in 1973. [See IV.H.2.]

2623.   "Checking up on Casey." Na 233.4 (1981) 99-100.
     CIA Director William Casey's deceptions make "us worry
about his competence as a deceiver" and "about the competence of
members of the Senate as confirmers."

2624.   Church, Frank. "Covert Action: Swampland of American
     Foreign Policy." BAS 32.2 (1976) 7-11.
     The CIA's disastrous covert activities, usually enacted out
of fear of communism or Marxism, have created only hostility.

2625.   The CIA and the Media. Washington, DC: U.S.
     GPO, 1978. 627.
     A report by the House of Representatives Select Committee
on Intelligence (the Pike Committee) on the relationship between
the CIA and journalists.

2626.   "CIAntics." NR 169.24 (1973) 7-8.
     Some US journalists abroad are CIA undercover agents.

2627.   "The CIA: Get the Leash On." CJR 18.6 (1980) 20-21.
     President Carter scuttled the proposed new intelligence
charter proposed by Senator Huddleston and the Senate Select
Committee on Intelligence, and ended attempts to reform the CIA,
including an end to the use of journalists.

2628.   "The CIA: Incorrigible." Prog 45.9 (1981) 9-10.
     The CIA is "a terrorist organization in design, purpose,
and execution."

2629.   "CIA, the Press and Central America." CAIB 21
     (Spring 1984) 7-23.
     Two essays on the extent of US-sponsored terrorism and the

way the US establishment media treat it. One essay appraises the
pro-US bias of The New York Times in reporting the 1984
Salvadoran and Nicaraguan elections, the second exposes the
covert pro-US propaganda in Time and Newsweek.

2630.   "CIA Studying Article by Post on Espionage."
           AG (May 22, 1986) 6A.
Even though the SU already knew about the CIA's high-tech
eavesdropping device sown in Soviet harbors by US submarines,
the CIA is threatening to prosecute the Washington Post and NBC
News for reporting the facts to the US public.

2631.   "C.I.A. Symbolism." Na 230.10 (1980) 292-293.
     The CIA continues to attack FOIA requirements in its desire
to avoid public accountability.

2632.   "CIA Threat of Prosecution of Press in Intelligence
           Leaks Draws Attacks." AG (May 8, 1986) 5A.
     The proper response by the government is to stop the leak.
One expert on the First Amendment observed that it would be a
"major turnabout in American history for a journalist to be
prosecuted for furnishing truthful information in news
articles."

2633. Cancelled.

2634.   Clarkson, Fred. "Behind the Supply Lines." CAIB 25
           (Winter 1986) 56, 50-53.
     "Both Congress and the public have been blatantly
manipulated by the administration and the CIA" in "the use of
private groups by military and intelligence agencies."

2635.   Covert Action In Chile 1963-1973: Staff Report.
           Senate Select Committee to Study Governmental Operations
           with Respect to Intelligence Activities. Washington, DC:
           GPO, 1975. 62.
     Sen. Frank Church leads an investigation into the
activities of the CIA in Chile.

2636.   Cranberg, Gilbert. "The Casey Offensive." CJR 25.2
           (1986) 18-19.
     CIA Director William Casey's threats to prosecute news
organizations for printing or airing allegedly secret
information is an "assault on open government" and possibly an
effort to establish an Official Secrets Act through Title 18,
Section 798, of the U.S. Code.

2637.   Dinges, John and Saul Landau. "The C.I.A.'s Link
           to Chile's Plot." Na 234.23 (1982) 712-13.
     The CIA possibly "concealed facts about its relation with
DINA, the Chilean secret police, that might have helped solve
the murder" of Chilean exile leader Orlando Letelier "quickly."
[See IV.H.2.]

2638.   Doolittle, Jerome. "Notes of a Spookwatcher: As

Ever, You Get What You Pay For." <u>Na</u> 235.16 (1982) 490.
Examples of how CIA payment for information can produce
distortion and lies.

2639.   Drinnon, Richard. "Who is Edward G. Lansdale."
         <u>Inq</u> 2.4 (February 5, 1979) 25-26.
A review of Lansdale's autobiography. Lansdale infiltrated
and influenced the politics of the Philippines and South Vietnam
for the CIA.

2640.   Equale, Tony. "CIA Manual Targets Priests." <u>NaR</u>
         9.2 (1985) 8.
Out of the 300 odd pages of the "infamous CIA <u>Manual</u>" about
the "psychological war against Nicaragua" only two people are
listed as "subjects of special attack," both priests, Miguel
d'Escoto and Fernando Cardenal. Revelation of the manual's
encouragement of assassination has embarrassed the Reagan
administration.

2641.   Eveland, Wilbur. <u>Ropes of Sand: American's Failure
         in the Middle East</u>. New York: Norton, 1980. 382.
"Presumably the CIA is entitled to lie before Congress,
violate the rights of American citizens, employ newspapers,
magazines, book publishers, press services, radio and T.V.
stations for propagandizing Americans and foreigners, as well as
to intervene without accountability in the affairs of sovereign
nations. Nonetheless, I still believe that the First Amendment
protects a citizen's right to criticize our government" (14, in
response to the CIA's efforts to censor this book). "The United
States must demonstrate to the Third World nations that we are
concerned foremost with the people of the Middle East and that
we do not regard that area as merely a source of oil or a
platform for military bases" (365).

2642.   Franck, Thomas M. and James J. Eisen. "Balancing
         National Security and Free Speech." <u>NYUJLP</u> 14
         (Winter 1982) 339-369.
The Supreme Court's support of the CIA's breach of contract
suit against Frank Snepp is "highly unsatisfactory," because it
contravenes the first amendment, which protects disclosure of
unclassified information.

2643.   Frazier, Howard, ed. <u>Uncloaking the CIA</u>. New York:
         Free, 1978. 288.
Twenty-six "presentations made at or prepared in connection
with the Conference on the CIA and World Peace held at Yale
University on April 5, 1975." "The CIA's smokescreen that it is
mainly involved in gathering information with only occasional
sallies into covert political operations and that it is only a
defensive response ('counterintelligence') to the much larger
operations of the Soviet KGB is indefensible. Its now notorious
practices--corruption, sabotage, assassination--are aimed
against the forces of reform and revolution in Third World
countries and in the service of the 'Pax Americana' of
repression and unequal distribution of wealth preferred by

American multinational corporations. . . .The intelligence
establishment's domestic operations show that it has tried out
for the role of gravedigger of liberty at home as well as
abroad" (3).

2644.   Freed, Donald and Fred Landis. Death in Washington:
          The Murder of Orlando Letelier. Westport, CT: Hill,
          1980. 254.
The authors charge that the assassination of the former
Chilean Ambassador to the US by officials of the Pinochet
military junta which rules Chile was known to the CIA and that
the CIA, State Department officials, and right-wing Americans
who helped overthrow the Allende government "also attempted to
cover up for the murder of Orlando Letelier."

2645.   Friedman, John. "Culture War II." Na 232.15
          (1981) 452-53.
The anticommunist organization Committee for the Free World
is supported by several foundations with "close ties to the
C.I.A.": the Smith Richardson Foundation and the Scaife Family
Charitable Trusts.

2646.   Friedman, John. "Press Fights CIA Curbs on
          Information." WJR 2.4 (1980) 11-12.
On efforts by the CIA, backed by the Justice Department, to
establish more exclusions from FOIA disclosure.

2647.   Friedman, John. "Public TV's C.I.A. Show." Na 231.3
          (1980) 73-77.
Right wing foundations--the Scaife Family Trusts and the
Smith Richardson Foundation--are funding PBS programs like
Night Watch at Langley on the CIA in conflict of interest.

2648.   "Future Secrets." Na 230.7 (1980) 197,212.
The proposed foreign intelligence charter bill (S.2284)
"would almost totally exempt" the CIA from the FOIA.

2649.   Garwood, Darrell. Under Cover: Thirty-Five Years
          of C.I.A. Deception. New York: Grove, 1985. 309.
          (Orig. American Shadow. Stafford, VA: Dan River,
          1980).
"It seems to me the present crisis in international affairs
exists not only because the CIA has largely succeeded in
undermining this country's once-treasured integrity" but because
it has shaped and "especially" frustrated "American foreign
policy" (Foreword by author). The sixteen chapters are divided
into I, "The CIA Abroad" (Gary Powers and U-2, the Bay of Pigs,
etc.), and II, "The CIA at Home" (failure of Congress,
infiltration of SDS, etc.). "It is important that we be
reminded of this history, because the record of our nation's
covert activities is largely a record of violations of law and
abuses of power. It contradicts the principles of justice and
nonintervention in the affairs of other nations which America
claims to uphold. . . .Most CIA covert action has been a

violation of our Neutrality Act. Most of it has violated agreements respecting the sovereignty of nations embodied in Article 2(4) of the United Nations Charter, which our government signed, and in United Nations General Assembly Resolutions 2131 (XX) of 1965 and 2625 (XXV) of 1970, which our government approved. All of it has been a betrayal of international trust. . . .The public lately has been led to believe that covert action to protect our national interests is legitimate," but "illegitimate use of force has earned only" the "contempt" of other nations (Introduction by Tom Gervasi).

2650.   Gelb, L.H. "The CIA and the Press: Bearing Out
         Seymour Hersh." NR 172.12 (1975) 13-16.
    Hersh correctly stated that the CIA conducted "a massive, illegal domestic intelligence operation during the Nixon Administration," in spite of CIA denials, well reported by the press, and attacks on his credibility by various journalists and officials.

2651.   "The Great Southern African War." CS 2.4 (Winter
         1976) 34-39.
    "Americans can substantially aid in the defeat of the Nixon-Kissinger Doctrine by demanding a more democratic foreign policy decided by the majority of the public rather than in corporate board rooms and the secret chambers of the CIA."

2652.   Halperin, Morton. "The CIA and Manipulation of the
         American Press." FP 3.5 (1978) 1-5.
    Discusses the CIA's "hidden impact on the press": 1) "use of the American and foreign press to influence events and opinions in the United States," and 2) "background investigations of journalists without their permission and knowledge."

2653.   Halperin, Morton. "The CIA on American Campuses:
         The Harvard Confrontation." FP 4.1 (1978) 1-4.
    Harvard investigated and countered the agency's covert activities.

2654.   Hanrahan, John.   "CIA Mind Control Experiments."
         SD 2.2 (1977) 28.
    More on CIA's use of "LSD, psycho-surgery and electroshock" and its failure to provide documentation on MKULTRA mind control experiments.

2655.   Herman, Edward S. "An Overview: U.S. Sponsorship of
         State Terrorism." CAIB 26 (Summer 1986) 27-33.
    Through the CIA and other mechanisms the government "aided the forces of state terrorism" by invasion, subversion, and counterinsurgency. US success is demonstrated by the military takeovers and rise of national security states.

2656.   Hermann, Kai. "Klaus Barbie: A Killer's Career."
         CAIB 25 (Winter 1986) 15-20.
    Documents Barbie's connections to the CIA.

435

2657.   Hertz, David. "Security Leak: Is It Espionage?"
     IREJ 9.3 (Summer 1986) 19-20.
CIA Director William Casey's threat to prosecute media that
broadcast or publish information about US covert intelligence
activities is an over-reaction. "The majority of leaking is
done for policy reasons."

2658.   Hinckle, Warren. "MSU: The University on the Make."
     Ram 4.12 (1966) 11-22.
CIA men "were hidden within the ranks of the Michigan State
University professors."

2659.   Hitchens, Christopher. "Minority Report." Na 239.16
     (1984) 502.
The CIA handbook on atrocities prepared for the Contras,
and other CIA wrongdoings.

2660.   Hitchens, Christopher. "Minority Report." Na 236.23
     (1983) 724.
Richard Nixon had the financial support of the Greek
dictators during the 1968 election. The dictatorship was itself
financed by the CIA. "Covert action not only undermines the
sovereignty of smaller nations" but "inevitably rebounds to
debauch American democracy as well."

2661.   Hitt, Jack. "Warning: CIA Censors at Work." CJR
     23.2 (1984) 44-46.
A look at "how the CIA has, for years, been censoring books
and articles" by its former employees. Censorship was informal
until the establishment of the Publications Review Board in
1977, which began censoring materials already in the public
domain, as in books by Frank Snepp and Ralph McGehee. President
Reagan's 1982 Executive Order 12356 intensified the censorship
by allowing intelligence agencies to reclassify "retrievable"
information that has become public.

2662.   Holzman, Franklyn D. "Dollars or Rubles: The CIA's
     Military Estimates." BAS 36.6 (1980) 23-27.
Comparisons of military spending in the US and the USSR,
published by the CIA, are misleading.

2663.   Honey, Martha. "Contra Polygraphs." Na 242.12
     (1986) 445.
CIA attempts to compel the Costa Rica-based Contra leaders
to take a lie-detector test have alienated them.

2664.   Honey, Martha, and Tony Avirgan. "The Carlos File."
     Na 241.10 (1985) 311-315.
The CIA and the Contras in Costa Rica. The CIA "is
involved in dirty tricks in Central America which are designed
to provoke U.S. intervention" in Nicaragua.

2665.   Kaplan, Carl, and Fred Halliday. "The Savak-C.I.A.
     Conection." Na 230.8 (1980) 229-230.

The CIA "had knowledge of instances of Savak torture," the
Agency "trained Savak agents in interrogation techniques," and
"knowledge of Savak torture was kept from the American public
for more than a quarter of a century."

2666.   Kelly, John. "Censored!" NaR 9 (Winter 1986) 55.
A list of writers and researchers who have voluntarily
submitted their work to CIA censors for review.

2667.   Kelly, John. "CIA Lies About Central America."
     CS 7.2 (1982) 22-27.
Criticism of CIA reports on El Salvador and Nicaragua by
the staff of the Subcommittee on Oversight and Evaluation of the
House Permanent Select Committee on Intelligence.

2668.   Kim, Young, ed. The Central Intelligence Agency:
     Problems of Secrecy in a Democracy. Lexington, MA:
     Heath, 1968. 113.
Twelve essays and the editor's introduction, divided into
four sections: I "Background, Power, and Danger of the CIA,"
II "Rationale and Defense of the CIA," III "Attacks on the CIA,"
IV "Need for Supervision and Control of the CIA." Three of the
essays deal with how the CIA has compromised the integrity of
the educational establishment.

2669.   Kondracke, Morton. "The CIA and 'Our Conspiracy.'"
     MORE 5 (May 1975) 10-12.
How then-CIA director William E. Colby persuaded some of
the major newspapers and newsmagazines not to run a story on the
CIA's attempt to raise a sunken Soviet submarine from the
Pacific Ocean floor.

2670.   LaFeber, Walter. "Lest We Forget the Bay of Pigs."
     Na 242.15 (1986) 537, 549.
The CIA-created Contras of 1986 resemble the CIA-created
invaders of Cuba of 1961. Neither is "an independent band of
dedicated patriots who will stem the tide of communism" as
President Kennedy claimed and as President Reagan claims.

2671.   Landau, Saul, and Craig Nelson. "The C.I.A. Rides
     Again." Na 234.9 (1982) 257, 274-5.
The CIA is secretly funneling funds to the Contras through
countries aligned with the US in order to destabilize Nicaragua.
[See IV.H.1.]

2672.   Landis, Fred. "CIA Psychological Warfare Operations:
     Case Studies in Chile, Jamaica, and Nicaragua." ScP
     (Jan.-Feb. 1982) 6-11, 29-37.
CIA methods for taking over a newspaper are studied through
the examples of Chile's El Mercurio, Jamaica's Daily Gleaner,
and Nicaragua's La Prensa. (Landis also wrote his dissertation
on "Psychological Warfare and Media Operations in Chile: 1970-
1973"; "Psychological Warfare in the Media: The Case of
Jamaica," 32 pp.; a series on La Prensa in Barricada, July 8-22;

and he contributed to "Covert Action," Vol. 7 of the 1975 Hearings of the Senate Church Committee and to "The CIA and the Media," 1977-78 Hearings of the House Intelligence Committee.)

2673.   Langguth, Arthur. Hidden Terrors. New York: Pantheon, 1978. 345.
CIA support of police terrorism in US client states, focusing upon the story of Dan Mitrione, the US police advisor in Uruguay executed in 1970 by the Tupamaros.

2674.   Lardner, George, Jr. "The Agency's Bill: Moynihan Unleashes the C.I.A." Na 230.6 (1980) 161, 176-178.
The Intelligence Reform Act of 1980 "amounts to an official secrets act." S.2216 "could have been written by the C.I.A.--as indeed much of it was."

2675.   Laurence, Philip, and Tracey Dewart. "The CIA Goes to College," NT 4.5 (1986) 21-2.
An article in Harvard's International Security journal was CIA-financed.

2676.   "Leash the C.I.A." Na 230.3 (1980) 69.
In spite of his campaign pledge to leash the CIA, Carter is seeking to eliminate the only reform of the CIA passed by Congress after Watergate--the Hughes-Ryan amendment.

2677.   Lee, Martin. "C.I.A.: Carcinogen." Na 234.22 (1982) 675.
The CIA's "multi-million-dollar project" to "develop and test psychotropic drugs" included "cancer-causing drugs to use in assassinating political opponents."

2678.   Lee, Martin, and Bruce Shlain. Acid Dreams: The CIA, LSD, and the Sixties Rebellion. New York: Grove, 1985. 343.
"Nearly every drug that appeared on the black market during the 1960s" had been "scrutinized, tested, and in some cases refined by CIA and army scientists" as part of a never substantiated claim by the CIA that "the Soviets and the Red Chinese might have been mucking about with LSD in the 1950s." The book is a study both of the CIA's "multimillion-dollar twenty-five-year quest to conquer the human mind" and of the psychedelic movement.

2679.   Lernoux, Penny. "C.I.A. Secret Missionaries." Na 230.16 (1980) 494-496.
On CIA use of clerics and missionaries as informants and for covert activities.

2680.   Lernoux, Penny. "Golden Gateway for Drugs: the Miami Connection." Na 238.6 (1984) 186-198.
"The C.I.A.-mob narcotics connection will not be broken by this Administration."

2681.   "Liberals and the Reagan Doctrine." Prog 50.10
        (1986) 11.
    In support of the Reagan Doctrine of opposing communist
governments everywhere, the CIA is helping overthrow the
government of Angola.

2682.   "Locking the Files." Na 238.14 (1984) 435-436.
    Further erosion of the FOIA. CIA operational files are
pertinent to "dirty tricks" in "progress today" and should be
open to the public.

2683.   Loory, Stuart H. "The CIA's Use of the Press:
        A 'Mighty Wurlitzer.'" CJR 13.3 (1974) 9-18.
    The CIA contracts with newsmen in order to obtain
information from news organizations and in order to leak untrue
or misleading news stories worldwide.

2684.   Mackenzie, Angus. "Better Late Than Never?" NR
        9.2 (1985) 12-13.
    The American Civil Liberties Union now opposes key portions
of the 1984 CIA Information Act which was enacted last year
"primarily because of ACLU support." The 1984 Act was intended
to speed up FOIA requests by exempting operational files
without decreasing significant access to the public, but the
speed-up did not occur and access did decrease.

2685.   Mackenzie, Angus. "A C.I.A.-A.C.L.U. Deal?: The
        Operational Files Exemption." Na 237.8 (1983)
        231-234.
    The ACLU joined the CIA and the Senate Intelligence
Committee in support of S.1324, which exempts the agency's
"operational files" from FOIA search and disclosure
requirements. [The ACLU later repudiated its agreement.]

2686.   Mackenzie, Angus. "Darker Cloaks, Longer Daggers:
        A New Law Protects Spies' Identities and Covers Up
        Their Dirty Work." Prog 26.6 (1982) 39-41.
    The Intelligence Identities Protection Act visits
"destruction" on press freedom and the public's need to know
about illegal activities in governmental agencies.

2687.   Mackenzie, Angus. "Welcome Reversal." Na 240.16
        (1985) 485.
    The ACLU now opposes a 1984 law tightening CIA secrecy
because the law "could be used to cover up domestic intelligence
operations."

2688.   Marchetti, Victor and John Marks. The CIA and the
        Cult of Intelligence. New York: Knopf, 1974; Dell,
        1980. 377.
    "What Victor Marchetti and John Marks did was a classic
vindication of the American constitutional theory that public
knowledge is essential to both democratic and effective
government" (from the Introduction by Anthony Lewis).

2689.   Marks, John. The Search for the 'Manchurian
          Candidate': The CIA and Mind Control. New York:
          Times, 1979. 242.
     An account of CIA drug experiments and an appeal for strict
controls on the CIA. The author compares the scientists who
performed these tests with the Nazi doctors who performed tests
on inmates at concentration camps and who were sentenced to
death for "crimes against humanity."

2690.   McGarvey, Patrick J. C.I.A.: The Myth and the
          Madness. New York: Saturday Review, 1972. 240.
     The CIA is "an insufferable bureaucratic morass with little
or no central direction, sorely needing drastic change."
Examples: one agent was transferred to an insignificant job
when he put forward evidence about MIG defenses in Eastern
Europe which contradicted exaggerated Air Force budget requests;
Thailand and South Korea were praised publicly by the US
government for "spontaneously" entering the Vietnam War, but
secretly it was strictly a financial deal costing the taxpayers
billions of dollars; etc. "It is a pervasive sickness."

2691.   McGehee, Ralph. "Back In The Saddle Again." Prog
          49.8 (1985) 32-33.
     Under the scrutiny of Congressional investigations, the CIA
"substantially reduce[d] its illegal operations. Now, the reins
on the CIA have been removed," and "we should anticipate gross
violations of the law and renewed attempts to build the powers
of a police state."

2692.   McGehee, Ralph. "The C.I.A. and the White Paper
          on El Salvador." Na 232.14 (1981) 423-25.
     The CIA invented situations and forged documents to bring
about the overthrow of the governments of Chile and Indonesia.
Now the same deceptions are occurring in El Salvador to defeat
the rebels. The CIA censored this article, and the author and
Na are suing for "unreasonable prior restraint."

2693.   McGehee, Ralph. Deadly Deceits: My Twenty-Five
          Years in the CIA. Berkeley: Meiklejohn Civil
          Liberties, 1983. 250.
     The CIA is "the covert arm of the President's" foreign
policy, and disinforming the public is one of its chief
responsibilities.

2694.   McGrory, Mary. "CIA's Casey Wants Press in the Dark."
          AG (May 30, 1986) 21A.
     Contrary to the Reagan administration's "professed
devotion" to freedom, it has acted consistently to reduce
individual liberties. Casey is one agent of this attack on
freedom.

2695.   Melanson, Philip. "The C.I.A.'s Secret Ties to Local
          Police." Na 236.12 (1983) 352, 364-68.
     President Reagan's Executive Order 12333 allowing the CIA

to conduct domestic intelligence operations encourages the
expansion of CIA/local police suppression of dissent.

2696.   Miller, Arthur S. "Carter and the CIA." _Prog_ 41.5
          (1977) 9-10.
     President Carter responded to press disclosure of CIA
bribery of King Hussein by tightening secrecy, revealing he has
"become a prisoner of 'the system.'"

2697.   Miller, Judith. "Gary Weissman's Catch 22." _Prog_
          41.1 (1977) 10.
     The CIA refuses to give Weissman the documents it illegally
compiled on him.

2698.   Nairn, Allan. "Behind the Death Squads." _Prog_ 48.5
          (1984) 20-29.
     Early in the 1960s, the CIA created "two official security
organizations" in El Salvador "that killed thousands of
peasants and suspected leftists over the next fifteen years."
These organizations developed the death squads ravaging El
Salvador today. The CIA, "in violation of U.S. law--continues
to provide training, support, and intelligence to security
forces directly involved in Death Squad activity."

2699.   Nairn, Allan. "Confessions of a Death Squad Officer."
          Prog 50.3 (1986) 26-29.
     A Salvadoran army officer who says he worked for the CIA
and participated in Death Squad assassinations contradicts
Reagan Administration and El Salvadoran denials of military
origination of death squads and of CIA torture training.

2700.   Neier, Aryeh. "The C.I.A. as Censor." _Na_ 230.20
          (1980) 617-620.
     CIA censors testifying before HR's Select Committee on
Intelligence regarding the Supreme Court's _Snepp_ decision
revealed that "their concern is with appearances rather than
with actual secrets," and with "appearing as a monolith and
inspiring fear."

2701.   Neier, Aryeh. "Frank Snepp: A Win for the CIA."
          _IC_ 9.4 (1980) 51-56.
     The author deplores the Supreme Court decision allowing the
CIA to censor Snepp's book about the CIA, for the decision
"appears to provide the government of the United States with a
power it has never previously enjoyed, or even claimed: the
power to censor the writings and speeches of all employees and
former employees." Henceforth "one of the two principal methods
Americans have had of learning of governmental abuses--whistle-
blowing by employees and former employees of the government--
will be simply curbed."

2702.   Nocera, Joseph. "Le Couvert Blown: William Colby
          en Francais." _WM_ 14.9 (1980) 11-19.
          Censorship by the CIA Publicaitons Review Board.

441

2703.   O'Keeffe, Mike. "Boulder: Three Hundred Protest CIA
     Recruitment; Police Riot." Guard 39.10 (1986) 3.
     Community in Action members protested CIA violations of
national and international laws throughout the world.

2704.   "Open Letter to the C.I.A." Na 235.12 (1982) 353.
     A defense of the FOIA against CIA attack by Director
Casey.

2705.   "Paper Reports Harvard Official to Resign; CIA Backed
     Work." AG (Jan. 2, 1986) 10A.
     The director of Harvard University's Center for Middle
Eastern Studies is resigning because he had secretly accepted
$45,000 from the CIA to finance a conference, and $107,000 for
a book on Saudi Arabia.

2706.   Peck, Keenen. "Strange Bedfellows: When the ACLU
     Teams up with the CIA." Prog 48.11 (1984) 28-31.
     By supporting a bill to exclude the CIA operational files
from FOIA scrutiny, the ACLU strengthened interests "wholly
inimical to the right of Americans."

2707.   Peck, Winslow. "The AFL-CIA Goes On Safari." CS
     2.3 (1975) 51-63.
     An overview of CIA-labor collaboration in Africa. "The
evidence indicates cooperation between the AFL-CIO and the
Central Intelligence Agency is perhaps the most strategic
element of continued multinational corporate power and
influence."

2708.   Peck, Winslow. "Clandestine Enforcement of U.S.
     Foreign Labor Policy." CS 2.1 (1974) 26-46, 48.
     Multinational corporations use intelligence to collect
information on anti-corporate forces worldwide (the SU, Third
World nationalism, national liberation movements), and they use
this intelligence clandestinely to achieve policies advantageous
to themselves. The corporations have their own intelligence
networks, but "the most important intelligence resource
available to them" is the CIA.

2709.   Peck, Winslow. "Death On Embassy Row." CS 3.2
     (1976) 8-15.
     The author claims that the CIA is covering up a "murder
web of Chilean Gestapo with false stories and terrorist
operations."

2710.   Pell, Eve. "Taking C.I.A. Critics to Court." Na
     233.12 (1981) 371-72.
     Former agent David Atlee Phillips's libel suits are part of
the "danger to anyone who attemts to write about illegal acts
committed by the intelligence community."

2711.   Perlo, Victor. "C.I.A. Numbers Game: the Myth of
     Soviet Superiority." Na 231.7 (1980) 201, 214-218.

CIA data alleging higher Soviet military spending are inaccurate and misleading. "The C.I.A.'s fictitious figures about comparative Soviet and U.S. military activities generate the political climate in which nuclear war is more likely."

2712.	Peterzell, Jay. "Can the CIA Spook the Press?" CJR 25.3 (1986) 29-34.
CIA Director Casey's efforts to censor the press under the espionage law is a "time bomb" endangering the First Amendment.

2713.	Peterzell, Jay. "No Bars for Mars at the C.I.A.?" Na 241.7 (1985) 193, 209.
CIA Director William Casey used CIA facilities to assist the business of a friend.

2714.	Pless, Laurance. "Snepp v. United States--Short Shrift for the Prior Restraint Doctrine." NCLR 59 (1981) 417-427.
A "future Supreme Court. . . must still consider the important constitutional questions raised, but not resolved, in Snepp" (CIA censorship of Decent Interval).

2715.	Poelchau, Warner, ed. White Paper Whitewash: Interviews with Philip Agee on the CIA and El Salvador. New York: Deep cover, 1981. 101 + 103 (2 Appendixes).
A refutation of the false "captured documents" used by the Reagan administration to support its claim of "indirect aggression" against El Salvador "by Communist powers acting through Cuba." The opening some 70 pages give background to CIA document falsification practices (Agee is an ex-CIA officer), and other CIA operations. The State Department White Paper on El Salvador, based upon the documents, is then analyzed, followed by the text of the "White Paper" and the text of the "Dissent Paper" (the views of current and former government officials).

2716.	Pollock, Richard. "In the Winter of 1957. . ." CMJ 6.1 (1980) 4,11.
For twenty years the CIA withheld information about a major nuclear waste accident which took place in the Soviet Union in the winter of 1957, because it pointed to US nuclear problems.

2717.	Prouty, Leroy Fletcher. The Secret Team: The CIA and Its Allies in Control of the United States and the World. Englewood Cliffs, NJ: Prentice, 1973. 496.
An analysis of the "inseparably intertwined" roles of secrecy in government and anticommunism "which have nurtured each other in a blind Pavlovian way." Part I examines "The Secret Team," the increasing "control over military and diplomatic operations at home and abroad by men whose activities are secret, whose budget is secret, whose very identities as often as not are secret." Part II, "The CIA: How it Runs," Part III, "The CIA: How It Is Organized," Part IV, "The CIA: Some Examples Throughout the World." "We must end the exploitation of secret intelligence by clandestine operations . . . . The CIA should be limited to the function of intelligence--

and not a bit more" (426).

2718.   Ray, Ellen, et al., eds. Dirty Work II: The CIA
     in Africa. Secaucus, NJ: Stuart, 1979. 523.
     Thirty-three essays on clandestine operations by the CIA in
Africa. Sean MacBride declares he felt compelled to write the
Preface because "all the values that made me admire the American
people were being eroded by the covert operations of the CIA and
kindred secret bodies." Two of the essays focus upon media
control; four on CIA use of academics and universities.

2719.   Ray, Ellen, et al. "Half a Billion Allocated: the
     C.I.A. Chooses a New Contra Leader." CAIB 26 (Summer
     1986) 25-26.
     Further evidence of CIA direction of contra forces
attacking Nicaragua and of the excess of $100 million being
approved by Congress for the "vile and illegal war."

2720.   Report to the President by the Commission on CIA
     Activities Within the United States. Washington:
     U.S. GPO, 1975. 299.
     The Rockefeller Commission report on suppression of dissent
concluded that "the great majority of the CIA's domestic
activities comply with its statutory authority," but some of its
actions during the past 28 years were "plainly unlawful and
constituted improper invasions upon the rights of Americans."

2721.   Richman, David. "CIA Silences a Whistle Blower." HR
     10.1 (1982) 24-27, 48-52.
     The CIA censored Frank Snepp's Decent Interval even though
it contained no classified material. Effective government has
been damaged because whistleblowing is "an integral part of our
constitutive process."

2722.   Robbins, Christopher. Air America: The Story of the
     CIA's Secret Airlines. New York: Putnam's, 1979. 323.
     One of the CIA's commercial proprietary corporations
created for Clandestine Services, or dirty tricks, Air America
became at one time "the largest airline in the world."

2723.   Roettinger, Philip C. "The Company, Then and Now."
     Prog 50.7 (1986) 50.
     In overthrowing the Guatemalan government in 1954 the CIA
told the same lie the Reagan administration is telling in trying
to overthrow the government of Nicaragua--that the subversion is
necessary to prevent a communist beachhead in the Western
Hemisphere.

2724.   Roosevelt, Kermit. Countercoup: The Struggle for the
     Control of Iran. New York: McGraw, 1979. 217.
     An account of the overthrow of the Iranian government of
Prime Minister, Dr. Mohammed Mossadegh, by Britain and the CIA.

2725.   Rositzke, Harry. The CIA's Secret Operations.

New York: Reader's Digest, Crowell, 1977. 286.
The CIA is "a pillar of the Imperial Presidency."

2726.   Rothschild, Matthew. "Central Employment Agency:
Students Respond to the C.I.A. Rush." Prog 48.2
(1984) 18-21.
"The CIA is enjoying a remarkable renaissance on American
college campuses." "Its image has been retouched" and
"remystified," and the students seek an interesting and well-
paying job.

2727.   Ryan, David. "United States vs. Marchetti and Alfred
A. Knopf, Inc. vs. Colby: Secrecy 2: First Amendment
O." HCLQ 3.4 (1976) 1073-1105.
Weighs the NYT/Pentagon Papers principles with the contract
theory applied to the Marchetti/Knopf case "to formulate a
standard for the enforcement of secrecy agreements that will
protect both the need for secrecy and First Amendment rights."

2728.   Salisbury, Harrison. Without Fear or Favor: "The
New York Times" and Its Times. New York: Times, 1980.
652.
A generally admiring history of the Times since the mid-
1950s, but also a study of the "American system of hypocrisy" as
revealed by Watergate, the Civil Rights struggle, and Vietnam,
and of "the CIA as a metaphor of homegrown, secret and out-of-
control bureaucracy" which for a time used the Times. The author
shows how biased is the Times in favor of people in power. For
example, the owner allowed a Central Intelligence Group (late the
CIA) man read private memos and letters from Times correspondents
without their knowledge; the newspaper sat on the Glomar
submarine story at the request of CIA officials; it submitted its
entire 1966 CIA series to John McCone, former director of the
agency, and made changes at his suggestion; etc.

2729.   Sandler, Norman. 28 Years of Looking the Other Way:
Congressional Oversight of the Central Intelligence
Agency, 1947-1975. Cambridge, MA: Center for
International Studies, 1975. 309.
Examines "the reasons behind Congress' inadequate oversight
of the Central Intelligence Agency" and makes suggestions "as to
ways in which the major legal and institutional obstacles to
effective oversight might be overcome. For governmental
agencies to function in a democratic society, there must be a
public accounting of their activities--at least to the elected
representatives of the electorate. This has not occurred in the
case of the CIA and other intelligence agencies. This study is
intended to explain why this has not occurred and how it might
in the future."

2730.   Schechter, Dan, et al. "The CIA is an Equal
Opportunity Employer." Ram 7.13 (1969) 25-33.
CIA methods dealing with "militant blackness."

445

2731.   Schwartz, Herman. "Agents Protection Act: A
    Constitutional Disaster." Na 235.1 (1982) 11-13.
    "For the first time in our country's history, private
citizens can be imprisoned for disclosing information lawfully
obtained from publicly available sources."

2732.   Scott, Peter Dale. "How Allen Dulles and the SS
    Preserved Each Other." CAIB 25 (Winter 1986) 4-14.
    "CIA personnel protected the convicted war criminal Barbie
and concealed him from French authorities." A recent U.S.
Justice Department report on the U.S. handling of the Barbie
case is designed "to blame low-level people in U.S. Army
Counterintelligence while suppressing the rather obvious
connections to the Gehlen organization and its then employers,
the CIA."

2733.   "Secret Panel Co-ordinates Covert Activities, Paper
    Says." AG (March 10, 1986) 7A.
    Summary of a Washington Post story of a new Reagan
administration "208 Committtee" established for covert military
activities around the world to guarantee White House and State
Department control over secret military operations which are
budgeted by the CIA "far exceeding $500 million."

2734.   Seitz, Michael H. "Purposeful Documentary." Prog
    46.1 (1982) 46-47.
    Rev. of On Company Business, a "chronicle of the CIA's most
ignoble operations" abroad--the subversion of Brazilian labor
unions, the attempt to buy an election in Chile and the
overthrow of its goverment, the training of Iranian and Latin
American police in torture methods, etc.

2735.   "Shielding the CIA." CJR 19.1 (1980) 25.
    The Supreme Court ruled that Frank Snepp, a former CIA
employee, could be placed under prior restraint even though his
book, Decent Interval, contained no classified information.

2736.   "'Snepp' Fallout." Na 230.11 (1980) 323-324.
    The Carter administration and the CIA. "The Snepp decision
has given the Government a potent weapon to silence critics from
within its own ranks," as the suit against John Stockwell
demonstrates.

2737.   "Snepp v. United States: The CIA Secrecy Agreement
    and the First Amendment." CLRv 81.3 (1980) 662-706.
    Rejects the CIA prior-approval procedure and proposes "an
alternative system that protects legitimate interests of the CIA
in a manner more consistent with First Amendment values."

2738.   Stanford, Phil. "Watergate Revisited." CJR 24.6
    (1986) 46-49.
    A generally favorable review of Jim Hougan's Watergate
book, Secret Agenda, which alleges that the Watergate break-in
was sabotaged by the CIA to protect its own operations. "The

importance of Hougan's book lies in the questions it raises
about all the old theories."

2739.   Stein, Jeffrey. "The Guild: Spooked Again?" CJR
          18.1 (1979) 6-10.
     Controversy over the Newspaper Guild's acceptance of CIA-
connected AIFLD's $100,000 for training Latin American
journalists.

2740.   Stein, Jeff. "Putting the C.I.A. 'Right':   Reagan's
          Plans for Intelligence." Na 231.2 (1980) 40-41.
     The Reagan-Republican plans for the CIA include checks on
liberals in the Agency, more covert action, weakening the FOIA
and privacy acts, etc.

2741.   Stern, Sol. "A Short Account of International Student
          Politics & the Cold War, with Particular Reference to the
          NSA, CIA, etc." Ram 7.10 (1968) 87-96.
     "It is widely known that the CIA has a number of
foundations which serve as direct fronts or as secret 'conduits'
that channel money from the CIA to preferred organizations."

2742.   Steven, Stewart. Operation Splinter Factor.
          Philadelphia: Lippincott, 1974.   249.
     "Operation Splinter Factor ["probably the foremost
intelligence battle of the Cold War"] represents the nadir of
American foreign-policy making during those bleak Cold War
years. It degraded the cause which it set out to serve and set
back the possibility of detente between East and West for a
generation." The author also deplores "the ability of our
intelligence agencies to escape all public accountability."
Operation Splinter Factor convinced Stalin that the Easten bloc
was riddled with Western agents and that the "American military
assault would not be long in coming" (161).

2743.   Stockwell, John. "A C.I.A. Trip--from Belief, to
          Doubt, to Despair." CM 12.5 (1979) 18-29.
     An attack on the C.I.A.'s anti-Soviet dogmatism and
clandestine operations by an ex-agent. He joined believing the
"simplistic" anticommunist line, but the lying, the covert
actions, the unaccountability, and the killing brought
disillusionment, and a conviction that the CIA was destroying
traditional US values of peace, human rights, and freedom.

2744.   Stockwell, John. In Search of Enemies: A CIA Story.
          New York: Norton, 1978.   285.
     The former chief of the CIA's task force to Angola tells
about how the CIA lied to Congress and "actively propagandized
the American public, with cruel results."

2745.   Stone, Peter. "High Times in the 'Political Risk'
          Business." Na 235.22 (1982) 673, 686-90.
     Many retired CIA agents enter the field of advising
multinational corporations regarding "political violence and

investment uncertainties around the world." One of the chief firms doing such consulting is IMAR, the International Management Analysis and Resources Corporation. Some corporations have established in-house political risk departments. At risk are some $200 billion in US corporate foreign investments.

2746.   "The Story of Donald Alvey." Prog 49.2 (1985) 11.
CIA and Army covert military activities against Nicaragua.

2747.   "Target: Sihanouk." CS 1.3 (1973) 5-22.
On the 20 years of covert war waged by the US intelligence community against Sihanouk of Cambodia. "We present this report as an example of secret government operations which have produced national shame."

2748.   "Two Down, 57,690 to Go." Prog 48.10 (1984) 11-12.
Two members of the US Army's Special Forces Unit of the Alabama National Guard were shot down over Nicaragua after attacking a school in a Huey helicopter.

2749.   "3 Tales of the CIA." Special Report. Ram 5.10
         (1967) 15-28.
CIA agents, student recruitment, and labor union manipulation. "The continued proliferation of the CIA, with its corrupting money and its alien philosophy" could "destroy our democratic society."

2750.   United States and Chile During the Allende Years,
         1970-1973: Hearings. House Subcommittee on Inter-
         American Affairs, 1975. Washington, DC: GPO, 1975.
         677.
Witnesses offer information on the relationship between the two countries, and reprints of articles on CIA activity in Chile are provided.

2751.   Van Houten, Margaret and Tim Butz. "The Inside
         Story Of The Overseas Educational Fund." CS 2.2 (1975)
         10-18.
How the Overseas Education Fund of the League of Women Voters is being used by the CIA.

2752.   Varner, Roy, and Wayne Collier. A Matter of Risk:
         The Incredible Inside Story of the CIA's Hughes Glomar
         Explorer Mission to Raise a Russian Submarine.
         New York: Random, 1978. 258.
The CIA spent over six years and over $550 million to raise a Golf-II submarine which sank in 1968, with minimal intelligence benefit and maximum "risk of military confrontation with the Soviet Union." Also, the "CIA committed numerous illegalities in keeping the project secret," and mission contractors were making "sizable profits" of 30 percent.

2753.   Waas, Murray. "The Case of the Flying Spies."

Na 234.7 (1982) 193, 203-06.
Evidence of CIA and Page Airways connections with the
gunrunning operations of two former CIA employees, Edwin Wilson
and Frank Terpil.

2754.   Waas, Murray. "Covert Charge." Na 234.24
         (1982) 738-9.
The CIA "secretly funneled some $7 million to West German
press baron Axel Springer in the early 1950s to help him build
his vast media empire and serve American geopolitical
interests." [See VII.A.]

2755.   Waas, Murray, and Jeff Chester. "Sworn Testimony."
         Na 233.4 (1981) 100-101.
CIA Director Casey was convicted of plagiarism in 1961 and
misled Senators about the conviction during confirmation
hearings in 1971.

2756.   Weaver, Maureen, and Hannah Roditi. "U.S. Covert
         Operations Against Nicaragua: A Public Forum."
         ON 6.6 (1982) 6-8.
A forum called in response to the Reagan administration's
plan to use CIA covert operations against Nicaragua.

2757.   "The Wilson-Terpil Case: The C.I.A. & the 'Rogue
         Agents.'" Na 233.18 (1981) 561, 563-65.
An introduction to two essays suggesting CIA "complicity"
in the shady deals of former agents Edwin Wilson and Frank
Terpil. The story of Wilson and Terpil "casts grave doubts on
not only the efficiency but also the integrity of the C.I.A. and
of our entire intelligence system."

2758.   Wise, David. "The Secret Committee Called '40.'"
         NYT (Jan. 19, 1975) E4.
A special committee of the national Security Council has a
part in approving the CIA's covert operations.

2759.   Wise, David, and Thomas Ross. The U-2 Affair.
         New York: Random, 1962. 269.
An account of the downing of the US reconnaissance plane
over the USSR in 1960 and the trial of its pilot Francis Gary
Powers. Powers is presented as a pawn in the hands of
overzealous technicians who allowed the game to exceed the bounds
originally established for it.

2760.   Wyden, Peter. Bay of Pigs: The Untold Story.
         New York: Simon, 1979. 352.
An account of the CIA's unsuccessful invasion of Cuba, "the
largest secret operation in U.S. history," the CIA "acting out
of control and independently." "If the reasons for the collapse
at the Bay of Pigs had not been covered up. . . the CIA might
perhaps have been curbed, and the country could have been spared
the intelligence scandals of the 1970s, the revelations of a
government agency routinely, daily, committing unconstitutional

acts against its own citizens in its own country" (7-8).

2761.   Yakovlev, N. Trans. Victor Schneierson and Dmitry
          Belyavsky. CIA Target: The USSR. USSR: Progress,
          1982. 279.
     The CIA's clandestine war against the Soviet Union, with
the aim of controlling the world. "[T]he ruling American
political tradition is intolerance"; thus, "the permanent
conflict between the U.S.A. and the rest of the world is in
fact inevitable. The function role of the CIA is to do what it
can to settle the conflict in America's favor" (9).

VI. D. National Security Agency 2762-2768

2762.   Ball, Desmond. A Suitable Piece of Real Estate:
          American Installations in Australia. Sydney, Aus.:
          Hale, 1980. 180.
     Australia is practically a preserve of the National
Security Agency which massively eavesdrops on worldwide and
Australian communications as part of the US nuclear war fighting
machine against the SU.

2763.   Bamford, James. "How I Got the N.S.A. Files. How
          Reagan Tried to Get Them Back." Na 235.15 (1982) 466-68.
     Documents revealing illegal use of electronic surveillance
by the NSA and the CIA were declassified and released by the
Justice Department. Two years later the two agencies demanded
their reclassification and President Reagan issued an Executive
Order to make it possible.

2764.   Bamford, James. The Puzzle Palace: A Report on
          America's Most Secret Agency. New York: Houghton;
          England: Penguin, 1983. 655.
     Profiles of the NSA leaderhip and analyses of the successes
and failures of the agency.

2765.   Miller, Arthur S. "Police State Tactic." Prog 42.9
          (1978) 9.
     In Halkin v. Helms the US Court of Appeals validated
warrantless wiretaps, "a police state tactic."

2766.   Preston, William, Jr. "The Puzzle Palace, Privacy,
          and Public Access to Information." ORK (Spring 1984)
          11-12.
     Criticism of the "immense Orwellian monstrosity" of the
National Security Agency (NSA), larger than the CIA or the FBI
and possessing "an unrivaled capacity to violate the privacy of
American citizens."

2767.   "U.S. Electronic Espionage: A Memoir." Ram
          (August 1972) 35-50.
     The article describes the activities of the super-secret
National Security Agency, which is said to provide an estimated
80% of all US intelligence information. A former senior NSA

analyst is interviewed about the NSA's intelligence-gathering activities.

2768.   Wirbel, Loring. "Somebody Is Listening: There's a
     Computer on the Line." <u>Prog</u> 44.11 (1980) 16-22.
     A description of the organization and activities of the NSA and its technological assistance to other intelligence organizations. "The secrecy that pervades the 'national security state,' threatening not only the liberties but also the lives of Americans, finds its ultimate expression in the National Security Agency and its computer systems."

VII. GLOBAL 2769-2943

Introduction

A. United States Information Order, Multinational Com-
    munications Corporations, Global Cultural Domina-
    tion   2769-2853

B. New World Information Order, "Free Flow" Contro-
    versy, UNESCO   2854-2897

C. Propaganda, United States Information Agency, Cold
    War   2898-2936

D. Foundations   2937-2943

INTRODUCTION

United States Information Order

Although the phenomenon is in dispute (Lee), the concept of
"media imperialism" in general and US media imperialism in particular have gained increasing adherents in recent years.
("Media imperialism" is defined as the process by which modern
communication media have created, maintained, and expanded world
systems of dominance and dependence.) The contributors to this
part of the bibliography treat US global communications expansion
as part of US world-wide economic, political, and military power.
As elsewhere in the bibliography, the studies focus mainly on the
period following World War II, but several studies offer a larger
historical context. Fejes (1983), for example, describes how by
1945 the "dominant position" of the US government-media corporations partnership in Latin America was so "unchallenged" that it
could "ignore" the problems there "while it turned its major
attention and efforts toward the problems of creating a new" US
economic, political, military, and communications order (25).

Mosco and Herman (1981) suggest broad areas for research into
US global communications power: the submarine cable, the earth-
orbiting satellite, the computer, advertising companies, traditional media (magazines, film, radio, tv), the wire services,
military telecommunications, banking telecommunications, energy
corporation telecommunications, etc. They ask such questions as,
regarding the wire services: Who owns and controls them? What
are their ties to other institutions of US multinational domination? And what impact do ownership and interlocking economic
relationships have on the news they distribute to the world?
Point-to-point communications combined with traditional mass
media, they argue, generate both "vast accumulation" and a "world
system of legitimation" for it.

New International Information Order

US global ascendancy, the leading factor in the developed-
undeveloped, North-South confrontation, is being played out in
the United Nations. The issues are extremely complex and bit-
terly contested. Ganley and Ganley explain Third World demands
for a New International Information Order in the context of their
struggle for a New Economic Order during the 1960s and 1970s,
which comes down to their desire for a redistribution of the
world's wealth. On most broad communications principles the US
and the developing nations agree, but over the definition and
function of "news" conflict arose. The Ganley's describe the
UNESCO Mass Media Resolution, based upon the Report of the
International Commission for the Study of Communication Problems
(the MacBride Commission) as an attempt to deal sympathetically
with "the perception of virtually all the developing countries"
that "they are being inundated with Western--primarily American--
media and information products, with no reciprocal flow from
them" (74-76). Against the Report stand US media in a strict

First Amendment stance. The 1980 MacBride "final report" at the UNESCO General Assembly meeting in Belgrade offered a compromise which "strongly endorsed" press freedoms, but also recommended "breaking up the five major news `cartels'" (79). The Ganleys appeal for more flexibility on both sides.

Propaganda War

The United States Information Agency became an independent agency of the executive branch in 1953. One of its missions is to achieve US foreign policy objectives by influencing foreign populations. It uses a variety of methods and media to achieve this objective. The "Media and Programs" section of the 1986 Report of the U.S. Advisory Commission on Public Diplomacy describes and assesses all of the propaganda activities of the USIA: Worldnet, RIAS (Radio in the American Sector), Television and Film Service, TV Satellite File, Video Library, Voice of America, the Wireless File, American Participants Program, Traveling Exhibits, National Endowment for Democracy, exchanges and international visitors, Arts America and Artistic Ambassador programs, U.S. Books Abroad, English teaching program, East-West Center, etc. (The Commission, headed by the president of The Heritage Foundation and including the Senior Editor of The National Review, pursues a strong Cold War program.) Quasi-government institutions like Radio Free Europe/Radio Liberty make up another important weapon in the propaganda war . And see VI items on CIA contributions.

Foundations

These selections present the foundations as desiring to benefit disadvantaged populations but in nationalistic and class-oriented ways. The Carnegie, Ford, and Rockefeller foundations wanted to help Third World peoples. But they also were concerned with establishing educational and cultural institutions which would "train indigenous leaders who would guide their societies along lines generally supportive of, or minimally not antagonistic to, the interests of the United States as defined by the foundation elites." These foundations are "class institutions that attempt to create a world order supportive of the interests of the class that they represent" (Berman 162). Asian scholarly studies were nurtured by foundations and government to service the growing needs of a US-dominated Asia (Judy Coburn).

Works Cited

Coburn, Judy. "Asian Scholars and Government: The Chrysan-themum on the Sword." America`s Asia. Ed. Edward Friedman and Mark Selden. New York: Pantheon, 1971. 67-107.

Lee, C.C. "Media Imperialism" Reconsidered: The Homogenizing of Television Culture. Beverly Hills: Sage, 1980.

VII. Global

VII. A. United States Information Order, Multinational
          Communications Corporations, Global Cultural
          Domination 2769-2853

2769.   Aldridge, Robert. "Jaws III: the Pentagon Sinks
          Its Teeth into the South Sea Islands." Prog 46.5
          (1982) 34-37.
     The military is attempting to persuade the people of Belau,
part of the United Nations Trust Territory of the Pacific
Islands under US administration, to allow installation of a
guerrilla-warfare training camp, airstrips for war planes, and
perhaps a Trident submarine base. But Belau has a nuclear-free
constitution.

2770.   Aldridge, Robert. "Subase Palau: The Deception
          Continues." GZ 4.4 (1986) 3-4.
     Accuses the navy of wanting to use the Micronesian islands
of Paulau as a forward base for Trident submarines in the
Pacific Ocean and of "skirting the issue and misleading the
public."

2771.   "American Imperium: 'Any Part of the Earth.'"
          Na 237.14 (1983) 417, 419-20.
     President Reagan is determined to "establish an imperial
presence in global politics."

2772.   Auxter, Thomas. "Cultural Pluralism and Regional
          Realities: A Report from the Inter-American Congress
          of Philosophy (Guadalajara, 1985)." AHV 2.3
          (1985) 86-88.
     On the efforts of Latin American and Canadian philosophers
"to put an end to the cultural legacy of colonialism and to
support cultural pluralism in the Americas," in contrast to the
uncertainty of US philosophers regarding US cultural and
political imperialism. Hostility at the Congress "may have been
a turning point for U.S. philosophers to realize how they are
perceived by others."

2773.   Barnet, Richard, and Ronald Muller. Global Reach:
          The Power of the Multinational Corporations. New
          York: Simon, 1974. 508.
     The growing concentration of power of the multinationals
includes their control of the mass media. "In the TV field
particularly, U.S.-based global [communications] firms dominate
underdeveloped countries," but the U.S. dominates other
communications media also (145-6). "The colossal power of the
global corporation to shape the societies of the underdeveloped
world is not a matter for debate" (147).

2774.   Bernstein, Barton, ed. Towards a New Past:
     Dissenting Essays in American History. New York:
     Pantheon, 1968. 364.
     Two essays describe US efforts to create and maintain a
world order conducive to the prosperity and power of the US.

2775.   Buchanan, Keith. "The Intellectual Pillage of the
     Third World." The Geography of Empire. Nottingham,
     UK: Bertrand Russell Peace Center, 1972. 19-39.
     Intellectual and cultural imperialism accompanies US
economic imperialism.

2776.   Caplan, Richard, and Scott L. Malcomson. "Giving
     the U.N. the Business." Na 243.4 (1986) 108-112.
     The "international business community, alone and in
partnership with the Reagan Administration, is engaged in an
active and effective assault on U.N. initiatives that are
perceived as threats to corporate profits."

2777.   Carmo, Alberto. "Brazil's Problems Today." DJ 2
     (1974) 17-20.
     The growing US control of Brazilian education and culture
partly through direct satellite educational programming.

2778.   Carmo, Alberto. "International Telephone and
     Telegraph--A Gigantic Multinational Octopus." DJ 9
     (1973) 15-18.
     The penetration of ITT into the communications systems of
the world, with focus upon Chile.

2779.   The Case Against Satellites. New York: The
     Network Project (Notebook 7), 1974. 30.
     Centralized corporate control over communications
technology has many negative effects--militarism, etc.

2780.   Chomsky, Noam. "Trilateral's Rx for Crisis:
     Governability Yes; Democracy No." SD 1.1
     (1977) 10-11.
     On the "class character of political rule," the many
"problems of democracy" in Trilateral countries, and their
relation to education, politics and the economy.

2781.   Chomsky, Noam, and Edward S. Herman. The Political
     Economy of Human Rights, Vol. I: The Washington
     Connection and Third World Fascism. Boston: South
     End, 1979. 441.
     A Prefatory Note gives an account of the suppression of the
first edition of the book. Ch. 1 a summary of conclusions, Ch. 2
"The Pentagon-CIA Archipelago," Chs. 3-4 on terror by US
client states worldwide, Ch. 5 on Indochina. "Brainwashing Under
Freedom" (66-83) on how the system shapes events and perception.

2782.   Cockcroft, Eva. "Abstract Expressionism: Weapon of

the Cold War." Artforum 12.10 (1974) 39-41.
The interconnected interests of U.S. avantguard art, the Museum of Modern Art, the CIA, and the Rockefellers.

2783.   Constantino, Renato.   "The Mis-Education of the
          Filipino."   JCA 1.1 (1970) 20-36.
Education as a weapon of colonial conquest and domination of the Philippines.

2784.   Dorfman, Ariel, and Armand Mattelart.   Trans. David
          Kunzle.   How to Read "Donald Duck": Imperialist
          Ideology in the Disney Comic. New York: International,
          1975. 112.
The "Disney utopia" "segregates spirit and matter, town and countryside, city folk and noble savages, monopolists of mental power and mono-sufferers of physical power, the morally flexible and the morally immobile, father and son, authority and submission, and well-deserved riches and equally well-deserved poverty" (98).

2785.   Faraone, Roque.   Mass Media in Latin America.
          ISAL Abstracts (Montevideo) 4.45 (1973).   30.
The structure and ownership of the media and its control by US interests; entertainment, advertising and anarchy of the capitalist media and its role as vehicle for the dominant ideology; etc. Bibliography of studies of the mass media by country.

2786.   Fejes, Fred.   "Media Imperialism: An Assessment."
          MCS 3 (1981) 281-289.
An examination of the new concept of "media imperialism," broadly defined as "the processes by which modern communication media have operated to create, maintain and expand systems of domination and dependence on a world scale." It is best understood as "a research approach" to problems of Third World development, generally termed the "dependency model."

2786a.   Fejes, Fred.   "The U.S. in Third World Communications:
          Latin America 1900-1945."   JM 86 (November 1983)
          1-29.
A study of "media imperialism" as a "historical phenomenon" through an examination of "the expansion of United States communication interests into Latin America." "In time the various mass media--first film, then newspapers and magazines, and lastly radio broadcasting--were integrated into the media structure of the United States. By 1945, United States hegemony in hemispheric communications was complete."

2787.   Fenton, Tom, and Mary Heffron, eds.   Third World
          Resource Directory: A Guide to Organizations and
          Publications. Maryknoll, NY: Orbis, 1984.   320.
"A guide to modern day prophets who are attempting to speak truth to the illegitimate use of U.S. corporate and govenmental power," to "reveal the private interests behind the

public policies," and to "counter disinformation campaigns and
publicize the other side of the story" (Foreword).

2788.   "Forms of Cultural Dependency: A Symposium." JoC
          15.2 (1975) 121-93.
Nine essays on US multinationals' control over Colombian TV
from 1953, colonialism of tourist promotion, standardization of
US film content for international sales, imposition of US and
European research values on Latin American research, etc.

2789.   Frappier, Jon. "Advertising: Latin America." RA
          3.4 (1969) 1-11.
US advertising in Latin America is expanding rapidly.

2790.   Frappier, Jon. "U.S. Media Empire Latin America."
          RA 2.19 (1968).
The ownership and control of the Latin American press,
radio and TV by US media and business interests.

2791.   Friedman, Edward and Mark Selden, eds. America's
          Asia: Dissenting Essays on Asian-American Relations.
          New York: Pantheon, 1971. 458.
"Asia is America's in three important ways": 1) "we impose
American categories to describe, evaluate, and direct Asian
experience," 2) we have "channeled, distorted, and suppressed
much that is Asia," and 3) we have ignored "much that is humane,
valuable, and worthy of emulation" in Asia.

2792.   Friel, Howard, and Michelle Joffroy. "The Continuing
          War: Media Manipulation in Costa Rica." CAIB 26
          (Summer 1986) 39-41.
The primary US anti-Nicaragua intervention in Costa Rica is
through the mass media, which are "owned and operated" by "the
upper classes." Through them, for seven years the Reagan
administration has mounted a propaganda and disinformation
campaign "to scare Costa Ricans into a hostile attitude toward
Nicaragua." [See IV. H. and VI. C.]

2793.   Ganley, Oswald, and Gladys Ganley. To Inform or to
          Control? The New Communications Networks. New York:
          McGraw, 1982. 250.
"A prime concern of the United States is to maintain" its
"military and economic security" and that of its allies.
"Communications and information must therefore work in harness
with this objective. . .High on the list" is "the aid and
protection of U. S. business and U.S. markets" (195-96). "This
book has pointed out the all-pervasiveness, variety, and
interdependence of the swiftly accelerating communications and
information resources and their importance to U.S. business
strategy and governmental policy. . . . Increasingly, all these
matters are uncomfortably merging because of the evolving
technologies" (205). The authors give a history of the
communication revolution, then turn to specific international
problem areas such as "free flow" vs. "balanced" news.

2794.　Gerbner, George, and Marsha Siefert, eds. <u>World Communications: A Handbook</u>. New York: Longman, 1984. 527.
Fifty-four essays divided into five parts: "Global Perspectives on Information," "Transnational Communications: The Flow of News and Images," "Telecommunications: Satellites and Computers," "Mass Communications: Development Within National Contexts," "Intergovernmental Systems: Toward International Policies." Many relevant essays: "U.S. Television Coverage of Foreign News," "Transnational Advertising: The Latin American Case," "International Circulation of U.S. Theatrical Films and Television Programming," "Remote Sensing by Satellite: Global Hegemony or Social Utility," etc.

2795.　<u>Global Salesman</u>. New York: The Network Project (Notebook 10), 1975. 30.
U.S. commercial television expansion and economic benefits to the networks.

2796.　Guback, Thomas. "American Interests in the British Film Industry." <u>OREB</u> 7.2 (1967) 7-21.
US film industry's control of British film production and distribution.

2797.　Guback, Thomas. "Film and Cultural Pluralism." <u>JAE</u> 5.2 (1971) 35-51.
US domination of European film production and distribution.

2798.　Guback, Thomas. "Film as International Business." <u>JoC</u> 24.1 (1974) 59-70.
How co-production arrangements are used by the US film industry to dominate the international flow of film and TV programs.

2799.　Guback, Thomas. <u>The International Film Industry: Western Europe and America Since 1945</u>. Bloomington: Indiana UP, 1969. 244.
"The object of this study is to uncover and analyze relationships between the American and European film industries, keeping in mind the financial stake American companies have in Europe"--i.e., the economic imperatives influencing the content of films. "The propaganda quality of film has also played a part in the American industry's policy in foreign operations," especially for Germany, first to combat Nazi ideology, then to indoctrinate West Germany "for its place in the Cold War. Hollywood's overriding concern for profit tended to work against the programs of our Military Government, and it was not until the film industry was, in effect, subsidized by Washington that it actively began distributing pictures in the West German market" (6).

2800.　Hachten, William. <u>Muffled Drums: The News Media in Africa</u>. Ames, Iowa: Iowa State UP, 1971. 314.

"The plight of Africa's news media is directly related to the circumstance that they are a Western import--a by-product of European colonialism." Today, "European influences still pervade news communication." Yet "the need to 'Africanize' the news media in both content and personnel is very real. . . . Until Africans themselves, and not Europeans, completely control the instruments of communication, the media are certain to be resented not only by government officials but by the public itself" (271-72).

2801.   Hamelink, Cees, ed. The Corporate Village: The Role of Transnational Corporations in International Communication. Rome: IDOC International, 1977. 233.
Forty texts and excerpts by twenty authors in seven sections: the global village, corporate interest in international communications, corporate concentration, cultural dependency, etc.

2802.   Harris, Phil. Reporting Southern Africa: Western News Agencies Reporting from Southern Africa. Paris: UNESCO, 1981. 168.
A study of news coverage of Rhodesia and South Africa by Reuters, the Associated Press, and United Press International. Ch. 1 gives a history of Western news agencies in southern Africa, Ch. 3, "Control of the News Media in Southern Africa," Ch. 4, "The News from Southern Africa," offers a content analysis of a week of coverage which reveals the pro-Western bias of the agencies (125) in its more positive representation of Great Britain and the US as compared to African nationalists.

2803.   Hayter, Teresa, and Catherine Watson. AID: Rhetoric and Reality. London: Pluto, 1985. 303.
A reexamination of Hayter's Aid As Imperialism with conclusions similar to those stated in the earlier book. "Governments of the rich countries of the West and their ruling class claim, with considerable hypocrisy, that they are providing 'aid' to help the Third World to escape from the underdevelopment and poverty which they and their predecessors created and continue to create. But much of this aid fails to alleviate poverty even in the immediate context in which it is provided; and its overall purpose is the preservation of a system which damages the interests of the poor in the Third World" (Introduction).

2804.   Hochman, Sandra. Satellite Spies. Indianapolis: Bobbs, 1976. 212.
On US domination of satellites--e.g., Western Union's Westar satellite. The author focuses upon government subsidies to favored corporations in the creation of "entrenched monopolies." That is, the taxpayers paid billions of dollars to develop satellites which were then turned over to selected companies which now decide what is covered and shown.

2805.   Horowitz, Andrew. "Domestic Communications

Satellites."   RadS 2.5 (1973) 36-40.
The US communications satellite program, the interlocking interests of the US military and monopoly aircraft and communications industries, etc.

2806.   Humberto, Maximo. "Yankee Television Control." The
          Chilean Road to Socialism. Ed. Dale L. Johnson.
          Garden City, NY: Anchor. 1973. 120-24.
Each TV network has its role in US control of Latin American TV, especially in the creation of mindless consumers.

2807.   Jacoby, Neil, et al. Bribery and Extortion in
          World Business: A Study of Corporate Political Payments
          Abroad. New York: Macmillan, 1977. 294.
The eight chapters are divided into a description, an analysis, and solutions of the problem.

2808.   Janus, Noreene. "Advertising and the Mass Media in
          the Era of the Global Corporation." Communication
          and Social Structure: Critical Studies in Mass Media
          Research. Ed. Emile McAnany, et al., eds. New York:
          Praeger, 1981. 287-316.
"The age of the global corporation is also the age of the globalization of Madison Avenue." The present system of world communications "favors the expansion of the transnational power structures." Advertising is "the most glaring form in which communication serves this end."

2809.   The Kissinger Study Of Southern Africa: National
          Security Study Memorandum 39. Ed. Mohamed El-Khawas
          and Barry Cohen. Westport, CT: Hill, 1976. 189.
The full text of the secret 1969 study of US options in southern Africa and facts about how US "security is planned through collaboration with racist and fascist regimes," to ensure availability of minerals and to stop "liberation movements that are anti-imperialist" (Preface), because "stability" "profitably serves the interests of US corporations" (27).

2810.   Kolosov, Yuri. "TV and International Law." DJ 11
          (1974) 21-4.
On issues debated in the UN concerning control of direct TV broadcast satellites.

2811.   Kwitny, Jonathan. Endless Enemies: The Making of an
          Unfriendly World. New York: Congdon, 1984. 435.
"Our efforts overseas have become more and more remote from the true interests of the American people, and the principles we stand for" because these interests and principles have been "habitually ignored by the geopolitical strategists who for thirty-five years have committed us to endless and counterproductive entanglements abroad" (4, 7).

2812.   Lent, John. "Imperialism via Q-Sorts." DJ 9

(1974) 14-17.
The monopolization of Asian communications research by the US, UK, France, and West Germany.

2813.   Lundestad, Geir. America, Scandinavia, and the
          Cold War, 1945-1949. New York: Columbia UP, 1980. 434.
"Expansion was the main tendency in the policies of the
United States." Even "if spurred by its fear of communist
expansion, the United States came to expand its own commitments
and influence on a larger scale than did the Soviet Union."

2814.   Madeley, John. "The Worldwide Explosion in Cigarette
          Advertising." Pr 9.2 (1981) 15.
The seven major companies are turning to the Third World
where regulation is less, and they are spending "around $2,500
million a year on advertising."

2815.   Marxism and the Mass Media: Towards a Basic
          Bibliography. Bagnolet, France: International
          Mass Media Research Center.
"An ongoing bibliographic research series to provide a
global, multi-lingual annotated documentation of past and
current marxist studies on all aspects of communications,"
including global subjects.

2816.   Mass Media Group. Speeches Given at the Seminar on
          Cultural Imperialism, Stockholm, October 1974. 47,
          mimeographed.
Speeches by Herbert Schiller, Sven Ekberg, Stefan DeVylder,
and Tapio Varis.

2817.   Mattelart, Armand. "Modern Communications
          Technologies and New Facets of Cultural Imperialism."
          CRPV 1 (1973) 9-26.
The union of US mass culture, the electronics and aerospace
corporations, the US war economy, and the militarization of
world science and education.

2818.   Mattelart, Armand. Trans. Michael Chanan.
          Multinational Corporations and the Control of Culture:
          The Ideological Apparatuses of Imperialism. New Jersey:
          Humanities, 1979 (orig. 1976). 304.
From the translator's Foreword: "There has been very little
work done so far on the evolution of what is now the fastest
growing sector of production in contemporary capitalism: the
electronics-based multinationals involved in communications and
the media, the companies responsible for the ideological
apparatus of imperialism which this book analyzes. Mattelart
explores new aspects of the concentration and centralisation of
capital, new patterns of production and consumption, new ways in
which cultural production and the media are subordinated to
capital, new forms of State practice in partnership with capital
in the era of the multinationals."

2819.   Mattelart, Armand. <u>Transnationals and the Third
World: The Struggle for Culture</u>. South Hadley, MA:
Bergin, 1983. 184.
Examination of the pervasive role of transnational firms as
"sociocultural investors"--producers of cultural commodities,
business culture, and new institutional models. The
relationships among these investors through their networks--
film, TV, advertising, publishing, news agencies, tourism, and
linguistics--are shown to affect the host countries in countless
ways.

2820.   Mattelart, Armand, and Daniel Waksman. "Plaza Sesamo
and an Alibi for the Author's Real Intentions." <u>DJ</u> 7/8
(1974) 21-25.
"Sesame Street" is a model for a world repressive education
system based upon technology, business values, and satellite
communications.

2821.   Mattelart, Armand, and Seth Siegelaub, eds.
<u>Communication and Class Struggle: 1. Capitalism,
Imperialism</u>. New York: International General;
Bagnolet, France: IMMRC, 1979.
First vol. of 2-vol. anthol.: 64 texts organized in four
sections, on basic concepts, the bourgeois ideology of
communication, the capitalist mode of communication, and
monopoly capitalism/imperialism and global ideological control.

2822.   McAnany, Emile, et al., eds. <u>Communication and
Social Structure</u>. New York: Praeger, 1981. 341.
The three essays in Part III, "Critical Research Issues in
International Mass Commmunication," and other essays in this
collection deal with US worldwide infrastructures of
telecommunication which serve the purposes of those who own and
control them. The economic structures both within the US and
abroad make change difficult.

2823.   Morse, Randy, and Larry Pratt. <u>Darkness at the End of
the Tunnel: A Radical Analysis of Canadian-American
Relations</u>. Toronto: New Hogtown, 1975. 39.
Pp. 17-32 on US communications and cultural domination of
Canada.

2824.   Naison, Mark. "Sports and the American Empire."
<u>RadA</u> 6.4 (1972) 95-120.
Post-WW II development of mass spectator sports, including
US sports relations with the Third World and blacks and their
role as a means of assimilating peoples into the interests of
the US.

2825.   Nelson, Joyce. "Caught in the Webs: Political
Economy of TV." <u>JC</u> 20 (1979) 31-33.
The global expansion of the conglomerate networks is an
important aspect of US corporate hegemony worldwide, often to
the detriment of other countries.

CONTROL OF INFORMATION

2826.   Read, William. America's Mass Media Merchants.
         Baltimore: Johns Hopkins U P, 1976. 209.
Supports the global penetration of US ideology, business,
and mass media, and the principle of "free flow" of information
over that of national sovereignty. "Through the market place
system by which America's mass media merchants communicate with
foreign consumers, both parties enjoy different, but useful
benefits" (181). The author surveys eight print media and two
visual: AP, UPI, NYTNS, WP-LATNS; Time, Newsweek,
Reader's Digest; motion pictures, telefilms.

2827.   Repo, Satu. "The American Comic Book: Proletarian
         Literature for Children." This Magazine 8.1 (1974)
         8-11.
The escapist contents of the three principal types of comic
(superheroes, mystery, and romance) affect the child negatively.

2828.   Rips, Geoffrey. "In Whose Interest? Big Labor's
         Foreign Policy." TO 79.7 (1986) 7-10.
A history of labor support of US, CIA, and corporate
foreign policy through such organizations as the American
Institute for Free Labor Development (AIFLD) and the Inter-
American Regional Organization of Workers (ORIT) which have
assisted in overthrowing democratic governments, aiding
dictatorships, and furthering the expansion of US
multinationals, using US money.

2829.   Rosenberg, Emily. Spreading the American Dream:
         American Economic and Cultural Expansion, 1890-1945.
         New York: Hill and Wang, 1982. 258.
Around the turn of the century the US--leaders in all walks
of life in alliance with government--agreed upon a set of values
the author labels "liberal developmentalism" to promote global
expansion. The problem was that these leaders confused freedom
in general with the particular sort of freedom found in the US,
which led to efforts toward global regulation and to the Cold
War.

2830.   Sampson, Anthony. The Sovereign State of ITT.
         New York: Stein, 1973. 335.
A history from 1920 to the present: relations with Nazi
Germany, telephone systems in Latin America, Cold War proponent,
domination of European telecommunications, overthrow of the
Allende government, etc.

2831.   Schiller, Herbert. "The Appearance of National
         Communications Policies: A New Arena for Social
         Struggle." Gaz 21.2 (1972) 82-94.
US domination of television and film production,
distribution, and technology, etc.

2832.   Schiller, Herbert. Communication and Cultural
         Domination. White Plains, NY: Sharpe, 1976. 126.
An account of America's efforts to dominate the world

465

culturally as well as economically. "The marketing system
developed to sell industry's outpouring of (largely inauthentic)
consumer goods is now applied as well to selling globally ideas,
tastes, preferences, and beliefs. In fact, in advanced
capitalism's present stage, the production and dissemination of
what it likes to term 'information' become major and
indispensable activities. . . in the overall system" (3).

2833.   Schiller, Herbert. "Information: America's New
        Global Empire." Ch 2.3 (1982) 30-35.
    An economic/information international order is developing
under US direction "almost without journalistic attention." The
Information Age enjoyed by the developed nations under the
banner of the "free flow of information" represents "a new kind
of domination," again "largely unreported" in the US.

2834.   Schiller, Herbert. Information and the Crisis
        Economy. Norwood, NJ: Ablex, 1984. 133.
    The worldwide conflict over control of information and
communication between the transnational corporate powers and
those fighting for a more democratic and egalitarian social
order is given renewed urgency by the deepening of two crises:
the race towards nuclear annihilation and the increasing
instability of the capitalist world economy. The new
information and communication technologies are being rapidly
introduced by the transnational corporations and their
government allies for economic and political purposes: to
increase corporate productivity and coordination globally and to
reinforce the power of States necessary to control social forces
unleashed by these developments. Above all other dangers in
these developments is the growth of information as a commodity
and the information gap between the rich and poor, which
Schiller sees as the core of the new order.

2835.   Schiller, Herbert. "Madison Avenue Imperialism."
        Communications in International Politics. Ed. R. L.
        Merritt. Urbana, IL: Illinois UP, 1972. 318-38.
    The increasing domination over world mass communications by
US multinational corporations.

2836.   Schiller, Herbert. Mass Communications and American
        Empire. Boston: Beacon, 1969. 170.
    "If conspiracy is absent in the American commercial
electronic invasion of the world, there is all the same a very
clear consciousness present of how to utilize communication for
both highly ideological and profitable ends" (105-06). Chs. 3,
4, and 5 explain the militarization of the domestic
communications complex. Ch. 6 treats global US electronic
expansion, and 7 the international commercialization of
broadcasting. Ch. 8 deals with the impact of the "developing
world under siege," 9 the structure of international
communications control, 10 a program for the democratic
reconstruction of mass communications.

466

2837.   Schiller, Herbert. "Waiting for Orders--Some Current
          Trends in Mass Communications Research in the United
          States." Gaz 1 (1974) 11-21.
     The increasing support of communications research as an arm
of US foreign and military planning.

2838.   Schonberger, Howard. "The Cold War and the American
          Empire in Asia." RHR 33 (1985) 139-154.
     A rev. of six books which describe the development of US
containment policies after WW II designed to achieve "US hegemony
in Asia and elsewhere." The US had "three interrelated aims in
Asia after the war: 1) integrating the region into the
American-dominated world capitalist economy; 2) thwarting the
power and influence of the Soviet Union; 3) channeling the
revolutions sweeping the European and former Japanese colonial
empires away from communism or, alternatively, repressing them"
(140).

2839.   Selvaggio, Kathy, and Tim Shorrock. "Which Side Are
          You On, AAFLI?" Na 242.6 (1986) 170-173.
     In the Philippines and South Korea "there is strong
evidence" that the Asian American Free Labor Institute, an
AFL/CIO agency funded by AID, "supports only" status quo labor
organizations.

2840.   Sklar, Holly. Reagan, Trilateralism and the
          Neoliberals: Containment and Intervention in the 1980s.
          Boston: South End, 1986. 64.
     Analyzes the dominant foreign policy options--Rollback,
"Moderate" Containment, and Neoliberal Containment--as advocated
by the Reagan administration, the Heritage Foundation,
Trilateral Commission, and Rockefeller Foundation Commission on
South Africa. The author tries to specify how far US elites
are willing to go in accommodating or opposing change abroad.

2841.   Smythe, Dallas. Dependency Road: Communications,
          Capitalism, Consciousness, and Canada. Norwood, NJ:
          Ablex, 1981. 347.
     Communications institutions produced the consciousness and
ideology necessary to the dependency of Canada upon the US: US
imperial policy, mass media and popular culture, the audience
commodity, the hegemony of big business, cultural submission and
media, etc. "This is a study of the process by which people
organized in the capitalist system produced a country called
Canada as a dependency of the United States, the center of the
core of the capitalist system," focusing on "the role of
communications institutions (press, magazines, books, films,
radio and television broadcasting, telecommunications, the arts,
sciences, and engineering) in producing the necessary
consciousness and ideology to seem to legitimate that
dependency."

2842.   Staple, Gregory. "The Assault on Intelsat." Na
          239.21 (1984) 665, 679-82.

The author's narrative of the competition between the
International Telecommunications Satellite Organization and US
entrepreneurs illuminates the power over international
communications enjoyed by the US.

2843.   Taylor, Peter. Smoke Ring: The Politics of Tobacco.
         London: Bodley Head, 1984. 328.
         Chs. 14 and 15 deal with the Third World.   "In the Third
World a new Smoke Ring is being forged which is even stronger
than the one in the West. It is made up of the same political
and economic links--employment, revenue, trade, advertising and
promotion--but it is stronger because the governments of many
developing countries are even more dependent on tobacco."

2844.   Tompkins, E. Berkeley. Anti-Imperialism in the
         United States: The Great Debate, 1890-1920.
         Philadelphia: U of Pennsylvania P, 1970. 344.
         The final decade of the nineteenth century "witnessed the
emergence of an American imperialist rationale."   The anti-
imperialist side of the debate and the decade between 1892 and
1902 are stressed.   The anti-imperialists argued that political
domination of another country or people (Hawaii, the
Philippines, Samoa, Guam, Puerto Rico) violated the principles
the US had traditionally championed--liberty, democracy,
equality, and self-government.

2845.   Tunstall, Jeremy. The Media are American. London:
         Constable; New York: Columbia UP, 1977. 352.
         "[T]he world, by adopting American media formats, has in
practice become hooked on American-style media."   The author
discusses news agencies, newspapers, magazines, films, radio,
television, records, paperback books, and advertising to show
how all "fit into a much larger jig-saw."   But Tunstall opposes
the "media imperialism" thesis of critics like Herbert Schiller.

2846.   "Unesco Walkout." Na 238.1 (1984) 4.
         The Reagan administration's decision to pull out of Unesco
is an assertion of US power, among other motives.

2847.   "U.N. Stopover." Na 239.10 (1984) 307-308.
         President Reagan's attacks on the United Nations exceeds
his presidential predecessors "in sheer destructiveness."

2848.   "Uruguay and Mass Media Today." JA (1974) 1-28.
         The role of the USIA and the CIA from 1967 to 1973 in
support of the Uruguayan ruling class control of media.

2849.   "The U.S.A. Threat to British Culture." Arena 2.8
         (1951) 1-56.
         Thirteen texts from a 1951 conference in London.

2850.   Varis, Tapio. "Global Traffic in Television." JoC
         24.1 (1974) 102-109.
         The dominance of the US and Great Britain in the sale of TV

programs and ideology to Europe and the developing countries.

2851.   Varis, Tapio. The Impact of Transnational
     Corporations on Communications (Transnational
     Communication Project, Tampere Report 1; General
     Outline). Tampere: Tampere Peace Reasearch
     Institute, 1975. 58.
     Conceptual framework, corporate structure, government
policies, trends, cases, etc.

2852.   Vayrynen, Raimo. "Military Uses of Satellite
     Communications." CRPV 1 (1973) 44-49.
     US development of satellite communications for military
uses.

2853.   Weeks, James L. "Comsat: The Technology for Ruling
     Global Communications." An End to Political Science:
     The Caucus Papers. Ed. Marvin Surkin and Alan Wolfe.
     New York: Basic, 1970. 215-240.
     Communications by satellite are rapidly changing the
international system and raising the question of who will rule
global communications? The US took the lead with its
Communications Satellite Corporation (Comsat), a government
chartered private monopoly corporation created by "the mixture of
the ambitions of the private corporations and the capabilities
developed by the government" (NASA). "The thesis of this essay
is that within the context of this global technology, the United
States via Comsat has pursued a nationalistic policy, using its
superiority in space technology to enhance its position in the
world. Technology is being used, in this case, as an instrument
of national power and expansion" (218).

VII. B. New World Information Order, "Free Flow" Controversy,
          UNESCO 2854-2897

2854.   Ainslie, Rosalynde. The Press in Africa:
     Communications Past and Present. New York: Walker,
     1967. 264.
     African editors and people must see the world through
foreign eyes, because foreign news is "dominated by four
countries, the United States, the Soviet Union, the United
Kingdom and France. . . .[N]ews flows from the developed to the
developing countries," and particularly from the US. But within
many countries the media are appendages of the state.

2855.   Altschull, J. Herbert. Agents of Power (previously
     cited).
     Ch. 9, "UNESCO: A New International Information Order,"
summarizes the "free flow" controversy between the US and Third
World nations: "at its root the quarrel is economic," "free
flow" to the US and her capitalist allies meaning "continued
domination of the channels of communications"; the term has
become "so emotionally charged that it has lost its value in
international dialogue" (213).

2856.   Biryukov, N.S. Television in the West and Its
          Doctrines. Tr. Yuri Sviridov. Moscow: Progress,
          1981. 207.
     Ch. 9, "'Free Flow of Information' and Television's
International Relations." The "free flow of information"
doctrine "is being used by the ruling circles of the capitalist
world to cover up the ideological expansion of imperialism,"
with the US "very much in the forefront."

2857.   Breyers, Bob. "Knowledge Is a Matter of Freedom."
          Pr 9.3 (1981) 27-8.
     On the conflict between the Third World and the developed
nations regarding the flow of information.

2858.   Dixler, Elsa. "Another Opening, Another Showcase for
          the Right." Na 239.21 (1984) 672-73.
     On the vigorous attack on UNESCO by the Heritage
Foundation.

2859.   Du Boff, Richard B. "Communications and Capitalism:
          Another 'Bias' of Technology." MR 34.4 (1982) 56-61.
     Rev. of Smythe's Dependency Road and Schiller's Who
Knows. "In our lifetime, monopoly over communications and the
output of information has become a control device equally as
important as trade and capital flows, international monetary
institutions, foreign aid, even military force." Schiller and
Smythe "show how the free flow of information is as thoroughly
deceptive a description of the impact of communications
technology on society as 'free trade' has been for the effects
of exports, imports, and foreign investment on economic
development. Just as 'international' trade consists of goods and
services produced by a handful of business firms identified with
the major industrial nations, so information is created,
managed, transmitted, stored, and retrieved by specific
corporations and groups of people--for profit."

2860.   Fascell, Dante B., ed. International News: Freedom
          Under Attack. Beverly Hills, CA: Sage, 1979. 320.
     Four essays in defense of the "free flow" principle as
"vital" to the "political, economic, and social structure of the
United States" and "of the Western World."

2861.   "The Global News Flow Controversy." AWPR 24.12
          (Dec. 1977) 31-37.
     Four short articles discuss the Third World's desire to
develop its own system of news gathering and dissemination (one
independent from Soviet and Western sources), tailored to the
needs of its own people.

2862.   Gottlieb, Bob. "Information Wars: Developing Nations
          Challenge U.S. Media Domination." MORE 8.5 (1978)
          34-36.
     A review of Herbert Schiller's Communication and Cultural
Domination and the House Subcommittee on International

Operations' <u>The Implications of International Communications
and Information</u>. In contrast to the Senate committee's defense
of US "free-flow" policy, Schiller explains the policy as
another element in US worldwide economic expansion.

2863.   Gronberg, Tom, and Kaarle Nordenstreng. "Approaching
         International Control of Satellite Communications."
         <u>CRPV</u> 1 (1973) 3-8.
A report of actions taken at UNESCO and elsewhere to
prevent the spread of U.S.-style communications.

2864.   Hall, Peter. "What's all the fuss about InterPress?"
         <u>CJR</u> 22.5 (1983) 53-57.
US opposition to Inter Press Service Third World News
Agency (IPS) on commercial and ideological grounds is part of US
opposition to the New International Information Order and
UNESCO.

2865.   "High Noon at UNESCO." <u>CJR</u> 19.2 (1980) 24-25.
         Comment on the MacBride report on Third World information.

2866.   Hirshberg, Peter. "The War Over Information." <u>WJR</u>
         2.2 (1980) 24-26.
Information is an immensely powerful and valuable
commodity, and the US is "the world's major information
supplier." Countries all around the planet are reacting against
what they perceive as US electronic and cultural imperialism.

2867.   <u>The Implications of International Communications and
         Information</u>. Subcommittee on International Operations
         of the Committee on Foreign Relations, United States
         Senate, 95th Congress, June 8-10, 1977. Washington, DC:
         GPO, 1977. 286.
A defense of US information free-flow policy.

2868.   <u>International Inventory of Television Programme
         Structure and the Flow of TV Programmes Between Nations</u>.
         UNESCO Research Institute and the Institute of Journalism
         and Mass Communications, Univ. of Tampere, Finland, 1973.
A platform of principles developed at the Tampere Symposium
to establish conditions for a "free flow of information," in
response to increasing hegemony over worldwide information by
Western countries, particularly the US.

2869.   Joyce, James A. "UNESCO Is Not the Problem:
         A Maligning Press Distorts the Truth." <u>Chm</u> 199
         (January 1985) 8-10.
The U.S. press has not reported the Reagan
administrations's hostility to UNESCO fairly. In fact, U.S.
"militray capitalism" seeks to control UNESCO as part of its
global expansion over the Third World. The Western "free press"
has deprived "the poor four-fifths of mankind from knowing the
facts" and has slandered UNESCO "for allegedly advocating
controls over the printed news," which is not true.

2870.   Lee, Philip, ed. Communication for All: The
          Churches and the New World Information and Communication
          Order. Maryknoll, NY: Orbis, 1986. 176.
"The media of information and communication has long been
dominated by the First World. The result has been a lack of
impartial information about the poorer, marginalized countries,
particularly those of the Third World, and inadequate analysis,
due to cultural bias, of Third World issues. In an effort to
combat this problem, a New World Information and Communication
Order (NWICO) has been proposed that aims to develop a more
democratic, decentralized, participatory communication system.
This book provides an examination of the world's present
communication system, the NWICO proposal, and the challenges that
NWICO presents to the churches."

2871.   Many Voices, One World: Towards a New More Just and
          More Efficient World Information and Communication
          Order. London: Kogan, 1980. 312.
The MacBride Report, named after the president of the
International Commission for the Study of Communication
Problems, Sean MacBride. The report establishes guidelines for
a New World Information and Communication Order (NWICO).

2872.   Massee, John. "UNESCO Defends MacBride Report."
          E&P 114 (1981) 42-52.
Presents UNESCO's arguments and assertions that the US
press had not reported the Belgrade General Conference
accurately.

2873.   Mattelart, Armand, Xavier Delcourt, and Michelle
          Mattelart. Tr. David Buxton. International
          Image Markets: In Search of an Alternative Perspective.
          London: Comedia, 1984. 122.
Advocates a "Latin audio-visual space" as an alternative to
Anglo-Saxon and especially US media.

2874.   McPhail, Thomas. Electronic Colonialism: The
          Future of International Broadcasting and Communication.
          Beverly Hills: Sage, 1981. 259.
The basic issue of the struggle by the Third World for a
New World Information Order (NWIO) is "freedom of the press
versus government control of the media." The free press
principle "has not led to a very perfect system of
international communication (distorted coverage, waste of media
in fostering development). The "story of this book" is "what the
Third World tried to do about these problems" and "how the
United States and other Western governments reacted."

2875.   Nordenstreng, Kaarle. "Mass Media and Developing
          Nations." DJ 1 (1975) 6-9.
The present international communications system is
unbalanced in favor of Western interests.

2876.   Nordenstreng, Kaarle, and Lauri Hannikainen.

The Mass Media Declaration of UNESCO. Norwood, NJ:
Ablex, 1984. 475.
Since 1980 the US has been on the attack against the
document adopted unanimously in November 22, 1978 called
Declaration on Fundamental Principles Concerning the
Contribution of the Mass Media to Strengthening Peace and
International Understanding, to the Promotion of Human Rights
and to Countering Racialism, Apartheid and Incitement to War.
The US claims that this statement and the "New International
Information Order" it envisions would establish government
controls over the news and free market economics. But this
volume "sharply contradicts" such "flagrant fabrication" in
defense of the old order of domination and submission. The book
is divided into three parts: the process of formulating the
Declaration, a review of international law applicable to the
subject, and the ethics of mass communication.

2877.   Nordenstreng, Kaarle, and Herbert Schiller.
"Helsinki: The New Equation." JoC 26.1 (1976) 130-4.
The new problems of the international flow of information
after the Helsinki accords.

2878.   Nordenstreng, Kaarle, and Tapio Varis. *Television
Traffic--a One-Way Street?: A Survey and Analysis
of the International Flow of Television Programme
Material*. Paris: UNESCO, 1974. 62.
The symposium "The International Flow of Television
Programmes" held in Tampere, Finland, 1973, focused upon the
one-way flow from the West.

2879.   Preston, William, Jr. "The Nature of Information:
Capitalist Commodity or Human Right?" ORK
(Spring 1985) 2-5.
Article looks at the issue of Reagan's position on UNESCO
and questions why there is "no investigative journalism on
Reagan's UNESCO policy."

2880.   Preston, William Jr. "The New World Information Order
Versus Cold War Communications." ORK 2 (Fall/Winter
1984-5) 6-10.
"Because the United States has long regarded international
communications as its own imperial resource and has linked its
supremacy in the field to victory in the struggle against the
Soviet Union, it will not be easy to accept the implicit
cultural equality the Third World espouses or an information
order free from its East-West context."

2881.   Raskin, A.H. "U.S. Coverage of the Belgrade UNESCO
Conference." JoC 31.4 (1981) 164-74.
The coverage was highly antagonistic, suspicious, and
biased, focusing on those aspects of the conference that
fulfilled the fears of editors and systematically excluding
opposing viewpoints.

2882.   Ray, Ellen. "Information Imperialism: U.S., U.K.
          Join Forces to Attack UNESCO." ORK 2 (Fall/Winter
          1984-85) 1-4.
     On opposition to the MacBride Commission Report, which
called for democratization of communication, defense of human
rights, support for people struggling for freedom and
independence, and reduction of inequalities in communication
capabilities. The Reagan administration found the report so
abhorrent that it withdrew from UNESCO, after a long-planned,
covert campaign to manipulate support for the withdrawal.

2883.   Schiller, Herbert. "Breaking the West's Media
          Monopoly." Na 241.8 (1985) 248-51.
     The U.N. and UNESCO are not trying "to establish a new
international information order that would limit the circulation
of ideas and impose a tyranny over the mind. . . .The only
successful world information order was achieved by the American
communications industry in the twenty-year period immediately
after World War II," a development in which the U.N. and UNESCO
collaborated. When Third World nations in the 1970s began to
question this one-way flow of information, "rarely were the
proceedings reported in the U.S. media."

2884.   Schiller, Herbert. "Freedom from the 'Free Flow.'"
          JoC 24.1 (1974) 110-116.
     The growing international resistance to the one-way flow of
information and values from the few powerful capitalist
countries, particularly the US, partly in reaction to U.S.
media monopoly use of the concept of "free flow" to continue
their economic and cultural penetration around the world.

2885.   Schiller, Herbert. "'Free Flow of Information' Aids
          U.S. Capitalism." ORK (Spring 1985) 4-5.
     The "powerful transnational corporate system, its marketing
apparatus, and the military presence around the globe that
protects it, are now each dependent almost totally on massive,
instantaneous, and international information flows."

2886.   Schiller, Herbert. "Genesis of the Free Flow of
          Information Principles." Crisis in International
          News: Policies and Practices. Ed. Jim Richstad
          and Michael Anderson. New York: Columbia UP, 1981.
          162-183.
     A study of the free flow of information concept in terms of
American capitalism's past and present imposition of
communication domination on the formerly colonial countries.
The ideal of the free flow of communication exists only for the
privileged.

2887.   Schiller, Herbert. "Mass Media and U.S. Foreign
          Policy." Stockholm: Mass Media Group, 1974. 1-16.
     The relation between media owners and foreign policy from
the 1940s to their use of UNESCO to promote "free flow of
information" for corporate purposes.

2888.	Schiller, Herbert.	"National Development Requires
	Some Social Distance." AR 27.1 (1967) 63-75.
	The power of the imperialist mass media and the need for
developing countries to control incoming political-cultural
messages.

2889.	Smith, Anthony. The Geopolitics of Information:
	How Western Culture Dominates the World. New York:
	Oxford UP, 1980. 192.
	On the domination of news by the four major Western news
agencies (Reuters, Agence France-Presse, AP, and UPI),
domination of communication another aspect of Western economic
domination. "Today information is power, and the United States
massively dominates the world of information." Very sympathetic
to Third World countries, but rejects the New International
Information Order demanded by many developing nations at many
UNESCO conferences.

2890.	Smith, Anthony. "The Global Data Bank: Information--
	the Newest Resource." Na 231.6 (1980) 169, 184-188.
	An explanation of the conflict between the undeveloped and
the developed nations over communications in a world in which
"distribution of the means of production and distribution of
information is grossly unequal." Part of the conflict, and a
growing one, is over the assignment of frequencies. The power
of IBM and AT&T threatens the very sovereignty and indigenous
control of underdeveloped nations.

2891.	Sussman, Leonard. "The Third World and the Fourth
	Estate." WJR 3.5 (1981) 36-39.
	An analysis of the conflict between Third World nations and
Western nations over the flow of information. The author seeks
ways to provide information more acceptable to Third World
governments, while maintaining the flow of information free from
governmental control.

2892.	"Toward a New World Information Order?" JIA 35.2
	(1981-82) 155-277.
	The entire issue is devoted to the information-order, free
flow controversy and contains statements of opposing points of
view.

2893.	Varis, Tapio. "Trends in International Television
	Flow." IPSR 7.3 (1986) 235-49.
	A survey of more than 50 countries for 1973 and 1983
reveals "a one-way traffic from a few exporting countries to the
rest of the world and the dominance of entertainment." The US
influence is strong everywhere outside the eastern bloc of
countries, and even they "import more western programming than
vice versa." "The United States imports relatively fewer
foreign programs than any other country."

2894.	Weaver, David H., et al. The News of the World in
	Four Major Wire Services. Schools of Journalism,

Indiana U and U of North Carolina, 1980. A study of the content of AP, UPI, Reuters, and Agence France-Presse stories during two weeks in 1979. Western coverage of the Third World concentrates on conflicts and crises, but these countries receive more international news than do the developed countries. Much of the coverage originates in the Third World countries. Western coverage follows the same patterns operating in covering the domestic scene, and these traditional judgments should be questioned.

2895.   Whitlam, Gough. "The United Kingdom, United Nations, and United States." ORK (Fall Winter 1984-85) 4-5.
Western media opposition to UNESCO helped spread the withdrawal of nations from it.

2896.   Yadava, Jaswant. Politics of News: Third World Perspective. New Delhi: Concept, 1984. 300.
Defenses of UNESCO and the New Information Order.

2897.   Zasursky, Y.N. "'Free Flow of Information': The Cold War and Reducing International Tension." DJ 3 (1974) 7-11.
The "free flow of information" imposes capitalist values on the rest of the world, as in the example of Chile.

VII. C. Propaganda, United States Information Agency, Cold War   2898-2936

2898.   Arbatov, Georgi. The War of Ideas in Contemporary International Relations: The Imperialist Doctrine, Methods, and Organization of Foreign Political Propaganda. Tr. David Skvirsky. Moscow: Progress, 1973. 313.
Analysis of psychological warfare in the leading capitalist countries, their "acts of ideological subversion" and "subversive propaganda" (14). Ch. 1 on the "Ideological Struggle"; 2, "The Crisis of Bourgeois Ideology"; 3, "Imperialism's Foreign Political Propaganda Today" (doctrine and methods of political propaganda). "To make up for its ideological weakness, the monopoly bourgeoisie is perfecting the methods and organisation of propaganda" (297).

2899.   "The Arsenal of Propaganda." Inq 6.5 (1983) 4-5.
In its passion to counter the SU, the USIA and its VOA and Radio Marti distort information and language.

2900.   Bennett, James R. "Soviet Scholars Look at U.S. Media." JoC 36.1 (1986) 126-32.
Four books, using US sources, document for socialist countries the workings and messages of an "imperialist" mass media.

2901.   Bird, Kai, and Max Holland. "Freedom House Journalists." Na 242.20 (1986) 720.

President Reagan's National Endowment for Democracy gave
$200,000 to Leonard Sussman's Freedom House to send out articles
supporting Reagan's foreign policy to "some 350 journalists in
fifty countries."

2902.   Bogart, Leo. Premises for Propaganda: The
U.S.I.A.'s Operating Assumptions in the Cold War.
New York: Free, 1976. 250.
[The publication history of this book is relevant to the
subject of this bibliography.] The book was commissioned by the
US Information Agency and then, because officials deemed it
sensitive, classified it and kept it locked up for twenty years,
perhaps because its effort to "convey the flavor of how
propaganda is actually produced" got too close to the
practitioners, their operational procedures, personnel, and
budget.

2903.   Campbell, John. The Foreign Affairs Fudge Factory.
New York: Basic, 1971. 292.
An indictment of the excessive size and fragmentation of
the Department of State and other organizations dealing with
foreign policy. Ch. 6, "The Intelligence and Propaganda
Complexes," sets forth the weaknesses of the CIA and the USIA
and suggests reforms. The author would abolish the USIA and
"move toward a BBC-type system."

2904.   Charles, Daniel. "Behind Closed Doors." Na 9.2
(1985) 40-42.
Charles Wick, United States Information Director, showed
himself "to be a true cold warrior" with his "aggressively
partisan instrument of propaganda" aimed at spreading the
deployment of Pershing missiles in Europe.

2905.   Chester, Jeff. "Reagan's Global Reach." CJR 23.6
(1985) 10-12.
National Security Decision Directive 130 (NSDD-130)
emphasizes international communications as "an integral part of
U.S. national security policy and strategy" and authorizes the
expansion of radio and TV programs, a new program for a joint
government-industry effort to strengthen U.S. book publishing
and marketing abroad, an increase of military psychological
operations, and other programs. USIA's "Worldnet," for example,
links TV studios in Washington to about forty embassies and
consulates overseas in order to bring administration
policymakers face to face with foreign journalists.

2906.   "CIA to Europe: Take the Missiles!" CS 7
(June-Aug. 1983) 12-14.
Reagan's "public diplomacy" propaganda in the US, in
Europe, and in the world ("Project Democracy").

2907.   Cook, Blanche. "First Comes the Lie: C.D. Jackson
and Political Warfare." RHR 31 (1984) 42-70.
Contemporary US propaganda greatly derives from a virtually

477

unknown propagandist under Eisenhower named C.D. Jackson, the
vicepresident of Time, Inc., and publisher of Fortune. His aim
was simple--to extend US power throughout the world in order to
create the "American Century."

2908.   Danaher, Kevin. In Whose Interest?: A Guide to
          U.S.-South Africa Relations. Washington, DC:
          Institute for Policy Studies, 1985.
     On the double standards and deceits of US-SA relations--the
rationalizations for business investment, the lies, half-truths,
and covert operations with which the US bolsters SA's regime.

2909.   David, Michael, and Pat Aufderheide. "All the
          President's Media." Ch 5.3 (1985) 20-24.
     New technology "holds the promise of being highly
democratic in giving more people an opportunity to communicate to
diverse audiences. But the reality is that government has the
money and the sophistication to mobilize the technology for its
purposes," nor has any group "mobilized modern technology more
determinedly for government purposes than the United States
Information Agency--the government's overseas propaganda arm."
Also, the Reagan administration has used the new technology "to
expand in quantum jumps the public-relations component of modern
diplomacy."

2910.   Elder, Robert E. The Information Machine: The
          United States Information Agency and American
          Foreign Policy. Syracuse: Syracuse UP, 1968. 356.
     The people of the US have "allowed their government to
fashion a powerful propaganda machine" as "a normal policy
tool." Viewed against the liabilities of an obsolescent nation-
state as the dominant political organizing device for resolving
international problems, the USIA "may be no more than a crude
prototype of future information machines," but it may contribute
to the evolution of that nation-state system "into a higher
political form" more relevant to contemporary needs and dangers.
This is a study of internal organization of USIA from 1963 to
1967.

2911.   Epstein, S. "Imperialism and Manipulating with
          Public Opinion." DJ 9 (1973) 4-5.
     US propaganda analyzed.

2912.   Evenson, Debra. "Cuban Listeners Tuning Out Message
          on Radio Marti." ITT 9 (July 10-23, 1985) 20.
     Reagan's $10 million "public service station" for Cuba
which began broadcasting on May 20, 1985, initially "shot itself
in the foot" by its "inept ultra-right propaganda and
uninteresting programming."

2913.   Goodfriend, Arthur. The Twisted Image. New York:
          St. Martin's, 1963. 264.
     A study of the United States Information Agency in India
and why it failed to communicate US aims and desires to the

Indian People, by a supporter of the Agency. He ends with
twelve recommendations for an effective Agency.

2914.   Gordon, George, and Irving A. Falk.   The War of
      Ideas: America's International Identity Crisis.
      New York: Hastings, 1973. 362.
A critique of US ad hoc foreign policy and its chaotic
foreign propaganda--the USIA, Radio Free Europe, Radio
Liberty. The authors recommend that all propaganda should be
under one agency.

2915.   Grey, Robin. "Inside the Voice of America." CJR
      21.1 (1982) 23-30.
Internal conflict within the VOA between the public affairs
officers, who consider the VOA a "psy-war instrument in the
Reagan administration's assault on the Soviet Union," and the
journalists, who favor information over propaganda, credibility
prior to ideological warfare.

2916.   Hale, Julian. Radio Power: Propaganda and
      International Broadcasting. Philadelphia: Temple,
      1975. 196.
"The BBC provides a model of radio propaganda broadcasting
[minimal interference in the internal affairs of foreign
countries] that puts it apart from the American and the
communist models [overt, direct propaganda], and at the other
end of the spectrum from the Nazi External Service [frenzy and
invective]" (xix).

2917.   Kaplan, Sheila. "Up, Up and Away with USIA." CC
      12.3 (1986) 7-8.
Contrary to the Gramm-Rudman budget cutting program,
President Reagan has proposed a 12 percent increase for the US
Information Agency for 1987 to a budget of nearly $960 million.

2918.   Lagnado, Lucette. "Behind Radio Marti: Anti-Castro
      PAC in Washington." Na 237.11 (1983) 332-333.
The National Coalition for a Free Cuba lobbies against
Castro on Capitol Hill. It was a major force behind the Radio
Marti bill and the $14 million for it the first year.

2919.   Landis, Fred. "Psychological Warfare in Chile: The
      CIA Makes Headlines." Liberation 19.3 (1975) 21-32.
The CIA used polling, advertising, language study, etc.
through the Chilean newspaper El Mercurio to overthrow Allende.

2920.   Lawson, John H. Film in the Battle of Ideas. New
      York: Masses & Mainstream, 1953. 126. Rptd. New York:
      Garland, 1985.
The Hollywood film industry is a propaganda arm for US
ideology: imperialism, anti-labor, class, gangster and soldier
glorification, distortion of history, etc.

2921.   Matusow, Barbara. "How Reagan Controls His Coverage

Abroad: The White House Writes the Lead."   WJR 6
(Sept. 1984) 43-46.
Reagan and his public relations aides as masters of the
staged event.

2922.   Meehan, Maureen.   "Briefing: U.S. Pre-empts Costa
Rican Airwaves." ITT 8.41 (1984) 5.
The US Voice of America has bought access to Costa Rican
radio in order to attack Nicaragua, in violation of the
Neutrality Act of Costa Rican Constitutional Law. Television
stations are also being built with similar arrangements and
purpose.

2923.   Nelson, Lars-Erik.   "Anti-Semitism and the Airwaves."
ForP 61 (1985-86) 180-96.
Radio Liberty (formerly run by the CIA), an outlet for
voices considered subversive in the Soviet Union, has been
excessively dominated by "anti-democratic forces" and "right-
wing views." It should be moved from Munich to New York or
Washington to ensure it reflects "American rather than emigre
values."

2924.   Newman, Bud, and Verne Williams.   "Foreign Travel on
USIA's Account." WJR 5.8 (1983) 50-54.
Some prominent journalists have traveled abroad courtesy of
the United States Information Service, but "most professional
organizations for journalists" condemn the practice. Recipients
of the free trips defend it, but the "program under Reagan has
come under criticism for an unwritten policy to send overseas
only those speakers whose views were in accord with the
administration's."

2925.   Riznik, J. Q.   "The Voice Of America--Who Listens?"
Na 163 (September 14, 1946) 295-296.
The United States Department of State considers short-wave
radio "a political weapon of prime importance and a competitive
necessity."

2926.   Rubin, Ronald I.   The Objectives of the U.S.
Information Agency: Controversies and Analysis.
New York: Praeger, 1966. 251.
A book on how to make the USIA more effective.

2927.   Sorensen, Thomas.   The Word War: The Story of
American Propaganda. New York: Harper, 1968. 337.
A defense of US global propaganda organized historically--
the beginnings in WWI, the "Murrow Years" (three chs.), etc.

2928.   United States Advisory Commission on Public
Diplomacy: 1986 Report. Washington, DC: United
States Advisory Commission on Public Diplomacy, 1986.
48.
A study of the propaganda activities of the US Information
Agency, which reinforce traditional diplomacy "by explaining U.

480

S. Policies to foreign publics." "Advanced communications
technology, growing audiences, and recognition by most world
leaders of the value of obtaining public support for their
statements and actions has given public diplomacy new
importance." A "Summary of Findings and Recommendations" is
followed by analysis of four areas: "Public Diplomacy and
Foreign Policy," "Media and Programs," "Educational and
Cultural," and "Management."

2929.   "The United States Information Agency: Pushing the
     Big Lie." LAER 6.7 (1972) 1-31.
The propaganda, psychological warfare, and
counterinsurgency activities of the USIA: promotion of US
business, periodicals, Voice of America, comic book in Latin
America, etc.

2930.   "USIA Plans Extending Use of TV." AG (January 28,
     1986) 6A.
The USIA has created a TV service it calls "Worldnet" to
reach cable television systems worldwide via satellite.

2931.   "VOA, 5 Countries Agree on Improving Equipment."
     AG (December 26, 1984) 11A.
The Voice of America (the broadcasting arm of the USIA)
"signed agreements with five nations for improving broadcast
equipment within their borders as part of a $1.5 billion
modernization program, and VOA is also pressing Israel for
permission "to set up installations there to broadcast to the
[Soviet] Central Asian republics."

2932.   Wake, Jim. "The Mideast: More Puzzling Than Ever."
     HI 4 (1985) 1-7.
"The United States government is extremely active in the
region" in arms and arms transfers, bases in Arab countries, and
"erecting a huge Voice of America radio transmitter in Israel,"
as part of its anti-Soviet foreign policy.

2933.   Wenger, Martha. "No Budget Cuts for RFE/RL." CS
     5.4 (1981) 22-24.
A description of Radio Free Europe/Radio Liberty.

2934.   Wenger, Martha. "USIA/ICA: Arrowhead of
     Penetration." CS 5.1 (1980-81) 5-13.
The goal of the International Communication Agency (ICA)
"is to influence and/or manipulate events in foreign countries
along lines favorable to U.S. corporate and government foreign
policy objectives. Concretely, those objectives translate to
economic rape by U.S. multinational corporations for many third
world countries, and military and cultural domination for
others."

2935.   Whitton, John B., and Arthur Larson. Propaganda:
     Towards Disarmament in the War of Words. Dobbs Ferry,
     NY: Oceana, 1964. 305. Pub. for The World Rule of Law

481

Center, Duke U.
"The main substance of this book is a legal analysis of the
rules, principles and remedies available to control propaganda
of a kind that threatens the peace." Part I sets forth the
problem in two chs., the reason for the increased danger of
propaganda and the evolution of propaganda as a national weapon
since the French Revolution. Part II (chs. 3-8) presents the
law as it pertains to war-mongering, subversive, and defamatory
propaganda by a state, and Part III offers "Remedies and
Improvements" (Chs. 9-17).

2936.   "Youth Council Backers Threaten Withdrawal Over
         Apartheid Issue." AG (Dec. 1, 1985) 10A.
    The United States Youth Council, paid for mainly by the
United States Information Agency ($406,000 annually), was formed
to "foster democratic ideals abroad and provide representatives
for international youth conferences" in "an ideological united
front."

VII. D. Foundations (see III. E.) 2937-2943

2937.   Arnove, Robert F., ed. Philanthropy and Cultural
         Imperialism: The Foundations at Home and Abroad.
         Bloomington: Indiana UP, 1982. 473.
    Fourteen essays mainly on the Carnegie, Rockefeller, and
Ford foundations in "the production of culture and the formation
of public policy" particularly in the "fields of education and
social science research." "A central thesis is that
foundations" like these "help maintain an economic and political
order, international in scope, which benefits the ruling-class
interests of philanthropists," a system which "has worked
against the interests of minorities, the working class, and
Third world peoples." Essays on legitimating industrial
capitalism, Rockefeller medicine in China, control over black
higher education, educational colonialism in Africa, the
reproduction of a conservative ideology through the social
sciences, etc.

2938.   Berman, Edward H. "Educational Colonialism in Africa:
         The Role of American Foundations, 1910-1945."
         Philanthropy and Cultural Imperialism. ed. Robert
         Arnove. Boston: Hall, 1980. 179-202.
    The Phelps-Stokes Fund policies in Africa (financed by the
Carnegie, Rockefeller, and other foundations) "were intended to
perpetuate indefinitely the unequal relationships characteristic
of the colonial situation" and "beneficial primarily to the
metropolitan powers."

2939.   Berman, Edward H. "The Foundations Role in American
         Foreign Policy: The Case of Africa, post 1945."
         Philanthropy and Cultural Imperialism. ed. Robert
         Arnove. Boston: Hall, 1980. 203-232.
    Ford, Carnegie, and Rockefeller foundation support for
African education and research enabled them "to spread their

common ideology across a greater range of local societies than heretofore," and "to appear in the guise of disinterested humanitarians." In fact, "education was perceived as the opening wedge ensuring an American presence in those African nations considered of strategic and economic importance to the governing and business elite of the United States."

2940.   Berman, Edward H. The Ideology of Philanthropy: The Influence of the Carnegie, Ford and Rockefeller Foundations on American Foreign Policy. Albany: State U of New York P, 1983. 227.
    "The archival materials, coupled with interviews with foundation personnel and those formerly associated with their overseas programs, gradually helped me to understand the foundations' role as silent partners in United States foreign policy determination and as vital cogs in the ideological support system of state capitalism. Indeed, these two major functions have been inseparable." The foundations "further these goals by encouraging certain ideas congruent with their objectives and by supporting those educational institutions which specialize in the production and dissemination of these ideas." The foundations function similarly to support the status quo of "the existing social order and the futherance of state capitalism" within the US. These foreign and domestic aims and activities further "the elaboration and extension of a worldview commensurate with the economic, military, and political hegemony" of US state capitalism here and abroad.

2941.   Brown, E. Richard. "Rockefeller Medicine in China: Professionalism and Imperialism." Philanthropy and Cultural Imperialism. Ed. Robert Arnove. Boston: Hall, 1980. 123-146.
    "The Rockefeller medical education programs, guided in their conception and development by imperialist objectives, were more concerned with building an elite professional stratum to carry out cultural and technological transformation than with meeting the health needs of each country."

2942.   Dixler, Elsa. "Another Opening, Another Showcase for the Right." Na 239.21 (1984) 672-73.
    The right-wing think tank, the Heritage Foundation, is leading the attack on UNESCO.

2943.   Fisher, Donald. "American Philanthropy and the Social Sciences: The Reproduction of a Conservative Ideology." Philanthropy and Cultural Imperialism. ed. Robert Arnove. Boston: Hall, 1980. 233-268.
    The Rockefeller foundation "determined that the social sciences in Britain should help preserve the economic structure, and the resulting social inequality, in British society and its overseas empire."

Contributors Index

(Numbers refer to entries, not pages.)

Abel, Elie, 1006
Abrams, Floyd, 1653
Abrams, Pamela, 1929
Ackley, Charles, 2188
Ackroyd, Carol, 1835
Adamic, Louis, 69
Adams, Gordon, 471
Adams, Robert, 1806
Adams, William, 666, 667, 1475
Adler, Allan, 2318
Adler, Richard, 1147
Agee, Philip, 2597, 2598, 2599, 2600
Agnew, Jean-Christopher, 1148
Ainslie, Rosalynde, 2854
Ajemian, Peter, 535, 536
Albert, Stewart, 2559
Alderman, Jeffrey, 2319
Aldrich, Pearl, 606
Aldridge, Robert, 2320, 2769, 2770
Allende, Hortensia, 2180
Allen, Henry, 789
Allen, Thomas, 1248
Allman, T.D., 1980
Alperovitz, Gar, 18
Alter, Jonathan, 2602
Altheide, David, 668
Altschull, J. Herbert, 19, 169, 2855
Alvarez, Robert, 538
Ambrose, Stephen, 2189, 2603
Ambrosio, Angela, 1322
Anawalt, H.C., 2604
Anderson, Dave, 2605
Anderson, Jack, 253, 670, 1543, 1544, 1654, 1807
Anderson, James, 1419
Anderson, Jon, 276, 2163
Anderson, Kent, 1149
Anderson, Marion, 2322
Anderson, Scott, 276
Anderson, William, 1586
Andres, Monica, 2606
Andrews, Bert, 70
Apple, Michael, 790, 791, 792, 793
Appleman, Daniel, 1476
Aptheker, Bettina, 794
Aptheker, Herbert, 71
Arana, Ana, 2174
Arbatov, Georgi, 2898
Archer, Dane, 473
Archer, Gleason, 1007
Arditti, Rita, 859
Arevalo, Juan, 2034

Arieff, Irwin, 539, 1096
Arisian, Khoren, 2383
Arkin, William, 235, 474, 2323, 2357
Arnett, Peter, 1981
Arno, Andrew, 671
Arnove, Robert, 2937
Aronowitz, Stanley, 415, 795
Aronson, James, 72, 78, 672, 673, 2514
Aronson, Steve, 1150
Arvidson, Cheryl, 2515
Asher, Thomas, 1323
Astor, Gerald, 1324
Atkin, Kenward, 540
Auerbach, Jerold, 2
Aufderheide, Pat, 277, 541, 607, 608, 1151, 1152, 1325, 1493,
  1656, 1657, 1658, 2239, 2909
Auletta, Ken, 1622
Auster, Albert, 1153
Austin, Anthony, 1946
Autin, Dianna, 2607
Auxter, Thomas, 2772
Avirgan, Tony, 2664
Avrich, Paul, 3
Axelrod, Daniel, 2203
Babington, Charles, 674
Badhwar, Inderjit, 1154
Bagdikian, Ben, 676, 889, 1008, 1009, 1010, 1011, 1155, 1430,
  1477, 1478, 1659, 1877
Bailey, George, 1982, 1983
Baker, Beth, 2516
Baker, Dorothy, 20
Baker, Russell, 1587
Baker, Samm, 1156
Baldwin, Deborah, 1431
Baldwin, Hanson, 1660
Ballard, Hoyt, 416
Ball, Desmond, 2762
Ball-Rokeach, Sandra, 609
Bamford, James, 2763, 2764
Baral, Jaya, 2190
Barber, Benjamin, 1012, 1013
Barber, James, 2189
Bardsley, Anne, 677
Barger, Harold, 1479
Bario, Joanne, 1661
Baritz, Loren, 860
Barker, Carol, 1662
Barmash, Isadore, 610
Barnett, Paul, 880
Barnett, Stephen, 1014
Barnet, Richard, 2773
Barnouw, Erik, 611, 612, 613, 614, 678, 1157
Barrett, Edward, 1158
Barrett, John, 615
Barrett, Marvin, 679, 680, 681, 682, 683, 684, 685, 686, 687

CONTRIBUTORS

Barron, Jerome, 542
Barry, Tom, 2041
Barsamian, David, 688
Barth, Alan, 73, 74
Barton, Laurence, 75
Bass, Carole, 890
Bass, Cyrus, 21
Bass, Paul, 890
Bates, Stephen, 1625
Batscha, Robert, 689
Battaglia, Frank, 1159
Baughman, James, 543
Bayley, Edwin, 255
Bazelon, David, 1015
Bean, Kevin, 475
Beaubien, Michael, 690
Beban, Richard, 278
Beck, Hubert, 882
Beck, Joan, 1326
Beck, Melvin, 2608
Becker, Robert, 691
Bedell, Sally, 1160
Begun, Jay, 1663
Behrens, Steven, 1161
Belair, Robert, 1839
Belfrage, Cedric, 76, 77, 78
Belknap, Michal, 79
Bell, Clark, 1162
Bell, Daniel, 80
Bello, Walden, 179
Bender, Paul, 1688
Bendiner, Robert, 81
Benjamin, Alan, 2172
Benjamin, Gerald, 1664
Bennett, James, 38, 274, 280, 281, 282, 414, 692, 694, 788, 796,
    797, 1163, 1164, 1327, 1328, 1329, 1330, 1331, 1332, 1474,
    1480, 1588, 1837, 2042, 2043, 2044, 2119, 2164, 2304, 2382,
    2609, 2900
Bennett, John, 2324
Bennett, Jonathan, 891, 544, 2325, 1665
Bennett, Lance, 695
Bensman, David, 1165
Bentley, Eric, 82
Berlowitz, Marvin, 798
Berman, Edward, 2938, 2939, 2940
Berman, Jerry, 2384, 2583
Berman, Larry, 1481
Bermann, Karl, 2120
Bernstein, Barton, 22, 23, 24, 83, 1930, 2774
Bernstein, Carl, 1642, 1652, 2610
Bernstein, Dennis, 1333, 2386
Berryman, Phillip, 2045, 2121, 2122
Bertrand, Claude-Jean, 696
Bertsch, Kenneth, 476
Beschloss, Michael, 1545

487

Bethell, Thomas, 1906
Betts, Richard, 2191
Biddle, Francis, 84
Bird, Kai, 1643, 1808, 1840, 2385, 2614, 2615, 2901
Birnbaum, John, 85
Biryukov, N.S., 616, 2856
Bishop, Dale, 283
Biskind, Peter, 86, 799, 1838, 1984, 2616
Bizzell, Patricia, 799
Black, George, 284, 2617
Blackburn, Robin, 800
Blackstock, Nelson, 2517
Blair, William, 87
Blakely, Robert, 1166, 1167
Blanchard, Robert, 1878
Blank, Susan, 2518
Blinken, Anthony, 2519
Blitt, Connie, 1333, 2386
Block, Herbert, 1589
Blum, Bill, 2522
Blum, Richard, 2387
Blume, Keith, 1623
Blyskal, Jeff, 697
Blyskal, Marie, 697
Boffey, Philip, 801
Bogart, Beth, 892
Bogart, Leo, 2902
Boggs, Timothy, 2449
Bok, Sissela, 893
Bolinger, Dwight, 894
Bollier, David, 545
Bonafede, Dom, 1336, 1482, 1483, 1484, 1907
Bonner, Raymond, 2165
Bonpane, Blase, 2046
Bontecou, Eleanor, 88
Boorstin, Daniel, 698
Boot, William, 285, 286, 698a, 1168, 1169, 1432, 1485
Bordewich, Fergus, 89, 1170
Borosage, Robert, 2389, 2618
Bossong, Ken, 1666
Bottome, Edgar, 25
Boudin, Leonard, 2520
Bowart, Walter, 2521
Bowlby, Rachel, 1171, 1192
Bowles, Samuel, 802
Boyd, James, 1654
Boyd-Barret, Oliver, 699
Boyer, Brian, 1841
Boyer, Paul, 90
Boyer, William, 2192
Boylan, James, 416a
Braestrup, Peter, 1985
Braeutigam, Ronald, 580
Bram, Steven, 2328
Branch, Taylor, 1762, 1947

CONTRIBUTORS

Brandt, Daniel, 2390
Branfman, Fred, 1948
Bray, Howard, 1172
Breckenridge, Adam, 1546
Breen, Myles, 700
Breitbart, Eric, 701
Brenkman, John, 1180
Brennan, Pat, 859
Brennan, Timothy, 1173
Brenner, Daniel, 546
Brenner, Philip, 2047
Brenton, Myron, 1433
Breyers, Bob, 2857
Brick, Allan, 2305
Bright, Charles, 287
Broad, William, 288
Broder, David, 1908
Brodeur, Paul, 1434, 1435
Brodhead, Frank, 289, 290, 350, 2166
Brody, Reed, 2124
Brooks, Julie, 2391
Broughton, Diane, 1175
Brown, Ben, 895
Brown, Cynthia, 2035, 2167, 2168
Brown, E. Richard, 2941
Brown, Harrison, 1809
Brown, Les, 547, 548, 549, 550, 551, 552, 1176, 1177, 1178, 1179,
    1436
Brown, Pamela, 26
Brown, Ralph, 91, 92
Brown, Robert, 1667
Brown, William, 1337
Browne, Malcolm, 1949
Brumberg, Abraham, 2125
Brush, Douglas, 1016
Brush, Judith, 1016
Buchanan, Keith, 2775
Buchwald, Art, 1590, 1591
Budiardjo, Carmel, 896
Buell, John, 1097
Bunce, Richard, 702, 1017
Bupp, Irvin, 417
Burbach, Roger, 2048
Burchett, Wilfred, 1931, 2329
Burger, Robert, 1668
Burkholder, Steve, 2392
Burnham, David, 897, 2393
Burnham, Walter, 418
Burns, E. Bradford, 2049, 2126
Burroughs, William, 617
Burrow, Marian, 898
Butts, Nina, 2306
Butz, Tim, 1842, 2751
Buxton, Edward, 1181
Cabestrero, Teofilo, 2127

Cade, Dozier, 93
Caldeira, Mark, 2620
Caldicott, Helen, 477, 1669
Caldwell, Terry, 2240
Callen, Earl, 2394
Cameron, Juan, 1670
Campbell, John, 2903
Camper, Natalie, 803
Cannon, Lou, 1486
Caplan, Lincoln, 1338
Caplan, Richard, 2776
Carleton, Don, 94
Carmo, Alberto, 2777, 2778
Carnoy, Martin, 805, 806
Carpenter, Tom, 553
Carr, Robert, 95
Carson, Hank, 2621
Carter, Bill, 1182
Cassidy, Robert, 1339
Castelli, Jim, 2395
Catto, Jessica, 2050
Caute, David, 96
Cavrak, Steve, 859
Ceplair, Larry, 97
Cerra, Frances, 1340
Chaberski, Stephen, 2523
Chace, James, 292, 2051
Chafee, Zachariah, 98
Chakrapani, Sumitra, 711
Chambers, John, 99
Chamorro, Edgar, 2129
Chaplan, Debra, 1183
Chapman, Frank, 798
Charles, Daniel, 2904
Charlton, Linda, 1341
Chavkin, Samuel, 2622
Chenoweth, Lawrence, 618
Chester, Jeff, 2755, 2905
Chittick, William, 1671
Chobanian, Peter, 1437
Chomsky, Noam, 28, 29, 619, 703, 704, 1672, 1979, 1986, 1987,
    1988, 1989, 1990, 1991, 2052, 2780, 2781
Christensen, Jack, 1844
Christenson, Reo, 1185
Christgau, John, 1845
Church, Frank, 2624
Churchill, Mae, 2396, 2545
Cirino, Robert, 620, 705, 706
Claney, Maura, 763
Clark, Blair, 2524
Clark, Jeff, 1343
Clark, Michael, 1992
Clark, Ramsey, 1932
Clarke, Peter, 707
Clarkson, Fred, 293, 409, 807, 2634

CONTRIBUTORS

Claybrook, Joan, 536, 1547, 1548
Clements, Tim, 808
Clevett, John, 1098
Clewett, John, 1438
Clifford, George, 1544
Clift, Eleanor, 1487
Cloherty, Jack, 1344
Clotfelter, James, 2193
Cloward, Richard, 583
Clubb, Edmund, 100
Cobb, Jean, 101, 1099
Cochran, Thomas, 2357
Cockburn, Alexander, 294, 295, 297, 708, 1488, 1489, 1673, 1933, 2053, 2130, 2398
Cockburn, Andrew, 296, 2241, 2242
Cockcroft, Eva, 2782
Coffin, Tristram, 2131, 2194
Cogley, John, 102
Cohen, Bernard, 1490
Cohen, Jerry, 446, 447
Cohen, Joshua, 2054, 2055
Cohen, Stanley, 709
Cohen, Stephen, 30, 298, 299, 300
Colby, Gerard, 1018
Coleman, James, 1019
Cole, Barry, 554
Cole, John, 1674
Cole, Lester, 104
Colhoun, Jack, 1847, 2525
Collier, Wayne, 2752
Collins, Joseph, 440, 2141
Collum, Danny, 105, 710, 1020
Comanor, William, 1186
Combs, James, 649, 754
Comendul, Michael, 1274
Commager, Henry, 106, 1549
Commoner, Barry, 900, 1624
Compaine, Benjamin, 1022
Coney, Cargill, 1491
Conrad, Peter, 1187
Conrad, Thomas, 2244
Constantino, Renato, 2783
Conway, Flo, 901
Cook, Blanche, 1551, 2907
Cook, Bruce, 107
Cook, David, 1188
Cook, Fay, 1910
Cook, Fred, 108, 256, 555, 2195, 2526, 2527, 2528, 2529
Cook, Richard, 1675
Cookson, Peter, 809
Cooney, James, 762
Coons, John, 810
Cooper, Marc, 302
Copelon, Rhonda, 1848
Cormier, Frank, 1911

Cornelius, Kay, 1189
Corning, Steve, 1879
Cornwell, Elmer, 1492
Corn, David, 1676
Corry, Steve, 2181
Countryman, Vern, 109
Courrier, Kathleen, 2196
Cowan, Paul, 1345, 2401
Cox, Arthur, 110, 303
Cox, Edward, 556
Cox, Harvey, 621
Crable, Richard, 1337
Cragan, John, 31
Cranberg, Gilbert, 1677, 2636
Crane, Sylvia, 111
Crespi, Irving, 1346
Critchlow, Donald, 1889
Croft, Jack, 1190
Cronkite, Walter, 1552
Crosby, Ned, 1810
Cros, Michele, 710a
Cross, Donna, 622
Croteau, David, 2197
Crowell, George, 304, 1592
Cunningham, Ann, 218
Curry, Beth, 1101
Curti, Merle, 1420
D'Agostino, Peter, 623
D'Ari, Paul, 1193
Dahl, Robert, 624, 1553
Dahlgren, Peter, 711, 1191, 1192
Dallek, Robert, 305
Dallin, Alexander, 306, 307
Danaher, Kevin, 2908
Danielson, Michael, 1024
Darknell, Frank, 1421
David, Michael, 1493, 2909
Davidon, Ann, 112
Davies, Peter, 902
Davis, Bill, 1025
Davis, Elmer, 113
Davis, Jon, 811
Davis, Rod, 308
Davis, William, 2403
Dawson, Jim, 1459
Day, Samuel, 1678
De Grasse, Robert, 2300
de Leseps, Suzanne, 1026
De Zutter, Henry, 1811
Deakin, James, 1912, 1913
Dean, John, 1644
Decter, Moshe, 271
Deeb, Gary, 1194
Deibel, Mary, 1195
Delcourt, Xavier, 2873

CONTRIBUTORS

Delgado, Richard, 1593
Deluca, Donald, 768
Demac, Donna, 1554
deMause, Lloyd, 309
DeMott, Benjamin, 625
Denison, Dave, 310, 311, 312
Dennis, Elissa, 2405
Denniston, Lyle, 1555
Derian, Jean-Claude, 417
DeSantis, Hugh, 4
Detzer, David, 1594
Devol, Kenneth, 1680
DeVolpi, Alexander, 1681
Dewart, Tracey, 2675
Diamond, Edwin, 712, 713, 714, 1027, 1625, 2332
Diamond, Sara, 479
Diamond, Sigmund, 2531, 2532
Dibble, Vernon, 2198
DiBernardo, Gail, 2533
Dickey, Christopher, 2133
Dickson, David, 812, 861
Dillon, Jay, 2333
Dinges, John, 2637
Diskin, Martin, 2058
Dissanayake, Wimal, 671
Divine, Robert, 1682
Dixler, Elsa, 2858, 2942
Dixon, Marlene, 115, 314, 903
Dobrin, Arthur, 2406
Dodge, Charlie, 1347, 1348
Doi, Kathy, 481
Dolan, Thomas, 2534
Domhoff, G. William, 416, 419, 420, 421, 422, 423, 1890
Donner, Frank, 315, 2407, 2408, 2409, 2410, 2535, 2536, 2537
Donovan, James, 2199
Donovan, Kevin, 1993
Doolittle, Jerome, 2638
Dorfman, Ariel, 1196, 2784
Dorfman, Ron, 626, 1994, 2411
Dorman, William, 116, 316, 317, 715, 716
Dorsen, Norman, 904, 1685, 1688
Dos Passos, John, 1349
Doudna, Christine, 1028
Douglass, Jim, 318
Dowie, Mark, 1494
Draper, Theodore, 32, 319, 2059
Dreier, Peter, 1029, 1197
Drew, Elizabeth, 1103, 1646
Drinnon, Richard, 2639
Drogin, Bob, 2334
Du Boff, Richard, 862, 2859
Duffy, Gloria, 320
Dugger, Ronnie, 321, 1495, 1496, 1497, 2060
Dujack, Stephen, 1350
Duker, Laurie, 482

493

CONTROL OF INFORMATION

Duncan, Donald, 117
Dunham, Corydon, 627
Durr, Clifford, 118
Dusek, Val, 813
Dwyer, Paula, 1104
Dye, Thomas, 424
Easterbrook, Gregg, 1105
Easton, Nina, 1106
Ebert, Allen, 324
Ecenbarger, William, 1813
Eckert, Charles, 1198
Edgar, Patricia, 717
Edmundson, Mark, 1199
Edsall, Thomas, 1030
Edwards, Richard, 1031
Egan, Jack, 1351
Ege, Konrad, 325, 326, 2169
Eggleston, Arthur, 119
Egleson, Nick, 2401
Ehrenreich, Barbara, 425
Ehrlich, Howard, 718
Eisen, James, 2642
Eisenberg, Carolyn, 33, 1891
Eisenhower, David, 2186
Eisler, Benita, 1200
Elder, Robert, 2910
Elias, Thomas, 1892
Elliff, John, 2538
Elliot, Dave, 426
Elliott, Philip, 1201
Ellison, Harlan, 1557
Ellul, Jacques, 628
Elsworth, Peter, 1849
Emerson, Steven, 863
Emerson, Thomas, 905
Emery, Walter, 557
Engel, Leonard, 120
Engelmayer, Sheldon, 1439
Englund, Steven, 97
Entman, Robert, 1995
Epstein, Benjamin, 90
Epstein, Edward, 719, 1558, 2412
Epstein, Jason, 1950
Epstein, Joshua, 2247
Epstein, S., 2911
Equale, Tony, 2640
Erickson, Paul, 1498
Ericson, Edward, 327, 906
Erlich, Reese, 495, 496
Ernst, Morris, 1032
Eshenaur, Ruth, 1951
Eskey, Kenneth, 1595
Etzioni, Amitai, 34, 1107
Evangelista, Matthew, 328
Evans, Frank, 121

Eveland, Wilbur, 2641
Evenson, Debra, 2912
Everett, Robert, 2248
Eversole, Pam, 1033
Ewen, Elizabeth, 1203
Ewen, Stuart, 1203, 1204, 1205
Ewing, David, 907, 1440
Fain, Jim, 2249
Fair, Elizabeth, 1353
Falbaum, Berl, 1689
Falk, Irving, 2914
Falk, Richard, 2200
Fallows, James, 2307
Faraone, Roque, 2785
Farhang, Mansour, 715
Farrell, James, 483, 1815
Fascell, Dante, 2860
Faulk, John, 122
Faulkner, Francis, 1996
Fausy, Verna, 1354
Fehrenbach, T. R., 1934
Feinberg, Lotte, 1690
Fejes, Fred, 2786, 2786a
Feld, Bernard, 2250
Feldman, Orna, 1206
Fenton, Tom, 2787
Ferber, Michael, 2251
Ferguson, LeRoy, 1880
Ferguson, Thomas, 1109, 1625a
Feuerlicht, Roberta, 257
Fieldhouse, Richard, 474
Fielding, Raymond, 721, 1207
Finder, Joseph, 329
Finn, Chester, 1691
Firestone, O. J., 1499
Fisher, Donald, 2943
Fisher, June, 1355
Fishman, Mark, 722
Fitzgerald, Ernest, 484
Fitzgerald, Frances, 814
Flaherty, Francis, 2414
Fleming, D.F., 5
Flippo, Chet, 1034, 1208
Flora, Jan, 2061
Flynn, Patricia, 2048
Flynt, Larry, 1596
Foley, Joseph, 1035
Foner, Philip, 6
Fontaine, Andre, 7
Ford, Daniel, 559
Ford, Sherman, 258
Fore, William, 560
Forest, Marsha, 123
Forster, Arnold, 124
Foss, Daniel, 441

Foster, Douglas, 125
Fox, Matthew, 1662
Fox, Richard, 1209
Franck, Thomas, 35, 1693, 2642
Frank, Robert, 2252
Frankel, Max, 1500
Franklin, Bruce, 815
Franklin, Marc, 1694
Franklin, Ruth, 1694
Frantzich, Stephen, 1881
Frappier, Jon, 2789, 2790
Frazier, Howard, 2643
Fredin, Eric, 707
Freed, Donald, 1596, 2644
Freeland, Richard, 126
Freeman, Joshua, 2542
Freifeld, Karen, 909
French, Scott, 2416
Frendreis, John, 1111
Freund, Charles, 1441, 1697
Fried, Emanuel, 910
Fried, Richard, 260
Friedman, Edward, 911, 2791
Friedman, John, 2645, 2646, 2647
Friedman, Robert, 485, 1357, 1698
Friedrich, Otto, 1816
Friel, Howard, 307, 486, 2792
Friendly, Fred, 723
Friendly, Jonathan, 2253
Fromartz, Samuel, 561
Fry, Ron, 942
Frye, Jerry, 1597
Fulbright, J. William, 2254
Fuller, John, 1699, 2335
Furgurson, Ernest, 912
Gabis, Stanley, 1700
Galbraith, John, 487
Galen, Michele, 1775
Galnoor, Itzhak, 1701
Gandy, Oscar, 427, 724
Ganley, Gladys, 2793
Ganley, Oswald, 2793
Gans, Herbert, 725, 726, 727
Garcia, Elise, 1112
Gardner, Corinna, 330
Gardner, Lloyd, 36
Garrison, Jim, 331
Garrison, Omar, 2417
Garrow, David, 2543
Gartner, Alan, 1598
Garwood, Darrell, 2649
Gaut, Greg, 37
Gaventa, John, 1210
Gavshon, Arthur, 332, 1893
Gay, Lance, 2255

CONTRIBUTORS

Geis, Michael, 1211
Gelb, L.H., 2650
Gelb, Leslie, 1501
Gelbspan, Ross, 2418
Geller, Henry, 562, 563
Gellhorn, Walter, 127
Gerbner, George, 2794
Gerdeman, Alice, 2062
Gervasi, Tom, 333, 728, 2256
Getlein, Frank, 2201, 2257, 2544
Gettleman, Marvin, 2171
Ghiglione, Loren, 1036
Gibson, William, 1997
Gilbert, James, 1817
Gillers, Stephen, 1685
Gilliam, Dorothy, 128
Gilpin, Robert, 864, 865
Gilson, Lawrence, 1702
Ginsberg, Benjamin, 1626
Giroux, Henry, 795, 816, 817, 818
Gitlin, Todd, 488, 629, 729, 1212, 1213
Gladstone, Brooke, 1161
Glasmeier, Amy, 2298
Glasser, Ira, 2493
Glessing, Robert, 630
Gliserman, Marty, 631
Gluck, Sidney, 334
Gofman, John, 913, 1358
Gold, Michael, 1442
Goldberg, Donald, 335
Goldman, Debra, 996
Goldman, Neal, 1703
Goldsen, Rose, 632, 1214
Goldstein, Jonathan, 1998
Goldstein, Robert, 8
Goldston, Robert, 261
Gollon, Peter, 489, 2336
Gonchar, Ruth, 1599
Goodell, Charles, 1851
Goodell, Rae, 1359
Goodfriend, Arthur, 2913
Goodman, David, 1704
Goodman, Julian, 1705
Goodman, Walter, 129
Gordon, Diana, 2545
Gordon, George, 2914
Gordon, Michael, 336
Gordon, Suzanne, 337
Gossage, Howard, 1215
Gottlieb, Bob, 2862
Goulart, Ron, 1216
Gould, Andrew, 2064
Gould, Christopher, 38, 2609
Goulden, Joseph, 490, 1952
Goulding, Phil, 2337

497

Graber, Doris, 633, 1037, 1627, 1628
Grady, Sandy, 1600
Graedon, Joe, 564
Graham, Fred, 633a, 1852
Grambart, James, 2338
Granato, Leonard, 1706
Grant, Mark, 1217
Gravel, Michael, 1953
Graves, Florence, 1114, 1115, 2546
Gravois, John, 565
Greeley, Bill, 1648
Green, Gil, 130
Green, Mark, 428, 1037a, 1360, 1601, 1882
Green, Philip, 820, 1894
Green, Timothy, 1218
Greenberg, Daniel, 914
Greene, Bob, 1602
Greer, Colin, 821
Gregory, Richard, 915
Grey, Robin, 2915
Griffee, Carol, 1361
Griffen, William, 1999, 2000
Griffin-Nolan, Edward, 2135
Griffith, Robert, 131, 262
Griffith, Thomas, 730
Grodzins, Morton, 1853
Gronberg, Tom, 2863
Gross, Bertram, 429
Grosscup, Beau, 39
Grossman, Karl, 916, 1707
Grossman, Lawrence, 822
Grossman, Michael, 1502, 1503, 1504
Grossman, Richard, 1373
Grossman, Zoltan, 1708
Grube, Joel, 609
Gruber, Carol, 1935
Gruening, Ernest, 1362
Guback, Thomas, 2796, 2797, 2798, 2799
Guerra, Joe, 430, 1363, 1364
Guilbaut, Serge, 132
Guilfoy, Christine, 1560
Gulden, Bob, 338
Guma, Greg, 1038
Gunn, Herb, 2136
Gusmao, Ivna, 2172
Guttman, Daniel, 1895
Gwyn, Robert, 133, 1219
Haberer, Joseph, 866
Hachten, William, 2800
Hahn, Dan, 1599, 1818
Haig, Alexander, 1505
Haight, Timothy, 1083
Haiman, Franklyn, 917
Hairston, Marc, 2258
Halberstam, David, 431, 1954

CONTRIBUTORS

Hale, Julian, 2916
Hall, Bob, 1220
Hall, Earl, 1896
Hall, Francoise, 40
Hall, Peter, 2864
Hall, Ross, 1221
Halliday, Fred, 29, 41, 339, 2665
Hallin, Daniel, 1506, 2001
Halloran, Richard, 2070
Halperin, David, 1603
Halperin, Morton, 1561, 1562, 1709, 1710, 1854, 2384, 2421, 2422, 2583
Halsey, A.H., 829
Halverson, Richard, 2259
Hamelink, Cees, 1039, 2801
Hannikainen, Lauri, 2876
Hanrahan, John, 2654
Hans, Dennis, 2071
Hansen, George, 1711
Hanson, C.T., 1116
Hanson, Elizabeth, 219
Hardee, Patty, 1883
Harger, Richard, 2423
Harker, Dave, 1040
Harnik, Peter, 1365
Harper, Fowler, 134
Harris, Amanda, 1712
Harris, Kevin, 823
Harris, Phil, 2802
Harris, Richard, 2002, 2424
Hart, Roderick, 1507
Hartley, John, 731
Hartman, Thomas, 491, 2260
Hartnett, Rodney, 883
Harty, Sheila, 824
Hartz, Louis, 432
Hartzell, Grace, 492
Harvey, Joan, 918
Haskell, Anne, 1508
Hatch, Richard, 919
Haug, Wolfgang, 1222
Havig, Alan, 1223
Hawes, William, 920
Hayakawa, S.I., 135
Hayden, Tom, 1884
Hayden, Trudy, 1443
Hayter, Teresa, 2803
Healy, Tim, 1444
Heffron, Mary, 2787
Heilbroner, Robert, 433
Heise, Juergen, 2261
Heller, Scott, 921
Hellinger, Dan, 2137
Hellman, Lillian, 137
Hellmann, John, 2003

499

Helmer, John, 826
Helmreich, Jonathan, 42
Hembree, Diana, 1470
Hennessee, Judith, 1224
Henry, J.S., 1366
Henry, William, 922
Henslin, James, 454
Hentoff, Nat, 340, 1713, 1714, 1855, 1856, 2401, 2425
Herken, Gregg, 43
Herman, Edward, 138, 307, 341, 732, 862, 867, 1041, 1990, 1991,
    2072, 2073, 2166, 2655, 2781
Hermann, Kai, 2656
Hersh, Seymour, 342, 1563, 2262, 2263, 2264, 2339, 2340
Hertsgaard, Mark, 1042
Hertsgaard, Mark, 343
Hertz, David, 2657
Herzon, Mary, 868
Hess, John, 1225
Hess, Judith, 634
Hess, Stephen, 1914, 1915, 1916
Heuvel, Katrina, 344
Hickey, Neil, 1445
Hiebert, Ray, 1629
Hilgartner, Stephen, 923
Hill, Doug, 566
Hinckle, Warren, 1966, 2658
Hirsch, Glenn, 1367
Hirshberg, Peter, 2866
Hitchens, Christopher, 493, 2138, 2547, 2659, 2660
Hitt, Jack, 2661
Hobbs, Malcolm, 140
Hoch, Paul, 2548
Hochberg, Lee, 1446
Hochman, Sandra, 434, 2804
Hoekstra, Douglas, 1510
Hoffman, Daniel, 1562, 1710
Hoffman, Lyla, 2202
Hoffman, Mike, 2074
Hoffman, Nicholas Von, 465, 1368, 1917
Hoffmann, Stanley, 345
Hofstadter, Richard, 924
Hogan, Bill, 1447, 1448
Hogan, J. Michael, 1511
Hohenberg, John, 1512
Holder, Dennis, 1226
Holderness, Mike, 1715
Holk, Richard, 2004
Holland, Max, 1643, 1808, 1840, 2139, 2385, 2614, 2615, 2901
Hollyday, Joyce, 2075
Holzman, Franklyn, 2662
Homer, Frederick, 2426, 2427
Honey, Martha, 2663, 2664
Horne, Gerald, 141
Horowitz, Andrew, 1227, 2805
Horowitz, Daniel, 1228

Horowitz, David, 44, 494, 495, 496, 1422, 1423
Horowitz, Irving, 1857
Horton, Forest, 1716
Hotaling, Edward, 2005
Houlding, Andrew, 2428
Hovsepian, Nubar, 1955
Howard, Bruce, 497
Howard, John, 1229
Howe, Barbara, 1424
Howell, Leon, 1450
Howell, Rex, 733
Hoyt, Michael, 733a, 1451
Huebner, Al, 925
Hughes, Joseph, 926
Hulbert, James, 1229
Hulser, Kathleen, 927
Humberto, Maximo, 2806
Hume, Brit, 1918, 2265
Hung, N. M, 2006
Hunt, Linda, 1717
Hunter, Jane, 1564
Hynds, Ernest, 1718
Immerman, Richard, 2076
Imwinkelried, Edward, 2238
Ingold, Beth, 1541
Irons, Peter, 2342
Isbell, Florence, 1719
Jackson, Dennis, 1330
Jackson, Nancy, 1859
Jacobs, Jim, 2440
Jacoby, Neil, 2807
Jaffe, Louis, 143
James, Goodman, 2419
James, Peter, 2441
Jamieson, Kathleen, 635, 1630
Janus, Noreene, 2808
Jencks, Richard, 567
Jensen, Jay, 2361
Jess, Paul, 1043
Jetter, Alexis, 2080
Jezer, Marty, 435
Joffe, Phyllis, 1044
Joffroy, Michelle, 2792
Johansen, Robert, 1513
Johnson, David, 1819
Johnson, Flora, 1230
Johnson, Giff, 1720
Johnson, Loch, 2442
Johnson, M.B., 1721
Johnson, Michael, 348
Johnson, Nicholas, 1045, 1046, 1231, 1232
Johnson, Paul, 2007
Johnson, R.W., 349
Johnstone, Diana, 350, 351
Jonas, Susanne, 2081

Jones, J. Harry, 46
Jones, Jeff, 352
Joseph, Nadine, 1369
Josephson, Matthew, 144
Joyce, James, 2869
Judis, John, 1820, 2443
Jungk, Robert, 1370
Jungmeyer, Paul, 827
Jussim, Daniel, 2444
Justice, William, 1860
Kahane, Howard, 636
Kahn, Albert, 9, 145, 1604
Kahn, David, 2445
Kaidy, Mitchell, 568
Kaiser, Robert, 1631
Kaku, Michio, 2203
Kalvelage, Carl, 1543
Kamen, Martin, 146
Kampf, Louis, 828
Kanfer, Stefan, 147
Kanter, Elliot, 2551
Kaplan, Carl, 2665
Kaplan, Craig, 930
Kaplan, Fred, 148, 2267, 2343
Kaplan, Joel, 1119
Kaplan, Sheila, 1120, 1121, 2268, 2917
Karabel, Jerome, 829
Karmen, Andrew, 1722, 1723
Karp, Walter, 436, 437, 735, 1371, 1565
Karpatkin, Marvin, 1566
Katel, Peter, 1452
Katznelson, Ira, 438
Kaufman, Joel, 1233
Kaye, Tony, 354, 355, 356
Kazis, Richard, 1373
Keegan, Paul, 1372
Kefauver, Estes, 1047
Keisling, Phillip, 2269
Kellermann, Bill, 2447
Kelley, Joseph, 2270
Kelley, Kevin, 931, 2182
Kelly, J.B., 932
Kelly, John, 149, 1605, 2082, 2271, 2552, 2666, 2667
Kelly, Kevin, 1514
Kelly, Orville, 1781
Kemper, Vicki, 736, 2140
Kennan, George, 45
Kennedy, Pam, 1725
Kenny, Robert, 150
Kenworthy, Eldon, 2083
Kern, Montague, 1515
Kernek, Sterling, 1586
Kesselman, Mark, 438
Kidder, Rushworth, 1897
Kiester, Sally, 1898

CONTRIBUTORS

Kilian, Michael, 2084
Kim, Young, 2668
Kimball, Penn, 2553, 2554
King, Jonathan, 933
Kinsley, Michael, 1048
Kinzer, Stephen, 2085
Kirby, Laurie, 934
Kirchwey, Freda, 151, 152, 153
Kirkhorn, Michael, 357
Klare, Michael, 154, 2086, 2204, 2205, 2272, 2308
Klausen, Paul, 155
Klugman, Craig, 1919
Knelman, F.H., 358
Kneupper, Charles, 1606
Knightly, Phillip, 1936, 1956
Knoll, Erwin, 1726, 1727, 1749, 2214, 2555, 2556, 2557
Koch, Lewis, 1861
Koger, Daniel, 2273
Kohn, Alfie, 2448
Koistinen, Paul, 497a
Kolko, Gabriel, 439
Kolodney, David, 1423
Kolosov, Yuri, 2810
Kondracke, Morton, 2669
Konecky, Eugene, 935
Konrad, George, 359
Kopkind, Andrew, 1049, 1234
Kosterlitz, Julie, 1123, 1124, 1125, 1126, 1127, 2274
Kotch, Jonathan, 569
Kotelchuch, David, 1453
Kotz, David, 1050
Koughan, Martin, 1235
Kovel, Joel, 360
Kowet, Don, 2344
Kozol, Jonathan, 830
Krasnow, Erwin, 570, 571
Kraus, Sidney, 1632
Krehm, William, 2088
Krepon, Michael, 1607, 1937
Kriesberg, Martin, 11
Krimsky, Sheldon, 869, 870
Kronenburg, Philip, 530
Krueger, Marlis, 936
Kuklick, Bruce, 47
Kumar, Martha, 1502, 1503
Kunstler, William, 2558, 2559
Kupferberg, Seth, 1454
Kurland, Philip, 1649
Kutler, Stanley, 156
Kwitny, Jonathan, 157, 2089, 2811
La Rocque, Gene, 1819
Labris, Roger, 336
Labunski, Richard, 572
Lacob, Miriam, 937
Ladd, Anthony, 1374

Ladd, Bruce, 2345
Lafeber, Walter, 2090, 2091, 2092, 2670
Lagemann, Ellen, 1425
Lagnado, Lucette, 2093, 2918
Laitner, Skip, 1728
Lake, Anthony, 1501
Lambro, Donald, 938
Lancaster, John, 1729
Landau, Fred, 2346
Landau, Jack, 1730, 1862
Landau, Saul, 361, 2637, 2671
Landis, Fred, 158, 362, 2644, 2672, 2919
Lane, Winthrop, 2309
Lang, Gladys, 737, 1650
Lang, Kurt, 737, 1650
Langer, John, 1236
Langguth, Arthur, 2673
Lanouette, William, 738
Lapp, Ralph, 2206, 2347
Lappe, Frances, 440, 2141
Laqueur, Walter, 739
Lardner, George, 2674
Lardner, Ring, 159
Larkin, Ralph, 441
Larson, Arthur, 2935
Larson, James, 740
Lasch, Christopher, 160, 498, 1237, 1238
Lasch, Robert, 48
Lash, Jonathan, 1567
Laski, Harold, 161
Lasswell, Harold, 162
Latham, Earl, 163
Lattimore, Owen, 264
Laurence, Philip, 2675
Lauter, Paul, 828
Law, Steven, 363
Lawrence, Ken, 1899, 2577
Lawson, John, 2920
Lawton, George, 2184
Lazarsfeld, Paul, 164
Le Duc, Don, 1733
Leab, Daniel, 165
Leamer, Laurence, 1731
Lears, T.J., 1239
Lech, Raymond, 2348
Ledbetter, James, 364
Lederer, William, 1732
Lee, Martin, 2677, 2678
Lee, Philip, 1295, 2870
Lefever, Ernest, 2275
Leggett, John, 941, 2183
Lehman, Bruce, 2449
Leiss, William, 1240
Lemann, Nicholas, 2349
Lemisch, Jesse, 831

CONTRIBUTORS

LeMond, Alan, 942
Lens, Sidney, 10, 49, 499, 1608, 2207, 2350, 2351, 2450
Lent, John, 2812
Lentricchia, Frank, 832
LeoGrande, William, 2094
Leone, Bruno, 1760
Lepkowski, Wil, 2310
Lernoux, Penny, 442, 2679, 2680
LeRoy, David, 741
Lesage, Julia, 2008
Lesher, Stephan, 742
Leubsdorf, Carl, 1516
Levenstein, Alan, 1241
Levi, Michael, 500
Levin, Harvey, 573
Levin, Jack, 1375
Levin, Murray, 12
Levine, Bruce, 2311
Levine, Greg, 2499
Levine, Robert, 1569
Levinson, Sanford, 820
Levitch, Joel, 943
Levy, Gerald, 833
Lewis, Anthony, 365, 501, 637, 1609, 1610, 2541
Lewis, Carolyn, 574
Lewis, Lionel, 944
Lewis, Phyllis, 2452
Lewis, Richard, 575
Lewis, Roger, 743
Lichtman, Richard, 834
Lifschultz, Lawrence, 166
Lightman, Richard, 167
Lindee, Susan, 502
Lindorff, Dave, 1863, 2453
Lindsay, Sue, 1734
Lindstrom, Duane, 1051
Lingeman, Richard, 945, 2561
Linsky, Martin, 743a
Liong, Liem, 896
Lippard, Lucy, 638
Lippmann, Walter, 13
Lipsitz, George, 443
Litwak, Leo, 946
Lloyd, Frank, 947
Lloyd, Rees, 948
Loader, Jayne, 503
Lobaco, Gina, 2522
Loeb, Paul, 504, 1611, 2173
Long, Franklin, 505, 2312
Longley, Lawrence, 570
Loory, Stuart, 2208, 2683
Lopez, Alfredo, 1735
Lord, Benjamin, 1052
Loving, Bill, 2276
Lowenstein, Douglas, 1633

Lowenthal, Max, 2562
Lowi, Theodore, 1864
Lubasch, Arnold, 168
Lukas, J. Anthony, 169
Lundberg, Ferdinand, 1054, 1054a
Lundestad, Geir, 2813
Lutz, William, 1376, 1377, 2277
Lyford, Joseph, 1736
Lynch, Joe, 50
Lynn, Joyce, 744
Lyon, Matthew, 1378
Lytle, Stewart, 2352, 2353
MacCann, Donnarae, 2209
MacColl, Gail, 1601
MacDonald, J. Fred, 2009
MacDougall, A. Kent, 1379, 1380, 1381
MacDougall, Allan, 1242
MacIver, Robert, 949
Mackenzie, Angus, 1737, 1738, 2455, 2563, 2684, 2685, 2686, 2687
Mackenzie, James, 1382, 1383, 1384
MacKenzie, Robert, 745, 746
MacKerron, Conrad, 950, 1739
Macy, John, 639
Madeley, John, 2814
Madsen, Axel, 1243
Magid, Larry, 951
Mahler, Richard, 367
Mailer, Norman, 171
Makhijani, Arjun, 368
Maland, Charles, 172
Malcomson, Scott, 2776
Mancini, Paolo, 1506
Mandel, Ernest, 640
Mander, Jerry, 1244, 1385
Mankiewicz, Frank, 1245
Mankin, Eric, 1246
Manley, John, 369
Mann, James, 2456
Manno, Jack, 2211, 2212
Manoff, Robert, 173, 174, 370, 747, 952, 1517, 1740, 1741
Manzione, Elton, 371
Marchand, Donald, 1716
Marchetti, Victor, 2688
Marchino, Michael, 175, 2354
Marciano, John, 2000, 2010
Margolius, Sidney, 1247
Marin, Peter, 2011
Marine, Gene, 576
Mark, Norman, 2278
Marker, Dennis, 953
Markowitz, Gerald, 2564
Markowitz, Norman, 176
Marks, John, 1957, 2618, 2688, 2689
Marks, Russell, 1426
Markusen, Ann, 2213

CONTRIBUTORS

Marnell, William, 1742
Marquis, Donald, 1248
Marrow, Anthony, 1823
Marshall, Jonathan, 2548
Marshall, Peter, 1444
Marshall, Rachell, 954
Marwick, Christine, 1743, 1744, 1865, 2457, 2458
Marx, Gary, 2459, 2460
Maslow, Jonathan, 2174
Massee, John, 2872
Massing, Michael, 577, 748, 1055, 1249, 1824, 2036, 2175, 2279
Mastro, Randy, 1386
Mastroberardino, Joy, 278, 2012
Mather, Kirtley, 177
Mathews, Anthony, 1745
Mathews, Jay, 1920
Mathewson, Judith, 1746
Mathias, Charles, 1570
Mathurin, Victor, 2013
Mattelart, Armand, 2784, 2817, 2818, 2819, 2820, 2821, 2873
Mattelart, Michelle, 2873
Matthews, Herbert, 2095
Matthews, Robert, 284
Matthiessen, Peter, 2565
Matusow, Allen, 265
Matusow, Barbara, 749, 1130, 2921
Maurer, Harry, 1058
May, Gary, 179
May, Ronald, 271
Mayer, Allan, 1387
Mayer, Milton, 2280
McAnany, Emile, 642, 2096, 2822
McAuliffe, Kevin, 643
McAuliffe, Mary, 180
McCartney, James, 1518, 1747
McCartney, Laton, 1388
McClellan, Grant, 1866
McClellan, Jim, 181
McClellan, Jimmie, 1885
McCombs, Maxwell, 1637
McDermott, John, 644
McFeatters, Ann, 1748
McGaffin, William, 1749, 2214
McGarvey, Patrick, 2690
McGehee, Fielding, 1750
McGehee, Ralph, 2691, 2692, 2693
McGilligan, Pat, 240
McGinniss, Joe, 1634
McGovern, George, 182, 1635
McGovern, James, 1056
McGrory, Mary, 1751, 2355, 2694
McIntyre, Mark, 955, 2265
McIntyre, Thomas, 183
McMahan, Jeff, 372, 1612
McNulty, Thomas, 2014

507

McPhail, Thomas, 2874
McQuaid, Kim, 1131
McWilliams, Carey, 51, 184, 185, 186, 187, 2566
McWorter, Gerald, 956
Mead, Judy, 1867
Means, Howard, 957
Mechling, Thomas, 1825
Medsger, Betty, 1250
Meehan, Eileen, 1057
Meehan, Maureen, 2922
Meeropol, Michael, 188
Meeropol, Robert, 188
Meiklejohn, Alexander, 1752
Melanson, Philip, 2695
Melman, Seymour, 444, 507, 507a, 507b, 2215
Melody, William, 1251
Meranto, Philip, 958
Merbaum, Richard, 1900
Merwin, W.S., 959
Merz, Charles, 13
Meyer, Karl, 189
Mickelson, Sig, 1519
Mickiewicz, Ellen, 750
Miles, Michael, 190, 960
Miles, Sara, 373
Miliband, Ralph, 52
Miller, Arthur, 961, 962, 2696, 2765
Miller, Judith, 2462, 2697
Miller, Merle, 191, 192
Miller, Steven, 374
Millis, Walter, 508
Millman, Joel, 1868, 2142, 2143, 2144
Mills, C. Wright, 53, 445
Mills, Kay, 1753
Minor, Dale, 1939
Minow, Newton, 1520
Mintz, Morton, 446, 447, 577a, 1252, 1455
Mirow, Kurt, 1058
Mische, Patricia, 375
Mitchell, David, 14
Mitchell, Greg, 963
Mitford, Jessica, 1958
Moberg, David, 376
Moffett, Toby, 1521
Mohr, Charles, 2015
Mollenhoff, Clark, 1755, 2281
Montague, Peter, 948
Mooney, Michael, 646
Moore, Michael, 1456
Moore, Ray, 647
Moore, Robin, 2016
Moore, Taylor, 2216
Moraes, Maria, 2184
Morales, Waltraud, 2145
Morano, Roy, 1059

CONTRIBUTORS

Morgan, Carol, 194
Morgan, Edward, 195
Morgan, Paul, 1826
Morgan, Richard, 1139, 1756, 2463
Moritz, Owen, 1757
Morland, Howard, 1758
Morley, Jefferson, 2129
Morley, Morris, 2146
Morris, Julie, 1253
Morris, Roger, 750a, 751, 1390, 1571, 2282
Morris, Scott, 1522
Morrison, David, 509
Morrissette, Walt, 2283
Morse, Randy, 2823
Mosco, Vincent, 578
Mosher, James, 579
Moxley, Bob, 835
Mueller, Claus, 448
Muller, Ronald, 2773
Munson, Richard, 1391, 1392
Muro, Mark, 1901
Murray, Robert, 15
Musil, Robert, 1613, 2217
Mutnick, Deborah, 2147
Muwakkil, Salim, 752
Myerson, Michael, 196
Mysak, Joseph, 1457
Nader, Ralph, 836
Nadler, Eric, 837
Naiman, Adeline, 2218
Nairn, Allan, 2176, 2465, 2698, 2699
Naison, Mark, 2824
Nash, Roderick, 1420
Nation, Fitzroy, 2097
Navasky, Victor, 197, 1254, 2466
Neier, Aryeh, 1759, 2568, 2700, 2701
Nelkin, Dorothy, 502, 2313
Nelson, Anne, 2617
Nelson, Craig, 2671
Nelson, Jack, 198, 964
Nelson, Jill, 1255
Nelson, Joyce, 2825
Nelson, Lars-Erik, 2356, 2923
Nelson, Lin, 1393
Nelson, Madeline, 1256
Nelson-Pallmeyer, Jack, 2098
Nemeth, Louis, 1394
Neuborne, Burt, 1688
Neuman, Robert, 753
Newcomb, Horace, 648
Newman, Bud, 2924
Newman, Dale, 753
Nicholas, Jeff, 1257
Nicholas, Ralph, 838
Nielsen, Waldemar, 1427

509

Nigut, Bill, 2534
Nimmo, Dan, 449, 649, 754, 755, 1921
Nix, Mindy, 1523
Noah, Timothy, 1060, 1258, 2284
Noble, David, 839
Nocera, Joseph, 2702
Nordenstreng, Kaarle, 2863, 2875, 2876, 2877, 2878
Norrgard, Lee, 229, 510, 511, 1115, 2274
Norris, Robert, 2357
Norsworthy, Kent, 2149
Norton, Chris, 2099, 2177
Novak, Michael, 1524
Noyes, Dan, 1004
Nugent, David, 710a
Nyhan, Michael, 1774
O'Connor, James, 840
O'Connor, John, 1259
O'Connor, Tom, 200
O'Keeffe, Mike, 2703
O'Leary, Brian, 871
O'Neill, Terry, 1760
O'Reilly, Kenneth, 2570, 2571
O'Reilly, William, 1261
O'Shaughnessy, Hugh, 2101
Oakes, John, 2100
Oberdorfer, Don, 1960
Obert, John, 183
Oettinger, Mal, 554
Ohanian, Susan, 1260
Ohmann, Richard, 841, 1395
Ola, Akinshiju, 2569
Ollman, Bertell, 842
Omeed, Ehsan, 716
Oppenheim, Jerrold, 1572, 1961
Orman, John, 1573
Oseth, John, 2468
Oshinsky, David, 266, 267
Osnos, Peter, 201
Ott, George, 202, 2285
Owen, Bruce, 580
Owen, David, 1262
Packard, Frank, 1061
Packard, Vance, 650, 965
Packer, Herbert, 203
Packwood, Bob, 581
Paden, Mary, 1784
Paine, Christopher, 512
Paletz, David, 651, 757, 1396, 1995
Pally, Marcia, 378
Panitt, Merrill, 1263
Parenti, Michael, 204, 205, 758, 2220
Parham, Paul, 2017
Park, Robert, 2358
Parker, Richard, 1458
Parnas, David, 2359

CONTRIBUTORS

Parsons, Marjorie, 1764
Patterson, Oscar, 2018, 2019
Patterson, Walter, 513
Payne, Anthony, 2103
Payne, Cril, 2572
Payne, Les, 966
Pearson, David, 2470
Pearson, Roberta, 1396
Pearson, Ted, 2185
Peck, Abe, 2020
Peck, Keenen, 1869, 2471, 2706
Peck, Winslow, 2707, 2708, 2709
Peele, Gillian, 450
Peinado, Jaime, 2150
Pell, Eve, 968, 2573, 2710
Pember, Don, 451
Penelope, Julia, 1397
Penick, J.L., 843
Pennington, Francis, 2472
Perkovich, George, 54
Perl, Peter, 1266
Perlo, Victor, 2711
Perry, Ralph, 206
Perry, Roland, 1525
Perry, Susan, 1459
Persell, Caroline, 809
Persky, Stan, 2104
Peters, Charles, 1762
Peterson, Ted, 2361
Peterson, Trev, 1763
Peterzell, Jay, 379, 1870, 2473, 2474, 2475, 2712, 2713
Petras, James, 2146
Petrusenko, Vitaly, 759
Pfeiffer, Richard, 2021
Phee, Molly, 514
Phelan, John, 969, 1267
Philip, Weiss, 1317
Phillips, Kevin, 1062
Picard, Robert, 1460, 2289
Pieragostini, Karl, 380
Pike, John, 381, 2290
Pike, Otis, 1614
Piliawsky, Monte, 884
Piller, Charles, 515, 2362
Pilpel, Harriet, 1764
Piven, Frances, 583
Pless, Laurance, 2714
Poelchau, Warner, 2715
Pollak, Richard, 1063, 2022
Pollan, Michael, 1269
Pollard, James, 1526
Pollock, Francis, 1270, 1461
Pollock, John, 2186, 2187
Pollock, Michele, 2187
Pollock, Richard, 584, 585, 586, 844, 1271, 1272, 1273, 1765,

511

1766, 2716
Polman, Jeffrey, 1038
Pool, Gail, 1274
Pool, Ithiel, 587
Pope, James, 1767
Porter, William, 1575
Post, Louis, 16
Potter, Charles, 268
Potter, Walt, 565
Powe, Scot, 1576
Powell, Jody, 1922
Powell, Walter, 1064
Powers, Richard, 2574
Powers, Ron, 970, 1275
Powledge, Fred, 971, 1065, 1768
Pratt, James, 1119
Pratt, Larry, 2823
Prendergast, Alan, 2291
Preston, Ivan, 1276
Preston, William, 452, 972, 1769, 1872, 2105, 2478, 2766, 2879, 2880
Preusch, Deb, 2041
Price, Sean, 973
Pringle, Peter, 207, 516, 2293, 2294
Pritt, Denis, 2479
Prouty, Leroy, 2717
Pruessen, Ronald, 55, 2106
Purpel, David, 818
Putney, Bryant, 1067
Pyadyshev, B., 517
Pyle, Christopher, 2480
Radecki, Thomas, 1828
Rader, Melvin, 208
Rafferty, Keven, 503
Rafferty, Pierce, 503
Randal, Judith, 975
Randall, Willard, 976
Rank, Hugh, 1277
Ransom, Harry, 209
Rapoport, Roger, 588, 977
Rasberry, Robert, 1827
Rashke, Richard, 1462
Raskin, A.H., 2881
Raskin, Marcus, 56
Ray, Ellen, 2718, 2719, 2882
Raymond, Chris, 1278
Raymond, Jack, 2221
Read, William, 589, 2826
Reardon, Betty, 2222
Redekop, John, 210
Reding, Andrew, 2152
Reece, Ray, 1398
Reel, Frank, 1068
Reeves, Thomas, 269
Reich, Charles, 453

CONTRIBUTORS

Reich, Robert, 518
Reidy, John, 1069
Reinhard, David, 211
Reinhold, Robert, 872
Reisig, Robin, 2482
Reitz, Sara, 1135
Relyea, Harold, 1528
Repo, Satu, 2827
Reston, James, 1529
Retboll, Torben, 979
Reuben, William, 383, 2576
Reynolds, Larry, 454
Rhea, John, 2364
Rice, Condoleezza, 307
Rice, Michael, 762
Rich, Jonathan, 389
Richelson, Jeffrey, 384, 2483
Richman, David, 2721
Richman, Sheldon, 2295
Rickover, Hyman, 1071
Ridder, Pamela, 1072
Ridgeway, James, 385, 455, 519, 1399, 1400, 1873, 2484
Riencourt, Amaury de, 1530
Riley, Kathy, 982
Ripmaster, Terence, 1773
Rips, Geoffrey, 873, 1615, 2485, 2828
Ritt, Martin, 212
Rivers, William, 546, 1774, 1923
Riznik, J.Q., 2925
Roach, Janet, 941
Roane, Stephen, 2296
Robbins, Christopher, 2722
Robbins, William, 980
Roberts, Gene, 198
Robinson, J.P., 1284
Robinson, Michael, 763, 764
Robinson, William, 2149
Robreno, Gustavo, 1616
Rodberg, Leonard, 2223
Rodgers, Raymond, 1874
Roditi, Hannah, 2756
Roe, Yale, 1279
Roediger, David, 213, 214
Roettinger, Philip, 2723
Rogers, Joel, 1109, 1625a, 2054, 2055
Rogge, O. John, 215
Rogin, Michael, 270
Roisen, Jill, 1775
Rokeach, Milton, 609
Rollins, Peter, 2024
Roman, James, 1280, 1282
Roos, Joe, 2486
Roose, Diana, 520
Roosevelt, Kermit, 2724
Rorty, James, 271

513

Rose, Ernest, 1074
Rosen, Jay, 386, 765
Rosenau, Neal, 1075, 2025, 2026
Rosenau, William, 2314
Rosenberg, Emily, 2829
Rosenberg, Howard, 2365
Rosenbloom, Joe, 199
Rosenson, Sarah, 999
Rosenthal, Bruce, 591, 1463
Rosenthal, Herma, 1401
Rosenzweig, Roy, 981
Roshco, Bernard, 1281, 1829
Rositzke, Harry, 2725
Ross, Caroline, 2577
Ross, Thomas, 2509, 2759
Rosset, Peter, 2154
Rossman, Michael, 845
Roszak, Theodore, 456, 846
Roth, Jeffrey, 982
Rothmyer, Karen, 387, 1428, 1962
Rothschild, Matthew, 592, 2726
Rothstein, Stanley, 847
Roubatis, Yiannas, 217
Rourke, Francis, 1504, 1776
Rovere, Richard, 272
Rowan, Carl, 388, 1777
Rowe, James, 1076
Rowland, Willard, 1281, 1281
Rowse, Arthur, 1402
Rubin, Barry, 766, 1778
Rubin, David, 218, 389, 390, 1283, 1403, 1779
Rubin, Ronald, 767, 2926
Rubin, Trudy, 1963
Ruby, Robert, 593, 1780
Rucker, Bryce, 1077
Rudolph, Frederick, 885
Ruether, Rosemary, 2107
Rushford, Gregory, 2487
Russell, Philip, 2178
Russett, Bruce, 219, 768
Russo, Anthony, 1904
Rustin, Richard, 1964
Ryan, David, 2727
Ryan, Geoffrey, 220, 221, 222, 983, 1577
Ryan, Michael, 944
Rydell, Robert, 457
Ryter, Mark, 2578, 2579
Sabato, Larry, 1136
Saffer, Thomas, 1781
Safire, William, 1137, 1782
Sahin, H., 1284
Said, Edward, 769, 874, 1940
Sale, Kirkpatrick, 984
Salisbury, Harrison, 2580, 2728
Sallach, David, 458

Salvaggio, Jerry, 655
Salzman, George, 522
Salzman, Lorna, 594
Sampson, Anthony, 1285, 2830
Sanders, Jane, 223
Sanders, Jerry, 224, 2108, 2366
Sandler, Norman, 2729
Sandman, Peter, 1784
Sarkesian, Sam, 523
Sarnoff, Irving, 656
Sarnoff, Thomas, 1569
Sartre, Jean-Paul, 57
Sayre, Nora, 58
Scardino, Albert, 1429
Schaap, William, 2109
Schaar, Stuart, 1955
Schandler, Herbert, 1965
Scharff, Ned, 1464
Schechter, Daniel, 987, 2730
Scheer, Robert, 391, 1966, 1969
Scheinin, Richard, 2297
Schiller, Anita, 985
Schiller, Dan, 459
Schiller, Herbert, 1078, 1079
Schiller, Herbert, 460, 524, 525, 985, 986, 1078, 1079, 2831, 2832, 2833, 2834, 2835, 2836, 2837, 2877, 2883, 2884, 2885, 2886, 2887, 2888
Schlesinger, Stephen, 2085
Schmidt, Benno, 595
Schneider, Keith, 596
Schneiders, Greg, 1886
Schneir, Miriam, 770, 2581
Schneir, Walter, 770, 2581
Schoenberger, Erica, 2298
Schonberg, Edward, 2488
Schonberger, Howard, 2838
Schorr, Daniel, 1080, 1578
Schrag, Peter, 988, 1287, 1967
Schrank, Jeffrey, 1288
Schrecker, Ellen, 225, 930
Schreiber, Mark, 2299
Schreibman, Fay, 667
Schudson, Michael, 771, 1289
Schulzinger, Robert, 1905
Schumach, Murray, 989
Schuman, Frederick, 59
Schuman, Pat, 875
Schwab, Priscilla, 1405
Schwartz, Berl, 2367
Schwartz, Herman, 1875, 2489, 2490, 2491, 2492, 2493, 2731
Schwartz, Richard, 2582
Schwartz, Robert, 1081
Schwartz, Wendy, 657
Schwarzlose, Richard, 772
Schwichtenberg, Cathy, 1286

Schwoch, James, 1082
Scott, John, 2224
Scott, Peter, 2732
Scott, Sue, 1826
Seaman, John, 226
Searle, Chris, 2110
Sears, John, 1636
Sedacca, Sandra, 2300
Seitz, Michael, 2734
Selcraig, James, 227
Selden, Mark, 911, 2791
Seldes, George, 228, 773, 774
Selig, Michael, 1290
Seltzer, Curtis, 1291
Selvaggio, Kathy, 2839
Sethi, S. Prakash, 1406
Sexton, Patricia, 848
Shaffer, Butler, 461
Shaheen, Jack, 990
Shaikh, Salim, 1465
Shannon, William, 1924
Shapiro, Bruce, 392
Sharkey, Jacqueline, 2155
Shattuck, John, 1789, 2495, 2583
Shawcross, William, 1968
Shaw, Donald, 1637
Shaw, Linda, 476
Shayon, Robert, 567, 1292
Shear, Marie, 2111
Shearer, Derek, 2223
Sheehan, Margaret, 764
Sheinbaum, Stanley, 1969
Sheinfeld, Lois, 2496
Sherrill, Robert, 1925, 2497, 2498
Shils, Edward, 1790
Shivpuri, Pyare, 331
Shlain, Bruce, 2678
Shore, Elliot, 526
Shorrock, Tim, 2839
Shoup, Laurence, 462
Showalter, Stuart, 2027
Shute, Nancy, 1407
Sibbison, Jim, 597, 1293
Sichel, Berta, 991
Siefert, Marsha, 2794
Siegel, Daniel, 2156
Siegel, Lenny, 2225
Siegelaub, Seth, 2821
Siegelman, Jim, 901
Siepmann, Charles, 598, 1294
Sigal, Leon, 775
Silverman, Milton, 1295
Silverstein, Brett, 1296, 1830
Silvert, Frieda, 936
Simmons, George, 229, 230

CONTRIBUTORS

Simmons, Steven, 599
Simon, Roger, 1297
Simon, Samuel, 571
Simons, Pamela, 1387
Singer, Benjamin, 2028
Singer, Michael, 876
Singleton, Kathy, 1942
Skardon, James, 776, 1792
Sklar, Holly, 2157, 2840
Sklar, Robert, 1298
Sklar, Zachary, 685
Skornia, Harry, 777, 1299, 1300, 1301, 1302
Slack, Jennifer, 463
Sloman, Larry, 1831
Sloyan, Patrick, 493
Small, William, 1970
Smith, Anthony, 658, 2889, 2890
Smith, Craig, 231
Smith, David, 886
Smith, Doug, 1832
Smith, Eleanor, 1303
Smith, Fred, 1793
Smith, F. Leslie, 2370
Smith, Jeffrey, 600
Smith, Merritt, 527
Smith, Michael, 528
Smith, Myron, 2302
Smith, Norma, 2158
Smith, Philip, 1902
Smith, Robert, 992
Smith, R.C., 1304
Smock, William, 394
Smuckler, Ralph, 1880
Smythe, Dallas, 2841
Snel, Alan, 1467
Sobel, David, 2499
Soble, Richard, 2440
Soloman, Goody, 600a
Solomon, Mark, 196
Solomon, Norman, 396
Solovitch, Sara, 659
Sonn, Bill, 1971
Sorensen, Jeff, 1468
Sorensen, Thomas, 2927
Sorkin, Michael, 232, 2585
Spear, Joseph, 1531
Spence, Jack, 2179
Sperber, Ann, 1469
Spiegelmen, Robert, 529
Spigelman, James, 516
Springer, Claudia, 2029
Spring, Joel, 849
Stanford, Phil, 1795, 2738
Staple, Gregory, 2842
Stares, Paul, 2226

517

Steenland, Sally, 650
Steger, Tina, 994
Steif, William, 233
Steinberg, Charles, 601
Steinert, Sylvia, 2371
Stein, Jeffrey, 2739, 2740
Stein, Loren, 1470
Stein, Meyer, 1972
Stein, Robert, 1796
Sterling, Christopher, 741, 1083
Sternberg, Steve, 1409
Stern, Laurence, 61
Stern, Sol, 1903, 2741
Stevenson, Russell, 1471
Steven, Stewart, 2742
Stiglin, Peter, 62
Stockman, David, 1533
Stockwell, John, 2743, 2744
Stoloff, Samuel, 397
Stone, I.F., 234, 235, 236, 237, 1797, 1798, 1943, 1973
Stone, Peter, 2372, 2745
Stranahan, Susan, 602
Streeter, Thomas, 603
Stringfellow, William, 2228
Strouse, Jean, 2030
Stuart, Lyle, 2587
Sturges, Gerald, 1799
Suall, Irvin, 238
Suid, Lawrence, 2031, 2374
Surkin, Marvin, 851
Sussman, Leila, 1305
Sussman, Leonard, 2891
Swaim, J. Carter, 995
Swan, Jon, 1468, 1472, 1800
Swerdlow, Joel, 1084, 1245, 1638
Swomley, John, 2229, 2303, 2315
Szulc, Tad, 1617, 2113
Tackwood, Louis, 2501
Tajima, Renee, 996
Talbot, David, 1139
Talbott, Strobe, 400,
Tamplin, Arthur, 1358
Tarasov, Konstantin, 2039
Tasini, Jonathan, 2589
Tate, Cassandra, 1085, 1306
Taylor, Peter, 604, 2843
Taylor, Terri, 1876
Tebbel, John, 1534
Thatcher, Rebecca, 2620
Theiler, Patricia, 1127, 1140, 1141, 1142
Theoharis, Athan, 131, 239, 240, 2502, 2590
Thielens, Wagner, 164
Thomas, Helen, 1535, 1579
Thomas, Jimmie, 2044, 2119
Thompson, David, 778

CONTRIBUTORS

Thompson, E.P., 2230
Thompson, Kenneth, 1536
Thompson, Thomas, 1834
Tirman, John, 2231
Tobias, Andrew, 1473
Tobis, David, 2081
Tolchin, Martin, 605
Tolchin, Susan, 605
Tolley, Howard, 2232
Tompkins, E. Berkeley, 2844
Torney-Purta, Judith, 852, 877
Torre, Marie, 1308
Toynbee, Arnold, 63
Trachtenberg, Alan, 464
Trager, Frank, 530
Traska, Maria, 779
Traub, James, 605a
Trillin, Calvin, 1086
Trinkl, John, 401
Truse, Kenneth, 1309
Tuchman, Gaye, 781, 782, 1310, 1311
Tucker, Nancy, 241
Tunstall, Jeremy, 1088, 2845
Turnbull, George, 2032
Turner, Kathleen, 1974
Turner, Richard, 1312
Turner, William, 2503, 2591
Tyler, Suzanne, 1887
Tyrrell, C. Merton, 531
Udell, Richard, 998, 999
Underhill, David, 878
Ungar, Sanford, 2592
Unger, Stephen, 1803
Valdez, Armando, 1313
Valentino, Linda, 2505
Van Allen, Judith, 576, 1089
Van Atta, Dale, 2506
Van Houten, Margaret, 1002, 2751
Vandermeer, John, 2154
Varis, Tapio, 2850, 2851, 2878, 2893
Varner, Roy, 2752
Vaughn, Robert, 243
Vayrynen, Raimo, 2852
Veblen, Thorstein, 887
Veenstra, Charles, 1888
Vernoff, Edward, 842
Villarejo, Don, 1090
Vinas, Angel, 2114
Vlanton, Elias, 217
Vogel, Amos, 651
Von Hoffman, Nicholas (see Hoffman)
Voran, Marilyn, 1314
Waas, Murray, 2753, 2754, 2755
Wagman, Robert, 1439, 2377
Wake, Jim, 2932

519

Waksman, Daniel, 2820
Waldman, Michael, 1882
Wald, Richard, 783
Walker, David, 1088
Wallace, Bill, 2507
Wallace, Mike, 1411
Wallack, Lawrence, 579
Wallis, Jim, 466, 2160
Walsh, Joan, 2593
Walton, Richard, 244
Ward, Larry, 1944
Warsh, David, 1975
Wasko, Janet, 1091
Wasserman, Harvey, 1003, 1092
Waterman, Richard, 1111
Watkins, Arthur, 273
Watson, Catherine, 2803
Watson, Goodwin, 245
Wattenmaker, Steve, 2115
Watters, Susan, 1926
Watts, Sarah, 1534
Weaver, David, 784, 2894
Weaver, Maureen, 404, 2756
Wechsler, James, 246
Weeks, James, 2853
Weinberg, Meyer, 662
Weinberg, Steve, 1029, 1144, 1581, 1582
Weinstein, Henry, 1412
Weinstein, James, 467, 1093
Weir, David, 1004
Weis, Lois, 793
Weisband, Edward, 35, 1693
Weisberger, Bernard, 247
Weisman, John, 1315
Weisman, Steven, 1538
Weiss, Andrea, 1804
Weiss, Ann, 1316
Weiss, Kenneth, 1145
Weiss, Philip, 785
Weiss, Ted, 405
Weisskopf, Victor, 65
Weissman, Steve, 1651
Welch, Richard, 66, 2116
Welch, Susan, 2033
Welles, Chris, 1318
Wells, Alan, 2040
Wenger, Martha, 406, 2933, 2934
Werden, Frieda, 786
Wertheimer, Fred, 1146, 1414
Westbrook, Robert, 1639
Westin, Alan, 248
Wexley, John, 249
Wheaton, Philip, 407
Whelan, Elizabeth, 1319
White, Leonard, 1330

CONTRIBUTORS

White, Richard, 2117
White, William, 630
Whiteside, Thomas, 1094
Whitlam, Gough, 2895
Whittemore, L.H., 1540
Whitton, John, 2935
Wicker, Tom, 1620
Wicklein, John, 533, 1005, 1095, 1804
Wieseltier, Leon, 2233
Wiesner, Jerome, 2234
Wilcox, Clair, 250
Wilhoit, G. Cleveland, 784
Wilkinson, Francis, 561
Williams, Cathleen, 880
Williams, Greg, 2235
Williams, Verne, 2924
Williams, William, 67
Willis, Donald, 1396
Willner, Barry, 1895
Wilner, Herbert, 946
Wilson, Christopher, 1320
Wilson, Thomas, 1186
Windt, Theodore, 1541
Winn, Marie, 663
Winsten, Jay, 1416
Wirbel, Loring, 2768
Wise, Arthur, 853
Wise, David, 1584, 2508, 2509, 2758, 2759
Witcover, Jules, 1976, 1977, 2379
Wittner, Lawrence, 68, 251
Witty, Susan, 664
Wofsy, Leon, 534
Wolf, Charles, 2236
Wolf, Louis, 409, 2600
Wolfe, Alan, 252, 468, 851, 2303a
Wolff, Robert, 854
Wolfson, Lewis, 1928
Wolf-Wasserman, Miriam, 855, 856
Wong, Sybil, 434
Wood, Barry, 857
Wood, David, 2380
Wood, Robin, 665
Woode, Allen, 1978
Woodmansee, Dave, 410
Woodward, Bob, 1642, 1652
Workman, John, 2161
Wright, Christopher, 865
Wright, J.S., 1640
Wyckoff, Gene, 1641
Wyden, Peter, 2760
Wylie, Jeanie, 2510
Yadava, Jaswant, 2896
Yakovlev, N., 2761
Yarmolinsky, Adam, 2237
Yates, Michael, 411

CONTROL OF INFORMATION

Yoakum, Robert, 1585
Yoffe, Emily, 413
Young, Jack, 709
Young, Peter, 2511
Young, T.R., 469
Yudof, Mark, 1542
Zachar, George, 1417
Zasursky, Y.N., 2897
Zeidner, M.A., 1418
Zillman, Donald, 2238
Zimroth, Peter, 2596
Zinn, Howard, 470, 858, 1979
Zion, Sidney, 787
Zubenko, Vyacheslav, 2039
Zuckerman, Laurence, 2512
Zuckerman, Solly, 2381

Subject Index

(Numbers refer to entries, not pages.)

2,4,5-T, 976
A Matter of Risk, 2752
A Public Trust, 701
A.C. Nielsen Company (see Nielsen ratings)
A. H. Robins Company, 1439, 1455, 1459
ABC News, 291, 1494
ABC World News Tonight, 354, 750
ABC, 294, 367, 614, 758, 1179, 1312, 1794, 2071
Abrams, Elliot, 1663, 2150
Abscam, FBI, 2463, 2530, 2558
abstract expressionism, anti-Sovietism, 132
academia (see education)
Acceptable Risks, 1312
access to information, 875, 985
access, broadcasting (see broadcasting)
access, corporations, 1020
accountability, 446, 447
Accuracy in Academia, 334, 364, 369, 385, 403, 921, 957, 1000
Accuracy in Media, 301, 413, 608, 664, 770, 952, 953, 1428, 1441
Accuracy in Media, PBS, 2012
ACCUtane, 1293
Acheson, Dean, 36
acid rain, 1037a
ACLU, 191, 908, 954, 1550, 1566, 1713, 1719, 1789, 1971, 2299,
    2394, 2418, 2453, 2478
ACLU, CIA, 2684, 2658, 2687, 2706
ACLU, FBI, 2513, 2568
acquisitive cognition, 1148
Action for Children's Television (ACT), 664
Adolph Coors Foundation, 1429
Advertising Council (see Public Service Ads, PSAs), 423, 497,
    566, 1323, 1357, 1367, 1376, 1387, 1395, 1412
advertising, II.D., III.C.D., 556, 613-14, 635-36, 650, 1089,
    2040
advertising, agencies, 614
advertising, cars, 1224, 1253
advertising, children, 1174, 1211, 1216, 1251
advertising, cigarettes, 2814
advertising, corporate advocacy, 2295
advertising, deceptive, 592, 1065, 1154, 1211, 1254, 1276, 1339,
    1350, 2299
advertising, endorsements, 1261
advertising, films, 1351
advertising, global, 2808
advertising, government, 1499, 1542
advertising, Latin America, 2789
advertising, political campaigning, 1625, 1630, 1634
advertising, public service, 1331
advertising, regulation, 1760
advertising, self-realization, 1239
advertising, sexuality, 1222

advertising, substantiation, 1406
advertising, tax deductibility, 1406
advertising, testimonials, 1217
advertising, tobacco, 604
Advisory Committee on Reactor Safeguards (see nuclear power),
   1728
advocacy advertising (see advertising, corporate advocacy), 471,
   1197
advocacy advertising, arms contractors, 485
AEC (see nuclear entries), 559, 575, 588, 977, 1687, 1699, 2335
AEC, censorship, 1655
Afghanistan, 75, 379, 742, 1475
AFL-CIO, 1308, 2811, 2936
AFL-CIO, CIA, 2707
AFL-CIO, foreign labor, 2839
AFL-CIO, foreign policy, 2828
Africa, American foundations, 2938, 2939
Africa, CIA, 2718
Africa, educational colonialism, 2937
Africa, Kissinger Study, 2809
Africa, press, 2854
Africa, U.S. relations, 2811
Africa, Western control of news media, 2800
Agca, Mehmet Ali (see Pope, assassination attempt), 275, 341, 351
Agee, Philip, 1874
Agence France-Presse, 699, 2889, 2894
Agency for International Development (AID), 2177, 2615, 2739,
   2803
agenda setting, 758, 775
Agent Orange, 1998
agents provocateurs, 2479, 2499, 2501
Agnew, Spiro, 680, 743a, 1768
Agnew, Spiro, censorship, 1556, 1557
Agnew, Spiro, newspapers, 1597
agribusiness, 440, 1073, 1221
Air America, 2722
Air Force, 2269, 2276
Air Force, espionage, 2441
Air Force Foreign Technology Division, 2441
Air Force Mafia, 2441
Air Force, public relations, 2298
airwaves ownership, 571
Albano Report, 341
Albuquerque Journal, 1452
alcohol advertising, 579
Alien and Sedition Acts, 2479
aliens, 1845, 1860
All in the Family, 1212
All My Children, 620
Allendé, Salvador, 1573, 2183, 2644
Alsop, Joseph, CIA, 2610
alternative press, 526, 743, 1951
Altman, Robert, 665
American Association of University Professors (AAUP), 225, 949
American Bar Association, FBI, 2560

American Broadcasting Company (see ABC)
American Civil Liberties Union (see ACLU)
American Committee for Cultural Freedom, 160
American Council on Science and Health, 1334, 1365
American Dream, 415, 649
American Electric Power Company, 1406
American Federation of Labor, 267
American Heritage, 981
American Indian Movement, FBI, 1842, 2551, 2565
American Institute for Free Labor Development (AIFLD), 2177,
    2739, 2828
American Labor Party, FBI, 2590
American League of Lobbyists, 1140
American Legal Foundation, 1441
American Medical Association, 1126
American National Standards Institute, 585
American Parade, 748
American Polygraph Association, 2444
American Security Council, 2108
American Specialty Metals Corporation, 1119
American Telegraph and Telephone (AT&T), 490
American Trucking Association, 1111
Americans for Energy Independence, 559
Americas Watch, 2035
Amerika, 294, 367
Amway Corporation, 901
anarchism, 8
anarchists, FBI, 2562
anchormen, Vietnam War, 1982, 1983
Andreas, Dwayne, 1121
Andropov, Yuri, 218
ANESAL, 2698
Angola, 39, 1562
Angola, CIA, 2651, 2681
Angola, Kissinger Study, 2809
Anti-Ballistic missile treaty, 25, 1522
anti-imperialism, 2844
anti-intellectualism, 924
anti-nuclear movement media coverage, 529
anti-nuclear movement, harassment, 1870, 2474
anti-nuclear movement (see nuclear freeze movement), 426
anti-Sovietism, I., 754, 1000, 2001
anti-submarine warfare, 2216
anti-war movement, disruption (see repression), 2423
anti-war publications, harassment, 2455, 2467
anticipatory criminality, 2105
anticommunism, I., 443, 465, 906, 944, 957, 973, 1018, 2001,
    2064, 2065, 2152, 2717
anticommunism, Cold War, I.C.1
anticommunism, conformity, I.C.2
anticommunism, disinformation, I.C.2
anticommunism, general history, I.A.
anticommunism, Hoover Institution, 1898, 1899
anticommunism, post-World War I, I.B.
anticommunism, post-World War II, I.C.

anticommunism, psychology, 309
anticommunism, repression, I.C.2
anticommunism, Ronald Reagan, I.D.
anticommunism, Senator Joseph McCarthy, I.C.3
antitrust (see monopoly), 446, 614, 1066, 1068, 1082, 1961, 1987
AP (Associated Press), 316, 699, 733, 1946, 2036, 2037, 2371,
    2889, 2894
AP, Africa, 2802, 2854
AP, CIA, 2610, 2625
Apocalypse Now, 2003, 2374
Apollo Program (see NASA), 2211
Appalachia, 912, 1210
Arab Americans, 760
Arabs, 990
Aramco, 863
Argentina, 1532, 2035
Arkansas Gazette, 2044
Armageddon, 1498
arms bazaars, 2204
arms contractors, industry (see military-industrial complex)
Arms Control and Disarmament Agency, 391
arms control, 320, 374, 375, 389, 400, 1513, 1537, 1699, 1779,
    2376
arms control treaties, verification, 2376
arms control violations, Soviet, 381, 412
arms control, communication, 2793
arms estimates, 1819, 1830
arms "gap" (see gap)
arms race, 25, 47, 287, 296, 313, 327, 330, 348, 359, 391, 1522,
    1613, 1812, 2214, 2234, 2290, 2300, 2347, 2351
arms race, advocacy, 521
arms race, government propaganda, 1593
arms race, nuclear, 33, 50, 303, 358, 360
arms research (iron triangle), II.C.&E.2, V.C., 477, 481, 505,
    519, 525
arms research, universities, 473
arms, economics, 507
Army Intelligence Command, 2461
Army Intelligence, 2394, 2463
Army, blacklist, 2461
Army, conscientious objectors, 2280
Army, Counterintelligence Branch, 2455
Army, germ warfare, 2264
Army, news management, 2319
Army, propaganda, 2293
Army, recruiting, 2270, 2283
Army, secrecy, 2327, 2334, 2339
Army, spying on host countries, 2464
Army, subversives file, 2461
Army, surveillance in 1960s, 2461
Army, weapons testing, 2327, 2356
Army, wiretaps, bugging, 2493
Aronson, James, 1994
art, Cold War, 2782
asbestos (see corporation, crime), 1037a, 1250, 1266, 1434, 1453

Asia, 911
Asia, imperialism, 2791, 2838
Asia, Western control of communications research, 2812
Asian-American Free Labor Institute, 2839
Asner, Ed, 1212
aspirin, 564
assassination manual, CIA, 2640, 2659
assassination, CIA, 2601, 2603, 2643, 2649, 2677
assassinations, 2503
Associated Press (see AP; news agencies)
AT&T, 614, 1048, 1082, 1084, 1087, 1449
AT&T, Third World, 2890
athletics (see sports), militarism, 2224
Atlantic Council of the United States, 462
atomic bomb, 18, 20, 43-44, 90, 173-74
atomic bomb, secrecy, 1741
Atomic Energy Act, 1653, 1684
Atomic Energy Commission (see AEC)
Atomic Energy Committee, 1655
Atomic Industrial Forum, 559, 1272, 1393, 1417
atomic testing, 1003, 1004, 1699, 1720
Atoms for Peace, 36
Attack on the Americas, 407
Australia, 700
Australia, NSA, 2762
authoritarianism, 962
authorities, 1670
automation, 2231
automobile, industry, 428, 1073
automobile, safety, 1547
Aviation Week, 2256, 2260
B-1 bomber, 512, 1114
B-36, 25
Babar, 1196
Babcock and Wilcox (see nuclear power; Three Mile Island), 559,
    602
Bakker, Jim, 901
Ballistic Missile Early Warning System, 2225
Bangladesh, 1544
banks, 423, 428, 442, 1037a, 1039, 1041, 1050, 1091
Barbados, 2097
Barbie dolls, 1216
Barbie, Klaus, CIA, 2656, 2732
Barrons, 404
Baruch, Bernard M., 36
Bay of Pigs invasion, 2092, 2603, 2649, 2717
Bay of Pigs invasion, CIA, 2760
BBC, 675
BBC, comparison with PBS, 1176
BBC, propaganda, 2916
Beacon Press, 1963
Bechtel Construction Company, 1004
Beggs, James, 698
behavior modification, 452, 988
Beilenson, Laurence, 391

Beirut massacre (marines), 393
Belau, military, 2769
Bentley, Elizabeth, 203, 2479
Benton, Senator William, 1880
Berlin crisis, 1515
Bernstein, Carl, 1642
Bethe, Hans 391
Bhopal (see corporation, crime), 1465
Big Brother, 452
Big Story, 1981, 1989
Biggers, Virginia, 94
bigotry, 924, 1864, 1935
bigotry, political, I. (see Sovietphobia), 144, 152, 167, 191,
   221, 238, 298, 315, 2015
bigotry, television, 660
Bill of Rights (see First Amendment), 230, 452, 1713, 2424
Billings, Warren, 1437
biological warfare, 515
biotechnology, 869
bipartisanship (see Contents; Congress), 432, 465, 1632, 1885
black bag jobs, IV.A.2., IV.B. (see break-ins; covert oper-
   ations), 2430, 2432
Black higher education, 1419
Black militants, CIA, 2730
Black Panther Party, 8, 719, 1651, 1843, 1852, 2430, 2436
Black Panthers, FBI, 2523, 2534, 2566, 2569
Black Panthers, trial, 2596
Black, Hugo, Justice (see First Amendment)
black/white thinking, Reagan, 1498
blacklisting, 86, 102, 107, 121-22, 147, 187, 191, 212, 225, 989,
   1566
blacklisting, Army, 2461
blacklisting, Attorney General, 127
blacklists, 614
Blacks Britannica, 1001
Blacks, 936
Blood and Sand, PBS, 1656
Bloom, Marshall, 2455
Blue Book, 598
Bolivia, 2039
Bonner, Raymond, 759a, 2175
book publishing, CIA, 2612
books, censorship, 2088
boosterism, 1169
Borchgrave, Arnaud de, 158
Boston State College, 789
Boy Scouts, 2223
Bradlee, Benjamin, 1495
Bradley Fighting Vehicle, 2327
Braestrup, Peter, 1986, 1989
Brazil, 2777
break-ins, 2502, 2508
break-ins, CIA, 2618
break-ins, FBI, 2572, 2588
breakfast cereals, 1211, 1216

breeder reactor, secret research, 2333
Brezhnev, Leonid, 218
bribery, 1133, 1138
bribery, Congress, 1882
bribery, FBI, 2572
Bridges, Harry, 2479
Bright, Bill, 901
BRILAB, 2463
Brinkley, David, 1923, 2071
Britain, racism, 1001
broadcasting (see news, television), 191, 449, 543, 547, 549,
    554, 595, 601, 603, 611, 612, 614, 655, 658, 689, 737, 738,
    917, 1048, 1130, 1325, 1680
broadcasting, conformity, 613, 617
broadcasting, corporate control, 683, 1157, 1301, 1346
broadcasting, minority, 642
broadcasting, presidency, 1476
broadcasting, regulation, 570, 572, 578
Broadway, 222
Brookings Institute (see think tanks), 462, 1889, 1902
Brookings Institute, corporations, 1890
brown lung (see corporation, crime), 1220
Brown, Norman, 456
Brutus, Dennis, 324
Buchanan, Patrick, 1495
Budenz, Louis, 203
bugging (see wiretaps), 1875, 2489, 2490, 2491, 2492, 2493, 2596
Bulgarian Connection (see Pope)
Bullitt, William C., 36
Bundy, McGeorge, 1946, 2199
Bureau of Narcotics and Dangerous Drugs, 2412
bureaucracy, 454
Burford, Anne, 600
Burt, Richard, NYT and government, 1909
Business Council, 423, 462, 1131
business journalism awards, 1318
Business Roundtable, 423, 462, 1037a, 1131
Business Week, 1256
business, deception, III. (see corporation, crime), 1247
Byrnes, James F., 23, 36
C-5A transport, 531
cable television, 578, 741, 1044
Caddell, Patrick, 1525
caffeine, 576
Caldwell, Earl, reporter's privacy, 1768, 1843, 1852
California Campaign to Enact Proposition 9, 1406
Cam Ne, 1964
Cambodia, 1562, 1563, 1947, 1957, 1968
Cambodia, CIA, 2643, 2747
campaign contributions, III.B., 1110, 1116, 1119, 1124, 1139
campaign contributions, corporate, 1139
campaign financing, 1103, 1118, 1127, 1640, 1647
Campus Crusade for Christ, 901
campus press, 542, 1768
campus press, right wing, 1429

Canada, 778
Canada, communications, 2793
Canada, cultural dependency, 2823, 2841
Canada, journalism, 1023
Canada, peace groups, 1812
cancer, 538, 980, 1442
cancer, radiation, 1781
cancer, tobacco, 604
Cannikin Papers, 1693
Canwell Committee (see McCarthyism), 208, 223
Capital Legal Foundation, 1450
capitalism, II., III., VII, 2, 433, 438, 439, 443, 454, 1197,
   1201, 1286
capitalism, class, 457-58
capitalism, communications, 2859, 2897
capitalism, literature, 1163
capitalism, state, 2940
capitalism, the family, 1237
Capra, Frank, 2029
Captains of Consciousness, 1204
Carnegie Commission on Higher Education, 819
Carnegie commissions on education, 1421
Carnegie Foundation for the Advancement of Teaching, 1425
Carnegie Foundation, 2937, 2940
Carney, Father James R., CIA, 2617
cartels (see multinational corporations), 1058
Carter administration, IV.A., 1532, 1719
Carter administration, CIA, 2736
Carter administration, deception, 1605
Carter administration, intelligence, 2468
Carter administration, Nicaragua, 2120
Carter, Jimmy, 25, 27, 89, 148, 449, 462, 649, 900, 1476, 1483,
   1484, 1516, 1789, 2201, 2210, 2267
Carter, Jimmy, campaigning, 1622, 1625, 1632
Carter, Jimmy, Central America, 2058
Carter, Jimmy, CIA, 2609, 2627, 2676, 2696
Carter, Jimmy, deregulation, 605
Carter, Jimmy, intelligence agencies, 2395, 2456, 2674
Carter, Jimmy, militarism, 2205
Carter, Jimmy, press, 1922
Carter, Jimmy, rhetoric, 1541
Carter, Jimmy, secrecy, 1744
cartoons, 955, 1589
Casey, William, CIA, 1495, 2623, 2657, 2694, 2712, 2713, 2755
Castro (see Bay of Pigs; Cuba), 1573
Castro, Fidel, CIA, 2649
Caucus for New Political Science, 851
CBS Evening News, 354, 1192
CBS News, 356, 2275
CBS Reports, 741
CBS, 189, 614, 674, 708, 726, 736, 748, 758, 764, 770, 1064,
   1179, 1445, 1469, 1648, 1768, 1793, 2271, 2370
CBS, CIA, 2610
CBS, Pentagon, 2332
CBW, 377, 406, 1998, 2293, 2362, 2678

CBW, Pentagon public relations, 2262
celebrities, 649, 1150
censorship, I., II.F., III.F., IV.A.B.C.G.2.a., 144, 173, 238,
    245, 250, 364, 369, 557, 559, 577, 581, 613, 629, 647, 706,
    741, 1018, 1206, 1272, 1495, 1645, 1653, 1655, 1684, 1698,
    1728, 1740, 1758, 1759, 1761, 1763, 1797, 1798, 1949, 1959,
    1961, 1964, 2063, 2261, 2504
censorship, academia, 85, 115, 155
censorship, books, 1190, 2088
censorship, CIA, 2602, 2604, 2606, 2613, 2630, 2632, 2636, 2641,
    2642, 2657, 2661, 2666, 2669, 2692, 2700, 2701, 2702, 2712,
    2714, 2721, 2735
censorship, corporations, 1231
censorship, FBI, 2515
censorship, Grenada invasion, 2112
censorship, international, 2860
censorship, newspapers, 1317
censorship, private, 542
censorship, television, 382, 1183, 1194, 1212, 1271, 1273, 1312
censorship, travel, 1874
Census Bureau, 961
Center for Constitutional Rights, 1683
Center for Defense Information, 296
Center for Strategic and International Studies, 2108
Central America, IV.H.2., 52, 276, 314, 373, 1619, 2372, 2811
Central America, CIA, 2629, 2667
Central Intelligence Agency (CIA), VI.C.
Challenger disaster (see NASA)
Chamber of Commerce, 237, 835, 1037a, 1352, 1356, 1378, 1380,
    1405
Chambers, Whittaker, 203
Chandler family, 1369
CHAOS, CIA, 2455, 2691
charter, FBI, 2583, 2593
Chase Manhattan Bank, 1256, 1403
chauvinism, 619, 2111
chemical industry, 582, 1138, 1772
chemical warfare (see CBW), 377, 406, 2293
Chernobyl disaster (see nuclear accidents), 333
Chesebrough-Pond, 1328
Chevron, 1175
Cheyenne helicopter, 531
Chiaie, Stefano Delle, 732
Chicago Conspiracy Trial of 1969 (Chicago Seven), 1861, 1950,
    2559
Chicago Tribune, 1515, 1633, 2033
Chicago, press, 2025
chieftains (corporate), 445
children, 652
children, advertising, 1147, 1184, 1211, 1216, 1251
children, militarism in books for, 2209
children, television, 569, 642, 660, 1184, 1313
children, war, 2232
Chile, 758, 1513, 1573, 2035, 2039, 2145, 2180, 2183, 2185, 2421,
    2430, 2437

Chile, CIA, 2618, 2622, 2635, 2637, 2643, 2644, 2709, 2750, 2919
Chile, information flow, 2897
Chile, ITT, 2778
China Syndrome, 559
China, 27, 179, 241, 1563, 2937
China, Rockefeller medical education, 2941
Chiquita Banana, IV.H., 980
Chitester, Robert, PBS, 1225
Christian apocalypse, 1498
Christian Broadcasting Network, 479, 901
Church Committee Report, 2415, 2438
Church Committee, VI., 2430, 2442, 2463, 2649
Church of Scientology, FBI, 2521
Church Rock disaster, 1003
Church, Frank, 2389, 2456
churches, New World Inf. and Comm. Order, 2870
churches, surveillance, 2386, 2403
CIA (see Contras)
CIA Information Act, 2684
CIA, VI.C., 8, 76, 149, 171, 267, 313, 379, 391, 393, 442, 526,
    553, 965, 1495, 1545, 1559, 1647, 1651, 1791, 1795, 1807, 1812,
    1857, 1866, 1873, 2039, 2085, 2092, 2106, 2129, 2144, 2180,
    2321, 2384, 2387, 2389, 2394, 2397, 2403, 2421, 2430, 2432,
    2442, 2447, 2455, 2456, 2468, 2934
CIA, biological poisons, 2431
CIA, Carter Administration, 1605
CIA, Central America, IV.H.2., 2076
CIA, Chile, 2919
CIA, covert operations, 2399
CIA, foreign policy, 2903
CIA, Guatemala, 2398
CIA, illegal operations, 2450
CIA, organized labor, 2828
CIA, PBS, 2647
CIA, Post Office, 2449
CIA, statistics, 1830
CIA, television, 614
CIA, Uruguay, 2848
cigarette advertising, 614, 894
cigarettes, Third World advertising, 2814
Cincinnati Gas and Electric Co., 553
Citizens Communications Center, 664
citizens' groups, 554
civil defense, 90, 145, 1608, 2301, 2354
civil disobedience, 1851
Civil False Claims Act, 1104
civil liberties, 23, 119, 215, 250, 383, 904, 908, 1562, 2478
civil liberties, CIA, 2609, 2694
civil liberties, electronic surveillance, 2414
Civil Preparedness Review, 175
civil rights, 141, 904, 960, 965
civilian orientation tours, Pentagon, 2223
Clandestine Services, CIA (see covert operations), 2722
Clark, Harry Kenneth, 340
class structure, 758, 1192, 1197, 1200, 2940

classification system (see secrecy), I., IV.A., B., C., 1584,
  1645, 1662, 1685, 1693, 1709, 1747, 2387, 2657
classified information, 1788, 1803
Clay, Lucius D., 36
Clayton, Will, 36
Clean Air Act, 1101, 1102
clergy, CIA, 2679
co-opting, Pentagon, 2292
coal industry, 1210, 1291
Coalition for Better Television, 1371
Cohn, Roy, 371
COINTELPRO (see FBI), 1651, 1873, 2430, 2436, 2455, 2463, 2517,
  2538, 2552, 2566, 2569, 2571, 2578, 2579, 2592
Cold War, I., 5, 7, 358-60, 372, 443, 508, 534, 758, 2076, 2116,
  2191, 2211, 2214, 2234, 2838
Cold War, Afro-American, 141
Cold War, art, 2782
Cold War, communications, 2793
Cold War, covert operations, 2742
Cold War, drugs, 2678
Cold War, ideology, 911
Cold War, modern art, 132
Cold War, NSA, 2762
Cold War, RAND, 1903
Cold War, surveillance, 2502, 2509
Colgate-Palmolive, 1307
college and school journalism (see campus press)
college trustees (see education), 883
Collins, Peter, 2142
Colombia, 2035
Colombia, cultural imperialism, 2788
colonialism, 141, 2772
colonialism, education, 2783
Colorado Tibetans, CIA covert operations, 1584
Colson, Charles, IV.B., 1651
Columbia Broadcasting System (see CBS)
Columbia U revolt, 878
Columbian Exposition of 1893, Chicago, 464
comic books, 620, 1216, 2827
comic strips, anticommunism, 164
commercial speech (see First Amendment), 632, 1408
commissions (see Grace Commission; Kissinger Report; presidency;
  Scranton Commission)
Committee for Economic Development, 423
Committee for Energy Awareness, 1321, 1363, 1382, 1383, 1384,1391
Committee for the Free World, 2645
Committee for the Preservation of Methodism, 94
Committee on Public Information, 1944
Committee on Sound American Education, 94
Committee on the Present Danger (see Sovietphobia), 25, 49, 224,
  391, 462, 2108
commodities (see consumer), 1240, 1286
commodity scientism, 528
Common Cause, 478, 1414, 1702
Communications Act of 1934, 572

Communications Act of 1950, 1495
communications research, U.S. foreign and military planning, 2837
communications, II.D.
communications, capitalism, 2859
communications, centralized corporate control, 2779
communications, Cold War, 2880
communications, concentration, 1081
communications, global control, 2822, 2831, 2833, 2836, 2842,
  2886, 2794
communications, imperialism, 2821
communications, international, 1078, 2801
communications, ITT, 2778
communications, politics, 1664
communications, technology, 1070, 2793, 2817
communications, Third World, 2786a
communications, transnationals, 2851
communications, U.S. foreign policy, 2905
communications, Western dominance, VII., 2875
Communist conspiracy trial (1949), 230
Communist Interference in El Salvador, 2169, 2170
Communist Party USA, 112, 130, 163, 243, 246, 2430, 2436, 2538
Community Antenna Television, 542
Community in Action, CIA, 2703
complex, II.
complex, censorship, deceit, disinformation, secrecy, II.F.
Comprehensive Test Ban Treaty (see nuclear test bans), 402
computers, 459, 524, 942, 992, 1195, 2393, 2793
computers, Congress, 1881
computers, data banks, 895, 961, 1002
computers, FBI, 2545, 2585
computers, surveillance, 2500
computers, voice recognition, 2768
Comsat, 1048, 2853
concentration camps, 1845, 1853
concentration camps, Emergency Detention Plan, FBI, 2577
concentration of power, I.-VII., 424, 429, 453, 454, 533, 1048,
  1065, 1073
concentration, media, 1066, 1078, 1081, 1094, 2818
Condon, Dr. Edward, 120
Conference Board, 423
confidential sources, 1718
confidentiality, 1800
conformity (see orthodoxy), 1086, 1196, 1620, 1798
conformity, corporations, 618
conformity, FBI, I., VI.B.
conformity, films, 634
conformity, mass media, II.D.
conglomerates (see concentration of power; monopoly), 1159
Congress for Cultural Freedom, 160, 2940
Congress, IV.D., 405, 438, 449, 1097, 1116, 1119, 1132, 1138,
  1561, 1657
Congress, CIA, 2729
Congress, ethics, 478
Congress, intelligence agencies, 2391, 2407
Congress, need to know, 1546

Congress, Nicaragua, 2147
Congress, PBS, 1879
Congress, Pentagon lying, 2287, 2378
Congress, television, 614
Congress, tobacco, 604
Congress, totalitarianism, 162
Connecticut, MIC, 475
conscientious objectors, 2027, 2280
consensus (see Contents; bipartisanship; power elite)
consensus politics (see bipartisanship), 465
conservatism (see Contents), 758
conspiracy laws, 1958
Constitution (see Bill of Rights; First Amendment), 904
constitutional limits on power, 1710
consumer, 1209, 1216
consumer advocacy, 1076
consumer culture, III.C.
consumer protection, 600a
consumer reporting, 1270
consumer sovereignty, 446
consumerism, 448, 2040
consumption, 1203
containment doctrine, anti-Sovietism, I., 23, 2840
content analysis, 667
contracting, military (see military-industrial complex), 471
Contras (see Nicaragua), 311, 2064, 2123, 2124, 2127, 2129, 2132,
    2133, 2135, 2136, 2144, 2153, 2155, 2659
Contras, CIA polygraphs, 2663
Contras, CIA, 2663, 2664, 2670, 2671, 2719
Contras, drug connection, 2680
Cook, Richard, 2325
Coplon, Judith, FBI, 2520
corporate crime, reporting (see corporation, crime), 1164
corporate deception, III., 553, 556, 594
corporate directors, 424
corporate power, 251
corporate sponsored conferences, 1295
corporate state, 438, 453, 454, 759, 900, 1192
corporate-government complex, II., 1497
Corporation for Public Broadcasting (CPB), 563, 926
corporation, II., III., VII., 219, 429, 439, 613, 972, 1009,
    1010, 1048
corporation, advocacy advertising, III.D., 430, 916, 1146, 1348,
    1352, 1353, 1360, 1361, 1364, 1366, 1367, 1370, 1380
corporation, broadcasting, 658
corporation, campaign contributions, III.B.
corporation, censorship, III.F.
corporation, concentration, III.A.
corporation, Congress, 1882
corporation, crime, 422, 428, 553, 556, 577a, 602, 662, 1037a,
    1104, 1190, 1197, 1266, 1278, 1332, 1434, 1439, 1442, 1446,
    1453, 1455, 1462, 1465
corporation, Equal Time Provision, 1343
corporation, Fairness Doctrine, 1343
corporation, federal chartering, 446

corporation, films, 1415
corporation, foreign bribery and extortion, 2807
corporation, foundations, III.E., VII.D.
corporation, free flow of information, 2887
corporation, freedom of speech, 1440
corporation, history, 464, 467, 470
corporation, image advertising, III.D.
corporation, lobbying, III.B., 472
corporation, monopolies, 1371
corporation, ownership, 1090
corporation, philanthropy, III.E.
corporation, private, 1448
corporation, product advertising, III.C.
corporation, public relations, III.D., 1337
corporation, secrecy, III.F., 1772
corporation, sponsors, III.C.
corporation, surveillance, III.F.
corporation, taxation, 1394
corporation, think tanks, 1890
corporation, tyranny, 1021
corporation, video press releases, 1401
corruption, government, 1107
cosmetics industry, 1148a
Cosmos 954 incident, 1735
Costa Rica, CIA, 2664
Costa Rica, control of mass media, 2792
Costa Rica, Voice of America, 2922
cotton industry, 1220
Council on Foreign Affairs, 1891, 1905
Council on Foreign Relations, 64, 423, 462
Council on the Arts, 910
counter culture, 456
counter-advertising, 601
Counterattack, 191
counterforce, 2320
counterinsurgency, V., VI.C., 2372
Counterintelligence Analysis Branch, Army, 2461
counterintelligence, V., VI., 2384
Counterspy, 2390
country songs, philosophy, 1611
courts, totalitarianism, 162
cover-up, 2502
cover-up, CIA, 2690
cover-up, Watergate, 1647, 1651, 1652,
covert operations, IV.A.2., V.D., VI., 1559, 1685, 2105, 2321,
     2399, 2400, 2407, 2421, 2430, 2483, 2649, 2660, 2674, 2717,
     2733, 2734
covert operations, CIA, 2597, 2608, 2618, 2624, 2743, 2746, 2756
covert operations, foreign policy, 2437
Cox, Archibald, 1650
credibility, 753, 1584
credit bureaus, 961
CREEP, 1647
crime (see corporation, crime)
Crime Control Act, 961

crime, FBI report, 2534, 2540
Criminal Code Reform Act of 1978, 1714
criminal justice, 904
crisis economy, information, 2834
Cronkite, Walter, 1192
cruise missile, 2294, 2328
cryptology, 2445
Cuba, 178, 1563, 1580, 2039, 2092, 2095, 2107, 2116, 2811
Cuba, CIA, 2603, 2608
Cuba, missile crisis, 35, 1477, 1515, 1594
Cullen, Hugh Roy, 94
cult of intelligence, 2688
cultural domination (see Contents; hegemony), 1180, 1992
cultural exchanges, 2928
cultural expansion, VII., 2786
Current News, 2297
curriculum, II.E.1.
Cvetic, Matt, 2479
cyclamates, 576
Czechoslovakian invasion, 35
Daily Gleaner, CIA, 2672
Dalkon Shield (see corporation, crime), 1439, 1455, 1459
Dallas Morning News, 310
daminozide, II.C., 537
Danforth Foundation, 1427
Dark Circle, 967, 996
Dartmouth Review, 1429
data banks (see computers), 2459
dataveillance, 2500
Davis, James R., 392
de Borchgrave, Arnaud, 351, 362, 409
De Palma, Brian, 665
DEA, 1661
Dean, John, 1651
Death in the West, tobacco, 604, 1206
Death of a Princess, censorship, 922, 932
death squads, 276, 2067, 2165, 2176
death squads, CIA, 2698, 2699
Debs, Eugene, 857
deception, mass media, II.D., 610
DeLoach, Cartha, FBI, 2592
Demetracopoulos, Elias, FBI & CIA, 2547
demilitarization, 2200
democracy, 209, 861, 1113, 1553
democracy, CIA, 2749
democracy, Hiroshima, 1741
democracy, Trilateral Commission, 2780
Democratic Business Council, 1125
Democratic Party, 260, 279, 420, 432, 1030
demonstrations, 904-05, 917, 1978
Dennis v. U.S. (1951), I.C., 1680
Department of Agriculture, 980
Department of Commerce, 1387
Department of Energy (see DOE)
Department of Health, Education, and Welfare (see HEW)

SUBJECT INDEX

Department of Housing and Urban Development (see HUD)
Department of Justice (see Justice Department)
department stores (see consumerism), 1171
deportation, 16, 114, 366
deportation, FBI, 2562
depth psychology, advertising, 650
deregulation, 605, 1111, 1134
deregulation, broadcasting, II.C., 560, 565, 568, 573, 587, 589,
  605a
DES, secrecy, 1679
detective/crime stories, 640
detention plans (see concentration camps), 2502
deterrence, 864, 2203
Dickey v. Alabama, 677
dictatorship, client state (see state terrorism), 1673
dictatorships, 1570, 1825
Dien Bien Phu, 2024
Dies, Martin, 94, 129, 220, 243
diplomacy, 4, 2932
diplomacy, Ronald Reagan, 1586
Directorate for Civil Disturbance Planning and Operations, 2461
disarmament (see arms control; nuclear disarmament; nuclear
  freeze)
disarmament, economics, 507
disarmament, politics, 508
disarmament, unilateral, 396
discrimination, education, 789, 790, 803, 809, 810, 826, 849
disinformation (see Contents), 290, 313, 1667, 2107, 2143, 2168,
  2178
disinformation, CIA, 2597, 2599, 2600
disinformation, FBI, 2578-79, 2592
disinformation, intelligence agencies, 2502
Disney, 460, 697
Disneyland, 1216
Disney World, 1374, 1411
dissent, 1958
dissent, repression, 1851, 2410, 2423, 2596, 2695
dissidents, CIA, 2643
dissidents, FBI, 2517, 2523, 2528
dissidents, Soviet, 89, 201
dissidents, surveillance, harrassment, VI., 2484, 2485, 2486,
  2512
DNA, 876
documentaries, 301, 614, 687, 746, 927, 943, 945, 970, 971, 996,
  1001, 1055, 1158, 1182, 1287, 1309, 1450, 2014
documentaries, broadcasting, 679, 785
DOE, 430, 685, 894, 950, 975, 998, 1398, 1707, 1715, 2335
DOE, distortion, 1808
DOE, nuclear weapons, 2196
DOE, secrecy, 1715
Doherty, William, 2739
Dolan, John, 901
Dole, Robert, 1121
domestic intelligence, CIA, 2695, 2720
Dominican Republic, invasion, 1939, 2059, 2113

Domino theory, 2104
Donald Duck (see Disney), 1196
Donald Duck, imperialist ideology, 2784
Donovan, Raymond, FBI (see corporation, crime), 1494
doublespeak (see Contents; disinformation; lying), 483, 1377,
    1397, 1832
doublespeak, government, 1813, 1816
doublespeak, nuclear, 1815
doublespeak, Pentagon, 2277
Douglas, Senator Paul, FBI, 2539
Dow Chemical, 941
Dow Jones, 1381
Dowling, Tom, 1432
Dr. Strangelove, 172
draft registration, 904
Dreiser, Theodore, 1171
drug abuse, 2412
drug enforcement agencies, 1558, 1872
Drug Enforcement Agency (see DEA)
drug industry, 1037a, 1409
drug promotion, 1295
drug traffic, 442
drugs, 1697
drugs, CIA, 2678, 2689
drugs, Office of National Narcotics Intelligence, 2412
Du Pont Company, 676, 1008, 1018, 1190
Duarte, Napoleon, IV.H.2.b., 2162
DuBois, W.E.B., 141, 214
due process, 907, 2478
Duke University, 863
Dulles, Allen, 2649
Dulles, John Foster, 2717
détente, 48
Earth Day, 680
East Africa, foundations, 2940
East Timor, state terrorism, 703, 896, 979
East-West Center, 2928
ecology (see environment), 40
economic blackmail, 916
economic justice, 904, 2098
economic planning, 427
Economic Recovery Tax Act, 1125
economics education, 1405
economists, 862, 867
economy, world, 1058
Edenic myth, 1337
education, II.E., 184, 250, 427, 438, 449, 454, 460, 498, 852,
    1221, 1356, 1362, 1378, 1380, 1935, 1998
education, alienation, 856
education, anticommunism, 123, 126, 143, 155, 161, 164, 208
education, Bill of Rights, 1713
education, boards and officers, II.E.3.
education, bureaucracy, 853
education, censorship in, 921
education, CIA, 2668, 2718, 2749

education, colonial weapon, 2783
education, corporate control, 855, 941, 1089
education, corporate training, 856
education, cultural imperialism, 2937, 2940
education, discrimination (see discrimination, education)
education, federal aid, 843, 846
education, foundations, CIA, 2730
education, government control, 855, 949
education, higher, 794, 807, 843
education, militarism, 2192, 2198, 2214, 2232, 2244, 2258
education, patriotism, 877
education, philanthropy, III.E.
education, presidency, 1691
education, repression, 903, 944
education, tests and measurements, 803, 850
education, Vietnam War, 1999
Edwards, James, 998
Ehrlichman, John, Watergate, 1644
Einstein, Albert, FBI, 2582
Eisenhower, Dwight D., 25, 525, 1584, 1755, 1946, 2106, 2603
Eisenhower, Dwight D., CIA, 2649
Eisenhower, Dwight D., farewell address, 2214
Eisenhower, Dwight D., foreign policy, 2811
Eisenhower, Dwight D., lying, 1545
Eisenhower, Dwight D., nuclear testing, 1682
Eisenhower, Dwight D., secrecy, 1551
El Mercurio, CIA, 2672
El Salvador, IV.H.2.b., 2035, 2039, 2046, 2061, 2111, 2291
El Salvador, CIA, 2692, 2698, 2699, 2715
El Salvador, elections, 2178
El Salvador, White Paper, 2715
elections of 1980, 686
elections, 649, 1109
elections, financing, 1629
elections, social control, 1626, 1630
elections, U.S.-staged (see El Salvador), 2166
electronic church (see religion), 649, 901
electronic communications, 533
electronic surveillance (see surveillance), 897, 942, 961, 965,
    988, 992, 1444, 1875
elite, social science (see education; hegemony; power elite), 860
Ellis, Thomas F., 674
Ellsberg, Daniel, 1651, 1967
Ellul, Jacques, 1827
Enemy Alien Act, 1845
energy (see DOE), 426, 455
energy corporations, 1139
Energy Research and Development Agency (ERDA), 844, 1766
Energy Research and Development Agency, censorship, 1765
Energy, Department of (see DOE), 2716
engineered consent, 650
English teaching, 2928
enjoinment, 1976
Enlai, Zhou, 2649
Entertainment Analysis Group, 1028

Entertainment Tonight, 354, 1199
entrapment, VI., 1872, 2417
environment, 1337
Environmental Protection Agency (see EPA)
EPA, 535, 537, 582, 590, 596, 597, 600, 1175, 1374, 1411, 1567, 1686, 1766, 1772
EPCOT (see Disney)
equal opportunities, 1386
Equal Time Rule, 549, 558, 706, 1343
Ervin, Senator Sam (see Watergate), 1650, 1878
Espionage Act, 1726, 1805, 2636
espionage, 383, 388, 1576, 1865, 2441
espionage, laws, 1562, 1693
espionage, private, 2416
Establishment (see power elite), 1620
establishment press, II.D., 758
ethics, intelligence agencies, 2483
euphemism, 1813, 1816, 1832
euphemism, nuclear, 2252
euphemism, Pentagon, 2380
Europe, film industry, 2797
evangelical religion (see religion), 906
Evans, Rowland, 1919
Executive Order 10450, 181
Executive Order 12291, 1565
Executive Order 12333, 2442, 2695
Executive Order 12356, 1788, 2661
Executive Order 9385, 181
executive power, IV.A., 1479
executive privilege, 1546, 1649, 1685. 1693, 1701, 1755
Exemption 1, FOIA, 1750
exiles, Central America, 1802
expansionism, cultural and economic, VII., 2813, 2829, 2862
Exxon, 863, 873, 1366
Face the Nation, 1523
Faces of War, 2080, 2087
fact-finding tours, 1120
Fair Deal, Brookings, 1889
Fairchild Industries, 434
Fairness Doctrine, 541, 542, 545, 551, 558, 567, 572, 577, 581, 599, 706, 723, 824, 1325, 1343, 1386, 1572, 1694
fallout, 1809, 2335
Fallows, James, 2267
FALN, 757
false advertising (see advertising)
Falwell, Jerry (see right wing, religions), 62, 901
Family, 1328
family, 424, 1237
family, television, 660
fanaticism (see right wing; Sovietphobia), 901
Fanjul family, 1121
Fanning, David, 785
fantasy chain, 649
Far Right (see right wing), 62, 210
Farber, M. A. (see Caldwell, Carl), reporter's sources, 1800,

1855
fascism, 429, 732
fascism, Third World, 2781
Fat Man, bomb, 1817
FBI, 8, 70, 74, 76, 108, 118, 168, 225, 240, 882, 910, 918, 935,
    942, 956, 1002, 1443, 1462, 1544, 1647, 1651, 1660, 1768, 1775,
    1787, 1801, 1807, 1845, 1857, 1866, 1873, 2020, 2384, 2387,
    2389, 2394, 2397, 2418, 2421, 2430, 2432, 2442, 2447, 2452,
    2455, 2456, 2460, 2463, 2468, 2680
FBI, alternative press, 2485
FBI, anticommunism, I.C.D., 130
FBI, burglary (break-ins), 2407, 2463
FBI, censorship, 1876
FBI, conference, 2463
FBI, criminal officials, 2544, 2550
FBI, domestic surveillance, 2436
FBI, illegal operations, 2450
FBI, informers, 2407
FBI, Oppenheimer, 83
FBI, Post Office, 2449
FBI, repression, VI.B., 2504
FBI, Socialist Workers Party, 2404
FBI, spying, 2502, 2509
FBI, wiretaps, bugging, 1840, 2407, 2428, 2493
FCC, 539, 541-43, 547-49, 551-52, 554, 557, 562, 565-66, 568-70,
    572-73, 578, 581, 598, 603, 642, 655, 662, 679-80, 723, 733,
    1064, 1108, 1130, 1174, 1233, 1293, 1295, 1408, 1657, 1753,
    1783
FCC, television, 614
FDA, 564, 576, 577a, 592, 596, 933, 1455, 1697
Federal Bureau of Alcohol, Tobacco, and Firearms, 579
Federal Bureau of Investigation (see FBI)
Federal Communications Commission (see FCC)
Federal Depository Library Program, 986
Federal Election Commission, 1746
Federal Emergency Management Agency (FEMA), 335, 391, 1869
Federal Home Loan Bank Board, 1110
Federal Trade Commission (see FTC)
Feldene, 592
feminism, militarism (see women), 2202
FHA, corruption, 1757
Fifth Amendment, 243, 2424
film industry, 234
film industry, bank support, 1091
film industry, global, 2796, 2797, 2798, 2799, 2826, 2831
film industry, ideology, 2920
filmmakers, 1055
filmmakers, independent, 940
films, 678, 917, 1351, 2845
films, anticommunist, 58
films, censorship, 1680, 2352, 2353, 2360
films, Central America, 2080
films, corporate advocacy, 1328
films, ideology, 665
films, monopoly, 1032

films, Pentagon, 2223
films, propaganda, 1944
films, Sovietphobia, 346, 378, 395, 401
films, Vietnam War, 1992, 2029
films, war, 2353
films, working class, 1153
films, WWII, 2029
Finger, Harold, 1391
fingerprinting, 992
Finpolity, 1054a
First Amendment, 72, 78, 87, 230-31, 243, 539, 541-42, 545, 567,
    571, 587, 589, 595, 632, 655, 669, 696, 741, 905, 954, 968,
    986, 994, 1015, 1035, 1118, 1408, 1653, 1680, 1681, 1694, 1698,
    1703, 1706, 1713, 1714, 1718, 1730, 1752, 1759, 1760, 1768,
    1774, 1800, 1971, 1977, 2238, 2370, 2401, 2424, 2454, 2642,
    2714, 2721
First Amendment, CIA, 2632, 2661, 2712, 2720, 2737
First Amendment, corporations, 1338, 1410
First Amendment, secrecy, 2727
First Amendment, surveillance, 2472
first strike, 2210, 2320, 2351
Fitzgerald, A. Ernest, 2324, 2355
flag (see patriotism), 852, 877, 1941
flexible response (see nuclear war), 25
Flint Journal, 1456
Florida State University, 951
FM radio, 578, 935
FOIA, 559, 961, 1551, 1552, 1555, 1685, 1690, 1692, 1696, 1712,
    1719, 1722, 1743, 1750, 1760, 1768, 1775, 1782, 1801, 1839,
    2261, 2335, 2392, 2394, 2446, 2455, 2546, 2674, 2701
FOIA, CIA, 2631, 2646, 2648, 2682, 2684, 2685, 2697, 2704, 2706
FOIA, Congress, 1725, 1878
FOIA, FBI, 2573
FOIA, presidential opposition, 1724
food additives, 576
Food and Drug Administration (see FDA)
food industry, 576, 1089, 1335
food processing, 980
food, 440, 600a, 980, 1065, 1159, 1221, 1314
Ford administration, intelligence, 2468
Ford Foundation, 64, 948, 1427, 2937, 2940
Ford Motor Company (see automobile, industry), 963, 1268
Ford Pinto (see automobile, safety; corporation, crime), 1037a,
    1268
Ford, Gerald, campaign debates, 1632
Ford, Gerald, intelligence, 2487
Ford, Gerald, press, 1924
Ford, Gerald, rhetoric, 1541
Ford, Gerald, secrecy, 1573
Ford, Gerald, Southern Africa, 2809
Foreign Intelligence Surveillance Act, 2462, 2649
Foreign Intelligence Surveillance Court, 2471
foreign intervention (see imperialism; interventionism)
foreign labor policy, 2708
foreign policy (see Contents), 57, 61, 345, 399, 768, 911, 991,

1511, 1571, 1671, 1773, 1824, 2104, 2108, 2146, 2437, 2651,
2811, 2813, 2840
foreign policy, CIA, 2693
foreign policy, communications, 2905
foreign policy, foundations, 2940
foreign policy, mass media, 2887
foreign policy, Pentagon, 2190
foreign policy, reform, 2903
foreign policy, values, 1513
Foreign Relations, 1891
Forrestal, James V., 36
Fort Jackson, deaths, 2334
Fort Monmouth, 259
Fortas, Abe, 264
foundations, III.E., VII.D., 424
foundations, CIA, 2741
Fourth Amendment, 87, 2408, 2412, 2424, 2430
framing, 758
fraud, 938
fraud, Pentagon, 2324
free enterprise propaganda, education, 1356
free flow of information, VII.B., 2793, 2816, 2826, 2833, 2845,
2856, 2860, 2862, 2866, 2867, 2868, 2882, 2883, 2884
free flow of information, capitalism, 2885, 2886, 2897
free flow of information, corporations, 2887
free market of ideas, 133
free press (see freedom, press)
free speech (see freedom, speech)
Freed, Donald, Death in Washington libel suit, 2710
Freedom House, 2901
freedom of choice, 1288
freedom of travel, 134
freedom, academic (see education), 187, 206, 223, 225, 364, 369,
403
freedom, information, 1693, 1767, 1771, 1774
freedom, press, 774, 982, 1657, 1713, 1730, 1798, 1800, 2330,
2874, 2879
freedom, speech, 8, 93, 546, 907, 917, 968, 1325, 1332, 1640,
1694, 1752, 1760, 1764, 1782, 1950, 2424
freeze movement (see nuclear freeze movement)
Frontline, PBS, 785
FTC, 428, 540, 556, 1130, 1135, 1174, 1229, 1254, 1375, 1408
FTC, tobacco, 604
Fulbright, J. William, 525, 542, 1548, 1946, 2243, 2302
Fulbright, J. William, CIA, 2649, 2668
fundamentalism (see religion), 62, 466, 1790
G.I. Joe, 1945
Gannett Co., 1085
gap, bomber, missile, 25, 148, 154, 182
Garfield, John, 243
garrison state, V.A. (see militarism; national security state;
Sovietphobia), 2188
Garvey, Marcus, FBI, 2589
Gemstone, Watergate, 1647, 1651
General Dynamics, 510, 698

General Electric, 417, 559
General Electric, television, 614
General Foods, 191
General Motors (see automobile), 532, 1165, 1394, 1456
general semantics, Cold War, 135
genetic research, 515, 1359
Geneva Summit (see arms control; nuclear freeze; nuclear test
  bans), 1495
genocide, 896
George, Wally, 302
Georgetown University, 1428
germ warfare (see CBW), 2264
Geyelin, Philip, 149
Gilded Age, 464
Ginsberg, Allen, 456
Gissing, George, 1171
global, VII., 457
Glomar Explorer mission, CIA, 2752
Gobots, militarism, 1945
Goldwater, Barry, 1946
Goodman, Paul, 456
Gorbachev, Mikhail, 318
Gorsuch, Anne, EPA, 1567
Gottlieb, Sidney, 2678
Gould Corp., 1104
government regulatory agencies (see regulatory agencies)
government, IV., 1107, 1109, 1138
government, access, 1702
government, accountability, 1702
government, advertising, 1542
government, bureaucracy, IV.C.
government, censorship, IV.C.1.
government, commissions, 535
government, corporate consultants, 1895
government, corruption, 1918
government, cover-up, IV.C.1.
government, disinformation, IV.C.2., 1542, 1587
government, lying, 1994, 2077, 2079, 2113, 2148
government, media, 1926
government, press officer, 1914, 1921
government, press, 771, 1770, 1787, 1928, 1970
government, propaganda, 1659
government, regulation of advertising, 1406
government, regulation of corporations, II.C.
government, regulation, II.C., 442
government, regulation, need for, 1772
government, repression, IV.C.3., VI.
government, secrecy, IV.C.1, 1939, 1994, 2092, 2105, 2113, 2180
government, surveillance, IV.C.3., VI.
government, waste, 1431
government-corporate complex, II., 2022
government-press conflict, 1721
Grace Commission, 535, 536, 728
Grace, J. Peter, 536
Graham, Billy, 758

grammar, Pentagon, 2277
grand juries, 1848, 1867, 2401, 2407, 2421
Gray, L. Patrick III, FBI, 2592
Great Britain, cultural influence, 2849
Great Britain, film industry, 2796
Great Britain, Rockefeller Foundation, 2943
Greece, 68, 217
Greece, CIA, 2660
greed (see corporation), 1160
Green Berets, 2003
Grenada, 310, 758, 995, 1565, 1932, 2050, 2060, 2110
Grenada, invasion, 2063, 2066, 2070, 2079, 2083, 2084, 2086,
    2089, 2097, 2101, 2102, 2103, 2105, 2109
Grenada, invasion, censorship, 2112
Griffiths, William E., 341
groupthink (see conformity; ideology; mass media), 649
Gruening, Ernest, 1946
Grumman Aircraft, 485
Guatemala, IV.H., 2035, 2046, 2065, 2067, 2068, 2069, 2076, 2085,
    2106, 2398, 2811
Guatemala, CIA, 2603, 2649, 2723
Guatemala, human rights, 2099
Guatemala, lobbying, 2081
Guiffrida, Louis, 335
guilt by association, FBI, 2562, 2571
Gulf of Tonkin Resolution, Vietnam War, 1946, 1952
gunrunning, CIA, 2753
H-bomb (see nuclear), 25, 1653, 1681, 1684, 1698, 1758, 1681,
    1758
Haig, Alexander, 1874
Haiti, IV.H., 1673
Haldeman, H.R., Watergate, 1644
Halkin v. Helms, 2765
Hanauer, Stephen, 559
Hanford Nuclear Reservation, 504, 975
Hargis, Billy James (see religion; Sovietphobia), 210, 226
Harrington, Michael, 2643
Harris Corp., 1104
Harrison, Jim, FBI, 2543
Hart, Gary, 1434
Harvard University, 949
Harvard University, CIA, 2621, 2653, 2675
Harvard University, FBI, 2531, 2532, 2590
Harvard University, Law School, 836
Harvest, NSA, 2768
Hawkins, Paula, 1104
Haymarket Riot, 3, 857
health and safety, 426-27, 544, 553, 559, 564, 577a, 579, 582,
    588, 590, 592, 724, 779, 916, 975, 980, 999, 1679, 1687
Hearst, William Randolph, 773, 1064
heart disease, 1355
hegemony (see Contents; conformity; indoctrination; orthodoxy),
    438, 441, 458, 460, 463, 467, 619, 764, 1290, 1986, 2940
hegemony, government-press, IV.F., 1917, 1926
hegemony, reporting dissent, 133

Helms, Jesse, 674, 736, 901, 2389
Helms, Richard, CIA, 2649
Helsinki Accords, 2860
Helsinki Accords, information flow, 2877
Hemingway, Ernest, FBI, 2561
Hentoff, Nat, 139
Henze, Paul, 341, 351
heptachlor, 561
Herald Publishing Co. v. Tornillo, 655
Herbert, Anthony, 2271
Heritage Foundation (see right wing), 332, 656, 770, 1428
Heritage Foundation, FBI, 2537
Heritage Foundation, foreign policy, 2840
Heritage Foundation, intelligence agencies, 2475
Heritage Foundation, NPR, 608, 786
Heritage Foundation, right wing, 1893, 1896, 1901, 1902, 2108
Heritage Foundation, UNESCO, 2858, 2942
Hernandez, John, 600
Hersh, Seymour, 2650
HEW, 181, 925, 1521
high school journalism, 994
high technology (see science), 2231
high technology, Pentagon, 518
high-tech industry, 2213
Hill Street Blues, 1212
Hinton, Deane, 2173
Hiroshima, 18, 20, 1741, 1817, 1930, 2329
Hiroshima, censorship, 1741
Hiroshima, secrecy, 1741
Hiss, Alger, 221, 2526
Hiss, Alger, FBI, 2576, 2590
history, falsification, 176, 194, 198, 858, 881, 915, 981, 2010
history, US, 2774
Hobby, Oveta, 94
Hollywood Ten, 96, 104, 147, 187, 243
Hollywood, 86, 97, 107, 197, 221-22, 649, 665, 1088, 1153
Hollywood, FBI, 2574
Honduras, IV.H., 2035, 2082, 2100
Hooker Chemical Company (see Love Canal; Occidental Petroleum
    Corp.; toxic chemicals; toxic waste), 1472
Hoover Institution, think tank, 1898, 1899, 1902
Hoover, J. Edgar, 96, 191, 555, 942, 2432, 2528, 2535, 2543
Hoover, J. Edgar, FBI public relations, 2574
Hostess Foods, 1241
House Committee on Un-American Activities (see HUAC)
House Internal Security Committee (HISC), 139
Houston, environment, 1446
Houston, Sovietphobia, 94
Howe, Russell W., 149
HUAC (1945-50), 95
HUAC, 70, 74, 76, 84, 96, 109, 111, 114, 121, 129, 137, 140, 150,
    159, 163, 220, 221, 225, 235, 243, 910, 1884
HUAC, FBI, 2571
HUAC, free speech, 1888
HUAC, hearings 1938-68, 82

HUAC, Hollywood, 104
HUAC, Texas, 94
HUD, 942
Hughes Aircraft, 532
Hughes-Ryan Amendment of 1974, 2674, 2676
human rights (see civil liberties; civil rights), 904, 2035,
    2061, 2069, 2099, 2118, 2150
human rights, Central America, 2052
humanitarian aid, 2634
hunger, 440, 710, 2098
Hunt, Howard, Watergate, 1647
Hunt, Nelson Bunker, 311, 371, 901
Hunter Project, intelligence, 2432
Huston Plan (see COINTELPRO; repression), 1647, 1651, 2430, 2432,
    2435, 2502, 2592
Huston, Tom Charles, 2432
Hutchins Commission, 669
IBM, 1087, 1388
IBM, Third World, 2890
ideology (see hegemony), I.-VII., 219, 287, 421, 422, 432, 438,
    458, 461, 463, 635, 640, 645, 651, 753, 758, 771, 781, 816,
    1049, 1620, 2001
ideology, consumption, 1203
ideology, corporate, 1093
ideology, education, 793
ideology, films, 665
ideology, journalists, 784
ideology, mass media, 629
ideology, television, 1213, 1286, 1311
ideology, think tanks, 1890
Iklé, Fred, 2372
illegal operations, VI.C.
illegal search and seizure, 1872
Immigration and Naturalization Service (see INS)
immigration, anticommunism (see sanctuary trial), 136
Imperial Presidency, 2725
imperialism, IV.G., VII., 23, 141, 289, 372, 457, 465, 470, 711,
    1549, 2008, 2016, 2330, 2772
imperialism, Asia, 2838
imperialism, communications, 2821, 2853
imperialism, corporate, 2828
imperialism, cultural, VII., 669, 2382, 2775, 2803, 2816-19,
    2826, 2836, 2841, 2845, 2856, 2862, 2866, 2869, 2882, 2884,
    2937-2943
imperialism, intellectual, 2775
imperialism, mass media, VII.A., 2888, 2900
imperialism, PBS, 1173
imperialism, presidency, 1479
imperialism, propaganda, 2898, 2907, 2911
imperialism, Southern Africa, 2809
imperialism, sports, 2824
imperialism, television, 614
independence myth, 758
India, USIA, 2913
indirect communication, advertising, 1211

Indochina, 1987, 1991, 2033, 2603
indocrination, 629
indoctrination, corporations, III.B.C.D.E., VII., 618
indoctrination, mass media, 606, 633
Indonesia, 896, 979
Indonesia, East Timor, 1672
Industrial Workers of the World (see IWW)
Industry Advisory Council (IAC), Pentagon, 520
inequality (see Contents; power elite), 1024
inequality, Central America, 2054
infant mortality, 1255
influence-peddling, III.B., 1137
information embargoes, censorship, 909
information revolution, 1057
information society, 1074, 1201
information sovereignty, 2826
information, access, 1548, 1568, 1662, 1688, 1698, 2109, 2860
information, classified, 1709, 1747
information, crisis economy, 2834
information, freedom, 1552, 1693, 1695, 1698, 1745, 2731
information, international flow, VII.B.
information, political control, 1668
information, Third World, 2890
information-based economy, 2833
informers (see repression), 2479, 2499
informers, FBI, 2530
Infowire, 1272
INS, 324, 2057, 2386, 2469
INS, El Diario-La Prensa, 1868
INS, Sanctuary Movement, 2425, 2429, 2465
INS, Socialist Workers Party, 2413
Institute for Constructive Capitalism, 1378
Institute for Contemporary Studies (see think tanks), 1428, 1892
Institute for Defense Analysis, NSA, 2768
Institute for Regional and International Studies, 2064
instrumental rationality, 1191
insurance industry, 1473
intellectuals, intelligentsia (see education), 270, 1988
intelligence agencies, I., VI., 524, 1645, 1750
intelligence agencies, destruction of public records, 2384
intelligence agencies, media, 2397
intelligence agencies, need for restraint, 2422
intelligence agencies, obstruction of justice, 2384
intelligence agencies, propaganda, 2397
intelligence agencies, regulation, 2468
intelligence gathering, domestic, 1756, 2418
intelligence gathering, Post Office, 2449
Intelligence Identities Protection Act, 2454, 2473, 2686
Intelligence Oversight Act, 2442
Intelligence Reform Act of 1980, 2674
intelligence, 1789, 2288, 2341
intelligence, countersubversive, 2407
intelligence, domestic, 2387, 2407, 2431, 2463
intelligence, domestic, CIA, 2650, 2687, 2695, 2720
intelligence, NSA, 2767

intelligence, political, 2458
Intelsat, 2853
Inter Press Service Third World News Agency, 2864
Inter-American Press Association, CIA, 2672
Inter-American Regional Organization of Workers, 2828
interlocking power, media-government (see Contents), 1906, 1910, 1917
interlocking power, the system (see Contents), II.A., 446, 447
interlocking power, think tanks, IV.E.
Internal Revenue Service (see IRS)
Internal Security Act of 1950, 250
internal security, I., 56, 2105, 2387
International Communication Agency, 2915, 2934
international expositions, 457
international law, Central America, 2052
international law, violation, I.D., IV.A., V., VI.(see imperialism; interventionism)
International Management Analysis and Research Corporation, CIA, 2745
International Monetary Fund, 2803
International Physicians for the Prevention of Nuclear War, 390
International Security, CIA, 2675
International Telecommunications Satellite Organization, 2842
International Workers of the World (see IWW)
interventionism, 289, 365, 1559, 2074, 2086, 2106, 2117, 2154, 2180, 2223, 2372, 2828, 2840
interventionism, Central America, 2052, 2053, 2054, 2055
interventionism, CIA, 2597, 2599, 2600, 2618
intimidation, 1569
intimidation, IRS, 1711
intolerance, 906
investigative journalism, 555, 686, 750a, 928, 929, 1230, 1954
investment institutions, 425
IRA, 757
Iran, 713, 715-16, 769, 1940
Iran, Carter Administration, 1605
Iran, CIA, 2603, 2607, 2724
Iran, embassy hostages, 694, 734, 742, 754, 1475, 1833, 1941
Iron Triangle, military-industrial complex (MIC), 471, 477, 1037a
IRS, 942, 1408, 1711, 1860, 2384, 2407, 2417, 2421, 2430, 2463
IRS, against political activists, 2433
IRS, Mother Jones, 2476
Irvine, Reed, Accuracy in Media, 413
Islam, 769
Israel, 1564
Issues and Answers, 1523
ITT, 1048, 1241, 1285, 1544, 1651, 2830
ITT, Chile, 2778
IWW, 8, 857
IWW, FBI, 2562
Jackson, C. D., The American Century, 2907
James, Henry, 1148
Japanese, 1845
Japanese-Americans, 1853
Japanese-Americans, WWII relocation (see concentration camps),

2342
jingoism (see chauvinism; nationalism; patriotism), 1517, 1935, 1941
John Birch Society, 80, 238
John Paul II (see Pope)
Johns-Manville Corp. (see asbestos; corporation, crime), 1434
Johnson administration, 1952
Johnson, Lyndon, 8, 24, 251, 543, 1496, 1604, 1807, 1878, 1960, 1965, 1974, 2001, 2199
Johnson, Lyndon, CIA, 2649
Johnson, Lyndon, deception, 1584
Johnson, Lyndon, foreign policy, 2811
Johnson, Lyndon, lying, 2059
Johnson, Lyndon, press, 1912
Johnson, Lyndon, secrecy, 1573
Johnson, Nicholas, 542, 547, 551
Joint Anti-Fascist Refugee Committee, 235
Joint Chiefs of Staff, 2199
journalism (see FOIA; media; news; press), 329, 416a, 747
journalism, broadcasting, 679, 680, 681, 682, 683, 684, 685, 686
journalism, business, 1318
journalism, corporate, 1514
journalism, education, 677, 807, 964
journalism, high school, 964
journalism, objectivity, 1620
journalism, secrecy, 1430
journalism, wealth, 1054
journalists, CIA, 2610, 2616, 2625, 2626
journalists, El Salvador, 2163, 2167
journalists, privacy, 2488
judiciary, 1689
justice and fairness, 2426
Justice Department, 114, 1976
Justice Department, Civil Disturbance Group, 942
Justice Department, repression, 1842
KAL 007, 285, 306, 342, 349, 353, 758, 1676, 1754, 1821, 2470
Kalmbach, Herbert, Watergate, 1647, 1651
Kamen, Martin, 134
Kelley, Clarence, FBI, 2592
Kellogg Foundation, 1427
Kennan, George F., 36, 44
Kennedy, Edward, 1922
Kennedy, John F., 25, 148, 649, 1515, 1660, 2001, 2003, 2092
Kennedy, John F., CIA, 2649
Kennedy, John F., Cuban missile crisis, 1594
Kennedy, John F., deception, 1584
Kennedy, John F., murder, FBI, 2548
Kennedy, John F., rhetoric, 1541
Kennedy, John F., secrecy, 1573
Kennedy, Robert, 2543
Kennedy, Robert, White House corps, 1908
Kent State University, 902, 1521
Kent State, coverup, 1973
Kerr-McGhee Corp. (see corporation, crime; radiation; toxic chemicals), 1333, 1462

KGB, 286, 362
Khadafy, Moammar, 1514, 1933
Khe Sanh, 2024
Khmer Rouge, 125
kick-backs, 1056
kickbacks, Congress, 1882
Kikoski, John F., 341
Kimball, Penn, FBI, 2524, 2546, 2553
Kimberly-Clark, 1212
King, Corita, corporate advocacy, 1332
King, Martin Luther, Jr., FBI, 2421, 2543, 2586
Kirkland, Lane (see AFL-CIO; unions), 2828
Kissinger Report, Central America, 1612, 2049, 2051, 2056, 2071, 2074, 2094, 2114, 2115
Kissinger, Henry, 39, 1563, 1571, 1617, 1968, 2002, 2008, 2043, 2443
Kissinger, Henry, FBI, 2594
Kissinger, Henry, intelligence, 2487
Kissinger, Henry, wiretaps, 1854
Klinghoffer, Leon, 760
Knight-Ridder (newspaper chain), 1461
Know Your Enemy--the Viet Cong, 2029
Kojak, 620
Koppel, Ted, 756
Korea, 1931
Korean Air Lines Flight 007 (see KAL 007)
Korean War, IV.G.1., 1934, 1936, 1939, 1942, 1943
Krogh, Egil "Bud", Watergate, 1651, 2412, 2432
Ku Klux Klan, 918, 2518
L.A. Free Press, 2020
La Prensa, IV.H.2.a., CIA, 2762
labor, 326
labor, organized (see AFL-CIO; unions)
Ladies' Home Journal, 1355
LaHaye, Tim, 901
Laird, Melvin, 1584
language debasement (see deception, mass media; doublespeak), 1667
language erosion, 2173
language, government, 1826
language, misuse, 2277
Lansdale, Edward G., CIA, 2639
Laos, 1515, 1573, 1584, 1948
Laos, CIA, 2618
Lara, Patricia, 2469
Lardner, Ring, 70
Latin America, IV.H., 23, 276
Latin America, advertising, 2789
Latin America, mass media, 2785, 2790
Latin America, television, 2806
Lautner, John, 203
Lavelle, Rita, EPA, 600
law (see international law), 454
Law Enforcement Assistance Administration, 2396
Law Enforcement Intelligence Unit (LEIU), disinformation, 2505,

2507
Lawrence Livermore National Laboratory (see arms race; nuclear
    bomb research; science), 288, 394, 481, 532, 2316
Lawson, John Howard, 243
lawyers, 424
Laxalt, Paul, 1494
Leach, Jim, 1113
League of Women Voters, CIA, 2751
leaks (see government; press), 1576, 1584
Lear, Norman, 1212
Lebanon, 283
Ledeen, Michael, 341
left wing, 180
legislative investigative committees, 905
legitimation, power elite (see ideology), 448, 651
leisure time (see advertising; consumerism), 1284
Let Poland Be Poland, 2915
Let's Make a Deal, 620
Letelier, Orlando, assassination, 2644, 2709
Levison, Stanley, FBI, 2543
Lewis, Sinclair, 1596
libel, 1450, 1782, 1962
liberal consensus (see bipartisanship), 467
liberal state, Brookings, 1889
liberalism, 432
liberals, 2391
Liberation News Service, 2455
liberation theology, IV.H., 2046, 2058
Liberty Federation, 479
liberty, speech (see freedom, speech), 696
libraries, 985
Libya, 708, 752, 1514, 1517, 1820
Libya, disinformation, 692
Liddy, G. Gordon, Watergate, 1647, 2412
lie detectors, 992
light water, 417
Lippmann, Walter, 1923
Little Boy, nuclear bomb, 1817
Litton Industry, 495, 496
lobbying, III.B. (see Iron Triangle), 532, 1037a, 1056, 1353,
    1354, 1359, 1702, 2801
lobbying, military contractors, 510, 512
lobbying, Pentagon, 2246, 2255
Lockheed Corporation (see military-industrial complex), 472, 532,
    698, 1128
London Times, Vietnam War, 2013
Lone Ranger, 1196
Long Commission, 393
Lord, Judge Miles, 1439
Los Alamos Scientific Laboratory (see Iron Triangle; Lawrence
    Livermore National Laboratory; science), 481
Los Angeles Police Department, 2453
Los Angeles police, intelligence, 2501
Los Angeles Times, 89, 431, 462, 758, 761, 1049, 1369, 2020
Los Angeles Times, sports, 620

Lou Grant, 1212
Love Boat, 1286
Love Canal (see Hooker Chemical Company), 743a, 1037a, 1472
loyalty, 122, 905
loyalty check, FBI, 2553, 2571
loyalty oath, 127, 131, 184-85, 191, 223, 225, 240, 883
loyalty programs, 23
Loyalty Review Board, 92, 118
loyalty-security program, 88, 91
LSD, CIA, 2678
Luce, Henry, 99, 669
LXO9, 2375
lying, 325
lying, CIA, 2690
lying, FBI, 2550
lying, government (see credibility; gap), 1584, 1604
M.I.T., military research, 2313
MacArthur, Douglas, 170
Macbride International Commission, 2874
MacBride Report, 2871
Mackenzie, Angus, 2467
Maddox, 1946
Madison Avenue, 1181, 1316
Mafia, 442
Mafia, narcotics connection, CIA, 2680
magazines, II.D., 2845
magazines, computer, 1274
magazines, mass-market, 1320
magazines, military technology, 2260
magazines, monopoly, 1038
magazines, technical, 1248
magazines, tobacco advertising, 1304, 1319
magazines, Vietnam, 2017
Magruder, Jeb, Watergate, 1647
mail opening, 8, 992, 2384, 2417, 2430, 2432, 2434, 2502
mail opening, CIA, 2649, 2720
mail opening, FBI, 2559
Mancuso, Frank, 1687
Mancuso, Thomas, radiation, 1687
Marcantonio, Congressman Vito, FBI, 2590
Marcuse, Herbert, 456, 542
marijuana, 1831
Marine Corps, 2192, 2217
marketing, 1195
Marks, Leonard, 2927
Marshall Islands, nuclear testing, 1781
Marshall, George C., 36
Marxism, education, 842
Marxism, media, 2815
Maryknoll, 2046
Marzani case, 236
mass communication, ownership (see concentration, mass media),
    1022
mass culture, 449
mass media, II.D.1., 451, 449, 1011, 1180, 1196, 1205, 2773

mass media, Costa Rica, 2792
mass media, developing countries, 2888
mass media, foreign policy, 2887
mass media, influence abroad, 2826
mass media, Latin America, 2785
mass media, multinationals, 2808
mass media, Third World, 2860
mass-consumption (see consumption), 1240
Masterpiece Theatre, 1173, 1341, 1347
MCA, 1064
McCarran-Walter Act, 77, 101, 134, 136, 250, 324, 352, 366, 1837, 1858, 2469
McCarthy, Senator Joseph, I.C.3, 8, 59, 74, 76, 80, 163, 221, 231, 243, 246, 251, 758, 774
McCarthy, Senator Joseph, 1952 campaign, 1880
McCarthyism, 51, 71, 78, 84, 86, 94, 111, 113, 126, 130-31, 142, 146, 190, 222, 225, 231, 239, 247, 405, 906, 1667, 2105, 2475
McCarthyism, FBI, academia, 2532
McCarthyism, FBI, VI.B., 2570, 2571
McCarthyism, global, 2076
McCarthyism, Washington, D.C., 106
McCord, James, 1647
McDonald, Larry, 371, 404
McDonnell Douglas Corporation, 485, 1457
McGehee, Ralph, 2661
McGill University, 903
McGovern, George, campaigning, 1635
McNamara, Robert, 2199
media conglomerates, 1062, 1064
media control, CIA, 2657, 2718
media coverage, business, 1165
media coverage, Central America, 2067, 2096, 2100, 2111, 2119, 2130
media coverage, Chile, 2184, 2185, 2186
media coverage, corporate crime, 1164, 1230, 1250, 1266, 1268, 1278
media coverage, El Salvador, 2162, 2164, 2172, 2174, 2175, 2179
media coverage, FOIA, 1722
media coverage, food industry, 1335
media coverage, foreign news, 2072, 2145
media coverage, freeze movement, 1509, 1537, 1669
media coverage, government, 1504, 1518, 1543
media coverage, health hazards, 1262, 1304, 1319
media coverage, human rights, 1532
media coverage, judiciary, 1689
media coverage, militarism, 2229
media coverage, military, 2259, 2275, 2328, 2371
media coverage, national defense, 2252
media coverage, Nicaragua, 2137, 2142, 2152
media coverage, nuclear power, 1273, 1290, 1306
media coverage, nuclear weapons, 1740
media coverage, peace movement, 1004, 1929
media coverage, Pentagon, 2267, 2284
media coverage, politics, 1508, 1641, 1648
media coverage, president, 1503, 1504, 1519

media coverage, privacy, 1723
media coverage, revolution, 2139, 2183
media coverage, secrecy, 1723
media coverage, strikes, 1291
media coverage, television, 947
media coverage, UNESCO, 2881, 2895
media coverage, unions, 1308
media coverage, Vietnam veterans, 2019
media coverage, Vietnam War, 1974, 1982, 1983, 1984, 2006, 2011,
  2273
media coverage, war, 614
media coverage, Washington, 1927
media coverage, weapons, 2241
media imperialism, 2786a
media, II.D.
media, access, 542, 572, 595, 1055, 1324, 1352, 1406, 1511
media, access, president, 1511, 1538
media, bias, 1185
media, complicity, 2022
media, concentration, 451, 1053, 1066, 1078, 1094
media, conformity, 2022
media, corporations, 1234
media, deception, 1200
media, diplomacy, 756
media, electronic, 1492
media, foreign news, 11, 13, 178, 241, 299, 308, 317, 329, 339,
  354, 356-57, 379, 979, 990
media, government, 1926
media, ideology, 688
media, Latin America, 2790
media, Marxism, 2815
media, monopoly, 758, 986, 1046, 1051, 1057, 1068, 1072, 1077,
  1088, 1095
media, ownership, 387, 1063, 1066, 1072, 1077, 1081, 1083
media, PACs, 1145
media, politics, 620
media, regulation, 546
media, self-censorship, 1460
media, Soviet Union, 354, 356-57
medical corporations, 876
medical profession, 454
medical research, doublespeak, 1418
medicines, 1233
Meese, Edwin, 1585, 1873
Meet the Press, 1523
Melady, Thomas P., 341
Mellon family, 1428
mercenaries, IV.H., VI.C., 2643
Mercury project (see NASA)
mergers (see monopoly), 428
Mexico, CIA, 2608
Mexico, news coverage, 751
Micronesia, nuclear testing, 1720
Middle East, 760, 990, 1475, 2932
Middle East, CIA, 2641

Mighty Oak test, 1715
militarism, I., II.B., IV.G., V.A., 28, 145, 239, 314, 499, 508,
    523, 534, 941, 986, 990, 1570, 1935, 2291
militarism, economy, 2213
militarism, racism, 2235
militarism, science and technology, 127
militarism, secrecy, 2383
militarism, sexism, 2222
militarism, toys, 1945
militarism, Truman, 153
military, V., 170
military, advisers, 2191
military, budget, 325, 2247, 2350
military, budget, lying, 2343, 2349
military, contractors, II.B., 476, 482, 531-32, 1133, 2214, 2231
military, education, 2315
military, estimates, CIA, 2662, 2711
military, information collection and processing, 2248
military, intelligence, 942, 2384, 2421
military, maneuvers, 1760
military, press, 491
military, repression of dissent, 2366
military, schools, 2315
military, security, 2070
military, spending, 1124
military, spending, economy, 2331
military, superiority, 348
military-education complex, 2214
military-industrial complex, II.B., 59, 218, 238, 454, 708, 839,
    2192, 2198, 2199, 2208, 2213, 2231, 2234, 2312
military-industrial complex, anticommunism, 127
military-industrial-education complex, 2308, 2311
Milk Fund, 1647
Miller, Arthur, 243
mind control, 988
mind control, CIA, 2654, 2689
mines, safety (see coal industry; corporation, crime), 1037a
mining, 750a
Minnesota Public Radio, 1226
Minow, Newton, FCC, 543, 662
Minute Women of the U.S.A., 94
Minuteman missile program, 531
Minutemen, 46
mirror image, Cold War, 135
MIRV (see nuclear weapons), 25
misrepresentation, 758
missile gap (see gap, bomber, missile)
missile technology (see military-industrial complex; science),
    2206
MIT, 873
Mitchell, John, Watergate, 1544, 1644, 1651
MK-ULTRA, CIA, 2678, 2691
Mobil Oil Corp., 863, 1246, 1324, 1329, 1330, 1341, 1366, 1380,
    1414
Mobil Oil, PBS, 922, 1173, 1347, 1368

Mobil Oil, propaganda, 1389
monopoly, II., III. (see concentration of power), 428, 440, 443,
    573, 614, 759, 1031, 1037a, 1047, 1050, 1057, 1060, 1067, 1070,
    1077, 1079, 1084, 1088, 1090, 1095, 1180, 1186, 1325
monopoly politics, 758
monopoly, energy, 455
monopoly, food, 1037a
monopoly, media, 655, 1055, 1079
monosodium glutamate, 576
Monroe Doctrine, IV.H., 63
moon landing, 2211
Moon, Reverend Sun Myung, 293, 387, 409
Mooney, Thomas, 1437
Moral Majority (see religion), 901
Morgan Guaranty Trust, 529
Morison, Samuel L., 1576
Morland, Howard, 1758, 1759
Morland, Howard, H-bomb, 1653, 1681, 1684, 1698, 1758, 1759
Morocco, 1656
Morse, Senator Wayne, 1878, 1946
Morton Thiokol, 1104
Mosqueda-Judd case, 958
Moss Subcommittee on Government, 2345
Moss, Robert, 158, 362
Mother Jones, 2476
motion pictures (see films)
motivational research, 650
Mountain Eagle, 912
Moynihan, Daniel Patrick, 2674
Mozambique, Kissinger Study, 2809
MTM, 1212
muckraking, 1654
Muir, Jean, 191
multinational corporations, VII., 424, 426, 470, 1255, 1285,
    1374, 2816
multinational corporations, advertising, 2808
multinational corporations, CIA, 2707, 2708
multinational corporations, cultural imperialism, 2818, 2819,
    2831
multinational corporations, domination of world communications,
    2835, 2850
multinational corporations, mass media, 2773, 2808
Mungo, Ray, 2455
Murrow, Edward R., 255, 614, 1145, 1469, 2927
museums, 813
MX Education Bureau, 511
MX missile, 218, 511, 1124, 1667, 2267, 2298
My Lai, 2188, 2261, 2339, 2340
myth, 449, 665, 758, 832
NAACP, anticommunism, 141
Nader, Ralph, 556, 1076
Nagasaki, 1817, 2329, 2936
NASA, 528, 698, 891, 1674, 1675, 1735, 1792, 2211, 2227, 2313,
    2325
NASA, Apollo disaster, 776

NASA, Challenger disaster, 502, 522, 891, 1675
NASA, militarization of space, 2197
NASA, secrecy, 1707
NASA, space shuttle journalists, 514
Nation, The, 2273
Nation, The, FBI, 2554
National Academy of Sciences, 801
National Association of Broadcasters, 539, 598, 1211
National Association of Realtors Political Action Committee, 1129
National Broadcasting Company (see NBC)
National Coalition for a Free Cuba, 2093, 2918
National Coalition on Television Violence, 1945
National Committee to Abolish HUAC, FBI, 2590
National Congressional Club, 674
National Data Center, 961
National Endowment for Democracy (see USIA), 2901, 2928
National Energy Plan, 900
National Freedom of Information Committee, 1695
National Geographic, 460
National Guardian, 78
National Highway Safety Administration, 1547
National Journalism Center, 837
National Law Enforcement Telecommunications System, 1002
National Lawyers Guild, 2134
National Lawyers Guild, FBI, 2590
national liberation movements, 2108
National Public Radio (NPR), 659, 688, 786, 935
National Public Radio, censorship, 698
National Reporter, 2390
National Security Agency (see NSA)
National Security Council (see NSC)
National Security Decision Directive 13 (NSDD 13), 391
National Security Decision Directive 84 (NSDD 84), 1737, 1786
National Security Decision Directive 130 (NSDD 130), 2385, 2905
National Security Seminars, 2223
national security state (NSS), 218, 240, 388, 530, 1570, 2065,
    2068, 2223
national security, I., II.B., IV., V., VI., 23, 173, 181, 191,
    209, 250, 320, 904, 997, 1509, 1552, 1561, 1562, 1584, 1688,
    1710, 1743, 1760, 1789, 1803, 2261, 2337, 2441, 2538
national security, censorship, 1763
national security, CIA, 2597, 2609
national security, Council on Foreign Affairs, 1905
national security, press, 2669
national security, secrecy, 1698
National Student Association, CIA, 2741
nationalism (see jingoism; patriotism), 457
NATO, 25, 720, 1733
natural gas, 1116
Naval Intelligence, VI.A., 2394
Naval Investigative Service, 2394
Naval Reactors Branch, 2333
NAVSTAR, Global Positioning System, 2225
Navy, 1004, 2216, 2223, 2296
Navy, lying, 2377

Navy, Micronesia nuclear tests, 1720
Navy, propaganda, 2285
Navy, public relations, 2268, 2295
Navy, secrecy, 2326, 2348, 2375
Nazi scientists, 1717
Nazis, 889, 972
Nazis, CIA, 2614, 2732
NBC, 614, 726, 758, 1179, 1389, 1495
NCLIS Task Force, 875
NCPAC, III.B., 901
Nelson, Jack, 1768
Nelson, Steve, 2479
Neoconservatives, 1937
Nestlé Corporation, 1255
NET (see PBS), 614
network news (see television), 75, 620, 735, 754, 763, 1705,
    2096, 2111, 2145
network news, interview shows, 355
Network Project, 434
network television, 543
neutralism, 1969
Neutrality Act, 2649
neutron bomb, 743a, 2266
Nevada, nuclear testing, 1781
New Deal, Brookings, 1889
New Economists, 862
New Globalism, 365
New International (World) Economic Order, 2819
New International (World) Information Order, VII.B., 669, 2819
New Leader, 2273
New Left, 33, 984, 2432, 2436
New Left, disruption, 2430
New Nobility, 531
New Republic, The, 1262, 2273
New Right, 183, 190, 276, 450, 906, 1962
New World (International) Information Order, VII.B.
New York Times v. Sullivan, 770
New York Times, 13, 89, 178, 313, 390, 462, 758, 761, 775, 780,
    934, 1256, 1390, 1466, 1515, 1812, 1923, 2020, 2033, 2037,
    2073, 2371
New York Times, Allendé overthrow, 2183
New York Times, campaign coverage, 1633
New York Times, CIA, 2610, 2625, 2629, 2649, 2728
New York Times, El Salvador, 2172
New York Times, government, 1909
New York Times, military, 2303a
New York Times, Progressive H-bomb case, 1684, 1698
New York Times, Vietnam War, 2001, 2013
news agencies, 690, 699, 716, 761, 764, 772, 778, 995, 1293,
    1490, 1822, 2036, 2037, 2874, 2894
news agencies, Africa, 2800, 2854
news agencies, domination, 2826, 2845, 2889
news agencies, Southern Africa, 2802
News Clipping and Analysis Service, 2297
news embargo, 2070

news leaks, White House (see leaks), 1505
news management (see Contents; journalism; media), 173, 200, 229, 329, 339, 379, 389, 747, 759, 771, 934, 1242, 1300, 1736, 1741, 1749, 1923, 1959, 2001
news management, Army, 2319
news management, government, 775
news management, presidential, 2345
news media, 424, 1197, 1760
news media, advertising, 1215
news media, business, 1242, 1256, 1281, 1318
news media, drugs, 1252
news media, First Amendment, 1703
news media, government, 1584
news media, presidency, 1575
news quarantines, 889
news releases, corporations, 633
news shows, "meet the press," 1523
news, II.D.2., 451, 629, 635-36, 649
news, CIA (see journalists, CIA), 2609, 2625
news, construction of, 781-82
news, consumer, 680
news, corporations, 684, 686
news, elections, 682
news, entertainment, 1275, 1281
news, environment, 680
news, foreign, 739, 766
news, government regulation, 686
news, international, 685, 2860, 2886
news, leaks, 2657, 2683, 2712, 2811
news, management (see news management)
news, manipulation, 1972
news, network (see network news)
news, oil, 685
news, radio, 620
news, Sunday morning shows, 749
news, suppression (see censorship), 1272, 1931, 2329
news, television, 1569
news, Western domination, 2889
newspapers, 34, 643, 771, 1014, 1060, 1067, 1170, 1230, 1718, 2845
newspapers, advertising, 1249
newspapers, business, 1250, 1270
newspapers, censorship, 955, 1220, 1317
newspapers, Central America, 2100
newspapers, Chile, 2186
newspapers, foreign, 762
newspapers, Houston, 1208
newspapers, monopoly, 1027, 1029, 1032, 1036-37, 1043
newspapers, nuclear power, 1306
newspapers, takeovers, CIA, 2672
newspapers, weekly, 1086
newsprint shortage, 1067
newsreels, 721, 1207
Newsweek, 316, 462, 486, 726, 758, 1256, 2044, 2629
Newsweek, influence abroad, 2826

Nicaragua, IV.H.2.a., 284, 666, 2035, 2039, 2046, 2061, 2082, 2111, 2372, 2398, 2410
Nicaragua, CIA, 2640, 2745, 2756
Nicaragua, MIG scare, 2158
Nicaraguan Democratic Force, 2133
Nielsen ratings, 1177, 1179
Nigeria, foundations, 2940
Nitze, Paul, 49
Nixon administration, lying, 1544
Nixon, Richard M. (see Watergate), 8, 25, 148, 190, 251, 588, 723, 779, 1476, 1512, 1531, 1543, 1544, 1549, 1566, 1569, 1584, 1604, 1643, 1644, 1648, 1651, 1818, 1960, 1961, 1968, 1988, 2001, 2008, 2025, 2412, 2443
Nixon, Richard M., 1968 campaign, 1634
Nixon, Richard M., censorship, 1557
Nixon, Richard M., CIA, 2738
Nixon, Richard M., dissent, 1521
Nixon, Richard M., education, 1691
Nixon, Richard M., foreign policy, 1617, 2811
Nixon, Richard M., intelligence, 2432
Nixon, Richard M., lying, 1563
Nixon, Richard M., national defense, 1819
Nixon, Richard M., news media, 1575, 1577
Nixon, Richard M., PBS, 701, 971, 1574
Nixon, Richard M., presidential myths, 1599
Nixon, Richard M., press, 1912
Nixon, Richard M., rhetoric, 1541
Nixon, Richard M., secrecy, 1563, 1573, 1947
Nixon, Richard M., Southern Africa, 2809
Nixon, Richard M., surveillance, 2508
Nixon, Richard M., TV licensing, 1859
Northern Ireland, 313, 1812
Novak, Robert, 1919
NRC, 533, 559, 584-86, 591, 593, 602, 908, 999, 1370, 1463, 1464
NRC, censorship, 1728
NRC, ineptitude, 1784
NRC, secrecy, 1666, 1739
NSA, VI.D., 1495, 2384, 2387, 2389, 2394, 2398, 2421, 2430, 2432, 2459, 2463
NSA, domestic intelligence, 2435
NSC paper #68 (NSC-68), 25, 49
NSC, 162, 1563, 2443
NSC, CIA, 2758
NSC, wiretaps, 1854
nuclear accidents, 333, 916, 1715
nuclear arms race (see arms race, nuclear)
nuclear bomb research 488
nuclear culture, 504
nuclear disarmament, 304
nuclear energy (see nuclear power), 417
Nuclear Energy Women, 1393
nuclear fallout, 2301
nuclear freeze movement, 404, 1509, 1537, 1667, 1669
nuclear industry, 967, 1003, 1097, 1098, 1132, 1273, 1438
nuclear industry, PBS, 996

nuclear industry, public relations, 1303, 1321, 1342
nuclear policy, 2320
nuclear policy, language, 1815
nuclear power elite, 516
nuclear power, 426, 526, 559, 575, 584-86, 588, 591, 594, 738,
    761, 900, 916, 923, 950, 977, 998-99, 1042, 1092, 1290, 1306,
    1353, 1358, 1361, 1363, 1364, 1370, 1372, 1382, 1391, 1393,
    1463, 1464, 2231
nuclear power, licensing, 1739
nuclear power, secrecy, 500, 1708, 1728, 1739
nuclear power, US and SU, 1708
nuclear proliferation, 1681
nuclear reactors, universities, 500
nuclear regime, 1741
Nuclear Regulatory Commission (see NRC)
nuclear safety, 602
nuclear secrecy, 516, 1715, 1739, 1740
nuclear superiority, 1781
nuclear test bans, 242, 297, 304, 318, 390, 402, 1488, 1682
nuclear testing, 242, 402, 508, 1592, 2365
nuclear testing, cancer, health, safety, 1699, 1720, 1781, 2335
nuclear testing, cover-up, 1781
nuclear testing, disinformation, 1809
nuclear testing, secrecy, 1682, 1699, 1715, 1720, 1734, 1766,
    1809, 2346
nuclear testing, sheep deaths, 2335
nuclear war, 207, 391, 1488, 2098, 2201
nuclear war, children, 145
nuclear war, limited, 2233, 2267, 2292
nuclear war, NSA, 2762
nuclear war, prevention, 2347
nuclear war, survival, 2354
nuclear waste, secrecy, 1678
nuclear weapons and energy, 513
nuclear weapons, 218, 476, 1553, 1740, 2196, 2307, 2316, 2347
nuclear weapons, advocacy, 503, 509
nuclear weapons, infrastructures, 474
nuclear weapons, National Museum exhibit, 1817
nuclear weapons, secrecy, 1740, 2326, 2357, 2381
nuclear winter, 25
nuclearism, 483, 516, 534
nutrition, 1065, 1159, 1221, 1296, 1314
nutritional guidelines, 898
O Group, 288
objectivity, 758, 878
obscenity laws (see censorship), 1764
Occidental Petroleum Corp., 1472
Odeh, Alex, 760
Odets, Clifford, 243
Odom, William, 1495
Office of Students and Youth, 1521
Official Secrets Act, 1495
official sources, 775, 2096, 2143
oil industry, 428, 455, 863, 1037a, 1056, 1134, 1208, 1329, 1340,
    1344, 1345, 1366, 1400, 1458, 2068

oligarchy (see power elite), 424, 436, 1054a
oligopoly, 1089
oligopoly, broadcasting, 603
oligopoly, mass media, 629
Olin Foundation, 363
Olin-Mathiesen, 941
Olympic boycott of 1980, 75
OMB, 986, 1481
On Company Business, CIA, 2734
OPEC (see oil industry), 1134
Operation Broiler, 2203
Operation Chaos, NSA, 2763
Operation Minaret, NSA, 2763, 2768
Operation Shamrock, NSA, 2768
Operation Sojourner, 2429
Operation Splinter Factor, 2742
Operation Wigwam, 1004
Oppenheimer, Robert, 83
optimism, official, 2015
ORDEN, CIA, 2698
organized crime, 1651
organized crime, FBI, 2527
organized labor (see unions)
Ortega, Daniel (see Nicaragua), 2130
orthodoxy (see hegemony), I.-VII., 198, 432
Orwell, George, 280, 452, 1704, 2869
Osgood, Charles, 2672
OSHA, safety, 544, 1220, 1278, 1442, 1665
Overseas Education Fund, CIA, 2751
ownership, II.-III., 423, 446
Pacific Gas and Electric, 1287
Pacific Legal Foundation, 1428
Pacific Stars and Stripes, 1975
Pacifica Foundation, 672, 1753
Pacifica Radio, 1441
pack journalism, 649
Packwood, Robert, 568
PACs, III.B., 115, 1097, 1100, 1101, 1102, 1111, 1112, 1113,
   1122, 1123, 1132, 1136, 1146, 1414, 1882
paid informants (see informers), CIA, 2638
Pajaro Dunes Conference, 804
Palestinians, 760, 931
Paley, William, 614
Palmer raids, I.A.B., 8, 17, 857
Panama Canal, 1511, 2090
Paper Tiger Television, 607, 638, 661
Paraguay, 2181
paranoia (see Sovietphobia), 261
parties, political (see bipartisanship), 437
passivity (see conformity), 1187, 1204
passports (see visa control), 134
Pastora, Eden (see Contras), 2144
patent monopoly, 1409
Patent Office (see U.S. Patent and Trademark Office)
patient package inserts (see advertising), 564

patriotism, 432, 465, 748, 852, 877, 1168, 1169, 1297, 1498, 1941, 2001
Paulau, Navy, 2770
payoffs, 1647
PBS, 54, 278, 301, 382, 601, 625, 626, 681, 684, 701, 741, 745-46, 939-40, 945, 971, 996, 1001, 1048, 1053, 1226, 1235, 1280, 1347
PBS, advertising, 1176, 1202, 1368
PBS, censorship, 892, 899, 919, 922, 927, 931, 932, 933, 939, 940, 945, 971, 996, 1001, 1257, 1271, 1303, 1656, 1658, 2012
PBS, CIA, 2647
PBS, commercialism, 1161, 1176
PBS, compared with BBC, 637
PBS, Congress, 1879
PBS, consumerism, 1155
PBS, control, 1235, 1281
PBS, corporate control, 1257, 1258, 1264, 1282, 1341
PBS, corporations, 899, 1151, 1257, 1258, 1264, 1282, 1315
PBS, documentaries, 687, 927
PBS, FCC, 1282
PBS, funding, 637, 653, 1235
PBS, imperialism, 1173
PBS, independent producers, 943
PBS, news, 672
PBS, Nixon, 1574
PBS, nuclear industry, 1303
PBS, political interference, 926
PBS, propaganda, 1225
PBS, reform, 639, 783, 1005, 1166, 1167
PBS, self-censorship, 1299
PBS, sponsorship, III.C., 1193
PBS, television, 947
PBS, unions, 1152, 1265
PBS, Vietnam War, 1980, 1984, 1997, 2007, 2011, 2012
PBS, White House, 1572
PCBs (see corporation, crime; toxic chemicals), 976
peace movement, 313, 376, 1929, 1978, 2207
Pearson, Drew, 1654, 1923
Peltier, Leonard, FBI, 2565
Pentagon Papers, 741, 1500, 1562, 1645, 1659, 1685, 1953, 1963, 1970, 1976, 1977, 1979, 1994, 1999
Pentagon Papers, RAND, 1904
Pentagon Propaganda Machine, The, 2302
Pentagon, V., 162, 224, 325, 454, 460, 471, 477, 533, 697, 871, 938, 1733, 1747, 1750, 1776, 1779, 1790, 1959, 1978
Pentagon, 1967 March on, 2461
Pentagon, accountability, 484
Pentagon, budget, 2220, 2245, 2257, 2272, 2349, 2350
Pentagon, censorship, V.D.
Pentagon, Central America, 2052
Pentagon, Congress, 2287
Pentagon, deception, 1948, 2264, 2278, 2324
Pentagon, disinformation, V.D.
Pentagon, education, V.C.
Pentagon, media, V.B.

Pentagon, news management, 2261
Pentagon, press, 2267, 2282, 2288, 2289, 2292, 2324
Pentagon, propaganda, 517, 681, 2199, 2214, 2223, 2250, 2254, 2263
Pentagon, public relations, V.B.
Pentagon, secrecy, V.D., 1948, 2082, 2109, 2261, 2264
Pentagon, statistics, 1819
Pentagon, surveillance of civilians, 2480
Pentagon, waste, 484
People's Dreadnought, 2467
periodicals (see magazines)
perjury, 2478
Perle, Richard, 391
persecution, 128
Pershing II, propaganda, 2904
Pershing missile, 2294
Peru, 2035
pesticides, 590, 959, 1175
Pfizer Corporation, 592
pharmaceutical industry, 1293, 1295, 1418
Phelps-Stokes Fund, Africa, 2938
philanthropy, 1052
philanthropy, cultural imperialism, 2937, 2938, 2939, 2940, 2941, 2943
Philip Morris, 1206
Phillipine revolt, 710
Phillipines, 2639, 2811
Phillipines, AFL-CIO, 2839
Phillipines, education, 2783
Phoenix Program, CIA, 2643
Physicians for Social Responsibility, FBI, 2563
Pike Committee, CIA, 2487, 2625
Pike Report, 2389
Pincus, Walter, 149
Pinkerton agents, 2479
pipeline technology, 2231
Pipes, Richard, 391
PL-5, 336
plant relocations, 1037a
Playboy, 620
plutocracy, 1107
plutonium (see nuclear power; radiation), 513, 1707, 2335
Plutonium, Element of Risk, 1257
plutonium, missing, 1765
Poland, 735
Poletown, 1037a
police state (see political prisoners; repression), 162
police state, CIA, 2508
police terrorism, CIA, 2673
police, 1811, 2478, 2481
police, anti-nuclear movement, 2474
police, behavior, 2478
police, history, 2478
police, intelligence units, 2402, 2440, 2453
police, political intelligence gathering, 2402, 2411

police, political repression, 2409, 2420
police, Red Squad, 2481
police, secret, 2501, 2509
police, surveillance, 2401
police, undercover operations, 2460
police, use of newsmen, 2411
policy process, 427
political advertising, 755
political campaigns, 1602
political candidates, packaging, 1639
political candidates, rhetoric, 1602
Political Information System, 1525
political parties, 1122
political police, VI. (see Red Squad), 2507, 2509
political prisoners, 159, 1838, 1851, 1853, 1858, 1861, 1871,
    2406, 2482, 2596
political prisoners, FBI, 2565
political science (see social science), 449, 878
political spying, 2691
politics, communications, 1664
Polk, George, 217
polls (see public opinion polls)
pollsters, 449
pollution, 600, 976, 1337, 1446, 1513
polygraphs, 1443, 1787, 2444, 2452
Pope, assassination attempt (see Agca), 275, 295, 313, 341, 351,
    758, 1619, 1812
popular culture, 1196, 1267, 1288
popular music, 1040
pornography, 1585
Portugal, 2183
Posner, Vladimir, 1794
Post Office (see Postal Service)
postal censorship (see mail opening), 1680
Postal Service, 743a, 1769
Potsdam, 18, 21, 36
poverty, 660, 693, 1024, 1030
power elite, I.-VII., 416, 420-24, 436, 439, 445-47, 454, 457-58,
    461, 487, 651
power elite, elections, 1625, 1630
power structure analysis, 1049
power, concentration (see Contents), 162
power, private centers, 905
Powers That Be, 1287
Powers, Francis Gary, U-2, 2759
Pratt, Elmo, FBI, 2569
presidency, IV.A., 438, 451, 460, 465, 1620, 1755
presidency, campaign reporting, 764
presidency, censorship, IV.A.2.
presidency, commissions, 574
presidency, Congress, 1887
presidency, control of information, 1474
presidency, cover-up, IV.A.2
presidency, disinformation, IV.A.3.
presidency, education, 1691

presidency, elections, IV.A.4.
presidency, imperial, 22
presidency, intelligence agencies, 2422
presidency, leaks, 1925
presidency, lying, 1912, 2345
presidency, media access, IV.A.1
presidency, media, 2909
presidency, news management, IV.A.1., 1911, 1925, 1928, 2345
presidency, news wire, 654
presidency, photo opportunities, 1925
presidency, press agents, 449
presidency, press conference, 1912, 1925
presidency, press, 1925, 1938
presidency, propaganda machine, 1584
presidency, public relations, IV.A.1.
presidency, secrecy, IV.A.2, 2345
presidency, television, 654, 680
presidency, TV networks, 1922
presidency, Vietnam War, 1995
Presidential Directive (PD), 84, 1760
Presidential Directive 58, 2201
Presidential Directive 59, 25, 148, 391, 2210, 2267, 2292
presidential power, IV.A., 1570, 1649, 1810, 2725
press (see news), 200, 233
Press and the Cold War, The, 1994
press conferences, 1749
press conferences, science, 1416
press conferences, White House, 1485, 1487, 1492, 1512, 1526, 1539, 1540
press corps, Pentagon, 2263, 2265
Press Councils, 741, 1063
press manipulation, CIA, 2652
press officer, government, 1914, 1915
press pools, 2070
press release as news, 1274, 1293, 1322, 1335
press release, corporation, 654
press releases, Congress, 1877, 1883
press responsibility, 78
press, agenda setting, presidential campaign, 1637
press, alternative, 1731
press, bias, 228-30, 317, 386, 1080
press, campaign coverage, 1880
press, censorship, 1964, 2473
press, Chicago, 2185
press, Chile, 2187
press, CIA, 2652, 2683, 2712
press, combat, 2253
press, corporations, 773
press, distortion, 308, 339
press, freedom (see freedom, press)
press, government harassment, 1862
press, government, 1543, 1721, 1928, 1970, 2337
press, Grenada invasion, 2083, 2102, 2109, 2112
press, human rights, 1532
press, influence, 768

press, intelligence agencies, 2387
press, national security, 2669
press, Nicaragua, 2139
press, objectivity, 1145
press, Pentagon, 2292, 2379
press, presidency, IV., 1482, 1925, 1983
press, source privacy, 1856, 1871
press, subpoena, 1841
press, underground, 1731
press, UNESCO, 2872, 2881
press, Vietnam War, 1949, 1954, 1960, 1964, 1972, 1974, 1987
press, Washington corps, IV.F.
press, White House corps, IV.F.
pressure groups, 1212
price-fixing (see corporation, crime), 428
print media, 661
prior restraint (see censorship), 1495, 1562, 1645, 1653, 1680,
    1681, 1684, 1698, 1706, 1718, 1742, 1759, 1763, 2604, 2642,
    2692, 2714
prior restraint, CIA, 2735
Privacy Act, 1839
privacy, 655, 897, 904, 907, 942, 961, 965, 992, 1433, 1443,
    1550, 1680, 1710, 1866, 2459, 2500
Privacy, Common Law of, 961
Privacy, Constitutional Law of, 961
privacy, invasion, 2417
private domain power, 1236
Proctor and Gamble, 1307
producers, independent, public broadcasting, 943
product advertising, III.C.
product labeling (see advertising), 1260
professors, McCarthyism (see education), 164
profit motive, 1160
programmed president, 1602
Progressive era, 439
Progressive Party, 141
Progressive, The, 1681, 1684, 1698, 1758, 1759
Progressive, The, H-bomb, FBI, 1653, 1681, 1684, 1698, 1758,
    1759, 1763, 2556
Project Censored, 997
Project Galileo, 1707
Project Sandwedge, 1647
propaganda (see conformity; indoctrination), 376, 628, 894-95,
    1197, 1219, 1342, 2452
propaganda, CIA, 2683, 2744
propaganda, government, 1659, 1660
propaganda, intelligence agencies, 2397
propaganda, international, VII.A.&C.
propaganda, Pentagon, 175, 1733
propaganda, presidential, 286, 343, 373, 1534
propaganda, Soviet, 242
Protestant churches, challenges to corporations, 1059
Protestantism, 1239
psychological warfare, 2907
psychological warfare, CIA, 2672

psychotropic drugs, CIA, 2677
public access, 1081
public affairs programming, 568, 970, 1170
Public Broadcasting System (see PBS)
Public Citizen's Health Research Group, 1293
Public Citizen, 1138
Public Disorder Intelligence Unit, 2453
public forum doctrine, 2238
public opinion polls, 1346, 1525
public opinion, 768
public relations (see Contents), 1056, 1353
public relations firms, 1825
public relations, corporate, 1359
public relations, FBI, 2595
public relations, fiction, 1349
public relations, oil industry, 1345
Public Service Ads (PSAs)(see Advertising Council), 1323, 1396
public sphere, 1201
public utilities, 808, 1362, 1375, 1392
public, knowledge and ignorance, 765
Publications Review Board, 2702
publishers, book, 1061, 1094
publishing, acquisitions and mergers, 1025
Puerto Rico, CIA, 2643
puffery (see advertising; public relations), 1181, 1274, 1276
quiz shows, corporate crime, 1149
R. J. Reynolds Tobacco Co., 1350
racism, 457, 855
racism, Britain, 1001
racism, militarism, 2235
radiation, 146, 513, 538, 559, 913, 916, 975, 1003, 1004, 1092,
    1435, 1462, 1468, 1682, 1687, 1707, 1728, 1734, 1741, 1758,
    2329, 2335
radiation, cancer, 1781
radiation, low level, 1781
radiation, secrecy, 1761, 1766, 1780
radical right (see right wing), 906
radicals, 2391
radio broadcasting, 1007
Radio Free Europe, 2914, 2933
Radio Liberty, 344, 2914, 2933
Radio Liberty, anti-semitism, 2923
Radio Marti, 2039, 2899, 2912, 2918
radio, 614, 935, 1305, 2845
radio, commercialization, 1223
radio, monopoly, 1032
radio, propaganda, 2916
radio, public interest, 1226, 1294
radioactivity (see radiation), 738
Rambo, 1945
Ramparts, 2455
RAND Corporation (see RAND)
RAND, 148, 1894, 1902, 1903, 2023
RAND, MIC, 1900
RAND, Pentagon Papers, 1904

Randall, Margaret, 352, 366, 1837, 2057
Rankin, John, 221
Rat, 2020
Rather, Dan, 952
RCA, 434, 1064
Reader's Digest, 295, 341, 351, 404, 618, 937, 1185, 1196, 1355, 1402
Reader's Digest, cultural imperialism, 2826, 2832
Reagan administration, 986, 1937
Reagan administration, Central America, 2122, 2146
Reagan administration, CIA, 2740
Reagan administration, covert operations, 2399
Reagan administration, deception, 1616
Reagan administration, El Salvador, 1612, 2165, 2169, 2171, 2176
Reagan administration, human rights, 2118
Reagan administration, intelligence gathering, 2404, 2410, 2468
Reagan administration, interventionism, 2086
Reagan administration, lying, 2140, 2143, 2160, 2165
Reagan administration, military budget, 2247
Reagan administration, news management, 2175
Reagan administration, Nicaragua, 1612, 2120, 2121, 2128, 2132, 2140, 2143, 2156, 2160, 2161
Reagan administration, PBS, 939, 1005
Reagan administration, press, 1495
Reagan administration, propaganda, 2122
Reagan administration, repression, 2405
Reagan administration, scandals, 1494
Reagan administration, secrecy and censorship, 2496
Reagan administration, surveillance, 2512
Reagan administration, UNESCO, 2879, 2895
Reagan administration, United Nations, 2776, 2847
Reagan administration, visa control, 2182
Reagan Doctrine, 1610, 2681
Reagan, Ronald (see Meese, Edwin)
Reagan, Ronald, 25, 62, 148, 429, 450, 466, 665, 891, 901, 937-38, 968, 991, 998, 1109, 1352, 1371, 1487, 1514, 1534, 1552, 1591, 1777, 1788, 1794, 1812, 1932, 1992, 2043, 2075, 2105, 2336, 2452
Reagan, Ronald, arms control, 1522, 1529, 1606, 1612
Reagan, Ronald, broadcasting, 550, 552
Reagan, Ronald, campaigning, 1611, 1625, 1631
Reagan, Ronald, cartoons, 1589
Reagan, Ronald, censorship, 1561, 1565
Reagan, Ronald, Central America, IV.H.2., 2047, 2052
Reagan, Ronald, CIA, 2661, 2694
Reagan, Ronald, Cold War, I.D., 1612
Reagan, Ronald, covert intelligence, 1850
Reagan, Ronald, deception, 1913
Reagan, Ronald, demonstrations, 1489
Reagan, Ronald, deregulation, 605
Reagan, Ronald, diplomacy, 1586
Reagan, Ronald, Executive Order No. 12356, 1581, 1582, 1583
Reagan, Ronald, FOIA, 1555, 1582
Reagan, Ronald, foreign policy, 2840
Reagan, Ronald, Grenada, 1612

Reagan, Ronald, health and safety, 1547, 1548
Reagan, Ronald, Heritage Foundation, 1896
Reagan, Ronald, Hoover Institution, 1898
Reagan, Ronald, human rights, 1612
Reagan, Ronald, hypocrisy, 1598
Reagan, Ronald, ideology (see right wing), 1486, 1497, 1603, 1610
Reagan, Ronald, imperialism, 1612, 2771
Reagan, Ronald, intelligence agencies, 2456
Reagan, Ronald, interventionism, 1529
Reagan, Ronald, lying, 1554, 1590, 1601, 1612, 1615, 2077, 2134, 2151, 2158, 2161
Reagan, Ronald, media manipulation, 2921
Reagan, Ronald, militarization, 2234
Reagan, Ronald, missiles, 1612
Reagan, Ronald, myth, 1486 1498
Reagan, Ronald, National Security Decision Directive 84, 1583
Reagan, Ronald, news leaks, 1505
Reagan, Ronald, news management, 1535
Reagan, Ronald, nuclear bomb testing, 1488, 1592
Reagan, Ronald, nuclear power, 1739
Reagan, Ronald, nuclear war, 1488
Reagan, Ronald, nuclear weapons, 1612
Reagan, Ronald, policy, 1612
Reagan, Ronald, press conferences, 1539
Reagan, Ronald, press, 1920
Reagan, Ronald, propaganda, 2901, 2906, 2909
Reagan, Ronald, public relations, 1527, 1607, 2131
Reagan, Ronald, repression, 1560
Reagan, Ronald, Reykjavik summit, 1609
Reagan, Ronald, rhetoric, 1480, 1498, 1541, 1588
Reagan, Ronald, secrecy and surveillance, 2495
Reagan, Ronald, secrecy, 1554, 1561, 1565
Reagan, Ronald, space shuttle, 2325
Reagan, Ronald, Star Wars, 1491, 1621
Reagan, Ronald, television, 1529
Reagan, Ronald, terrorism, 1619
Reagan, Ronald, think tanks, 1891
Reagan, Ronald, tobacco, 604
Reagan, Ronald, totalitarianism, 1596
Reaganism, 1269
Reaganomics, 1600
real estate industry, 1189
Rebozo, Bebe, 1651
recruiting, 2299, 2377
recruiting, CIA, 2605, 2620
Red Brigades, 757
Red Channels, 191-92
Red Lion Broadcasting Co. v. FCC, 542, 655, 741, 1680, 2370
Red Scare, 12, 15, 70, 94, 100, 227
Red Squad, Chicago, 2557
red-baiting, 220, 443, 758
red-squads, 315
redlining, 1037a
Reel, A. Frank, 2361
Rees, John, 371

referendum process, 1386
reform, 562-63
regulation, 1037a, 1065, 1566
regulation, oil industry, 1330
regulatory agencies, II.C., 538, 544, 580, 594, 1360, 1548, 1554
religion, 454, 649
religion, broadcasting, 686
religion, right wing, 450, 466, 479
religious fundamentalism, 901
religious right, 1760
Reporter, The, 2273
reporters and reporting, investigative, 679
repression, 2, 8, 12, 314, 340, 366, 397, 465, 468, 526, 633a,
   918, 948-49, 951, 956, 962, 978, 1437, 1560, 1566, 1655, 1731,
   2098, 2105, 2426, 2441
repression, academia (see education)
repression, by allies (see state terrorism), 2097
repression, government, 156
repression, news, 1660
repression, police, 315
repression, political, 2409, 2413, 2420, 2448, 2451, 2457, 2467,
   2476
repression, technology, 1835
Republican Party, 211, 260, 432, 450, 1651
Research and Development Association, 591
research, II.E. (see science), 1998
research, military, 2258
research, university, 494
Resources for the Future Institute, corporations, 1890
Reuters (see news agencies), 699, 2889, 2895
Reuters, Southern Africa, 2802
Revenue Ruling 78-160, 1738
revolution, news, 1075
revolving door, 525
revolving door, government-media, 2249
revolving door, Pentagon and contractors, 480, 2214
Reykjavik, 398
rhetoric, political, 1498
rhetoric, presidential, 1492, 1507, 1541
Rhodesia, 39, 690
Rhodesia, Kissinger Study, 2809
Rhodesia, Western news agencies, 2802
Rickover, Admiral Hyman, 2333
Riding, Alan, 2175
right to know, 169, 1561, 1562, 1670, 1688, 1718, 1742, 2261
right to publish, 1718
right wing, 124, 158, 238, 314, 315, 327, 332, 362, 404, 423,
   450, 656-57, 664, 758, 770, 921, 937, 944, 952, 968, 1371,
   1428, 1596, 1807, 2108, 2942
right wing, censorship, 608
right wing, Central America, 2052
right wing, Heritage Foundation, 1893, 1896, 1901
right wing, media, 691
right wing, religions, 1760
right wing, students, 973

right wing, television, 1212
right wing, think tanks, IV.E., 1897
right wing, tobacco, 604
riots, 1811, 1968
Ritt, Martin, 212
Robertson, Pat, 466, 479, 901
Robeson, Paul, 128, 213, 243
Rockefeller Commission, CIA, 2649, 2720
Rockefeller Foundation, 925, 1427, 2937, 2940
Rockefeller Foundation, Britain, 2943
Rockefeller, David, 424, 1256, 1403
Rockefeller, Nelson, 2412
Rockwell International, 512, 1114
Rodino, Peter, 1650
Rogers Commission, 1675
Rogers, William P., 1563
Rosenberg, Julius and Ethel, 188, 216, 249, 1712
Rosenberg-Sobell case, FBI, 2564, 2581
Rostow, Eugene, 391
Rostow, Walter, 2199
ROTC, 2223, 2305, 2309, 2315
Rowan, Carl, 2927
ruling class (see power elite), 1050, 1052, 1054, 1079, 1093,
  1246
Rusk, Dean, 1946, 2199
sabotage, CIA, 2643
Safe Energy Communication Council, 1391
safety (see asbestos; atomic testing; automobile, safety; cancer;
  corporation, crime; FDA; mines, safety; nuclear safety; radia-
  tion), 963, 1548
SALT I, 25
SALT II, 49
SALT II, press, 336
SALT talks, 182
SALT treaties, 320, 374, 1563
San Francisco Chronicle, 2033
San Francisco Examiner, 1515
San Francisco to Moscow Peace Walk, 133
Sanctuary Movement, 2403, 2425, 2465
sanctuary trial, 2057
Sanderson, James, 600
Sandinistas, IV.H.2.a.
satellite communications, 1048, 2805
satellites, 2289, 2779, 2793, 2842
satellites, control, 2804, 2810, 2863
satellites, direct educational programming, 2777
satellites, military, 2852
Saturday Evening Post, 618
Saturday Review, advertising awards, 1331
Saudi Arabia, 863, 932
Savak torture, CIA, 2665
Savio, Robert, 2864
Scaife Family Charitable Trusts, 2645
Scaife Foundation, 363, 1429, 1450
Scaife, Richard Mellon, 1004, 1428, 1441, 1962

Scalia, Judge Antonin, 1782
Schanberg, Sidney, 780, 1466
Schaufelberger, Albert, 2173
Schenk v. U.S. (1919), 1680
Schlesinger, James, 2267
Schmertz, Herbert, 1341, 1347
Schorr, Daniel, 742
Schultz, George, 2062
science news, 1416
science, 411, 454, 812, 1803, 2038
science, anticommunism, 127
science, arms research, 489
science, censorship, 1655
science, government, 914, 2445
science, militarization, 2231
science, military secrecy, 2368
science, military, 2310, 2336, 2381
science, neutrality of, 859
science, secrecy, 2358
science, social control, 859
science, society, 861
scientists, 177, 221, 224, 250
scientists, arms, 477
scientists, Cold War, 864
scientists, disarmament, 864
scientists, government, 865-66
scientists, public trust, 869
scientists, RAND, 1894
Scorsese, Martin, 665
Scranton Commission (see commissions), 1973
SDI (see Star Wars), 1805, 2258, 2305, 2312, 2325
SDI, deception, 2359
SDI, finances, 2336
SDS, CIA, 2649
Seabrook, 1092
search and seizure, FBI, 2533, 2562, 2588
search and seizure, 2424
search warrants, journalists, 2488, 2494
Seberg, Jean, FBI, 2567
second-strike, 25
secrecy, II.F., III.F., IV.A.2.C.1., V.D., VI., 42, 92, 146, 162,
   169, 173, 181, 388, 531, 559, 561, 676, 759, 871, 875, 905,
   1098, 1645, 1646, 1681, 1797, 2039
secrecy, anticommunism, 131
secrecy, arms research, 473
secrecy, CIA, 2597, 2599, 2600, 2619, 2690, 2717, 2720, 2744
secrecy, CIA, Intelligence Identities Protection bill, 2598
secrecy, corporate, 1073, 1085, 1090
secrecy, foundations, 1427
secrecy, government, 1939, 1994
secrecy, intelligence, VI., 2483
secrecy, nuclear, 1678
secrecy, Pentagon surveillance, 2480
secrecy, Pentagon, 484, 1948
secrecy, presidential, 1477, 1484, 1535, 1536, 1643

secrecy, science, 127
secrecy, Vietnam War, 1968
Secret Army Organization, 1651
secret files, FBI, 2547, 2549, 2553, 2571
secret police, FBI, VI.B., 2555, 2571
Secret Service, 1536, 2384, 2463
Section 140C, Pentagon secrecy, 2318
secular humanism, 327
secularization, 1239
security classifications, 2288
Security Council Directive 130, 1493
security leaks, 1760
security, loyalty-security program, I.
Segretti, Donald, Watergate, 1647
Selected Acquisition Report, intelligence, 2364
self-censorship, 758, 1086, 1190, 1220, 1262, 1266, 1319, 1578,
   2022, 2666
self-help books, 618
self-incrimination, 2424
Selling of the Pentagon, The, 1878, 2302, 2363, 2370, 2373
semantic differential, CIA, 2672
semiconductors, 2231
Senate Foreign Relations Committee, 1946
Sesame Street, 620
Sesame Street, global education, 2820
Seventeen, 945
sexism, 855, 1205
sexism, militarism, 2222
Sgt. York anti-aircraft gun, 2356
Sheehan, Neil, 1994
Shell, 1366
Sheridan tank, 531
Signal Corps, 527
Sihanouk, CIA, 2747
Silkwood, Karen, 1462
Silverman, Fred, 1160, 1212
Singlaub, John, 311, 2064
SIOP, 207, 2203
Sirica, John, 1650
situation comedies, 652, 1298
Sixty Minutes, 966, 1243, 2271
Smith Act (Alien Registration Act of 1940), I.C.D., 79, 81, 151,
   230, 2404, 2479
Smith Richardson Foundation, 2645
Smith Richardson Foundation, CIA, 2647
Smith, C. Arnholt, 1651
Smith, Samantha, FBI, 2549
Smith, William French, secrecy, 2419
smoking (see tobacco), 1350
Snepp, Frank, CIA, 1791, 2602, 2604, 2642, 2661, 2701, 2714,
   2721, 2735, 2736
social control (see conformity; hegemony; indoctrination)
social responsibility, corporations, 1059, 1071
social science (see political science), 527, 800, 827, 936
social science, conservative ideology, 2937

social science, corporate use of, 860
Social Security, 743a
social services, 744
social theorists, 1237
socialism, 14, 232, 432
socialism, FBI, 2517
Socialist Workers Party, FBI, 87, 168, 933, 2404, 2413, 2430,
   2436, 2588
socialization, media (see conformity; hegemony; ideology; indoc-
   trination), 651
soft news, 748
Sojourners magazine, surveillance, 2512
Sojourners, 953
solar energy, 900, 1092, 1139, 1398, 1516
Soldier of Fortune, 2064, 2291
Somoza Debayle, Anastasio, 2139, 2145
Son Tay affair, 1584
Sostre, Martin, 2406
South Africa, 39, 966, 987, 1564
South Africa, relations with U.S., 2908
South Africa, United States Youth Council, 2936
South Africa, Western news agencies, 2802
South America, IV.H.3.
South Korea, AFL-CIO, 2839
Southern University, Baton Rouge, 956
Soviet Military Power, 313, 2290
Soviet nuclear accident, CIA, 2716
Soviet Peace Committee, 396
Soviet television news, 750
Soviet threat, 196, 202, 252, 280, 296, 305, 322, 328, 331, 1830,
   2285, 2290, 2350, 2371, 2376, 2711
Soviet Union, CIA, 2506, 2761
Soviet Union, foreign policy, 60
Soviet Union, imperialism, 307, 331
Soviet Union, media coverage, 299, 300, 308, 317, 356-57
Soviet Union, treaty violations, 336
Sovietphobia, I. (see Red Squad), 758, 918, 1548, 1824, 1994,
   2033, 2104, 2223, 2250, 2307, 2553, 2689, 2828
Sovietphobia, censorship, 1729
Sovietphobia, CIA, 2608, 2610
Sovietphobia, FBI, 2537, 2563, 2571, 2588, 2593
Sovietphobia, Harvard, 2531
Sovietphobia, president, 1493
space flight, 1792
space program, 506, 528
space shuttle, 410, 891, 1707, 2211, 2227, 2325
space shuttle, militarization, 1675, 2197, 2369
space shuttle, plutonium, 1707
space, militarization, 2197, 2212, 2226, 2227, 2289
Spacetrack, 2225
speakers' bureaus, 2223
special interests, 436
Special Operations Forces, 2321, 2372
special privilege, 436
spies, police, 2481, 2485

sponsor (see broadcasting), 777
sports, 498, 649
sports, imperialism, 2824
sportswriters, 1317
Springer, Axel, CIA, 2754
Sputnik, 44
spy dust, 286
spying, 1545, 2461
SSDD 130, 2909
St. Louis Post-Dispatch, 1515
Standard Oil, 863, 1397, 1399
standing army, 2188
Stanford Daily, press privacy, 1800, 2494
Stanford University, 954
Stans, Maurice, 1651
Stanton, Frank, 2370
star system, 1267
Star Wars, 288, 328, 350, 384, 394, 532, 1491, 1603, 1621, 1808,
   1814, 2211, 2212, 2258, 2300, 2305
Star Wars, deception, 2359
Star Wars, research, 489, 492
state capitalism, II., III., IV., 460
State Department, 2062, 2170, 2174
State Department, fragmentation, 2903
State Department, secrecy, 1748
state religion (state capitalism, Pentagon state), 619
state terrorism, 2060
state terrorism, Central America, 2052
state terrorism, CIA, 2615, 2628
state, corporations, 426
statism, 173-74
statistics, 753
statistics, government, 1595
statistics, propaganda, 1830
Stealth airplane, 2279, 2338
steel industry, 428
sterilization, 925
Sterling, Claire, 295, 341, 351
stock, 425
Stockman, David, 1600, 1614
Stockwell, John, CIA, 2661
Stone, I. F., 1797, 1798
Strategic Air Commmand, 1968
Strategic Defense Initiative (SDI) (see Star Wars)
Strauss, Lewis, 83
strip mining, ads, 1339
student press, 982
student protest, 936, 958, 960
Students for a Better America, 361
Students for a Democratic Society, 984, 2432
subliminal persuasion, CIA, 2672
subliminal politics, 449
submarine bases, 2769, 2770
subpoena, press, 1841
subsidized information, 427, 775

subversion of foreign governments, CIA, 2649
subversion, I., 69, 2387
Subversive Activities Control Board, 2479
sugar, 1121
Sullivan, William, FBI, 2592
Superman, 1216
suppression (see repression), 449, 586
Supreme Court, 685, 1677, 1680, 1764
Supreme Court, CIA, 2701
surveillance, VI., 8, 240, 315, 388, 633a, 904, 1550, 1710, 1845,
    2417, 2418, 2423, 2453, 2459, 2504, 2509, 2510
surveillance, Army, 2461
surveillance, Bible, 2447
surveillance, Black Panthers, 2523
surveillance, CIA, 2720
surveillance, computer, 2393
surveillance, demonstrations, 2510
surveillance, domestic, 2393, 2410, 2436, 2451
surveillance, electronic, 2384, 2401, 2408, 2416, 2417, 2432,
    2452, 2459
surveillance, electronic, civil liberties, 2414
surveillance, electronic, Foreign Intelligence Surveillance Act,
    2490
surveillance, electronic, NSA, 2768
surveillance, FBI of ACLU, 2513
surveillance, FBI, VI.B., 2516, 2517, 2528, 2537, 2538
surveillance, FBI, press credentials, 2514
surveillance, government, 2455, 2472
surveillance, MIC, 524
surveillance, military, 2387, 2407
surveillance, NSA, 2763
surveillance, of civilian groups, VI., 2507
surveillance, Pentagon, 2480
surveillance, police, 2401, 2402, 2411, 2460, 2478, 2481
surveillance, political, 2457, 2498, 2500, 2502, 2509
surveillance, space, CIA and NSA, 2511
surveillance, technology, 2387
surveillance, telephone, 2416
Swaggart, Jimmy, 62
Symbionese Liberation Army, 2183
symbol, 832
symbolism, presidential, 1524
Taiwan, 1834
talk shows, 620
Taylor, General Maxwell, 2199
Team B, Reagan, 391
technocracy, 456, 506, 2228, 2940
technology, 427, 459
technology, control, 1079, 1095
technology, information, 469
technology, police state (see repression), 1835
technology, repression (see computers), 1849
Ted Bates Advertising Co., 1241
telecommunications, 524, 655, 1039
telecommunications, decontrol, 1074

telecommunications, White House, 1476
telematics, 459
television, "meet the press" programs, 1311
television, 282, 437, 551, 577, 609, 614, 649, 652, 737, 748,
   763, 770, 1177, 1187, 1199, 1244, 1279, 1290, 1796, 2040, 2845
television, acquisitions and mergers, 1027
television, advertising, 1188
television, bias, 2096
television, cable, 1436 (note)
television, censorship, 899, 919-20, 922, 939-40, 945, 970-71,
   996, 1183, 1194, 1212, 1312, 1557, 2370
television, children, 614, 1174, 1184, 1211, 1216, 1251, 1311,
   1313, 1945
television, China, 614
television, CIA, 614
television, Cold War, 614
television, commercialism, 614, 1178, 1193, 1214, 1218, 1259,
   1275
television, commercials, 614, 1217, 1296, 1297, 1309
television, conformity, 615, 647
television, Congress, 614, 1886
television, consumerism, 1302
television, control, 1227, 1232
television, corporate control, 1263
television, corporate sponsors, 614
television, corporations, 1069
television, Cuba, 614
television, documentaries, 614, 1287, 1309
television, dominance, 2850
television, Eisenhower, 614
television, elections, 682
television, evangelism, 62
television, family, 663
television, FCC, 614
television, General Electric, 614
television, Hollywood, 614
television, ideology, 616, 1311
television, imperialism, 614
television, indoctrination, 632
television, instructional, 822
television, international news, 666
television, Latin America, 666, 2806
television, monopoly, 1026-27, 1033, 1045
television, Moscow Olympics, 666
television, multinationals, 2773
television, Navy, 614
television, networks, 316, 354, 462, 603, 614, 741, 758, 761,
   1055, 1068, 1096, 1158, 1160, 1212, 1227, 1298, 1475, 1961
television, networks, global expansion, 2795, 2825
television, news, 545, 667-68, 757, 777, 1191, 1192, 1227, 1245,
   1275, 1569, 2024
television, news, presidential elections, 1623, 1624, 1637, 1638
television, news, sponsor control, 1300
television, Nixon, 614
television, pathogenesis, 663

television, Pentagon, 614
television, personality system, 1236
television, political campaigns, 1641
television, political conventions, 614
television, preachers, 466
television, president, 1478, 1506, 1519
television, presidential campaigns, 1628, 1634, 1636
television, prime time, 657, 660, 1212, 1245, 1269
television, programming, 1298
television, programs, international flow, 2878
television, public access, 661
television, public interest, 1292
television, quiz scandal, 662
television, sacrifice of social life, 1284
television, Senator McCarthy, I.C.3., 614
television, Seven Station Rule, 573
television, sponsors, III.C., 662, 777, 1212, 1245, 1259, 1263
television, sports, 614
television, talk shows, 1310, 1311
television, terrorism, 666
television, Third World, 666
television, unions, 1454
television, USSR, 614
television, Vietnam War, IV.G.2, 666, 1982, 1983, 2001, 2009,
    2014, 2018
television, violence, 1096, 1245, 1945
television, war, 614
television, Watergate, 1648
television, Westinghouse, 614
Teller, Dr. Edward, 288, 394
Temple, Shirley, 1198
tenure, 883
Terpil, Frank, CIA, 2757
terrorism, 276, 281, 684, 732, 757, 758, 1619, 1812, 1820, 1828,
    1857, 2044, 2427, 2928
terrorism, Reagan administration, 1618
terrorism, Senate Subcommittee, 2497
terrorism, state, 281, 323, 2068, 2655
terrorism, workshops for police, 392
Test Ban Treaty, 25
test bans, nuclear (see nuclear testing)
testing, educational (see education, tests and measurements)
Tet Offensive, 742, 1960, 1965, 1985, 1989, 2001, 2015
Tet Offensive, press, 1981
Texaco, 863
Texas Un-American Activities Committee, 94
textbooks, 194, 198, 636, 911, 1362
textbooks, Vietnam War, 1993, 2000, 2010
The Spike (see Borchgrave, Arnaud de; Moss, Robert), 362
think tanks, IV.E., 149, 199, 224, 423, 462, 499, 526, 710-11,
    1367, 2108, 2199
third parties (see bipartisanship), 1624, 1885
Third World War, The, 322
Third World, 1255, 2781
Third World, CIA (see interventionism), 2597

Third World, cigarette advertising, 2814
Third World, cultural imperialism, 2816
Third World, foundations, 2940
Third World, imperialism, 2803
Third World, information flow, VII.B., 740, 2860, 2865, 2869,
    2888, 2891, 2894
Third World, news gathering, 2861
Third World, tobacco, 2843
Thomas, J. Parnell, 234, 243
thought control (see Contents; advertising; anticommunism; black-
    listing; censorship; classification system; COINTELPRO; corpo-
    ration, advocacy advertising; disinformation; doublespeak; edu-
    cation; HUAC; secrecy; wiretaps), 1844
Three Mile Island (see nuclear accidents), 333, 559, 574, 593,
    602, 685, 713, 738, 742, 754, 761, 1003, 1092, 1372, 1438
Three Mile Island, NRC, 1784
Three Mile Island, secrecy, 1780
Three-M Corporation, 544
Tiger Cruises, Navy, 2268
Time, 232, 316, 431, 462, 486, 726, 758, 1256, 1355, 1923, 2044,
    2629
Time, CIA, 2610
Time, Inc., 1034, 1169
Time, Inc., propaganda, 2907
Time, influence abroad, 2826
tobacco advertising, 993, 1326
tobacco industry, 1162, 1262
tobacco, 604, 1206
tobacco, cancer, 1319, 1442
tobacco, smokeless, 933
tobacco, Third World, 2843
Tolson, Clyde, 2432
torture, 1776, 2035
totalitarianism (see repression; state terrorism), 1584, 1596
toxic chemicals, 537, 561, 582, 590, 596-97, 600, 743a, 880, 976,
    1312, 2430
toxic waste disposal, 1004
toxic waste, 1037a, 1407, 1472
transnational corporations (see multinational corporations), 2801
travel bans (see visa control), 904
travel, freedom, 195, 1874
traveling art shows, 2223
trials, political, 1958
Trilateral Commission, 25, 462, 1988, 2780, 2840
Truman Doctrine, 44, 126
Truman, Harry S. (see Cold War), 22-24, 36, 153, 239-40, 244,
    1755, 2106
Truman, Harry S., wiretaps, 1840
Trumbo, Dalton, 243
Truong, David, 1847, 1955, 2525
TRW, 1104
Turner Joy, 1946
Turner, Ted, 386, 674
TV Guide, 282, 460, 1283
two-party system (see bipartisanship), 420, 436

Tylenol, 754
U-2 (see Eisenhower, Dwight D.), 1545, 2603, 2717, 2759
U-2 incident, CIA, 2649
U.N. information officer, 767
U.S. Committee for Energy Awareness, 1404
U. S., Constitution, First Amendment (see First Amendment)
U.S. Information Agency (see USIA)
U.S. Patent and Trademark Office, 1799
U.S.News & World Report, 2044
U.S.S. Indianapolis, cover-up, 2348
UHF, 601, 1068
Ulasewicz, Tony, 1647
Unclassified Controlled Nuclear Information Law, 2318
Uncounted Enemy, 2344
undercover agents, 2499, 2501, 2509
undercover operations, 2460
underground press, 672, 741, 743, 1768, 2020, 2485
unemployment, military spending, 2322
UNESCO, 2819, 2855, 2857, 2858, 2860, 2863-66, 2869, 2874, 2879,
    2880, 2882, 2883, 2885, 2887, 2891, 2895, 2896, 2942
UNESCO, Belgrade General Conference, 2872
UNESCO, communications, 2793
UNESCO, mass media declaration, 2876
UNESCO, press, 2872, 2881
UNESCO, U.S. pullout, 2846
UNESCO, VII.B., 233, 669, 995
Unification Church, 276
union busting, 1037a
Union Carbide, 596, 1465
Union of Concerned Scientists, 559
union press, censorship by corporations, 1451
unions, 6, 8, 14, 103, 119, 267, 426, 438, 443, 733a, 758, 857,
    1153, 1291, 1305, 1308, 1437
unions, CIA, 2643, 2749
unions, FBI, 2562
unions, MIC, 525
unions, repression, 1018
unions, television, 1454
Unique War, The, 2029
Uniroyal, 1175
Unitarian Universalist Association, 1963
United Fruit Company, 2085, 2811
United Nations Charter, Article 2(4), 2649
United Nations, 656, 767, 2847
United Nations, assault by international business, 2776
United Press International (see UPI, news agencies)
United States Department of Agriculture (USDA), 561
United States Information Agency (see USIA), VII.C.
United States Youth Council, support of South Africa, 2936
United Technologies Corporation, 475, 638
universities, 225, 424, 854, 936, 960, 978
universities, boards of trustees, 882-85, 949
universities, CIA, 2643, 2653, 2658, 2675, 2705, 2726
universities, corporate control of, 868, 872-73, 876, 880,
    886-87, 958

universities, government control of, 872, 879
universities, military industrial complex, 2192
universities, models for, 854
universities, Pentagon, 530
universities, secrecy, 2358
universities, Star Wars, 870
University of California, 184, 949
University of California, Davis, 361
University of Colorado, 1971
University of Pennsylvania, 1998
University of Seattle, 208
University of Southern Mississippi, 884
University of Texas at Austin, 973
University of Texas, 397
University of Texas, SDI, 2305
University of Washington, 187, 958
UPI (see news agencies), 316, 699, 764, 2036, 2037, 2142, 2168,
    2889, 2894
UPI, Africa, 2854
UPI, CIA, 2610, 2625
UPI, Southern Africa, 2802
upper class indicators, 423
uranium mining, 42, 1003, 1781
uranium, missing, 1765
Uruguay, 2035
Uruguay, USIA and CIA media control, 2848
used-car dealers, 1141
USIA, VII.C., 1493, 1959, 1999, 2902, 2903, 2905, 2909, 2910,
    2914, 2924, 2926, 2927, 2928, 2930, 2934, 2936
USIA, funding, 2917
USIA, India, 2913
USIA, propaganda, 2899
USIA, Uruguay, 2848
utilities (see public utilities; utilities industry)
utilities industry, 455, 1410
Valenti, Jack, 1432
Van Doren, Charles, 662
Vatican II, 2046
VDT, 1468, 1470
Velde, Harold, 243
VHF, 1068
video games, militarism and sexism, 2218
videotapes, 1016
Vietnam crises, 1515
Vietnam lobby, 1966
Vietnam Veterans, 2019
Vietnam Village Reborn, 2029
Vietnam War, IV.G.2., 8, 251, 377, 703, 741, 758, 1501, 1549,
    1563, 1651, 1861, 1936, 1939, 2006, 2011, 2190, 2199, 2211,
    2271, 2273, 2339, 2345, 2469
Vietnam War protest, FBI, 2517
Vietnam War, films, 2029
Vietnam War, PBS, 1980, 1984
Vietnam War, RAND, 1903, 1904
Vietnam War, Xmas bombing, 1563

Vietnam, 1847, 2639
Vietnam, CIA, 2643
Vietnam: A Television History, 1984, 1997, 2006, 2011, 2016
vigilantes, 122
Village Voice, 643
Vincent, John Carter, 179
violence, 1945, 2188
violent crimes, 631
visa control (see censorship), 101, 134, 136, 904, 2182, 2469
Voice of America, 2915, 2925, 2928, 2931
Voice of America, Costa Rica, 2922
von Braun, Wernher, 2211
Vremya (Time), 750
VVAW, 2430, 2436
Wall Street Journal, 462, 758-759a, 1256, 1322, 1381
Wall Street, 1028
Wallace, Henry, 120, 244
Walsh Commission (1915), higher education, 1424
Walt Disney Productions (see Disney)
Walter, Francis S., 243
Walters, Barbara, 684
Walters, Vernon A., 1824
war cartoons, 1945
war correspondents, 1936, 1943, 1956, 1972
war economy (see militarism; military-industrial complex)
war films, Pentagon, 2353, 2360, 2374
war news, 2032, 2033
War Powers Resolution, 1887, 1968
war toys, 1216, 1945
war, low intensity, 2149
warfare state, 2194, 2195
warlords, 445
Warnke, Paul, 391
wars, IV.G., 1205
Washington Post Co., 1859
Washington Post, 89, 149, 246, 409, 413, 431, 758, 761, 775,
    1049, 1060, 1172, 1515, 1578, 1643, 1727, 1922, 2033, 2044,
    2630
Washington Post, campaign coverage, 1633
Washington Post, censorship, 1727
Washington Post, Progressive H-bomb case, 1684, 1698
Washington Press Corps, IV.F.
Washington Star, 1169, 1432
Waste Management, Inc., public relations, 1407
waste, 938
waste, government, 536
Watergate, IV.B., 169, 438, 719, 1234, 1546, 1549, 1584, 1795,
    1826, 1827, 2432, 2477, 2738
Watt, James, 1567
Watts, Alan, 456
wealth, 1107, 1269, 1702
weapons evaluation, 2367
weapons gap, 745
weapons testing, 2356
Weekly, 1797

Weinberger, Caspar, 2371
Weinberger, Caspar, distortion, 2343
welfare system, 438, 583
WESTAR, 434
Western Electric, 490
Western Goals Foundation, 371
western hero, 2003
Western Union, 434, 1048
Westinghouse Broadcasting Company, 614, 1332
Westinghouse, 417, 559, 2333
Westmoreland, General William C., 770, 1450, 1962, 2015
Westmoreland, General William C., lawsuit against CBS, 2344
whistleblowing, 1431, 1438, 1467, 1685, 1714, 1751, 2355, 2441, 2701, 2721
White House (see presidency), IV.A., 697, 1807, 1810
White House news service, 995
White House "Plumbers", Watergate, 1563, 1647
White House, press corps, 1502, 1536, 1540
White Nights, 277
White Papers, 2811
White, Theodore H., 99
Why We Fight, 2029
Wick, Charles, 1494
Wick, Charles, missile deployment, 2904
Widener, Don, 1287
Wildmon, Reverend Donald, 1371
Wilkinson, Frank, FBI, 2522
Wilson, Edwin, CIA, 2757
wire services (see news agencies)
Wireless File, 2928
wiretaps (see bugging), 8, 248, 1444, 1563, 1875, 2408, 2417, 2428, 2462, 2489, 2491, 2493, 2502, 2508, 2509, 2596, 2765
wiretaps, CIA, 2720
wiretaps, FBI, 2515, 2528, 2559, 2572, 2588, 2591
Wirthlin, Richard, 1525
witch hunt, 120, 220, 2105
witch hunt, academia, 164
With the Contras, 2135
Women's Action for Nuclear Disarmament, 1669
women, unemployment and military spending, 2322
Wood, John S., 243
Woodward, Bob, 1642, 2712
working class, 443
working class, films, 1153
World Administrative Radio Conference, 2793
World Anti-Communist League, 276, 311-12, 368
World Bank, 2802, 2940
World News Tonight, 1494, 2142
World War II, films, 202
World, 892
Worldnet, 1493, 2905, 2909, 2930
Wounded Knee (see American Indian Movement)
WW I, 1935
WW III, 2301
xenophobia, I., 1790

Yalta, 319
Yamashita, Tomoyuki, 2361
yellow rain, 377, 406, 412, 758
Young Socialist Alliance, 2404
Your Tour in Vietnam, 2029
Zaire, 2811
Zimbabwe, 690
Zola, Émile, 1171